Writing Arguments: A Rhetoric with Readings

With Selections from Rhetorical Grammar

A Custom Edition

Taken from:
Writing Arguments: A Rhetoric with Readings,
Brief Ninth Edition
by John D. Ramage, John C. Bean, and June Johnson

Rhetorical Grammar: Grammatical Choices, Rhetorical Effects,
Sixth Edition
by Martha Kolln and Loretta Gray

Taken from:

Writing Arguments: A Rhetoric with Readings, Brief Ninth Edition
by John D. Ramage, John C. Bean, and June Johnson
Copyright © 2012, 2010, 2007, 2004 by Pearson Education, Inc.
Published by Pearson
Upper Saddle River, New Jersey 07458

Rhetorical Grammar: Grammatical Choices, Rhetorical Effects, Sixth Edition
by Martin Kolln and Loretta Gray
Copyright © 2010, 2007, 2003 by Pearson Education, Inc.
Published by Longman
New York, New York 10036

This special edition published in cooperation with Pearson Learning Solutions.

All trademarks, service marks, registered trademarks, and registered service marks are the property of their respective owners and are used herein for identification purposes only.

Pearson Learning Solutions, 501 Boylston Street, Suite 900, Boston, MA 02116
A Pearson Education Company
www.pearsoned.com

Printed in the United States of America

1 2 3 4 5 6 7 8 9 10 V311 16 15 14 13 12 11

000200010271265950

SW

ISBN 10: 1-256-41662-2
ISBN 13: 978-1-256-41662-3

Brief Contents

READINGS AND VISUAL ARGUMENTS

Detailed Contents

Taken from: *Writing Arguments: A Rhetoric with Readings,* Brief Ninth Edition, by Ramage

17 Citing and Documenting Sources   383

Appendix Informal Fallacies   404

Taken from: *Rhetorical Grammar: Grammatical Choices, Rhetorical Effects,*
Sixth Edition, by Kolln

Preface

Through eight editions, *Writing Arguments* has established itself as a leading college textbook in argumentation. By focusing on argument as dialogue in search of solutions to problems instead of as pro-con debate with winners and losers, *Writing Arguments* treats argument as a process of inquiry as well as a means of persuasion. Users and reviewers have consistently praised the book for teaching the critical thinking skills needed for *writing* arguments: how to analyze the occasion for an argument; how to ground an argument in the values and beliefs of the targeted audience; how to develop and elaborate an argument; and how to respond sensitively to objections and alternative views. The text is available in three versions—a regular edition, which includes an anthology of readings; a brief edition, which offers the complete rhetoric without the anthology; and a concise edition with fewer readings and examples—to support many instructional approaches and course designs. We are pleased that in this ninth edition, we have made many improvements while retaining the text's signature strengths.

What's New in the Ninth Edition?

Based on our continuing research into argumentation theory and pedagogy, as well as on the advice of users, we have made significant improvements in the ninth edition that increase the text's flexibility for teachers and its appeal to students. We have made the following major changes:

■ **Expanded and updated treatment of integrating source material into arguments.** The previous edition's brief coverage of the use of sources has been expanded into a new chapter that will be appreciated by teachers who combine argumentation with research writing. Chapter 16, "Incorporating Sources into Your Own Argument," provides more thorough instruction to help students summarize, paraphrase, and quote sources properly. Examples of strong and weak syntheses are given a new visual treatment to help students more clearly understand how to fold the ideas and words of others into their own writing effectively and accurately. Its updated treatment of plagiarism and the ethical use of sources in the academic community incorporates the latest rhetorical research into students' often unintentional misuse of sources, including patchwriting.

■ **Expanded coverage of Rogerian argument.** In Chapter 7, a new section on Rogerian argument reflects recent rhetorical scholarship on Rogerian communication by emphasizing inquiry, writers' examination of their own values, and the establishment of an open, collaborative problem-solving relationship with the audience. A new student example of a Rogerian letter, charts that highlight features of delayed-thesis and Rogerian arguments, and a new exercise with visuals help students practice and apply these concepts.

- **New visual examples throughout the text.** New images in several Examining Visual Arguments boxes, a new student PowerPoint proposal, and new editorial cartoons provide up-to-date examples of visual argument. In addition, a new analysis of a television commercial models critical reading of visual examples, and new For Class Discussion activities offer more exercises that students can use to analyze and write about how visual arguments work (Chs. 3, 7, 9, and 12–14).

- **New multimodal writing assignment options.** The ninth edition includes several new writing assignment options that ask students to integrate verbal and visual arguments. These include revising an argument to use images that appeal to *pathos*, creating a visual argument based on a well-known or iconic image, creating an editorial cartoon, and developing PowerPoint slides to support an oral presentation (Chs. 6, 9, 14).

- **Four new professional readings and five new student essays throughout the text.** New readings about topics such as carrying guns on campus, building a mosque at Ground Zero, changing college meal plans that discriminate against women, and watching comedy shows to get the news have been chosen for their illustrative power and student interest.

- **Streamlined coverage of definition and resemblance arguments.** We have combined the eighth edition's separate treatment of definition and resemblance arguments, streamlining coverage into one chapter to better highlight their common features as types of categorical arguments.

What Hasn't Changed? The Distinguishing Features of *Writing Arguments*

Building on earlier success, we have preserved the signature features of earlier editions praised by students, instructors, and reviewers:

- **Focus throughout on writing arguments.** Grounded in composition theory, this text combines explanations of argument with exploratory writing activities, sequenced writing assignments, and class-tested discussion tasks with the aim of helping students produce their own strong arguments. The text emphasizes the critical thinking that underlies effective arguments, particularly the skills of critical reading, of active questioning and listening, of believing and doubting, and of developing effective reasons and evidence to support claims.

- **Emphasis on argument as a rhetorical act.** Analyzing audience, understanding the real-world occasions for argument, and appreciating the context and genre of arguments are all treated as equally important rhetorical considerations. Focusing on both the reading and the writing of arguments, the text emphasizes the critical thinking that underlies effective arguments, particularly the skills of critical reading, of rhetorical analysis, of believing and doubting, of empathic listening, of active questioning, and of negotiating ambiguity and seeking synthesis.

- **Integration of four different approaches to argument.** This text uses
  - the Toulmin system as a means of inventing and analyzing arguments;
  - the enthymeme as a logical structure rooted in the beliefs and values of the audience;
  - the classical concepts of *logos, pathos*, and *ethos* as persuasive appeals; and
  - stasis theory (called claim types) as an aid to inventing and structuring arguments through the understanding of generic argumentative moves associated with different categories of claims.
- **Generous treatment of the research process.** Coverage includes guidance for finding sources, reading and evaluating them rhetorically, taking notes, integrating source material, and citing sources using two academic citation systems: MLA and APA.
- **Well-sequenced writing assignments.** The text provides a variety of sequenced writing assignments that include
  - an argument summary
  - a "supporting-reasons" argument
  - a classical argument
  - a delayed-thesis or Rogerian argument
  - a rhetorical analysis of a written argument
  - a rhetorical analysis of a visual argument
  - an advocacy ad
  - a short argument incorporating quantitative data
  - an editorial cartoon
  - a definition argument
  - a causal argument
  - an evaluation or ethical argument
  - a proposal argument
  - an advocacy poster
  - a speech with PowerPoint slides
- **"For Class Discussion" and "Examining Visual Arguments" exercises.** These class-tested activities, which teach critical thinking and build argumentative skills, are designed to produce active class discussion and debate. All "For Class Discussion" exercises can be used either for whole-class discussions or for collaborative group tasks.
- **Effective and engaging student and professional arguments.** The ninth edition contains 12 written arguments and 42 visual arguments drawn from public and academic arenas as well as 16 student essays and 2 student visual arguments to illustrate argumentative strategies and stimulate discussion, analysis, and debate.

Our Approaches to Argumentation

Our interest in argumentation grows out of our interest in the relationship between writing and thinking. When writing arguments, writers are forced to lay bare their thinking processes in an unparalleled way, grappling with the complex interplay between inquiry and persuasion, between issue and audience. In an effort to engage students in the kinds of critical thinking that argument demands, we draw on four major approaches to argumentation:

1. **The enthymeme as a rhetorical and logical structure.** This concept, especially useful for beginning writers, helps students "nutshell" an argument as a claim with one or more supporting *because* clauses. It also helps them see how real-world arguments are rooted in assumptions granted by the audience rather than in universal and unchanging principles.
2. **The three classical types of appeal—***logos, ethos,* **and** *pathos.* These concepts help students place their arguments in a rhetorical context focusing on audience-based appeals; they also help students create an effective voice and style.
3. **Toulmin's system of analyzing arguments.** Toulmin's system helps students see the complete, implicit structure that underlies an enthymeme and develop appropriate grounds and backing to support an argument's reasons and warrants. It also highlights the rhetorical, social, and dialectical nature of argument.
4. **Stasis theory concerning types of claims.** This approach stresses the heuristic value of learning different patterns of support for different types of claims and often leads students to make surprisingly rich and full arguments.

Throughout the text these approaches are integrated and synthesized into generative tools for both producing and analyzing arguments.

Structure of the Text

Writing Arguments provides a sound pedagogical framework for the teaching of argument while giving instructors the flexibility to use what they need. Part One begins with an overview of argument and a chapter on reading arguments and exploring issues. Part Two examines the elements of writing arguments: the enthymeme (a claim with reasons); the rhetorical appeals of *logos, ethos,* and *pathos*; Toulmin's system for analyzing arguments; the use of evidence; acknowledging and responding to alternative views; and using delayed-thesis and Rogerian approaches. In Part Three, the focus shifts to analyzing written and visual arguments. Part Four provides a deeper understanding of definition, resemblance, causal, evaluation, and proposal arguments. Part Five shows students how to use sources in support of an argument by evaluating, integrating, citing, and documenting them properly. An appendix on logical fallacies is a handy section where all the major informal fallacies are treated at once for easy reference.

Supplements

The Instructor's Manual, Ninth Edition, includes the following features:

- Discussion of planning decisions an instructor must make in designing an argument course: for example, how to use readings; how much to emphasize Toulmin or claim type theory; how much time to build into the course for invention, peer review of drafts, and other writing instruction; and how to select and sequence assignments.
- For new instructors, a helpful discussion of how to sequence writing assignments and how to use a variety of collaborative tasks in the classroom to promote active learning and critical thinking.
- Four detailed syllabi that support a variety of course structures and emphases.
- An independent, highly teachable introductory lesson on the Toulmin schema and an additional exercise giving students practice using Toulmin to generate argument frames.
- Chapter-by-chapter teaching tips, responses to the For Class Discussion exercises, and sample quizzes.
- Suggestions for encouraging students to explore how visual arguments mold public thinking about issues and controversies.
- Helpful suggestions for using the exercises in Part Four on critiquing readings. By focusing on rhetorical context as well as on the strengths and weaknesses of these arguments, our suggestions will help students connect their reading of arguments to their writing of arguments.
- A list of anthology readings that employ each claim type, either as a major claim or as a substantial portion of the argument.
- An analysis of anthology readings that points out striking connections among readings, suggesting how the readings participate in larger societal argumentative conversations, but that also connects the anthology to the rhetoric portion of the text. Using a bulleted, quick-reference format, each analysis briefly discusses (1) the core of the argument, (2) the major or dominant claims of the argument, (3) the argument's use of evidence and argumentative strategies, (4) the appeals to *ethos* and *pathos* in the argument, and (5) the argument's genre.

MyCompLab

The only online application to integrate a writing environment with proven resources for grammar, writing, and research, MyCompLab gives students help at their fingertips as they draft and revise. Instructors have access to a variety of assessment tools including commenting capabilities, diagnostics and study plans, and an e-portfolio. Created after years of extensive research and in partnership with faculty and students across the country, MyCompLab offers a seamless and flexible teaching and learning environment built specifically for writers.

Interactive Pearson eText

An e-Text version of *Writing Arguments,* Ninth Edition, is also available in MyCompLab. This dynamic online version of the text is integrated throughout MyCompLab to create an enriched, interactive learning experience for writing students.

CourseSmart

Students can subscribe to *Writing Arguments,* Ninth Edition, as a CourseSmart eText (at CourseSmart.com). The site includes all of the book's content in a format that enables students to search the text, bookmark passages, save their own notes, and print reading assignments that incorporate lecture notes.

Acknowledgments

We are happy for this opportunity to give public thanks to the scholars, teachers, and students who have influenced our approach to composition and argument. For this edition, we owe special thanks to our colleagues who helped us revise the anthology of *Writing Arguments:* Hilary Hawley and Anthony Warnke of Seattle University, Alison Cardinal and Kit Bean of South Seattle Community College, and Tamara Fish of the University of Houston. We also thank Stephen Bean for his research support on issues related to food and environmental politics.

We also want to thank our talented students who contributed their ideas, research, and time to this edition, especially Colleen Fontana for her writing of the new Rogerian letter on gun control legislation in Chapter 7; Chris Moore for his argument evaluating *The Daily Show* and *The Colbert Report* as good news shows; and Megan Johnson for her practical proposal on campus food options. Additionally, we are grateful to all our students whom we have been privileged to teach in our writing classes and to our other students who have enabled us to include their arguments in this text. Their insights and growth as writers have inspired our ongoing study of rhetoric and composition.

We thank too the many users of our texts who have given us encouragement about our successes and offered helpful suggestions for improvements. Particularly we thank the following scholars and teachers who reviewed this revision of *Writing Arguments* in its various stages: Kaye Brown, Owensboro Community and Technical College; Michael Callaway, Mesa Community College; Joyce A. A. Camper, Howard University; Jason Dockter, Lincoln Land Community College; Renee Field, Moberly Area Community College; April Gentry, Savannah State University; Kent Gordon, University of Central Oklahoma; Rachel C. Jackson, University of Oklahoma; Karla Saari Kitalong, Michigan Technological University; A. Abby Knoblauch, Kansas State University; Maria Anderson Knudtson, University of Nebraska at Omaha; Marsha A. Rutter, Southwestern College; Kay Siebler, Missouri Western State University; Paula Tran, University of Texas at San Antonio; and Theresa P. Trela, West Texas A&M University.

We are especially grateful to our editor, Lauren Finn, whose keen understanding of the needs of argument instructors and whose commitment to producing the most useful texts has guided us with her support and professional expertise. Finally, we owe our deepest thanks to Marion Castellucci, our development editor, without whom we could not maintain the pace and quality of our textbook revisions. Marion's invaluable mastery of both the big picture and the specific dimensions of this work and her calmness, encouragement, and wit have shepherded this project at every point.

As always, we want to conclude by thanking our families. John Bean thanks his wife, Kit, also a professional composition teacher, and his children Matthew, Andrew, Stephen, and Sarah, all of whom have grown to adulthood since he first began writing textbooks. Our lively conversations at family dinners, which now include spouses and grandchildren, have kept him engaged in arguments that matter about how to create a just, humane, and sustainable world. June Johnson thanks her husband, Kenneth Bube, a mathematics professor and researcher, and her daughter, Janie Bube, now viewing this text as a college student. Ken and Janie have played major roles in the ongoing family analysis of argumentation in the public sphere and of specific arguments on wide-ranging issues. They have also made it possible for her to meet the demands and challenges of continuing to infuse new ideas and material into this text in each revision.

John C. Bean
June Johnson

PART ONE
Overview of Argument

These stills from the film *Under the Same Moon* (2007) depict the painful separation and longing for connection of an immigrant mother in the United States and her young son, Carlitos, left behind in Mexico. The telephone booth and the furtive, precious calls symbolize the plight of families divided by economics and immigration policy. The film's appeals to our emotions are discussed in Michael Banks's exploratory essay in Chapter 2, pages 50–56.

1

Argument: An Introduction

At the outset of a book on argument, we ought to explain what an argument is. Instead, we're going to explain why no universally accepted definition is possible. Over the centuries, philosophers and rhetoricians have disagreed about the meaning of the term and about the goals that arguers should set for themselves. This opening chapter introduces you to some of these controversies.

We begin by asking what we mean by argument, suggesting what argument isn't as well as what it is. We then proceed to three defining features of argument: it requires writers or speakers to justify their claims, it is both a product and a process, and it combines elements of truth seeking and persuasion. Next, we explore more deeply the relationship between truth seeking and persuasion by asking questions about the nature of "truth" that arguments seek. Finally, we give you an example of a successful arguing process. Our goal is to show you various ways of thinking about argument as a way of helping you become a more powerful arguer yourself. In this chapter, you will learn to:

- Explain what argument is
- Describe the features of argument

What Do We Mean by Argument?

Let's begin by examining the inadequacies of two popular images of argument—fight and debate.

Argument Is Not a Fight or a Quarrel

To many, the word *argument* connotes anger and hostility, as when we say, "I just got in a huge argument with my roommate," or "My mother and I argue all the time." What we picture here is heated disagreement, rising pulse rates, and an urge to slam doors. Argument imagined as fight conjures images of shouting talk-show guests, flaming bloggers, or fist-banging speakers.

But to our way of thinking, argument doesn't imply anger. In fact, arguing is often pleasurable. It is a creative and productive activity that engages us at high levels of inquiry and critical thinking, often in conversation with people we like and respect. For your primary image of argument, we invite you to think not of a shouting match on cable news but of a small group of reasonable people seeking the best solution to a problem. We will return to this image throughout the chapter.

Argument Is Not Pro-Con Debate

Another popular image of argument is debate—a presidential debate, perhaps, or a high school or college debate tournament. According to one popular dictionary, *debate* is "a formal contest of argumentation in which two opposing teams defend and attack a given proposition." Although formal debate can develop critical thinking, its weakness is that it can turn argument into a game of winners and losers rather than a process of cooperative inquiry.

For an illustration of this weakness, consider one of our former students, a champion high school debater who spent his senior year debating the issue of prison reform. Throughout the year he argued for and against propositions such as "The United States should build more prisons" and "Innovative alternatives to prison should replace prison sentences for most crimes." We asked him, "What do you personally think is the best way to reform prisons?" He replied, "I don't know. I haven't thought about what I would actually choose."

Here was a bright, articulate student who had studied prisons extensively for a year. Yet nothing in the atmosphere of pro-con debate had engaged him in truth-seeking inquiry. He could argue for and against a proposition, but he hadn't experienced the wrenching process of clarifying his own values and taking a personal stand. As we explain throughout this text, argument entails a desire for truth; it aims to find the best solutions to complex problems. We don't mean that arguers don't passionately support their own points of view or expose weaknesses in views they find faulty. Instead, we mean that their goal isn't to win a game but to find and promote the best belief or course of action.

Arguments Can Be Explicit or Implicit

Before proceeding to some defining features of argument, we should note also that arguments can be either explicit or implicit. An *explicit* argument directly states its controversial claim and supports it with reasons and evidence. An *implicit* argument, in contrast, may not look like an argument at all. It may be a bumper sticker, a billboard, a poster, a photograph, a cartoon, a vanity license plate, a slogan on a T-shirt, an advertisement, a poem, or a song lyric. But like an explicit argument, it persuades its audience toward a certain point of view.

Consider the striking photograph in Figure 1.1—a baby wearing a bib labeled "POISON." This photograph enters a conversation about the safety of toys and other baby products sold in the United States. In recent years, fears about toy safety have come mostly from two sources: the discovery that many toys imported from China contained lead paint and the discovery that a substance used to make plastics pliable and soft—called *phthalates* (pronounced "thalates")—may be harmful. Phthalates have been shown to interfere with hormone production in rat fetuses and, based on other rodent studies, may produce some kinds of cancers and other ailments. Because many baby products contain phthalates—bibs, edges of cribs, rubber duckies, and any

FIGURE 1.1 An implicit argument against phthalates

number of other soft, rubbery toys—parents worry that babies can ingest phthalates by chewing on these toys.

The photograph of the baby and bib makes the argumentative claim that baby products are poisonous; the photograph implicitly urges viewers to take action against phthalates. But this photograph is just one voice in a surprisingly complex conversation. Is the bib in fact poisonous? Such questions were debated during a recent campaign to ban the sale of toys containing phthalates in California. A legislative initiative sparked intense lobbying from both child-advocacy groups and representatives of the toy industry. At issue were a number of scientific questions about the risk posed by phthalates. To what extent do studies on rats apply to humans? How much exposure to phthalates should be considered dangerous? (Experiments on rats used large amounts of phthalates—amounts that, according to many scientists, far exceed anything a baby could absorb by chewing on a toy.) Also at issue is the level of health risks a free market society should be willing to tolerate. The European Union, operating on the "precautionary principle," and citing evidence that such toys *might* be dangerous, has banned toys containing phthalates. The U.S. government sets less strict standards than does the European Union. A federal agency generally doesn't ban a substance unless it has been *proven* harmful to humans, not merely suspected of being harmful. In defense of free markets, the toy and chemical industries accused opponents of phthalates of using "junk science" to produce scary but inaccurate data.

Our point in summarizing the toxic toy controversy is to demonstrate the persuasive roles of both implicit and explicit arguments.

In contrast to the implicit argument made in Figure 1.1, Dr. Louis W. Sullivan, who was secretary of health and human services under the Clinton administration, makes an explicit argument in a letter to the governor of California. Sullivan opposes the bill banning phthalates, claiming that scientific agencies charged with public safety haven't found phthalates harmful. Instead, he supports an alternative "Green Chemistry Initiative" that would make public policy decisions based on "facts, not fear."

Let the Facts Decide, Not Fear: Ban AB 1108

LOUIS W. SULLIVAN, M.D.

Dear Governor Schwarzenegger:

As a physician and public servant who has worked in the field of medicine and public health all my life, I am writing to urge your veto of AB 1108, a bill that would ban the use of compounds used to make vinyl toys and childcare products soft and flexible. AB 1108 widely misses the mark on the most fundamental underpinning of all good public health policy—sound science.

AB 1108 ignores a recent, comprehensive review of the safety of vinyl toys conducted by the U.S. Consumer Product Safety Commission. The CPSC took a long, hard look at the primary softener used in children's toys and concluded that vinyl toys containing this compound are safe as used. In fact, its experts warned that using substitutes could make toys more brittle and less safe.

The CPSC's conclusions are reinforced by the findings of many scientific bodies around the globe—including the European Union's European Chemicals Bureau, the U.S. National Toxicology Program, and the U.S. Centers for Disease Control and Prevention. At a time when public officials are trying to deal with the serious issue of lead paint in toys imported from China, California lawmakers should not confuse the safety of these softening compounds in vinyl toys with that issue. Signing AB 1108 will do nothing to resolve the lead paint in toys issue.

California needs public health policies based on science. That's why I resoundingly support your Green Chemistry Initiative. This is a coordinated, comprehensive strategy for addressing possible risk from products—in a holistic, science-based fashion—that would serve the interests of California families and their children.

5   I urge you to reject AB 1108 and allow your health and safety experts, not legislators, to make judgments about the chemicals in our environment—based on facts, not fear.

Sincerely,

Louis W. Sullivan, M.D.
U.S. Secretary of Health & Human Services 1989–1993
President Emeritus, Morehouse School of Medicine

■ ■ ■ **FOR CLASS DISCUSSION**   Implicit and Explicit Arguments

1. Any argument, whether implicit or explicit, tries to influence the audience's stance on an issue, moving the audience toward the arguer's claim. Arguments work on us psychologically as well as cognitively, triggering emotions as well as thoughts and ideas. How would you describe the differences in the way that the photograph with the bib labeled "poison" (Figure 1.1) and the letter from Sullivan "work on us"?

2. Assume that you are explaining implicit arguments to an international exchange student who is not yet familiar with U.S. politics and popular culture. Each of the implicit arguments in Figures 1.2–1.6 makes a claim on its audience, trying to get viewers to adopt the arguer's position, perspective, belief, or point of view on an issue. For each argument, answer the following questions for your new international friend:

   a. What conversation does this argument join? What is the issue or controversy? What is at stake?

   b. What is the argument's claim? That is, what value, perspective, belief, or position does the argument ask its viewers to adopt?

   c. What is an opposing or alternative view? What views is the argument pushing against?

   d. How does the argument try to do its work on the brains or hearts of the audience?

FIGURE 1.2 These colors don't run

FIGURE 1.3 These colors don't run the world

FIGURE 1.4 Assisted suicide isn't "natural"

FIGURE 1.5 The climate change controversy

FIGURE 1.6 Arizona tan block

The Defining Features of Argument

We turn now to examine arguments in more detail. (Unless we say otherwise, by *argument* we mean explicit arguments that attempt to supply reasons and evidence to support their claims.) This section examines three defining features of such arguments.

Argument Requires Justification of Its Claims

To begin defining argument, let's turn to a humble but universal site of disagreement: the conflict between a parent and a teenager over rules. In what way and in what circumstances do such conflicts constitute arguments?

Consider the following dialogue:

YOUNG PERSON (*racing for the front door while putting coat on*):   Bye. See you later.

PARENT: Whoa! What time are you planning on coming home?

YOUNG PERSON (*coolly, hand still on doorknob*):   I'm sure we discussed this earlier. I'll be home around 2 A.M. (*The second sentence, spoken very rapidly, is barely audible.*)

PARENT (*mouth tightening*):   We did *not* discuss this earlier and you're *not* staying out till two in the morning. You'll be home at twelve.

At this point in the exchange, we have a quarrel, not an argument. Quarrelers exchange antagonistic assertions without any attempt to support them rationally. If the dialogue never gets past the "Yes-you-will/No-I-won't" stage, it either remains a quarrel or degenerates into a fight.

Let us say, however, that the dialogue takes the following turn:

YOUNG PERSON (*tragically*):   But I'm *sixteen years old!*

Now we're moving toward argument. Not, to be sure, a particularly well-developed or cogent one, but an argument all the same. It's now an argument because one of the quarrelers has offered a reason for her assertion. Her choice of curfew is satisfactory, she says, *because* she is sixteen years old, an argument that depends on the unstated assumption that sixteen-year-olds are old enough to make decisions about such matters.

The parent can now respond in one of several ways that will either advance the argument or turn it back into a quarrel. The parent can simply invoke parental authority ("I don't care—you're still coming home at twelve"), in which case argument ceases. Or the parent can provide a reason for his or her view ("You will be home at twelve because your dad and I pay the bills around here!"), in which case the argument takes a new turn.

So far we've established two necessary conditions that must be met before we're willing to call something an argument: (1) a set of two or more conflicting assertions and (2) the attempt to resolve the conflict through an appeal to reason.

But good argument demands more than meeting these two formal requirements. For the argument to be effective, an arguer is obligated to clarify and support the reasons presented. For example, "But I'm sixteen years old!" is not yet a clear support for the assertion "I should be allowed to set my own curfew." On the surface, Young Person's argument seems absurd. Her parent, of all people, knows precisely how old she is. What makes it an argument is that behind her claim lies an unstated assumption—all sixteen-year-olds are old enough to set their own curfews. What Young Person needs to do now is to support that assumption.* In doing so, she must anticipate the sorts of questions the assumption will raise in the minds of her parent: What is the legal status of sixteen-year-olds? How psychologically mature, as opposed to chronologically mature, is Young Person? What is the actual track record of Young Person in being responsible? and so forth. Each of these questions will force Young Person to reexamine and clarify her assumptions about the proper degree of autonomy for sixteen-year-olds. And her responses to those questions should in turn force the parents to reexamine their assumptions about the dependence of sixteen-year-olds on parental guidance and wisdom. (Likewise, the parents will need to show why "paying the bills around here" automatically gives them the right to set Young Person's curfew.)

As the argument continues, Young Person and Parent may shift to a different line of reasoning. For example, Young Person might say: "I should be allowed to stay out until 2 A.M. because all my friends get to stay out that late." (Here the unstated assumption is that the rules in this family ought to be based on the rules in other families.) The parent might in turn respond, "But I certainly never stayed out that late when I was your age"—an argument assuming that the rules in this family should follow the rules of an earlier generation.

As Young Person and Parent listen to each other's points of view (and begin realizing why their initial arguments have not persuaded their intended audience), both parties find themselves in the uncomfortable position of having to examine their own beliefs and to justify assumptions that they have taken for granted. Here we encounter one of the earliest meanings of the term *to argue,* which is "to clarify." As an arguer begins to clarify her own position on an issue, she also begins to clarify her audience's position. Such clarification helps the arguer see how she might accommodate her audience's views, perhaps by adjusting her own position or by developing reasons that appeal to her audience's values. Thus Young Person might suggest an argument like this:

> I should be allowed to stay out until two on a trial basis because I need enough freedom to demonstrate my maturity and show you I won't get into trouble.

The assumption underlying this argument is that it is good to give teenagers freedom to demonstrate their maturity. Because this reason is likely to appeal to her parent's own values (the parent wants to see his or her daughter grow in maturity) and because it is tempered by the qualifier "on a trial basis" (which reduces

---

*Later in this text we will call the assumption underlying a line of reasoning its *warrant* (see Chapter 4).

some of the threat of Young Person's initial demands), it may prompt productive discussion.

Whether or not Young Person and Parent can work out a best solution, the preceding scenario illustrates how argument leads people to clarify their reasons and provide justifications that can be examined rationally. The scenario also illustrates two specific aspects of argument that we will explore in detail in the next sections: (1) Argument is both a process and a product. (2) Argument combines truth seeking and persuasion.

Argument Is Both a Process and a Product

As the preceding scenario revealed, argument can be viewed as a *process* in which two or more parties seek the best solution to a question or problem. Argument can also be viewed as a *product,* each product being any person's contribution to the conversation at a given moment. In an informal discussion, the products are usually short, whatever time a person uses during his or her turns in the conversation. Under more formal settings, an orally delivered product might be a short, impromptu speech (say, during an open-mike discussion of a campus issue) or a longer, carefully prepared formal speech (as in a PowerPoint presentation at a business meeting or an argument at a public hearing for or against a proposed city project).

Similar conversations occur in writing. Roughly analogous to a small-group discussion is an exchange of the kind that occurs regularly online through informal chat groups or more formal blog sites. In an online discussion, participants have more thinking time to shape their messages than they do in a real-time oral discussion. Nevertheless, messages are usually short and informal, making it possible over the course of several days to see participants' ideas shift and evolve as conversants modify their initial views in response to others' views.

Roughly equivalent to a formal speech would be a formal written argument, which may take the form of an academic argument for a college course; a grant proposal; an online posting; a guest column for the op-ed* section of a newspaper; a legal brief; a letter to a member of Congress; or an article for an organizational newsletter, popular magazine, or professional journal. In each of these instances, the written argument (a product) enters a conversation (a process)—in this case, a conversation of readers, many of whom will carry on the conversation by writing their own responses or by discussing the writer's views with others. The goal of the community of writers and readers is to find the best solution to the problem or issue under discussion.

Op-ed stands for "opposite-editorial." It is the generic name in journalism for a signed argument that voices the writer's opinion on an issue, as opposed to a news story that is supposed to report events objectively, uncolored by the writer's personal views. Op-ed pieces appear in the editorial-opinion section of newspapers, which generally features editorials by the resident staff, opinion pieces by syndicated columnists, and letters to the editor from readers. The term *op-ed* is often extended to syndicated columns appearing in newsmagazines, advocacy Web sites, and online news services.

Argument Combines Truth Seeking and Persuasion

In thinking about argument as a product, the writer will find herself continually moving back and forth between truth seeking and persuasion—that is, between questions about the subject matter (What is the best solution to this problem?) and about audience (What do my readers already believe or value? What reasons and evidence will most persuade them?). Back and forth she'll weave, alternately absorbed in the subject of her argument and in the audience for that argument.

Neither of the two focuses is ever completely out of mind, but their relative importance shifts during different phases of the development of a paper. Moreover, different rhetorical situations place different emphases on truth seeking versus persuasion. We could thus place arguments on a kind of continuum that measures the degree of attention a writer gives to subject matter versus audience. (See Figure 1.7.) At the far truth-seeking end of the continuum might be an exploratory piece that lays out several alternative approaches to a problem and weighs the strengths and weaknesses of each with no concern for persuasion. At the other end of the continuum would be outright propaganda, such as a political campaign advertisement that reduces a complex issue to sound bites and distorts an opponent's position through out-of-context quotations or misleading use of data. (At its most blatant, propaganda obliterates truth seeking; it will do anything, including the knowing use of bogus evidence, distorted assertions, and outright lies, to win over an audience.) In the middle ranges of the continuum, writers shift their focuses back and forth between truth seeking and persuasion but with varying degrees of emphasis.

As an example of a writer focusing primarily on truth seeking, consider the case of Kathleen, who, in her college argument course, addressed the definitional question "Is American Sign Language (ASL) a 'foreign language' for purposes of meeting the university's foreign language requirement?" Kathleen had taken two years of ASL at a community college. When she transferred to a four-year college, the chair of the foreign languages department at her new college would not allow her ASL proficiency to count for the foreign language requirement. ASL isn't a "language," the chair said summarily. "It's not equivalent to learning French, German, or Japanese."

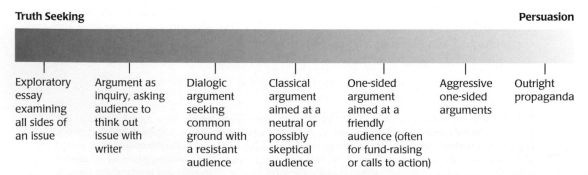

FIGURE 1.7 Continuum of arguments from truth seeking to persuasion

Kathleen disagreed, so she immersed herself in developing her argument. While doing research, she focused almost entirely on subject matter, searching for what linguists, neurologists, cognitive psychologists, and sociologists had said about the language of deaf people. Immersed in her subject matter, she was only tacitly concerned with her audience, whom she thought of primarily as her classmates and the professor of her argument class—people who were friendly to her views and interested in her experiences with the deaf community. She wrote a well-documented paper, citing several scholarly articles, that made a good case to her classmates (and the professor) that ASL is indeed a distinct language.

Proud of the big red A the professor had placed on her paper, Kathleen decided for a subsequent assignment to write a second paper on ASL—but this time aiming it directly at the chair of foreign languages and petitioning him to accept her ASL proficiency for the foreign language requirement. Now her writing task fell closer to the persuasive end of our continuum. Kathleen once again immersed herself in research, but this time focused not on subject matter (whether ASL is a distinct language) but on audience. She researched the history of the foreign language requirement at her college and discovered some of the politics behind it (an old foreign language requirement had been dropped in the 1970s and reinstituted in the 1990s, partly—a math professor told her—to boost enrollments in foreign language courses). She also interviewed foreign language teachers to find out what they knew and didn't know about ASL. She discovered that many teachers thought ASL was "easy to learn," so that accepting ASL would allow students a Mickey Mouse way to avoid the rigors of a "real" foreign language class. Additionally, she learned that foreign language teachers valued immersing students in a foreign culture; in fact, the foreign language requirement was part of her college's effort to create a multicultural curriculum.

This new understanding of her target audience helped Kathleen reconceptualize her argument. Her claim that ASL is a real language (the subject of her first paper) became only one section of her second paper, much condensed and abridged. She added sections showing the difficulty of learning ASL (to counter her audience's belief that learning ASL is easy), showing how the deaf community forms a distinct culture with its own customs and literature (to show how ASL would meet the goals of multiculturalism), and showing that the number of transfer students with ASL credits would be negligibly small (to allay fears that accepting ASL would threaten enrollments in language classes). She ended her argument with an appeal to her college's public emphasis (declared boldly in its mission statement) on eradicating social injustice and reaching out to the oppressed. She described the isolation of deaf people in a world where almost no hearing people learn ASL, and she argued that the deaf community on her campus could be integrated more fully into campus life if more students could "talk" with them. Thus the ideas included in her new argument— the reasons selected, the evidence used, the arrangement and tone—all were determined by her primary focus on persuasion.

Our point, then, is that all along the continuum, writers attempt both to seek truth and to persuade, but not necessarily with equal balance. Kathleen could not have written her second paper, aimed specifically at persuading the chair of foreign languages, if she hadn't first immersed herself in truth-seeking research that convinced her that ASL is indeed a distinct language. Nor are we saying that her second argument was better than her first. Both fulfilled their purposes and met the needs of their intended audiences. Both involved truth seeking and persuasion, but the first focused primarily on subject matter whereas the second focused primarily on audience.

Argument and the Problem of Truth

The tension that we have just examined between truth seeking and persuasion raises an ancient issue in the field of argument: Is the arguer's first obligation to truth or to winning the argument? And just what is the nature of the truth to which arguers are supposed to be obligated?

In Plato's famous dialogues from ancient Greek philosophy, these questions were at the heart of Socrates' disagreement with the Sophists. The Sophists were professional rhetoricians who specialized in training orators to win arguments. Socrates, who valued truth seeking over persuasion and believed that truth could be discovered through philosophic inquiry, opposed the Sophists. For Socrates, Truth resided in the ideal world of forms, and through philosophic rigor humans could transcend the changing, shadowlike world of everyday reality to perceive the world of universals where Truth, Beauty, and Goodness resided. Through his method of questioning his interlocutors, Socrates would gradually peel away layer after layer of false views until Truth was revealed. The good person's duty, Socrates believed, was not to win an argument but to pursue this higher Truth. Socrates distrusted rhetoricians because they were interested only in the temporal power and wealth that came from persuading audiences to the orator's views.

Let's apply Socrates' disagreement with the Sophists to a modern instance. Suppose your community is divided over the issue of raising environmental standards versus keeping open a job-producing factory that doesn't meet new guidelines for waste discharge. The Sophists would train you to argue any side of this issue on behalf of any lobbying group willing to pay for your services. If, however, you followed the spirit of Socrates, you would be inspired to listen to all sides of the dispute, peel away false arguments, discover the Truth through reasonable inquiry, and commit yourself to a Right Course of Action.

But what is the nature of Truth or Right Action in a dispute between jobs and the environment? The Sophists believed that truth was determined by those in power; thus they could enter an argument unconstrained by any transcendent beliefs or assumptions. When Socrates talked about justice and virtue, the Sophists could reply contemptuously that these were fictitious concepts invented by the weak to protect themselves from the strong. Over the years, the Sophists' relativist beliefs became so repugnant to people that the term *sophistry* became synonymous with trickery in argument.

However, in recent years the Sophists' critique of a transcendent Universal Truth has been taken seriously by many philosophers, sociologists, and other thinkers who doubt Socrates' confident belief that arguments, properly conducted, necessarily arrive at a single Truth. For these thinkers, as for the Sophists, there are often different de-grees of truth and different kinds of truths for different situations or cultures. From this perspective, when we consider questions of interpretation or value, we can never demonstrate that a belief or assumption is true—not through scientific observation, not through reason, and not through religious revelation. We get our beliefs, according to these contemporary thinkers, from the shared assumptions of our particular cultures. We are condemned (or liberated) to live in a pluralistic, multicultural world with com-peting visions of truth.

If we accept this pluralistic view of the world, do we then endorse the Sophists' radical relativism, freeing us to argue any side of any issue? Or do we doggedly pursue some modern equivalent of Socrates' truth?

Our own sympathies are with Socrates, but we admit to a view of truth that is more tentative, cautious, and conflicted than his. For us, truth seeking does not mean finding the "Right Answer" to a disputed question, but neither does it mean a valueless relativism in which all answers are equally good. For us, truth seeking means taking responsibility for determining the "best answer" or "best solution" to the question for the good of the whole community when taking into consideration the interests of all stakeholders. It means making hard decisions in the face of uncertainty. This more ten-tative view of truth means that you cannot use argument to "prove" your claim, but only to make a reasonable case for your claim. One contemporary philosopher says that argument can hope only to "increase adherence" to ideas, not absolutely convince an audience of the necessary truth of ideas. Even though you can't be certain, in a Socratic sense, that your solution to the problem is the best one available, you must ethically take responsibility for the consequences of your claim and you must seek jus-tice for stakeholders beyond yourself. You must, in other words, forge a personal stance based on your examination of all the evidence and your articulation of values that you can make public and defend.

To seek truth, then, means to seek the best or most just solution to a problem while observing all available evidence, listening with an open mind to the views of all stakeholders, clarifying and attempting to justify your own values and assump-tions, and taking responsibility for your argument. It follows that truth seeking often means delaying closure on an issue, acknowledging the pressure of alternative views, and being willing to change one's mind. Seen in this way, learning to argue effec-tively has the deepest sort of social value: It helps communities settle conflicts in a rational and humane way by finding, through the dialectic exchange of ideas, the best solutions to problems without resorting to violence or to other assertions of raw power.

■ ■ ■ ■ **FOR CLASS DISCUSSION** Role-Playing Arguments

On any given day, the media provides evidence of the complexity of living in a plural-istic culture. Issues that could be readily decided in a completely homogeneous culture raise questions in a society that has fewer shared assumptions. Choose one of the following cases as the subject for a "simulation game" in which class members present the points of view of the people involved.

Case 1: College Athletes Caught in Tangled Web

As the following newspaper excerpt shows, social networking Web sites such as Facebook create conflicts between free speech and the reputations of people and institutions in the public domain.

> College students across the country have been cited or disciplined for content they posted on social networking Web sites such as MySpace and Facebook, including such things as criticism of a student government candidate (at the University of Central Florida), complaints about the theater department (Cowley College in Kansas), or vulgar comments about a teaching assistant (Syracuse).
>
> "College administrators are very nervous about this huge new forum," said Greg Lukianoff, president of the Foundation for Individual Rights in Education.
>
> The most nervous of those might be coaches and athletic directors, whose student-athletes are under a more intense public spotlight than the general student body and who usually are required to adhere to more stringent policies and rules of conduct. One distasteful picture of a prominent football player on the Internet could be seen by anybody and might end up on the front page of a newspaper. It's why some athletic departments have stricter policies about such sites and restrict usage as part of individual team rules.

Your task: Imagine an open meeting on your campus on the issue of students' free speech rights versus the rights of your college or university and its athletic departments to establish rules and monitor students' online social network pages. Hold a meeting in which classmates play the following roles: (a) a student athlete who has been warned to remove from his Facebook profile a photograph of himself chugging beer at fraternity party; (b) students who are not on athletic teams but are concerned about institutionally imposed restrictions on students' freedom; (c) a faculty member who feels he has been libeled on a former student's Facebook page; (d) a women's basketball coach who forbids student athletes on her teams from having personal online social networking accounts; (e) a tennis coach who establishes clear team policies for postings on students' sites; (f) the athletic director, who is considering buying tracking technology to monitor athletes' online social networking pages; (g) a representative of the American Civil Liberties Union who supports student rights and free speech; and (h) the dean of students, who is concerned for the reputation of the institution and for the future well-being of students who might be embarrassed by current postings or endangered by disclosing too much personal information.

Case 2: Homeless Hit the Streets to Protest Proposed Ban

> The homeless stood up for themselves by sitting down in a peaceful but vocal protest yesterday in [name of city].
>
> About 50 people met at noon to criticize a proposed set of city ordinances that would ban panhandlers from sitting on sidewalks, put them in jail for repeatedly urinating in public, and crack down on "intimidating" street behavior.
>
> "Sitting is not a crime," read poster boards that feature mug shots of [the city attorney] who is pushing for the new laws. [...] "This is city property; the police want to tell us we can't sit here," yelled one man named R. C. as he sat cross-legged outside a pizza establishment.

Your task: Imagine a public hearing seeking reactions to the proposed city ordinance. Hold a mock hearing in which classmates play the following roles: (a) a homeless person; (b) an annoyed merchant; (c) a shopper who avoids places with homeless people; (d) a citizen advocate for the homeless; (e) the city attorney.

A Successful Process of Argumentation: The Well-Functioning Committee

We have said that neither the fist-banging speaker nor the college debate team represents our ideal image of argument. The best image for us, as we have implied, is a well-functioning small group seeking a solution to a problem. In professional life such small groups usually take the form of committees.

We use the word *committee* in its broadest sense to indicate all sorts of important work that grows out of group conversation and debate. The Declaration of Independence is essentially a committee document with Thomas Jefferson as the chair. Similarly, the U.S. Supreme Court is in effect a committee of nine judges who rely heavily, as numerous books and articles have demonstrated, on small-group decision-making processes to reach their judgments and formulate their legal briefs.

To illustrate our committee or small-group model for argument, let's briefly consider the workings of a university committee on which coauthor John Ramage once served, the University Standards Committee. The Arizona State University (ASU) Standards Committee plays a role in university life analogous to that of the Supreme Court in civic life. It's the final court of appeal for ASU students seeking exceptions to various rules that govern their academic lives (such as registering under a different catalog, waiving a required course, or being allowed to retake a course for the third time).

The issues that regularly come before the committee draw forth all the argument types and strategies discussed throughout this text. For example, the different argument claim types discussed in Part Four regularly surface during committee deliberations, as shown in the following list:

- **Definition issues:** Is math anxiety a "learning disability" for purposes of exempting a student from a math requirement?
- **Resemblance issues:** How is this case similar to a case from the same department that we considered last semester?
- **Cause/consequence issues:** What were the causes of this student's sudden poor performance during spring semester? What will be the consequences of approving or denying her appeal?
- **Evaluation issues:** What criteria need to be met before we allow a student to graduate under a previous catalog?
- **Proposal issues:** Should we make it a policy to allow course X to substitute for course Y in the General Studies requirements?

On any given day, the committee's deliberations show how dialogue can lead to clarification of thinking. On many occasions, committee members' initial views shift as they study the specifics of individual cases and listen to opposing arguments from their colleagues. What allows this committee to function as well as it does is the fundamental civility of its members and their collective concern that their decisions be just. Because of the importance of these decisions to students' lives, committee members are willing to concede a point to another member in the name of reaching a better decision and to view the deliberations as an ongoing process of negotiation rather than a series of win-lose debates.

To give you firsthand experience at using argument as a process of clarification, we conclude this chapter with an actual case that came before the University Standards Committee in the early 1990s, when Ramage was a member of the committee. We invite you to read the following letter, pretending that you are a member of the University Standards Committee, and then proceed to the exercises that follow.

Petition to Waive the University Mathematics Requirement

Standards Committee Members,

I am a 43-year-old member of the Pawnee Tribe of Oklahoma and a very nontraditional student currently pursuing Justice Studies at the Arizona State University (ASU) College of Public Programs. I entered college as the first step toward completion of my goal—becoming legal counsel for my tribe, and statesman.

I come before this committee in good faith to request that ASU suspend, in my special case, its mathematics requirement for undergraduate degree completion so I may enter the ASU college of Law during Fall 1993. The point I wish to make to this committee is this: I do not need algebraic skills; I will never use algebra in my intended profession; and, if forced to comply with ASU's algebra requirement, I will be needlessly prevented from graduating in time to enter law school next fall and face an idle academic year before my next opportunity in 1994. I will address each of these points in turn, but a few words concerning my academic credentials are in order first.

Two years ago, I made a vow of moral commitment to seek out and confront injustice. In September of 1990, I enrolled in college. Although I had only the benefit of a ninth grade education, I took the General Equivalency Diploma (GED) examination and placed in the top ten percent of those, nationwide, who took the test. On the basis of this score I was accepted into Scottsdale Community College (SCC). This step made me the first in my entire family, and practically in my tribe, to enter college. During my first year at SCC I maintained a 4.0 GPA, I was placed on the President's list twice, was active in the Honors Program, received the Honors Award of Merit in English Humanities, and was conferred an Honors Scholarship (see attached) for the Academic year of 1991–1992 which I declined, opting to enroll in ASU instead.

At the beginning of the 1991 summer semester, I transferred to ASU. I chose to graduate from ASU because of the courses offered in American Indian studies, an important field ignored by most other Universities but necessary to my commitment. At ASU I currently maintain a 3.6 GPA, although my cumulative GPA is closer to 3.9, I am a member of the Honors and Justice Colleges, was appointed to the Dean's List, and awarded ASU's prestigious Maroon and Gold Scholarship twice. My academic standing is impeccable. I will enter the ASU College of Law to study Indian and criminal law during the Fall of 1993—if this petition is approved. Upon successful completion of my juris doctorate I will return to Oklahoma to become active in the administration of Pawnee tribal affairs as tribal attorney and advisor, and vigorously prosecute our right to sovereignty before the Congress of the United States.

5   When I began my "college experience," I set a rigid time schedule for the completion of my goal. By the terms of that self-imposed schedule, founded in my belief that I have already wasted many productive years, I allowed myself thirty-five months in which to achieve my Bachelor of Science degree in Justice Studies, for indeed justice is my concern, and another thirty-six months in which to earn my juris doctorate—summa cum laude. Consistent with my approach to all endeavors, I fell upon this task with zeal. I have willingly assumed the burden of carrying substantial academic loads during fall, spring and summer semesters. My problem now lies in the fact that in order to satisfy the University's math requirement to graduate I must still take MAT-106 and MAT-117. I submit that these mathematics courses are irrelevant to my goals, and present a barrier to my fall matriculation into law school.

Upon consideration of my dilemma, the questions emerged: Why do I need college algebra (MAT-117)? Is college algebra necessary for studying American Indian law? Will I use college algebra in my chosen field? What will the University gain or lose, from my taking college algebra—or not? I decided I should resolve these questions.

I began my inquiry with the question: "Why do I need college algebra (MAT-117)?" I consulted Mr. Jim _____ of the Justice College and presented this question to him. He referred to the current ASU catalog and delineated the following answer: I need college algebra (1) for a minimum level of math competency in my chosen field, and (2) to satisfy the university math requirement in order to graduate. My reply to the first answer is this: I already possess ample math skills, both practical and academic; and, I have no need for algebra in my chosen field. How do I know this? During the spring 1992 semester at ASU I successfully completed introductory algebra (MAT-077), scoring the highest class grade on one test (see attached transcript and test). More noteworthy is the fact that I was a machine and welding contractor for fifteen years. I used geometry and algebra commonly in the design of many welded structures. I am proficient in the use of Computer Assisted Design (CAD) programs, designing and drawing all my own blueprints for jobs. My blueprints and designs are always approved by city planning departments. For example, my most recent job consisted of the manufacture, transportation and installation of one linear mile of anodized, aluminum handrailing at a luxury resort condo on Maui, Hawaii. I applied extensive use of math to calculate the amount of raw materials to order, the logistics of mass production and transportation for both men and materials from Mesa to Maui, the job site installation itself, and cash flow. I have successfully completed many jobs of this nature—all without a mathematical hitch. As to the application of math competency in my chosen field, I can guarantee this committee that there will not be a time in my practice of Indian law that I will need algebra. If an occasion ever occurs that I need algebra, I will hire a mathematician, just as I would an engineer if I need engineering, or a surgeon if I need an operation.

I then contacted Dr. _____ of the ASU Mathematics Department and presented him with the same question: "Why do I need college algebra?" He replied: (1) for a well rounded education; (2) to develop creative thinking; and (3) to satisfy the university math requirement in order to graduate. Responding to the first answer, I have a "well rounded education." My need is for a specific education in justice and American Indian law. In fact, I do not really need the degree to practice Indian law as representative of my tribe, just the knowledge. Regarding the second, I do not need to develop my creative thinking. It has been honed to a keen edge for many years. For example, as a steel contractor, I commonly create huge, beautiful and intricate structures from raw materials. Contracting is not my only experience in creative thinking. For twenty-five years I have also enjoyed the status of being one of this country's foremost designers and builders of racebikes. Machines I have designed and brought into existence from my imagination have topped some of Japan and Europe's best engineering efforts. To illustrate this point, in 1984 I rode a bike of my own design to an international victory over Honda, Suzuki, Laverda, BMW and Yamaha. I have excelled at creative thinking my entire life—I called it survival.

Expanding on the question of why I need college algebra, I contacted a few friends who are practicing attorneys. All responded to my question in similar manner. One, Mr. Billy _____, Esq., whose law firm is in Tempe, answered my two questions as follows: "When you attended law school, were there any courses you took which required algebra?" His response was "no." "Have you ever needed algebra during the many years of your practice?" Again, his response was "no." All agreed there was not a single occasion when they had need for algebra in their professional careers.

10   Just to make sure of my position, I contacted the ASU College of Law, and among others, spoke to Ms. Sierra _____. I submitted the question "What law school courses will I encounter in which I will need algebra?" The unanimous reply was, they knew of none.

I am not proposing that the number of credit hours I need for graduation be lowered. In fact, I am more than willing to substitute another course or two in its place. I am not trying to get out of anything hard or distasteful, for that is certainly not my style. I am seeking only to dispose of an unnecessary item in my studies, one which will prevent me from entering law school this fall—breaking my stride. So little holds up so much.

I agree that a young adult directly out of high school may not know that he needs algebraic skills. Understandably, he does not know what his future holds—but I am not that young adult. I claim the advantage. I know precisely what my future holds and that future holds no possibility of my needing college algebra.

Physically confronting injustice is my end. On reservations where government apathy allows rapacious pedophiles to pose as teachers; in a country where a million and a half American Indians are held hostage as second rate human beings whose despair results in a suicide, alcohol and drug abuse rate second to no other people; in prisons where helpless inmates are beaten like dogs by sadistic guards who should be the inmates—this is the realm of my chosen field—the disenfranchised. In this netherworld, algebra and justice exist independently of one another.

In summary, I am convinced that I do not need college algebra for a minimum level of math competency in my chosen field. I do not need college algebra for a well rounded education, nor to develop my creative thinking. I do not need algebra to take the LSAT. I do not need algebra for any courses in law school, nor will I for any purpose in the practice of American Indian law. It remains only that I need college algebra in order to graduate.

15 I promise this committee that ASU's integrity will not be compromised in any way by approving this waiver. Moreover, I assure this committee that despite not having a formal accreditation in algebra, I will prove to be nothing less than an asset to this University and its Indian community, both to which I belong, and I will continue to set a standard for integrity, excellence and perseverance for all who follow. Therefore, I ask this committee, for all the reasons described above, to approve and initiate the waiver of my University mathematics requirement.

[Signed] Gordon Adams

■ ■ ■ **FOR CLASS DISCUSSION** Responding to Adams's Argument

1. Before class discussion, decide how you would vote on this issue. Should this student be exempted from the math requirement? Write out the reasons for your decision.
2. Working in small groups or as a whole class, pretend that you are the University Standards Committee, and arrive at a group decision on whether to exempt this student from the math requirement.
3. After the discussion, write for five to ten minutes in a journal or notebook describing how your thinking evolved during the discussion. Did any of your classmates' views cause you to rethink your own? Class members should share with each other their descriptions of how the process of argument led to clarification of their own thinking.

We designed this exercise to help you experience argument as a clarifying process. But we had another purpose. We also designed the exercise to stimulate thinking about a problem we introduced at the beginning of this chapter: the difference between argument as clarification and argument as persuasion. Is a good argument necessarily a persuasive argument? In our opinion, this student's letter to the committee is a *good* argument. The student writes well, takes a clear stand, offers good reasons for his position, and supports his reasons with effective evidence. To what extent, however, is the letter a *persuasive* argument? Did it win its case? You know how you and your classmates stand on this issue. But what do you think the University Standards Committee at ASU actually decided during its deliberations?

We will return to this case in Chapter 4.

Conclusion

In this chapter we have explored some of the complexities of argument, showing you why we believe that argument is a matter not of fist banging or of win-lose debate but of finding, through a process of rational inquiry, the best solution to a problem or issue. What is our advice for you at the close of this introductory chapter? Briefly, to see the purpose of argument as truth seeking as well as persuasion. We suggest that throughout the process of argument you seek out a wide range of views, that you especially welcome views different from your own, that you treat these views respectfully, and that you see them as intelligent and rationally defensible. (Hence you must look carefully at the reasons and evidence on which they are based.)

Our goal in this text is to help you learn skills of argument. If you choose, you can use these skills, like the Sophists, to argue any side of any issue. Yet we hope you won't. We hope that, like Socrates, you will use argument for truth seeking and that you will consequently find yourself, on at least some occasions, changing your position on an issue while writing a rough draft (a sure sign that the process of arguing has complicated your views). We believe that the skills of reason and inquiry developed through the writing of arguments can help you get a clearer sense of who you are. If our culture sets you adrift in pluralism, argument can help you take a stand, to say, "These things I believe." In this text we will not pretend to tell you what position to take on any given issue. But as a responsible being, you will often need to take a stand, to define yourself, to say, "Here are the reasons that choice A is better than choice B, not just for me but for you also." If this text helps you base your commitments and actions on reasonable grounds, then it will have been successful.

For support in learning this chapter's content, follow this path in **MyCompLab:** Resources ⇒ Writing ⇒ Writing Purposes ⇒ Writing to Argue or Persuade. Review the instructions and multimedia resources about argument, and then complete the exercises and click on Gradebook to measure your progress.

Argument as Inquiry
Reading and Exploring

2

In the previous chapter we explained that argument is both a process and a product, both inquiry and persuasion. In this chapter, we focus on inquiry as the entry point into argumentative conversations. Although our social environment is rich with these conversations—think of the oral, visual, print, and hypertext arguments that surround us—argument in the early twenty-first century is often degraded into talk-show shouting matches or antagonistic sound bites and "talking points." This reductive trend has elicited the concern of many cultural critics, journalists, rhetoricians, scholars, and citizens. Journalist Matt Miller recently posed the questions, "Is it possible in America today to convince anyone of anything he doesn't already believe?...[A]re there enough places where this mingling of minds occurs to sustain a democracy?"* How can argument's role as a community's search for the best answers to disputed questions be emphasized? How can arguers participate in a "mingling of minds" and use argument productively to seek answers to problems?

We believe that the best way to reinvigorate argument is to approach the reading and writing of arguments as an exploratory process. To do so means to position ourselves as inquirers as well as persuaders, engaging thoughtfully with alternative points of view, truly listening to other perspectives, examining our own values and assumptions, and perhaps even changing our views. Rhetorician Wayne Booth proposes that when we enter an argumentative conversation, we should first ask, "When should I change my mind?" rather than, "How can I change your mind?"†

In this chapter, we present some practical strategies for reading and exploring arguments in an open-minded and sophisticated way. You will learn to play what rhetorician Peter Elbow calls the believing and doubting game, in which a thinker systematically stretches her thinking by willing herself to believe positions that she finds threatening and to doubt positions that she instinctively

---

*Matt Miller, "Is Persuasion Dead?" *New York Times* 4 June 2005, A29.
†Wayne Booth raised these questions in a featured session with Peter Elbow titled "Blind Skepticism vs. the Rhetoric of Assent: Implications for Rhetoric, Argument, and Teaching," presented at the CCCC annual convention, Chicago, Illinois, March 2002.

accepts.* The thinker's goal is to live with questions, to acknowledge uncertainty and complexity, and to resist settling for simple or quick answers. In this chapter, you will learn to:

- Use a variety of means to find complex, puzzling issues to explore
- Place a text in its rhetorical context
- Read to believe an argument's claims
- Read to doubt an argument's claims
- Think dialectically

Although we present these strategies separately here, as you become familiar with them you will use them automatically and often implement several at once. In this chapter, we show how one student, Michael Banks, jumped into the puzzling, complex problem of illegal immigration and used these strategies to guide his thoughtful exploration of various viewpoints and texts.

Finding Issues to Explore

The mechanisms by which you enter a controversy will vary, but most likely they will include reflecting on your experiences or reading. Typically, the process goes like this: Through reading or talking with friends, you encounter a contested issue on which you are undecided or a viewpoint with which you disagree. Your curiosity, confusion, or concern then prompts you to learn more about the issue and to determine your own stance. In this section we examine some strategies you can use to find issues worth exploring.

Do Some Initial Brainstorming

As a first step, make an inventory of issues that interest you. Many of the ideas you develop may become subject matter for arguments that you will write later in this course. The chart on page 25 will help you generate a productive list.

Once you've made a list, add to it as new ideas strike you and return to it each time you are given a new argumentative assignment.

Be Open to the Issues All around You

We are surrounded by argumentative issues. You'll start noticing them everywhere once you get attuned to them. You will be invited into argumentative conversations by posters, bumper stickers, blog sites, newspaper editorial pages, magazine articles, the sports section, movie reviews, song lyrics, and so forth. When you read or listen, watch for "hot spots"—passages or moments that evoke strong agreement, disagreement, or confusion. As an illustration of how arguments are all around us, try the following exercise on the issue of illegal immigration.

---

*Peter Elbow, *Writing without Teachers* (New York: Oxford University Press, 1973), 147–90.

Brainstorming Issues to Explore

What You Can Do	How It Works
Make an inventory of the communities to which you belong. Consider classroom communities; clubs and organizations; residence hall, apartment, neighborhood, or family communities; church/synagogue or work communities; communities related to your hobbies or avocations; your city, state, region, nation, and world communities.	Because arguments arise out of disagreements within communities, you can often think of issues for argument by beginning with a list of the communities to which you belong.
Identify controversies within those communities. Think both big and small: ■ Big issue in world community: What is the best way to prevent destruction of rain forests? ■ Small issue in residence hall community: Should quiet hours be enforced?	To stimulate thinking, use prompts such as these: ■ People in this community frequently disagree about _____ . ■ Within my work community, Person X believes _____ ; however, this view troubles me because _____ . ■ In a recent residence hall meeting, I didn't know where I stood on _____ . ■ The situation at _____ could be improved if _____.
Narrow your list to a handful of problematic issues for which you don't have a position; share it with classmates. Identify a few issues that you would like to explore more deeply. When you share with classmates, add their issues to yours.	Sharing your list with classmates stimulates more thinking and encourages conversations. The more you explore your views with others, the more ideas you will develop. Good writing grows out of good talking.
Brainstorm a network of related issues. Any given issue is always embedded in a network of other issues. To see how open-ended and fluid an argumentative conversation can be, try connecting one of your issues to a network of other issues including subissues and side issues.	Brainstorm questions that compel you to look at an issue in a variety of ways. For example, if you explored the controversy over whether toys with phthalates should be banned (see Chapter 1), you might generate questions such as these about related issues: ■ How dangerous are phthalates? ■ Is the testing that has been done on rats adequate or accurate for determining the effects on humans? ■ Is the European "precautionary principle" a good principle for the United States to follow? ■ To what extent are controversies over phthalates similar to controversies over steroids, genetically modified foods, nitrites in cured meat, or mercury in dental fillings?

■ ■ ■   **FOR CLASS DISCUSSION**   Responding to Visual Arguments about Immigration

Suppose, in your casual reading, you encounter some photos and political cartoons on the U.S. problems with illegal immigration (see Figures 2.1–2.4). Working individually or in small groups, generate exploratory responses to these questions:

1. What claim is each cartoon or photo making?
2. What background information about the problems of illegal immigration do these cartoons and photos assume?
3. What network of issues do these visual texts suggest?
4. What puzzling questions do these visual texts raise for you?

FIGURE 2.1 Protest photo

FIGURE 2.2 Protest photo

FIGURE 2.3 Political cartoon on immigration and labor

FIGURE 2.4 Another political cartoon on immigrant labor

Explore Ideas by Freewriting

Freewriting is useful at any stage of the writing process. When you freewrite, you put fingers to keyboard (or pen to paper) and write rapidly *nonstop,* usually five to ten minutes at a stretch, without worrying about structure, grammar, or correctness. Your goal is to generate as many ideas as possible without stopping to edit your work. If you can't think of anything to say, write "relax" or "I'm stuck" over and over until new ideas emerge. Here is how Michael Banks did a freewrite in response to the cartoon in Figure 2.3.

Michael's Freewrite

This cartoon made me think about what jobs immigrant workers do. Come to think of it when I traveled with my dad on a business trip, all the chamber maids at the hotel were immigrants speaking Spanish. How ridiculous to think of replacing hotel housekeepers with robots! Yes, it's true that mechanization has taken away lots of jobs, but to think that all service jobs requiring low education could be easily done by machines is completely unrealistic. Relax think relax think relax. What other kinds of work do immigrants do? In my home region of Southern California a lot of the low pay work was done by Mexicans. My high school service group took free lunches to immigrants waiting for work in front of a Home Depot. It seemed that they would take any kind of job. Although lots of men were standing around, they seemed orderly and eager to work. Were these men illegal? The men who built the retaining wall in my neighbors' backyard and rolled out the sod lawn were immigrants and could have been illegal. Immigrants are willing to work hard. I wonder why there aren't enough jobs in Mexico. Why are we so dependent on immigrant labor? This low-skill work has to be done by someone. Why won't our homeless people or unemployed people in the United States take these low-skill jobs? Would American citizens take these jobs if they paid more? I can't help thinking that our whole economy would change if we cut way back on immigrant labor. Also all the efforts to limit immigration such as building the wall along the border have been super expensive and not effective. We can't build a wall over 1,900 miles long. Many of the ways we try to solve our immigration problem seem to be as out of touch as this cartoon.

Explore Ideas by Idea Mapping

Another good technique for exploring ideas is *idea mapping.* When you make an idea map, draw a circle in the center of a page and write some trigger idea (a broad topic, a question, or working thesis statement) in the center of the circle. Then record your ideas on branches and subbranches extending from the center circle. As long as you pursue one train of thought, keep recording your ideas on that branch. But when that line of thinking gives out, start a new branch. Often your thoughts will jump back and forth between branches. That's a major advantage of "picturing" your thoughts; you can see them as part of an emerging design rather than as strings of unrelated ideas.

Idea maps usually generate more ideas, though less well-developed ones, than freewrites. Figure 2.5 shows an idea map that student Michael Banks created on the issue of illegal immigration after class discussion of the photographs and cartoons in Figures 2.1–2.4.

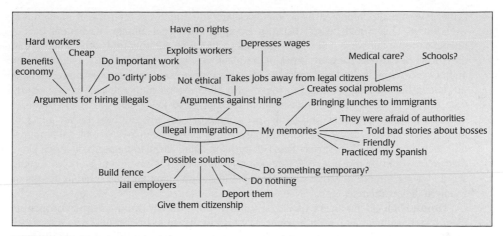

FIGURE 2.5 Michael's idea map

Explore Ideas by Playing the Believing and Doubting Game

The believing and doubting game, a term coined by rhetorician Peter Elbow, is an excellent way to imagine views different from your own and to anticipate responses to those views.

- **As a believer, your role is to be wholly sympathetic to an idea.** You must listen carefully to the idea and suspend all disbelief. You must identify all the ways in which the idea may appeal to different audiences and all the reasons for believing the idea. The believing game can be difficult, even frightening, if you are asked to believe an idea that strikes you as false or threatening.
- **As a doubter, your role is to be judgmental and critical, finding fault with an idea.** The doubting game is the opposite of the believing game. You do your best to find counterexamples and inconsistencies that undermine the idea you are examining. Again, it is can be threatening to doubt ideas that you instinctively want to believe.

When you play the believing and doubting game with an assertion, simply write two different chunks, one chunk arguing for the assertion (the believing game) and one chunk opposing it (the doubting game). Freewrite both chunks, letting your ideas flow without censoring. Or, alternatively, make an idea map with believing and doubting branches. Here is how student writer Michael Banks played the believing and doubting game with an assertion about stopping illegal immigration: "Employers of illegal immigrants should be jailed."

Michael's Believing and Doubting Game

Believe: If we really want to stop illegal immigration, then we should jail employers who hire illegals. What draws illegal immigrants to this country is the money they can make, so if the government eliminated these jobs by jailing the employers then illegal immigration would stop. This would be just because employers of illegal immigrants benefit by not having to pay a fair wage and what's more they often do this hiring under the table so that they don't pay taxes. They are breaking laws and deserve to go to jail. By avoiding taxes and not providing medical insurance etc., they cost every American taxpayer more, and it is not fair to law abiding citizens. Employers also often exploit immigrant laborers, because they have nobody to be held accountable to. They also lower the wages of American workers. Their actions can cause rifts in communities already troubled by an influx of immigration. Like anybody else who supports illegal activity, employers of illegal immigration should be jailed. If employers faced charges for hiring illegal immigrants, it seems likely that there would be much less of a market for the services of immigrant workers. I could see this being a more effective way to combat illegal immigration than building fences or trying to deport them all.

   Doubt: Jailing employers of illegal immigrants probably would stop some people from hiring undocumented immigrants, but I doubt it would be a reliable long-term solution. Especially for people who only hire a few immigrants at a time, it would likely be hard to prosecute them. Besides, I'm not convinced there is anything necessarily wrong with the employer's actions in hiring undocumented immigrants. If the government cannot enforce its own immigration laws, employers shouldn't be forced to do so for them. Many businesses, especially in agriculture, absolutely depend on good workers who will work long hours in hot fields to pick fruit and vegetables. Employers can't possibly be expected to do background checks on every employee. Moreover, if undocumented workers weren't available, the fruit wouldn't get picked. To send the employers to jail would mean to cause horrible disruption to much of our food supply. We are lucky to have these workers. The United States has a long history of people capitalizing on good business opportunities when the opportunity presents itself, and that's just what illegal immigrants are. It does not make sense to jail people for taking advantage of cheap and motivated labor.

Although Michael sees the injustice of paying workers substandard wages, he sees that much of our economy depends on this cheap labor. Playing the believing and doubting game has helped him articulate his dilemma and see the issue in more complex terms.

■ ■ ■   **FOR CLASS DISCUSSION**   Playing the Believing and Doubting Game
Individual task: Choose one or more of the following controversial claims and play the believing and doubting game with it, through either freewriting or idea mapping.
Group task: Working in pairs, in small groups, or as a whole class, share your results with classmates.

1. A student should report a fellow student who is cheating on an exam or plagiarizing an essay.
2. Women should be assigned to combat duty equally with men.
3. Athletes should be allowed to take steroids and human growth hormone under a doctor's supervision.
4. Illegal immigrants already living in the United States should be granted amnesty and placed on a fast track to U.S. citizenship.

Placing Texts in a Rhetorical Context

In the previous section, we suggested strategies for finding issues and entering argumentative conversations. Once you join a conversation, you will typically read a number of different arguments addressing your selected issue. The texts you read may be supplied for you in a textbook, anthology, or course pack, or you may find them yourself through library or Internet research. In this section and the ones that follow, we turn to productive strategies for reading arguments. We begin by explaining the importance of analyzing a text's rhetorical context as a preliminary step prior to reading. In subsequent sections, we explain powerful strategies for reading an argument—reading to believe, reading to doubt, and placing texts in conversation with each other through dialectic thinking.

As you read arguments on a controversy, try to place each text within its rhetorical context. It is important to know, for example, whether a blog that you are reading appears on Daily Kos (a liberal blog site) or on Little Green Footballs (a conservative blog site). In researching an issue, you may find that one article is a formal policy proposal archived on the Web site of an economics research institute, whereas another is an op-ed piece by a nationally syndicated columnist or a letter to the editor written by someone living in your community. To help you reconstruct a reading's rhetorical context, you need to understand the genres of argument as well as the cultural and professional contexts that cause people to write arguments. We'll begin with the genres of argument.

Genres of Argument

To situate an argument rhetorically, you should know something about its genre. A *genre* is a recurring type or pattern of argument such as a letter to the editor, a political cartoon, or the home page of an advocacy Web site. Genres are often categorized by recurring features, formats, and styles. The genre of any given argument helps determine its length, tone, sentence complexity, level of informality or formality, use of visuals, kinds of evidence, depth of research, and the presence or absence of documentation.

When you read arguments reprinted in a textbook such as this one, you lose clues about the argument's original genre. (You should therefore note the information about genre provided in our introductions to readings.) Likewise, you can lose clues about genre when you download articles from the Internet or from licensed databases such as LexisNexis or ProQuest. (See Chapter 15 for explanations of these research tools.) When you do your own research, you therefore need to be aware of the original genre of the text you are reading: was this piece originally a newspaper editorial, a blog, an organizational white paper, a scholarly article, a student paper posted to a Web site, or something else?

In the chart on pages 32–34, we identify most of the genres of argument through which readers and writers carry on the conversations of a democracy.

Cultural Contexts: Who Writes Arguments and Why?

A democratic society depends on the lively exchange of ideas—people with different points of view creating arguments for their positions. Now that you know something about the genre of arguments, we ask you to consider who writes arguments and why.

Genres of Argument

Genre	Explanation and Examples	Stylistic Features
Personal correspondence	■ Letters or e-mail messages ■ Often sent to specific decision makers (complaint letter, request for an action)	■ Style can range from a formal business letter to an informal note
Letters to the editor	■ Published in newspapers and some magazines ■ Provide a forum for citizens to voice views on public issues	■ Very short (fewer than three hundred words) and time sensitive ■ Can be summaries of longer arguments, but often focus in "sound bite" style on one point
Newspaper editorials and op-ed pieces	■ Published on the editorial or op-ed ("opposite-editorial") pages ■ Editorials promote views of the newspaper owners/editors ■ Op-ed pieces, usually written by professional columnists or guest writers, range in bias from ultraconservative to socialist (see pages 350–352 in Chapter 15) ■ Often written in response to political events or social problems in the news	■ Usually short (500–1,000 words) ■ Vary from explicit thesis-driven arguments to implicit arguments with stylistic flair ■ Have a journalistic style (short paragraphs) without detailed evidence ■ Sources usually not documented
Articles in public affairs or niche magazines	■ Usually written by staff writers or freelancers ■ Appear in public affairs magazines such as *National Review* or *The Progressive* or in niche magazines for special-interest groups such as *Rolling Stone* (popular culture), *Minority Business Entrepreneur* (business), or *The Advocate* (gay and lesbian issues) ■ Often reflect the political point of view of the magazine	■ Often have a journalistic style with informal documentation ■ Frequently include narrative elements rather than explicit thesis-and-reasons organization ■ Often provide well-researched coverage of various perspectives on a public issue
Articles in scholarly journals	■ Peer-reviewed articles published by nonprofit academic journals subsidized by universities or scholarly societies ■ Characterized by scrupulous attention to completeness and accuracy in treatment of data	■ Usually employ a formal academic style ■ Include academic documentation and bibliographies ■ May reflect the biases, methods, and strategies associated with a specific school of thought or theory within a discipline

Genre	Explanation and Examples	Stylistic Features
Legal briefs and court decisions	■ Written by attorneys or judges ■ "Friend-of-the-court" briefs are often published by stakeholders to influence appeals courts ■ Court decisions explain the reasoning of justices on civic cases (and often include minority opinions)	■ Usually written in legalese, but use a logical reasons-and-evidence structure ■ Friend-of-the-court briefs are sometimes aimed at popular audiences
Organizational white papers	■ In-house documents or PowerPoint presentations aimed at influencing organizational policy or decisions or giving informed advice to clients ■ Sometimes written for external audiences to influence public opinion favorable to the organization ■ External white papers are often posted on Web sites or sent to legislators	■ Usually desktop or Web published ■ Often include graphics and other visuals ■ Vary in style from the dully bureaucratic (satirized in *Dilbert* cartoons) to the cogent and persuasive
Blogs and postings to chat rooms and electronic bulletin boards	■ Web-published commentaries, usually on specific topics and often intended to influence public opinion ■ Blogs (Web logs) are gaining influence as alternative commentaries to the established media ■ Reflect a wide range of perspectives	■ Often blend styles of journalism, personal narrative, and formal argument ■ Often difficult to determine identity and credentials of blogger ■ Often provide hyperlinks to related sites on the Web
Public affairs advocacy advertisements	■ Published as posters, fliers, Web pages, or paid advertisements ■ Condensed verbal/visual arguments aimed at influencing public opinion ■ Often have explicit bias and ignore alternative views	■ Use succinct "sound bite" style ■ Employ document design, bulleted lists, and visual elements (graphics, photographs, or drawings) for rhetorical effect
Advocacy Web sites	■ Usually identified by the extension ".org" in the Web site address ■ Often created by well-financed advocacy groups such as the NRA (National Rifle Association) or PETA (People for the Ethical Treatment of Animals) ■ Reflect the bias of the site owner ■ For further discussion of reading and evaluating Web sites, see Chapter 15, pages 362–363	■ Often contain many layers with hyperlinks to other sites ■ Use visuals and verbal text to create an immediate visceral response favorable to the site owner's views ■ Ethically responsible sites announce their bias and purpose in an "About Us" or "Mission Statement" link on the home page

(Continued)

Genre	Explanation and Examples	Stylistic Features
Visual arguments	■ Political cartoons, usually drawn by syndicated cartoonists ■ Other visual arguments (photographs, drawings, graphics, ads), usually accompanied by verbal text	■ Make strong emotional appeals, often reducing complex issues to one powerful perspective (see Chapter 9)
Speeches and PowerPoint presentations	■ Political speeches, keynote speeches at professional meetings, informal speeches at hearings, interviews, business presentations ■ Often made available via transcription in newspapers or on Web sites ■ In business or government settings, often accompanied by PowerPoint slides	■ Usually organized clearly with highlighted claim, supporting reasons, and transitions ■ Accompanying PowerPoint slides designed to highlight structure, display evidence in graphics, mark key points, and sometimes provide humor
Documentary films	■ Formerly nonfiction reporting, documentary films now range widely from efforts to document reality objectively to efforts to persuade viewers to adopt the filmmaker's perspective or take action ■ Usually cost less to produce than commercial films and lack special effects ■ Cover topics such as art, science, and economic, political, and military crises	■ Often use extended visual arguments, combined with interviews and voice-overs, to influence as well as inform viewers ■ The filmmaker's angle of vision may dominate, or his or her perspective and values may be more subtle

In reconstructing the rhetorical context of an argument, consider how any given writer is spurred to write by a motivating occasion and by the desire to change the views of a particular audience. In this section, we'll return to our example of illegal immigration. The following list identifies the wide range of writers, cartoonists, filmmakers, and others who are motivated to enter the conversation about immigration.

Who Writes Arguments about Immigration and Why?

■ **Lobbyists and advocacy groups.** Lobbyists and advocacy groups commit themselves to a cause, often with passion, and produce avidly partisan arguments aimed at persuading voters, legislators, government agencies, and other decision makers. They often maintain advocacy Web sites, buy advertising space in newspapers and magazines, and lobby legislators face-to-face. For example, the immigrant advocacy group La Raza defends immigrant rights, whereas the Federation for American Immigration Reform (FAIR) fights to end illegal immigration and rallies people to pressure businesses not to hire undocumented workers.

- **Legislators, political candidates, and government officials.** Whenever new laws, regulations, or government policies are proposed, staffers do research and write white papers recommending positions on an issue. Often these are available on the Web. On the perplexing problem of illegal immigration, numerous staff researchers for legislators, political candidates, and government officials have produced white papers on the practicality of extending a wall along the U.S.-Mexican border, of beefing up border patrol to increase national security, and of offering temporary guest worker visas to immigrant laborers.

- **Business professionals, labor union leaders, and bankers.** Business spokespeople often try to influence public opinion in ways that support corporate or business interests, whereas labor union officials support wage structures favorable to union members. Typically businesspeople produce "corporate image" advertisements, send white papers to legislators, or write op-ed pieces that frame issues from a business perspective, whereas labor unions produce arguments favorable to workers. Professionals that could profit from undocumented labor (fruit growers, winemakers, landscapers, construction companies, and so forth) or could be harmed by it (labor unions) are active participants in the public controversy.

- **Lawyers and judges.** Immigration issues are frequently entangled in legal matters. Lawyers write briefs supporting their clients' cases. Sometimes lawyers or legal experts not directly connected to a case, particularly law professors, file "friend-of-the-court" briefs aimed at influencing the decision of judges. Finally, judges write court opinions explaining their decisions on a case. As more illegal immigrants are deported and others die trying to cross the border, more legal professionals are writing about these cases.

- **Media commentators.** Whenever immigration issues are in the news, media commentators (journalists, editorial writers, syndicated columnists, bloggers, political cartoonists) write articles and blogs or op-ed pieces on the issue or produce editorial cartoons, filtering their arguments through the perspective of their own political views. For example, conservative commentator Lou Dobbs is known for his strong stand on keeping illegal immigrants out of the country.

- **Professional freelance or staff writers.** Some of the most thoughtful analyses of public issues are composed by freelance or staff writers for public forum magazines such as *Atlantic Monthly, The Nation, Ms., The National Review, The New Yorker,* and many others. Arguments about immigration policy reform and immigrants' integration into American society surface whenever the topic seems timely to magazine editors.

- **Think tanks.** Because today many political, economic, and social issues are very complex, policy makers and commentators often rely on research institutions or think tanks to supply statistical studies and in-depth investigation of problems. These think tanks range across the political spectrum, from conservative (the Hoover Institute, the Heritage Foundation) or libertarian (the Cato Institute) to the centrist or liberal (the Brookings Institution, the Pew Foundation, the Economic Policy Institute). They usually maintain many-layered Web sites that include background on research writers, recent publications, and archives of past publications, including policy statements and white papers. Recently the conservative Center for

Immigration Studies published articles on the cost to Americans of legal and illegal immigration; the Center for American Progress, a liberal think tank, outlined the important features for a reform of the U.S. immigration system.

- **Scholars and academics.** College professors play a public role through their scholarly research, contributing data, studies, and analyses to public debates. Scholarly research differs substantially from advocacy argument in its systematic attempt to arrive at the best answers to questions based on the full examination of relevant data. Much scholarship investigates the patterns of immigrant participation in American political life, the relationship between crime and immigration, possibilities of worker solidarity, and the cost of products and services if the United States were to raise the minimum wage substantially. Scholarly research is usually published in refereed academic journals rather than in popular magazines.

- **Independent and commercial filmmakers.** Testifying to the growing popularity of film and its power to involve people in issues, documentary filmmakers often reflect on issues of the day, and commercial filmmakers often embed arguments within their dramatic storytelling. The global film industry is adding international perspectives as well. Many recent documentary and dramatic films present the experiences of immigrants and undocumented workers and their struggle to fit into American society while preserving their cultural roots. For instance, the documentary film *Farmingville,* shown on PBS, follows the antagonism among immigrant day laborers, homeowners, and other residents of the town of Farmingville on Long Island, New York, and depicts the town debating the practicality of establishing a hiring site to remove day laborers from the streets.

- **Citizens and students.** Engaged citizens influence social policy through letters, contributions to advocacy Web sites, guest editorials for newspapers, blogs, and speeches in public forums. Students also write for university communities, present their work at undergraduate research conferences, and influence public opinion by writing to political leaders and decision makers. For example, students involved in a service-learning project tutoring children of immigrant laborers might write to spread their knowledge of immigrants' educational needs.

Analyzing Rhetorical Context and Genre

The background we have just provided about the writers and genres of argument will help you situate arguments in their rhetorical context. When you encounter any argumentative text, whether reprinted in a textbook or retrieved through your own library and Web research, use the following guide questions to analyze its rhetorical context:

Questions about Rhetorical Context and Genre

1. What genre of argument is this? How do the conventions of that genre help determine the depth, complexity, and even appearance of the argument?
2. Who is the author? What are the author's credentials and what is his or her investment in the issue?
3. What audience is he or she writing for?

4. What motivating occasion prompted the writing? The motivating occasion could be a current event, a crisis, pending legislation, a recently published alternative view, or another ongoing problem.

5. What is the author's purpose? The purpose could range from strong advocacy to inquiring truth seeker (analogous to the continuum from persuasion to truth seeking discussed in Chapter 1, page 12).

6. What information about the publication or source (magazine, newspaper, advocacy Web site) helps explain the writer's perspective or the structure and style of the argument?

7. What is the writer's angle of vision? By angle of vision, we mean the filter, lens, or selective seeing through which the writer is approaching the issue. What is left out from this argument? What does this author not see? (Chapter 5, pages 94–96, discusses how angle of vision operates in the selection and framing of evidence.)

This rhetorical knowledge becomes important in helping you select a diversity of voices and genres of argument when you are exploring an issue. Note how Michael Banks makes use of his awareness of rhetorical context in his exploratory paper on pages 50–56.

■ ■ ■ **FOR CLASS DISCUSSION**   Placing Readings in Their Rhetorical Context
Find two recent arguments on the illegal immigration issue.* Your arguments should (1) represent different genres and (2) represent different kinds of arguers (syndicated newspaper columnists, bloggers, freelance magazine writers, scholars, and so forth). You can find your arguments in any of these places:

- In magazines: news commentary/public affairs magazines or niche magazines
- On the Web: on Web sites for think tanks, advocacy organizations, or blogs
- In newspapers: local, regional, or national

For each argument, answer the "Questions about Rhetorical Context and Genre" on pages 36–37. Then share your findings with classmates.   ■ ■ ■

Reading to Believe an Argument's Claims

Once you have established the rhetorical context of an argument, you are ready to begin reading. We suggest that you read arguments in the spirit of the believing and doubting game, beginning with "believing," in which you practice what psychologist Carl Rogers calls *empathic listening*. Empathic listening requires that you see the world through the author's eyes, temporarily adopt the author's beliefs and values, and suspend your skepticism and biases long enough to hear what the author is saying.

To illustrate what we mean by reading to believe, we will continue with our example of illegal immigration. As you may have discovered through prior experience, reading, and examining the cartoons and photos at the beginning of this chapter, this issue

---

*For help on how to find articles through Web or licensed database searches, see Chapter 15.

includes many related issues: Why do millions of foreigners risk their lives to come illegally to the United States? How can the United States reduce the number of illegal immigrants? What should the United States do about the people currently living in the United States illegally? Does the U.S. economy need the workforce represented by these undocumented workers? The following article, "Amnesty?" by Roman Catholic priest and professor of philosophy John F. Kavanaugh, appeared in the March 10, 2008, issue of *America,* a Jesuit publication that describes itself as "the only national Catholic weekly magazine in the United States." Please read this article carefully in preparation for the exercises and examples that follow.

Amnesty?
Let Us Be Vigilant and Charitable
JOHN F. KAVANAUGH

Let's call her María. She was illegally brought into the United States at the age of 2. Now 27, she is a vital member of her parish and has three young children. María was recently deported to Ciudad Juárez, where, in the last 15 years, 600 young women have been kidnapped, raped, murdered and buried in the desert. Luckily, she was able to find a way into the United States, again illegally, to be with her children. If she is discovered again, she will spend five years in a U.S. federal prison.

My Jesuit friend and neighbor, Dick Vogt, has told me of people like María and many others of the 12 to 14 million "undocumented aliens." She is not necessarily typical of the masses who have illegally entered this country. Some, no doubt, are drunks and dealers; many are incarcerated for other crimes than their immigrant status. But most have come at great risk to their lives, because their lives were already at risk from poverty and displacement. They want to make a living, form a family, and help their families back home.

The Catholic bishops of Mexico pointed out in January that the recent surge of immigration is a direct effect of the North American Free Trade Agreement. Open trade, while benefiting the most powerful and technologically advanced, has threatened poor farmers and their small rural communities. They cannot compete with heavily subsidized U.S.

and Canadian producers. It is this phenomenon that drives so many to leave their homeland for a livelihood in the United States, despite, as the bishops put it, "its anti-humane immigration program."

The U.S. bishops, witnessing everything from evictions in California to employment raids in Massachusetts, have stirred the consciences of their dioceses and taken stands in conscience of their own. The bishop of Oklahoma City and 10 of his pastors have publicly professed defiance of a punitive state law that makes felons of all who "aid, assist, or transport any undocumented person." The bishops of Missouri have expressed their alarm over politicians "who vie to see who can be tougher on illegal immigrants." Cognizant of the economic pressures on many families in rural Mexico, they call for a more compassionate, fair, and realistic reform of our immigration system, including education and humanitarian assistance to all children, "without regard to legal status."

5   There has been some resistance to the bishops' proposals and some resentment. It is reminiscent of the outrage directed by anti-immigrant groups toward last year's immigration reform bill, a very harsh measure that they nonetheless condemned for proposing what they called amnesty.

Some of the resentment is understandable. There are householders, especially on the border, who have had their land and yards trashed. Residents of some towns feel flooded with immigrants they cannot engage or manage. A few businesspersons who have refused to hire undocumented or cheaper labor have lost sales and customers.

But this does not explain the seething hostility that can be read in some nativist opinion columns and popular books or heard on radio talk shows: "They are criminals, felons; and that's that."

"They have broken the law." This is an interesting standard of ethics, justice or charity for a nation that sees itself as Judeo-Christian and humane. It is puzzling that we do not think of the Good Samaritan or of the "least of our brothers and sisters" in Matthew 25, or of the passage from Leviticus that the Missouri bishops quote: "The stranger who sojourns with you shall be to you as the native among you, and you shall love him as yourself."

As for making the law our bottom line, do Christians know how many times Jesus was in trouble with the law? Do they know that the natural law tradition, articulated in the work of Thomas Aquinas, holds an unjust law to be no law at all? Do they forget that our nation was founded upon an appeal to a higher law than positive law, an appeal shared by the labor movement, by Martin Luther King Jr., and by Elizabeth Cady Stanton and Susan B. Anthony?

10   A nation has every right to secure its borders. Unrestrained immigration will hurt our country, the immigrants, and their homeland. So let us indeed protect our borders (even though that will not solve the problem of those who enter legally and overstay their visa). Let us also honestly face the multiple causes of illegal immigration. As an excellent position paper from the Center for Concern notes, illegal immigration involves many factors: trade negotiation, the governments involved, the immigrants who break the law by entering our country, employers who take advantage of them, corporate leaders who profit from them, and consumers who benefit from lower food and service costs.

We must devise ways to offer legal status to anyone who contributes to our common good, whether as a future citizen or a temporary guest worker. If that means using the dirty word "amnesty," so be it.

As to those who sojourn in our midst, let us be vigilant if they are threats and charitable if they are friends. It would be a good, if unusual, move if our legislators had the imagination to call for citizen panels before which an illegal immigrant could request amnesty, leniency, and a path to citizenship based on his or her contribution to the community, solid employment record, faithful payment of taxes, family need, and crime-free record.

Instead of fearing some abstract horde of millions, we might see the faces of people like María and hear their stories. If we turn them away, we will have to face the fact that we are not so much a nation of Judeo-Christian values as a punitive and self-interested people hiding under the protection of lesser, human-made laws.

Summary Writing as a Way of Reading to Believe

One way to show that you have listened well to an article is to summarize its argument in your own words. A summary (also called an *abstract,* a *précis,* or a *synopsis*) presents only a text's major points and eliminates supporting details. Writers often incorporate summaries of other writers' views into their own arguments, either to support their own views or to represent alternative views that they intend to oppose. (When opposing someone else's argument, writers often follow the template "Although X contends that [summary of X's argument], I argue that _____.") Summaries can be any length, depending on the writer's purpose, but usually they range from several sentences to one or two paragraphs. To maintain your own credibility, your summary should be as neutral and fair to that piece as possible.

To help you write an effective summary, we recommend the following steps:

Step 1: *Read the argument for general meaning.* Don't judge it. Put your objections aside; just follow the writer's meaning, trying to see the issue from the writer's perspective. Try to adopt the writer's values and belief system. Walk in the writer's shoes.

Step 2: *Reread the article slowly, writing brief* does *and* says *statements for each paragraph (or group of closely connected paragraphs).* A *does* statement identifies a paragraph's function, such as "summarizes an opposing view," "introduces a supporting reason," "gives an example," or "uses statistics to support the previous point." A *says* statement summarizes a paragraph's content. Your challenge in writing *says* statements is to identify the main idea in each paragraph and translate that idea into your own words, most likely condensing it at the same time. This process may be easier with an academic article that uses long, developed paragraphs headed by clear topic sentences than with more informal, journalistic articles such as Kavanaugh's that use shorter, less developed paragraphs. What follows are *does* and *says* statements for the first six paragraphs of Kavanaugh's article:

Does/Says Analysis of Kavanaugh's Article

Paragraph 1: *Does:* Uses a vivid example to introduce the injustice of the current treatment of illegal immigrants. *Says:* The U.S. government is separating productive, long-term illegal immigrants from their families, deporting them, exposing them to dangerous conditions, and threatening them with felony charges.

Paragraph 2: *Does:* Puts the problem of illegal immigrants in a larger, international context. *Says:* Although some illegal immigrants are involved in criminal activities, most have been pushed here by poverty and loss of opportunity in their own countries and have come to the United States seeking a better life for themselves and their families.

Paragraph 3: *Does:* Further explores the reasons behind the increase in immigration rates. *Says:* Catholic bishops have spoken out against the North American Free Trade Agreement and corporate interests, which have sought their own trade benefits at the expense of poor farmers and rural communities.

Paragraph 4: *Does:* Presents a sketch of Catholic leaders protesting the recent crackdowns on illegal immigrants. *Says:* U.S. bishops are protesting recent punitive laws against illegal immigrants and advocating for "a more compassionate, fair, and realistic reform of our immigration system."

Paragraph 5: *Does:* Sketches some opposing views. *Says:* Anti-immigration groups and others object to humane treatment of illegal immigrants, seeing it as akin to amnesty.

Paragraph 6: *Does:* Recognizes the validity of some opposing views. *Says:* The problems of some groups of Americans, including homeowners living on the border and businesses trying not to hire illegally, need to be heard.

■ ■ ■ **FOR CLASS DISCUSSION**   Writing *Does/Says* Statements
Working individually or in small groups, write *does* and *says* statements for the remaining paragraphs of Kavanaugh's article.   ■ ■ ■

> **Step 3**: *Examine your* does *and* says *statements to determine the major sections of the argument.* Create a list of the major points (and subpoints) that must appear in a summary in order to represent that argument accurately. If you are visually oriented, you may prefer to make a diagram, flowchart, or scratch outline of the sections of Kavanaugh's argument.
>
> **Step 4**: *Turn your list, outline, flowchart, or diagram into a prose summary.* Typically, writers do this in one of two ways. Some start by joining all their *says* statements into a lengthy paragraph-by-paragraph summary and then prune it and streamline it. They combine ideas into sentences and then revise those sentences to make them clearer and more tightly structured. Others start with a one-sentence summary of the argument's thesis and major supporting reasons and then flesh it out with more supporting ideas. Your goal is to be as neutral and objective as possible by keeping your own response to the writer's ideas out of your summary. To be fair to the writer, you also need to cover all the writer's main points and give them the same emphasis as in the original article.
>
> **Step 5**: *Revise your summary until it is the desired length and is sufficiently clear, concise, and complete.* Your goal is to spend your words wisely, making every word count. In a summary of several hundred words, you will often need transitions to indicate structure and create a coherent flow of ideas: "Kavanaugh's second point is that…," or "Kavanaugh concludes by…." However, don't waste words with meaningless transitions such as "Kavanaugh goes on to say…." When you incorporate a summary into your own essay, you must distinguish that author's views from your own by using *attributive tags* (expressions such as "Kavanaugh asserts" or "according to Kavanaugh"). You must also put any directly borrowed wording in quotation marks. Finally, you must cite the original author using appropriate conventions for documenting sources.

What follows are two summaries of Kavanaugh's article—a one-paragraph version and a one-sentence version—by student writer Michael Banks. Michael's one-paragraph version illustrates the MLA documentation system in which page numbers for direct quotations are placed in parentheses after the quotation and complete bibliographic information is placed in a Works Cited list at the end of the paper. See Chapter 17 for a complete explanation of the MLA and APA documentation systems.

Michael's One-Paragraph Summary of Kavanaugh's Argument

In his article "Amnesty?" from *America* magazine John F. Kavanaugh, a Jesuit priest and professor of philosophy at St. Louis University, questions the morality of the current U.S. treatment of undocumented immigrants and advocates for a frank dealing with "the multiple causes of illegal immigration" (39). He points out that most immigrants are not criminals but rather hard-working, family-oriented people. He attributes recent increases in immigration to the North American Free Trade Agreement and the poverty it causes among rural Mexican farmers. Kavanaugh reports that recently U.S. bishops have protested the "anti-humane" treatment of immigrants and called for "compassionate, fair, and realistic reform" (38). He also mentions the anti-immigration groups, residents on the border, and business owners who have resisted the bishops and any treatment that resembles "amnesty." Kavanaugh's piece culminates with his argument that a nation that identifies itself as "Judeo-Christian and humane" should follow biblical teaching, "higher law," and the courageous example of leaders such as Martin Luther King, Jr., in challenging unjust laws (39). Admitting that unrestrained immigration would help nobody, Kavanaugh exhorts the country to move constructively toward "legal status to anyone who contributes to our common good" (39) and suggests a radically new solution to the problem: a citizen panel for the review of an immigrant's legal status. He concludes by stating that turning away undocumented immigrants is an immoral act motivated by self-interest.

Work Cited

Kavanaugh, John F. "Amnesty?" *America* 10 Mar. 2008: 8. Rpt. in *Writing Arguments: A Rhetoric with Readings.* John D. Ramage, John C. Bean, and June Johnson. 9th ed. New York: Pearson Longman, 2012: 38–39. Print.

Michael's One-Sentence Summary of Kavanaugh's Argument

In his article in *America*, Jesuit professor of philosophy John F. Kavanaugh questions the morality of the current treatment of undocumented immigrants in the United States, arguing that in a Judeo-Christian nation anyone who contributes positively to their community should be afforded some level of legal status.

Practicing Believing: Willing Your Own Belief in the Writer's Views

Although writing an accurate summary of an argument shows that you have listened to it effectively and understood it, summary writing by itself doesn't mean that you have actively tried to enter the writer's worldview. Before we turn in the next section to doubting an argument, we want to stress the importance of believing it. Rhetorician Peter Elbow reminds us that before we critique a text, we should try to "dwell with" and "dwell in" the writer's ideas—play the believing game—in order to "earn" our right to criticize.* He asserts, and we agree, that this use of the believing game to engage with strange, threatening, or unfamiliar views can lead to a deeper understanding and may provide a new vantage point on our own knowledge, assumptions, and values. To believe a writer and dwell with his or her ideas, find places in the text that resonate positively for you, look for values and beliefs you hold in common (however few), and search for personal experiences and values that affirm his or her argument.

Reading to Doubt

After willing yourself to believe an argument, will yourself to doubt it. Turn your mental energies toward raising objections, asking questions, expressing skepticism, and withholding your assent. When you read as a doubter, you question the writer's logic,

---

*Peter Elbow, "Bringing the Rhetoric of Assent and the Believing Game Together—Into the Classroom," *College English,* 67.4 (March 2005), 389.

the writer's evidence and assumptions, and the writer's strategies for developing the argument. You also think about what is *not* in the argument by noting what the author has glossed over, unexplained, or left out. You add a new layer of marginal notes, articulating what is bothering you, demanding proof, doubting evidence, challenging the author's assumptions and values, and so forth. Writing your own notes helps you read a text actively, bringing your own voice into conversation with the author.

■ ■ ■ **FOR CLASS DISCUSSION**   Raising Doubts about Kavanaugh's Argument

Return now to Kavanaugh's article and read it skeptically. Raise questions, offer objections, and express doubts. Then, working as a class or in small groups, list all the doubts you have about Kavanaugh's argument. ■ ■ ■

Now that you have doubted Kavanaugh's article, compare your questions and doubts to some raised by student writer Michael Banks.

Michael's Doubts about Kavanaugh's Article

■ Kavanaugh's introductory paragraph seems sensational. María's situation is disturbing, but I doubt that every deported immigrant is likely to be "kidnapped, raped, murdered, and buried in the desert" as he seems to be insinuating.

■ His argument often seems to be based too much upon vague statements about the opposition. He talks about "some resentment," "some towns," "a few people," and "some hateful columns," but he doesn't provide specifics. He also doesn't provide any specific data about the effects of NAFTA, which seems like something he really should have provided.

■ In his second paragraph, he says that María's story "is not necessarily typical of the masses who have illegally entered" the U.S. and that "many are incarcerated for other crimes than their immigrant status." However, he never considers the rate of criminal behavior of illegal immigrants in further detail. Are illegal immigrants more likely to commit crimes? This might be the start of an argument against him.

■ His references to opinion columns and popular books and radio talk shows seem to suggest that the majority of opposition to immigration reform is simplistic and ignorant. He only pays lip service to a few "understandable" objections. There must be more to the opposition than this. It would be particularly interesting to find an ethical justification for an anti-immigration stance.

■ Perhaps because he's a member of the Society of Jesus, he draws hardly any line at all between church and state. However, most U.S. citizens I know believe that government should be secular. This contrasts harshly with his notion that the U.S. self-identifies as "Judeo-Christian" and limits his audience to people who would probably already agree with him. If we remove religion from the equation, the capitalistic values behind NAFTA and immigration policy seem much more understandable. I would need to investigate the economic impact of illegal immigration. Who really benefits the most from it? Who's really harmed?

These are only some of the objections that might be raised against Kavanaugh's argument. The point here is that doubting as well as believing is a key part of the exploratory process and purpose. *Believing* takes you into the views of others so that you can expand your views and perhaps see them differently and modify or even change them. *Doubting* helps protect you from becoming overpowered by others' arguments and teaches you to stand back, consider, and weigh points carefully. It also leads you to new questions and points you might want to explore further.

Thinking Dialectically

This chapter's final strategy—thinking dialectically to bring texts into conversation with each other—encompasses all the previous strategies and can have a powerful effect on your growth as a thinker and arguer. The term *dialectic* is associated with the German philosopher Georg Wilhelm Friedrich Hegel, who postulated that each thesis prompts an opposing thesis (which he calls an "antithesis") and that the conflict between these views can lead thinkers to a new claim (a "synthesis") that incorporates aspects of both views. Dialectic thinking is the philosophical underpinning of the believing and doubting game, pushing us toward new and better ideas. As Peter Elbow puts it, "Because it's so hard to let go of an idea we are holding (or more to the point, an idea that's holding us), our best hope for leverage in learning to doubt such ideas is *to take on different ideas*."*

This is why expert thinkers actively seek out alternative views—not to shout them down but to listen to them. If you were an arbitrator, you wouldn't settle a dispute between A and B on the basis of A's testimony only. You would also insist on hearing B's side of the story (and perhaps also C's and D's if they are stakeholders in the dispute). Dialectic thinking means playing ideas against each other, creating a tension that forces you to keep expanding your perspective. It helps you achieve the "mingling of minds" that we discussed in the introduction to this chapter.

As you listen to differing views, try to identify sources of disagreement among arguers, which often fall into two categories: (1) disagreement about the facts of the case and (2) disagreement about underlying values, beliefs, or assumptions. We saw these disagreements in Chapter 1 in the conversation about phthalates in children's toys. At the level of facts, disputants disagreed about the amount of phthalates a baby might ingest when chewing a rubber toy or about the quantity of ingested phthalates needed to be harmful. At the level of values, disputants disagreed on the amount of risk that must be present in a free market economy before a government agency should ban a substance. As you try to determine your own position on an issue, consider what research you might have to do to resolve questions of fact; also try to articulate your own underlying values, beliefs, and assumptions.

Questions to Stimulate Dialectic Thinking

As you consider multiple points of view on an issue, try using the following questions to promote dialectic thinking:

---

*Peter Elbow, "Bringing the Rhetoric of Assent and the Believing Game Together—Into the Classroom," *College English* 67.4 (March 2005), 390.

Questions to Promote Dialectic Thinking

1. What would writer A say to writer B?
2. After I read writer A, I thought _____; however, after I read writer B, my thinking on this issue had changed in these ways: _____.
3. To what extent do writer A and writer B disagree about facts and interpretations of facts?
4. To what extent do writer A and writer B disagree about underlying beliefs, assumptions, and values?
5. Can I find any areas of agreement, including shared values and beliefs, between writer A and writer B?
6. What new, significant questions do these texts raise for me?
7. After I have wrestled with the ideas in these two texts, what are my current views on this issue?

Responding to questions like these—either through class discussion or through exploratory writing—can help you work your way into a public controversy. Earlier in this chapter you read John Kavanaugh's article expressing a Catholic, pro-immigrant, anti-corporate view of immigrants. Now consider an article expressing a quite different point of view, "Why Blame Mexico?" by freelance journalist Fred Reed, published in *The American Conservative* on March 10, 2008. We ask you to read the article and then use the preceding questions to stimulate dialectic thinking about Kavanaugh versus Reed.

■ ■ ■   **FOR CLASS DISCUSSION**   Practicing Dialectic Thinking with Two Articles
Individual task: Freewrite your responses to the preceding questions, in which Kavanaugh is writer A and Reed is writer B. **Group task:** Working as a whole class or in small groups, share your responses to the two articles, guided by the dialectic questions.   ■ ■ ■

Why Blame Mexico?

FRED REED

To grasp American immigration policy, one needs only remember that the United States frowns on smoking while subsidizing tobacco growers.

We say to impoverished Mexicans, "See this river? Don't cross it. If you do, we'll give you good jobs, drivers licenses, citizenship for your kids born here, school for said kids, public assistance, governmental documents in Spanish for your convenience, and a much better future. There is no penalty for getting caught. Now, don't cross this river, hear?"

How smart is that? We're baiting them. It's like putting out a salt lick and then complaining when deer come. Immigrant parents would be irresponsible not to cross.

The problem of immigration, note, is entirely self-inflicted. The U.S. chose to let them in. It didn't have to. They came to work. If Americans hadn't hired them, they would have gone back.

We have immigration because we want immigration. Liberals favor immigration because it makes them feel warm and fuzzy and from a genuine streak of decency. Conservative Republican businessmen favor immigration, frequently *sotto voce*, because they want cheap labor that actually shows up and works.

It's a story I've heard many times—from a landscaper, a construction firm, a junkyard owner, a group of plant nurserymen. "We need Mexicans." You could yell "Migra!" in a lot of restaurants in Washington, and the entire staff would disappear out the back door. Do we expect businessmen to vote themselves out of business? That's why we don't take the obvious steps to control immigration. (A $1,000 a day fine for hiring illegals, half to go anonymously to whoever informed on the employer would do the trick.)

In Jalisco, Mexico, where I live, crossing illegally is regarded as casually as pirating music or smoking a joint and the coyotes who smuggle people across as a public utility, like light rail. The smuggling is frequently done by bribing the border guards, who are notoriously corrupt.

Why corrupt? Money. In the book *De Los Maras a Los Zetas,* by a Mexican journalist, I find an account of a tunnel he knew of that could put 150 illegals a day across the border. (I can't confirm this.) The price of passage is about $2,000 a person. That's $300,000 a day, tax-free. What does a border guard make? (And where can I find a shovel?) The author estimated that perhaps 40 tunnels were active at any given time. Certainly some are. A woman I know says she came up in a restaurant and just walked out the door. Let's hear it for Homeland Security.

There is much noise about whether to grant amnesty. The question strikes me as cosmetic. We are not going to round up millions of people and physically throw them across the border. Whether we should doesn't matter. It's fantasy. Too many people want them here or don't care that they are here or don't want to uproot families who have established new lives here. Ethnic cleansing is ugly.

Further, the legal Latino population is just starting to vote. A bumper crop of Mexican-American kids, possessed of citizenship, are growing headlong toward voting age. These people cannot be thrown out, even in principle.

People complain that Mexico doesn't seal the borders. Huh? Mexico is a country, not a prison. It has no obligation to enforce American laws that America declines to enforce. Then there was the uproar when some fast-food restaurant in the U.S. began accepting pesos. Why? Mexican border towns accept dollars. Next came outrage against Mexico because its consulates were issuing ID cards to illegals, which they then used to get drivers licenses. Why outrage? A country has every right to issue IDs to its citizens. America doesn't have to accept them. If it does, whose problem is that?

If you want to see a reasonable immigration policy, look to Mexico. You automatically get a 90-day tourist visa when you land. To get residency papers, you need two things apart from photographs, passport, etc. First, a valid tourist visa to show that you entered the country legally. Mexico doesn't do illegal aliens. Second, a demonstrable income of $1,000 a month. You are welcome to live in Mexico, but you are going to pay your own way. Sounds reasonable to me.

You want a Mexican passport? Mexico allows dual citizenship. You (usually) have to be a resident for five years before applying. You also have to speak Spanish. It's the national language. What sense does it make to have citizens who can't talk to anybody?

It looks to me as though America thoughtlessly adopted an unwise policy, continued it until reversal became approximately impossible, and now doesn't like the results. It must be Mexico's fault.

Three Ways to Foster Dialectic Thinking

In this concluding section, we suggest three ways to stimulate and sustain the process of dialectic thinking: Effective discussions in class, over coffee, or online; a reading log in which you make texts speak to each other; or a formal exploratory essay. We'll look briefly at each in turn.

Effective discussions   Good, rich talk is one of the most powerful ways to stimulate dialectic thinking and foster a "mingling of minds." The key is to keep these discussions from being shouting matches or bully pulpits for those who like to dominate the airtime. Discussions are most productive if people are willing to express different points of view or to role-play those views for the purpose of advancing the conversation. Try Rogerian listening, in which you summarize someone else's position before you offer your own, different position. (See Chapter 7 for more explanation of Rogerian listening.) Probe deeply to discover whether disagreements are primarily about facts and evidence or about underlying values and beliefs. Be respectful of others' views, but don't hesitate to point out where you see problems or weaknesses. Good discussions can occur in class, in late-night coffee shops, or in online chat rooms or on discussion boards.

Reading Logs   In our classes, we require students to keep reading logs or journals in which they use freewriting and idea mapping to explore their ideas as they encounter multiple perspectives on an issue. One part of a journal or reading log should include summaries of each article you read. Another part should focus on your own dialectic thinking as you interact with your sources while you are reading them. Adapt the questions for promoting dialectic thinking on page 45.

A Formal Exploratory Essay   A formal exploratory essay tells the story of an intellectual journey. It is both a way of promoting dialectical thinking and a way of narrating one's struggle to negotiate multiple views. The keys to writing successful exploratory essays are: (1) choosing an issue to explore on which you don't have an answer or position (or on which you are open to changing your mind); (2) wrestling with an issue or problem by resisting quick, simple answers and by exploring diverse perspectives; and (3) letting your thinking evolve and your own stance on the issue grow out of this exploration.

Exploratory essays can be powerful thinking and writing experiences in their own right, but they can also be a valuable precursor to a formal argument. Many instructors assign a formal exploratory paper as the first stage of a course research project—what we might call a "thesis-seeking" stage. (The second stage is a formal argument that converts your exploratory thinking into a hierarchically organized argument using reasons and evidence to support your claim.) Although often used as part of a research project, exploratory essays can also be low-stakes reflective pieces narrating the evolution of a writer's thinking during a class discussion.

An exploratory essay includes these thinking moves and parts:

- The essay is opened and driven by the writer's issue question or research problem—not a thesis.
- The introduction to the essay presents the question and shows why it interests the writer, why it is significant, and why it is problematic rather than clear-cut or easy to resolve.
- The body of the essay shows the writer's inquiry process. It demonstrates how the writer has kept the question open, sincerely wrestled with different

views on the question, accepted uncertainty and ambiguity, and possibly rede-fined the question in the midst of his or her reading and reflection on multiple perspectives.

- The body of the essay includes summaries of the different views or sources that the writer explored and often includes believing and doubting responses to them.
- In the essay's conclusion, the writer may clarify his or her thinking and discover a thesis to be developed and supported in a subsequent argument. But the conclusion can also remain open because the writer may not have discovered his or her own position on the issue and may acknowledge the need or desire for more exploration.

One of the writing assignment options for this chapter is a formal exploratory paper. Michael Banks's exploratory essay on pages 50–56 shows how he explored different voices in the controversy over illegal immigration.

Conclusion

This chapter has focused on inquiry as a way to enrich your reading and writing of arguments. This chapter has offered five main strategies for deep reading: (1) Use a variety of questions and prompts to find an issue to explore; (2) place readings in their rhetorical context; (3) read as a believer; (4) read as a doubter; and (5) think dialectically. This chapter has also shown you how to summarize an article and incorporate summaries into your own writing, using attributive tags to distinguish the ideas you are summarizing from your own. It has explained why a reading's rhetorical context (purpose, audience, and genre) must be considered in any thoughtful response to an argument. Finally, it has emphasized the importance of dialectic thinking and has offered the exploratory essay as a way to encourage wrestling with multiple perspectives rather than seeking early closure.

WRITING ASSIGNMENT   An Argument Summary or a Formal Exploratory Essay

Option 1: An Argument Summary   Write a 250-word summary of an argument selected by your instructor. Then write a one-sentence summary of the same argument. Use as models Michael Banks's summaries of John Kavanaugh's argument on immigration (pages 41 and 42).

Option 2: A Formal Exploratory Essay   Write an exploratory essay in which you narrate in first-person, chronological order the evolution through time of your thinking about an issue or problem. Rather than state a thesis or claim, begin with a question or problem. Then describe your inquiry process as you worked your way through sources or different views. Follow the guidelines for an exploratory paper shown on page 49. When you cite the sources you have considered, be sure to use attributive tags so that the reader can distinguish between your own ideas and those of the sources you have

Organization Plan for an Exploratory Essay

Introduction (one to several paragraphs)	• Establish that your question is complex, problematic, and significant. • Show why you are interested in it. • Present relevant background on your issue. Begin with your question or build up to it, using it to end your introductory section.
Body section 1: First view or source	• Introduce your first source and show why you started with it. • Provide rhetorical context and information about it. • Summarize the source's content and argument. • Offer your response to this source, including both believing and doubting points. • Talk about what this source contributes to your understanding of your question: What did you learn? What value does this source have for you? What is missing from this source that you want to consider? Where do you want to go from here?
Body section 2: Second view or source	• Repeat the process with a new source selected to advance the inquiry. • Explain why you selected this source (to find an alternative view, pursue a subquestion, find more data, and so forth). • Summarize the source's argument. • Respond to the source's ideas. Look for points of agreement and disagreement with other sources. • Show how your cumulative reading of sources is shaping your thinking or leading to more questions.
Body sections 3, 4, 5, etc.	• Continue exploring views or sources.
Conclusion	• Wrap up your intellectual journey and explain where you are now in your thinking and how your understanding of your problem has changed. • Present your current answer to your question based on all that you have learned so far, or explain why you still can't answer your question, or explain what research you might pursue further.

summarized. If you use research sources, use MLA documentation for citing ideas and quotations and for creating a Works Cited at the end (see Chapter 17).

Explanation and Organization

An exploratory essay could grow out of class discussion, course readings, field work and interviews, or simply the writer's role-playing of alternative views. In all cases, the purpose of an exploratory paper is not to state and defend a thesis. Instead, its purpose is to think dialectically about multiple perspectives, narrating the evolution through time of the writer's thought process. Many students are inspired by the open, "behind-the-scenes" feel of an exploratory essay. They enjoy taking readers on the same intellectual and emotional journey they have just traveled. A typical organization plan for an exploratory essay is shown on page 49. ■

Reading

What follows is Michael Banks's exploratory essay on the subject of illegal immigration. His research begins with the articles by Kavanaugh and Reed that you have already read and discussed. He then moves off in his own direction.

Should the United States Grant Legal Status to Undocumented Immigrant Workers?

MICHAEL BANKS (STUDENT)

Introduction shows the writer's interest and investment in the issue, which, in this case, began with personal experience.

Having grown up in the California Bay Area, I have long been aware of illegal immigration. In high school, I volunteered through a school program to deliver free lunches to Mexican workers waiting for day jobs at popular hiring sites such as local hardware stores. One time we even went out to one of the farm fields to deliver lunches, and some of the workers scattered when they saw us coming. Apparently they thought we were police or immigration officials. Although the relationships were not deep or lasting, I had the opportunity to talk with some of the workers in my stumbling high school Spanish, and they would tell me about some of their bad experiences such as employers who wouldn't pay them what was promised. They had no recourse to file a complaint because they lacked legal status. Our program supervisor often stressed the importance of recognizing the workers as friends or equals rather than as charity cases. I often wondered how they could work with such low wages and still live a dignified life. However, my experiences did not push me to consider deeply the reality of being an illegal immigrant.

Writer presents the problem he is going to investigate. He shows why the problem is complex, significant, and difficult to resolve. The introduction shows his genuine perplexity.

Writer states his research question.

Writer explains his starting point, introduces his first source, and gives some rhetorical context for it.

Writer summarizes the article.

Writer includes believing and doubting points as he discusses what he learned from this article and how it influenced his thinking on his research question.

Here the writer doubts the article and challenges some of its ideas.

With this background, I entered our class discussions sympathetic towards the immigrants. However, I also recognized that the cheap labor they provided allowed Americans to keep food prices affordable or to find workers for any kind of hard day-labor job such as landscaping or digging up a backyard septic system. I am still not sure whether illegal immigrants are taking away jobs that Americans want, but I do know that I and most of my college friends would not be willing to work low-paying summer jobs picking tomatoes or weeding lettuce. For this exploratory essay, I wanted to look more deeply into this complicated ethical and economic dilemma. I set for myself this question: What is the best way for the United States to handle the problem of illegal immigration?

My exploration began with an article that our instructor assigned to the whole class: "Amnesty?" from *America* magazine by John F. Kavanaugh, a Jesuit priest and professor of philosophy at St. Louis University. In this article, Kavanaugh questions the morality of the current U.S. treatment of undocumented immigrants. He points out that most immigrants are not criminals but rather hard-working, family-oriented people. He attributes recent increases in immigration to the North American Free Trade Agreement and the poverty it causes among rural Mexican farmers. He also notes that anti-immigration groups have a "seething hostility" (39) for these persons and strongly resist any granting of amnesty or legal status. Kavanaugh disagrees with these groups, arguing that a nation that identifies itself as "Judeo-Christian and humane" should follow biblical teaching, "higher law," and the courageous example of leaders such as Martin Luther King, Jr., in challenging unjust laws (39). Although admitting that unrestrained immigration would help nobody, Kavanaugh exhorts the country to give "legal status to anyone who contributes to our common good" (39). He recommends that a citizen panel be used to review an immigrant's status and make recommendations for amnesty.

I found Kavanaugh's article to be quite persuasive. This article could particularly inspire its Catholic readers, and I too had an easy time agreeing with much of what Kavanaugh says. In fact, he reminded me of the director of my high school outreach program. I like the argument that people who contribute to the community should not be labeled as "illegal" as if they are in the same category as thieves or welfare cheaters. But I wasn't yet convinced that the laws governing immigration were "unjust" in the same way that segregation laws were unjust. It seems to me that a country has the right to control who enters the country, but doesn't have the right to make certain people sit in the back of the bus. So the references to Martin Luther King's fighting unjust laws didn't quite connect with me. So I was still caught in the dilemma. Also, I saw some other major problems with Kavanaugh's argument. First, it may not be fair to apply Judeo-Christian ethics to everyone in the country, especially considering our Constitutional separation of church and state. His appeal to religious beliefs may be appropriate to persuade Christians to volunteer for a cause but not to change a secular nation's laws. Also, his solution of having a citizen panel seemed impractical, especially for handling the number of illegal immigrants. Finally, Kavanaugh doesn't address the economic side of this argument. He didn't help me see what the disadvantages would be to granting amnesty to millions of undocumented workers.

Writer moves to his next source and provides some rhetorical context, including information about the author.

Writer summarizes the article.

5   My next article, which the class also read together, was from *The American Conservative* titled "Why Blame Mexico?" by Fred Reed. According to Reed's biographical sketch on the Web ("Fred on Everything: Biography"), Reed is an ex-marine, former scientist, wanderer and world traveler, former law-enforcement columnist for the *Washington Times,* and a freelance journalist currently living in Mexico. He is known for his provocative columns. Reed's article was hard to summarize because it jumps around and is very sarcastic. His overall view is best exemplified by his very first statement: "To grasp American immigration policy, one needs only remember that the United States frowns on smoking while subsidizing tobacco growers" (45). Reed argues that illegal immigration occurs not mainly because there are millions of impoverished Mexicans in need of work, but because liberals feel good about tolerating them and because "[c]onservative Republican businessmen favor immigration…because they want cheap labor that actually shows up and works" (45). Reed points out that Mexico itself is clear and consistent in its own immigration policies: Immigrants into Mexico must possess clear residency papers, must have regular monthly earnings, and must be fluent in Spanish. In contrast to Kavanaugh, who focuses on immigrants, Reed focuses on the Americans who hire them; without Americans wanting cheap labor, immigrants would have no reason to cross the border. He takes it for granted that illegal immigrants should not be given legal status. Reed offers no solutions for the tangled mess of U.S. treatment of illegal immigrants, but underscores the fact that it is this country's self-created problem.

Writer shows his dialectical thinking, as he weighs the ideas of this source against those in his first article. He explores points of disagreement between these two sources.

Writer shows how he is wrestling with the ideas in this source.

Reed's article pulled me back away from Kavanaugh's call for amnesty. It made me see more clearly the entangled economic issues. Many American citizens *want* a source of cheap labor. Reed, in contrast, wants to eliminate cheap labor. If we followed the logical path that Reed seems to propose, we'd start jailing employers in order to cut off the job supply. At this point in my research, the status quo seemed to be a better situation. If cheap labor is so important to America's economy and if a low paying job in the United States is better than no job, perhaps some kind of legal status other than amnesty and citizenship would help resolve the situation. My head was spinning because I could picture all my classmates who would disagree with my last sentence! At this point, I felt I needed to explore other approaches to this controversy.

The day after I read the Reed article, I was talking with a friend who suggested I watch a recent movie about immigration called *Under the Same*

Moon. I figured it would be a fun diversion, if nothing else, and rented it. The movie tells the tale of a nine-year-old boy, Carlitos, who lives with his grandmother until she dies and then sets out to cross the border illegally to find his mother, who has been working several jobs at once as an undocumented immigrant for four years in Los Angeles. The dramatic story— shown from the dual perspective of mother and son—highlights many of the dangers faced by the immigrants themselves: separation from family members and support networks, exploitation by border-crossing agencies, INS raids on job sites, and dangerous jobs such as picking pesticide-coated tomatoes, just to name a few. The main characters' immigrant laborer status also draws attention to the undeniable humanity of immigrants.

This film works powerfully to create sympathy for illegal immigrants but without the explicit religious coating provided by Kavanaugh. I cannot help but admire the sacrifices made by immigrant workers who leave behind children and family in order to try to provide a brighter future for their loved ones. In cases where immigrants are separated from their young children, granting these parents legal status could help unite families more quickly and could ease the great pain that comes with being separated while allowing them the opportunity to forge a better life. On the other hand, families would also be reunited if the parents were sent back to Mexico. The great sympathy I feel for illegal immigrants doesn't necessarily mean that granting amnesty and citizenship is the best solution. While the film evokes compassion for individual immigrants, it does not address the magnitude of the problem.

I had heard about a number of films about illegal immigration and immigrants' experiences and wanted to continue with another film, so I headed back to Blockbuster and asked one of the workers if he could point me towards a recent documentary on illegal immigration. What I came up with was *A Day Without a Mexican,* a mock documentary, or "mockumentary." The movie's plot imagines the complete disappearance of the entire Latino population in California, both legal and illegal. The state grinds to a complete halt, widespread panic occurs, and homes, restaurants, supermarkets, orchards, farms, schools, and construction services are completely dysfunctional. The story and structure of the film viciously satirize antiimmigrant organizations, the news media, the border patrol, and waffling politicians. I visited the movie's Web site to search for further information, as I was curious about its reception. The Latino audience saw this film as a hit; it took in the second best per screen average the weekend it was released in Southern California. According to the general sales manager of Televisa Cine, *A Day Without a Mexican*'s success "underscores that there is not only a broad Hispanic audience who wants to see this film, but also a significant crossover audience," while the director, Sergio Arau, and lead actress/screenwriter, Yareli Arizmendi, add "we still believe we can change the world one screen at a time" ("Missing José Found").

Writer explains his movement to his next source.

He summarizes the plot of the film.

Writer discusses and analyzes the ideas in the film by presenting believing and doubting points.

Writer mentions problems the source raises for him.

Writer explains his choice of another film.

A brief summary prepares for his discussion.

Writer presents some information about the rhetorical context of this film, including statements from the director and details about how it was first received.

10   The film's success at the box office suggests to me that Arau and
Arizmendi have revealed the important truth that Latino immigration
makes California a better place. The comic film works by exaggeration, but
its image of a helpless California without immigrants is easy to believe.
Since California, and presumably the rest of the country, relies so heavily
upon its immigrants, it would make very little sense to create new immigration policies that made the status quo worse. Perhaps a solution might lie in
somehow recognizing the worth of immigrants, as *A Day Without a
Mexican* suggests is important, while maintaining the status quo of paying
them wages lower than American standards. A moral dilemma remains,
however, because this approach places economics above justice.

At this stage, I decided to review some of the possible "solutions" that I
had encountered so far to the illegal immigration problem. One solution,
based on our valuing the humanity of immigrants, is to offer them amnesty,
legal status, and eventual citizenship. Another, based on our valuing the
economic benefits of cheap labor, is to keep the status quo. Still another
solution is to get rid of illegal aliens altogether either by deporting them or
by jailing their employers and thus eliminating their source of income. None
of these options appealed to me. In search of another approach, I decided to
head for the library to do more research. A friendly reference librarian suggested that I start with a couple of overview articles from *CQ Researcher.*
These articles, which I just skimmed, provided some background information, statistical data on immigration, and summaries of different bills before
Congress. I found my head swimming with so many little details that I
began losing the big picture about an actual direction I wanted to go.
However, one idea that kept emerging from the *CQ Researcher* was the
possibility of guest worker programs. I decided I wanted to find out more
about what these programs were. With the reference librarian's guidance, I
used *Academic Search Complete* to find a number of articles on guest
worker programs. I also entered "guest worker program" into Google and
found a number of bloggers supporting or attacking guest worker programs.

I focused first on an editorial, "That's Hospitality," from *The New Republic,*
a news commentary magazine that is in the political center, neither domi-
nantly liberal nor conservative. The editorial opposes a congressional bill that
would establish a guest worker program wherein businesses could hire foreigners as "guest workers" for up to six years. These workers would be
granted temporary legal status, but they would have to return to their home
country when the six years were up. Although supporters of the bill called it
"humane" and "compassionate," the editorial writer opposes it because it is
"un-American." No other group of immigrants, the editorial states, has been
treated this way—as second class transients who had no opportunity to make a
full life in America. The article compares this proposed guest worker program
to similar programs in Europe after WWII, where workers from Eastern
Europe or Turkey came to countries like Germany or Netherlands and stayed

Writer responds to this source and explains the current status of his thinking about his research question. He looks for points of agreement among this source and others he has consulted.

but never assimilated. What the article supports instead is an alternative bill that grants "temporary worker" status but allows workers to apply for a green card after six years and for citizenship after five more years.

This article excited me because it seemed to promote a compromise that turned undocumented workers who were afraid of getting caught and deported into persons with legal status and with the hope of eventually becoming citizens. It shared the pro-immigrant spirit of Kavanaugh and *Under the Same Moon* but didn't directly undermine the economic benefits provided by cheap labor. Rather than offering direct amnesty, it specified a waiting period of at least eleven years before a person could apply for citizenship. Although this article did not specify how the United States might manage the volume and rate of people seeking guest worker and then citizen status, I thought that this proposal would be the position I would like to argue for in a later, persuasive paper.

Writer decides to continue exploring his question by looking at a source that opposes his preceding one. He gives information about the rhetorical context of this source, particularly about the blogger.

He summarizes the ideas in his blog.

Writer shows how this source has challenged the ideas in the preceding source, complicated the issue, and raised important questions for him.

But I decided next to look at the negative side of a guest worker program and was amazed at how many anti-immigration groups hated this bill. One provocative blog, "Guest Worker Program Illusion," is by a freelance writer, Frosty Woolridge, who maintains his own Web site aimed at combating "overpopulation and immigration." According to his blog site he has written hundreds of articles for seventeen national and two international magazines and has been an invited speaker on environmental issues at many universities. Woolridge favors strict border enforcement and deportation of anyone who has illegally entered the country. He sees all forms of guest worker programs as amnesty that will lead to overpopulation and an increasing welfare burden on middle-class Americans who try to provide services for the guest workers. He also argues that the guest workers will suppress wages for American workers. His strategy is to point out all the problems that the guest worker program will open up: Can the guest worker bring his or her family? Will children born to guest workers automatically be U.S. citizens? Must the states provide tax payer-supported schools and hospital services for the guest workers? If so, must the schools be bilingual? Will guest workers pay social security taxes and thus become eligible for social security? Will they be eligible for Workers Compensation if they get hurt on the job? Will their older children get in-state rates at public universities? Will their younger children be covered by child labor laws? Will they actually leave after six years or simply revert back to undocumented illegal status?

Although he has not fully worked out his answer to his research question, he sums up how his views have evolved. He explains how his reading and thinking have deepened and clarified his views on this issue.

15   All these problems raised by Woolridge were never mentioned in *The New Republic* editorial, and they severely dampened my spirits. As I end this exploratory paper, I still have a number of articles left to read and much left to learn, but I think I have a pretty good grasp of what the issues and disagreements are. I definitely think that the plan supporting a guest worker program with the chance of eventual citizenship is the best approach. But it has to be linked with other approaches also, including ways to improve the economies of Mexico and other Latin American countries so that poor people wouldn't have to come to the United States to find work. My hope is that

He sketches a path he might follow in further exploration of his question.

many of the objections raised by Woolridge are solvable. I have realized from my inquiry that my heart is with the immigrants and that I don't share Woolridge's desire to close America off from future immigration.

A Works Cited page in MLA format lists the sources consulted and discussed in this essay.

Works Cited

A Day Without a Mexican. Dir. Sergio Arau. Xenon Pictures, 2004. DVD.

Kavanaugh, John F. "Amnesty?" *America* 10 Mar. 2008: 8. Print.

"Missing José Found: Walks His Way to Box Office Success Throughout Southern California." *ADWAM News*. A Day Without a Mexican, n.d. Web. 12 July 2008.

Reed, Fred. "Why Blame Mexico?" *American Conservative* 10 Mar. 2008: 35. Print.

"That's Hospitality." *New Republic* 17 Apr. 2006: 7. *Academic Search Complete*. Web. 30 Aug. 2008.

Under the Same Moon. Dir. Patricia Riggen. Perf. Adrián Alonso, Kate del Castillo, and Eugenio Derbez. Twentieth Century Fox, 2008. DVD.

Woolridge, Frosty. "Guest Worker Program Illusion." *Newswithviews.com*. N.p., 2 Dec. 2005. Web. 22 May 2008.

PART TWO
Writing an Argument

This still from the *Tomb Raider* video game series features main character Lara Croft engaged in one of her typical combats with humans, beasts, or supernatural creatures. Lara, an adventurer and archeologist, represents both a sexualized and an empowered woman. Women and violent video games are the focus of student Carmen Tieu's argument developed in Chapters 3–5; however, Carmen explores gender roles from the perspective of a woman playing a "male" video game, *Halo*.

3

The Core of an Argument
A Claim with Reasons

In Part One we explained that argument combines truth seeking with persuasion. Part One, by highlighting the importance of exploration and inquiry, emphasizes the truth-seeking dimension of argument. The suggested writing assignments in Part One included a variety of exploratory tasks: freewriting, playing the believing and doubting game, and writing a formal exploratory essay. In Part Two we show you how to convert your exploratory ideas into a thesis-governed classical argument that uses effective reasons and evidence to support its claims. Each chapter in Part Two focuses on a key skill or idea needed for responsible and effective persuasion. In this chapter, you will learn to:

- Describe the key elements of classical argument
- Explain the rhetorical appeals
- Distinguish between issue and information questions and between genuine and pseudoarguments
- Describe the basic frame of an argument

The Classical Structure of Argument

Classical argument is patterned after the persuasive speeches of ancient Greek and Roman orators. In traditional Latin terminology, the main parts of a persuasive speech are the *exordium,* in which the speaker gets the audience's attention; the *narratio,* which provides needed background; the *propositio,* which is the speaker's claim or thesis; the *partitio,* which forecasts the main parts of the speech; the *confirmatio,* which presents the speaker's arguments supporting the claim; the *confutatio,* which summarizes and rebuts opposing views; and the *peroratio,* which concludes the speech by summing up the argument, calling for action, and leaving a strong, lasting impression. (Of course, you don't need to remember these tongue-twisting Latin terms. We cite them only to assure you that in writing a classical argument, you are joining a time-honored tradition that links back to the origins of democracy.)

Let's go over the same territory again using more contemporary terms. We provide an organization plan showing the structure of a classical argument on page 59, which shows these typical sections:

- **The introduction.** Writers of classical argument typically begin with an attention grabber such as a memorable scene, illustrative story, or startling statistic. They continue the introduction by focusing the issue—often

Organization Plan for an Argument with a Classical Structure

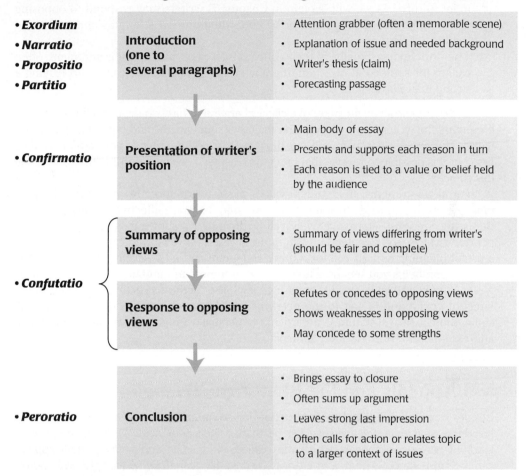

- *Exordium*
- *Narratio*
- *Propositio*
- *Partitio*

Introduction (one to several paragraphs)
- Attention grabber (often a memorable scene)
- Explanation of issue and needed background
- Writer's thesis (claim)
- Forecasting passage

- *Confirmatio*

Presentation of writer's position
- Main body of essay
- Presents and supports each reason in turn
- Each reason is tied to a value or belief held by the audience

- *Confutatio*

Summary of opposing views
- Summary of views differing from writer's (should be fair and complete)

Response to opposing views
- Refutes or concedes to opposing views
- Shows weaknesses in opposing views
- May concede to some strengths

- *Peroratio*

Conclusion
- Brings essay to closure
- Often sums up argument
- Leaves strong last impression
- Often calls for action or relates topic to a larger context of issues

by stating it directly as a question or by briefly summarizing opposing views—and providing needed background and context. They conclude the introduction by presenting their claim (thesis statement) and forecasting the argument's structure.

- **The presentation of the writer's position.** The presentation of the writer's own position is usually the longest part of a classical argument. Here writers present the reasons and evidence supporting their claims, typically choosing reasons that tie into their audience's values, beliefs, and assumptions. Usually each reason is developed in its own paragraph or sequence of paragraphs. When a paragraph introduces a new reason, writers state the reason directly and then support it with evidence or a chain of ideas. Along the way, writers guide their readers with appropriate transitions.

- **The summary and critique of alternative views.** When summarizing and responding to opposing views, writers have several options. If there are several opposing arguments, writers may summarize all of them together and then compose a single response, or they may summarize and respond to each argument in turn. As we will explain in Chapter 7, writers may respond to opposing views either by refuting them or by conceding to their strengths and shifting to a different field of values.

■ **The conclusion.** Finally, in their conclusion, writers sum up their argument, often calling for some kind of action, thereby creating a sense of closure and leaving a strong final impression.

In this organization, the body of a classical argument has two major sections—the one presenting the writer's own position and the other summarizing and critiquing alternative views. The organization plan and our discussion have the writer's own position coming first, but it is possible to reverse that order. (In Chapter 7 we consider the factors affecting this choice.)

For all its strengths, an argument with a classical structure may not always be your most persuasive strategy. In some cases, you may be more effective by delaying your thesis, by ignoring alternative views altogether, or by showing great sympathy for opposing views (see Chapter 7). Even in these cases, however, the classical structure is a useful planning tool. Its call for a thesis statement and a forecasting statement in the introduction helps you see the whole of your argument in miniature. And by requiring you to summarize and consider opposing views, the classical structure alerts you to the limits of your position and to the need for further reasons and evidence. As we will show, the classical structure is a particularly persuasive mode of argument when you address a neutral or undecided audience.

Classical Appeals and the Rhetorical Triangle

Besides developing a template or structure for an argument, classical rhetoricians analyzed the ways that effective speeches persuaded their audiences. They identified three kinds of persuasive appeals, which they called *logos, ethos,* and *pathos.* These appeals can be understood within a rhetorical context illustrated by a triangle with points labeled *message, writer or speaker,* and *audience* (see Figure 3.1). Effective arguments pay attention to all three points on this *rhetorical triangle.*

As Figure 3.1 shows, each point on the triangle corresponds to one of the three persuasive appeals:

■ *Logos* (Greek for "word") focuses attention on the quality of the message—that is, on the internal consistency and clarity of the argument itself and on the logic of its reasons and support. The impact of *logos* on an audience is referred to as its *logical appeal.*

■ *Ethos* (Greek for "character") focuses attention on the writer's (or speaker's) character as it is projected in the message. It refers to the credibility of the writer. *Ethos* is often conveyed through the writer's investment in his or her claim, through the fairness with which the writer considers alternative views, through the tone and style of the message, and even through the message's professional appearance on paper or screen, including correct grammar, flawless proofreading, and appropriate formats for citations and bibliography. In some cases, *ethos* is also a function of the writer's

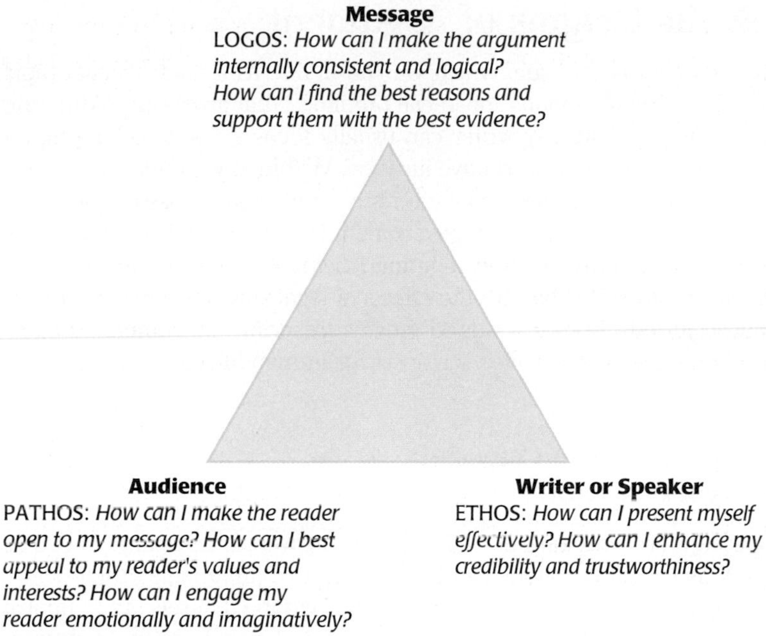

Message
LOGOS: *How can I make the argument internally consistent and logical? How can I find the best reasons and support them with the best evidence?*

Audience
PATHOS: *How can I make the reader open to my message? How can I best appeal to my reader's values and interests? How can I engage my reader emotionally and imaginatively?*

Writer or Speaker
ETHOS: *How can I present myself effectively? How can I enhance my credibility and trustworthiness?*

FIGURE 3.1 The rhetotical triangle

reputation for honesty and expertise independent of the message. The impact of *ethos* on an audience is referred to as the *ethical appeal* or *appeal from credibility.*

- **Pathos** (Greek for "suffering" or "experience") focuses attention on the values and beliefs of the intended audience. It is often associated with emotional appeal. But *pathos* appeals more specifically to an audience's imaginative sympathies—their capacity to feel and see what the writer feels and sees. Thus, when we turn the abstractions of logical discourse into a tangible and immediate story, we are making a pathetic appeal. Whereas appeals to *logos* and *ethos* can further an audience's intellectual assent to our claim, appeals to *pathos* engage the imagination and feelings, moving the audience to a deeper appreciation of the argument's significance.

A related rhetorical concept, connected to the appeals of *logos, ethos,* and *pathos,* is that of *kairos,* from the Greek word for "right time," "season," or "opportunity." This concept suggests that for an argument to be persuasive, its timing must be effectively chosen and its tone and structure in right proportion or measure. You may have had the experience of composing an argumentative e-mail and then hesitating before clicking the "send" button. Is this the right moment to send this message? Is my audience ready to hear what I'm saying? Would my argument be more effective if I waited for a couple of days? If I send this message now, should I change its tone and content? This attentiveness to the unfolding of time is what is meant by *kairos.* We will return to this concept in Chapter 6, when we consider *ethos* and *pathos* in more depth.

Given this background on the classical appeals, let's turn now to *logos*—the logic and structure of arguments.

Issue Questions as the Origins of Argument

At the heart of any argument is an issue, which we can define as a controversial topic area such as "the labeling of biotech foods" or "racial profiling," that gives rise to differing points of view and conflicting claims. A writer can usually focus an issue by asking an issue question that invites at least two alternative answers. Within any complex issue—for example, the issue of abortion—there are usually a number of separate issue questions: Should abortions be legal? Should the federal government authorize Medicaid payments for abortions? When does a fetus become a human being (at conception? at three months? at quickening? at birth?)? What are the effects of legalizing abortion? (One person might stress that legalized abortion leads to greater freedom for women. Another person might respond that it lessens a society's respect for human life.)

Difference between an Issue Question and an Information Question

Of course, not all questions are issue questions that can be answered reasonably in two or more differing ways; thus not all questions can lead to effective arguments. Rhetoricians have traditionally distinguished between *explication,* which is writing that sets out to inform or explain, and *argumentation,* which sets out to change a reader's mind. On the surface, at least, this seems like a useful distinction. If a reader is interested in a writer's question mainly to gain new knowledge about a subject, then the writer's essay could be considered explication rather than argument. According to this view, the following questions about teenage pregnancy might be called information questions rather than issue questions:

> How does the teenage pregnancy rate in the United States compare with the rate in Sweden? If the rates are different, why?

Although both questions seem to call for information rather than for argument, we believe that the second one would be an issue question if reasonable people disagreed on the answer. Thus, different writers might agree that the teenage pregnancy rate in the United States is seven times higher than the rate in Sweden. But they might disagree about why. One writer might emphasize Sweden's practical, secular sex-education courses, leading to more consistent use of contraceptives among Swedish teenagers. Another writer might point to the higher use of oral contraceptives among teenage girls in Sweden (partly a result of Sweden's generous national health program) and to less reliance on condoms for preventing pregnancy. Another might argue that moral decay in the United States or a breakdown of the traditional family is at fault. Thus, underneath the surface of what looks like a simple explication of the "truth" is really a controversy.

How to Identify an Issue Question

You can generally tell whether a question is an issue question or an information question by examining your purpose in relationship to your audience. If your relationship to your audience is that of teacher to learner, so that your audience hopes to gain new information, knowledge, or understanding that you possess, then your question is probably an information question. But if your relationship to your audience is that of advocate to decision maker or jury, so that your audience needs to make up its mind on something and is weighing different points of view, then the question you address is an issue question.

Often the same question can be an information question in one context and an issue question in another. Let's look at the following examples:

- **How does a diesel engine work?** (This is probably an information question, because reasonable people who know about diesel engines will probably agree on how they work. This question would be posed by an audience of new learners.)
- **Why is a diesel engine more fuel efficient than a gasoline engine?** (This also seems to be an information question, because all experts will probably agree on the answer. Once again, the audience seems to be new learners, perhaps students in an automotive class.)
- **What is the most cost-effective way to produce diesel fuel from crude oil?** (This could be an information question if experts agree and you are addressing new learners. But if you are addressing engineers and one engineer says process X is the most cost-effective and another argues for process Y, then the question is an issue question.)
- **Should the present highway tax on diesel fuel be increased?** (This is certainly an issue question. One person says yes; another says no; another offers a compromise.)

■ ■ ■ **FOR CLASS DISCUSSION**   Information Questions versus Issue Questions

Working as a class or in small groups, try to decide which of the following questions are information questions and which are issue questions. Many of them could be either, depending on the rhetorical context. For such questions, create hypothetical contexts to show your reasoning.

1. What percentage of public schools in the United States are failing?
2. Which is more addictive, marijuana or alcohol?
3. What is the effect on children of playing first-person-shooter games?
4. Is genetically modified corn safe for human consumption?
5. Should a woman with newly detected breast cancer opt for a radical mastectomy (complete removal of the breast and surrounding lymph tissue) or a lumpectomy (removal of the malignant lump without removal of the whole breast)?

■ ■ ■

Difference between a Genuine Argument and a Pseudo-Argument

Although every argument features an issue question with alternative answers, not every dispute over answers is a rational argument. Rational arguments require two additional factors: (1) reasonable participants who operate within the conventions of reasonable behavior and (2) potentially sharable assumptions that can serve as a starting place or foundation for the argument. Lacking one or both of these conditions, disagreements remain stalled at the level of pseudo-arguments.

Pseudo-Arguments: Committed Believers and Fanatical Skeptics

A reasonable argument assumes the possibility of growth and change; disputants may modify their views as they acknowledge strengths in an alternative view or weaknesses in their own. Such growth becomes impossible—and argument degenerates to pseudo-argument—when disputants are fanatically committed to their positions. Consider the case of the fanatical believer and the fanatical skeptic.

From one perspective, committed believers are admirable persons, guided by unwavering values and beliefs. Committed believers stand on solid rock, unwilling to compromise their principles or bend to the prevailing winds. But from another perspective, committed believers can seem rigidly fixed, incapable of growth or change. When committed believers from two clashing belief systems try to engage in dialogue with each other, a truth-seeking exchange of views becomes difficult. They talk past each other; dialogue is replaced by monologue from within isolated silos. Once committed believers push each other's buttons on global warming, guns, health care, taxes, religion, or some other issue, each disputant resorts to an endless replaying of the same prepackaged arguments. Disagreeing with a committed believer is like ordering the surf to quiet down. The only response is another crashing wave.

In contrast to the committed believer, the fanatical skeptic dismisses the possibility of ever believing anything. Skeptics often demand proof where no proof is possible. So what if the sun has risen every day of recorded history? That's no proof that it will rise tomorrow. Short of absolute proof, which never exists, fanatical skeptics accept nothing. In a world where the most we can hope for is increased audience adherence to our ideas, the skeptic demands an ironclad, logical demonstration of our claim's rightness.

A Closer Look at Pseudo-Arguments: The Lack of Shared Assumptions

As we have seen, rational argument degenerates to pseudo-argument when there is no possibility for listening, learning, growth, or change. In this section, we look more closely at a frequent cause of pseudo-arguments: lack of shared assumptions.

Shared Assumptions and the Problem of Ideology   As our discussion of committed believers suggests, reasonable argument is difficult when the disputants have differing "ideologies," which is an academic word for belief systems or worldviews. We all have our own ideologies. We all look at the world through a lens shaped by our life's experiences. Our beliefs and values are shaped by our family background, our friends, our culture, our particular time in history, our race or ethnicity, our gender or sexual orientation, our social class, our religion, our education, and so forth. Because we tend to think that our particular lens for looking at the world is natural and universal rather than specific to ourselves, we must be aware that persons who disagree with us may not share our deepest assumptions and beliefs. To participate in rational argument, we and our audience must seek *shared assumptions*—certain principles or values or beliefs that can serve as common ground.

The failure to find shared assumptions often leads to pseudo-arguments, particularly if one disputant makes assumptions that the other disputant cannot accept. Such pseudo-arguments often occur in disputes arising from politics or religion. For example, consider differences within the Christian community over how to interpret the Bible. Some Christian groups choose a straightforward, literal interpretation of the Bible as God's inerrant word while other groups read some passages metaphorically or mythically and focus on the paradoxes, historical contexts, and interpretive complexities of the Bible; still other Christian groups read it as an ethical call for social justice. Members of these different Christian groups may not be able to argue rationally about, say, evolution or gay marriage because they have very different ways of reading Biblical passages and invoking the authority of the Bible. Similarly, within other religious traditions, believers may also differ about the meaning and applicability of their sacred texts to scientific issues and social problems.

Similar disagreements about assumptions occur in the political arena as well. (See the discussions of "angle of vision" and "degree of advocacy" in Chapter 15, page 354.) Our point is that certain religious or political beliefs or texts cannot be evoked for evidence or authority when an audience does not assume the belief's truth or does not agree on the way that a given text should be read or interpreted.

Shared Assumptions and the Problem of Personal Opinions   Lack of shared assumptions also dooms arguments about purely personal opinions—for example, someone's claim that opera is boring or that pizza is better than nachos. Of course, a pizza-versus-nachos argument might be possible if the disputants assume a shared criterion about nutrition. For example, a nutritionist could argue that pizza is better than nachos because pizza provides more balanced nutrients per calorie. But if one of the disputants responds, "Nah, nachos are better than pizza because nachos taste better," then he makes a different assumption—"My sense of taste is better than your sense of taste." This is a wholly personal standard, an assumption that others are unable to share.

■ ■ ■ **FOR CLASS DISCUSSION**   Reasonable Arguments versus Pseudo-Arguments

The following questions can all be answered in alternative ways. However, not all of them will lead to reasonable arguments. Try to decide which questions will lead to reasonable arguments and which will lead only to pseudo-arguments.

1. Are the *Star Wars* films good science fiction?
2. Is it ethically justifiable to capture dolphins and train them for human entertainment?
3. Should cities subsidize professional sports venues?
4. Is this abstract oil painting created by a monkey smearing paint on a canvas a true work of art?
5. Are nose rings and tongue studs attractive?

■ ■ ■

Frame of an Argument: A Claim Supported by Reasons

We said earlier that an argument originates in an *issue question,* which by definition is any question that provokes disagreement about the best answer. When you write an argument, your task is to take a position on the issue and to support it with reasons and evidence. The *claim* of your essay is the position you want your audience to accept. To put it another way, your claim is your essay's *thesis statement,* a one-sentence summary answer to your issue question. Your task, then, is to make a claim and support it with reasons.

What Is a Reason?

A *reason* (also called a *premise*) is a claim used to support another claim. In speaking or writing, a reason is usually linked to the claim with connecting words such as *because, since, for, so, thus, consequently,* and *therefore,* indicating that the claim follows logically from the reason.

Let us take an example. In one of our recent classes, students heatedly debated the ethics of capturing wild dolphins and training them to perform in marine parks or "swim with dolphins" programs. One student had recently seen the 2009 documentary *The Cove,* about the gory dolphin hunts in Japan in which dolphins are killed en masse by fishermen and some are captured for display in shows around the world. Another student cited the 1960s family show *Flipper,* featuring a dolphin working harmoniously with—and often saving—his human friends. One student commented that his sister fell in love with marine biology on a family vacation in Hawaii when she swam with a dolphin, gave signals for the dolphin's jump, and touched its rubbery skin during a "swim with dolphins" program. In response, a few students remarked that the only ethical way to experience dolphins is with a pair of binoculars from a boat. Here are the frameworks the class developed for two alternative positions on this issue:

One View

CLAIM: The public should not support the commercial use of captured dolphins.

REASON   1: Aquariums, marine parks, and "swim with dolphins" programs separate dolphins from their natural habitat and social groups.

REASON 2:   The unnatural environment of aquariums, marine parks, and dolphin programs places great stress on dolphins.

REASON 3:   Aquariums, marine parks, and dolphin programs are mainly big businesses driven by profit.

REASON 4:   What these aquariums, marine parks, and "swim with" programs call "education about dolphins" is just a series of artificial, exploitive tricks taught through behavior modification.

REASON 5:   Marine parks and programs create a commercial market for dolphins, which directly or indirectly encourages dolphin hunts and captures.

REASON 6:   Marine parks and programs promote an attitude of human dominance over animals.

Alternative View

CLAIM: The public should continue to support aquariums, marine parks, and "swim with dolphins" programs.

REASON 1: These parks and programs observe accreditation standards for animal welfare, health, and nutrition, and monitor the well-being of their dolphins.

REASON 2: These marine parks and "swim with" programs enable scientists and veterinarians to study dolphin behavior in ways not possible with field studies in the wild.

REASON 3: While creating memorable family entertainment, these parks and programs provide environmental education and teach appreciation for dolphins.

REASON 4: Accredited programs do not endorse dolphin hunts and have self-sustaining breeding programs to avoid the need for dolphin hunts.

REASON 5: In their training of dolphins, these programs emphasize animal husbandry and animal enrichment to exercise dolphins' intelligence and abilities.

REASON 6: Marine parks and "swim with dolphins" programs support research and conservation.

Formulating a list of reasons in this way breaks your argumentative task into a series of subtasks. It gives you a frame for building your argument in parts. In the previous example, the frame for the argument opposing commercial use of dolphins suggests five different lines of reasoning a writer might pursue. A writer might use all five reasons or select only two or three, depending on which reasons would most persuade the intended audience. Each line of reasoning would be developed in its own separate section of the argument. For example, you might begin one section of your argument with the following sentence: "The public should not support these dolphin programs because they teach dolphins clownish tricks and artificial behaviors, which they pass off as 'education about dolphins.'" You would then provide examples of the tricks and stunts that dolphins are taught, explain how these contrast with dolphins' natural behaviors, and offer examples of erroneous facts or information about dolphins supplied by these programs. You might also need to support the underlying assumption that it is good for the public to acquire *real knowledge* about dolphins in the wild. (How one articulates and supports the underlying assumptions of an argument will be developed in Chapter 4 when we discuss warrants and backing.) You would then proceed in the same way for each separate section of your argument.

To summarize our point in this section, the frame of an argument consists of the claim (the thesis statement of the essay), which is supported by one or more reasons, which are in turn supported by evidence or sequences of further reasons.

■ ■ ■ **FOR CLASS DISCUSSION** Using Images to Support an Argument

In Chapter 1, we talked about implicit and explicit arguments and introduced you to some visual arguments. The photographs in Figures 3.2 and 3.3 are typical ways that dolphins are depicted in public discussions about dolphins. In groups or as a whole class, examine the photographs carefully and describe the image of dolphins that each photo is portraying. Then determine which claim, and more specifically, which reason or reasons, you think each image best supports. Which reason or reasons could each image be used to refute? Work out explanations for your thinking.

■ ■ ■

FIGURE 3.2 Typical photo from a "swim with dolphins" program

FIGURE 3.3 Jumping bottlenose dolphins

Expressing Reasons in Because Clauses

Chances are that when you were a child, the word *because* contained magical explanatory powers. Somehow *because* seemed decisive. It persuaded people to accept your view of the world; it changed people's minds. Later, as you got older, you discovered that *because* only introduced your arguments and that it was the reasons following *because* that made the difference. Still, *because* introduced you to the powers potentially residing in the adult world of logic.

Of course, there are many other ways to express the logical connection between a reason and a claim. Our language is rich in ways of stating *because* relationships:

- The public should not support marine parks and "swim with dolphins" programs because these programs place great stress on dolphins by separating them from their natural habitat and social groups.
- Marine parks and "swim with dolphin" programs place great stress on dolphins by separating them from their natural habitat and social groups. Therefore the public should not support the captivity of dolphins.
- Marine parks and "swim with dolphin" programs place great stress on dolphins by separating them from their natural habitat and social groups, so the public should not support these programs.
- One reason that the public should not support marine parks or "swim with dolphins" programs is that these programs place great stress on dolphins by separating them from their natural habitat and social groups.
- My argument that the public should not support marine parks and "swim with dolphins" programs is based mainly on the grounds that these programs place great stress on dolphins by separating them from their natural habitat and social groups.

Even though logical relationships can be stated in various ways, writing out one or more *because* clauses seems to be the most succinct and manageable way to clarify an argument for oneself. We therefore suggest that sometime in the writing process, you create a *working thesis statement* that summarizes your main reasons as because clauses attached to your claim.* Just when you compose your own working thesis statement depends largely on your writing process. Some writers like to plan out their whole argument from the start and often compose their working thesis statements with *because* clauses before they write their rough drafts. Others discover their arguments as they write. And sometimes it is a combination of both. For these writers, an extended working

---

*A working thesis statement opposing the commercial use of captured dolphins might look like this: *The public should not support the commercial use of captured dolphins because marine parks and "swim with dolphins" programs place great stress on dolphins by separating them from their natural habitat and social groups; because these parks and programs are mainly big businesses driven by profit; because they create inaccurate and incomplete educational information about dolphins; because they create a commercial market for dolphins that directly or indirectly encourages dolphin hunts and captures; and because they promote an attitude of human dominance over animals.* You might not put a bulky thesis statement like this into your essay; rather, a working thesis statement is a behind-the-scenes way of summarizing your argument so that you can see it whole and clear.

thesis statement is something they might write halfway through the composing process as a way of ordering their argument when various branches seem to be growing out of control. Or they might compose a working thesis statement at the very end as a way of checking the unity of the final product.

Whenever you write your extended thesis statement, the act of doing so can be simultaneously frustrating and thought provoking. Composing *because* clauses can be a powerful discovery tool, causing you to think of many different kinds of arguments to support your claim. But it is often difficult to wrestle your ideas into the *because* clause shape, which sometimes seems to be overly tidy for the complex network of ideas you are trying to work with. Nevertheless, trying to summarize your argument as a single claim with reasons should help you see more clearly what you have to do.

■ ■ ■ **FOR CLASS DISCUSSION**   Developing Claims and Reasons

Try this group exercise to help you see how writing *because* clauses can be a discovery procedure. Divide into small groups. Each group member should contribute an issue that he or she would like to explore. Discussing one person's issue at a time, help each member develop a claim supported by several reasons. Express each reason as a *because* clause. Then write out the working thesis statement for each person's argument by attaching the *because* clauses to the claim. Finally, try to create *because* clauses in support of an alternative claim for each issue. Recorders should select two or three working thesis statements from the group to present to the class as a whole.   ■ ■ ■

Conclusion

This chapter has introduced you to the structure of classical argument, to the rhetorical triangle (message, writer or speaker, and audience), and to the classical appeals of *logos, ethos,* and *pathos.* It has also shown how arguments originate in issue questions, how issue questions differ from information questions, and how arguments differ from pseudo-arguments. At the heart of this chapter we explained that the frame of an argument is a claim supported by reasons. As you generate reasons to support your own arguments, it is often helpful to articulate them as *because* clauses attached to the claim.

In the next chapter we will see how to support a reason by examining its logical structure, uncovering its unstated assumptions, and planning a strategy of development.

WRITING ASSIGNMENT   An Issue Question and Working Thesis Statements

Decide on an issue and a claim for a classical argument that you would like to write. Write a one-sentence question that summarizes the controversial issue that your claim addresses. Then draft a working thesis statement for your proposed argument. Organize the thesis as a claim with bulleted *because* clauses for reasons. You should have at least two reasons, but it is okay to have three or four. Also include an *opposing thesis statement*—that is, a claim with *because* clauses for an alternative position on your issue.

Recall that in Part One we emphasized exploratory writing as a way of resisting closure and helping you wrestle with multiple perspectives. Now we ask you to begin a process of closure by developing a thesis statement that condenses your argument into a claim with supporting reasons. However, as we emphasize throughout this text, drafting itself is an *exploratory process*. Writers almost always discover new ideas when they write a first draft; as they take their writing project through multiple drafts, their views may change substantially. Often, in fact, honest writers can change positions on an issue by discovering that a counterargument is stronger than their own. So the working thesis statement that you submit for this assignment may evolve substantially once you begin to draft.

In this chapter, as well as in Chapters 4 and 5, we will follow the process of student writer Carmen Tieu as she constructs an argument on violent video games. During earlier exploratory writing, she wrote about a classroom incident in which her professor had described video game playing as gendered behavior (overwhelmingly male). The professor indicated his dislike for such games, pointing to their antisocial, dehumanizing values. In her freewrite, Carmen described her own enjoyment of violent video games—particularly first-person-shooter games—and explored the pleasure that she derived from beating boys at *Halo 2*. She knew that she wanted to write an argument on this issue. What follows is Carmen's submission for this assignment.

Carmen's Issue Question and Working Thesis Statements

Issue Question: Should girls be encouraged to play first-person-shooter video games?

My claim: First-person-shooter (FPS) video games are great activities for girls

- because beating guys at their own game is empowering for girls
- because being skilled at FPS games frees girls from feminine stereotypes
- because they give girls a different way of bonding with males
- because they give girls new insights into a male subculture

Opposing claim: First-person-shooter games are a bad activity for anyone, especially girls,

- because they promote antisocial values such as indiscriminate killing
- because they amplify the bad, macho side of male stereotypes
- because they waste valuable time that could be spent on something constructive
- because FPS games could encourage women to see themselves as objects ■

4

The Logical Structure of Arguments

In Chapter 3 you learned that the core of an argument is a claim supported by reasons and that these reasons can often be stated as *because* clauses attached to a claim. In the present chapter we examine the logical structure of arguments in more depth. You will learn to:

- Explain the logical structure of argument
- Use the Toulmin system to analyze and plan arguments

An Overview of *Logos:* What Do We Mean by the "Logical Structure" of an Argument?

As you will recall from our discussion of the rhetorical triangle, *logos* refers to the strength of an argument's support and its internal consistency. *Logos* is the argument's logical structure. But what do we mean by "logical structure"?

Formal Logic versus Real-World Logic

First of all, what we *don't* mean by logical structure is the kind of precise certainty you get in a philosophy class in formal logic. Logic classes deal with symbolic assertions that are universal and unchanging, such as "If all ps are qs and if r is a p, then r is a q." This statement is logically certain so long as p, q, and r are pure abstractions. But in the real world, p, q, and r turn into actual things, and the relationships among them suddenly become fuzzy. For example, p might be a class of actions called "Sexual Harassment," while q could be the class called "Actions That Justify Dismissal from a Job." If r is the class "Telling Off-Color Stories," then the logic of our p–q–r statement suggests that telling off-color stories (r) is an instance of sexual harassment (p), which in turn is an action justifying dismissal from one's job (q).

Now, most of us would agree that sexual harassment is a serious offense that might well justify dismissal from a job. In turn, we might agree that telling off-color stories, if the jokes are sufficiently raunchy and are inflicted on an unwilling audience, constitutes sexual harassment. But few of us would want to say categorically that all people who tell off-color stories are harassing their listeners and ought to be fired. Most of us would want to know the particulars of the case before making a final judgment.

In the real world, then, it is difficult to say that *r*s are always *p*s or that every instance of a *p* results in *q*. That is why we discourage students from using the word *prove* in claims they write for arguments (as in "This paper will prove that euthanasia is wrong"). Real-world arguments seldom *prove* anything. They can only make a good case for something, a case that is more or less strong, more or less probable. Often the best you can hope for is to strengthen the resolve of those who agree with you or weaken the resistance of those who oppose you.

The Role of Assumptions

A key difference, then, between formal logic and real-world argument is that real-world arguments are not grounded in abstract, universal statements. Rather, as we shall see, they must be grounded in beliefs, assumptions, or values granted by the audience. A second important difference is that in real-world arguments, these beliefs, assumptions, or values are often unstated. So long as writer and audience share the same assumptions, it's fine to leave them unstated. But if these underlying assumptions aren't shared, the writer has a problem.

To illustrate the nature of this problem, consider one of the arguments we introduced in the last chapter.

> The public should not support marine parks and "swim with dolphins" programs because these programs separate dolphins from their natural habitat and social groups.

On the face of it, this is a plausible argument. But the argument is persuasive only if the audience agrees with the writer's assumption that it is wrong to separate wild animals from their natural habitats and social groups. What if you believed that confinement of wild animals is not always harmful or stressful to the animals, that the knowledge derived from the capture of wild animals enables humans to preserve the natural environment for these animals, and that the benefits to be gained from the captivity of a small number of wild animals outweigh the animals' loss of freedom? If this were the case, you might believe that dolphin programs have positive consequences so long as the marine parks strive to provide humane conditions for the animals, with minimal stress. If these were your beliefs, the argument wouldn't work for you because you would reject the underlying assumption. To persuade you with this line of reasoning, the writer would have to defend this assumption, showing why it is unwise or unethical to remove animals from their free and wild conditions.

The Core of an Argument: The Enthymeme

The previous core argument ("The public should not support marine parks and 'swim with dolphins' programs because these programs separate dolphins from their natural habitat and social groups") is an incomplete logical structure called an *enthymeme*. Its persuasiveness depends on an underlying assumption or belief that the audience must accept. To complete the enthymeme and make it effective, the audience must willingly supply a missing premise—in this case, that it is wrong to separate wild animals from their natural environments. The Greek philosopher Aristotle showed how successful enthymemes root the speaker's argument in assumptions, beliefs, or values held by the audience. The word *enthymeme* comes from the Greek *en* (meaning "in") and *thumos* (meaning "mind"). Listeners or readers must have in mind an assumption, belief, or value that lets them willingly supply the missing premise. If the audience is unwilling to supply the missing premise, then the argument fails. Our point is that successful arguments depend both on what the arguer says and on what the audience already has "in mind."

To clarify the concept of "enthymeme," let's go over this same territory again, this time more slowly, examining what we mean by "incomplete logical structure." The sentence "The public should not support marine parks and 'swim with dolphins' programs because these programs separate dolphins from their natural habitat and social groups" is an enthymeme. It combines a claim (the public should not support marine parks and "swim with dolphins" programs) with a reason expressed as a *because* clause (because these programs separate dolphins from their natural habitat and social groups). To render this enthymeme logically complete, the audience must willingly supply a missing assumption—that it is wrong to separate wild animals from their natural environments. If your audience accepts this assumption, then you have a starting place on which to build an effective argument. If your audience doesn't accept this assumption, then you must supply another argument to support it, and so on until you find common ground with your audience.

To sum up:

1. Claims are supported with reasons. You can usually state a reason as a *because* clause attached to a claim (see Chapter 3).
2. A *because* clause attached to a claim is an incomplete logical structure called an enthymeme. To create a complete logical structure from an enthymeme, the underlying assumption (or assumptions) must be articulated.
3. To serve as an effective starting point for the argument, this underlying assumption should be a belief, value, or principle that the audience grants.

Let's illustrate this structure by putting the previous example into schematic form.

ENTHYMEME

CLAIM The public should not support marine parks and "swim with dolphins" programs

REASON because these programs seperate dolphins from their natural habitat and social groups.

Audience must supply this assumption

UNDERLYING ASSUMPTION
Wild animals should remain free in their natural habitats and social groups.

■ ■ ■   **FOR CLASS DISCUSSION**   Identifying Underlying Assumptions

Working individually or in small groups, identify the unstated assumption that the audience must supply in order to make the following enthymemes persuasive.

Example

Enthymeme: Rabbits make good pets because they are gentle.

Underlying assumption: Gentle animals make good pets.

1. We shouldn't elect Joe as committee chair because he is too bossy.
2. Drugs should not be legalized because legalization would greatly increase the number of drug addicts.
3. Airport screeners should use racial profiling because doing so will increase the odds of stopping terrorists.
4. Racial profiling should not be used by airport screeners because it violates a person's civil rights.
5. We should strengthen the Endangered Species Act because doing so will preserve genetic diversity on the planet.
6. The Endangered Species Act is too stringent because it severely damages the economy.

■ ■ ■

Adopting a Language for Describing Arguments: The Toulmin System

Understanding a new field usually requires us to learn a new vocabulary. For example, if you were taking biology for the first time, you'd have to learn dozens and dozens of new terms. Luckily, the field of argument requires us to learn a mere handful of new terms. A particularly useful set of argument terms, one we'll be using occasionally throughout the rest of this text, comes from philosopher Stephen Toulmin. In the 1950s, Toulmin rejected the prevailing models of argument based on formal logic in favor of a very audience-based courtroom model.

Toulmin's courtroom model differs from formal logic in that it assumes that (1) all assertions and assumptions are contestable by "opposing counsel" and that (2) all final "verdicts" about the persuasiveness of the opposing arguments will be rendered by a neutral third party, a judge or jury. As writers, keeping in mind the "opposing counsel" forces us to anticipate counterarguments and to question our assumptions. Keeping in mind the judge and jury reminds us to answer opposing arguments fully, without rancor, and to present positive reasons for supporting our case as well as negative reasons for disbelieving the opposing case. Above all else, Toulmin's model reminds us not to construct an argument that appeals only to those who already agree with us. In short, it helps arguers tailor arguments to their audiences.

The system we use for analyzing arguments combines Toulmin's language with Aristotle's concept of the enthymeme. It builds on the system you have already been practicing. We simply need to add a few key terms from Toulmin. The first term is Toulmin's *warrant,* the name we will now use for the underlying assumption that turns an enthymeme into a complete, logical structure as shown at the top of the next page.

Audience must accept this warrant ⟶

WARRANT
Wild animals should remain free in their natural habitats and social groups.

Toulmin derives his term *warrant* from the concept of "warranty" or "guarantee." The warrant is the value, belief, or principle that the audience has to hold if the soundness of the argument is to be guaranteed or warranted. We sometimes make similar use of this word in ordinary language when we say, "That is an unwarranted conclusion," meaning one has leaped from information about a situation to a conclusion about that situation without any sort of general principle to justify or "warrant" that move. Thus the warrant—once accepted by the audience—"guarantees" the soundness of the argument.

But arguments need more than claims, reasons, and warrants. These are simply one-sentence statements—the frame of an argument, not a developed argument. To give body and weight to our arguments and make them convincing, we need what Toulmin calls *grounds* and *backing*. Let's start with grounds. Grounds are the supporting evidence that causes an audience to accept your reason. Grounds are facts, data, statistics, causal links, testimony, examples, anecdotes—the blood and muscle that flesh out the skeletal frame of your enthymeme. Toulmin suggests that grounds are "what you have to go on" in an argument—the stuff you can point to and present before a jury. Here is how grounds fit into our emerging argument schema:

ENTHYMEME

CLAIM The public should not support marine parks and "swim with dolphins" programs

REASON because these programs separate dolphins from their natural habitat and social groups.

Grounds support the reason ⟶ **GROUNDS**

Evidence and arguments showing difference between dolphin behavior in the wild and in captivity and the stress caused by this difference:

• In the wild, dolphins swim in pods around forty miles a day in the open ocean whereas marine park tanks provide only a tiny fraction of that space.

• Evidence that the echoes from concrete pools, the music of dolphin shows, and the applause and noise of audiences are stressful and harmful

• Statistics about the excessive number of performances or about the levels of stress hormones produced in dolphins

In many cases, successful arguments require just these three components: a claim, a reason, and grounds. If the audience already accepts the unstated assumption behind the reason (the warrant), then the warrant can safely remain in the background, unstated and unexamined. But if there is a chance that the audience will question or doubt the warrant, then the writer needs to back it up by providing an argument in its support. *Backing* is the argument that supports the warrant. It may require no more than one or two sentences or as much as a major section in your argument. Its goal is to persuade the audience to accept the warrant. Here is how *backing* is added to our schema:

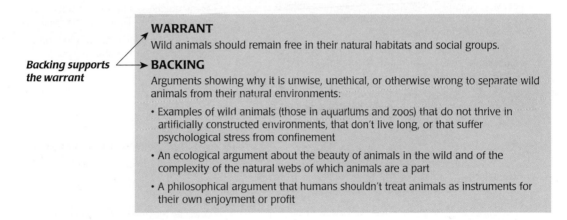

WARRANT

Wild animals should remain free in their natural habitats and social groups.

Backing supports the warrant

BACKING

Arguments showing why it is unwise, unethical, or otherwise wrong to separate wild animals from their natural environments:

• Examples of wild animals (those in aquariums and zoos) that do not thrive in artificially constructed environments, that don't live long, or that suffer psychological stress from confinement

• An ecological argument about the beauty of animals in the wild and of the complexity of the natural webs of which animals are a part

• A philosophical argument that humans shouldn't treat animals as instruments for their own enjoyment or profit

Toulmin's system next asks us to imagine how a resistant audience would try to refute our argument. Specifically, the adversarial audience might challenge our reason and grounds by arguing that dolphins in captivity are not as stressed as we claim (evidence provided by veterinarians, caretakers, or animal trainers verifying that most dolphins in captivity are in good health). Or the adversary might attack our warrant and backing by showing how the captivity of some wild animal might save the species from extinction or how animals are often saved from illness and predators by caring humans. An adversary might attack our philosophical or spiritual arguments by saying that the same reasoning, taken to its logical conclusion, would eliminate zoos and require all humans to become vegetarians or vegans. An adversary might even argue that dolphins enjoy being with humans and have the same capacity to be animal companions as dogs or cats.

In the case of the argument opposing dolphins in captivity, an adversary might offer one or more of the following rebuttals.

Writer must anticipate these attacks from skeptics

ENTHYMEME

CLAIM The public should not support marine parks and "swim with dolphins" programs

REASON because these programs separate dolphins from their natural habitat and social groups.

GROUNDS

Evidence and arguments showing stressful difference between dolphin behavior in the wild and in captivity:

• In the wild, dolphins swim in pods around forty miles a day in the open ocean whereas marine park tanks provide only a tiny fraction of that space.

• Evidence that the echoes from concrete pools, music of dolphin shows, and the applause and noise of audiences are stressful and harmful

• Statistics about the excessive number of performances or about the levels of stress hormones produced in dolphins

POSSIBLE CONDITIONS OF REBUTTAL
A skeptic can attack the reason and grounds

• Argument that these programs must observe strict accreditation standards for animal welfare, health, and nutrition

• Programs exercise dolphins' intelligence and abilities and build on their natural behaviors.

• Many dolphins in these programs have been bred in captivity, so they aren't "wild."

• The education and entertainment provided by these programs promote concern for dolphins.

WARRANT

Wild animals should remain free in their natural habitats and social groups.

BACKING

Arguments showing why it is unwise, unethical, or otherwise wrong to separate wild animals from their natural environments:

• Examples of wild animals (those in aquariums and zoos) that do not thrive in artificially constructed environments, that don't live long, or that suffer psychological stress from confinement

• An ecological argument about the beauty of animals in the wild and of the complexity of the natural webs of which animals are a part

• A philosophical argument that humans shouldn't treat animals as instruments for their own enjoyment or profit

POSSIBLE CONDITIONS OF REBUTTAL
A skeptic can attack the warrant and backing

• The natural habitat is not always the best environment for wild animals.

• Captivity may preserve a species or lengthen the lifespan of individual animals.

• Scientists have been able to conduct valuable studies of dolphins in captivity, which would have been impossible with dolphins in the wild.

As this example shows, adversarial readers can question an argument's reasons and grounds or its warrant and backing or sometimes both. Conditions of rebuttal remind writers to look at their arguments from the perspective of skeptics. The same principle can be illustrated in the following analysis of an argument that cocaine and heroin should be legalized.

ENTHYMEME

CLAIM Cocaine and heroin should be legalized

REASON because legalization would eliminate the black market in drugs.

GROUNDS

Statistical evidence and arguments showing how legalization would end the black market:

• Statistics and data showing the size of the current black market

• Examples, anecdotes, and facts showing how the black market works

• Causal explanation showing that selling cocaine and heroin legally in state-controlled stores would lower price and eliminate drug dealers

WARRANT

Eliminating the black market in drugs is good.

BACKING

Statistics and examples about the ill effects of the black market:

• The high cost of the black market to crime victims

• The high cost to taxpayers of waging the war against drugs

• The high cost of prisons to house incarcerated drug dealers

• Evidence that huge profits make drug dealing more attractive than ordinary jobs

CONDITIONS OF REBUTTAL
Attacking the reason and grounds

Arguments showing that legalizing cocaine and heroin would not eliminate the black market in drugs:

• Perhaps taxes on the drugs would keep the costs above black market prices.

• Perhaps new kinds of illegal designer drugs would be developed and sold on the black market.

CONDITIONS OF REBUTTAL
Attacking the warrant and backing

Arguments showing that the benefits of eliminating the black market are outweighed by the costs:

• The number of new drug users and addicts would be unacceptably high.

• The health and economic cost of treating addiction would be too high.

• The social costs of selling drugs legally in stores would bring harmful changes to our cultural values.

Toulmin's final term, used to limit the force of a claim and indicate the degree of its probable truth, is *qualifier*. The qualifier reminds us that real-world arguments almost never prove a claim. We may say things such as *very likely, probably,* or *maybe* to indicate the strength of the claim we are willing to draw from our grounds and warrant. Thus if there are exceptions to your warrant or if your grounds are not very strong, you will have to qualify your claim. For example, you might say, "Except for limited cases of scientific research, dolphins should not be held in captivity," or "With full awareness of the potential dangers, I suggest we consider the option of legalizing drugs as a way of ending the ill effects of the black market." In our future displays of the Toulmin scheme we will omit the qualifiers, but you should always remember that no argument is 100 percent persuasive.

■ ■ ■ **FOR CLASS DISCUSSION** Developing Enthymemes with the Toulmin Schema
Working individually or in small groups, imagine that you have to write arguments developing the six enthymemes listed in the For Class Discussion exercise on page 75. Use the Toulmin schema to help you determine what you need to consider when

developing each enthymeme. We suggest that you try a four-box diagram structure as a way of visualizing the schema. We have applied the Toulmin schema to the first enthymeme: "We shouldn't elect Joe as committee chair because he is too bossy."

ENTHYMEME

CLAIM We shouldn't elect Joe as committee chair
REASON because he is too bossy.

GROUNDS

Evidence of Joe's bossiness:

- Examples of the way he dominates meetings—doesn't call on people, talks too much
- Testimony about his bossiness from people who have served with him on committees
- Anecdotes about his abrasive style

WARRANT
Bossy people make bad committee chairs.

BACKING
Problems caused by bossy committee chairs:

- Bossy people don't inspire cooperation and enthusiam.
- Bossy people make others angry.
- Bossy people tend to make bad decisions because they don't incorporate advice from others.

CONDITIONS OF REBUTTAL
Attacking the reason and grounds

Evidence that Joe is not bossy or is only occasionally bossy:

- Counterevidence showing his collaborative style
- Testimony from people who have liked Joe as a leader and claim he isn't bossy; testimony about his cooperativeness and kindness
- Testimony that anecdotes about Joe's bossiness aren't typical

CONDITIONS OF REBUTTAL
Attacking the warrant and backing

- Arguments that bossiness can be a good trait
  - Sometimes bossy people make good chairpersons.
  - Argument that this committee needs a bossy person who can make decisions and get things done
- Argument that Joe has other traits of good leadership that outweigh his bossiness

Using Toulmin's Schema to Determine a Strategy of Support

So far we have seen that a claim, a reason, and a warrant form the frame for a line of reasoning in an argument. Most of the words in an argument, however, are devoted to grounds and backing.

For an illustration of how a writer can use the Toulmin schema to generate ideas for an argument, consider the following case. In April 2005, the Texas house of representatives passed a bill banning "sexually suggestive" cheerleading. Across the nation, evening television show comics poked fun at the bill, while newspaper editorialists debated its wisdom and constitutionality. In one of our classes, however, several students, including one who had earned a high school varsity letter in competitive cheerleading, defended the bill by contending that provocative dance moves hurt the athletic image of cheerleading. In the following example, which draws on ideas developed in class discussion, we create a hypothetical student writer (we'll call her Chandale) who argues in defense of the Texas bill. Chandale's argument is based on the following enthymeme:

> The cheerleading bill to ban suggestive dancing is good because it promotes a view of female cheerleaders as athletes rather than exotic dancers.

Chandale used the Toulmin schema to brainstorm ideas for developing her argument. Here are her notes:

Chandale's Planning Notes Using the Toulmin Schema

Enthymeme: The cheerleading bill to ban suggestive dancing is good because it promotes a view of female cheerleaders as athletes rather than exotic dancers.

Grounds: First, I've got to use evidence to show that cheerleaders are athletes.

- Cheerleaders at my high school are carefully chosen for their stamina and skill after exhausting two-week tryouts.
- We begin all practices with a mile run and an hour of warm-up exercises—also expected to work out on our own for at least an hour on weekends and on days without practice.
- We learned competitive routines and stunts consisting of lifts, tosses, flips, catches, and gymnastic moves. This requires athletic ability! We'd practice these stunts for hours each week.
- Throughout the year cheerleaders have to attend practices, camps, and workshops to learn new routines and stunts.
- Our squad competed in competitions around the state.
- Competitive cheerleading is a growing movement across the country—University of Maryland has made it a varsity sport for women.
- Skimpy uniforms and suggestive dance moves destroy this image by making women eye candy like the Dallas Cowboys cheerleaders.

Warrant: It is a good thing to view female cheerleaders as athletes.

Backing: Now I need to make the case that it is good to see cheerleaders as athletes rather than as eye candy.

- Athletic competition builds self-esteem, independence, a powerful sense of achievement— contributes to health, strength, conditioning.
- Competitive cheerleading is one of the few sports where teams are made up of both men and women. (Why is this good? Should I use this?)
- The suggestive dance moves turn women into sex objects whose function is to be gazed at by men—suggests that women's value is based on their beauty and sex appeal.
- We are talking about HIGH SCHOOL cheerleading—very bad early influence on girls to model themselves on Dallas Cowboys cheerleaders or sexy MTV videos of rock stars.
- Junior high girls want to do what senior high girls do—suggestive dance moves promote sexuality way too early.

Conditions of Rebuttal: Would anybody try to rebut my reasons and grounds that cheer-leading is an athletic activity?

■ No. I think it is obvious that cheerleading is an athletic activity once they see my evidence.

■ However, they might not think of cheerleading as a sport. They might say that the University of Maryland just declared it a sport as a cheap way to meet Title IX federal rules to have more women's sports. I'll have to make sure that I show this is really a sport.

■ They also might say that competitive cheerleading shouldn't be encouraged because it is too dangerous—lots of serious injuries including paralysis have been caused by mistakes in doing flips, lifts, and tosses. If I include this, maybe I could say that other sports are dangerous also—and it is in fact danger that makes this sport so exciting.

Would anyone doubt my warrant and backing that it is good to see female cheerleaders as athletes?

■ Yes, all those people who laughed at the Texas legislature think that people are being too prudish and that banning suggestive dance moves violates free expression. I'll need to make my case that it is bad for young girls to see themselves as sex objects too early.

The information that Chandale lists under "grounds" is what she sees as the facts of the case—the hard data she will use as evidence to support her contention that cheerleading is an athletic activity. The paragraph that follows shows how this argu-ment might look when placed in written form.

First Part of Chandale's Argument

Although evening television show comedians have made fun of the Texas legislature's desire to ban "suggestive" dance moves from cheerleading routines, I applaud this bill because it pro-motes a healthy view of female cheerleaders as athletes rather than showgirls. I was lucky enough to attend a high school where cheerleading is a sport, and I earned a varsity letter as a cheerleader. To get on my high school's cheerleading squad, students have to go through an exhausting two-week tryout of workouts and instruction in the basic routines; then they are chosen based on their stamina and skill. Once on the squad, cheerleaders begin all practices with a mile run and an hour of grueling warm-up exercises and are expected to exercise on their own on weekends. As a result of this regimen, cheerleaders achieve and maintain a top level of physical fitness. In addition, to get on the squad, students must be able to do hand-stands, cartwheels, handsprings, high jumps, and the splits. Each year the squad builds up to its complex routines and stunts consisting of lifts, tosses, flips, catches, and gymnastic moves that only trained athletes can do. In tough competitions at the regional and state levels, the cheerleading squad demonstrates its athletic talent. This view of cheerleading as a competi-tive sport is also spreading to colleges. As reported recently in a number of newspapers, the University of Maryland has made cheerleading a varsity sport, and many other universities are following suit. Athletic performance of this caliber is a far cry from the sexy dancing that many high school girls often associate with cheerleading. By banning suggestive dancing in cheerleading routines, the Texas legislature creates an opportunity for schools to emphasize the athleticism of cheerleading.

As you can see, Chandale has plenty of evidence for arguing that competitive cheerleading is an athletic activity quite different from sexy dancing. But how effective is this argument as it stands? Is this all she needs? The Toulmin schema encourages writers to include—if needed for the intended audience—explicit support for their warrants as well as attention to conditions for rebuttal. Because the overwhelming national response to the Texas law was ridicule at the perceived prudishness of the legislators, Chandale decides to expand her argument as follows:

Continuation of Chandale's Argument

Whether we see cheerleading as a sport or as sexy dancing is an important issue for women. The erotic dance moves that many high school cheerleaders now incorporate into their routines show that they are emulating the Dallas Cowboys cheerleaders or pop stars on MTV. Our already sexually saturated culture (think of the suggestive clothing marketed to little girls) pushes girls and women to measure their value by their beauty and sex appeal. It would be far healthier, both physically and psychologically, if high school cheerleaders were identified as athletes. For women and men both, competitive cheerleading can build self-esteem, pride in teamwork, and a powerful sense of achievement, as well as promote health, strength, and fitness.

Some people might object to competitive cheerleading by saying that cheerleading isn't really a sport. Some have accused the University of Maryland of making cheerleading a varsity sport only as a cheap way of meeting Title IX requirements. But anyone who has watched competitive cheerleading, and imagined what it would be like to be thrown high into the air, knows instinctively that this is a sport indeed. In fact, other persons might object to competitive cheerleading because it is too dangerous, with potential for very severe injuries including paralysis. Obviously the sport is dangerous—but so are many sports, including football, gymnastics, diving, and trampoline. The danger and difficulty of the sport is part of its appeal. Part of what can make cheerleaders as athletes better role models for girls than cheerleaders as erotic dancers is the courage and training needed for success. Of course, the Texas legislators might not have had athleticism in mind when they banned suggestive dancing. They might only have been promoting their vision of morality. But at stake are the role models we set for young girls. I'll pick an athlete over a Dallas Cowboys cheerleader every time.

Our example suggests how a writer can use the Toulmin schema to generate ideas for an argument. For evidence, Chandale draws primarily on her personal experiences as a cheerleader/athlete and on her knowledge of popular culture. She also draws on her reading of several newspaper articles about the University of Maryland's making cheerleading a varsity sport. (In an academic paper rather than a newspaper editorial, she would need to document these sources through formal citations.) Although many arguments depend on research, many can be supported wholly or in part by your own personal experiences, so don't neglect the wealth of evidence from your own life when searching for data. A more detailed discussion of evidence in arguments occurs in Chapter 5.

■ ■ ■ **FOR CLASS DISCUSSION**   Reasons, Warrants, and Conditions of Rebuttal

1. Working individually or in small groups, consider ways you could use evidence to support the stated reason in each of the following partial arguments.

    a. Another reason to oppose a state sales tax is that it is so annoying.

    b. Rap music has a bad influence on teenagers because it promotes disrespect for women.

    c. Professor X is an outstanding teacher because he (she) generously spends so much time outside of class counseling students with personal problems.

2. Now create arguments to support the warrants in each of the partial arguments in exercise 1. The warrants for each of the arguments are stated below.

a. Support this warrant: We should oppose taxes that are annoying.

b. Support this warrant: It is bad to promote disrespect for women.

c. Support this warrant: Time spent counseling students with personal problems is an important criterion for identifying outstanding teachers.

3. Using Toulmin's conditions of rebuttal, work out a strategy for refuting either the stated reasons or the warrants or both in each of the preceding arguments.

The Power of Audience-Based Reasons

As we have seen, both Aristotle's concept of the enthymeme and Toulmin's concept of the warrant focus on the arguer's need to create what we will now call "audience-based reasons." Whenever you ask whether a given piece of writing is persuasive, the immediate rejoinder should always be, "Persuasive to whom?" What seems like a good reason to you may not be a good reason to others. Finding audience-based reasons means finding arguments whose warrants the audience will accept—that is, arguments effectively rooted in your audience's beliefs and values.

Difference between Writer-Based and Audience-Based Reasons

To illustrate the difference between writer-based and audience-based reasons, consider the following hypothetical case. Suppose you believed that the government should build a dam on the nearby Rapid River—a project bitterly opposed by several environmental groups. Which of the following two arguments might you use to address environmentalists?

1. The government should build a dam on the Rapid River because the only alternative power sources are coal-fired or nuclear plants, both of which pose greater risk to the environment than a hydroelectric dam.
2. The government should build a hydroelectric dam on the Rapid River because this area needs cheap power to attract heavy industry.

Clearly, the warrant of argument 1 ("Choose the source of power that poses least risk to the environment") is rooted in the values and beliefs of environmentalists, whereas the warrant of argument 2 ("Growth of industry is good") is likely to make them wince. To environmentalists, new industry means more congestion, more smokestacks, and more pollution. However, argument 2 may appeal to out-of-work laborers or to the business community, to whom new industry means more jobs and a booming economy.

From the perspective of logic alone, arguments 1 and 2 are both sound. They are internally consistent and proceed from reasonable premises. But they will affect different audiences very differently. Neither argument proves that the government should build the dam; both are open to objection. Passionate environmentalists, for example, might counter argument 1 by asking why the government needs to build any power plant at all. They could argue that energy conservation would obviate the need for a new power plant. Or they might argue that building a dam would hurt the environment in ways unforeseen by dam supporters. Our point, then, isn't that argument 1 will persuade environmentalists. Rather, our point is that argument 1 will be more persuasive than argument 2 because it is rooted in beliefs and values that the intended audience shares.

Let's consider a second example by returning to Chapter 1 and student Gordon Adams's petition to waive his math requirement. Gordon's central argument, as you will recall, was that as a lawyer he would have no need for algebra. In Toulmin's terms, Gordon's argument looks like this:

ENTHYMEME

CLAIM I should be exempted from the algebra requirement

REASON because in my chosen field of law I will have no need for algebra.

Stated explicitly in Gordon's argument

GROUNDS

Testimony from lawyers and others that lawyers never use algebra

Fully developed in Gordon's argument

WARRANT

General education requirements should be based on career utility (that is, if a course is not needed for a particular student's career, it shouldn't be required).

Left unstated in Gordon's argument

BACKING

Arguments that career utility should be the chief criterion for requiring general education courses

Missing from Gordon's argument

In our discussions of this case with students and faculty, students generally vote to support Gordon's request, whereas faculty generally vote against it. And in fact, the University Standards Committee rejected Gordon's petition, thus delaying his entry into law school.

Why do faculty and students differ on this issue? Mainly they differ because faculty reject Gordon's warrant that general education requirements should serve students' individual career interests. Most faculty believe that general education courses, including math, provide a base of common learning that links us to the past and teaches us modes of understanding useful throughout life.

Gordon's argument thus challenges one of college professors' most cherished beliefs—that the liberal arts and sciences are innately valuable. Further, it threatens his immediate audience, the committee, with a possible flood of student requests to waive other general education requirements on the grounds of their irrelevance to a particular career choice.

How might Gordon have created a more persuasive argument? In our view, Gordon might have prevailed had he accepted the faculty's belief in the value of the math requirement and argued that he had fulfilled the "spirit" of that requirement through alternative means. He could have based his argument on an enthymeme like this:

> I should be exempted from the algebra requirement because my experience as a contractor and inventor has already provided me with equivalent mathematical knowledge.

Following this audience-based approach, he would drop all references to algebra's uselessness for lawyers and expand his discussion of the mathematical savvy he acquired on the job. This argument would honor faculty values and reduce the faculty's fear of setting a bad precedent. Few students are likely to have Gordon's background, and those who do could apply for a similar exemption without threatening the system. Again, this argument might not have won, but it would have gotten a more sympathetic hearing.

■ ■ ■ **FOR CLASS DISCUSSION**   Audience-Based Reasons

Working in groups, decide which of the two reasons offered in each instance would be more persuasive to the specified audience. Be prepared to explain your reasoning to the class. Write out the implied warrant for each *because* clause and decide whether the specific audience would likely grant it.

1. Audience: people who advocate a pass/fail grading system on the grounds that the present grading system is too competitive

   a. We should keep the present grading system because it prepares people for the dog-eat-dog pressures of the business world.

   b. We should keep the present grading system because it tells students that certain standards of excellence must be met if individuals are to reach their full potential.

2. Audience: young people ages fifteen to twenty-five

   a. You should become a vegetarian because an all-vegetable diet will help you lower your cholesterol.

   b. You should become a vegetarian because doing so will help eliminate the suffering of animals raised in factory farms.

3. Audience: conservative proponents of "family values"

   a. Same-sex marriages should be legalized because doing so will promote public acceptance of homosexuality.

   b. Same-sex marriages should be legalized because doing so will make it easier for gay people to establish and sustain long-term, stable relationships.   ■ ■ ■

Conclusion

Chapters 3 and 4 have provided an anatomy of argument. They have shown that the core of an argument is a claim with reasons that usually can be summarized in one or more *because* clauses attached to the claim. Often, it is as important to articulate and support the underlying assumptions in your argument (warrants) as it is to support the stated reasons because a successful argument should be rooted in your audience's beliefs and values. In order to plan an audience-based argument strategy, arguers can use the Toulmin schema, which helps writers discover grounds, warrants, and backing for their arguments and test them through conditions of rebuttal. Finally, we showed how the use of audience-based reasons helps you keep your audience in mind from the start whenever you design a plan for an argument.

WRITING ASSIGNMENT   Plan of an Argument's Details

This assignment asks you to return to the working thesis statement that you created for the brief writing assignment in Chapter 3. From that thesis statement extract one of your enthymemes (your claim with one of your *because* clauses). Write out the warrant for your enthymeme. Then use the Toulmin schema to brainstorm the details you might use (grounds, backing, conditions of rebuttal) to convert your enthymeme into a fleshed-out argument. Use as your model Chandale's planning notes on pages 81–82.

Like the brief assignment for Chapter 3, this is a process-oriented brainstorming task aimed at helping you generate ideas for one part of your classical argument. You may end up changing your ideas substantially as you compose the actual argument. What follows is Carmen's submission for this assignment.

Carmen's Plan for Part of Her Argument

Enthymeme: First-person-shooter (FPS) video games are great activities for girls because playing these games gives girls new insights into male subculture.

Grounds: I've got to show the insights into male subculture I gained.

- The guys who play these video games are intensely competitive.
  - They can play for hours without stopping—intense concentration.
  - They don't multitask—no small talk during the games; total focus on playing.
  - They take delight in winning at all costs—they boast with every kill; they call each other losers.
- They often seem homophobic or misogynist.
  - They put each other down by calling opponents "faggot" and "wussy," or other similar names that are totally obscene.
  - They associate victory with being macho.

Warrant: It is beneficial for a girl to get these insights into male subculture.

Backing: How can I show these benefits?

- Although I enjoy winning at FPS games, as a girl I feel alienated from this male subculture.
- I'm glad that I don't feel the need to put everyone else down.
- It was a good learning experience to see how girls' way of bonding is very different from that of boys; girls tend to be nicer to each other rather than insulting each other.
- The game atmosphere tends to bring out these traits; guys don't talk this way as much when they are doing other things.

- This experience helped me see why men may progress faster than women in a competitive business environment—men seem programmed to crush each other and they devote enormous energy to the process.
- What else can I say? I need to think about this further.

Conditions of Rebuttal: Would anybody try to rebut my reasons and grounds?

- I think my evidence is pretty convincing that males put each other down, concentrate intensely, use homophobic or misogynist insults, etc.
- However, some guys may say, "Hey, I don't talk that way," etc.
- Maybe people would say that my sample is biased.

Would anyone try to rebut my warrant and backing?

- Skeptics may say that girls are just as mean to each other as guys are, but girls display their meanness in a different way. ■

For additional writing, reading, and research resources, go to www.mycomplab.com

Using Evidence Effectively   5

In Chapters 3 and 4 we introduced you to the concept of *logos*—the logical structure of reasons and evidence in an argument—and showed you how an effective argument advances the writer's claim by linking its supporting reasons to one or more assumptions, beliefs, or values held by the intended audience. In this chapter, we turn to the uses of evidence in argument. By "evidence," we mean all the verifiable information a writer might use as support for an argument, such as facts, observations, examples, cases, testimony, experimental findings, survey data, statistics, and so forth. In Toulmin's terms, evidence is part of the "grounds" or "backing" of an argument in support of reasons or warrants.

In this chapter, we show you how to use evidence effectively. We begin by explaining some general principles for the persuasive use of evidence. Next we describe and illustrate various kinds of evidence and then present a rhetorical way to think about evidence, particularly the way writers select and frame evidence to support the writer's reasons while simultaneously guiding and limiting what the reader sees. By understanding the rhetorical use of evidence, you will better understand how to use evidence ethically, responsibly, and persuasively in your own arguments. We conclude the chapter by suggesting strategies to help you gather evidence for your arguments, including advice on conducting interviews and using questionnaires. You will learn to:

- Evaluate evidence for persuasiveness
- Select, frame, and use different types of evidence in a responsible, ethical manner
- Gather evidence from interviews, surveys, and questionnaires.

The Persuasive Use of Evidence

Consider a target audience of educated, reasonable, and careful readers who approach an issue with healthy skepticism, open-minded but cautious. What demands would such readers make on a writer's use of evidence? To begin to answer that question, let's look at some general principles for using evidence persuasively.

Apply the STAR Criteria to Evidence

Our open-minded but skeptical audience would first of all expect the evidence to meet what rhetorician Richard Fulkerson calls the STAR criteria:*

Sufficiency: Is there enough evidence?

Typicality: Is the chosen evidence representative and typical?

Accuracy: Is the evidence accurate and up-to-date?

Relevance: Is the evidence relevant to the claim?

Let's examine each in turn.

Sufficiency of Evidence   How much evidence you need is a function of your rhetorical context. In a court trial, opposing attorneys often agree to waive evidence for points that aren't in doubt in order to concentrate on contested points. The more a claim is contested or the more your audience is skeptical, the more evidence you may need to present. If you provide too little evidence, you may be accused of *hasty generalization* (see Appendix 1), a reasoning fallacy in which a person makes a sweeping conclusion based on only one or two instances. On the other hand, if you provide too much evidence your argument may become overly long and tedious. You can guard against having too little or too much evidence by appropriately qualifying the claim your evidence supports.

> **Strong claim:** Working full time seriously harms a student's grade point average. (much data needed—probably a combination of examples and statistical studies)
>
> **Qualified claim:** Working full time often harms a student's grade point average. (a few representative examples may be enough)

Typicality of Evidence   Whenever you select evidence, readers need to believe the evidence is typical and representative rather than extreme instances. Suppose that you want to argue that students can combine full-time work with full-time college and cite the case of your friend Pam, who pulled a straight-A grade average while working forty hours per week as a night receptionist in a small hotel. Your audience might doubt the typicality of Pam's case since a night receptionist can often use work hours for studying. What about more typical jobs, they'll ask, where you can't study while you work?

Accuracy of Evidence   Evidence can't be used ethically unless it is accurate and up-to-date, and it can't be persuasive unless the audience believes in the writer's credibility. As a writer, you must be scrupulous in using the most recent and accurate evidence you can find. Faith in the accuracy of a writer's data is one function of *ethos*—the audience's confidence in the writer's credibility and trustworthiness (see Chapter 6, pages 111–112).

Relevance of Evidence   Finally, evidence will be persuasive only if the reader considers it relevant to the contested issue. Consider the following student argument: "I deserve an A in this course because I worked exceptionally hard." The student then cites substantial evidence of how hard he worked—a log of study hours, copies of multiple drafts of papers, testimony from friends, and so forth. Such evidence is ample support for the claim

---

*Richard Fulkerson, *Teaching the Argument in Writing* (Urbana, IL: National Council of Teachers of English, 1996), 44–53. In this section, we are indebted to Fulkerson's discussion.

"I worked exceptionally hard" but is irrelevant to the claim "I deserve an A." Although some instructors may give partial credit for effort, the criteria for grades usually focus on the quality of the student's performance, not the student's time spent studying.

Use Sources That Your Reader Trusts

Another way to enhance the persuasiveness of your evidence is, whenever possible, to choose data from sources you think your readers will trust. Because questions of fact are often at issue in arguments, readers may be skeptical of certain sources. When you research an issue, you soon get a sense of who the participants in the conversation are and what their reputations tend to be. Knowing the political biases of sources and the extent to which a source has financial or personal investment in the outcome of a controversy will also help you locate data sources that both you and your readers can trust. Citing evidence from a peer-reviewed scholarly journal is often more persuasive than citing evidence found on an advocacy Web site. Similarly, citing a conservative magazine such as the *National Review* may be unpersuasive to liberal audiences, just as citing a Sierra Club publication may be unpersuasive to conservatives. (See Chapter 15 for further discussion of how to evaluate research sources from a rhetorical perspective.)

Rhetorical Understanding of Evidence

In the previous section we presented some general principles for effective use of evidence. We now want to deepen your understanding of how evidence persuades by asking you to consider more closely the rhetorical context in which evidence operates. We'll look first at the kinds of evidence used in arguments and then show you how writers select and frame evidence for persuasive effect.

Kinds of Evidence

Writers have numerous options for the kinds of evidence they can use in an argument, including personal-experience data, research findings, and hypothetical examples. To explain these options, we present a series of charts that categorize different kinds of evidence, illustrate how each kind might be worked into an argument, and comment on the strengths and limitations of each.

Data from Personal Experience   One powerful kind of evidence comes from personal experience:

Example	Strengths and Limitations
Despite recent criticism that Ritalin is overprescribed for hyperactivity and attention-deficit disorder, it can often seem like a miracle drug. My little brother is a perfect example. Before he was given Ritalin, he was a terror in school…. [Tell the "before" and "after" story of your little brother.]	■ Personal-experience examples help readers identify with writer; they show writer's personal connection to the issue. ■ Vivid stories capture the imagination and appeal to *Pathos*. ■ Skeptics may sometimes argue that personal-experience examples are insufficient (writer is guilty of hasty generalization), not typical, or not adequately scientific or verifiable.

Data from Observation or Field Research   You can also develop evidence by personally observing a phenomenon or by doing your own field research:

Example	Strengths and Limitations
The intersection at Fifth and Montgomery is particularly dangerous because pedestrians almost never find a comfortable break in the heavy flow of cars. On April 29, I watched fifty-seven pedestrians cross the street. Not once did cars stop in both directions before the pedestrian stepped off the sidewalk onto the street. [Continue with observed data about danger.]	■ Field research gives the feeling of scientific credibility. ■ It increases typicality by expanding database beyond example of one person. ■ It enhances *ethos* of the writer as personally invested and reasonable. ■ Skeptics may point to flaws in how observations were conducted, showing how data are insufficient, inaccurate, or nontypical.

Data from Interviews, Questionnaires, Surveys   You can also gather data by interviewing stakeholders in a controversy, creating questionnaires, or doing surveys. (See pages 102–103 for advice on how to conduct this kind of field research.)

Example	Strengths and Limitations
Another reason to ban laptops from classrooms is the extent to which laptop users disturb other students. In a questionnaire that I distributed to fifty students in my residence hall, a surprising 60 percent said that they are annoyed by fellow students' sending e-mail, paying their bills, or surfing the Web while pretending to take notes in class. Additionally, I interviewed five students who gave me specific examples of how these distractions interfere with learning. [Report the examples.]	■ Interviews, questionnaires, and surveys enhance the sufficiency and typicality of evidence by expanding the database beyond the experiences of one person. ■ Quantitative data from questionnaires and surveys often increase the scientific feel of the argument. ■ Surveys and questionnaires often uncover local or recent data not available in published research. ■ Interviews can provide engaging personal stories, thus enhancing *pathos*. ■ Skeptics can raise doubts about research methodology, questionnaire design, or typicality of interview subjects.

Data from Library or Internet Research   For many arguments, evidence is derived from reading, particularly from library or Internet research. Part Five of this text helps you conduct effective research and incorporate research sources into your arguments:

Example	Strengths and Limitations
The belief that a high-carbohydrate–low-fat diet is the best way to lose weight has been challenged by research conducted by Walter Willett and his colleagues in the department of nutrition at the Harvard School of Public Health. Willett's research suggests that complex carbohydrates such as pasta and potatoes spike glucose levels, increasing the risk of diabetes. Additionally, some fats—especially monounsaturated and polyunsaturated fats found in nuts, fish, and most vegetable oils—help lower "bad" cholesterol levels (45).*	■ Researched evidence is often powerful, especially when sources are respected by your audience; writers can spotlight source's credentials through attributive tags (see Chapter 16, pages 376–378). ■ Researched data may take the form of facts, examples, quotations, summaries of research studies, and so forth (see Chapters 15 and 16). ■ Skeptics might doubt the accuracy of facts, the credentials of a source, or the research design of a study. They might also cite studies with different results. ■ Skeptics might raise doubts about sufficiency, typicality, or relevance of your research data.

Testimony   Writers frequently use testimony when direct data are either unavailable or highly technical or complex. Testimonial evidence can come from research or from interviews:

Example	Strengths and Limitations
Although the Swedish economist Bjorn Lomborg claims that acid rain is not a significant problem, many environmentalists disagree. According to David Bellamany, president of the Conservation Foundation, "Acid rain does kill forests and people around the world, and it's still doing so in the most polluted places, such as Russia" (qtd. in *BBC News*).	■ By itself, testimony is generally less persuasive than direct data. ■ Persuasiveness can be increased if source has impressive credentials, which the writer can state through attributive tags introducing the testimony (see Chapter 16, pages 376–378). ■ Skeptics might undermine testimonial evidence by questioning credentials of source, showing source's bias, or quoting a countersource.

Statistical Data   Many contemporary arguments rely heavily on statistical data, often supplemented by graphics such as tables, pie charts, and graphs. (See Chapter 9 for a discussion of the use of graphics in argument.)

Example	Strengths and Limitations
Americans are delaying marriage at a surprising rate. In 1970, 85 percent of Americans between ages twenty-five and twenty-nine were married. In 2010, however, only 45 percent were married (U.S. Census Bureau).	■ Statistics can give powerful snapshots of aggregate data from a wide database. ■ They are often used in conjunction with graphics (see pages 202–208). ■ They can be calculated and displayed in different ways to achieve different rhetorical effects, so the reader must be wary (see pages 100–101). ■ Skeptics might question statistical methods, research design, and interpretation of data.

*Parenthetical citations in this example and the next follow the MLA documentation system. See Chapter 17 for a full discussion of how to cite and document sources.

Hypothetical Examples, Cases, and Scenarios   Arguments occasionally use hypothetical examples, cases, or scenarios, particularly to illustrate conjectured consequences of an event or to test philosophical hypotheses:

Example	Strengths and Limitations
Consider what might happen if we continue to use biotech soybeans that are resistant to herbicides. The resistant gene, through cross-pollination, might be transferred to an ordinary weed, creating an out-of-control superweed that herbicides couldn't kill. Such a superweed could be an ecological disaster.	■ Scenarios have strong imaginative appeal. ■ They are persuasive only if they seem plausible. ■ A scenario narrative often conveys a sense of "inevitability" even if the actual scenario is unlikely; hence rhetorical effect may be illogical. ■ Skeptics might show the implausibility of the scenario or offer an alternative scenario.

Reasoned Sequence of Ideas   Sometimes arguments are supported with a reasoned sequence of ideas rather than with concrete facts or other forms of empirical evidence. The writer's concern is to support a point through a logical progression of ideas. Such arguments are conceptual, supported by linked ideas, rather than evidential. This kind of support occurs frequently in arguments and is often intermingled with evidentiary support.

Example	Strengths and Limitations
Embryonic stem cell research, despite its promise in fighting diseases, may have negative social consequences. This research encourages us to place embryos in the category of mere cellular matter that can be manipulated at will. Currently we reduce animals to this category when we genetically alter them for human purposes, such as engineering pigs to grow more human-like heart valves for use in transplants. Using human embryos in the same way—as material that can be altered and destroyed at will—may benefit society materially, but this quest for greater knowledge and control involves a reclassifying of embryos that could potentially lead to a devaluing of human life.	■ These sequences are often used in causal arguments to show how causes are linked to effects or in definitional or values arguments to show links among ideas. ■ They have great power to clarify values and show the belief structure on which a claim is founded. ■ They can sketch out ideas and connections that would otherwise remain latent. ■ Their effectiveness depends on the audience's acceptance of each link in the sequence of ideas. ■ Skeptics might raise objections at any link in the sequence, often by pointing to different values or outlining different consequences.

Angle of Vision and the Selection and Framing of Evidence

You can increase your ability to use evidence effectively—and to analyze how other arguers use evidence—by becoming more aware of a writer's rhetorical choices when using evidence to support a claim. Where each of us stands on an issue is partly a function of our own critical thinking, inquiry, and research—our search for the best solution to a problem. But it is also partly a function of who we are as people—our values and beliefs as formed by the particulars of our existence such as our family history, education, gender and sexual orientation, age, class, and ethnicity. In other words, we don't enter the argumentative arena like disembodied computers arriving at our claims through a value-free calculus. We enter with our own ideologies, beliefs, values, and guiding assumptions.

These guiding assumptions, beliefs, and values work together to create a writer's "angle of vision." (Instead of "angle of vision," we could also use other words or metaphors such as *perspective, bias, lens,* or *filter*—all terms that suggest that our way of seeing the world is shaped by our values and beliefs.) A writer's angle of vision, like

EXAMINING VISUAL ARGUMENTS

Angle of Vision

Because of nationally reported injuries and near-death experiences resulting from stage diving and crowd surfing at rock concerts, many cities have tried to ban mosh pits. Critics of mosh pits have pointed to the injuries caused by crowd surfing and to the ensuing lawsuits against concert venues. Meanwhile, supporters cite the almost ecstatic enjoyment of crowd-surfing rock fans who seek out concerts with "festival seating."

These photos display different angles of vision toward crowd surfing. Suppose you were writing a blog in support of crowd surfing. Which image would you include in your posting? Why? Suppose alternatively that you were blogging against mosh pits, perhaps urging local officials to outlaw them. Which image would you choose? Why?

Analyze the visual features of these photographs in order to explain how they are constructed to create alternative angles of vision on mosh pits.

Crowd surfing in a mosh pit

An alternative view of a mosh pit

a lens or filter, helps determine what stands out for that writer in a field of data—that is, what data are important or trivial, significant or irrelevant, worth focusing on or worth ignoring.

To illustrate the concept of selective seeing, we ask you to consider how two hypothetical speakers might select different data about homeless people when presenting speeches to their city council. The first speaker argues that the city should increase its services to the homeless. The second asks the city to promote tourism more aggressively. Their differing angles of vision will cause the two speakers to select different data about homeless people and to frame these data in different ways. (Our use of the word *frame* derives metaphorically from a window frame or the frame of a camera's viewfinder. When you look through a frame, some part of your field of vision is blocked off, while the material appearing in the frame is emphasized. Through framing, a writer maximizes the reader's focus on some data, minimizes the reader's focus on other data, and otherwise guides the reader's vision and response.)

Because the first speaker wants to increase the council's sympathy for the homeless, she frames homeless people positively by telling the story of one homeless man's struggle to find shelter and nutritious food. Her speech focuses primarily on the low number of tax dollars devoted to helping the homeless. In contrast, the second speaker, using data about lost tourist income, might frame the homeless as "panhandlers" by telling the story of obnoxious, urine-soaked winos who pester shoppers for handouts. As arguers, both speakers want their audience to see the homeless from their own angles of vision. Consequently, lost tourist dollars don't show up at all in the first speaker's argument, whereas the story of a homeless man's night in the cold doesn't show up in the second speaker's argument. As this example shows, one goal writers have in selecting and framing evidence is to bring the reader's view of the subject into alignment with the writer's angle of vision. The writer selects and frames evidence to limit and control what the reader sees.

To help you better understand the concepts of selection and framing, we offer the following class discussion exercise to give you practice in a kind of controlled laboratory setting. As you do this exercise, we invite you to observe your own processes for selecting and framing evidence.

■ ■ ■ **FOR CLASS DISCUSSION**   Creating an Angle of Vision by Selecting Evidence

Suppose that your city has scheduled a public hearing on a proposed ordinance to ban mosh pits at rock concerts. (See the Examining Visual Arguments feature on page 95, where we introduced this issue.) Among the possible data available to various speakers for evidence are the following:

- Some bands, such as Nine Inch Nails, specify festival seating that allows a mosh pit area.
- A female mosher writing on the Internet says: "I experience a shared energy that is like no other when I am in the pit with the crowd. It is like we are all a bunch of atoms bouncing off of each other. It's great. Hey, some people get that feeling from basketball games. I get mine from the mosh pit."

- A student conducted a survey of fifty students on her campus who had attended rock concerts in the last six months. Of the respondents, 80 percent thought that mosh pits should be allowed at concerts.
- Narrative comments on these questionnaires included the following:
  - Mosh pits are a passion for me. I get an amazing rush when crowd surfing.
  - I don't like to be in a mosh pit or do crowd surfing. But I love festival seating and like to watch the mosh pits. For me, mosh pits are part of the ambience of a concert.
  - I know a girl who was groped in a mosh pit, and she'll never do one again. But I have never had any problems.
  - Mosh pits are dangerous and stupid. I think they should be outlawed.
  - If you are afraid of mosh pits, just stay away. Nobody forces you to go into a mosh pit! It is ridiculous to ban them because they are totally voluntary. They should just post big signs saying, "City assumes no responsibility for accidents occurring in mosh pit area."
- A teenage girl suffered brain damage and memory loss at a 1998 Pearl Jam concert in Rapid City, South Dakota. According to her attorney, she hadn't intended to body surf or enter the mosh pit but "got sucked in while she was standing at its fringe."
- Twenty-four concert deaths were recorded in 2001, most of them in the area closest to the stage where people are packed in.
- A twenty-one-year-old man suffered cardiac arrest at a Metallica concert in Indiana and is now in a permanent vegetative state. Because he was jammed into the mosh pit area, nobody noticed he was in distress.
- In 2005, a blogger reported breaking his nose on an elbow; another described having his lip ring pulled out. Another blogger on the same site described having his lip nearly sliced off by the neck of a bass guitar. The injury required seventy-eight stitches. In May 2008, fifty people were treated at emergency rooms for mosh pit injuries acquired at a Bamboozle concert in New Jersey.
- According to a 2008 ABC news special, a company specializing in crowd management at rock festivals estimated "that 10,000 people have been injured in and around mosh pits in the last decade." The company said further "that the most injuries incurred from mosh pits aren't actually by the moshers but by innocent bystanders."

Tasks: Working individually or in small groups, complete the following tasks:

1. Compose two short speeches, one supporting the proposed city ordinance to ban mosh pits and one opposing it. How you use these data is up to you, but be able to explain your reasoning in the way you select and frame them. Share your speeches with classmates.
2. After you have shared examples of different speeches, explain the approaches that different classmates employed. What principle of selection was used? If arguers included evidence contrary to their positions, how did they handle it, respond to it, minimize its importance, or otherwise channel its rhetorical effect?

3. In the first task, we assigned you two different angles of vision—one supporting the ordinance and one opposing it. If you had to create your own argument on a proposal to ban mosh pits and if you set for yourself a truth-seeking goal—that is, finding the best solution for the problem of mosh pit danger, one for which you would take ethical responsibility—what would you argue? How would your argument use the list of data we provided? What else might you add?

Rhetorical Strategies for Framing Evidence

What we hope you learned from the preceding exercise is that an arguer consciously selects evidence from a wide field of data and then frames these data through rhetorical strategies that emphasize some data, minimize others, and guide the reader's response. Now that you have a basic idea of what we mean by framing of evidence, here are some strategies writers can use to guide what the reader sees and feels.

Strategies for Framing Evidence

- **Controlling the space given to supporting versus contrary evidence**: Depending on their audience and purpose, writers can devote most of their space to supporting evidence and minimal space to contrary evidence (or omit it entirely). Thus people arguing in favor of mosh pits may have used lots of evidence supporting mosh pits, including enthusiastic quotations from concert-goers, while omitting (or summarizing very rapidly) the data about the dangers of mosh pits.

- **Emphasizing a detailed story versus presenting lots of facts and statistics**: Often, writers can choose to support a point with a memorable individual case or with aggregate data such as statistics or lists of facts. A memorable story can have a strongly persuasive effect. For example, to create a negative view of mosh pits, a writer might tell the heartrending story of a teenager suffering permanent brain damage from being dropped on a mosh pit floor. In contrast, a supporter of mosh pits might tell the story of a happy music lover turned on to the concert scene by the rush of crowd surfing. A different strategy is to use facts and statistics rather than case narratives—for example, data about the frequency of mosh pit accidents, financial consequences of lawsuits, and so forth. The single-narrative case often has a more powerful rhetorical effect, but it is always open to the charge that it is an insufficient or nonrepresentative example. Vivid anecdotes make for interesting reading, but by themselves they may not be compelling logically. In contrast, aggregate data, often used in scholarly studies, can provide more compelling, logical evidence but sometimes make the prose wonkish and dense.

- **Providing contextual and interpretive comments when presenting data**: When citing data, writers can add brief contextual or interpretive comments that act as lenses over the readers' eyes to help them see the data from the writer's perspective. Suppose you want to support mosh pits, but also want to admit that mosh pits are dangerous. You could make that danger seem irrelevant or inconsequential by saying: "It is true that occasional mosh pit accidents happen, just as accidents happen in any kind of recreational activity such as swimming or weekend softball games." The concluding phrase frames the danger of mosh pits by comparing it to other recreational accidents that don't require special laws or regulations. The implied argument is this: banning mosh pits because of an occasional accident would be as silly as banning recreational swimming because of occasional accidents.

■ **Putting contrary evidence in subordinate positions:** Just as a photographer can place a flower at the center of a photograph or in the background, a writer can place a piece of data in a subordinate or main clause of a sentence. Note how the structure of the following sentence minimizes emphasis on the rarity of mosh pit accidents: "Although mosh pit accidents are rare, the danger to the city of multimillion-dollar liability lawsuits means that the city should nevertheless ban them for reasons of fiscal prudence." The factual data that mosh pit accidents are rare is summarized briefly and tucked away in a subordinate *although* clause, while the writer's own position is elaborated in the main clause where it receives grammatical emphasis. A writer with a different angle of vision might say, "Although some cities may occasionally be threatened with a lawsuit, serious accidents resulting from mosh pits are so rare that cities shouldn't interfere with the desires of music fans to conduct concerts as they please."

■ **Choosing labels and names that guide the reader's response to data:** One of the most subtle ways to control your readers' response to data is to choose labels and names that prompt them to see the issue as you do. If you like mosh pits, you might refer to the seating arrangements in a concert venue as "festival seating, where concertgoers have the opportunity to create a free-flowing mosh pit." If you don't like mosh pits, you might refer to the seating arrangements as "an accident-inviting use of empty space where rowdies can crowd together, slam into each other, and occasionally punch and kick." The labels you choose, along with the connotations of the words you select, urge your reader to share your angle of vision.

■ **Using images (photographs, drawings) to guide the reader's response to data:** Another strategy for moving your audience toward your angle of vision is to include a photograph or drawing that portrays a contested issue from your perspective. You've already tried your hand at selecting mosh pit photographs that make arguments through their angle of vision. (See page 95.) Most people agree that the first photo supports a positive view of mosh pits. The crowd looks happy and relaxed (rather than rowdy or out of control), and the young woman lifted above the crowd smiles broadly, her body relaxed, her arms extended. In contrast, the second photo emphasizes muscular men (rather than a smiling and relaxed woman) and threatens danger rather than harmony. The crowd seems on the verge of turning ugly. (See Chapter 9 for a complete discussion of the use of visuals in argument.)

■ **Revealing the value system that determines the writer's selection and framing of data:** Ultimately, how a writer selects and frames evidence is linked to the system of values that organize his or her argument. If you favor mosh pits, you probably favor maximizing the pleasure of concertgoers, promoting individual choice, and letting moshers assume the risk of their own behavior. If you want to forbid mosh pits, you probably favor minimizing risks, protecting the city from lawsuits, and protecting individuals from the danger of their own out-of-control actions. Sometimes you can foster connections with your audience by openly addressing the underlying values that you hope your audience shares with you. You can often frame your selected data by stating explicitly the values that guide your argument.

Special Strategies for Framing Statistical Evidence

Numbers and statistical data can be framed in so many ways that this category of evidence deserves its own separate treatment. By recognizing how writers frame numbers to support the story they want to tell, you will always be aware that other stories are also possible. Ethical use of numbers means that you use reputable sources for your basic data, that you don't invent or intentionally distort numbers for your own purposes, and that you don't ignore alternative points of view. Here are some of the choices writers make when framing statistical data:

- **Raw numbers versus percentages.** You can alter the rhetorical effect of a statistic by choosing between raw numbers and percentages. In the summer of 2002, many American parents panicked over what seemed like an epidemic of child abductions. If you cited the raw number of these abductions reported in the national news, this number, although small, could seem scary. But if you computed the actual percentage of American children who were abducted, that percentage was so infinitesimally small as to seem insignificant. You can apply this framing option directly to the mosh pit case. To emphasize the danger of mosh pits, you can say that twenty-four deaths occurred at rock concerts in a given year. To minimize this statistic, you could compute the percentage of deaths by dividing this number by the total number of people who attended rock concerts during the year, certainly a number in the several millions. From the perspective of percentages, the death rate at concerts is extremely low.
- **Median versus mean.** Another way to alter the rhetorical effect of numbers is to choose between the median and the mean. The mean is the average of all numbers on a list. The median is the middle number when all the numbers are arranged sequentially from high to low. In 2006 the mean annual income for retired families in the United States was $41,928—not a wealthy amount but enough to live on comfortably if you owned your own home. However, the median income was only $27,798, a figure that gives a much more striking picture of income distribution among older Americans. This median figure means that half of all retired families in the United States had annual incomes of $27,798 or less. The much higher mean income indicates that many retired Americans are quite wealthy. This wealth raises the average of all incomes (the mean) but doesn't affect the median.
- **Unadjusted versus adjusted numbers.** Suppose your boss told you that you were getting a 5 percent raise. You might be happy—unless inflation rates were running at 6 percent. Economic data can be hard to interpret across time unless

the dollar amounts are adjusted for inflation. This same problem occurs in other areas. For example, comparing grade point averages of college graduates in 1970 versus 2012 means little unless one can somehow compensate for grade inflation.

■ **Base point for statistical comparisons.** In 2008, the stock market was in precipitous decline if one compared 2008 prices with 2007 prices. However, the market still seemed vigorous and healthy if one compared 2008 with 2002. One's choice of the base point for a comparison often makes a significant rhetorical difference.

■ ■ ■   **FOR CLASS DISCUSSION**   Using Strategies to Frame Statistical Evidence

A proposal to build a new ballpark in Seattle, Washington, yielded a wide range of statistical arguments. All of the following statements are reasonably faithful to the same facts:

■ The ballpark would be paid for by raising the sales tax from 8.2 percent to 8.3 percent during a twenty-year period.

■ The sales tax increase is one-tenth of 1 percent.

■ This increase represents an average of $7.50 per person per year—about the price of a movie ticket.

■ This increase represents $750 per five-person family over the twenty-year period of the tax.

■ For a family building a new home in the Seattle area, this tax will increase building costs by $200.

■ This is a $250 million tax increase for the residents of the Seattle area.

How would you describe the costs of the proposed ballpark if you opposed the proposal? How would you describe the costs if you supported the proposal?   ■ ■ ■

Gathering Evidence

We conclude this chapter with some brief advice on ways to gather evidence for your arguments. We begin with a list of brainstorming questions that may help you think of possible sources for evidence. We then provide suggestions for conducting interviews and creating surveys and questionnaires, since these powerful sources are often overlooked by students. For help in conducting library and Internet research—the most common sources of evidence in arguments—see Part Five: "The Researched Argument."

Creating a Plan for Gathering Evidence

As you begin contemplating an argument, you can use the following checklist to help you think of possible sources for evidence.

A Checklist for Brainstorming Sources of Evidence

■ What personal experiences have you had with this issue? What details from your life or the lives of your friends, acquaintances, or relatives might serve as examples or other kinds of evidence?

- What observational studies would be relevant to this issue?
- What people could you interview to provide insights or expert knowledge on this issue?
- What questions about your issue could be addressed in a survey or questionnaire?
- What useful information on this issue might encyclopedias, specialized reference books, or the regular book collection in your university library provide? (See Chapter 15.)
- What evidence might you seek on this issue using licensed database indexing sources for magazines, newspapers, and scholarly journals? (See Chapter 15.)
- How might an Internet search engine help you research this issue? (See Chapter 15.)
- What evidence might you find on this issue from reliable statistical resources such as U.S. Census Bureau data, the Centers for Disease Control, or *Statistical Abstract of the United States*? (See Chapter 15.)

Gathering Data from Interviews

Conducting interviews is a useful way not only to gather expert testimony and important data but also to learn about alternative views. To make interviews as productive as possible, we offer these suggestions.

- **Determine your purpose.** Consider why you are interviewing the person and what information he or she is uniquely able to provide.
- **Do background reading.** Find out as much as possible about the interviewee before the interview. Your knowledge of his or her background will help establish your credibility and build a bridge between you and your source. Also, equip yourself with a good foundational understanding of the issue so that you will sound informed and truly interested in the issue.
- **Formulate well-thought-out questions but also be flexible.** Write out beforehand the questions you intend to ask, making sure that every question is related to the purpose of your interview. However, be prepared to move in unexpected directions if the interview opens up new territory. Sometimes unplanned topics can end up being the most illuminating and useful.
- **Come well prepared for the interview.** As part of your professional demeanor, be sure to have all the necessary supplies (notepaper, pens, pencils, perhaps a tape recorder, if your interviewee is willing) with you.
- **Be prompt and courteous.** It is important to be punctual and respectful of your interviewee's time. In most cases, it is best to present yourself as a listener seeking clarity on an issue rather than an advocate of a particular position or an opponent. During the interview, play the believing role. Save the doubting role for later, when you are looking over your notes.
- **Take brief but clear notes.** Try to record the main ideas and be accurate with quotations. Ask for clarification of any points you don't understand.
- **Transcribe your notes soon after the interview.** Immediately after the interview, while your memory is still fresh, rewrite your notes more fully and completely.

When you use interview data in your writing, put quotation marks around any direct quotations. In most cases, you should also identify your source by name and indicate his or her title or credentials—whatever will convince the reader that this person's remarks are to be taken seriously.

Gathering Data from Surveys or Questionnaires

A well-constructed survey or questionnaire can provide lively, current data that give your audience a sense of the popularity and importance of your views. To be effective and responsible, however, a survey or questionnaire needs to be carefully prepared and administered, as we suggest in the following guidelines.

- **Include both closed-response questions and open-response questions.** To gain useful information and avoid charges of bias, you will want to include a range of questions. Closed-response questions ask participants to check a box or number on a scale and yield quantitative data that you can report statistically, perhaps in tables or graphs. Open-response questions elicit varied responses and often short narratives in which participants offer their own input. These may contribute new insights to your perspective on the issue.
- **Make your survey or questionnaire clear and easy to complete.** Consider the number, order, wording, and layout of the questions in your questionnaire. Your questions should be clear and easy to answer. The neatness and overall formal appearance of the questionnaire will also invite serious responses from your participants.
- **Explain the purpose of the questionnaire.** Respondents are usually more willing to participate if they know how the information gained from the questionnaire will benefit others. Therefore, it is a good idea to state at the beginning of the questionnaire how it will be used.
- **Seek a random sample of respondents in your distribution of the questionnaire.** Think out where and how you will distribute and collect your questionnaire to ensure a random sampling of respondents. For example, if a questionnaire about the university library went only to dorm residents, then you wouldn't learn how commuting students felt.
- **Convert questionnaires into usable data by tallying and summarizing responses.** Tallying the results and formulating summary statements of the information you gathered will yield material that might be used as evidence.

Conclusion

Effective use of evidence is an essential skill for arguers. In this chapter we introduced you to the STAR criteria and other strategies for making your data persuasive. We showed you various kinds of evidence and then examined how a writer's angle of vision influences the selection and framing of evidence. We also described framing strategies for emphasizing evidence, de-emphasizing it, and guiding your reader's response to it. Finally, we concluded with advice on how to gather evidence, including the use of interviews, surveys, and questionnaires.

WRITING ASSIGNMENT A Microtheme or a Supporting-Reasons Argument

Option 1: A Microtheme   Write a one- or two-paragraph argument in which you support one of the following enthymemes, using evidence from personal experience, field observation, interviews, or data from a brief questionnaire or survey. Most of your microtheme should support the stated reason with evidence. However, also include a brief passage supporting the implied warrant. The opening sentence of your microtheme should be the enthymeme itself, which serves as the thesis statement for your argument. (Note: If you disagree with the enthymeme's argument, recast the claim or the reason to assert what you want to argue.)

1. Reading fashion magazines can be detrimental to teenage girls because such magazines can produce an unhealthy focus on beauty.
2. Surfing the Web might harm your studying because it causes you to waste time.
3. Service-learning courses are valuable because they allow you to test course concepts within real-world contexts.
4. Summer internships in your field of interest, even without pay, are the best use of your summer time because they speed up your education and training for a career.
5. Any enthymeme (a claim with a *because* clause) of your choice that can be supported without library or Internet research. (The goal of this microtheme is to give you practice using data from personal experience or from brief field research.) You may want to have your instructor approve your enthymeme in advance.

Option 2: A Supporting-Reasons Argument   Write an argument that uses at least two reasons to support your claim. Your argument should include all the features of a classical argument except the section on summarizing and responding to opposing views, which we will cover in Chapter 7. This assignment builds on the brief writing assignments in Chapter 3 (create a thesis statement for an argument) and Chapter 4 (brainstorm support for one of your enthymemes using the Toulmin schema). We now ask you to expand your argument frame into a complete essay.

A *supporting-reasons argument* is our term for a classical argument without a section that summarizes and responds to opposing views. Even though alternative views aren't dealt with in detail, the writer usually summarizes an opposing view briefly in the introduction to provide background on the issue being addressed. Follow the explanations and organization chart for a classical argument as shown on page 59, but omit the section called "summary and critique of opposing views."

Like a complete classical argument, a supporting-reasons argument has a thesis-governed structure in which you state your claim at the end of the introduction, begin body paragraphs with clearly stated reasons, and use effective transitions throughout to keep your reader on track. In developing your own argument, place your most important, persuasive, or interesting reason last, where it will have the greatest impact on your readers. This kind of tightly organized structure is sometimes called a *self-announcing* or *closed-form* structure because the writer states his or her claim before beginning the body of the argument and forecasts the structure that is to follow. In contrast, an *unfolding* or *open-form* structure doesn't give away the writer's position until late in the essay. (We discuss delayed-thesis arguments in Chapter 7.)

In writing a self-announcing argument, students often ask how much of the argument to summarize in the thesis statement. Consider your options:

- You might announce only your claim:

  The public should not support the commercial use of captured dolphins.

- You might forecast a series of parallel reasons:

  There are several reasons why the public should not support the commercial use of captured dolphins.

- You might forecast the actual number of reasons:

  This paper presents four reasons why the public should not support the commercial use of captured dolphins.

- Or you might forecast the whole argument by including your *because* clauses with your claim:

  The public should not support the commercial use of captured dolphins because marine parks and "swim with dolphins" programs place direct stress on dolphins by separating them from their natural habitat and social groups; because they spread inaccurate and incomplete educational information about dolphins; because they create a commercial market for dolphins that directly or indirectly encourages dolphin hunts and captures; and because they promote an attitude of human dominance over animals.

This last thesis statement forecasts not only the claim, but also the supporting reasons that will serve as topic sentences for key paragraphs throughout the body of the paper.

No formula can tell you precisely how much of your argument to forecast in the introduction. However, these suggestions can guide you. In writing a self-announcing argument, forecast only what is needed for clarity. In short arguments, readers often need only your claim. In longer arguments, however, or in especially complex ones, readers appreciate your forecasting the complete structure of the argument (claim with reasons). ■

Reading

What follows is Carmen Tieu's supporting-reasons argument. Carmen's earlier explorations for this assignment are shown at the end of Chapters 3 and 4 (page 71 and page 87).

Why Violent Video Games Are Good for Girls

CARMEN TIEU (STUDENT)

It is ten o'clock P.M., game time. My entire family knows by now that when I am home on Saturday nights, ten P.M. is my gaming night when I play my favorite first-person-shooter games, usually *Halo 3,* on Xbox Live. Seated in my mobile chair in front of my family's 42-inch flat screen HDTV, I log onto Xbox Live. A small message in the bottom of the screen appears with the words "Kr1pL3r is online," alerting me that one of my male friends is online and already playing. As the game loads, I send Kr1pL3r a game invite, and he joins me in the pre-game room lobby.

In the game room lobby, all the players who will be participating in the match are chatting aggressively with each other: "Oh man, we're gonna own you guys so bad." When a member of the opposing team notices my gamer tag, "embracingapathy," he begins to insult me by calling me various degrading, gay-associated names: "Embracing apa-what? Man, it sounds so emo. Are you some fag? I bet you want me so bad. You're gonna get owned!" Players always assume from my gamer tag that I am a gay male, never a female. The possibility that I am a girl is the last thing on their minds. Of course, they are right that girls seldom play first-person-shooter games. Girls are socialized into activities that promote togetherness and talk, not high intensity competition involving fantasized shooting and killing. The violent nature of the games tends to repulse girls. Opponents of violent video games typically hold that these games are so graphically violent that they will influence players to become amoral and sadistic. Feminists also argue that violent video games often objectify women by portraying them as sexualized toys for men's gratification. Although I understand these objections, I argue that playing first-person-shooter games can actually be good for girls.

First, playing FPS games is surprisingly empowering because it gives girls the chance to beat guys at their own game. When I first began playing *Halo 2,* I was horrible. My male friends constantly put me down for my lack of skills, constantly telling me that I was awful, "but for a girl, you're good." But it didn't take much practice until I learned to operate the two joy sticks with precision and with quick instinctual reactions. While guys and girls can play many physical games together, such as basketball or touch football, guys will always have the advantage because on average they are taller, faster, and stronger than females. However, when it comes to video games, girls can compete equally because physical strength isn't required, just quick reaction time and manual dexterity—skills that women possess in abundance. The adrenaline rush that I receive from beating a bunch of testosterone-driven guys at something they supposedly excel at is exciting; I especially savor the look of horror on their faces when I completely destroy them.

Since female video gamers are so rare, playing shooter games allows girls to be freed from feminine stereotypes and increases their confidence. Culture generally portrays females as caring, nonviolent, and motherly beings who are not supposed to enjoy FPS games with their war themes and violent killings. I am in no way rejecting these traditional female values since I myself am a compassionate, tree-hugging vegan. But I also like to break these stereotypes. Playing video games offers a great way for females to break the social mold of only doing "girly" things and introduces them to something that males commonly enjoy. Playing video games with sexist males has also helped me become more outspoken. Psychologically, I can stand up to aggressive males because I know that I can beat them at their own game. The confidence I've gotten from excelling at shooter games may have even carried over into the academic arena because I am majoring in chemical engineering and have no fear whatsoever of intruding into the male-dominated territory of math and science. Knowing that I can beat all the guys in my engineering classes at *Halo* gives me that little extra confidence boost during exams and labs.

5   Another reason for girls to play FPS games is that it gives us a different way of bonding with guys. Once when I was discussing my latest *Halo 3* matches with one of my regular male friends, a guy whom I didn't know turned around and said, "You play *Halo*? Wow, you just earned my respect." Although I was annoyed that this guy apparently didn't respect women in general, it is apparent that guys will talk to me differently now that I can play video games. From a guy's perspective I can also appreciate why males find video games so addicting. You get joy from perfecting your skills so that your high-angle grenade kills become a thing of beauty. While all of these skills may seem trivial to some, the acknowledgment of my skills from other players leaves me with a perverse sense of pride in knowing that I played the game better than everyone else. Since I have started playing, I have also noticed that it is much easier to talk to males about lots of different subjects. Talking video games with guys is a great ice-breaker that leads to different kinds of friendships outside the realm of romance and dating.

Finally, playing violent video games can be valuable for girls because it gives them insights into a disturbing part of male subculture. When the testosterone starts kicking in, guys become blatantly homophobic and misogynistic. Any player, regardless of gender, who cannot play well (as measured by having a high number of kills and a low number of deaths) is made fun of by being called gay, a girl, or worse. Even when some guys finally meet a female player, they will also insult her by calling her a lesbian or an ugly fat chick that has no life. Their insults towards the girl will dramatically increase if she beats them because they feel so humiliated. In their eyes, playing worse than a girl is embarrassing because girls are supposed to be inept at FPS games. Whenever I play *Halo* better than my male friends, they often comment on how "it makes no sense that we're getting owned by Carmen."

When males act like such sexist jerks it causes one to question if they are always like this. My answer is no because I know, first hand, that when guys like that are having one-on-one conversations with a female, they show a softer side, and the macho side goes away. They don't talk about how girls should stay in the kitchen and make them dinner, but rather how they think it is cool that they share a fun, common interest with a girl. But when they are in a group of males their fake, offensive macho side comes out. I find this phenomenon troubling because it shows a real problem in the way boys are socialized. To be a real "man" around other guys, they have to put down women and gays in activities involving aggressive behavior where men are supposed to excel. But they don't become macho and aggressive in activities like reading and writing, which they think of as feminine. I've always known that guys are more physically aggressive than women, but until playing violent video games I had never realized how this aggression is related to misogyny and homophobia. Perhaps these traits aren't deeply ingrained in men but come out primarily in a competitive male environment. Whatever the cause, it is an ugly phenomenon, and I'm glad that I learned more about it. Beating guys at FPS games has made me a more confident woman while being more aware of gender differences in the way men and women are socialized. I joined the guys in playing *Halo,* but I didn't join their subculture of ridiculing women and gays.

For additional writing, reading, and research resources, go to www.mycomplab.com

Moving Your Audience
Ethos, Pathos, and *Kairos*

In Chapters 4 and 5 we focused on *logos*—the logical structure of reasons and evidence in argument. Even though we have treated *logos* in its own chapters, an effective arguer's concern for *logos* is always connected to *ethos* and *pathos* (see the rhetorical triangle introduced in Chapter 3, page 61). By seeking audience-based reasons—so that an arguer connects her message to the assumptions, values, and beliefs of her audience—she appeals also to *ethos* and *pathos* by enhancing the reader's trust and by triggering the reader's sympathies and imagination.

In this chapter, you will learn to:

- Use the persuasive appeals of *ethos, pathos,* and *kairos* to move your audience
- Improve the effectiveness of your arguments through deeper understanding of audience-based reasons

Ethos and *Pathos* as Persuasive Appeals: An Overview

At first, one may be tempted to think of *logos, ethos,* and *pathos* as "ingredients" in an essay, like spices you add to a casserole. But a more appropriate metaphor might be that of different lamps and filters used on theater spotlights to vary lighting effects on a stage. Thus if you switch on a *pathos* lamp (possibly through using more concrete language or vivid examples), the resulting image will engage the audience's sympathy and emotions more deeply. If you overlay an *ethos* filter (perhaps by adopting a different tone toward your audience), the projected image of the writer as a person will be subtly altered. If you switch on a *logos* lamp (by adding, say, more data for evidence), you will draw the reader's attention to the logical appeal of the argument. Depending on how you modulate the lamps and filters, you shape and color your readers' perception of you and your argument.

Our metaphor is imperfect, of course, but our point is that *logos, ethos,* and *pathos* work together to create an impact on the reader. Consider, for example, the different impacts of the following arguments, all having roughly the same logical appeal.

1. People should adopt a vegetarian diet because doing so will help prevent the cruelty to animals caused by factory farming.
2. If you are planning to eat chicken tonight, please consider how much that chicken suffered so that you could have a tender and juicy meal.

Commercial growers cram the chickens so tightly together into cages that they never walk on their own legs, see sunshine, or flap their wings. In fact, their beaks must be cut off to keep them from pecking each other's eyes out. One way to prevent such suffering is for more and more people to become vegetarians.

3. People who eat meat are no better than sadists who torture other sentient creatures to enhance their own pleasure. Unless you enjoy sadistic tyranny over others, you have only one choice: become a vegetarian.

4. People committed to justice might consider the extent to which our love of eating meat requires the agony of animals. A visit to a modern chicken factory—where chickens live their entire lives in tiny, darkened coops without room to spread their wings—might raise doubts about our right to inflict such suffering on sentient creatures. Indeed, such a visit might persuade us that vegetarianism is a more just alternative.

Each argument has roughly the same logical core:

ENTHYMEME

CLAIM People should adopt a vegetarian diet

REASON because doing so will help prevent the cruelty to animals caused by factory farming.

GROUNDS

• Evidence of suffering in commercial chicken farms, where chickens are crammed together and lash out at one another

• Evidence that only widespread adoption of vegetarianism will end factory farming

WARRANT

If we have an alternative to making animals suffer, we should use it.

But the impact of each argument varies. The difference between arguments 1 and 2, most of our students report, is the greater emotional power of argument 2. Whereas argument 1 refers only to the abstraction "cruelty to animals," argument 2 paints a vivid picture of chickens with their beaks cut off to prevent their pecking each other blind. Argument 2 makes a stronger appeal to *pathos* (not necessarily a stronger argument), stirring feelings by appealing simultaneously to the heart and to the head.

The difference between arguments 1 and 3 concerns both *ethos* and *pathos.* Argument 3 appeals to the emotions through highly charged words such as *torture, sadists,* and *tyranny.* But argument 3 also draws attention to its writer, and most of our students report not liking that writer very much. His stance is self-righteous and insulting. In contrast, argument 4's author establishes a more positive *ethos.* He establishes rapport by assuming his audience is committed to justice and by qualifying his argument with the conditional term *might.* He also invites sympathy for the chickens' plight—an appeal to *pathos*—by offering a specific description of chickens crammed into tiny coops.

Which of these arguments is best? They all have appropriate uses. Arguments 1 and 4 seem aimed at receptive audiences reasonably open to exploration of the issue, whereas arguments 2 and 3 seem designed to shock complacent audiences or to rally a group of True Believers. Even argument 3, which is too abusive to be effective in most instances, might work as a rallying speech at a convention of animal liberation activists.

Our point thus far is that *logos, ethos,* and *pathos* are different aspects of the same whole, different lenses for intensifying or softening the light beam you project onto the screen. Every choice you make as a writer affects in some way each of the three appeals. The rest of this chapter examines these choices in more detail.

How to Create an Effective *Ethos:* The Appeal to Credibility

The ancient Greek and Roman rhetoricians recognized that an argument would be more persuasive if the audience trusted the speaker. Aristotle argued that such trust resides within the speech itself, not in the prior reputation of the speaker. In the speaker's manner and delivery, tone, word choice, and arrangement of reasons, in the sympathy with which he or she treats alternative views, the speaker creates a trustworthy persona. Aristotle called the impact of the speaker's credibility the appeal from *ethos.* How does a writer create credibility? We suggest four ways:

- **Be knowledgeable about your issue.** The first way to gain credibility is to *be* credible—that is, to argue from a strong base of knowledge, to have at hand the examples, personal experiences, statistics, and other empirical data needed to make a sound case. If you have done your homework, you will command the attention of most audiences.
- **Be fair.** Besides being knowledgeable about your issue, you need to demonstrate fairness and courtesy to alternative views. Because true argument can occur only where people may reasonably disagree with one another, your *ethos* will be strengthened if you demonstrate that you understand and empathize with other points of view. There are times, of course, when you may appropriately scorn an opposing view. But these times are rare, and they mostly occur when you address audiences predisposed to your view. Demonstrating empathy to alternative views is generally the best strategy.
- **Build a bridge to your audience.** A third means of establishing credibility—building a bridge to your audience—has been treated at length in our earlier discussions of audience-based reasons. By grounding your argument in shared values and assumptions, you demonstrate your goodwill and enhance your image as a trustworthy person respectful of your audience's views. We mention audience-based reasons here to show how this aspect of *logos*—finding the reasons that are most rooted in the audience's values—also affects your *ethos* as a person respectful of your readers' views.

■ **Demonstrate professionalism.** Finally, you can enhance your *ethos* by the professionalism revealed in your manuscript itself: Appropriate style, careful editing and proofreading, accurate documentation, and adherence to the genre conventions expected by your audience all contribute to the image of the person behind the writing. If your manuscript is sloppy, marred by spelling or grammatical errors, or inattentive to the tone and style of the expected genre, your own credibility will be damaged.

How to Create *Pathos:* The Appeal to Beliefs and Emotions

Before the federal government outlawed unsolicited telephone marketing, newspapers published flurries of articles complaining about annoying telemarketers. Within this context, a United Parcel Service worker, Bobbi Buchanan, wanted to create sympathy for telemarketers. She wrote a *New York Times* op-ed piece entitled "Don't Hang Up, That's My Mom Calling," which begins as follows:

> The next time an annoying sales call interrupts your dinner, think of my 71-year-old mother, LaVerne, who works as a part-time telemarketer to supplement her social security income. To those Americans who have signed up for the new national do-not-call list, my mother is a pest, a nuisance, an invader of privacy. To others, she's just another anonymous voice on the other end of the line. But to those who know her, she's someone struggling to make a buck, to feed herself and pay her utilities—someone who personifies the great American way.

The editorial continues with a heartwarming description of LaVerne. Buchanan's rhetorical aim is to transform the reader's anonymous, depersonalized image of telemarketers into the concrete image of her mother: a "hardworking, first generation American; the daughter of a Pittsburgh steelworker; survivor of the Great Depression; the widow of a World War II veteran; a mother of seven, grandmother of eight, great-grandmother of three...." The intended effect is to alter our view of telemarketers through the positive emotions triggered by our identification with LaVerne.

By urging readers to think of "my mother, LaVerne" instead of an anonymous telemarketer, Buchanan illustrates the power of *pathos,* an appeal to the reader's emotions. Arguers create pathetic appeals whenever they connect their claims to readers' values, thus triggering positive or negative emotions depending on whether these values are affirmed or transgressed. Pro-life proponents appeal to *pathos* when they graphically describe the dismemberment of a fetus during an abortion. Proponents of improved women's health and status in Africa do so when they describe the helplessness of wives forced to have unprotected sex with husbands likely infected with HIV. Opponents of oil exploration in the Arctic National Wildlife Refuge (ANWR) do so when they lovingly describe the calving grounds of caribou.

Are such appeals legitimate? Our answer is yes, if they intensify and deepen our response to an issue rather than divert our attention from it. Because understanding is a matter of feeling as well as perceiving, *pathos* can give access to nonlogical, but not necessarily nonrational, ways of knowing. *Pathos* helps us see what is deeply at stake in an issue, what matters to the whole person. Appeals to *pathos* help readers walk in the writer's shoes. That is why arguments are often improved through the use of stories that make issues come alive or sensory details that allow us to see, feel, and taste the reality of a problem.

Appeals to *pathos* become illegitimate, we believe, when they confuse an issue rather than clarify it. Consider the case of a student who argues that Professor Jones ought to raise his grade from a D to a C, lest he lose his scholarship and be forced to leave college, shattering the dreams of his dear old grandmother. To the extent that students' grades should be based on performance or effort, the student's image of the dear old grandmother is an illegitimate appeal to *pathos* because it diverts the reader from rational to irrational criteria. The weeping grandmother may provide a legitimate motive for the student to study harder but not for the professor to change a grade.

Although it is difficult to classify all the ways that writers can create appeals from *pathos,* we will focus on four strategies: concrete language; specific examples and illustrations; narratives; and connotations of words, metaphors, and analogies. Each of these strategies lends "presence" to an argument by creating immediacy and emotional impact.

Use Concrete Language

Concrete language—one of the chief ways that writers achieve voice—can increase the liveliness, interest level, and personality of a writer's prose. When used in argument, concrete language typically heightens *pathos.* For example, consider the differences between the first and second drafts of the following student argument:

First Draft

People who prefer driving a car to taking a bus think that taking the bus will increase the stress of the daily commute. Just the opposite is true. Not being able to find a parking spot when in a hurry to be at work or school can cause a person stress. Taking the bus gives a person time to read or sleep, etc. It could be used as a mental break.

Second Draft (Concrete Language Added)

Taking the bus can be more relaxing than driving a car. Having someone else behind the wheel gives people time to chat with friends or cram for an exam. They can balance their checkbooks, do homework, doze off, read the daily newspaper, or get lost in a novel rather than foam at the mouth looking for a parking space.

In this revision, specific details enliven the prose by creating images that trigger positive feelings. Who wouldn't want some free time to doze off or to get lost in a novel?

Use Specific Examples and Illustrations

Specific examples and illustrations serve two purposes in an argument. They provide evidence that supports your reasons; simultaneously, they give your argument presence and emotional resonance. Note the flatness of the following draft arguing for the value of multicultural studies in a university core curriculum:

First Draft

Another advantage of a multicultural education is that it will help us see our own culture in a broader perspective. If all we know is our own heritage, we might not be inclined to see anything bad about this heritage because we won't know anything else. But if we study other heritages, we can see the costs and benefits of our own heritage.

Now note the increase in "presence" when the writer adds a specific example:

Second Draft (Example Added)

Another advantage of multicultural education is that it raises questions about traditional Western values. For example, owning private property (such as buying your own home) is part of the American dream. However, in studying the beliefs of American Indians, students are confronted with a very different view of private property. When the U.S. government sought to buy land in the Pacific Northwest from Chief Sealth, he is alleged to have replied:

> The president in Washington sends words that he wishes to buy our land. But how can you buy or sell the sky? The land? The idea is strange to us. If we do not own the freshness of the air and the sparkle of the water, how can you buy them?[…] We are part of the earth and it is part of us.[…] This we know: The earth does not belong to man, man belongs to the earth.

Our class was shocked by the contrast between traditional Western views of property and Chief Sealth's views. One of our best class discussions was initiated by this quotation from Chief Sealth. Had we not been exposed to a view from another culture, we would have never been led to question the "rightness" of Western values.

The writer begins his revision by evoking a traditional Western view of private property, which he then questions by shifting to Chief Sealth's vision of land as open, endless, and unobtainable as the sky. Through the use of a specific example, the writer brings to life his previously abstract point about the benefit of multicultural education.

Use Narratives

A particularly powerful way to evoke *pathos* is to tell a story that either leads into your claim or embodies it implicitly and that appeals to your readers' feelings and imagination. Brief narratives—whether true or hypothetical—are particularly effective as opening attention grabbers for an argument. To illustrate how an introductory narrative (either a story or a brief scene) can create pathetic appeals, consider the following first paragraph to an argument opposing jet skis:

> I dove off the dock into the lake, and as I approached the surface I could see the sun shining through the water. As my head popped out, I located my cousin a few feet away in a rowboat waiting to escort me as I, a twelve-year-old girl, attempted to swim across the mile-wide, pristine lake and back to our dock. I made it, and that glorious summer day is one of my most precious memories. Today, however, no one would dare attempt that swim. Jet skis have taken over this small lake where I spent many summers with my grandparents. Dozens of whining jet skis crisscross the lake, ruining it for swimming, fishing, canoeing,

rowboating, and even waterskiing. More stringent state laws are needed to control jet skiing because it interferes with other uses of lakes and is currently very dangerous.

This narrative makes a case for a particular point of view toward jet skis by winning our identification with the writer's experience. She invites us to relive that experience with her while she also taps into our own treasured memories of summer experiences that have been destroyed by change.

Opening narratives to evoke *pathos* can be powerfully effective, but they are also risky. If they are too private, too self-indulgent, too sentimental, or even too dramatic and forceful, they can backfire on you. If you have doubts about an opening narrative, read it to a sample audience before using it in your final draft.

Use Words, Metaphors, and Analogies with Appropriate Connotations

Another way of appealing to *pathos* is to select words, metaphors, or analogies with connotations that match your aim. We have already described this strategy in our discussion of the "framing" of evidence (Chapter 5, pages 94–96). By using words with particular connotations, a writer guides readers to see the issue through the writer's angle of vision. Thus if you want to create positive feelings about a recent city council decision, you can call it "bold and decisive"; if you want to create negative feelings, you can call it "haughty and autocratic." Similarly, writers can use favorable or unfavorable metaphors and analogies to evoke different imaginative or emotional responses. A tax bill might be viewed as a "potentially fatal poison pill" or as "unpleasant but necessary economic medicine." In each of these cases, the words create an emotional as well as intellectual response.

■ ■ ■ **FOR CLASS DISCUSSION**   Incorporating Appeals to *Pathos*
Outside class, rewrite the introduction to one of your previous papers (or a current draft) to include more appeals to *pathos*. Use any of the strategies for giving your argument presence: concrete language, specific examples, narratives, metaphors, analogies, and connotative words. Bring both your original and your rewritten introductions to class. In pairs or in groups, discuss the comparative effectiveness of these introductions in trying to reach your intended audience.   ■ ■ ■

Using Images for Emotional Appeal

One of the most powerful ways to engage an audience emotionally is to use photos or other images. (Chapter 9 focuses exclusively on visual rhetoric—the persuasive power of images.) Although many written arguments do not lend themselves to visual illustrations, we suggest that when you construct arguments you consider the potential of visual support. Imagine that your argument were to appear in a newspaper, in a magazine, or on a Web site where space would be provided for one or two visuals. What photographs or drawings might help persuade your audience toward your perspective?

When images work well, they are analogous to the verbal strategies of concrete language, specific illustrations, narratives, and connotative words. The challenge in using visuals is to find material that is straightforward enough to be understood without elaborate explanations, that is timely and relevant, and that clearly adds impact to a specific part of your argument. As an example, suppose you are writing an argument supporting fund-raising efforts to help a third-world country that has recently experienced a natural catastrophe. To add a powerful appeal to *pathos*, you might consider incorporating into your argument the photograph shown in Figure 6.1 of the cleanup efforts in Port-au-Prince, Haiti, after the January 2010 earthquake. A photograph such as this one can evoke a strong emotional and imaginative response as well as make viewers think.

■ ■ ■ **FOR CLASS DISCUSSION**   **Analyzing Images as Appeals to *Pathos***
Working in small groups or as a whole class, share your responses to the following questions:

1. How would you describe the emotional/imaginative impact of Figure 6.1?
2. Many disaster-relief photos seek to convey the magnitude of the destruction and suffering, sometimes shockingly, by depicting destroyed buildings, mangled bodies, and images of human misery. How is your response to Figure 6.1 similar to or different from your response to commonly encountered close-up photographs of grief-stricken victims or to distance shots of widespread destruction? To what extent is Figure 6-1's story-with the woman carrying a basket juxtaposed against

FIGURE 6.1 Cleanup in Port-au-Prince, Haiti, after the 2010 earthquake

the enormous mechanical shovel—different from the more typical photographs of destroyed buildings or anguished faces?

Kairos: The Timeliness and Fitness of Arguments

To increase your argument's effectiveness, you need to consider not only its appeals to *logos, ethos,* and *pathos,* but also its *kairos*—that is, its timing, its appropriateness for the occasion. *Kairos* is one of those wonderful words adopted from another language (in this case, ancient Greek) that is impossible to define, yet powerful in what it represents. In Greek, *kairos* means "right time," "season," or "opportunity." It differs subtly from the ordinary Greek word for time, *chronos,* the root of our words "chronology" and "chronometer." You can measure *chronos* by looking at your watch, but you measure *kairos* by sensing the opportune time through psychological attentiveness to situation and meaning. To think *kairotically* is to be attuned to the total context of a situation in order to act in the right way at the right moment. By analogy, consider a skilled base runner who senses the right moment to steal second, a wise teacher who senses the right moment to praise or critique a student's performance, or a successful psychotherapist who senses the right moment to talk rather than listen in a counseling session. *Kairos* reminds us that a rhetorical situation is not stable and fixed, but evolves as events unfold or as audiences experience the psychological ebbs and flows of attention and care. Here are some examples that illustrate the range of insights contained by the term *kairos:*

- If you write a letter to the editor of a newspaper, you usually have a one- or two-day window before a current event becomes "old news" and is no longer interesting. An out-of-date letter will be rejected, not because it is poorly written or argued but because it misses its *kairotic* moment. (Similar instances of lost timeliness occur in class discussions: On how many occasions have you wanted to contribute an idea to class discussion, but the professor doesn't acknowledge your raised hand? When you finally are called on, the *kairotic* moment has passed.)

- Bobbi Buchanan's "Don't Hang Up, That's My Mom Calling," which we used to illustrate *pathos* (page 112), could have been written only during a brief historical period when telemarketing was being publicly debated. Moreover, it could have been written only late in that period, after numerous writers had attacked telemarketers. The piece was published in the *New York Times* because the editor received it at the right *kairotic* moment.

- A sociology major is writing a senior capstone paper for graduation. The due date for the paper is fixed, so the timing of the paper isn't at issue. But *kairos* is still relevant. It urges the student to consider what is appropriate for such a paper. What is the "right way" to produce a sociology paper at this moment in the history of the discipline? Currently, what are leading-edge versus trailing-edge questions in sociology? What theorists are now in vogue? What research methods would most impress a judging committee? How would a good capstone paper written in 2010 differ from one written a decade earlier?

As you can see from these examples, *kairos* concerns a whole range of questions connected to the timing, fitness, appropriateness, and proportions of a message within

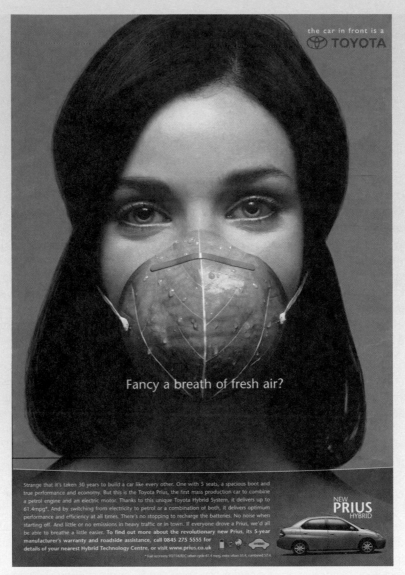

Logos, Ethos, Pathos, and *Kairos*

Increasing sales of Toyota's Prius, a hybrid car that runs on both electricity and gasoline, confirm that American consumers are willing to switch from SUVs to more energy-efficient cars. As this advertisement for the Prius shows, energy-efficient cars are connected to a constellation of issues, including the need to decrease carbon emissions because of pollution-caused health problems and environmental concern for cleaner energy.

How does this ad attempt to move its audience? Analyze the ad's visual and verbal appeals to *logos, ethos, pathos,* and *kairos.*

an evolving rhetorical context. There are no rules to help you determine the *kairotic* moment for your argument, but being attuned to *kairos* will help you "read" your audience and rhetorical situation in a dynamic way.

■ ■ ■ **FOR CLASS DISCUSSION** Analyzing an Argument from the Perspectives
of *Kairos, Logos, Ethos,* and *Pathos*

Your instructor will select an argument for analysis. Working in small groups or as a whole class, analyze the assigned argument first from the perspective of *kairos* and then from the perspectives of *logos, ethos,* and *pathos.*

1. As you analyze the argument from the perspective of *kairos,* consider the following questions:
   a. What is the motivating occasion for this argument? That is, what causes this writer to put pen to paper or fingers to keyboard?
   b. What conversation is the writer joining? Who are the other voices in this conversation? What are these voices saying that compels the writer to add his or her own voice? How was the stage set to create the *kairotic* moment for this argument?
   c. Who is the writer's intended audience and why?
   d. What is the writer's purpose? Toward what view or action is the writer trying to persuade his or her audience?
   e. To what extent can various features of the argument be explained by your understanding of its *kairotic* moment?
2. Now analyze the same argument for its appeals to *logos, ethos,* and *pathos.* How successful is this argument in achieving its writer's purpose?   ■ ■ ■

How Audience-Based Reasons Enhance *Logos, Ethos,* and *Pathos*

We conclude this chapter by returning to the concept of audience-based reasons that we introduced in Chapter 4. Audience-based reasons enhance *logos* because they are built on underlying assumptions (warrants) that the audience is likely to accept. But they also enhance *ethos* and *pathos* by helping the writer identify with the audience, entering into their beliefs and values. To consider the needs of your audience, you can ask yourself the following questions:

Questions for Analyzing Your Audience

What to Ask	Why to Ask It
1. *Who is your audience?*	Your answer will help you think about audience-based reasons.
	■ Are you writing to a single person, a committee, or the general readership of a newspaper, magazine, blog site, and so forth?

(Continued)

What to Ask	Why to Ask It
	■ Are your readers academics, professionals, fellow students, general citizens, or people with specialized background and interests? ■ Can you expect your audience to be politically and culturally liberal, middle of the road, conservative, or all over the map? What about their religious views? ■ How do you picture your audience in terms of social class, ethnicity, gender, sexual orientation, age, and cultural identity? ■ To what extent does your audience share your own interests and cultural position? Are you writing to insiders or outsiders with regard to your own values and beliefs?
2. *How much does your audience know or care about your issue?*	Your answer can especially affect your introduction and conclusion: ■ Do your readers need background on your issue or are they already in the conversation? ■ If you are writing to specific decision makers, are they currently aware of the problem you are addressing? If not, how can you get their attention? ■ Does your audience care about your issue? If not, how can you get them to care?
3. *What is your audience's current attitude toward your issue?*	Your answer will help you decide the structure and tone of your argument. ■ Are your readers already supportive of your position? Undecided? Skeptical? Strongly opposed? ■ What other points of view besides your own will your audience be weighing?
4. *What will be your audience's likely objections to your argument?*	Your answer will help determine the content of your argument and will alert you to extra research you may need. ■ What weaknesses will audience members find? ■ What aspects of your position will be most threatening to them and why? ■ How are your basic assumptions, values, or beliefs different from your audience's?
5. *What values, beliefs, or assumptions about the world do you and your audience share?*	Your answer will help you find common ground with your audience. ■ Despite different points of view on this issue, where can you find common links with your audience? ■ How might you use these links to build bridges to your audience?

To see how a concern for audience-based reasons can enhance *ethos* and *pathos,* suppose that you support racial profiling (rather than random selection) for determining who receives intensive screening at airports. Suppose further that you are writing a guest op-ed column for a liberal campus newspaper and imagine readers repulsed by the notion of racial profiling (as indeed you are repulsed too in most cases). It's important from the start that you understand and acknowledge the interests of those opposed to your position. The persons most likely targeted by racial profiling would be Middle Eastern males as well as black males with African passports, particularly those from African nations with large Islamic populations. These persons will be directly offended by racial profiling at airports. From the perspective of social justice, they can rightfully object to the racial stereotyping that lumps all people of Arabic, Semitic, or African appearance into the category "potential terrorists." Similarly, African Americans and Hispanics, who frequently experience racial profiling by police in U.S. cities, may object to further extension of this hated practice. Also, most political liberals, as well as many moderates and conservatives, may object to the racism inherent in selecting people for airport screening on the basis of ethnicity or country of origin.

What shared values might you use to build bridges to those opposed to racial profiling at airports? You need to develop a strategy to reduce your audience's fears and to link your reasons to their values. Your thinking might go something like this:

Problem: How can I create an argument rooted in shared values? How can I reduce fear that racial profiling in this situation endorses racism or will lead to further erosion of civil liberties?

Bridge-building goals: I must try to show that my argument's goal is to increase airline safety by preventing terrorism like that of 9/11/01. My argument must show my respect for Islam and for Arabic and Semitic peoples. I must also show my rejection of racial profiling as normal police practice.

Possible strategies:

- Stress the shared value of protecting innocent people from terrorism.
- Show how racial profiling significantly increases the efficiency of secondary searches. (If searches are performed at random, then we waste time and resources searching people who are statistically unlikely to be terrorists.)
- Argue that airport screeners must also use indicators other than race to select people for searches (for example, traits that might indicate a domestic terrorist).
- Show my respect for Islam.
- Show sympathy for people selected for searching via racial profiling and acknowledge that this practice would normally be despicable except for the extreme importance of airline security, which overrides personal liberties in this case.
- Show my rejection of racial profiling in situations other than airport screening—for example, stopping African Americans for traffic violations more often than whites and then searching their cars for drugs or stolen goods.
- Perhaps show my support of affirmative action, which is a kind of racial profiling in reverse.

These thinking notes allow you to develop the following plan for your argument.

- Airport screeners should use racial profiling rather than random selection to determine which people undergo intensive screening
  - because doing so will make more efficient use of airport screeners' time, increase the odds of finding terrorists, and thus lead to greater airline safety (*WARRANT: Increased airline safety is good;* or, at a deeper level, *The positive consequences of increasing airline safety through racial profiling outweigh the negative consequences.*)
  - because racial profiling in this specific case does not mean allowing it in everyday police activities nor does it imply disrespect for Islam or for Middle Eastern or African males (WARRANT: *Racial profiling is unacceptable in everyday police practices. It is wrong to show disrespect for Islam or Middle Eastern or African males.*)

As this plan shows, your strategy is to seek reasons whose warrants your audience will accept. First, you will argue that racial profiling will lead to greater airline safety, allowing you to stress that safe airlines benefit all passengers. Your concern is the lives of hundreds of passengers as well as others who might be killed in a terrorist attack. Second, you plan to reduce adversaries' resistance to your proposal by showing that the consequences aren't as severe as they might fear. Using racial profiling in airports would not justify using it in urban police work (a practice you find despicable) and it would not imply disrespect for Islam or Middle Eastern or African males. As this example shows, your focus on audience—on the search for audience-based reasons—shapes the actual invention of your argument from the start.

■ ■ ■ **FOR CLASS DISCUSSION**   **Planning an Audience-Based Argumentative Strategy**

1. How does the preceding plan for an argument supporting racial profiling make appeals to *ethos* and *pathos* as well as to *logos*?
2. Working individually or in small groups, plan an audience-based argumentative strategy for one or more of the following cases. Follow the thinking process used by the writer of the racial-profiling argument: (1) state several problems that the writer must solve to reach the audience, and (2) develop possible solutions to those problems.
   a. An argument for the right of software companies to continue making and selling violent video games: aim the argument at parents who oppose their children's playing these games.
   b. An argument to reverse grade inflation by limiting the number of As and Bs a professor can give in a course: aim the argument at students who fear getting lower grades.
   c. An argument supporting the legalization of cocaine: aim the argument at readers of *Reader's Digest,* a conservative magazine that supports the current war on drugs.   ■ ■ ■

Conclusion

In this chapter, we have explored ways that writers can strengthen the persuasiveness of their arguments by creating appeals to *ethos* and *pathos,* by being attentive to *kairos,* and by building bridges to their readers through audience-based reasons. Arguments are more persuasive if readers trust the credibility of the writer and if the argument appeals to readers' hearts and imaginations as well as to their intellects. Sometimes images such as drawings or photographs may reinforce the argument by evoking strong emotional responses, thus enhancing *pathos*. Additionally, attentiveness to *kairos* keeps the writer attuned to the dynamics of a rhetorical situation in order to create the right message at the right time. Finally, all these appeals come together when the writer explicitly focuses on finding audience-based reasons.

WRITING ASSIGNMENT Revising a Draft for *Ethos, Pathos,* and Audience-Based Reasons

Part 1: Choose an argument that you have previously written or that you are currently drafting. Revise the argument with explicit focus on increasing its appeals to *ethos, pathos,* and *logos* via audience-based reasons and other strategies. Consider especially how you might improve *ethos* by building bridges to the audience or improve *pathos* through concrete language, specific examples, metaphors, or connotations of words. Finally, consider the extent to which your reasons are audience-based.

Or

Multimodal option: Imagine an argument that you have previously written or are currently drafting that could be enhanced with effective photographs or images. Revise your argument to include these images, perhaps creating a desktop published document that wraps text around visuals chosen to enhance *pathos.* Other multimodal possibilities include transforming your argument into a speech supported by PowerPoint images (see Chapter 14, pages 341–343), into a poster argument (see Chapter 9, page 201 and Chapter 14, page 324), or even into a podcast that includes music.

Part 2: Attach to your revision or transformed project a reflective letter explaining the choices you made in revising your original argument or in transforming it using a multimodal approach. Describe for your instructor the changes or transformations you made and explain how or why your new version enhances your argument's effectiveness at moving its audience. ∎

PEARSON
mycomplab   For additional writing, reading, and research resources, go to
www.mycomplab.com

7 Responding to Objections and Alternative Views

In the previous chapter we discussed strategies for moving your audience through appeals to *ethos, pathos,* and *kairos.* In this chapter we examine strategies for addressing opposing or alternative views—whether to omit them, refute them, concede to them, or incorporate them through compromise and conciliation. In this chapter, you will learn to:

- Make choices about an argument's structure, content, and tone depending on whether your audience is sympathetic, neutral, or resistant to your views
- Use argument as a collaborative, problem-solving communication to open up new channels of understanding between you and your audience

One-Sided, Multisided, and Dialogic Arguments

Arguments are said to be one-sided, multisided, or dialogic:

- *A **one-sided argument*** presents only the writer's position on the issue without summarizing and responding to alternative viewpoints.
- *A **multisided argument*** presents the writer's position, but also summarizes and responds to possible objections and alternative views.
- *A **dialogic argument*** has a much stronger component of inquiry in which the writer presents himself as uncertain or searching, the audience is considered a partner in the dialogue, and the writer's purpose is to seek common ground, perhaps leading to a consensual solution to a problem. (See our discussion in Chapter 1 of argument as truth seeking versus persuasion, pages 12–14.)

One-sided and *multisided* arguments often take an adversarial stance in that the writer regards alternative views as flawed or wrong and supports his own claim with a strongly persuasive intent. Although multisided arguments can be adversarial, they can also be made to feel *dialogic*, depending on the way the writer introduces and responds to alternative views.

At issue, then, is the writer's treatment of alternative views. Does the writer omit them (a one-sided argument), summarize them in order to rebut them (an adversarial kind of multisided argument), or summarize them in order to acknowledge their validity, value, and force (a more dialogic kind of multisided argument)? Each of these approaches can be appropriate for certain occasions, depending on your purpose, your confidence in your own stance, and your audience's resistance to your views.

How can one determine the kind of argument that would be most effective in a given case? As a general rule, one-sided arguments occur commonly when an issue is not highly contested. If the issue is highly contested, then one-sided arguments tend to strengthen the convictions of those who are already in the writer's camp, but alienate those who aren't. In contrast, for those initially opposed to a writer's claim, a multisided argument shows that the writer has considered other views, and thus reduces some initial hostility. An especially interesting effect can occur with neutral or undecided audiences. In the short run, one-sided arguments are often persuasive to a neutral audience, but in the long run, multisided arguments have more staying power. Neutral audiences who have heard only one side of an issue tend to change their minds when they hear alternative arguments. By anticipating and rebutting opposing views, a multisided argument diminishes the surprise and force of subsequent counterarguments. If we move from neutral to highly resistant audiences, adversarial approaches—even multisided ones—are seldom effective because they increase hostility and harden the differences between writer and reader. In such cases, more dialogic approaches have the best chance of establishing common ground for inquiry and consensus.

In the rest of this chapter we will show you how your choice of writing one-sided, multisided, or dialogic arguments is a function of how you perceive your audience's resistance to your views as well as your level of confidence in your own views.

Determining Your Audience's Resistance to Your Views

When you write an argument, you must always consider your audience's point of view. One way to imagine your relationship to your audience is to place it on a scale of resistance ranging from strong support of your position to strong opposition (see Figure 7.1). At the "Accord" end of this scale are like-minded people who basically agree with your position on the issue. At the "Resistance" end are those who strongly disagree with you, perhaps unconditionally, because their values, beliefs, or assumptions sharply differ from your own. Between "Accord" and "Resistance" lies a range of opinions. Close to your position will be those leaning in your direction but with less conviction than you have. Close to the resistance position will be those basically opposed to your view but willing to listen to your argument and perhaps willing to

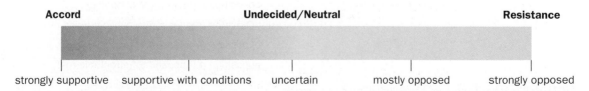

FIGURE 7.1 Scale of resistance

acknowledge some of its strengths. In the middle are those undecided people who are still sorting out their feelings, seeking additional information, and weighing the strengths and weaknesses of alternative views.

Seldom, however, will you encounter an issue in which the range of disagreement follows a simple line from accord to resistance. Often resistant views fall into different categories so that no single line of argument appeals to all those whose views are different from your own. You thus have to identify not only your audience's resistance to your ideas but also the causes of that resistance.

Consider, for example, the issues surrounding publicly financed sports stadiums. In one city, a ballot initiative asked citizens to agree to an increase in sales taxes to build a new retractable-roof stadium for its baseball team. Supporters of the initiative faced a complex array of resisting views (see Figure 7.2). Opponents of the initiative could be placed into four categories. Some simply had no interest in sports, cared nothing about baseball, and saw no benefit in building a huge, publicly financed sports facility. Another group loved baseball and followed the home team passionately, but was philosophically opposed to subsidizing rich players and owners with taxpayer money. This group argued that the whole sports industry needed to be restructured so that stadiums were paid for out of sports revenues. Still another group was opposed to tax hikes in general. It focused on the principle of reducing the size of government and of using tax revenues only for essential services. Finally, another powerful group supported baseball and supported the notion of public funding of a new stadium but opposed the kind of retractable-roof stadium specified in the initiative. This group wanted an old-fashioned, open-air stadium like Baltimore's Camden Yards or Cleveland's Jacobs Field.

Writers supporting the initiative found it impossible to address all of these resisting audiences at once. If a supporter of the initiative wanted to aim an argument at sports haters, he or she could stress the spinoff benefits of a new ballpark (for example, the new ballpark would attract tourist revenue, renovate a deteriorating downtown neighborhood, create jobs, make sports lovers more likely to vote for public subsidies of the arts, and so forth). But these arguments would be irrelevant to those who

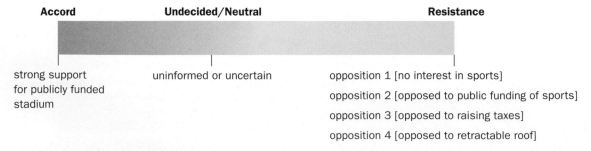

FIGURE 7.2 Scale of resistance, baseball stadium issue

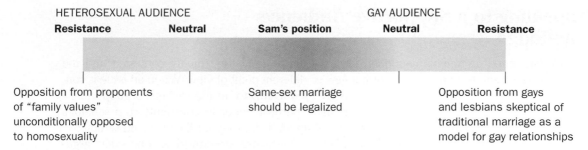

FIGURE 7.3 Scale of resistance for same-sex-marriage issue

wanted an open-air stadium, who opposed tax hikes categorically, or who objected to public subsidy of millionaires.

Another kind of complexity occurs when a writer is positioned between two kinds of resisting views. Consider the position of student writer Sam, a gay man who wished to argue that gay and lesbian people should actively support legislation to legalize same-sex marriage (see Figure 7.3). Most arguments that support same-sex marriage hope to persuade conservative heterosexual audiences, who tend to disapprove of homosexuality and stress traditional family values. But Sam imagined writing for a gay magazine such as the *Harvard Gay and Lesbian Review* or *The Advocate,* and he wished to aim his argument at liberal gay and lesbian activists who opposed traditional marriage on different grounds. These thinkers, critiquing traditional marriage for the way it stereotypes gender roles and limits the freedom of partners, argued that heterosexual marriage is not a good model for relationships in the gay community. These people constituted an audience 180 degrees removed from the conservative proponents of family values, who oppose same-sex marriage on moral and religious grounds.

In writing his early drafts, Sam was stymied by his attempt to address both audiences at once. Only after he blocked out the conservative "family values" audience and imagined an audience of what he called "liberationist" gays and lesbians was he able to develop a consistent argument. (You can read Sam's essay on pages 301–303.)

The baseball stadium example and the same-sex-marriage example illustrate the difficulty of adapting your argument to your audience's position on the scale of resistance. Yet doing so is important because you need a stable vision of your audience before you can determine an effective content, structure, and tone for your argument. As we showed in Chapter 4, effective content derives from choosing audience-based reasons that appeal to your audience's values, assumptions, and beliefs. As we show in the rest of this chapter, an effective structure and tone are often a function of where your audience falls on the scale of resistance. The next sections show how you can adjust your arguing strategy depending on whether your audience is supportive, neutral, or hostile.

Appealing to a Supportive Audience: One-Sided Argument

One-sided arguments commonly occur when an issue isn't highly contested and the writer's aim is merely to put forth a new or different point of view. When an issue is contested, however, one-sided arguments are used mainly to stir the passions of supporters—to convert belief into action by inspiring a party member to contribute to a senator's campaign or a bored office worker to sign up for a change-your-life weekend seminar.

Typically, appeals to a supportive audience are structured as one-sided arguments that either ignore opposing views or reduce them to "enemy" stereotypes. Filled with motivational language, these arguments list the benefits that will ensue from the reader's donations to the cause and the horrors just around the corner if the other side wins. One of the authors of this text recently received a fund-raising letter from an environmental lobbying group declaring, "It's crunch time for the polluters and their pals on Capitol Hill." The "corporate polluters" and "anti-environment politicians," the letter continues, have "stepped up efforts to roll back our environmental protections—relying on large campaign contributions, slick PR firms and well-heeled lobbyists to get the job done before November's election." This letter makes the reader feel part of an in-group of good guys fighting the big business "polluters." Nothing in the letter examines environmental issues from business's perspective or attempts to examine alternative views fairly. Because the intended audience already believes in the cause, nothing in the letter invites readers to consider the issues more thoroughly. Rather, the letter's goal is to solidify support, increase the fervor of belief, and inspire action. Most appeal arguments make it easy to act, ending with an 800 phone number to call, a Web site to visit, a tear-out postcard to send in, or a congressperson's address to write to.

Appealing to a Neutral or Undecided Audience: Classical Argument

The in-group appeals that motivate an already supportive audience can repel a neutral or undecided audience. Because undecided audiences are like jurors weighing all sides of an issue, they distrust one-sided arguments that caricature other views. Generally the best strategy for appealing to undecided audiences is the classically structured argument described in Chapter 3 (pages 58–60).

What characterizes the classical argument is the writer's willingness to summarize opposing views fairly and to respond to them openly—either by trying to refute them or by conceding to their strengths and then shifting to a different field of values. Let's look at these strategies in more depth.

Summarizing Opposing Views

The first step toward responding to opposing views in a classical argument is to summarize them fairly. Follow the *principle of charity,* which obliges you to avoid loaded, biased, or "straw man" summaries that oversimplify or distort opposing arguments, making them easy to knock over.

Consider the difference between an unfair and a fair summary of an argument. In the following example, a hypothetical supporter of genetically engineered foods intends to refute the argument of organic-food advocate Lisa Turner, who opposes all forms of biotechnology.

Unfair Summary of Turner's Argument

In a biased article lacking scientific understanding of biotechnology, natural-foods huckster Lisa Turner parrots the health food industry's party line that genetically altered crops are Frankenstein's monsters run amok. She ignorantly claims that consumption of biotech foods will lead to worldwide destruction, disease, and death, ignoring the wealth of scientific literature showing that genetically modified foods are safe. Her misinformed attacks are scare tactics aimed at selling consumers on overpriced "health food" products to be purchased at boutique organic-food stores.

Fair Summary of Turner's Argument

In an article appearing in a nutrition magazine, health food advocate Lisa Turner warns readers that much of our food today is genetically modified using gene-level techniques that differ completely from ordinary crossbreeding. She argues that the potential, unforeseen, harmful consequences of genetic engineering offset the possible benefits of increasing the food supply, reducing the use of pesticides, and boosting the nutritional value of foods. Turner asserts that genetic engineering is imprecise, untested, unpredictable, irreversible, and also uncontrollable because of animals, insects, and winds.

In the unfair summary, the writer distorts and oversimplifies Turner's argument, creating a straw man argument that is easy to knock over because it doesn't make the opponent's best case. In contrast, the fair summary follows the "principle of charity," allowing the strength of the opposing view to come through clearly.

■ ■ ■ **FOR CLASS DISCUSSION**   Distinguishing Fair from Unfair Summaries

Working in small groups or as a whole class, analyze the differences between the two summaries.

1. What makes the first summary unfair? How can you tell?
2. In the unfair summary, what strategies does the writer use to make the opposing view seem weak and flawed? In the fair summary, how is the opposing view made strong and clear?
3. In the unfair summary, how does the writer attack Turner's motives and credentials? This attack is sometimes called an *ad hominem* argument ("against the person"—see Appendix 1 for a definition of this reasoning fallacy) in that it attacks the arguer rather than the argument. How does the writer treat Turner differently in the fair summary?
4. Do you agree with our view that arguments are more persuasive if the writer summarizes opposing views fairly rather than unfairly? Why?

■ ■ ■

Refuting Opposing Views

Once you have summarized opposing views, you can either refute them or concede to their strengths. In refuting an opposing view, you attempt to convince readers that its argument is logically flawed, inadequately supported, or based on erroneous assumptions. In refuting an argument, you can rebut (1) the writer's stated reason and grounds, (2) the writer's warrant and backing, or (3) both. Put in less specialized language, you can rebut a writer's reasons and evidence or the writer's underlying assumptions. Suppose, for example, that you wanted to refute this argument:

We shouldn't elect Joe as committee chair because he is too bossy.

We can clarify the structure of this argument by showing it in Toulmin terms:

ENTHYMEME

CLAIM We shouldn't elect Joe as committee chair

REASON because he is too bossy.

WARRANT

Bossy people make bad committee chairs.

One way to refute this argument is to rebut the stated reason that Joe is too bossy. Your rebuttal might go something like this:

I disagree that Joe is bossy. In fact, Joe is very unbossy. He's a good listener who's willing to compromise, and he involves others in decisions. The example you cite for his being bossy wasn't typical. It was a one-time circumstance that doesn't reflect his normal behavior. [The writer could then provide examples of Joe's cooperative nature.]

Or you could concede that Joe is bossy but rebut the argument's warrant that bossiness is a bad trait for committee chairs:

I agree Joe is bossy, but that is just the trait we need now. This committee hasn't gotten anything done for six months and time is running out. We need a decisive person who can come in, get the committee organized, assign tasks, and get the job done.

Let's now illustrate these strategies in a more complex situation. Consider the controversy inspired by a *New York Times Magazine* article titled "Recycling Is Garbage." Its author, John Tierney, argued that recycling is not environmentally sound and that it is cheaper to bury garbage in a landfill than to recycle it. Tierney argued that recycling wastes money; he provided evidence that "every time a sanitation department crew picks up a load of bottles and cans from the curb, New York City loses money." In Toulmin's terms, one of Tierney's arguments is structured as shown on p. 131.

A number of environmentalists responded angrily to Tierney's argument, challenging either his reason, his warrant, or both. Those refuting the reason offered counterevidence showing that recycling isn't as expensive as Tierney claimed. Those refuting the warrant said that even if the costs of recycling are higher than the costs of burying wastes in a landfill, recycling still benefits the environment by reducing the amount of virgin materials taken from nature. These critics, in effect, offered a new warrant: We should dispose of garbage in the way that best saves the world's resources.

ENTHYMEME

CLAIM Recycling is bad policy

REASON because it costs more to recycle
material than to bury it in a landfill.

GROUNDS

• Evidence of the high cost of recycling [Tierney
says it costs New York City $200 more per ton
for recyclables than trash.]

WARRANT

We should dispose of garbage in the least
expensive way.

Strategies for Rebutting Evidence

Whether you are rebutting an argument's reasons or its warrant, you will frequently
need to question a writer's use of evidence. Here are some strategies you can use:

- **Deny the truth of the data.** Arguers can disagree about the facts of a case. If you
  have reasons to doubt a writer's facts, call them into question.
- **Cite counterexamples and countertestimony.** You can often rebut an argument
  based on examples or testimony by citing counterexamples or countertestimony
  that denies the conclusiveness of the original data.
- **Cast doubt on the representativeness or sufficiency of examples.** Examples
  are powerful only if they are believed to be representative and sufficient. Many
  environmentalists complained that John Tierney's attack on recycling was based
  too largely on data from New York City and that it didn't accurately take into
  account more positive experiences of other cities and states. When data from
  outside New York City were examined, the cost-effectiveness and positive environmental impact of recycling seemed more apparent.
- **Cast doubt on the relevance or recency of the examples, statistics, or testimony.** The best evidence is up-to-date. In a rapidly changing universe, data that
  are even a few years out-of-date are often ineffective. For example, as the demand
  for recycled goods increases, the cost of recycling will be reduced. Out-of-date
  statistics will skew any argument about the cost of recycling.
- **Question the credibility of an authority.** If an opposing argument is based on
  testimony, you can undermine its persuasiveness if you show that a person
  being cited lacks current or relevant expertise in the field. (This is different from
  the *ad hominem* fallacy discussed in the Appendix because it doesn't attack the
  personal character of the authority but only the authority's expertise on a specific matter.)

- **Question the accuracy or context of quotations.** Evidence based on testimony is frequently distorted by being either misquoted or taken out of context. Often scientists qualify their findings heavily, but these qualifications are omitted by the popular media. You can thus attack the use of a quotation by putting it in its original context or by restoring the qualifications in its original source.
- **Question the way statistical data were produced or interpreted.** Chapter 5 provides fuller treatment of how to question statistics. In general, you can rebut statistical evidence by calling into account how the data were gathered, treated mathematically, or interpreted. It can make a big difference, for example, whether you cite raw numbers or percentages or whether you choose large or small increments for the axes of graphs.

Conceding to Opposing Views

In writing a classical argument, a writer must sometimes concede to an opposing argument rather than refute it. Sometimes you encounter portions of an argument that you simply can't refute. For example, suppose you support the legalization of hard drugs such as cocaine and heroin. Adversaries argue that legalizing hard drugs will increase the number of drug users and addicts. You might dispute the size of their numbers, but you reluctantly agree that they are right. Your strategy is thus not to refute the opposing argument but to concede to it by admitting that legalization of hard drugs will promote heroin and cocaine addiction. Having made that concession, your task is then to show that the benefits of drug legalization still outweigh the costs you've just conceded.

As this example shows, the strategy of a concession argument is to switch from the field of values employed by the writer you disagree with to a different field of values more favorable to your position. You don't try to refute the writer's stated reason and grounds (by arguing that legalization will *not* lead to increased drug usage and addiction) or the writer's warrant (by arguing that increased drug use and addiction is not a problem). Rather, you shift the argument to a new field of values by introducing a new warrant, one that you think your audience can share (that the benefits of legalization—eliminating the black market and ending the crime, violence, and prison costs associated with procurement of drugs—outweigh the costs of increased addiction). To the extent that opponents of legalization share your desire to stop drug-related crime, shifting to this new field of values is a good strategy. Although it may seem that you weaken your own position by conceding to an opposing argument, you may actually strengthen it by increasing your credibility and gaining your audience's goodwill. Moreover, conceding to one part of an opposing argument doesn't mean that you won't refute other parts of that argument.

Example of a Student Essay Using Refutation Strategy

The following extract from a student essay is the refutation section of a classical argument appealing to a neutral or undecided audience. In this essay, student writer Marybeth Hamilton argues for continued taxpayer support of First Place, an alternative public school for homeless children that also provides job counseling and mental health services for families. Because running First Place is costly and because it can accommodate only 4 percent of her city's homeless children, Marybeth recognizes that her audience may object to continued public funding. Consequently, to reach the neutral or skeptical members of her audience, she devotes the following portion of her argument to summarizing and refuting opposing views.

From "First Place: A Healing School for Homeless Children"

MARYBETH HAMILTON (STUDENT)

... As stated earlier, the goal of First Place is to prepare students for returning to mainstream public schools. Although there are many reasons to continue operating an agency like First Place, there are some who would argue against it. One argument is that the school is too expensive, costing many more taxpayer dollars per child than a mainstream school. I can understand this objection to cost, but one way to look at First Place is as a preventative action by the city to reduce the future costs of crime and welfare. Because all the students at First Place are at risk for educational failure, drug and alcohol abuse, or numerous other long-term problems, a program like First Place attempts to stop the problems before they start. In the long run, the city could be saving money in areas such as drug rehabilitation, welfare payments, or jail costs.

Others might criticize First Place for spending some of its funding on social services for the students and their families instead of spending it all on educational needs. When the city is already making welfare payments and providing a shelter for the families, why do they deserve anything more? Basically, the job of any school is to help a child become educated and have social skills. At First Place, students' needs run deep, and their entire families are in crisis. What good is it to help just the child when the rest of the family is still suffering? The education of only the child will not help the family out of poverty. Therefore, First Place helps parents look for jobs by providing job search help including assistance with résumés. They even supply clothes to wear to an interview. First Place also provides a parent support group for expressing anxieties and learning coping skills. This therapy helps parents deal with their struggles in a productive way, reducing the chance that they will take out their frustration on their child. All these "extras" are an attempt to help the family get back on its feet and become self-supporting.

Another objection to an agency like First Place is that the short-term stay at First Place does no long-term good for the student. However, in talking with Michael Siptroth, a teacher at First Place, I learned that the individual attention the students receive helps many of them catch up in school quite quickly. He reported that some students actually made a three-grade-level improvement in one year. This improvement definitely contributes to the long-term good of the student, especially in the area of self-esteem. Also, the students at First Place are in desperate situations. For most, any help is better than no help. Thus First Place provides extended day care for the children so they won't have to be unsupervised at home while their parents are working or looking for work. For example, some homeless children live in motels on Aurora Avenue, a major highway that is overrun with fast cars, prostitutes, and drugs. Aurora Avenue is not a safe place for children to play, so the extended day care is important for many of First Place's students.

Finally, opponents might question the value of removing students from mainstream classrooms. Some might argue that separating children from regular classrooms is not good because it further highlights their differences from the mainstream children. Also, the separation period might cause additional alienation when the First Place child does return to a mainstream school. In reality, though, the effects are quite different. Children at First Place are sympathetic to each other. Perhaps for the first time in their lives, they do not have to be on the defensive because no one is going to make fun of them for being homeless; they are all homeless. The time spent at First Place is usually a time for catching up to the students in mainstream schools. When students catch up, they have one fewer reason to be seen as different from mainstream students. If the students stayed in the mainstream school and continued to fall behind, they would only get teased more.

5   First Place is a program that merits the community's ongoing moral and financial support. With more funding, First Place could help many more homeless children and their families along the path toward self-sufficiency. While this school is not the ultimate answer to the problem of homelessness, it is a beginning. These children deserve a chance to build their own lives, free from the stigma of homelessness, and I, as a responsible citizen, feel a civic and moral duty to do all I can to help them.

■ ■ ■   **FOR CLASS DISCUSSION**   Refutation Strategies

1. Individually or in groups, analyze the refutation strategies that Marybeth employs in her argument.

   a. Summarize each of the opposing reasons that Marybeth anticipates from her audience.

   b. How does she attempt to refute each line of reasoning in the opposing argument? Where does she refute her audience's stated reasons? Where does she refute a warrant? Where does she concede to an opposing argument but then shift to a different field of values?

   c. How effective is Marybeth's refutation? Would you as a city resident vote for allotting more public money for this school? Why or why not?

2. Examine each of the following arguments, imagining how the enthymeme could be fleshed out with grounds and backing. Then attempt to refute each argument.

Suggest ways to rebut the reason or the warrant or both, or to concede to the argument and then switch to a different field of values.

a. Signing the Kyoto treaty (pledging that the United States will substantially lower its emission of greenhouse gases) is a bad idea because reducing greenhouse emissions will seriously harm the American economy.

b. Majoring in engineering is better than majoring in music because engineers make more money than musicians.

c. The United States should reinstitute the draft because doing so is the only way to maintain a large enough military to defend American interests in several different trouble spots in the world.

d. The United States should build more nuclear reactors because nuclear reactors will provide substantial electrical energy without emitting greenhouse gases.

e. People should be allowed to own handguns because owning handguns helps them protect their homes against potentially violent intruders.

Appealing to a Resistant Audience: Dialogic Argument

Whereas classical argument is effective for neutral or undecided audiences, it is often less effective for audiences strongly opposed to the writer's views or for arguments that lean toward the inquiry end of the argument continuum. Because resistant audiences hold values, assumptions, or beliefs widely different from the writer's, they are often unswayed by classical argument, which attacks their worldview too directly. Writers, too, may recognize that progress toward communication on some values-laden issues may require them to take a more open, problem-solving approach. On issues such as abortion, gun control, gay rights, or the role of religion in the public sphere, the distance between a writer and a resistant audience can be so great that dialogue seems impossible. In these cases the writer's goal may be simply to open dialogue by seeking common ground—that is, by finding places where the writer and audience agree. For example, pro-choice and pro-life advocates may never agree on a woman's right to an abortion, but they may share common ground in wanting to reduce teenage pregnancy. There is room, in other words, for conversation, if not for agreement.

Because of these differences in basic beliefs and values, the goal of dialogic argument is seldom to convert resistant readers to the writer's position. The best a writer can hope for is to reduce somewhat the level of resistance, perhaps by increasing the reader's willingness to listen as preparation for future dialogue. In this section and the next, we introduce you to two kinds of dialogic argument—delayed-thesis argument, which is particularly helpful at reducing the resistance of hostile audiences, and Rogerian argument, a communicating and thinking strategy that can enlarge the writer's as well as the readers's view of a conflicted issue.

Delayed-Thesis Argument as Both Exploration and Persuasion

Unlike a classical argument, a delayed-thesis argument assumes an exploratory approach to a subject. With some issues, you may want to convey that you are still thinking out your position, finding your way through a thicket of alternative views and the complexities of the issue. You yourself may be pulled in multiple directions and may have arrived at your position after pondering different views. In addition, your readers' resistance to your views means that they may be turned off if you forthrightly plunge into your claim and reasons. Under these rhetorical conditions, a delayed-thesis argument enables you to engage your audience in a dialogic exploration of the problem before you argue a thesis. Instead of declaring a claim and reasons early in the argument, you may work your way slowly to your claim, devoting a large part of the argument to examining different views and re-creating your own inquiry into the subject.

Let's look at an example of a delayed-thesis argument, examining its form and its emotional impact. (For another example of a delayed-thesis argument, see Ellen Goodman's commentary piece "Womb for Rent—for a Price" on pages 170–171.) The following op-ed piece by syndicated columnist Ross Douthat appeared in the *New York Times* during the public debates about the building of a Muslim community center near Ground Zero in lower Manhattan. Note how Douthat takes a nonthreatening tone and pulls readers into his exploration of the issue.

Islam in Two Americas

ROSS DOUTHAT

Writer frames the controversy as a conflict of American identities, two divergent ways that the country thinks of itself.

There's an America where it doesn't matter what language you speak, what god you worship or how deep your New World roots run. An America where allegiance to the Constitution trumps ethnic differences, language barriers and religious divides. An America where the newest arrival to our shores is no less American than the ever-so-great granddaughter of the Pilgrims.

But there's another America as well, one that understands itself as a distinctive culture, rather than just a set of political propositions. This America speaks English, not Spanish or Chinese or Arabic. It looks back to a particular religious heritage: Protestantism originally, and then a Judeo-Christian consensus that accommodated Jews and Catholics as well.

Writer establishes the problem and its timeliness and invites his readers to contemplate it with him.

These two understandings of America, one constitutional and one cultural, have been in tension throughout our history. They're in tension in the controversy over the Islamic mosque and cultural center scheduled to go up two blocks from ground zero.

Writer explores the problem from several perspectives, first, the inclusive constitutional America, which defends the right of all religious groups to worship as they please.

Writer shows his awareness of the problem's complexity by exploring the second perspective, the melting-pot America, which emphasizes its Judeo-Christian heritage.

Writer keeps the problem open as he examines how these two identities functioned in American history.

Writer finally presents his own viewpoint, his thesis-claim that Muslims should not build a community center near Ground Zero.

He briefly develops his claim.

He argues that by not building near Ground Zero, American Muslims would signal their disassociation from Islamic terrorist groups and their respect for the national pain caused by 9/11.

He sums up his argument by restating his thesis-claim in larger terms that leave readers with his thinking.

The first America views the project as the consummate expression of our nation's high ideals. "This is America," President Barack Obama intoned last week, "and our commitment to religious freedom must be unshakeable." The construction of the mosque, Mayor Michael Bloomberg told New Yorkers, is as important a test of the principle of religious freedom "as we may see in our lifetimes."

5 The second America begs to differ. It sees the project as an affront to the memory of 9/11, and a sign of disrespect for the values of a country where Islam has only recently become part of the public consciousness. And beneath these concerns lurks the darker suspicion that Islam in any form may be incompatible with the American way of life.

Both understandings of this country have wisdom to offer, and both have been necessary to the American experiment's success. During the great waves of 19th-century immigration, the insistence that new arrivals adapt to Anglo-Saxon culture was crucial to their swift assimilation.

The same was true in religion. The steady pressure to conform to American norms eventually persuaded the Mormons to abandon polygamy, smoothing their assimilation into the American mainstream. Nativist concerns about Catholicism's illiberal tendencies inspired American Catholics to prod their church toward a recognition of the virtues of democracy, making it possible for generations of immigrants to feel unambiguously Catholic and American.

So it is today with Islam. The first America is correct to insist on Muslims' absolute right to build and worship where they wish. But the second America is right to press for something more from Muslim Americans—particularly from figures like Feisal Abdul Rauf, the imam behind the mosque—than simple protestations of good faith.

Too often, American Muslim institutions have turned out to be entangled with ideas and groups that most Americans rightly consider beyond the pale. Too often, American Muslim leaders strike ambiguous notes when asked to disassociate themselves completely from illiberal causes.

10 For Muslim Americans to integrate fully into our national life, they'll need leaders who don't describe America as "an accessory to the crime" of 9/11 (as Rauf did shortly after the 2001 attacks), or duck questions about whether groups like Hamas count as terrorist organizations (as Rauf did in June). They'll need leaders whose antennas are sensitive enough to recognize that the quest for inter-religious dialogue is ill served by throwing up a high-profile mosque two blocks from the site of a mass murder committed in the name of Islam.

They'll need leaders, in other words, who understand that while the ideals of the first America protect the *e pluribus*, it's the demands the second America makes of new arrivals that help create the *unum*.

FIGURE 7.4 Marchers in support of the Islamic culture center at Ground Zero

In this delayed-thesis argument, Ross Douthat, a conservative columnist writing for the liberal *New York Times,* asks readers to think with him about the fierce clash of views over building a Muslim community center near Ground Zero. Douthat wants to reach typical *New York Times* readers, who are apt to support the Muslim project based on their liberal views of tolerance and religious freedom. As the photos taken during the protests show (see Figures 7.4–7.7), this proposal elicited powerful emotions. Douthat enters this public debate calmly, admits the legitimacy of different opposing views, and only toward the end of the argument states his own position.

If Douthat had chosen to write a classical argument, he would have declared his position in the first paragraph, perhaps with a thesis statement like this:

> Muslim Americans should not build their community center near Ground Zero because doing so represents disrespect for America's core cultural identity and insensitivity to Americans' national pain caused by Islamic terrorists.

With this thesis, readers would have no initial doubt where Douthat stands. However, this in-your-face thesis would activate the emotional objections of readers who support the Islamic community center and might prevent them from even reading the piece. In contrast, both liberal and conservative readers can get drawn into the building momentum of Douthat's delayed-thesis version and appreciate its subtlety and surprise.

FIGURE 7.5 People protesting the Islamic culture center at Ground Zero

Writing a Delayed-Thesis Argument

Clearly, where you place your claim can affect your argument's impact on its audience. We should note, however, that a delayed-thesis argument is not simply a classical argument turned upside down. Instead, it promotes dialogue with the audience rather than compels readers to accept the writer's views. It strives to enrich and complicate the discussion as well as present a view of an issue. It entails some risk to the writer because it leaves space only at the end of the argument for developing the writer's claim. However, it may lead the writer and readers to a deeper understanding of the issue, provide clarification, and promote further discussion.

Although there is no set form, the organization plan on page 141 shows characteristic elements often found in delayed-thesis arguments.

FIGURE 7.6 People protesting the Islamic culture center at Ground Zero

FIGURE 7.7 People defending the rights of Muslims

Organization Plan for a Delayed-Thesis Argument

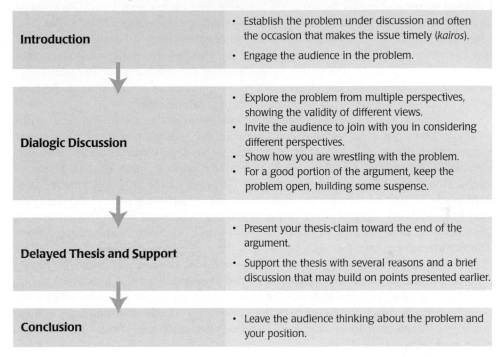

Introduction	• Establish the problem under discussion and often the occasion that makes the issue timely (*kairos*). • Engage the audience in the problem.
Dialogic Discussion	• Explore the problem from multiple perspectives, showing the validity of different views. • Invite the audience to join with you in considering different perspectives. • Show how you are wrestling with the problem. • For a good portion of the argument, keep the problem open, building some suspense.
Delayed Thesis and Support	• Present your thesis-claim toward the end of the argument. • Support the thesis with several reasons and a brief discussion that may build on points presented earlier.
Conclusion	• Leave the audience thinking about the problem and your position.

A More Open-Ended Approach: Rogerian Argument

We now turn to a more complex kind of dialogic argument: *Rogerian argument.* All dialogic arguments emphasize problem solving, collaborative thinking, and negotiation with a resistant audience. But Rogerian argument, besides delaying its thesis, works to change the writer as well as the reader. Rogerian argument is named after psychotherapist Carl Rogers, who developed a communication strategy for helping people resolve differences.* The Rogerian strategy emphasizes "empathic listening," which Rogers defined as the ability to see an issue sympathetically from another person's perspective or "frame of reference." He trained people to withhold judgment of another person's ideas until after they had listened attentively to the other person, understood that person's reasoning, appreciated that person's values, and respected that person's humanity—in short, walked in that person's shoes. What Carl Rogers understood is that traditional methods of argumentation are threatening. Because Rogerian argument stresses the psychological as well as the logical dimensions of argument, it is particularly effective when dealing with emotion-laden issues.

---

*See Carl Rogers's essay "Communication: Its Blocking and Its Facilitation" in his book *On Becoming a Person* (Boston: Houghton Mifflin, 1961), 329–37. For a fuller discussion of Rogerian argument, see Richard Young, Alton Becker, and Kenneth Pike, *Rhetoric: Discovery and Change* (New York: Harcourt Brave, 1972).

With Rogerian communication, the writer tries to reduce the sense of difference between writer and reader by releasing her tight hold on her own views. Particularly, she tries to show that *both writer and resistant audience share many basic values.* This search for common ground often has the psychological effect of enlarging, complicating, or deepening the writer's own worldview. By acknowledging that she has empathy for the audience's views, the writer makes it easier for the audience to listen to her views. Ideally, this mutual listening leads to a compromise or synthesis or, at the least, better understanding and more open channels of communication.

Essential to successful Rogerian argument, besides the art of listening, is the ability to point out areas of agreement between the writer's and reader's positions. For example, if you, as a supporter of alternative energy, oppose offshore or wilderness drilling, and you are arguing with someone who is in favor of maximizing oil exploration, you are caught in an impasse. However, if the problem you are both confronting is that of increasing available energy resources, you might reduce tension and establish conditions for problem solving. You might begin this process by summarizing your reader's position sympathetically, stressing your shared values. You might say, for example, that you also value energy independence, that you appreciate recent advances in safe oil drilling, and that you are disturbed by people who deny our country's vast energy needs. You also agree that it is unrealistic to pretend that we can dispense with our oil needs overnight. Your effort to understand your audience's views and to build bridges between you and your audience will encourage dialogue and make it more likely that your audience will listen when you offer your perspective.

Rogers's communication strategies have been the subject of intense debate among scholars. On the one hand, some rhetoricians don't like the term "Rogerian *argument*," preferring instead "Rogerian *rhetoric*" or "Rogerian *communication*." These theorists say that Rogerian listening isn't a form of argument or persuasion at all. Rather, its goal is increased mutual understanding and enlarged perspectives on reality for both writer and audience. According to rhetorician Nathaniel Teich, Rogerian rhetoric seeks to foster discovery of others' perspectives and revision of both parties' worldviews.*

In contrast to this perspective, other scholars view Rogerian argument as a means of manipulating resistant audiences. According to this view, the best way to persuade a hostile audience is to adopt a nonthreatening tone and approach, treat the opponent's views sympathetically, and then lure the opponent into accepting your views. The problem with this perspective is that it is purely instrumental and reduces Rogerian argument to a technique, a clever means to an end.

Our view of Rogerian argument forges a middle path between these two perspectives. We emphasize argument as a process of inquiry and treat Rogerian argument as dialogic problem solving in which the writer negotiates with the audience in a mutual search for provisional solutions.

---

*For one of the most thorough analyes of Carl Rogers's influence on rhetoric and composition, see Nathaniel Teich's scholarly anthology *Rogerian Perspectives: Collaborative Rhetoric for Oral and Written Communication* (Norwood, NJ: Ablex Publishing Corporation, 1992).

Rogerian Argument as Growth for the Writer

One of the key features of Rogerian argument is the open relationship it establishes between the writer and the subject; it recasts argument as a process of growth for the writer. Because Rogerian argument asks the writer to listen to the opponent's views—views that the writer may find uncomfortable or threatening—it promotes inquiry and self-reflection, a more tentative and exploratory approach to the subject than the writer takes in classical argument or delayed-thesis argument. Rogerian argument urges writers to play Peter Elbow's "believing game," where the writer must try "to get inside the head of someone" who holds unwelcome ideas.* (See our discussion of the believing and doubting game in Chapter 2, pages 29–30.) This "dwelling in" unappealing ideas often compels writers to articulate their own values and to achieve a new understanding of them. Extending Elbow's strategy and emphasizing the connection between values and identity, rhetorician James Baumlin argues that Rogerian argument creates "a realm of plural selves or identities" in the process of taking on "another's beliefs and worldview" through role-playing.† Rogerian argument thus promotes a writer's self-examination and exploration of multiple perspectives on a problem. This double process of exploration and reflection can in turn lead to a change of mind or at least a deeper understanding of a problem.

Rogerian Argument as Collaborative Negotiation

A second key feature of Rogerian argument is its altered argumentative purpose and attitude toward the audience. In the absence of the possibility of persuading a resistant audience to accept the writer's views, the writer seeks different goals through a relationship with the audience. These goals include reducing antagonism toward those with different beliefs, initiating small steps in understanding, cultivating mutual respect, and encouraging further problem solving—in short, nurturing conditions for future exchanges. Thus Rogerian argument particularly lends itself to rhetorical situations involving complex, emotionally volatile issues. Rogerian argument is appropriate whenever writers are seeking to open up communication with a resistant audience and are themselves willing to work toward a synthesis of views.

Writing a Rogerian Argument

A major thrust of Rogerian argument is building bridges between writer and audience. Because Rogers's principles originated as a communication strategy between two parties in conversation, Rogerian argument most commonly takes the form of a letter or an open letter directed to a specific person or group. For example, the audience for a Rogerian argument might be a particular person whom the writer already knows, a

---

*For more suggestions on how to encourage empathic listening, see Elbow's "Bringing the Rhetoric of Assent and the Believing Game Together—and into the Classroom," *College English* 67.4 (March 2005), 389.
†For more discussion of the relationship between role-playing, understanding, and identity, see James S. Baumlin's "Persuasion, Rogerian Rhetoric, and Imaginative Play," *Rhetoric Society Quarterly* 17.1 (Winter 1987), 36.

speaker the writer has recently heard, or the author of an article that the writer has recently read. In all these cases, the writer is disturbed by the audience's views and hopes to open up dialogue. Rogerian argument will most likely include the features shown in the chart below, although not necessarily in any set form.

Organization Plan for a Rogerian Argument

Introduction	• Address the audience and identify the problem that you and your audience want to solve. • Possibly, show the timeliness (*kairos*) of the problem. • Try to establish a friendly or cordial relationship with the audience. • Possibly include information that shows your familiarity with the audience.
Summary of the Audience's Views	• Summarize the audience's views in a fair and neutral way that the audience would accept. • Show that you understand the audience's position. • Also show an understanding of, and respect for, the audience's values and beliefs; the goal of this "saying back" (Rogers's term) is to summarize these views in a way that will be entirely acceptable to the audience.
Common Ground	• Identify common ground you share with your audience. • Demonstrate your growth through empathic consideration of views that you would otherwise find threatening or unwelcome. • Show understanding of the audience's views by "indwelling" with them and perhaps by extending them to other situations through new examples. • Show how your views have been enlarged by empathic listening to the audience's ideas.
Contribution of New Points to the Negotiation	• Respectfully propose your own way of looking at this issue. • Through a respectful and inquiring tone, encourage the audience to listen and work with you to solve the problem.
Conclusion	• Possibly propose a synthesis of the two positions, discuss how both parties gain from an enlarged vision, or invite the audience to ongoing negotiation.

In the following example of a Rogerian argument, student writer Colleen Fontana responds to an article written by Robert A. Levy, a senior fellow for constitutional studies at the Cato Institute, a libertarian think tank. In this open letter, Colleen conducts a collaborative discussion directed toward solving the problem of gun violence.* Annotations in the margins indicate how Colleen is practicing Rogerian principles.

An Open Letter to Robert Levy in Response to His Article "They Never Learn"

COLLEEN FONTANA (STUDENT)

Dear Robert Levy,

Writer addresses the audience.

Writer identifies the problem, shows its current timeliness (kairos), and establishes a cordial relationship with the audience.

My recent interest in preventing gun violence led me to find your article "They Never Learn" in *The American Spectator* about the mass shooting at Virginia Tech in 2007. I was struck by the similarities between that incident and the recent shooting in Tucson, Arizona, where a young man gunned down U.S. Representative Gabrielle Giffords and nineteen others in a supermarket parking lot. Although your article came several years before this Arizona incident, we can see that gun violence remains an enduring issue. I have long struggled with the question of how we can reduce gun-related violence without detracting from an individual's right to own a gun. Your article shed new light on this question for me.

Summary: In neutral, fair terms, the writer summarizes the audience's previous argument, the article to which she is responding.

Your article stresses the need for something different from our nation's current gun policies. You assert that the solution lies, not in stricter gun control policies, but rather in "liberalized laws." According to you, Mr. Levy, it was primarily the existence of anti-gun laws on the Virginia Tech campus that prevented an armed citizen from saving the victims of the 2007 shooting. You comment that "gun control does not work. It just prevents weaker people from defending themselves against stronger predators." Your article gives detailed examples of studies that have substantiated that stricter gun laws have not resulted in lower murder rates. You also cite evidence that fewer crimes are likely to happen if the victim brandishes a gun, even if he or she never fires it. According to your

---

*We are indebted to Doug Brent for his insight that Rogerian arguments can often be addressed to the author of an article that a reader finds disturbing. See "Rogerian Rhetoric: Ethical Growth Through Alternative Forms of Argumentation." In *Argument Revisited; Argument Redefined,* eds. Barbara Emmel, Paula Resch, and Deborah Tenney, (Thousand Oaks, CA: Sage, 1996), 81.

article, stricter gun laws are doing nothing to help society, and your solution lies in relaxed laws, allowing more responsible citizens to carry concealed weapons.

Common ground: Writer identifies common values that she shares with her audience; she demonstrates empathic listening; she imagines instances where the audience's values make the most sense.

Living on a college campus myself, I identify immediately with your concern for preventing school shootings. I appreciate that you are concerned with the safety of the students and the public, and I agree that there exists a need for greater safety on school campuses. I also agree that current gun laws are not effective, as is shown by the number of gun-related deaths that happen annually. Even though such laws exist, they are not likely to stop "crazed fanatics undeterred by laws against murder," as you say, from committing certain crimes. I particularly agree with you when you discuss the right of self-defense. I struggle with laws that forbid carrying a gun because I believe in the right of self-defense. As you mentioned in your article, instances do occur in which civilians carrying guns have the ability to save themselves and others. Although I have not experienced this situation personally, I have read of brave acts of self-defense and intervention. For example, my research turned up an article by John Pierce on Minneapolis' *Examiner.com,* "It Takes a Gun to Stop a Gunman." In this article Pierce describes an occurrence in Richmond, Virginia, in July of 2009 where a store owner and several customers were saved from an armed robber by a civilian in the store who happened to be carrying a firearm. Even though Pierce is a long-time gun rights advocate and an NRA-certified instructor, the points he brought up were striking. If that civilian hadn't been carrying a gun in that store on that day, then everyone in the store might have been killed by the robber. This realization resonates with me. I imagine myself in that store, and I know I would have been quite grateful that he was carrying a weapon that saved my life. Reading this story has forced me to think of the responsibility many gun-owning citizens must feel—a responsibility to protect not only themselves but those around them as well. A similar event happened recently in New York where a person attempting to rob a jewelry shop was shot by the owner in an act of self-defense. His neighbors regard him as a hero (Kilgannon).

Writer moves respectfully to presenting her own questions and differing perspectives on the problem. Note her tone of negotiation and her willingness to engage in further discussion.

While I agree with you that self-defense is an important right and that armed citizens can sometimes prevent the death of innocent people, I wonder whether the possibility of allowing more guns in public through liberalized gun laws is the best solution. Is there a chance more guns in the hands of more people would foster a more danger-prone climate both from accidents and from sudden fits of rage? I was surprised to learn in a recent *New York Times* article by Charles M. Blow that for every ten people in America there are nine guns. Among major nations, according to a U.N. study, we have both the highest ratio of guns to people and the highest incidence of violence. If liberalizing gun ownership will lead to even more guns, then my concern is that there will be a higher chance of children finding a loaded gun in a parent's bed stand or of deaths caused by gang warfare or from momentary rage in an escalating fight between neighbors. Such danger could also exist on school campuses if guns were allowed. On a campus where drinking nurtures the party scene, I worry that rowdy people waving a gun perhaps as a joke might turn a party into a tragedy. Do you have any ideas, Mr. Levy, for reducing gun accidents or irresponsible use of firearms if they are widely available?

Writer expresses a second concern, one that Levy did not mention: assault weapons.

I found your point about owning a firearm for self-defense really thought provoking. But even if Virginia Tech had allowed guns on campus, what are the odds that an armed student or teacher would have been at the right place at the right time with an actual chance of shooting the gunman? Only in the movies are good guys and heroes *always* on the spot and capable of taking the right action to protect potential victims. Although I can really see your point about using handguns for self-defense, I don't think self-defense can be used as a justification for assault weapons or automatic weapons with large clips. If guns were freely allowed on campuses, perhaps massacres such as Virginia Tech might occur more often. Or is there a way to allow people to carry concealed handguns on campus but still to forbid rifles, shotguns, or other weapons more useful for massacres than for self-defense?

Writer concludes her letter with a reiteration of the mutual concerns she shares with her audience; she acknowledges how her perspectives have been widened by Levy's views; she seeks to keep the channel of communication open; and she expresses interest in further problem solving.

After reading your article I have more understanding of the arguments in favor of guns, and I continue to ponder the ethical and practical issues of gun control versus the right to self-defense. You have underscored for me the importance of our continuing to seek means of preventing these terrible massacres from happening in our nation's schools. You have also opened my eyes to the fact that no amount of enforcement of gun laws can deter determined people from using guns to harm others. I am not sure, however, that your proposal to eliminate gun control laws is the best solution, and I am hoping that you might be willing to consider some of my reasons for fearing guns, especially assault weapons and automatic weapons that can be fired like machine guns. Perhaps we could both agree that pursuing responsible gun ownership is a step in the right direction so that we reduce the number of accidents, keep guns away from children, and reduce access to guns capable of unleashing mass murder. I am hopeful that with our common concern over the current ineffectiveness of gun laws and the desire for safety in our schools, we can find a reasonable solution while still preserving the human right of self-defense.

Sincerely,

Colleen Fontana

Works Cited

Blow, Charles M. "Obama's Gun Play." *New York Times.* New York Times, 21 Jan. 2011. Web. 21 Mar. 2011.

Kilgannon, Cory. "After Shooting, Merchant Is Hero of Arthur Avenue." *New York Times.* New York Times, 12 Feb. 2011. Web. 21 Mar. 2011.

Levy, Robert A. "They Never Learn." *American Spectator.* American Spectator, 25 Apr. 2007. Web. 13 Mar. 2011.

Pierce, John. "It Takes a Gun to Stop a Gunman." *Examiner.com.* Clarity Digital Group, 15 July 2009. Web. 15 Mar. 2011.

■ ■ ■ **FOR CLASS DISCUSSION**   **Listening Empathically and Searching for Common Ground**
A proposal to construct an Islamic community center near Ground Zero in Manhattan sparked intense emotional outbursts and public protests (the issue discussed in Ross Douthat's delayed-thesis argument "Islam in Two Americas" on pages 136–137). Protesters took different positions on this issue depending on their values and beliefs. Protesters even disagreed about what was at stake: Patriotism? Religious freedom? Respect for those who died when the World Trade Center towers collapsed? Anger at Muslims in general? The photos in Figures 7.4–7.7 portray some of these protesters and their views.

Working individually or in groups, choose the photo that represents the position on this controversy with which you most disagree. Then imagine that you are conducting a Rogerian discussion with the people in the photo and follow these thinking and writing steps:

1. What are your own views about the construction of an Islamic community center two blocks from Ground Zero? What's at stake for you in allowing or denying this proposal? Explore your own values.
2. Write a summary of the views you think the people in the photo hold. Write your summary in fair, neutral language that indicates your understanding and that would make your summary acceptable to the people you oppose.
3. Then write a common-grounds paragraph in which you go beyond summary to show your understanding of the values held by these people. Consider how these views might be valid. Demonstrate your empathy, and add an example of your own that shows how your views and those of the people in the photo could intersect.   ■ ■ ■

Conclusion

This chapter explains strategies for addressing alternative views. When intending to engage supportive audiences in a cause, writers often compose one-sided arguments. Neutral or undecided audiences generally respond most favorably to classical argument, which uses strong reasons in support of its claim while openly summarizing alternative views and responding to them through rebuttal or concession. Strongly resistant audiences typically respond most favorably to dialogic strategies, such as delayed-thesis or Rogerian argument, which seeks common ground with an audience, aims at reducing hostility, and takes a more inquiring or conciliatory   stance. Rogerian argument, especially, envisions both writer and reader undergoing mutual change.

WRITING ASSIGNMENT   A Classical Argument or a Rogerian Letter

Option 1: A Classical Argument   Write a classical argument following the explanations in Chapter 3, pages 58–60, and using the guidelines for developing such an argument throughout Chapters 3–7. Depending on your instructor's preferences, this argument could be on a new issue, or it could be a final stage of an argument in progress throughout Part 2. This assignment expands the supporting-reasons assignment from Chapter 5 by adding sections that summarize opposing views and respond to them through refutation or concession. For an example of a classical argument, see " 'Half-Criminals' or Urban Athletes? A Plea for Fair Treatment of Skateboarders" by David Langley (pages 150–152).

Option 2: A Rogerian Letter   Write a Rogerian argument in the form of a letter addressed to a specific person, either someone you know, someone you have heard deliver a speech, or the author of an article that has disturbed you. As you generate ideas for your argument, take stock of what you know about your audience and summarize his or her views in a way that your audience would find satisfactory. As you explore what your audience values and believes in, also explore how your own values differ. Where do you agree with your audience? Under what conditions would you find your audience's values acceptable? Follow the suggestions in the chart that explains the elements of Rogerian argument on page 145 for determining a purpose and structure for your argument. Depending on the distance between your views and your audience's, your goal may be simply to plant in your audience a willingness to consider your perspective. For examples of Rogerian argument, see Colleen Fontana's "Open Letter to Robert Levy" on pages 145–148 and Rebekah Taylor's "Letter to Jim" on pages 152–153. Your instructor may ask you to attach a reflective response in which you describe how your experience of writing this Rogerian letter differed from your experience of writing classical arguments. ■

Readings

Our first student essay illustrates a classical argument. This essay grew out of a class discussion about alternative sports, conflicts between traditional sports and newer sports (downhill skiing versus snowboarding), and middle-age prejudices against groups of young people.

"Half-Criminals" or Urban Athletes? A Plea for Fair Treatment of Skateboarders
(A Classical Argument)
DAVID LANGLEY (STUDENT)

For skateboarders, the campus of the University of California at San Diego is a wide-open, huge, geometric, obstacle-filled, stair-scattered cement paradise. The signs posted all over campus read, "No skateboarding, biking, or rollerblading on campus except on Saturday, Sunday, and holidays." I have always respected these signs at my local skateboarding spot. On the first day of 1999, I was skateboarding here with my hometown skate buddies and had just landed a trick when a police officer rushed out from behind a pillar, grabbed me, and yanked me off my board. Because I didn't have my I.D. (I had emptied my pockets so I wouldn't bruise my legs if I fell—a little trick of the trade), the officer started treating me like a criminal. She told me to spread my legs and put my hands on my head. She frisked me and then called in my name to police headquarters.

"What's the deal?" I asked. "The sign said skateboarding was legal on holidays."

"The sign means that you can only *roll* on campus," she said.

But that's *not* what the sign said. The police officer gave one friend and me a warning. Our third friend received a fifty-dollar ticket because it was his second citation in the last twelve months.

5   Like other skateboarders throughout cities, we have been bombarded with unfair treatment. We have been forced out of known skate spots in the city by storeowners and police, kicked out of every parking garage in downtown, compelled to skate at strange times of day and night, and herded into crowded skateboard parks. However, after I was searched by the police and detained for over twenty minutes in my own skating sanctuary, the unreasonableness of the treatment of skateboarders struck me. Where are skateboarders supposed to go? Cities need to change their unfair treatment of skateboarders because skateboarders are not antisocial misfits as popularly believed, because the laws regulating skateboarding are ambiguous, and because skateboarders are not given enough legitimate space to practice their sport.

Possibly because to the average eye most skateboarders look like misfits or delinquents, adults think of us as criminal types and associate our skateboards with antisocial behavior. But this view is unfair. City dwellers should recognize that skateboards are a natural reaction to the urban environment. If people are surrounded by cement, they are going to figure out a way to ride it. People's different environments have always produced transportation and sports to suit the conditions: bikes, cars, skis, ice skates, boats, canoes, surfboards. If we live on snow, we are going to develop skis or snowshoes to move around. If we live in an environment that has flat panels of cement for ground with lots of curbs and stairs, we are going to invent an ingeniously designed flat board with wheels. Skateboards are as natural to cement as surfboards are to water or skis to snow. Moreover, the resulting sport is healthful, graceful, and athletic. A fair assessment of skateboarders should respect our elegant, nonpolluting means of transportation and sport, and not consider us hoodlums.

A second way that skateboarders are treated unfairly is that the laws that regulate skateboarding in public places are highly restrictive, ambiguous, and open to abusive application by police officers. My being frisked on the UCSD campus is just one example. When I moved to Seattle to go to college, I found the laws in Washington to be equally unclear. When a sign says "No Skateboarding," that generally means you will get ticketed if you are caught skateboarding in the area. But most areas aren't posted. The general rule then is that you can skateboard so long as you do so safely without being reckless. But the definition of "reckless" is up to the whim of the police officer. I visited the front desk of the Seattle East Precinct and asked them exactly what the laws against reckless skateboarding meant. They said that skaters are allowed on the sidewalk as long as they travel at reasonable speed and the sidewalks aren't crowded. One of the officers explained that if he saw a skater sliding down a handrail with people all around, he would definitely arrest the skater. What if there were no people around, I asked? The officer admitted that he might arrest the lone skater anyway and not be questioned by his superiors. No wonder skateboarders feel unfairly treated.

One way that cities have tried to treat skateboarders fairly is to build skateboard parks. Unfortunately, for the most part these parks are no solution at all. Most parks were designed by nonskaters who don't understand the momentum or gravity pull associated with the movement of skateboards. For example, City Skate, a park below the Space Needle in Seattle, is very appealing to the eye, but once you start to ride it you realize that the transitions and the verticals are all off, making it unpleasant and even dangerous to skate there. The Skate Park in Issaquah, Washington, hosts about thirty to fifty skaters at a time. Collisions are frequent and close calls, many. There are simply too many people in a small area. The people who built the park in Redmond, Washington, decided to make a huge wall in it for graffiti artists "to tag on" legally. They apparently thought they ought to throw all us teenage "half-criminals" in together. At this park, young teens are nervous about skating near a gangster "throwing up his piece," and skaters become dizzy as they take deep breaths from their workouts right next to four or five cans of spray paint expelling toxins in the air.

Of course, many adults probably don't think skateboarders deserve to be treated fairly. I have heard the arguments against skateboarders for years from parents, storeowners, friends, police officers, and security guards. For one thing, skateboarding tears up public and private property, people say. I can't deny that skating leaves marks on handrails and benches, and it does chip cement and granite. But in general skateboarders help the environment more than they hurt it. Skateboarding places are not littered or tagged up by skaters. Because skaters need smooth surfaces and because any small object of litter can lead to painful accidents, skaters actually keep the environment cleaner than the average citizen does. As for the population as a whole, skateboarders are keeping the air a lot cleaner than many other commuters and athletes such as boat drivers, car drivers, and skiers on ski lifts. In the bigger picture, infrequent repair of curbs and benches is cheaper than attempts to heal the ozone.

10   We skateboarders aren't going away, so cities are going to have to make room for us somewhere. Here is how cities can treat us fairly. We should be allowed to skate when others are present as long as we skate safely on the sidewalks. The rules and laws should be

clearer so that skaters don't get put into vulnerable positions that make them easy targets for tickets. I do support the opening of skate parks, but cities need to build more of them, need to situate them closer to where skateboarders live, and need to make them relatively wholesome environments. They should also be designed by skateboarders so that they are skater-friendly and safe to ride. Instead of being treated as "half-criminals," skaters should be accepted as urban citizens and admired as athletes; we are a clean population, and we are executing a challenging and graceful sport. As human beings grow, we go from crawling to walking; some of us grow from strollers to skateboards.

To illustrate a conciliatory or Rogerian approach to an issue, we show you student writer Rebekah Taylor's argument written in response to this assignment. Rebekah chose to write a Rogerian argument in the form of a letter. An outspoken advocate for animal rights on her campus, Rebekah addressed her letter to an actual friend, Jim, with whom she had had many long philosophical conversations when she attended a different college. Note how Rebekah "listens" empathically to her friend's position on eating meat and proposes a compromise action.

A Letter to Jim
(A Rogerian Argument)
REBEKAH TAYLOR (STUDENT)

Dear Jim,

I decided to write you a letter today because I miss our long talks. Now that I have transferred colleges, we haven't had nearly enough heated discussions to satisfy either of us. I am writing now to again take up one of the issues we vehemently disagreed on in the past—meat-based diets.

Jim, I do understand how your view that eating meat is normal differs from mine. In your family, you learned that humans eat animals, and this view was reinforced in school where the idea of the food pyramid based on meat protein was taught and where most children had not even heard of vegetarian options. Also, your religious beliefs taught that God intended humans to have ultimate dominion over all animals. For humans, eating meat is part of a planned cycle of nature. In short, you were raised in a family and community that accepted meat-based diets as normal, healthy, and ethically justifiable whereas I was raised in a family that cared very deeply for animals and attended a church that frequently entertained a vegan as a guest speaker.

Let me now briefly reiterate for you my own basic beliefs about eating animals. As I have shared with you, my personal health is important to me, and I, along with other vegetarians and vegans, believe that a vegetarian diet is much more healthy than a meat diet. But my primary motivation is my deep respect for animals. I have always felt an overpowering sense of compassion for animals and intense sorrow and regret for the injuries that humans inflict upon them. I detest suffering, especially when it is forced upon creatures that cannot speak out against it. These deep feelings led me to become a vegetarian at the age of 5. While lying in bed one night, I looked up at the poster of a silky-white harbor seal that had always hung on my wall. As I looked at the face of that seal, I made a connection between that precious animal on my wall and the animals that had been killed for the food I ate every day. In the dim glow of my Strawberry Shortcake night light, I promised those large, dark seal eyes that I would never eat animals again. Seventeen years have passed now and that promise still holds true. Every day I feel more dedicated to the cause of animal rights around the world.

I know very well that my personal convictions are not the same as yours. However, I believe that we might possibly agree on more aspects of this issue than we realize. Although we would not be considered by others as allies on the issue of eating meat, we do share a common enemy—factory farms. Although you eat animal products and I do not, we both share a basic common value that is threatened by today's factory farms. We both disapprove of the unnecessary suffering of animals.

5   Though we might disagree on the morality of using animals for food at all, we do agree that such animals should not be made to suffer. Yet at factory farms, billions of animals across the world are born, live, and die in horribly cramped, dark, and foul-smelling barns. None of these animals knows the feeling of fresh air, or of warm, blessed sunlight on their backs. Most do not move out of their tight, uncomfortable pens until the day that they are to be slaughtered. At these factory farms, animals are processed as if they were inanimate objects, with no regard for the fact that they do feel fear and pain.

It is because of our shared opposition to animal suffering that I ask you to consider making an effort to buy meat from small, independent local farmers. I am told by friends that all supermarkets offer such meat options. This would be an easy and effective way to fight factory farms. I know that I could never convince you to stop eating meat, and I will never try to force my beliefs on you. As your friend, I am grateful simply to be able to write to you so candidly about my beliefs. I trust that regardless of what your ultimate reaction is to this letter, you will thoughtfully consider what I have written, as I will thoughtfully consider what you write in return.

Sincerely,

Rebekah

PART THREE
Analyzing Arguments

This advocacy poster fuses three big contemporary public controversies: environmentalism, sustainability, and vegetarianism. What tactics does this poster use to appeal to viewers' emotions and dramatize its claim that meat eating is destroying the world? Chapters 8 and 9 provide guidance for conducting rhetorical analyses of verbal and visual texts that work in a complex way, as this one does.

8 Analyzing Arguments Rhetorically

In Part Two of this book, we explained thinking and writing strategies for composing your own arguments. Now in Part Three we show you how to use your new rhetorical knowledge to conduct in-depth analyses of other people's arguments. To analyze an argument rhetorically means to examine closely how it is composed and what makes it an effective or ineffective piece of persuasion. A rhetorical analysis identifies the text under scrutiny, summarizes its main ideas, presents some key points about the text's rhetorical strategies for persuading its audience, and elaborates on these points.

Becoming skilled at analyzing arguments rhetorically will have multiple payoffs for you.

In this chapter, you will learn to:

- Critically examine the rhetorical features of arguments
- Construct essays that analyze the rhetorical effectiveness of arguments

By themselves, rhetorical analyses are common assignments in courses in critical thinking and argument. Rhetorical analysis also plays a major role in constructing arguments. Writers often work into their own arguments summaries and rhetorical analyses of other people's arguments—particularly in sections dealing with opposing views. This chapter focuses on the rhetorical analysis of written arguments, and the next one (Chapter 9) equips you to analyze visual arguments.

Thinking Rhetorically about a Text

The suggested writing assignment for this chapter is to write your own rhetorical analysis of an argument selected by your instructor (see page 168). This section will help you get started by showing you what it means to think rhetorically about a text.

Before we turn directly to rhetorical analysis, we should reconsider the key word *rhetoric*. In popular usage, *rhetoric* often means empty or deceptive language, as in, "Well, that's just rhetoric." Another related meaning of *rhetoric* is decorative or artificial language. The Greek Stoic philosopher Epictetus likened rhetoric to hairdressers fixing hair*—a view that sees

_____
*Chaim Perelman, "The New Rhetoric: A Theory of Practical Reasoning." In *Professing the New Rhetorics: A Sourcebook,* eds. Theresa Enos and Stuart C. Brown (Englewood Cliffs, NJ: Prentice Hall, 1994), 149.

rhetoric as superficial decoration. Most contemporary rhetoricians, however, adopt the larger view of rhetoric articulated by Greek philosopher Aristotle: the art of determining what will be persuasive in every situation. Contemporary rhetorician Donald C. Bryant has described rhetoric in action as "the function of adjusting ideas to people and of people to ideas."* Focusing on this foundational meaning of rhetoric, this chapter will show you how to analyze a writer's motivation, purpose, and rhetorical choices for persuading a targeted audience.

Most of the knowledge and skills you will need to write an effective rhetorical analysis have already been provided in Parts One and Two of the text. You have already learned how to place a text in its rhetorical context (Chapter 2), and from Chapters 3–7 you are already familiar with such key rhetorical concepts as audience-based reasons, the STAR criteria for evidence, and the classical appeals of *logos, ethos,* and *pathos.* This chapter prepares you to apply these argument concepts to the arguments you encounter.

■ ■ ■   **FOR CLASS DISCUSSION**   An Initial Exercise in Rhetorical Analysis

In the following exercise, consider the strategies used by two different writers to persuade their audiences to act against climate change. The first is from the opening paragraphs of an editorial in the magazine *Creation Care: A Christian Environmental Quarterly.* The second is from the Web site of the Sierra Club, an environmental action group. Please study each passage and then proceed to the questions that follow.

Passage 1

As I sit down to write this column, one thing keeps coming to me over and over: "Now is the time; now is the time."

In the New Testament the word used for this type of time is *kairos.* It means "right or opportune moment." It is contrasted with *chronos,* or chronological time as measured in seconds, days, months, or years. In the New Testament *kairos* is usually associated with decisive action that brings about deliverance or salvation.

The reason the phrase, "Now is the time" kept coming to me over and over is that I was thinking of how to describe our current climate change moment.

The world has been plodding along in chronological time on the problem of climate change since around 1988. No more.

Simply put: the problem of climate change has entered *kairos* time; its *kairos* moment has arrived. How long will it endure? Until the time of decisive action to bring about deliverance comes—or, more ominously, until the time when the opportunity for decisive action has passed us by. Which will we choose? Because we do have a choice.

—Rev. Jim Ball, Ph.D., "It's *Kairos* Time for Climate Change: Time to Act," *Creation Care: A Christian Environmental Quarterly* (Summer 2008), 28.

---

*Donald C. Bryant, "Rhetoric: Its Functions and Its Scope." In *Professing the New Rhetorics: A Sourcebook,* eds. Theresa Enos and Stuart C. Brown (Englewood Cliffs, NJ: Prentice Hall, 1994), 282.

Passage 2

[Another action that Americans must take to combat global warming is to transition] to a clean energy economy in a just and equitable way. Global warming is among the greatest challenges of our time, but also presents extraordinary opportunities to harness home-grown clean energy sources and encourage technological innovation. These bold shifts toward a clean energy future can create hundreds of thousands of new jobs and generate billions of dollars in capital investment. But in order to maximize these benefits across all sectors of our society, comprehensive global warming legislation must auction emission allowances to polluters and use these public assets for public benefit programs.

Such programs include financial assistance to help low and moderate-income consumers and workers offset higher energy costs as well as programs that assist with adaptation efforts in communities vulnerable to the effects of climate change. Revenue generated from emissions allowances should also aid the expansion of renewable and efficient energy technologies that quickly, cleanly, cheaply, and safely reduce our dependence on fossil fuels and curb global warming. Lastly, it is absolutely vital that comprehensive global warming legislation not preempt state authority to cut greenhouse gas emissions more aggressively than mandated by federal legislation.

—Sierra Club, "Global Warming Policy Solutions," 2008, http://www.sierraclub.org/

Group task: Working in small groups or as a whole class, try to reach consensus answers to the following questions:

1. How do the strategies of persuasion differ in these two passages?
2. Explain these differences in terms of targeted audience and original genre.
3. How effective is each argument for its intended audience?
4. Would either argument be effective for readers outside the intended audience?

Questions for Rhetorical Analysis

Conducting a rhetorical analysis asks you to bring to bear on an argument your knowledge of argument and your repertoire of reading strategies. The chart of questions for analysis on pages 159–160 can help you examine an argument in depth. Although a rhetorical analysis will not include answers to all of these questions, using some of these questions in your thinking stages can give you a thorough understanding of the argument while helping you generate insights for your own rhetorical analysis essay.

An Illustration of Rhetorical Analysis

To illustrate rhetorical analysis in this section and in the student example at the end of the chapter, we will use two articles on reproductive technology, a subject that continues to generate arguments in the public sphere. By *reproductive technology* we mean scientific advances in the treatment of infertility such as egg and sperm donation, artificial insemination, in vitro fertilization, and surrogate motherhood. Our first article, from a decade ago, springs from the early and increasing popularity of these technological options. Our second article—to be used in our later student example—responds to the recent globalization of this technology.

Questions for Rhetorical Analysis

What to Focus On	Questions to Ask	Applying These Questions
The *kairotic* moment and writer's motivating occasion	■ What motivated the writer to produce this piece? ■ What social, cultural, political, legal, or economic conversations does this argument join?	■ Is the writer responding to a bill pending in Congress, a speech by a political leader, or a local event that provoked controversy? ■ Is the writer addressing cultural trends such as the impact of science or technology on values?
Rhetorical context: Writer's purpose and audience	■ What is the writer's purpose? ■ Who is the intended audience? ■ What assumptions, values, and beliefs would readers have to hold to find this argument persuasive? ■ How well does the text suit its particular audience and purpose?	■ Is the writer trying to change readers' views by offering a new interpretation of a phenomenon, calling readers to action, or trying to muster votes or inspire further investigations? ■ Does the audience share a political or religious orientation with the writer?
Rhetorical context: Writer's identity and angle of vision	■ Who is the writer and what is his or her profession, background, and expertise? ■ How does the writer's personal history, education, gender, ethnicity, age, class, sexual orientation, and political leaning influence the angle of vision? ■ What is emphasized and what is omitted in this text? ■ How much does the writer's angle of vision dominate the text?	■ Is the writer a scholar, researcher, scientist, policy maker, politician, professional journalist, or citizen blogger? ■ Is the writer affiliated with conservative or liberal, religious or lay publications? ■ Is the writer advocating a stance or adopting a more inquiry-based mode? ■ What points of view and pieces of evidence are "not seen" by this writer?
Rhetorical context: Genre	■ What is the argument's original genre? ■ What is the original medium of publication? How does the genre and the argument's place of publication influence its content, structure, and style?	■ How popular or scholarly, informal or formal is this genre? ■ Does the genre allow for in-depth or only sketchy coverage of an issue? ■ (See Chapter 2, pages 31–36, for detailed explanations of genre.)
***Logos* of the argument**	■ What is the argument's claim, either explicitly stated or implied? ■ What are the main reasons in support of the claim? Are the reasons audience-based? ■ How effective is the writer's use of evidence? How is the argument supported and developed? ■ How well has the argument recognized and responded to alternative views?	■ Is the core of the argument clear and soundly developed? Or do readers have to unearth or reconstruct the argument? ■ Is the argument one-sided, multisided, or dialogic? ■ Does the argument depend on assumptions the audience may not share? ■ What evidence does the writer employ? Does this evidence meet the STAR criteria? (See pages 90–91.)

(Continued)

What to Focus On	Questions to Ask	Applying These Questions
Ethos of the argument	■ What *ethos* does the writer project? ■ How does the writer try to seem credible and trustworthy to the intended audience? ■ How knowledgeable does the writer seem in recognizing opposing or alternative views and how fairly does the writer respond to them?	■ If you are impressed or won over by this writer, what has earned your respect? ■ If you are filled with doubts or skepticism, what has caused you to question this writer? ■ How important is the character of the writer in this argument?
Pathos of the argument	■ How effective is the writer in using audience-based reasons? ■ How does the writer use concrete language, word choice, narrative, examples, and analogies to tap readers' emotions, values, and imaginations?	■ What examples, connotative language, and uses of narrative or analogy stand out for you in this argument? ■ Does this argument rely heavily on appeals to *pathos*? Or is it more brainy and logical?
Writer's style	■ How do the writer's language choices and sentence length and complexity contribute to the impact of the argument? ■ How well does the writer's tone (attitude toward the subject) suit the argument?	■ How readable is this argument? ■ Is the argument formal, scholarly, journalistic, informal, or casual? ■ Is the tone serious, mocking, humorous, exhortational, confessional, urgent, or something else?
Design and visual elements	■ How do design elements—layout, font sizes and styles, and use of color—influence the effect of the argument? (See Chapter 9 for a detailed discussion of these elements.) ■ How do graphics and images contribute to the persuasiveness of the argument?	■ Do design features contribute to the logical or the emotional/imaginative appeals of the argument? ■ How would this argument benefit from visuals and graphics or some different document design?
Overall persuasiveness of the argument	■ What features of this argument contribute most to making it persuasive or not persuasive for its target audience and for you yourself? ■ How would this argument be received by different audiences? ■ What features contribute to the rhetorical complexity of this argument? ■ What is particularly memorable, disturbing, or problematic about this argument? ■ What does this argument contribute to its *kairotic* moment and the argumentative controversy of which it is a part?	■ For example, are appeals to *pathos* legitimate and suitable? Does the quality and quantity of the evidence help build a strong case or fall short? ■ What specifically would count as a strength for the target audience? ■ If you differ from the target audience, how do you differ and where does the argument derail for you? ■ What gaps, contradictions, or unanswered questions are you left with? ■ How does this argument indicate that it is engaged in a public conversation? How does it "talk" to other arguments you have read on this issue?

At this point, please read the following article, "Egg Heads" by Kathryn Jean Lopez, and then proceed to the discussion questions that follow. Lopez's article was originally published in the September 1, 1998, issue of the biweekly conservative news commentary magazine *National Review*.

Egg Heads

KATHRYN JEAN LOPEZ

Filling the waiting room to capacity and spilling over into a nearby conference room, a group of young women listen closely and follow the instructions: Complete the forms and return them, with the clipboard, to the receptionist. It's all just as in any medical office. Then they move downstairs, where the doctor briefs them. "Everything will be pretty much normal," she explains. "Women complain of skin irritation in the local area of injection and bloating. You also might be a little emotional. But, basically, it's really bad PMS."

This is not just another medical office. On a steamy night in July, these girls in their twenties are attending an orientation session for potential egg donors at a New Jersey fertility clinic specializing in in-vitro fertilization. Within the walls of IVF New Jersey and at least two hundred other clinics throughout the United States, young women answer the call to give "the gift of life" to infertile couples. Egg donation is a quietly expanding industry, changing the way we look at the family, young women's bodies, and human life itself.

It is not a pleasant way to make money. Unlike sperm donation, which is over in less than an hour, egg donation takes the donor some 56 hours and includes a battery of tests, ultrasound, self-administered injections, and retrieval. Once a donor is accepted into a program, she is given hormones to stimulate the ovaries, changing the number of eggs matured from the usual one per month up to as many as fifty. A doctor then surgically removes the eggs from the donor's ovary and fertilizes them with the designated sperm.

Although most programs require potential donors to undergo a series of medical tests and counseling, there is little indication that most of the young women know what they are getting themselves into. They risk bleeding, infection, and scarring. When too many eggs are matured in one cycle, it can damage the ovaries and leave the donor with weeks of abdominal pain. (At worst, complications may leave her dead.) Longer term, the possibility of early menopause raises the prospect of future regret. There is also some evidence of a connection between the fertility drugs used in the process and ovarian cancer.

5   But it's good money—and getting better. New York's Brooklyn IVF raised its "donor compensation" from $2,500 to $5,000 per cycle earlier this year in order to keep pace with St. Barnabas Medical Center in nearby Livingston, New Jersey. It's a bidding war. "It's obvious why we had to do it," says Susan Lobel, Brooklyn IVF's assistant director. Most New York–area IVF programs have followed suit.

Some infertile couples and independent brokers are offering even more for "reproductive material." The International Fertility Center in Indianapolis, Indiana, for instance, places ads in the *Daily Princetonian* offering Princeton girls as much as $35,000 per cycle. The National Fertility Registry, which, like many egg brokerages, features an online catalogue for couples to browse in, advertises $35,000 to $50,000 for Ivy League eggs. While donors are normally paid a flat fee per cycle, there have been reports of higher payments to donors who produce more eggs.

College girls are the perfect donors. Younger eggs are likelier to be healthy, and the girls themselves frequently need money—college girls have long been susceptible to classified ads offering to pay them for acting as guinea pigs in medical research. One 1998 graduate of the University of Colorado set up her own website to market her eggs. She had watched a television show on egg donation and figured it "seemed like a good thing to do"—especially since she had spent her money during the past year to help secure a country-music record deal. "Egg donation would help me with my school and music expenses while helping an infertile couple with a family." Classified ads scattered throughout cyberspace feature similar offers.

The market for "reproductive material" has been developing for a long time. It was twenty years ago this summer that the first test-tube baby, Louise Brown, was born. By 1995, when the latest tally was taken by the Centers for Disease Control, 15 percent of mothers in this country had made use of some form of assisted-reproduction technology in conceiving their children. (More recently, women past menopause have begun to make use of this technology.) In 1991 the American Society for Reproductive Medicine was aware of 63 IVF programs offering egg donation. That number had jumped to 189 by 1995 (the latest year for which numbers are available).

Defenders argue that it's only right that women are "compensated" for the inconvenience of egg donation. Brooklyn IVF's Dr. Lobel argues, "If it is unethical to accept payment for loving your neighbor, then we'll have to stop paying babysitters." As long as donors know the risks, says Glenn McGee of the University of Pennsylvania's Center for Bioethics, this transaction is only "a slightly macabre version of adoption."

10   Not everyone is enthusiastic about the "progress." Egg donation "represents another rather large step into turning procreation into manufacturing," says the University of Chicago's Leon Kass. "It's the dehumanization of procreation." And as in manufacturing, there is quality control. "People don't want to say the word any more, but there is a strong eugenics issue inherent in the notion that you can have the best eggs your money can buy," observes sociology professor Barbara Katz Rothman of the City University of New York.

The demand side of the market comes mostly from career-minded baby-boomers, the frontiers women of feminism, who thought they could "have it all." Indeed they *can* have it all—with a little help from some younger eggs. (Ironically, feminists are also among its strongest critics; *The Nation*'s Katha Pollitt has pointed out that in egg donation and surrogacy, once you remove the "delusion that they are making babies for other women," all you have left is "reproductive prostitution.")

Unfortunately, the future looks bright for the egg market. Earlier this year, a woman in Atlanta gave birth to twins after she was implanted with frozen donor eggs. The same technology has also been successful in Italy. This is just what the egg market needed, since it avoids the necessity of coordinating donors' cycles with recipients' cycles. Soon, not only will infertile couples be able to choose from a wider variety of donor offerings, but in some cases donors won't even be needed. Young women will be able to freeze their own eggs and have them thawed and fertilized once they are ready for the intrusion of children in their lives.

There are human ovaries sitting in a freezer in Fairfax, Virginia. The Genetics and IVF Institute offers to cut out and remove young women's ovaries and cryopreserve the egg-containing tissue for future implantation. Although the technology was originally designed to give the hope of fertility to young women undergoing treatment for cancer, it is now starting to attract the healthy. "Women can wait to have children until they are well established in their careers and getting a little bored, sometime in their forties or fifties," explains Professor Rothman. "Basically, motherhood is being reduced to a good leisure-time activity."

Early this summer, headlines were made in Britain, where the payment of egg donors is forbidden, when an infertile couple traveled to a California clinic where the woman could be inseminated with an experimental hybrid egg. The egg was a combination of the recipient's and a donor's eggs. The clinic in question gets its eggs from a Beverly Hills brokerage, the Center for Surrogate Parenting and Egg Donation, run by Karen Synesiou and Bill Handel, a radio shock-jock in Los Angeles. Miss Synesiou recently told the London *Sunday Times* that she is "interested in redefining the family. That's why I came to work here."

15   The redefinition is already well under way. Consider the case of Jaycee Buzzanca. After John and Luanne Buzzanca had tried for years to have a child, an embryo was created for them, using sperm and an egg from anonymous donors, and implanted in a surrogate mother. In March 1995, one month before the baby was born, John filed for divorce. Luanne wanted child support from John, but he refused—after all, he's not the father. Luanne argued that John is Jaycee's father legally. At this point the surrogate mother, who had agreed to carry a baby for a stable two-parent household, decided to sue for custody.

Jaycee was dubbed "Nobody's Child" by the media when a California judge ruled that John was not the legal father nor Luanne the legal mother (neither one was genetically related to Jaycee, and Luanne had not even borne her). Enter Erin Davidson, the egg donor, who claims the egg was used without her permission. Not to be left out, the sperm donor jumped into the ring, saying that his sperm was used without his permission, a claim he later dropped. In March of this year, an appeals court gave Luanne custody and decided that John is the legal father,

making him responsible for child support. By contracting for a medical procedure resulting in the birth of a child, the court ruled, a couple incurs "the legal status of parenthood." (John lost an appeal in May.) For Jaycee's first three years on earth, these people have been wrangling over who her parents are.

In another case, William Kane left his girlfriend, Deborah Hect, 15 vials of sperm before he killed himself in a Las Vegas hotel in 1991. His two adult children (represented by their mother, his ex-wife) contested Miss Hect's claim of ownership. A settlement agreement on Kane's will was eventually reached, giving his children 80 percent of his estate and Miss Hect 20 percent. Hence she was allowed three vials of his sperm. When she did not succeed in conceiving on the first two tries, she filed a petition for the other 12 vials. She won, and the judge who ruled in her favor wrote, "Neither this court nor the decedent's adult children possess reason or right to prevent Hect from implementing decedent's pre-eminent interest in realizing his 'fundamental right' to procreate with the woman of his choice." One day, donors may not even have to have lived. Researchers are experimenting with using aborted female fetuses as a source of donor eggs.

And the market continues to zip along. For overseas couples looking for donor eggs, Bill Handel has the scenario worked out. The couple would mail him frozen sperm of their choice (presumably from the recipient husband); his clinic would use it to fertilize donor eggs, chosen from its catalogue of offerings, and reply back within a month with a frozen embryo ready for implantation. (Although the sperm does not yet arrive by mail, Handel has sent out embryos to at least one hundred international customers.) As for the young women at the New Jersey clinic, they are visibly upset by one aspect of the egg-donation process: they can't have sexual intercourse for several weeks after the retrieval. For making babies, of course, it's already obsolete.

■ ■ ■ **FOR CLASS DISCUSSION** **Identifying Rhetorical Features**
Working in groups, develop responses to the following questions:

1. How does Lopez appeal to *logos*? What is her main claim and what are her reasons? What does she use for evidence? What ideas would you have to include in a short summary?
2. What appeals to *pathos* does Lopez make in this argument? How well are these suited to the conservative readers of the *National Review*?
3. How would you characterize Lopez's *ethos*? Does she seem knowledgeable and credible? Does she seem fair to stakeholders in this controversy?
4. Choose an additional focus from the "Questions for Rhetorical Analysis" on pages 159–160 to apply to "Egg Heads." How does this question expand your understanding of Lopez's argument?
5. What strikes you as problematic, memorable, or disturbing in this argument?

■ ■ ■

A Rhetorical Analysis of "Egg Heads"

Now that you have identified some of the rhetorical features of "Egg Heads," we offer our own notes for a rhetorical analysis of this argument.

Rhetorical Context   As we began our analysis, we reconstructed the rhetorical context in which "Egg Heads" was published. In the late 1990s, a furious debate about egg donation rippled through college and public newspapers, popular journalism, Web sites, and scholarly commentary. This debate had been kicked off by several couples placing ads in the newspapers of the country's most prestigious colleges, offering up to $50,000 for the eggs of brilliant, attractive, athletic college women. Coinciding with these consumer demands, advances in reproductive technology provided an increasing number of complex techniques to surmount the problem of infertility, including fertilizing eggs in petri dishes and implanting them into women through surgical procedures. These procedures could use either a couple's own eggs and sperm or donated eggs and sperm. All these social and medical factors created the *kairotic* moment for Lopez's article and motivated her to protest the increasing use of these procedures. (Egg donation, surrogate motherhood, and the potential dehumanizing of commercial reproduction continue to be troubling and unresolved controversies across many genres, as you will see when you read Ellen Goodman's op-ed piece at the end of this chapter and student Zachary Stumps's rhetorical analysis of it.)

Genre and Writer   When we considered the genre and writer of this article and its site of publication, we noted that this article appeared in the *National Review*, which describes itself as "America's most widely read and influential magazine and Web site for Republican/conservative news, commentary, and opinion." It reaches "an affluent, educated, and highly responsive audience of corporate and government leaders, the financial elite, educators, journalists, community and association leaders, as well as engaged activists all across America" (http://www.nationalreview.com). According to our Internet search, Kathryn Jean Lopez is known nationally for her conservative journalistic writing on social and political issues. Currently the editor of *National Review Online*, she has also published in the *Wall Street Journal,* the *New York Post,* and the *Washington Times.* This information told us that in her article "Egg Heads," Lopez is definitely on home territory, aiming her article at a conservative audience.

Logos   Turning to the *logos* of Lopez's argument, we decided that the logical structure of Lopez's argument is clear throughout the article. Her claim is that egg donation and its associated reproductive advances have harmful, long-reaching consequences for society. Basically, she argues that egg donation and reproductive technology represent bad scientific developments for society because they are potentially harmful to the long-range health of egg donors and because they lead to an unnatural dehumanizing of human sexuality. She states a version of this last point at the end of the second paragraph: "Egg donation is a quietly expanding industry, changing the way we look at the family, young women's bodies, and human life itself" (page 161).

The body of her article elaborates on each of these reasons. In developing her reason that egg donation endangers egg donors, Lopez lists the risks but doesn't supply supporting evidence about the frequency of these problems: damage to the ovaries, persistent pain, early menopause, possible ovarian cancer, and even death. She supports her claim about "the expanding industry" by showing how the procedures have become commercialized. To show the popularity of these procedures as well as their commercial value, she quotes a variety of experts such as directors of in vitro clinics, fertility centers, bioethicists, and the American Society for Reproductive Medicine. She also cleverly bolsters her own case by showing that even liberal cultural critics agree with her views about the big ethical questions raised by the reproductive-technology business. In addition to quoting experts, Lopez has sprinkled impressive numbers and vivid examples throughout the body of her argument that give her argument momentum as it progresses from the potential harm to young egg donors to a number of case studies that depict increasingly disturbing ethical problems.

Pathos   Much of the impact of this argument, we noted, comes from Lopez's appeals to *pathos*. By describing in detail the waiting rooms for egg donors at fertility clinics, Lopez relies heavily on pathetic appeals to move her audience to see the physical and social dangers of egg donation. She conveys the growing commercialism of reproductive technology by giving readers an inside look at the egg-donation process as these young college women embark on the multistep process of donating their eggs. These young women, she suggests in her title "Egg Heads," are largely unaware of the potential physical dangers to themselves and of the ethical implications and consequences of their acts. She asserts that they are driven largely by the desire for money. Lopez also appeals to *pathos* in her choice of emotionally loaded and often cynical language, which creates an angle of vision opposing reproductive technology: 'turning procreation into manufacturing'; 'reproductive prostitution'; "the intrusion of children in their lives"; 'motherhood … reduced to a good leisure-time activity'; "aborted female fetuses as a source of donor eggs"; and intercourse as an "obsolete" way to make babies (pages 162, 163).

Audience   Despite Lopez's success at spotlighting serious medical and ethical questions, her lack of attention to alternative views and the alarmism of her language caused us to wonder: Who might find this argument persuasive and who would challenge it? What is noticeably missing from her argument—and apparently from her worldview—is the perspective of infertile couples hoping for a baby. Pursuing our question, we decided that a provocative feature of this argument—one worthy of deeper analysis—is the disparity between how well this argument is suited to its target audience and yet how unpersuasive it is for readers who do not share the assumptions, values, and beliefs of this primary audience.

To Lopez's credit, she has attuned her reasons to the values and concerns of her conservative readers of the *National Review*, who believe in traditional families, gender differences, and gender roles. Opposed to feminism as they understand it, this audience sanctions careers for women only if women put their families first. Lopez's choice of evidence and her orchestration of it are intended to play to her audience's fears that science has uncontrollably fallen into the hands of those who have little regard for the sanctity of the family or traditional motherhood. For example, in playing strongly to the values of her conservative readers, Lopez belabors the physical, social, and ethical dangers of egg donation, mentioning worst-case scenarios; however, these appeals to *pathos* will most likely strike other readers who do some investigating into reproductive technology as overblown. She emphasizes the commercialism of the process as her argument moves from college girls as egg donors to a number of sensationalist case studies that depict intensifying ethical ambiguity. In other words, both the *logos* and the *pathos* of her argument skillfully focus on details that tap her target audience's values and beliefs and feed that audience's fears and revulsion.

Use of Evidence   For a broader or skeptical audience, the alarmism of Lopez's appeals to *pathos,* her use of atypical evidence, and her distortion of the facts weaken the *logos* and *ethos* of her argument. First, Lopez's use of evidence fails to measure up to the STAR criteria (that evidence should be sufficient, typical, accurate, and relevant). She characterizes all egg donors as young women seeking money. But she provides little evidence that egg donors are only out to make a buck. She also paints these young women as shortsighted, uninformed, and foolish. Lopez weakens her *ethos* by not considering the young women who have researched the process and who may be motivated, at least in part, by compassion for couples who can't conceive on their own. Lopez also misrepresents the people who are using egg donation, placing them all into two groups: (1) wealthy couples eugenically seeking designer babies with preordered special traits and (2) feminist career, women. She directs much of her criticism toward this latter group: "The demand side of the market comes mostly from career-minded baby-boomers, the frontierswomen of feminism, who thought they could 'have it all'" (page 162). However, readers who do a little research on their own, as we did, will learn that infertility affects one in seven couples; that it is often a male and a female problem, sometimes caused by an incompatibility between the husband's and the wife's reproductive material; and that most couples who take the big step of investing in these expensive efforts to have a baby have been trying to get pregnant for a number of years. Rather than being casual about having children, they are often deeply desirous of children and depressed about their inability to conceive. In addition, far from being the sure thing and quick fix that Lopez suggests, reproductive technology has a success rate of only 50 percent overall and involves a huge investment of time, money, and physical discomfort for women receiving donor eggs.

Another way that Lopez violates the STAR criteria is her choice of extreme cases. For readers outside her target audience, her argument appears riddled with straw man and slippery-slope fallacies. (See the Appendix, "Informal Fallacies," pages 404–411.) Her examples become more bizarre as her tone becomes more hysterical. Here are some specific instances of extreme, atypical cases:

- her focus on careerwomen casually and selfishly using the service of young egg donors
- the notorious case of Jaycee Buzzanca, dubbed "Nobody's Child" because her adoptive parents who commissioned her creation divorced before she was born
- the legal contest between a dead man's teen girlfriend and his ex-wife and adult children over his vials of sperm
- the idea of taking eggs from aborted female fetuses

By keeping invisible the vast majority of ordinary couples who go to fertility clinics out of last-hope desperation, Lopez uses extreme cases to create a "brave new world" intended to evoke a vehement rejection of these reproductive advances. These skeptical readers would offer the alternative view of the sad, ordinary couples of all ages sitting week after week in fertility clinics, hoping to conceive a child through the "miracle" of these reproductive advances and grateful to the young women who have contributed their eggs.

Concluding Points   In short, we concluded that Lopez's angle of vision, although effectively in sync with her conservative readers of the *National Review,* exaggerates and distorts her case against these reproductive advances. Lopez's traditional values and slanting of the evidence undermine her *ethos,* limit the value of this argument for a wider audience, and compel that audience to seek out alternative sources for a more complete view of egg donation.

Conclusion

To analyze a text rhetorically means to determine how it works: what effect it has on readers and how it achieves or fails to achieve its persuasiveness. Assignments involving rhetorical analysis are present in courses across the curriculum, and analyzing texts rhetorically is a major step in constructing your own arguments. In this chapter, we showed you how to apply your understanding of argument concepts, such as the influence of genre and appeals to *logos, ethos,* and *pathos,* to examining the strength of verbal texts. We conclude with a student's rhetorical analysis written for the assignment in this chapter.

WRITING ASSIGNMENT A Rhetorical Analysis

Write a thesis-driven rhetorical analysis essay in which you examine the rhetorical effectiveness of an argument specified by your instructor. Unless otherwise stated, direct your analysis to an audience of your classmates. In your introduction, establish the argumentative conversation to which this argument is contributing. Briefly summarize the argument and present your thesis highlighting two or more rhetorical features of the argument that you find central to the effectiveness or ineffectiveness of this argument. To develop and support your own points, you will need to include textual evidence in the form of examples or short quotations from the argument. Use attributive tags to distinguish your ideas from those of the writer of the argument. Use MLA documentation to cite points and quotations in your essay and in a Works Cited list at the end. Think of your rhetorical analysis as a way to shine a spotlight on important aspects of this argument and to make the argument understandable and interesting for your readers. A student paper written for this assignment is shown at the end of this chapter—Zachary Stumps's analysis of Ellen Goodman's "Womb for Rent."

Generating Ideas for Your Rhetorical Analysis

To develop ideas for your essay, you might follow these steps:

Step1	How to Do It
Familiarize yourself with the article you are analyzing.	Read your article several times. Divide it into sections to understand its structure.
Place the article in its rhetorical context.	Follow the strategies in Chapter 2 and use the "Questions for Rhetorical Analysis" on pages 159–160.
Summarize the article.	Follow the steps in Chapter 2 on pages 39–40. You may want to produce a longer summary of 150–200 words as well as a short, one-sentence summary.
Reread the article, identifying "hot spots."	Note hot spots in the article—points that impress you, disturb you, confuse you, or puzzle you.
Use the "Questions for Rhetorical Analysis" on pages 159–160.	Choose several of these questions and freewrite responses to them.
From your notes and freewriting, identify the focus for your analysis.	Choose several features of the article that you find particularly important and that you want to discuss in depth in your essay. Identify points that will bring something new to your readers and that will help them see this article with new understanding. You may want to list your ideas and then look for ways to group them together around main points.
Write a thesis statement for your essay.	Articulate your important points in one or two sentences, setting up these points clearly for your audience.

In finding a meaningful focus for your rhetorical analysis essay, you will need to create a focusing thesis statement that avoids wishy-washy formulas such as, "This argument has some strengths and some weaknesses." To avoid a vapid thesis statement, focus on the complexity of the argument, the writer's strategies for persuading the target audience, and the features that might impede its persuasiveness for skeptics. These thesis statements articulate how their writers see the inner workings of these arguments as well as the arguments' contributions to their public conversations.

> Lopez's angle of vision, although effectively in sync with her conservative readers of the *National Review*, exaggerates and distorts her case against these reproductive advances, weakening her *ethos* and the value of her argument for a wider audience. [This is the thesis we would use if we were writing a stand-alone essay on Lopez.]

> In his editorial "Why Blame Mexico?" published in *The American Conservative*, Fred Reed's irony and hard-hitting evidence undercut his desire to contrast the United States' hypocritical and flawed immigration policies with Mexico's successful ones.

> In his editorial "Amnesty?" in the Jesuit news commentary *America*, John F. Kavanaugh makes a powerful argument for his Catholic and religious readers; however, his proposal based on ethical reasoning may fail to reach other readers.

To make your rhetorical analysis of your article persuasive, you will need to develop each of the points stated or implied in your thesis statement using textual evidence, including short quotations. Your essay should show how you have listened carefully to the argument you are analyzing, summarized it fairly, and probed it deeply.

Organizing Your Rhetorical Analysis

A stand-alone rhetorical analysis can be organized as shown below. ■

Organization Plan for a Rhetorical Analysis of an Argument

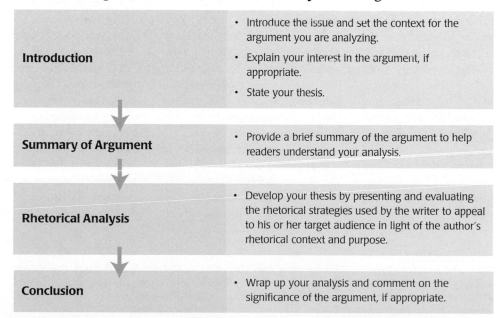

Introduction	• Introduce the issue and set the context for the argument you are analyzing. • Explain your interest in the argument, if appropriate. • State your thesis.
Summary of Argument	• Provide a brief summary of the argument to help readers understand your analysis.
Rhetorical Analysis	• Develop your thesis by presenting and evaluating the rhetorical strategies used by the writer to appeal to his or her target audience in light of the author's rhetorical context and purpose.
Conclusion	• Wrap up your analysis and comment on the significance of the argument, if appropriate.

Readings

Our first reading is by journalist Ellen Goodman, whose columns are syndicated in U.S. newspapers by the Washington Post Writers Group. This column, which appeared in 2008, is analyzed rhetorically by student Zachary Stumps in our second reading.

Womb for Rent—For a Price

ELLEN GOODMAN

BOSTON—By now we all have a story about a job outsourced beyond our reach in the global economy. My own favorite is about the California publisher who hired two reporters in India to cover the Pasadena city government. Really.

There are times as well when the offshoring of jobs takes on a quite literal meaning. When the labor we are talking about is, well, labor.

In the last few months we've had a full nursery of international stories about surrogate mothers. Hundreds of couples are crossing borders in search of lower-cost ways to fill the family business. In turn, there's a new coterie of international workers who are gestating for a living.

Many of the stories about the globalization of baby production begin in India, where the government seems to regard this as, literally, a growth industry. In the little town of Anand, dubbed "The Cradle of the World," 45 women were recently on the books of a local clinic. For the production and delivery of a child, they will earn $5,000 to $7,000, a decade's worth of women's wages in rural India.

5   But even in America, some women, including Army wives, are supplementing their income by contracting out their wombs. They have become surrogate mothers for wealthy couples from European countries that ban the practice.

This globalization of baby-making comes at the peculiar inter-section of a high reproductive technology and a low-tech work force. The biotech business was created in the same petri dish as Baby Louise, the first IVF baby. But since then, we've seen conception outsourced to egg donors and sperm donors. We've had motherhood divided into its parts from genetic mother to gestational mother to birth mother and now contract mother.

We've also seen the growth of an international economy. Frozen sperm is flown from one continent to another. And patients have become medical tourists, searching for cheaper health care whether it's a new hip in Thailand or an IVF treatment in South Africa that comes with a photo safari thrown in for the same price. Why not then rent a foreign womb?

I don't make light of infertility. The primal desire to have a child underlies this multinational Creation, Inc. On one side, couples who choose surrogacy want a baby with at least half their own genes. On the other side, surrogate mothers, who are rarely implanted with their own eggs, can believe that the child they bear and deliver is not really theirs.

As one woman put it, "We give them a baby and they give us much-needed money. It's good for them and for us." A surrogate in Anand used the money to buy a heart operation for her son. Another raised a dowry for her daughter. And before we talk about the "exploitation" of the pregnant woman, consider her alternative in Anand: a job crushing glass in a factory for $25 a month.

10   Nevertheless, there is—and there should be—something uncomfortable about a free market approach to baby-making. It's easier to accept surrogacy when it's a gift from one woman to another. But we rarely see a rich woman become a surrogate for a poor family. Indeed, in Third World countries, some women sign these contracts with a fingerprint because they are illiterate.

For that matter, we have not yet had stories about the contract workers for whom pregnancy was a dangerous occupation, but we will. What obligation does a family that simply contracted for a child have to its birth mother? What control do—should—contractors have over their "employees'" lives while incubating "their" children? What will we tell the offspring of this international trade?

"National boundaries are coming down," says bioethicist Lori Andrews, "but we can't stop human emotions. We are expanding families and don't even have terms to deal with it."

It's the commercialism that is troubling. Some things we cannot sell no matter how good "the deal." We cannot, for example, sell ourselves into slavery. We cannot sell our children. But the surrogacy business comes perilously close to both of these deals. And international surrogacy tips the scales.

So, these borders we are crossing are not just geographic ones. They are ethical ones. Today the global economy sends everyone in search of the cheaper deal as if that were the single common good. But in the biological search, humanity is sacrificed to the economy and the person becomes the product. And, step by step, we come to a stunning place in our ancient creation story. It's called the marketplace.

Critiquing "Womb for Rent—For a Price"

1. What is Goodman's main claim and what are her reasons? In other words, what ideas would you have to include in a short summary?
2. What appeals to *pathos* does Goodman make in this argument? How do these appeals function in the argument?
3. Choose an additional focus from the "Questions for Rhetorical Analysis" to apply to "Womb for Rent—For a Price." How does this question affect your perspective of Goodman's argument?
4. What strikes you as problematic, memorable, or disturbing in this argument?

Our second reading shows how student writer Zachary Stumps analyzed the Ellen Goodman article.

A Rhetorical Analysis of Ellen Goodman's "Womb for Rent—For a Price"

ZACHARY STUMPS (STUDENT)

Introduction provides context and poses issue to be addressed.

With her op-ed piece "Womb for Rent—For a Price," published in the *Seattle Times* on April 11, 2008 (and earlier in the *Boston Globe*), syndicated columnist Ellen Goodman enters the murky debate about reproductive technology gone global. Since Americans are outsourcing everything else, "Why not then rent a foreign womb?" (170) she asks. Goodman, a

Pulitzer Prize–winning columnist for the Washington Post Writers Group, is known for helping readers understand the "tumult of social change and its impact on families," and for shattering "the mold of men writing exclusively about politics" ("Ellen Goodman"). This op-ed piece continues her tradition of examining social change from the perspective of family issues.

Goodman launches her short piece by asserting that one of the most recent and consequential "jobs" to be outsourced is having babies. She explains how the "globalization of baby production" (170) is thriving because it brings together the reproductive desires of people in developed countries and the bodily resources of women in developing countries like India. Briefly tracing how both reproductive technology and medical tourism have taken advantage of global possibilities, Goodman acknowledges that the thousands of dollars Indian women earn by carrying the babies of foreign couples represent a much larger income than these women could earn in any other available jobs. After appearing to legitimize this global exchange, however, Goodman shifts to her ethical concerns by raising some moral questions that she says are not being addressed in this trade. She concludes with a full statement of her claim that this global surrogacy is encroaching on human respect and dignity, exploiting business-based science, and turning babies into products.

In this piece, Goodman's delay of her thesis has several rhetorical benefits: it gives Goodman space to present the perspective of poor women, enhanced by her appeals to *pathos,* and it invites readers to join her journey into the complex contexts of this issue; however, this strategy is also risky because it limits the development of her own argument.

Instead of presenting her thesis up front, Goodman devotes much of the first part of her argument to looking at this issue from the perspective of foreign surrogate mothers. Using the strategies of *pathos* to evoke sympathy for these women, she creates a compassionate and progressively minded argument that highlights the benefits to foreign surrogate mothers. She cites factual evidence showing that the average job for a woman in Anand, India, yields a tiny "$25 a month" gotten through the hard work of "crushing glass in a factory" (170), compared to the "$5,000 to $7,000" made carrying a baby to term (170). To carry a baby to term for a foreign couple represents "a decade's worth of women's wages in rural India" (170). Deepening readers' understanding of these women, Goodman cites one woman who used her earnings to finance her son's heart operation and another who paid for her daughter's dowry. In her fair presentation of these women, Goodman both builds her own positive *ethos* and adds a dialogic dimension to her argument by helping readers walk in the shoes of otherwise impoverished surrogate mothers.

The second rhetorical benefit of Goodman's delayed thesis is that she 5 invites readers to explore this complex issue of global surrogacy with her before she declares her own view. To help readers understand and think through this issue, she relates it to two other familiar global topics: outsourcing and medical tourism. First, she introduces foreign surrogacy as one of the latest forms of outsourcing: "This globalization of baby-making comes at the peculiar intersection of a high reproductive technology and a low-tech work force" (170). Presenting these women as workers, she explains that women in India are getting paid for "the production and delivery of a child" (170) that is analogous to the production and delivery of sneakers or bicycle parts. Goodman also sets this phenomenon in the context of global medical tourism. If people can pursue lower-cost treatment for illnesses and health conditions in other countries, why shouldn't an infertile couple seeking to start a family not also have such access to these more affordable and newly available means? This reasoning provides a foundation for readers to begin understanding the many layers of the issue.

Shows how the delayed-thesis structure creates two perspectives in conflict

The result of Goodman's delayed-thesis strategy is that the first two-thirds of this piece seem to justify outsourcing surrogate motherhood. Only after reading the whole op-ed piece can readers see clearly that Goodman has been dropping hints about her view all along through her choice of words. Although she clearly sees how outsourcing surrogacy can help poor women economically, her use of market language such as "production," "delivery," and "labor" carry a double meaning. On first reading of this op-ed piece, readers don't know if Goodman's punning is meant to be catchy and entertaining or serves another purpose. This other purpose becomes clear in the last third of the article when Goodman forthrightly asserts her criticism of the commercialism of the global marketplace that promotes worldwide searching for a "cheaper deal": "humanity is sacrificed to the economy and the person becomes the product" (171). This is a bold and big claim, but does the final third of her article support it?

Restates the third point in his thesis: lack of space limits development of Goodman's argument

In the final five paragraphs of this op-ed piece, Goodman begins to develop the rational basis of her argument; however, the brevity of the op-ed genre and her choice not to state her view openly initially have left Goodman with little space to develop her own claim. The result is that she presents some profound ideas very quickly. Some of the ethically complex ideas she introduces but doesn't explore much are these:

- The idea that there are ethical limits on what can be "sold"
- The idea that surrogate motherhood might be a "dangerous occupation"
- The idea that children born from this "international trade" may be confused about their identities.

Discusses examples of ideas raised by Goodman but not developed

Goodman simply has not left herself enough space to develop these issues and perhaps leaves readers with questions rather than with changed views. I am particularly struck by several questions. Why have European countries banned surrogacy in developing countries and why has the United States not banned this practice? Does Goodman intend to argue that the United States should follow Europe's lead? She could explore more how this business of finding illiterate women to bear children for the wealthy continues to exploit third-world citizens much as sex tourism exploits women in the very same countries. It seems to perpetuate a tendency for the developed world to regard developing countries as a poor place of lawlessness where practices outlawed in the rest of the world (e.g., child prostitution, slave-like working conditions) are somehow tolerable. Goodman could have developed her argument more to state explicitly that a woman who accepts payment for bearing a baby becomes an indentured servant to the family. Yet another way to think of this issue is to see that the old saying of "a bun in the oven" is more literal than metaphoric when a woman uses her womb as a factory to produce children, a body business not too dissimilar to the commercialism of prostitution. Goodman only teases readers by mentioning these complex problems without producing an argument.

Conclusion

Still, although Goodman does not expand her criticism of outsourced surrogate motherhood or explore the issues of human dignity and rights, this argument does introduce the debate on surrogacy in the global marketplace, raise awareness, and begin to direct the conversation toward a productive end of seeking a responsible, healthy, and ethical future. Her op-ed piece lures readers into contemplating deep, perplexing ethical and economic problems and lays a foundation for readers to create an informed view of this issue.

Works Cited

Uses MLA format to list sources cited in the essay

"Ellen Goodman." *Postwritersgroup.com.* Washington Post Writer's Group, 2008. Web. 19 May 2008.

Goodman, Ellen. "Womb for Rent—For a Price." *Seattle Times* 11 Apr. 2008: B6. Rpt. in *Writing Arguments.* John D. Ramage, John C. Bean, and June Johnson. 9th ed. New York: Pearson Longman, 2012. Print.

For additional writing, reading, and research resources, go to www.mycomplab.com

Analyzing Visual Arguments

9

To see how images can make powerful arguments, consider the rhetorical persuasiveness of the "polar bear" marching in a small town parade (Figure 9.1). Sponsored by local environmentalists advocating action against global warming, the polar bear uses arguments from *logos* (drawing on audience knowledge that climate change threatens polar bears), *pathos* (evoking the bears' vulnerability), and *ethos* (conveying the commitment of the citizens group). Delighting children and adults alike, the bear creates a memorable environmental argument.

This chapter is aimed at increasing your ability to analyze visual arguments and use them rhetorically in your own work. In this chapter, you will learn to:

- Analyze visual arguments, including ads, posters, and cartoons
- Use visuals in your own arguments
- Display numeric data in graphs and charts

FIGURE 9.1 A visual argument about climate change

Understanding Design Elements in Visual Argument

To understand how visual images can produce an argument, you need to understand the design elements that work together to create a visual text. In this section we'll explain and illustrate the four basic components of visual design: use of type, use of space and layout, use of color, and use of images and graphics.

Use of Type

Type is an important visual element of written arguments. Variations in type, such as size, boldface, italics, or all caps, can direct a reader's attention to an argument's structure and highlight main points. In arguments designed specifically for visual impact, such as posters or advocacy advertisements, type is often used in eye-catching and meaningful ways. In choosing type, you need to consider the typeface or font style, the size of the type, and formatting options. The main typefaces or fonts are classified as serif, sans serif, and specialty type. Serif type has little extensions on the letters. (This text is set in serif type.) Sans serif type lacks these extensions. Specialty type includes script fonts and special symbols. In addition to font style, type comes in different sizes. It is measured in points, with 1 point equal to $\frac{1}{72}$ of an inch. Most text-based arguments consisting mainly of body text are written in 10- to 12-point type, whereas more image-based arguments may use a mixture of type sizes that interacts with the images for persuasive effect. Type can also be formatted using bold, italics, underlining, or shading for emphasis. Table 9.1 shows examples of type styles, as well as their typical uses.

The following basic principles for choosing type for visual arguments can help you tachieve your overall goals of readability, visual appeal, and suitability.

Table 9.1 Examples and Uses of Type Fonts

Font Style	Font Name	Example	Use
Serif fonts	Times New Roman Courier New Bookman Old Style	Use type wisely. Use type wisely. Use type wisely.	Easy to read; good for long documents, good for *body type*, or the main verbal parts of a document
Sans serif fonts	Arial Century Gothic	Use type wisely. Use type wisely.	Tiring to read for long stretches; good for *display type* such as headings, titles, slogans
Specialty fonts	*Zapf Chancery* Onyx MT	*Use type wisely.* Use type wisely.	Difficult to read for long stretches; effective when used sparingly for playful or decorative effect

Principles for Choosing Type for Visual Arguments

1. If you are creating a poster or advocacy advertisement, you will need to decide how much of your argument will be displayed in words and how much in images. For the text portions, choose *display type* (sans serif) or specialty fonts for titles, headings, and slogans, and *body or text type* (serif) for longer passages of text.
2. Make type functional and appealing by using only two or three font styles per document.
3. Use consistent patterns of type (similar type styles, sizes, and formats) to indicate relationships among similar items or different levels of importance.
4. Choose type to project a specific impression (a structured combination of serif and sans serif type to create a formal, serious, or businesslike impression; sans serif and specialty type to create a casual, informal, or playful impression, and so forth).

Besides these general principles, rhetorical considerations of genre and audience expectations should govern decisions about type. Text-based arguments in scholarly publications generally use plain, conservative fonts with little variation, whereas text-based arguments in popular magazines may use more variations in font style and size, especially in headings and opening leads. Visual arguments such as posters, fliers, and advocacy ads exploit the aesthetic potential of type.

Use of Space or Layout

A second component of visual design is layout, which is critical for creating the visual appeal of an argument and for conveying meaning. Even visual arguments that are mainly textual should use space very purposefully. By spacing and layout we mean all of the following points:

- Page size and type of paper
- Proportion of text to white space
- Proportion of text to image(s) and graphics
- Arrangement of text on page (space, margins, columns, size of paragraphs, spaces between paragraphs, justification of margins)
- Use of highlighting elements such as bulleted lists, tables, sidebars, boxes
- Use of headings and other means of breaking text into visual elements

In arguments that don't use visuals directly, the writer's primary visual concern is document design, in which the writer tries to meet the conventions of a genre and the expectations of the intended audience. For example, Julee Christianson's researched argument on pages 272–277 is designed to meet the document conventions of the American Psychological Association (APA). Note the use of a plain, conventional typeface (for easy reading); double spacing and one-inch margins (to leave room for editorial marking and notations); and special title page, headers, and page number locations (to meet expectations of readers familiar with APA documents—which all look exactly the same).

But in moving from verbal-only arguments to visual arguments that use visual elements for direct persuasive effect—for example, posters, fliers, or advocacy ads—creative use of layout is vital. Here are some ideas to help you think about the layout of a visual argument.

Principles for Laying Out Parts of a Visual Text

1. Choose a layout that avoids clutter and confusion by limiting how much text and how many visual items you put on a page.
2. Focus on creating coherence and meaning with layout.
3. Develop an ordering or structuring principle that clarifies the relationships among the parts.
4. Use layout and spacing to indicate the importance of items and to emphasize key ideas. Because Western readers read from left to right and top to bottom, top and center are positions that readily draw readers' eyes.

An Analysis of a Visual Argument Using Type and Spatial Elements

To illustrate the persuasive power of type and layout, we ask you to consider Figure 9.2, which shows an advocacy ad sponsored by a coalition of organizations aimed at fighting illegal drugs.

This ad, warning about the dangers of the drug Ecstasy, uses different sizes of type and layout to present its argument. The huge word "Ecstasy" first catches the reader's attention. The first few words at the top of the ad, exuding pleasure, lull the reader with the congruence between the pleasurable message and the playful type. Soon, however, the reader encounters a dissonance between the playful type and the meaning of the words: *dehydrate, hallucinate, paranoid,* and *dead* name unpleasant ideas. By the end of the ad, readers realize they have been led through a downward progression of ideas, beginning with the youth culture's belief that Ecstasy creates wonderfully positive feelings and ending with the ad's thesis that Ecstasy leads to paranoia, depression, and death. The playful informality of the font styles and the unevenly scattered layout of the type convey the seductiveness and unpredictability of the drug. The ad concedes that the first effects are "fall[ing] in love with the world" but implies that what comes next is increasingly dark and dangerous. At the end of the ad, in the lines of type near the bottom, the message and typestyle are congruent again. The question "Does that sound harmless to you?" marks a shift in type design and layout. The designer composed this section of the ad in conventional fonts centered on the page in a rational, businesslike fashion. This type design signals a metaphoric move from the euphoria of Ecstasy to the ordered structure of everyday reality, where the reader can now consider rationally the drug's harm. The information at the bottom of the ad identifies the ad's sponsors and gives both a Web address and a telephone number to call for more information about Ecstasy and other illegal drugs.

■ ■ ■ **FOR CLASS DISCUSSION**   Comparing the Rhetorical Appeal of Two Advocacy Ads
This exercise asks you to examine Figure 9.3, an advocacy ad sponsored by Common Sense for Drug Policy, and to compare it to the ad in Figure 9.2. Figure 9.3 also

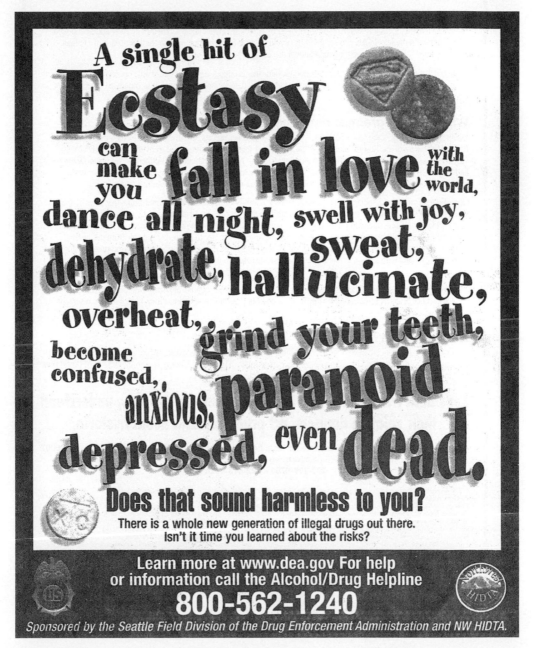

FIGURE 9.2 Advocacy advertisement warning against Ecstasy

What We Know About Ecstasy

What is Ecstasy?

Ecstasy, MDMA,[1] is a semi-synthetic drug patented by Merck Pharmaceutical Company in 1914 and abandoned for 60 years. In the late 1970s and early 1980s psychiatrists and psychotherapists in the US used it to facilitate psychotherapy.[2] In 1985 its growing recreational use caused the DEA to criminalize it.

Ecstasy's effects last 3 to 6 hours. It is a mood elevator that produces feelings of empathy, openness and well-being. People who take it at all night "rave" dances say they enjoy dancing and feeling close to others. It does not produce violence or physical addiction.[3]

What are the greatest risks from Ecstasy?

Death is a possibility when using MDMA. According to coroner reports, there were nine Ecstasy-related deaths (three of these involved Ecstasy alone) in 1998.[4] Some of these deaths are related to overheating. MDMA slightly raises body temperature. This is potentially lethal in hot environments where there is vigorous dancing and the lack of adequate fluid replacement.[5] Many of these tragic deaths were preventable with simple harm reduction techniques such as having free water available and rooms where people can rest and relax.

One of the recent risks associated with Ecstasy is the possibility of obtaining adulterated drugs that may be more toxic than MDMA. Some of the reported deaths attributed to Ecstasy are likely caused by other, more dangerous drugs.[6] Deaths from adulterated drugs are another consequence of a zero tolerance approach. While we do not encourage Ecstasy use, we recommend that the drug be tested for purity to minimize the risk from adulterated drugs by those who consume it.[7] However, MDMA itself has risks. For example, it raises blood pressure and heart rate. Persons with known cardiovascular or heart disease should not take MDMA.

Recent studies have indicated that individuals who have used MDMA may have decreased performance in memory tests compared to nonusers. These studies are presently controversial because they involved people who used a variety of other drugs. Furthermore, it is difficult to rule out possible pre-existing differences between research subjects and controls.[8]

What is a rave?

Raves are all-night dance parties popular with young people that feature electronic music. A variety of drug use, from alcohol to nicotine, and including ecstasy, occurs at raves. Hysteria is leading to criminalization of raves, thus pushing them underground and into less safe and responsible settings.

Let's deal with legal and illegal drugs knowledgeably, understand their relative dangers, act prudently and avoid hysteria.

Kevin B. Zeese, President, Common Sense for Drug Policy, 3220 N Street, NW #141, Washington, DC 20007
www.csdp.org * www.DrugWarFacts.org * www.AddictintheFamily.org * info@csdp.org
202-299-9780 * 202-518-4028 (fax)

1, 3 & 4 - methylenedioxymethamphetamine. 2 - Greer G. and Tolbert R., A Method of Conducting Therapeutic Sessions with MDMA. In Journal of Psychoactive Drugs 30 (1998) 4:371.379. For research on the therapeutic use of MDMA see: www.maps.org. 3 - Beck J. and Rosenbaum M., Pursuit of Ecstasy: The MDMA Experience. Albany: State University of New York Press, 1994. 4 - Drug Abuse Warning Network, Office of Applied Studies, Substance Abuse and Mental Health Services Administration, Report of March 21, 2000. (This was a special report because the published report only includes drugs where there were over 10 deaths.) 5 - C.M. Milroy; J.C. Clark; A.R.W. Forrest, Pathology of deaths associated with "ecstasy" and "eve" misuse, Journal of Clinical Pathology Vol 49 (1996) 149-153. 6 - Laboratory Pill Analysis Program, DanceSafe. For results visit www.DanceSafe.org. See also, Byard RW et al., Amphetamine derivative fatalities in South Australia—is "Ecstasy" the culprit?, American Journal of Forensic Medical Pathology, 998 (Sep) 19(3): 261-5. 7 - DanceSafe provides testing equipment and a testing service which can be used to determine what a substance is. See www.DanceSafe.org. 8 - E. Gouzoulis-Mayfrank; J. Daumann; F. Tuchtenhagen; S. Pelz; S. Becker; H.J. Kunert; B. Fimm; H. Sass; Impaired cognitive performance in drug-free users of recreational ecstasy (MDMA), by Journal Neurol Neurosurg Psychiatry Vol 68, June 2000, 719-725; K.I.Bolla; U.D.; McCann; G.A. Ricaurte; Memory impairment in abstinent MDMA ('Ecstasy') users, by Neurology Vol 51, Dec 1998, 1532-1537.

FIGURE 9.3 Common Sense for Drug Policy advocacy ad

focuses on the drug Ecstasy and also uses type and layout to convey its points. (This ad appeared in the liberal magazine *The Progressive.*) Individually or in groups, study this advocacy ad and then answer the following questions.

1. What is the core argument of this ad? What view of drug use and what course of action are this ad promoting? What similarities and differences do you see between the argument about Ecstasy in this ad and the ad in Figure 9.2?
2. What are the main differences in the type and layout of the two ads in Figures 9.2 and 9.3? To what extent do the ad makers' choices about type and layout match the arguments made in each ad?
3. How would you analyze the use of type and layout in Figure 9.3? How does this ad use typestyles to convey its argument? How does it use layout and spacing?
4. The ad in Figure 9.2 appeared in the weekly entertainment section of the *Seattle Times,* a newspaper with a large general readership, whereas the ad in Figure 9.3 appeared in a liberal news commentary magazine. In what ways is each ad designed to reach its audience?

Use of Color

A third important element of visual design is use of color, which can contribute significantly to the visual appeal of an argument and move readers emotionally and imaginatively. In considering color in visual arguments, writers are especially controlled by genre conventions. For example, academic arguments use color minimally, whereas popular magazines often use color lavishly. The appeal of colors to an audience and the associations that colors have for an audience are also important. For instance, the psychedelic colors of 1960s rock concert posters would probably not be effective in poster arguments directed toward conservative voters. Color choices in visual arguments often have crucial importance, including the choice of making an image black-and-white when color is possible. As you will see in our discussions of color throughout this chapter, makers of visual arguments need to decide whether color will be primarily decorative (using colors to create visual appeal), functional (for example, using colors to indicate relationships), realistic (using colors like a documentary photo), aesthetic (for example, using colors that are soothing, exciting, or disturbing), or some intentional combination of these.

Use of Images and Graphics

The fourth design element includes images and graphics, which can powerfully condense information into striking and memorable visuals; clarify ideas; and add depth, liveliness, and emotion to your arguments. A major point to keep in mind when using images is that a few simple images may be more powerful than complicated and numerous images. Other key considerations are (1) how you intend an image to work in your argument (for example, to convey an idea, illustrate a point, or evoke an emotional response) and (2) how you will establish the relationship between the image or graphic and the verbal text. Because using images and graphics effectively is especially challenging, we devote the rest of this chapter to explaining how images and graphics can be incorporated into visual arguments. We treat the use of photographs and drawings in the next main section and the use of quantitative graphics in the final section.

An Analysis of a Visual Argument Using All the Design Components

Before we discuss the use of images and graphics in detail, we would like to illustrate how all four of the design components—use of type, layout, color, and images—can reinforce and support each other to achieve a rhetorical effect. Consider the "Save the Children" advocacy ad from an April 2011 edition of *Newsweek* (Figure 9.4). This advocacy ad highlights the design features of image, color, and layout, with type used to interpret and reinforce the message delivered by the other features. The layout of the page highlights the connection between the adorable baby on the left side of the page and the female health care worker on the right. The "story" of the ad is told in unobtrusive text (in small white font), which leads the readers' eyes from the baby's face to the heart of the health worker. Interestingly from a design perspective, a third figure, probably the baby's mother, is just partly visible in the form of a hands holding the baby. The text itself celebrates the effectiveness of this local health healer, identified by name: "To show you all of the seriously ill children that local health worker Khalada Yesmin helped save this year, we'd need 122 more pages." At the bottom of the page, text conveys the call to action in the form of memorable tag lines "HELP ONE. SAVE MANY"; and "See where the good goes at GoodGoes.org."

This advocacy ad works on readers by blending three themes—the universal appeal of babies; the beneficial effects of educating local workers, particularly, women; and the symbolic meaning of helping/healing hands—to convey how those of us in the developed world can provide aid that empowers people in developing countries to help themselves. These themes are portrayed through various visual strategies. In this ad, a baby, the health worker, and a third figure outside the frame of the photo (probably the baby's mother) sit on a woven mat, inside a structure. (Information on the Web site for "Save the Children" and the clothing of the people suggest that this scene takes place in Bangladesh.) The use of bright colors, creating a feeling of warmth and love, the arrangement of the figures, and the close-up shots of the baby and health worker draw viewers into the scene. The close-up, slightly low-angle shot accentuates faces, hands, feet and traditional clothing. The blurred background suggests palm trees and the doorway to a house. The building is, most likely, the home of the mother and baby, which the health worker is visiting on her rounds. The baby, wearing an orange-beaded blouse or smock, pink shorts or skirt, and a necklace of purple beads, sits and smiles alertly at the health worker, in dark clothing and a red headscarf, who is engrossed in taking the baby's temperature. She seems to be holding the thermometer under the baby's arm with one hand and holding a watch with the other. Her focus on her task conveys her expertise; she knows what she is doing, an idea reinforced by the caption, which tells us that this health worker, Khalada Yesmin, "has helped 122 sick children this year." This caption and the prominence of hands in this photo— Khalada Yesmin's hands, the baby's hand, and the mother's hands supporting the

To show you all of the seriously ill children that local health worker Khalada Yesmin helped save this year, we'd need 122 more pages.

HELP ONE. **SAVE MANY.**
See where the good goes at **GoodGoes.org**

Ad Council

Save the Children.

FIGURE 9.4 Save the Children advocacy ad

baby—accentuate the idea of direct, grassroots aid that is improving the lives of mothers and children in a community through compassion and knowledge. The slogans at the bottom of the ad "Help one. Save many" and "See where the good goes" extend this network of help to viewers of the ad. If we contribute money to the training and medical supplies of health workers like Khalada Yesmin, we will help expand the web of aid.

In choosing to make this ad portray a positive, upbeat scene of medical success, instead of portraying scenes of pneumonia, malaria, malnutrition, or other diseases that the "seriously ill" children mentioned suffer from, the designers of this ad gave a memorable embodiment to the ideas in the words "help," "save," and "good." Perhaps most importantly, unlike some global ads, this one empowers people in the developing world. Rather than depict them as victims or helpless people in backward countries, this ad shows them—through the image of Khalada Yesmin and the eagerness of the people she is helping—as primary agents in the improvements in their lives. Rather than take control and rush in to solve problems, viewers in developed countries are invited to contribute to this success, figuratively lending a hand through financial support.

The Compositional Features of Photographs and Drawings

Now that we have introduced you to the four major elements of visual design—type, layout, color, and images—we turn to an in-depth discussion of photographic images and drawings. Used with great shrewdness in product advertisements, photos and drawings can be used with equal shrewdness in posters, fliers, advocacy ads, and Web sites. When an image is created specifically for an argument, almost nothing is left to chance. Although such images are often made to seem spontaneous and "natural," they are almost always composed: designers consciously select the details of staging and composition as well as manipulate camera techniques (filters, camera angle, lighting) and digital or chemical development techniques (airbrushing, merging of images). Even news photography can have a composed feel. For example, public officials often try to control the effect of photographs by creating "photo ops" (photographing opportunities), wherein reporters are allowed to photograph an event only during certain times and from certain angles. Political photographs appearing in newspapers are often press releases officially approved by the politician's staff. (See the campaign photographs later in this chapter on pages 191–192) To analyze a photograph or drawing, or to create visual images for your own arguments, you need to think both about the composition of the image and about the camera's relationship to the subject. Because drawings produce a perspective on a scene analogous to that of a camera, design considerations for photographs can be applied to drawings as well. The following list of questions can guide your analysis of any persuasive image.

- **Type of photograph or drawing:** Is the image documentary-like (representing a real event), fictionlike (intending to tell a story or dramatize a scene), or conceptual (illustrating or symbolizing an idea or theme)? The two photos of mosh pits—a girl shown crowd surfing and an unruly, almost menacing mosh pit crowd (Chapter 5, page 95)—are documentary photos capturing real events in action. In contrast, the drawing of the lizards in the Earthjustice ad in Figure 9.5 is both a fictional narrative telling a story and a conceptual drawing illustrating a theme.

Just then, the three lizards came home and found Goldilocks eating their porridge...

IT'S JUST NOT THE SAME WITHOUT BEARS.

Once upon a time there were over 100,000 grizzly bears in the lower 48 states. Now, there are less than a thousand grizzly bears left. The health of the grizzly is dependent on vast, undisturbed, wild lands. When bears disappear, other species will follow. Bears are such an important part of our wilderness, history, and culture that it's hard to imagine a world without them in the picture.

Grizzly bears are a threatened species, protected by the Endangered Species Act. But some special interests are pushing the U.S. Fish and Wildlife Service to remove Yellowstone grizzlies from the endangered species list. Why? They want to open up wild lands around Yellowstone

National Park to destructive logging, mining, off-road vehicle use, and development.

You can help protect our wilderness and grizzly bears. Please take a moment to contact Secretary Bruce Babbitt, Department of Interior, 1849 C St. NW, Washington DC 20240, or email Bruce_Babbitt@os.doi.gov – Tell him to keep grizzly bears on the Endangered Species List and that grizzly bears need more protection, not less.

Earthjustice Legal Defense Fund is working tirelessly to protect the grizzly bears and the wilderness they stand for. If we all work together, the grizzly bears will live happily ever after.

HELP KEEP BEARS IN THE PICTURE

www.earthjustice.org

EARTHJUSTICE
LEGAL DEFENSE FUND
1-800-584-6460

designed by **Sustain**

FIGURE 9.5 Earthjustice advocacy ad

- **Distance from the subject:** Is the image a close-up, medium shot, or long shot? Close-ups tend to increase the intensity of the image and suggest the importance of the subject; long shots tend to blend the subject into the background. In the baby photograph opposing phthalates in children's toys (Chapter 1, page 4), the effect of the baby's wearing a "poison" bib is intensified by the close-up shot without background. Contrast that close-up with the long shot shown in the photograph taken in Port-au-Prince, Haiti, after the 2010 earthquake (Chapter 6, page 116). The distance of the camera from the woman carrying a basket and the other huddled figures in the shadows makes them look small in contrast to the earth-moving machine brought in to grapple with the rubble of fallen buildings. While the photo captures the magnitude of the disaster, it also shows the woman carrying on with her life.

- **Orientation of the image and camera angle:** Is the camera (or artist) positioned in front of or behind the subject? Is it positioned below the subject, looking up (a low-angle shot)? Or is it above the subject, looking down (a high-angle shot)? Front-view shots, such as those of Carlitos and his mother in the stills from *Under the Same Moon* (page 1), tend to emphasize the persons being photographed. In contrast, rear-view shots often emphasize the scene or setting. A low-angle perspective tends to make the subject look superior and powerful, whereas a high-angle perspective can reduce the size—and by implication, the importance—of the subject. A level angle tends to imply equality. The high-angle shot of the girl in the mosh pit (page 95) emphasizes the superiority of the camera and the harmlessness of the mosh pit. In contrast, the low-angle perspective of the lizards in the Earthjustice advocacy ad in Figure 9.5 emphasizes the power of the lizards and the inferiority of the viewer.

- **Point of view:** Does the camera or artist stand outside the scene and create an objective effect as in the Haiti photograph on page 116? Or is the camera or artist inside the scene as if the photographer or artist is an actor in the scene, creating a subjective effect as in the drawing of the lizards in Figure 9.5?

- **Use of color:** Is the image in color or in black and white? Is this choice determined by the restrictions of the medium, (such as images designed to run in black and white in newspapers) or is it the conscious choice of the photographer or artist? Are the colors realistic or muted? Have special filters been used (a photo made to look old through the use of brown tints)? The bright colors in the lizard and Goldilocks drawing in Figure 9.5 resemble illustrations in books for children.

- **Compositional special effects:** Is the entire image clear and realistic? Is any portion of it blurred? Is it blended with other realistic or nonrealistic images (a car ad that blends a city and a desert; a body lotion ad that merges a woman and a cactus)? Is the image an imitation of some other famous image such as a classic painting (as in parodies)? The Earthjustice ad in Figure 9.5, the story of the polar bear in the Nissan Leaf ad in Figures 9.6–9.11, and the poster for the Wal-Mart movie in Figure 9.16 make visual associations with children's stories or other popular stories.

- **Juxtaposition of images:** Are several different images juxtaposed, suggesting relationships between them? Juxtaposition can suggest sequential or causal relationships or can metaphorically transfer the identity of a nearby image or background to the subject (as when a bath soap is associated with a meadow). This technique is frequently used in public relations to shape viewers' perceptions of political figures, as when Barack Obama was photographed with a huge American flag at a campaign appearance (page 192) to counter Republican Party charges that he was not "American enough."

- **Manipulation of images:** Are staged images made to appear real, natural, documentary-like? Are images altered with airbrushing? Are images actually composites of a number of images (for instance, using images of different women's bodies to create one perfect model in an ad or film)? Are images cropped for emphasis? What is left out? Are images downsized or enlarged?

- **Settings, furnishings, props:** Is the photo or drawing an outdoor or indoor scene? What is in the background and foreground? What furnishings and props, such as furniture, objects in a room, pets, and landscape features, help create the scene? What social associations of class, race, and gender are attached to these settings and props? Note, for example, how the designers of *America's Army*, the army video game, used a few simple props to create a gritty, urban street fighting scene (Figure 9.17). The burned-out vehicle hull suggests the aftermath of days of street fighting, whereas the telephone or power poles in the middle of a narrow, deserted street suggest a poor city in a third-world country.

- **Characters, roles, actions:** Does the photo or drawing tell a story? Are the people in the scene models? Are the models instrumental (acting out real-life roles) or are they decorative (extra and included for visual or sex appeal)? What are the facial expressions, gestures, and poses of the people? What are the spatial relationships of the figures? (Who is in the foreground, center, and background? Who is large and prominent?) What social relationships are implied by these poses and positions? In the "Save the Children" advocacy ad shown in Figure 9.4, the pose of the health worker and the baby—the health worker intently treating the baby and the baby happily trusting the health worker—tells the story of successful health care.

- **Presentation of images:** Are images separated from each other in a larger composition or connected to each other? Are the images large in proportion to verbal text? How are images labeled? How does the text relate to the image(s)? Does the image illustrate the text? Does the text explain or comment on the image? For example, the poster advocating vegetarianism (page 155) effectively juxtaposes words and images. The top is dominated by a question: "Think you can be a meat-eating environmentalist?" The "answer" is the image of a world with a big bite taken out of it. The text beneath the image, "Think again …," makes sense only after the viewer has interpreted the image. In contrast, the coat hanger hook dominates the advocacy ad on page 311.

FIGURE 9.6 Nissan Leaf ad: Glacier melting and calving ice bergs

FIGURE 9.7 Nissan Leaf ad: Polar bear floating on shrinking sea ice

FIGURE 9.8 Nissan Leaf ad: Polar bear walking on railroad tracks

FIGURE 9.9 Nissan Leaf ad: Polar bear walking along a highway

FIGURE 9.10 Nissan Leaf ad: Polar bear walking through a suburb

FIGURE 9.11 Nissan Leaf ad: Polar bear hugging car owner

An Analysis of a Visual Argument Using Images

To show you how images can be analyzed, let's examine the advertisement for Nissan's new electric car, the Nissan Leaf. Stills for this television ad are shown in Figures 9.6–9.11. You can see the whole one-minute ad on YouTube, where the fluid sequence of frames gives the full effect. With this ad's debut during a National Football League broadcast in fall 2010, Nissan boldly entered the global controversy over global warming and climate change, casting the iconic polar bear and the Nissan Leaf owner as heroes in a dramatic narrative intended to portray environmental consciousness and responsible consumerism.

This ad links a series of images in a suspenseful story of a long journey culminating in a dramatic encounter. The ad begins with frames of dripping ice melt and a crumbling glacier crashing into the ocean. The next frame shows a polar bear lying on a small floating island of ice, succeeded by a long view of calved icebergs, fragments of the glacier. The camera follows the polar bear swimming, with views of its powerful body above and below the water, until it arrives on land. From there, the polar bear takes a long journey: walking through northern forests; sheltering in a concrete culvert under a train trestle; walking along a train track; padding along a country highway, where it growls at a passing diesel truck; sitting and observing the brilliant lights of a big city at night; traveling across a massive suspension bridge into the city; walking through the city; and finally, walking down a suburban street. In the final frames, a bright blue Nissan Leaf sits in the wide driveway of a comfortable suburban home. Suddenly, the polar bear appears from behind the Nissan Leaf and surprises its owner, who has just come out of his house dressed in a sports coat and carrying a briefcase, presumably heading out for his commute to his white-collar job. As the bear rises on its hind legs, towering above the man, the astonished owner is met not by an attack but by a bear hug: the bear's thank-you for the driver's act of environmental responsibility in buying this electric car. The final frame includes the only text of the ad, which invites viewers to check out the features of the Nissan Leaf on the Web site. A musical soundtrack accompanies the images, with the only other sounds the honk of the truck and the growl of the bear in response. Noticeably absent from this ad is any specific information about the car itself, such as its five-passenger carrying capacity, its zero emissions, and its hundred-mile distance per charge.

The ad uses visual narrative to convey both a causal and an ethical argument. Through vivid, memorable scenes—the glacier calving, the bear afloat, the bear swimming—the ad taps viewers' knowledge of recent scientific accounts of the increased rate of glacial melting and the vanishing sea ice. The ad argues that these events are real, immediate, and threatening. By implication, it argues that the high volume of carbon dioxide emissions from gasoline-powered vehicles—in other words, human actions—has caused this increased rate of melting and destruction of polar bears' habitat. It asks viewers to fill in the links in the causal chain: large amounts of carbon dioxide emissions from internal combustion engines in cars and trucks have contributed to an increase in temperatures, which has sped up the rate at which glaciers and sea ice are melting. This increased rate of melting has in turn decreased the number of seals who usually live on the sea ice and thus reduced the food supply of polar bears. The ad reminds viewers that polar bears are endangered and need human aid. The ad's ethical argument is that humans can help polar bears and the environment by buying electric Nissan Leafs.

The ad's effect is enhanced by its positive *ethos* and its powerful appeals to *pathos*. By making these causal links through bold images and a memorable story, Nissan has staked its claim as a leader in producing alternative-fuel vehicles. In our view, the ad makes brilliant use of visual images, drawing on the most famous environmental icons in the global warming debate: the melting glacier and the polar bear. (See the photograph of the parade polar bear at the beginning of this chapter on page 175.) While news reports of declining polar bear populations arouse concern in some people, numbers can be vague and abstract. Many more people will be stirred by the heroic character of the lone bear making a long journey. This visual narrative taps viewers' familiarity with other animal stories, often featured on Animal Planet and the Discovery Channel, that blend environmental education and entertainment. But the Nissan ad pushes further by creatively drawing on Disney-like, anthropomorphic movies in which a wild creature becomes a friend of humans. Any Inuit will testify that polar bears are intimidating and dangerous, but this ad constructs an environmental fantasy, eliciting viewers' compassion for the heroic bear. It creates a kind of inverted "call of the wild" narrative: Instead of a captured or domesticated animal finding its way back to its wilderness home, this wild creature, endowed with knowledge and filled with gratitude, courageously finds its way to civilization on a mission to thank the Nissan Leaf owner. The ad cultivates warm feelings toward the bear through juxtaposing its isolation against the background of our technologically transformed and urbanized environment—the diesel truck; the concrete culvert; the impressive bridge; the vast, illuminated city; the well-cultivated suburban neighborhood. The ad enhances the character of the bear by showing it take time to watch a delicately flitting butterfly and exchange a glance with a raccoon, a wild creature at home in the city. As viewers are engrossed with the travels of this bear, they wonder, "Where is it going? What will happen?" The genius of the ad is that it casts the bear as an ambassador of the threatened environment and makes viewers care about the bear. It also converts the Nissan Leaf owner into an environmental hero. The implied ethical argument is that the right moral action is to drive a Nissan Leaf and thus save the environment. Viewers, identifying with the awestruck Nissan owner, will feel, "I want to be an environmental hero, too."

In this sense, the ad follows a problem-solution scenario. Nissan has skillfully enlisted the main symbols of global warming in the service of promoting its new electric car. It has, of course, greatly oversimplified an environmental problem and skirted major issues such as the problem of producing the electricity necessary to charge the Nissan Leaf, the environmental costs of producing the cars themselves, and the drop-in-the-bucket effect of replacing only a tiny portion of gasoline cars with electric vehicles. However, the ad works by suppressing these concerns and implying instead that the individual consumer can make a substantial difference in saving the environment.

■ ■ ■ **FOR CLASS DISCUSSION** Analyzing Photos
Rhetorically

1. The techniques for constructing photos come into play prominently in news photography. In this exercise, we ask you to examine four photographs of American presidential candidates or presidents. Working individually or in groups, study the four photos in Figures 9.12 through 9.15, and then answer the following questions:

   a. What camera techniques and composition features do you see in each photo?

   b. What do you think is the dominant impression of each photo? In other words, what is each photo's implicit argument?

2. In 2004, the photograph of the Democratic candidate John Kerry (running against Republican George W. Bush) "backfired." Republicans reversed the intended impact of the photograph and used it to ridicule Kerry.

   a. What is the intended effect of the Kerry photograph, which is from a windsurfing video showing Kerry zigzagging across the water?

   b. How might the Kerry photograph (and the windsurfing video) produce an unintended effect that opens the candidate to ridicule from the opposing party? (Suggestion: Enter "Kerry windsurfing photo" into your Web search engine. For another example of a campaign photograph that backfired, search for "Michael Dukakis tank photo.")

3. President Bush and Vice-President Cheney nurtured their image as western men and

FIGURE 9.12 Presidential candidate John Kerry windsurfing

FIGURE 9.13 President Bush and Vice-President Cheney riding in a track

FIGURE 9.14 Vice-presidential candidate
Sarah Palin

FIGURE 9.15 Presidential candidate Barack
Obama making a speech

ranchers, Bush from Texas and Cheney from Wyoming. How might this photo contribute to that image?

4. Sarah Palin, former Governor of Alaska, was John McCain's vice-presidential running mate in the 2008 election against Barak Obama and Joe Biden. In addition to portraying herself as a soccer mom and a family values advocate, Sarah Palin cultivates the image of rugged outdoors woman. How might this photo of Sarah Palin enhance her image? To what groups of voters would it most appeal?

5. The poster shown in Figure 9.16 is for the documentary film *Wal-Mart: The High Cost of Low Prices*, produced in 2005 by filmmaker and political activist Robert Greenwald. According to its Web site, the movie features "the deeply personal stories and everyday lives of families and communities struggling to survive in a Wal-Mart world."

Working individually or in groups, answer the following questions:

a. What compositional features and drawing techniques do you see in this image? What is striking or memorable about the visual features?

b. How would you state the argument made by this image?

c. The effect of this image derives partly from what cultural analysts call "intertextuality." By this term, analysts mean the way that a viewer's reading of an image depends on familiarity with a network of "connected" images—in this case, familiarity with posters for Godzilla films from the 1950s as well as Wal-Mart's conventional use of the smiley face. How does this drawing use viewers' cultural knowledge of Godzilla and of smiley faces to create an image of Wal-Mart? Why is this monster wearing a suit? Why does it have five or more arms? Why is this monster destroying a suburb or housing area rather than a city of skyscrapers? In short, what does it retain of conventional Godzilla images, what does it

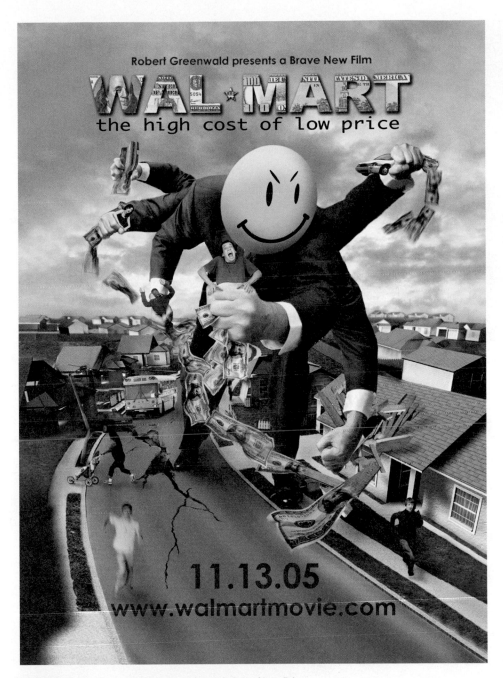

FIGURE 9.16 Poster for *Wal-Mart: The High Cost of Low Prices*

FIGURE 9.17 Urban assault scene, *America's Army* video game

change, and why? Similarly, how is the monster's smiley face similar to and different from the traditional Wal-Mart smiley face?

6. The images in Figures 9.17 and 9.18 are screen captures from the very popular PC action game *America's Army*, created by the U.S. Army. This "virtual soldiering" game, which is a free download from the Web site http://www.americasarmy.com, claims to "provide players with the most authentic military experience available."

   a. In these screen captures from the game, what is the effect of the action's distance from the subject and the point of view of the viewer/player?

   b. How do color and composition affect the visual appeal of these images?

   c. What impressions do settings, characters, and roles convey?

   d. Based on these two scenes from the game, why do you think this game has provoked heated public discussion? How effective do you think this game is as a recruitment device?

The Genres of Visual Argument

We have already mentioned that verbal arguments today are frequently accompanied by photographs or drawings that contribute to the text's persuasive appeal. For example, a verbal argument promoting U.N. action to help AIDS victims in Africa might be accompanied by a photograph of a dying mother and child. However, some genres of

FIGURE 9.18 Village scene, *America's Army* video game

argument are dominated by visual elements. In these genres, the visual design carries most of the argumentative weight; verbal text is used primarily for labeling, for focusing the argument's claim, or for commenting on the images. In this section we describe specifically these highly visual genres of argument.

Posters and Fliers

To persuade audiences, an arguer might create a poster designed for placement on walls or kiosks or a flier to be passed out on street corners. Posters dramatically attract and direct viewers' attention toward a subject or issue. They often seek to rally supporterte a strong stance on an issue, and call people to action. For example, during World War II, posters asked Americans to invest in war bonds and urged women to join the workforce to free men for active combat. During the Vietnam War, famous posters used slogans such as "Make Love, Not War" or "Girls say yes to boys who say no" to increase national resistance to the war.

The hallmark of an effective poster is the way it focuses and encodes a complex meaning in a verbal-visual text, often with one or more striking images. These images are often symbolic—for example, using children to symbolize family and home, a soaring bird to symbolize freedom, or three firefighters raising the American flag over the World Trade Center rubble on September 11, 2001, to symbolize American heroism, patriotism, and resistance to terrorism. These symbols derive potency from the values they share with their target audience. Posters tend to use words sparingly, either as slogans or as short, memorable directives. This terse verbal text augments the message encoded in an eye-catching, dominant image.

As an example of a contemporary poster, consider the poster on page 155, which is a call to stop eating red meat in order to protect the earth. This poster uses compositional special effects, depicting the earth from outer space against the backdrop of the Milky Way. The grain, color, and texture of pieces of red meat are superimposed over the continents of North and South America, where viewers expect to see the familiar greens and browns of Earth's surface. The impact of the poster is intensified by the big bite that has been taken out of Alaska, western Canada, and the West Coast of the United States. The substitution of meat for land and the presence of the bitten-out piece of the earth convey the message of immediate destruction. Framing this image of the earth on the top and bottom are a question and an imperative, phrased in casual but confrontational language: "Think you can be a meat-eating environmentalist? Think again!" The summary caption of the poster urges readers to become vegetarians. As you can see, this poster tries to shock and push readers toward a more radical environmentalism—one without meat.

Fliers and brochures often use visual elements similar to those in posters. An image might be the top and center attraction of a flier or the main focus of the front cover of a brochure. However, unlike posters, fliers and brochures offer additional space for verbal arguments, which often present the writer's claim supported with bulleted lists of reasons. Sometimes pertinent data and statistics, along with testimony from supporters, are placed in boxes or sidebars.

Public Affairs Advocacy Advertisements

Public affairs advocacy advertisements share with posters an emphasis on visual elements, but they are designed specifically for publication in newspapers and magazines and, in their persuasive strategies, are directly analogous to product advertisements. Public affairs advocacy ads are usually sponsored by a corporation or an advocacy organization and often have a more time-sensitive message than do posters and a more immediate and defined target audience. Designed as condensed arguments aimed at influencing public opinion on civic issues, these ads are characterized by their brevity, audience-based appeals, and succinct, "sound bite" style. Often, in order to sketch out their claim and reasons clearly and concisely, they employ headings and subheadings, bulleted lists, different sizes and styles of type, and a clever, pleasing layout on the page. They usually have an attention-getting slogan or headline such as "MORE KIDS ARE GETTING BRAIN CANCER. WHY?" or "STOP THE TAX REVOLT JUGGERNAUT!" And they usually include a call to action, whether it be a donation, a letter of protest to legislators, or an invitation to join the advocacy group.

The balance between verbal and visual elements in an advocacy advertisement varies. Some advocacy ads are verbal only, with visual concerns focused on document design (for example, an "open letter" from the president of a corporation appearing as a full-page newspaper ad). Other advocacy ads are primarily visual, using images and other design elements with the same shrewdness as advertisements. We looked closely at advocacy ads in this chapter when we examined the Ecstasy ads (Figures 9.2 and 9.3) and the Save the Children ad (Figure 9.4). These use text and images in different ways to present their messages.

As another example of a public affairs advocacy ad, consider the ad in Chapter 14, page 311, that attempts to counter the influence of the pro-life movement's growing campaign against abortion. As you can see, this ad is dominated by one stark image: a question mark formed by the hook of a coat hanger. The shape of the hook draws the reader's eye to the concentrated type centered below it. The hook carries most of the weight of the argument. Simple, bold, and harsh, the image of the hanger, tapping readers' cultural knowledge, evokes the dangerous scenario of illegal abortions performed crudely by nonmedical people in the dark backstreets of cities. The ad wants viewers to think of the dangerous last resorts that desperate women would have to turn to if they could not obtain abortions legally. The hanger itself creates a visual pun: As a question mark, it conveys the ad's dilemma about what will happen if abortions are made illegal. As a coat hanger, it provides the ad's frightening answer to the printed question— desperate women will return to backstreet abortionists who use coat hangers as tools.

■ ■ ■   **FOR CLASS DISCUSSION**   **Analyzing an Advocacy Ad Rhetorically**

Reexamine the Earthjustice public affairs advocacy ad shown in Figure 9.5 on page 185. This ad defends the presence of grizzly bears in Yellowstone National Park as well as other wilderness areas in the Rocky Mountains. In our classes, this ad has yielded rich discussion of its ingenuity and complexity.

Working individually or in groups, conduct your own examination of this ad using the following questions:

1. What visual features of this ad immediately attract your eyes? What principles for effective use of type, layout, color, and image does this ad exemplify?
2. What is the core argument of this ad?
3. Why did Earthjustice use the theme of Goldilocks? How do the lizards function in this ad? Why does the ad *not* have any pictures of grizzlies or bears of any kind?
4. How would you design an advocacy ad for the preservation of grizzly bears? What visuals would you use? After discussing the Earthjustice advocacy ad, explore the rhetorical appeals of a product advertisement such as the one that appears in Chapter 6 on page 118. The designers of this Toyota ad have made key choices in the use of the main image, the woman with the face mask. How does this product ad work to convey its argument? Consider questions about its use of type, layout, and image; about the core of its argument; and about its appeals to *ethos, pathos,* and *kairos.*

■ ■ ■

Cartoons

An especially charged kind of visual argument is the editorial or political cartoon and its extended forms, the comic strip and the graphic novel. Cartoonist and author Will Eisner identifies the key elements of this art form as "design, drawing, caricature and writing" and describes how storytelling is broken up in "sequenced segments" called "panels or frames"* that the artist arranges to tell the story. Here we will focus on the political cartoon, which usually uses a single frame. British cartoonist Martin Rowson calls himself "a visual journalist" who employs "humor to make a journalistic point."† Political cartoons are often mini-narratives portraying an issue dramatically, compactly, and humorously. They employ images and a few well-chosen words to dramatize conflicts and problems. Using caricature, exaggeration, and distortion, a cartoonist distills an issue down to an image that boldly reveals the creator's perspective on an issue.

"Scrub that previous message Houston. There is no, I repeat no intelligent life on Mars."

FIGURE 9.19 *American Idol* Cartoon

The purpose of political cartoons is usually satire, or, as cartoonist Rowson says, "afflicting the comfortable and comforting the afflicted."‡ Because they are so condensed and are often connected to current affairs, political cartoons are particularly dependent on the audience's background knowledge of cultural and political events. When political cartoons work well, through their perceptive combination of image and words, they flash a brilliant, clarifying light on a perspective or open a new lens on an issue, often giving readers a shock of insight.

As an illustration, note the cartoon in Figure 9.19, which was posted on the cartoon Web site index http://www.cartoonstock.com. The setting of the cartoon takes place on Mars and features caricatures of an American astronaut and Martians. The cartoon focuses on the moment the astronaut realizes that the "intelligent life" he has discovered on Mars is sitting in front of a television broadcasting the popular reality show *American Idol*. The cartoon's comic science fiction narrative tells a "before I

---

*Will Eisner explains the codes of comics as communication in *Comics & Sequential Art* (Tamarac, FL: Poorhouse Press, 1985), 38.
†"Biographies: Martin Rowson." *The British Cartoon Archive*. The British Cartoon Archives-University of Kent, n.d. Web. 2 June 2009.
‡"The Truth Told in Jest: Interview: Martin Rowson." *Morning Star*. Morning Star Online, 31 July 2007 Web. 6 June 2011.

thought … but now I think" story: once, we wondered if there was life on Mars; then we encountered life-forms; then we realized that these beings are fascinated by *American Idol*. Through exaggeration, the cartoon humorously speaks to the vast global (and now interplanetary) range of television broadcasting as well as to the hyperbolic popularity of *American Idol*. Highlighting a social-cultural subject, it voices a biting critique of the quality of the show by asserting its low intellectual content, thus implying that anyone enamored of this show or habituated to watching it must not be very smart. A deeper question the cartoon suggests is "What impression of ourselves are we humans transmitting into space?"

■ ■ ■   **FOR CLASS DISCUSSION**   Analyzing Cartoons

1. Cartoons can often sum up a worldview in a single image. The political cartoons in Chapter 2 on page 27 underscore the complexity of the economic role of illegal immigrants. The cartoons in Chapter 1 on pages 8 respond to the gulf between those who accept and those who deny the problem of climate change and to the motivation behind Arizona's recent state law to control illegal immigration. What mini-narrative does each convey? What is each cartoon arguing? How does each cartoon use caricature, exaggeration, or distortion to convey its perspective?

2. Cartoons can provide insight into how the public is lining up on issues. Choose a current issue such as health care reform, dependence on foreign oil, the state of the job market, reduced government spending on public education, or identity theft. Then, using an online cartoon index such as Daryl Cagle's Professional Cartoonists Index (http://www.cagle.com) or a Web search of your own, find several cartoons that capture different perspectives on your issue. What is the mini-narrative, the main claim, and the use of caricature, exaggeration, or distortion in each? How is *kairos*, or timeliness, important to each cartoon?

■ ■ ■

Web Pages

So far we have only hinted at the influence of the World Wide Web in accelerating the use of visual images in argument. The hypertext design of Web pages, along with the Web's complex mix of text and image, has changed the way many writers think of argument. The home page of an advocacy site, for example, often has many features of a poster argument, with hypertext links to galleries of images on the one hand and to verbal arguments on the other. These verbal arguments themselves often contain photographs, drawings, and graphics. The strategies discussed in this chapter for analyzing and interpreting visual texts also apply to Web pages.

Because the Web is such an important tool in research, we have placed our main discussion of Web sites in Chapter 15, pages 354–357. On these pages you will find our explanations for reading, analyzing, and evaluating Web sites.

Constructing Your Own Visual Argument

The most common visual arguments you are likely to create are posters, fliers, and public affairs advocacy ads. You may also decide that in longer verbal arguments, the use of visuals or graphics could clarify your points while adding visual variety to your paper. The following guidelines will help you apply your understanding of visual elements to the construction of your own visual arguments.

Guidelines for Creating Visual Arguments

1. **Genre:** Determine where this visual argument is going to appear (on a bulletin board, passed out as a flier, imagined as a one-page magazine or newspaper spread, or as a Web page).

2. **Audience-based appeals:** Determine who your target audience is.
   - What values and background knowledge of your issue can you assume that your audience has?
   - What specifically do you want your audience to think or do after reading your visual argument?
   - If you are promoting a specific course of action (sign a petition, send money, vote for or against a bill, attend a meeting), how can you make that request clear and direct?

3. **Core of your argument:** Determine what clear claim and reasons will form the core of your argument; decide whether this claim and these reasons will be explicitly stated or implicit in your visuals and slogans.
   - How much verbal text will you use?
   - If the core of your argument will be largely implicit, how can you still make it readily apparent and clear for your audience?

4. **Visual design:** What visual design and layout will grab your audience's attention and be persuasive?
   - How can font sizes and styles, layout, and color be used in this argument to create a strong impression?
   - What balance and harmony can you create between the visual and verbal elements of your argument? Will your verbal elements be a slogan, express the core of the argument, or summarize and comment on the image(s)?

5. **Use of images:** If your argument lends itself to images, what photo or drawing would support your claim or have emotional appeal? (If you want to use more than one image, be careful that you don't clutter your page and confuse your message. Simplicity and clarity are important.)
   - What image would be memorable and meaningful to your audience? Would a photo image or a drawing be more effective?
   - Will your image(s) be used to provide evidence for your claim or illustrate a main idea, evoke emotions, or enhance your credibility and authority?

As an example of a poster argument, consider the "Heather's Life" poster in Figure 9.20, sponsored by Heather Lerch's parents and TxtResponsibly.org. This poster, which appears on the TxtResponsibily.org Web site, reaches out to young drivers and their parents, especially, and makes effective use of both images and text. The images at first puzzle and then shock (Heather looking happy and attractive at the top of the poster with her demolished car shown below). The connection between the images is made clear by the attention-grabbing text, which combines a causal narrative with a proposal/plea. This ad joins the national conversation about the dangers of dis-

FIGURE 9.20 Poster argument warning against texting while driving

tracted driving and urges drivers to comply with new laws making it illegal to text and drive. TxtResponsibly.org invites viewers to contribute their consciousness-raising stories to its "Be a part of the solution" campaign.

■ ■ ■ **FOR CLASS DISCUSSION**   Developing Ideas for a Poster Argument
This exercise asks you to do the thinking and planning for a poster argument to be displayed on your college or university campus. Working individually, in small groups, or as a whole class, choose an issue that is controversial on your campus (or in your town or city), and follow the Guidelines for Creating Visual Arguments on page 200 to envision the view you want to advocate on that issue. What might the core of your argument be? Who is your target audience? Are you representing a group, club, or other organization? What image(s) might be effective in attracting and moving this audience? Possible issues might be commuter parking; poor conditions in the computer lab; student reluctance to use the counseling center; problems with dorm life, financial aid programs, or intramural sports; ways to improve orientation programs for new students, work-study programs, or travel-abroad opportunities; or new initiatives such as study groups for the big lecture courses or new service-learning opportunities.

■ ■ ■

Using Information Graphics in Arguments

Besides images in the form of photographs and drawings, writers often use quantitative graphics to support arguments using numbers. In Chapter 5 we introduced you to the use of quantitative data in arguments. We discussed the persuasiveness of numbers and showed you ways to use them responsibly in your arguments. With the availability of spreadsheet and presentation programs, today's writers often create and import quantitative graphics into their documents. These visuals—such as tables, pie charts, and line or bar graphs—can have great rhetorical power by making numbers tell a story at a glance. In this section, we'll show you how quantitative graphics can make numbers speak. We'll also show you how to analyze graphics, incorporate them into your text, and reference them effectively.

How Tables Contain a Variety of Stories

Data used in arguments usually have their origins in raw numbers collected from surveys, questionnaires, observational studies, scientific experiments, and so forth. Through a series of calculations, the numbers are combined, sorted, and arranged in a meaningful fashion, often in detailed tables. Some of the tables published by the U.S. Census Bureau, for example, contain dozens of pages. The more dense the table, the more their use is restricted to statistical experts who pore over the data to analyze their meanings. More useful to the general public are midlevel tables contained on one or two pages that report data at a higher level of abstraction.

Consider, for example, Table 9.2, published by the U.S. Census Bureau and based on the 2010 census. This table shows the marital status of people age 15 and older, broken into gender and age groupings, in March 2010. It also provides comparative data on the "never married" percentage of the population in March 2010 and March 1970.

TABLE 9.2 Marital Status of People 15 Years and Over by Age and Sex: March 1970 and March 2010
(Numbers in thousands, except for percentages.)

Characteristic	Total	March 2010 Number							March 1970 percent never married[a]
		Married spouse present	Married spouse absent	Separated	Divorced	Widowed	Never married	Percent never married	
Both Sexes									
Total 15 years old and over	242,047	120,768	3,415	5,539	23,742	14,341	74,243	30.7	24.9
15 to 19 years old	21,079	178	109	151	60	22	20,559	97.5	93.9
20 to 24 years old	21,142	2,635	202	309	195	17	17,765	84.0	44.5
25 to 29 years old	21,445	7,793	406	594	766	60	11,826	55.1	14.7
30 to 34 years old	19,623	10,896	337	632	1,447	72	6,239	31.8	7.8
35 to 44 years old	40,435	25,729	733	1,331	4,697	345	7,599	18.8	5.9
45 to 54 years old	44,373	28,619	703	1,295	6,951	1,080	5,725	12.9	6.1
55 to 64 years old	35,381	23,621	463	763	5,750	1,923	2,861	8.1	7.2
65 years old and over	38,569	21,276	461	465	3,875	10,823	1,668	4.3	7.6
Males									
Total 15 years old and over	117,686	60,384	1,789	2,352	9,981	2,974	40,206	34.2	28.1
15 to 19 years old	10,713	61	55	62	30	8	10,498	98.0	97.4
20 to 24 years old	10,677	946	86	123	49	3	9,469	88.7	54.7
25 to 29 years old	10,926	3,343	220	224	318	21	6,800	62.2	19.1
30 to 34 years old	9,759	5,143	188	246	593	28	3,561	36.5	9.4
35 to 44 years old	20,066	12,614	392	578	1,998	81	4,402	21.9	6.7
45 to 54 years old	21,779	14,280	367	539	3,063	284	3,246	14.9	7.5
55 to 64 years old	16,980	11,958	244	343	2,465	424	1,545	9.1	7.8
65 years old and over	16,786	12,039	237	237	1,464	2,124	685	4.1	7.5
Females									
Total 15 years old and over	124,361	60,384	1,626	3,187	13,760	11,368	34,037	27.4	22.1
15 to 19 years old	10,365	118	55	90	30	13	10,061	97.1	90.3
20 to 24 years old	10,465	1,708	116	185	146	14	8,296	79.3	35.8
25 to 29 years old	10,519	4,451	186	370	448	39	5,026	47.8	10.5
30 to 34 years old	9,864	5,753	150	386	854	44	2,678	27.1	6.2
35 to 44 years old	20,369	13,115	341	753	2,698	264	3,198	15.7	5.2
45 to 54 years old	22,594	14,339	337	756	3,889	794	2,479	11.0	4.9
55 to 64 years old	18,401	11,663	220	420	3,284	1,499	1,315	7.1	6.8
65 years old and over	21,783	9,238	224	227	2,412	8,700	983	4.5	7.7

[a]The 1970 percentages include 14-year-olds, and thus are for 14+ and 14–19.

Source: U.S. Census Bureau, *Current Population Survey,* March 2010 and March 1970.

Take a few moments to peruse the table and be certain you know how to read it. You read tables in two directions: from top to bottom and from left to right. Always begin with the title, which tells you what the table contains and includes elements from both the vertical and the horizontal dimensions of the table. In this case the vertical dimension presents demographic categories for people "15 years old and over" for both sexes, for males, and for females. Each of these gender categories is subdivided into age categories. The horizontal dimension provides information about "marital status." Seven of the columns give total numbers (reported in thousands) for March 2010. The eighth column gives the "percent never married" for March 2010, while the last column gives the "percent never married" for March 1970. To make sure you know how to read the table, pick a couple of rows at random and say to yourself what each number means. For example, the first row under "Both sexes" gives total figures for the entire population of the United States age 15 and older. In March 2010 there were 242,047,000 people age 15 and older (remember that the numbers are presented in thousands). Of these, 120,768,000 were married and living with their spouses. As you continue across the columns, you'll see that 3,415,000 people were married but not living with their spouses (a spouse may be stationed overseas or in prison; or a married couple may be maintaining a "commuter marriage" with separate households in different cities). Continuing across the columns, you'll see that 5,539,000 people were separated from their spouses, 23,742,000 were divorced, and 14,341,000 were widowed, and an additional 74,243,000 were never married. In the next-to-last column, the number of never-married people is converted to a percentage: 30.7 percent. Finally, the last column shows the percentage of never-married people in 1970: 24.9 percent. These last two columns show us that the number of unmarried people in the United States rose 5.8 percentage points since 1970.

Now that you know how to read the table, examine it carefully to see the kinds of stories it tells. What does the table show you, for example, about the percentage of married people age 25–29 in 1970 versus 2010? What does it show about different age-related patterns of marriage in males and females? By showing you that Americans are waiting much later in life to get married, a table like this initiates many causal questions for analysis and argument. What happened in American culture between 1970 and 2010 to explain the startling difference in the percentage of married people within, say, the 20–24 age bracket? In 2010 only 16 percent of people in this age bracket were married (we converted "unmarried" to "married" by subtracting 84 from 100). However, in 1970, 55.5 percent of people in this age bracket were married.

Using a Graph to Tell a Story

Table 9.2, as we have seen, tells the story of how Americans are postponing marriage. However, one has to tease out the story from the dense columns of numbers. To focus on a key story and make it powerfully immediate, you can create a graph.

Bar Graphs   Suppose you are writing an argument in which you want to show that the percentage of married women in the 20–29 age bracket has dropped significantly since 1970. You could tell this story through a bar graph (Figure 9.21).

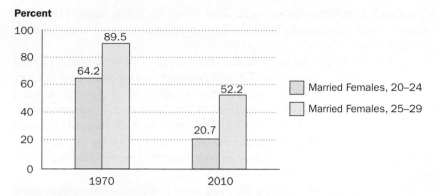

FIGURE 9.21 Percentage of married females ages 20–29, 1970 and 2010

Source: U.S. Census Bureau, *Current Population Survey,* March 2010.

Bar graphs use bars of varying length, extending either horizontally or vertically, to contrast two or more quantities. As with any graphic presentation, you must create a comprehensive title. In the case of bar graphs, titles tell readers what is being compared to what. Most bar graphs also have "legends," which explain what the different features on the graph represent. Bars are typically distinguished from each other by use of different colors, shades, or patterns of crosshatching. The special power of bar graphs is that they can help readers make quick comparisons.

Pie Charts   Another vivid kind of graph is a pie chart or circle graph, which depicts different percentages of a total (the pie) in the form of slices. Pie charts are a favorite way of depicting the way parts of a whole are divided up. Suppose, for example, that you wanted your readers to notice the high percentage of widows among women age 65 and older. To do so, you could create a pie chart (Figure 9.22) based on the data in the last row of Table 9.2. As you can see, a pie chart shows at a glance how the whole of something is divided into segments. However, the effectiveness of pie charts diminishes as you add more slices. In most cases, you'll begin to confuse readers if you include more than five or six slices.

Line Graphs   Another powerful quantitative graphic is a line graph, which converts numerical data into a series of

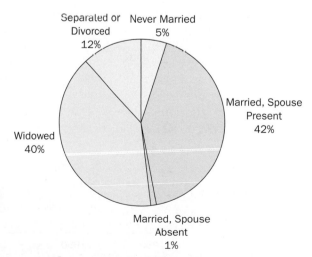

FIGURE 9.22 Marital status of females age 65 and older, 2010

Source: U.S. Census Bureau, *Current Population Survey,* March 2010.

points on a grid and connects them to create flat, rising, or falling lines. The result gives us a picture of the relationship between the variables represented on the horizontal and vertical axes.

Suppose you wanted to tell the story of the rising number of separated/divorced women in the U.S. population. Using Table 9.2, you can calculate the percentage of separated/divorced females in 2010 by adding the number of separated females (3,187,000) and the number of divorced females (13,760,000) and dividing that sum by the total number of females (124,361,000). The result is 13.6 percent. You can make the same calculations for 2000, 1990, 1980, and 1970 by looking at U.S. census data from those years (available on the Web or in your library). The resulting line graph is shown in Figure 9.23.

To determine what this graph is telling you, you need to clarify what's represented on the two axes. By convention, the horizontal axis of a graph contains the predictable, known variable, which has no surprises—what researchers call the "independent variable." In this case the horizontal axis represents the years 1970–2010 arranged predictably in chronological order. The vertical axis contains the unpredictable variable, which forms the graph's story—what researchers call the "dependent variable"—in this case, the percentage of separated or divorced females. The ascending curve tells the story at a glance.

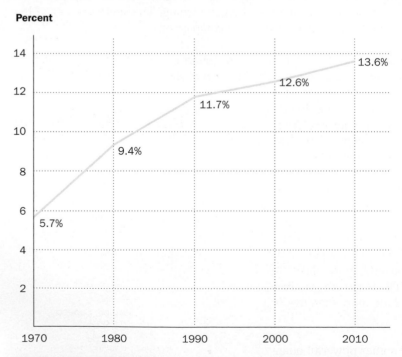

FIGURE 9.23 Percentage of females age 15 and older who were separated or divorced, 1970–2010

Source: U.S. Census Bureau, *Current Population Survey,* March 2010.

Note that with line graphs, the steepness of the slope (and hence the rhetorical effect) can be manipulated by the intervals chosen for the vertical axis. Figure 9.23 shows vertical intervals of 2 percent. The slope could be made less dramatic by choosing intervals of, say, 10 percent and more dramatic by choosing intervals of 1 percent.

Incorporating Graphics into Your Argument

Today, writers working with quantitative data usually use graphing software that automatically creates tables, graphs, or charts from data entered into the cells of a spreadsheet. For college papers, some instructors may allow you to make your graphs with pencil and ruler and paste them into your document.

Designing the Graphic   When you design your graphic, your goal is to have a specific rhetorical effect on your readers, not to demonstrate all the bells and whistles available on your software. Adding extraneous data to the graph or chart or using such features as a three-dimensional effect can often distract from the story you are trying to tell. Keep the graphic as uncluttered and simple as possible and design it so that it reinforces the point you are making.

Numbering, Labeling, and Titling the Graphic   In newspapers and popular magazines, writers often include graphics in boxes or sidebars without specifically referring to them in the text itself. However, in academic and professional workplace writing, graphics are always labeled, numbered, titled, and referred to directly in the text. By convention, tables are listed as "Tables," whereas line graphs, bar graphs, pie charts, or any other kinds of drawings or photographs are labeled as "Figures." Suppose you create a document that includes four graphics—a table, a bar graph, a pie chart, and a photograph. The table would be labeled as Table 1. The rest would be labeled as Figure 1, Figure 2, and Figure 3.

In addition to numbering and labeling, every graphic needs a comprehensive title that explains fully what information is being displayed. Look back over the tables and figures in this chapter and compare their titles to the information in the graphics. In a line graph showing changes over time, for example, a typical title will identify the information on both the horizontal and vertical axes and the years covered. Bar graphs also have a "legend" explaining how the bars are coded if necessary. When you import the graphic into your own text, be consistent in where you place the title—either above the graphic or below it.

Referencing the Graphic in Your Text   Academic and professional writers follow a referencing convention called *independent redundancy*. The general rule is this: The graphic should be understandable without the text; the text should be understandable without the graphic; the text should repeat the most important information in the graphic. An example is shown in Figure 9.24.

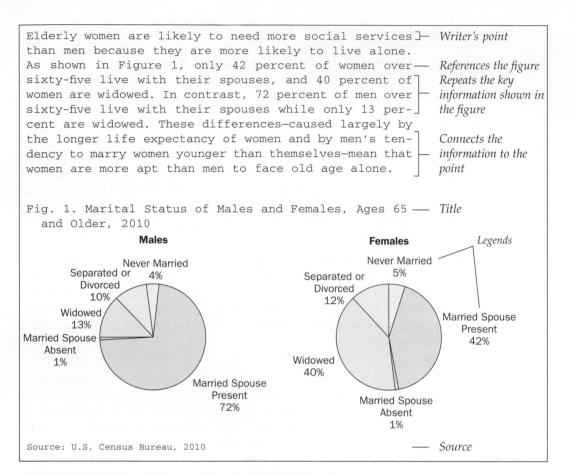

Elderly women are likely to need more social services — *Writer's point*
than men because they are more likely to live alone.
As shown in Figure 1, only 42 percent of women over — *References the figure*
sixty-five live with their spouses, and 40 percent of — *Repeats the key*
women are widowed. In contrast, 72 percent of men over — *information shown in*
sixty-five live with their spouses while only 13 per- — *the figure*
cent are widowed. These differences—caused largely by
the longer life expectancy of women and by men's ten- — *Connects the*
dency to marry women younger than themselves—mean that — *information to the*
women are more apt than men to face old age alone. — *point*

Fig. 1. Marital Status of Males and Females, Ages 65 — *Title*
and Older, 2010

Males   **Females**   *Legends*

Never Married 4%
Separated or Divorced 10%
Widowed 13%
Married Spouse Absent 1%
Married Spouse Present 72%

Never Married 5%
Separated or Divorced 12%
Married Spouse Present 42%
Widowed 40%
Married Spouse Absent 1%

Source: U.S. Census Bureau, 2010 — *Source*

FIGURE 9.24 Example of a student text with a referenced graph

Conclusion

In this chapter we have explained the challenge and power of using visuals in arguments. We have examined the components of visual design—use of type, layout, color, and images—and shown how these components can be used for persuasive effect in arguments. We have also described the argumentative genres that depend on effective use of visuals—posters and fliers, advocacy advertisements, cartoons, and Web pages—and invited you to produce your own visual argument. Finally, we showed you that graphics can tell a numeric story in a highly focused and dramatic way. Particularly, we explained the functions of tables, bar graphs, pie charts, and line graphs, and showed you how to reference graphics and incorporate them into your own prose.

WRITING ASSIGNMENT   A Visual Argument Rhetorical Analysis, a Visual Argument, or a Microtheme Using Quantitative Data

Option 1: Writing a Rhetorical Analysis of a Visual Argument   Write a thesis-driven rhetorical analysis essay in which you examine the rhetorical effectiveness of a visual argument, either one of the visual arguments in this text or one specified by your instructor. Unless otherwise stated, direct your analysis to an audience of your classmates. In your introduction, establish the argumentative conversation to which this argument is contributing. Briefly summarize the argument and describe the visual text. Present your thesis, highlighting two or more rhetorical features of the argument that you find central to the effectiveness or ineffectiveness of this argument. To develop and support your own points, you will need to include visual features and details (such as color, design, camera angle, framing, and special effects) as well as short quotations from any verbal parts of the argument.

Option 2: Multimodal Assignment: A Poster Argument   Working with the idea of a poster argument that you explored in For Class Discussion on page 202, use the visual design concepts and principles presented on page 200, your understanding of visual argument and the genre of poster arguments, and your own creativity to produce a poster argument that can be displayed on your campus or in your town or city. Try out the draft of your poster argument on people who are part of your target audience. Based on these individuals' suggestions for improving the clarity and impact of this visual argument, prepare a final version of your poster argument.

Option 3: Multimodal Assignment: Intertextual Visual Argument   Often, visual arguments rely on what scholars call "intertextual associations." By "intertextual" (literally "between texts"), we mean that an image gets its power by drawing on ideas or emotions associated with other images that are part of our cultural background. A good example is the anti–Wal-Mart poster (Figure 9.16), in which the image of the smiley face corporate executive destroying a city depends for its effect on our cultural knowledge of Godzilla. Examples of frequently used intertextual images include the Statue of Liberty, the Uncle Sam "I Want You" recruitment poster, Adam and Eve in the garden with an apple or snake, Rosie the Riveter, the raising of the flag on Iwo Jima, and the Rodin sculpture *The Thinker*. Intertextual associations can also be drawn from fairy tales, legends, or popular culture, as in the Earthjustice poster's reference to Goldilocks and the Three Bears on page 185. For this assignment, create an idea for a poster or bumper sticker that would depend on an intertextual association for its persuasive effect. Think of an idea or behavior that you would like to promote and then link your persuasive purpose to an image from history, popular culture, or fairy tales that would speak to your audience and enliven your message. Finally, write a short reflection explaining the challenge of creating an intertextual visual argument. Possible ideas for an intertextual visual argument might include silencing cell phones in public places, buying local food, voting for a certain candidate, changing a school policy, supporting or criticizing skateboarders, admiring or mocking video game players, opposing Facebook addiction, defending an art form you value, supporting or criticizing car drivers who are angry at bikers, attacking employers' fixation on dress codes, and so forth.

Option 4: Multimodal Assignment: Cartoon   Choose a controversial issue important to you and create a single-frame political cartoon that presents your perspective on the issue in a memorable way. Use the cartoon strategies of mini-narrative, caricature, exaggeration, distortion, and the interaction between image and text.

Option 5: A Microtheme Using a Quantitative Graphic   Write a microtheme that tells a story based on data you select from Table 9.2 or from some other table provided by your instructor or located by you. Include in your microtheme at least one quantitative graphic (table, line graph, bar graph, pie chart), which should be labeled and referenced according to standard conventions. Use as a model the short piece shown in Figure 9.24 on page 208. ■

For additional writing, reading, and research resources, go to www.mycomplab.com

PART FOUR

Arguments in Depth

Types of Claims

A shortage of body organs and long waiting lists have motivated some people to make personal appeals to the public on billboards like this one. In Chapter 13, a reading and the "Critiquing" exercise on pages 309–310 ask you to think about the evaluation and ethical issues involved in advertising for organs and in the selling and trading of body organs.

10 An Introduction to the Types of Claims

In Parts One, Two, and Three of this text, we showed how argument entails both inquiry and persuasion. We explained strategies for creating a compelling structure of reasons and evidence for your arguments (*logos*), for linking your arguments to the beliefs and values of your audience (*pathos*), and for establishing your credibility and trustfulness (*ethos*). We also explained how to do a rhetorical analysis of both verbal and visual texts.

Now in Part Four we examine arguments in depth by explaining five types of claims, each type having its own characteristic patterns of development and support. Because almost all arguments use one or more of these types of claims as "moves" or building blocks, knowing how to develop each claim type will advance your skills in argument. The claims we examine in Part Four are related to an ancient rhetorical concept called *stasis,* from a Greek term meaning "stand," as in "to take a stand on something." There are many competing theories of stasis, so no two rhetoricians discuss stasis in exactly the same way. But all the theories have valuable components in common.

In Part Four we present our own version of stasis theory, or, to use more ordinary language, our own approach to argument based on the types of claims.

In this chapter, which presents an overview of claim types, you will learn to:

- Use strategies based on claim types to help you focus an argument, generate ideas for it, and structure it persuasively
- Recognize how different claim types work together in hybrid arguments, thus increasing your flexibility as an arguer

An Overview of the Types of Claims

To appreciate what a study of claim types can do, imagine one of those heated but frustrating arguments in which the question at issue keeps shifting. Everyone talks at cross-purposes, each speaker's point unconnected to the previous speaker's. Suppose your heated discussion is about the use of steroids. You might get such a discussion back on track if one person says: "Hold it for a moment. What are we actually arguing about here? Are we arguing about whether steroids are a health risk or whether steroids should be banned from sports? These are two different issues. We can't debate both at once." Whether she recognizes it or not, this person is applying the concept of claim types to get the argument focused.

212

To understand how claim types work, let's return to the concept of stasis. A stasis is an issue or question that focuses a point of disagreement. You and your audience may agree on the answer to question A and so have nothing to argue about. Likewise you may agree on the answer to question B. But on question C you disagree. Question C constitutes a stasis where you and your audience diverge. It is the place where disagreement begins, where as an arguer you take a stand against another view. Thus you and your audience may agree that steroids, if used carefully under a physician's supervision, pose few long-term health risks but still disagree on whether steroids should be banned from sports. This last issue constitutes a stasis, the point where you and your audience part company.

Rhetoricians have discovered that the kinds of questions that divide people have classifiable patterns. In this text we identify five broad types of claims—each type originating in a different kind of question. The following chart gives you a quick overview of these five types of claims, each of which is developed in more detail in subsequent chapters in Part Four. It also shows you a typical structure for each type of argument. Note that the first three claim types concern questions of truth or reality, whereas the last two concern questions of value. You'll appreciate the significance of this distinction as this chapter progresses.

Claims about Reality, Truth, or the Way Things Are

Claim Type and Generic Question	Examples of Issue Questions	Typical Methods for Structuring an Argument
Definitional arguments: *In what category does this thing belong?* (Chapter 11)	■ Is sleep deprivation torture? ■ Is an expert video game player an athlete?	■ Create a definition that establishes criteria for the category. ■ Use examples to show how the contested case meets the criteria.
Resemblance arguments: *To what is this thing similar?* (Chapter 11)	■ Is opposition to gay marriage like opposition to interracial marriage? ■ Is steroid use to improve strength similar to LASIK surgery to improve vision?	■ Let the analogy or precedent itself create the desired rhetorical effect. [or] ■ Elaborate on the relevant similarities between the given case and the analogy or precedent.
Causal arguments: *What are the causes or consequences of this phenomenon?* (Chapter 12)	■ What are the causes of autism? ■ What might be the consequences of requiring a national ID card?	■ Explain the links in a causal chain going from cause to effect. [or] ■ Speculate about causes (consequences) or propose a surprising cause (consequence).

Claims about Values

Claim Type and Generic Question	Examples of Issue Questioins	Typical Methods for Structuring an Arguement
Evaluation and ethical arguments: *What is the worth or value of this thing?* (Chapter 13)	▪ Is behavior modification a good therapy for anxiety? ▪ Is it ethical to use steroids in sports?	▪ Establish the criteria for a "good" or "ethical" member of this class or category. ▪ Use examples to show how the contested case meets the criteria.
Proposal arguments: *What action should we take?* (Chapter 14)	▪ Should the United States enact a single-payer health care system? ▪ To solve the problem of prison overcrowding, should we legalize possession of drugs?	▪ Make the problem vivid. ▪ Explain your solution. ▪ Justify your solution by showing how it is motivated by principle, by good consequences, or by resemblance to a previous action the audience approves.

■ ■ ■ **FOR CLASS DISCUSSION** Identifying Types of Claims

Working as a class or in small groups, read the following questions and decide which claim type is represented by each. Sometimes the claim types overlap or blend together, so if the question fits two categories, explain your reasoning.

1. Should overnight camping be permitted in this state park?
2. Is taking Adderall to increase concentration for an exam a form of cheating?
3. Will an increase in gas taxes lead to a reduction in road congestion?
4. Is depression a learned behavior?
5. Were the terrorist attacks of September 11, 2001, more like Pearl Harbor (an act of war) or more like an earthquake (a natural disaster)?
6. How effective is acupuncture in reducing morning sickness?
7. Is acupuncture quackery or real medicine?
8. Should cities use tax dollars to fund professional sports arenas?
9. Are Mattel toy factories sweatshops?
10. Why are couples who live together before marriage more likely to divorce than couples who don't live together before marriage? ■ ■ ■

Using Claim Types to Focus an Argument and Generate Ideas: An Example

Having provided an overview of the types of claims, we now show you some of the benefits of this knowledge. First of all, understanding claim types will help you focus an argument by asking you to determine what's at stake between you and your audience. Where do you and your audience agree and disagree? What are the questions at issue? Second, it will help you generate ideas for your argument by suggesting the kinds of reasons, examples, and evidence you'll need.

To illustrate, let's take a hypothetical case—one Isaac Charles Little (affectionately known as I. C. Little), who desires to chuck his contact lenses and undergo the new LASIK procedure to cure his nearsightedness. LASIK, or laser in-situ keratomileusis, is a surgical treatment for myopia. Sometimes known as "flap and zap" surgery, it involves using a laser to cut a thin layer of the cornea and then flattening it. It's usually not covered by insurance and is quite expensive.

I. C. Little has two different arguments he'd like to make: (1) he'd like to talk his parents into helping him pay for the procedure, and (2) he'd like to join with others who are trying to convince insurance companies that the LASIK procedure should be covered under standard medical insurance policies. In the discussions that follow, note how the five types of claims can help I. C. identify points of disagreement for each audience and simultaneously suggest lines of argument for persuading each one. Note, too, how the questions at issue vary for each audience.

Making the LASIK Argument to Parents

First imagine what might be at stake in I. C.'s discussions with his parents. Here is how thinking about claim types will help him generate ideas:

- **Definition argument:** Because I. C.'s parents will be concerned about the safety of LASIK surgery, the first stasis for I. C.'s argument is a question about categories: Is LASIK a safe procedure? I. C.'s mom has read about serious complications from LASIK and has also heard that ophthalmologists prefer patients to be at least in their midtwenties or older, so I. C. knows he will have to persuade her that the procedure is safe for twenty-year-olds.
- **Resemblance argument:** I. C. can't think of any resemblance questions at issue.
- **Causal argument:** Both parents will question I. C.'s underlying motivation for seeking this surgery. "Why do you want this LASIK procedure?" they will ask. (I. C.'s dad, who has worn eyeglasses all his life, will not be swayed by cosmetic desires. "If you don't like contacts," he will say, "just wear glasses.") Here I. C. needs to argue the good consequences of LASIK. Permanently correcting his nearsightedness will improve his quality of life and even his academic and professional options. I. C. decides to emphasize his desire for an active, outdoor life, and especially his passion for water sports, where his need for contacts is a serious handicap. He is even thinking of majoring in marine biology, so LASIK surgery would help him professionally. He says that wearing scuba equipment is easier without worrying about contact lenses or corrective goggles.
- **Evaluation argument:** When the pluses and minuses are weighed, is LASIK a good way to treat nearsightedness? Is it also a good way for his parents to spend family money? Would the results of the surgery be beneficial enough to justify

the cost and the risks? In terms of costs, I. C. might argue that even though the procedure is initially expensive (from $1,000 to $4,000), over the years he will save money by not needing glasses or contacts. The convenience of seeing well in the water and not being bothered by glasses or contacts while hiking and camping constitutes a major benefit. (Even though he thinks he'll look cooler without glasses, he decides not to mention the cosmetic benefits because his dad thinks wearing glasses is fine.)

■ **Proposal argument:** Should I. C.'s parents pay for a LASIK procedure to treat their son's nearsightedness? (All the previous points of disagreement are subissues related to this overarching proposal issue.)

This example shows that writers often need to argue issues of reality and truth in order to make claims about values. In this particular case, I. C. would need to convince his parents (1) that the procedure is safe (definition argument), (2) that the consequences of the procedure would be beneficial recreationally and professionally (causal argument), and (3) that the benefits outweigh the costs (evaluation argument). Only then would I. C. be able to persuade his parents (4) that he should have LASIK surgery with their financial help (proposal claim). Almost all arguments combine subarguments in this way so that lower-order claims provide supporting materials for addressing higher-order claims.

Making the LASIK Argument to Insurance Companies

The previous illustration focused on parents as audience. If we now switch audiences, we can use our claim types to identify different questions at issue. Let's suppose I. C. wants to persuade insurance companies to cover the LASIK procedure. He imagines his primary audience as insurance company executives, along with the general public and state legislators, who may be able to influence them. Again, I. C. generates ideas by considering the claim types.

■ **Definition argument:** For this audience the issue of safety is no longer relevant. (They share I. C.'s belief that LASIK is a safe procedure.) What's at stake is another definition issue: Should LASIK be considered "cosmetic surgery" (as insurance companies contend) or "medically justifiable surgery" (as I. C. contends)? This definitional question constitutes a major stasis. I. C. wants to convince his audience that LASIK belongs in the category of "medically justifiable surgery" rather than "cosmetic surgery." He will need to define "medically justifiable surgery" in such a way that LASIK can be included.

■ **Resemblance argument:** Does LASIK more resemble a face-lift (not covered by insurance) or plastic surgery to repair a cleft palate (covered by insurance)?

■ **Causal argument:** What will be the consequences to insurance companies and to the general public of making insurance companies pay for LASIK? Will there be an overwhelming crush of claims for LASIK surgery? Will there be a corresponding decrease in claims for eye exams, contacts, and glasses? What will happen to the cost of insurance?

- **Evaluation argument:** Would it be good for society as a whole if insurance companies had to pay for LASIK?
- **Proposal argument:** Should insurance companies be required to cover LASIK?

As this analysis shows, the questions at issue change when you consider a different audience. Now the chief question at issue is definition: Is LASIK cosmetic surgery or medically justifiable surgery? I. C. does not need to argue that the surgery is safe (a major concern for his parents); instead he must establish criteria for "medically justifiable surgery" and then argue that LASIK meets these criteria. Again note how the higher-order issues of value depend on resolving one or more lower-order issues of reality and truth.

Note also that any of the claim type examples just described could be used as the major focus of an argument. If I. C. were not concerned about a values issue (his proposal claims), he might tackle only a reality/truth issue. He could, for example, focus an entire argument on a definition question about categories: "Is LASIK safe?" (an argument requiring him to research the medical literature). Likewise he could write a causal argument focusing on what might happen to optometrists and eyeglass manufacturers if the insurance industry decided to cover LASIK.

The key insight here is that when you develop an argument, you may have to work through issues of reality and truth before you can tackle a values issue and argue for change or action. Before you embark on writing an evaluation or proposal argument, you must first consider whether you need to resolve a lower-order claim based on reality and truth.

Hybrid Arguments: How Claim Types Work Together in Arguments

As the LASIK example shows, hybrid arguments can be built from different claim types. A writer might develop a proposal argument with a causal subargument in one section, a resemblance subargument in another section, and an evaluation subargument in still another section. Although the overarching proposal argument follows the typical structure of a proposal, each of the subsections follows a typical structure for its own claim type.

Some Examples of Hybrid Arguments

The examples on page 218 show how these combinations of claim types can play out in actual arguments. (For more examples of these kinds of hybrid arguments, see Chapter 14, pages 320–321, where we explain how lower-order claims about reality and truth can support higher-order claims about values.)

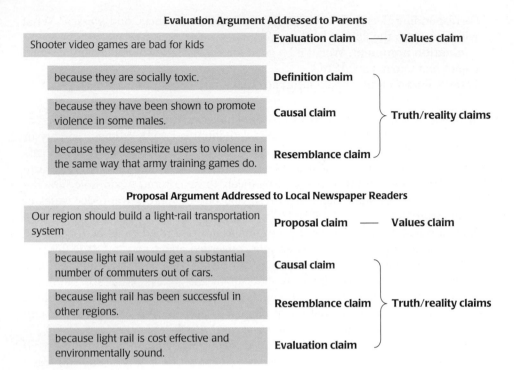

Evaluation Argument Addressed to Parents

Shooter video games are bad for kids	Evaluation claim — Values claim
because they are socially toxic.	Definition claim
because they have been shown to promote violence in some males.	Causal claim ⎫ Truth/reality claims
because they desensitize users to violence in the same way that army training games do.	Resemblance claim ⎭

Proposal Argument Addressed to Local Newspaper Readers

Our region should build a light-rail transportation system	Proposal claim — Values claim
because light rail would get a substantial number of commuters out of cars.	Causal claim
because light rail has been successful in other regions.	Resemblance claim ⎬ Truth/reality claims
because light rail is cost effective and environmentally sound.	Evaluation claim

■ ■ ■ **FOR CLASS DISCUSSION** Exploring Different Claim Types and Audiences

1. Select an issue familiar to most members of the class—perhaps a current campus issue or an issue prominent in the local or national news—and generate possible issue questions and arguments using the claim types. Take as your models our discussion of I. C. Little's arguments about LASIK surgery. Consider how a writer or speaker might address two different audiences on this issue, with a different purpose for each audience.

2. The following is the table of contents for a "friend of the court" legal brief opposing a contested Missouri law outlawing sale of violent video games to minors. How would you classify the claims put forward in this brief?

   - What is the overarching claim of this legal brief? What claim type is it?
   - What are the claim types for major sections I, II, and III?
   - How might you recast section III's title to state its implied claim more explicitly
   - How does the "friend of the court" brief try to rebut the argument against violent video games shown in the example above?

No. 02-3010
In the
United States Court of Appeals for the Eighth Circuit
INTERACTIVE DIGITAL SOFTWARE ASS'N, et al.
Plaintiffs - Appellants,
v.
ST. LOUIS COUNTY, et al.

Defendants - Appellees

BRIEF *AMICI CURIAE* OF THIRTY-THREE MEDIA SCHOLARS
IN SUPPORT OF APPELLANTS, AND SUPPORTING REVERSAL

CONTENTS

An Extended Example of a Hybrid Argument

As the previous examples illustrate, different claim types often serve as building blocks for larger arguments. We ask you now to consider a more extended example. Read the following op-ed piece arguing the proposal claim that "the New York City Council should ban car alarms." Note how the reasons are different claim type subarguments that develop the overall proposal claim.

As you can see, the thesis of Friedman's op-ed piece is a proposal claim, and the article follows the typical problem-solution structure of proposal arguments. Although the whole argument follows a proposal shape, the individual pieces—the various subarguments that support the main argument—comprise different kinds of claim types with their own characteristic structures.

All That Noise for Nothing

AARON FRIEDMAN

Main proposal claim: City Council should ban car alarms

Early next year, the New York City Council is supposed to hold a final hearing on legislation that would silence the most hated of urban noises: the car alarm. With similar measures having failed in the past, and with Mayor Michael R. Bloomberg withholding his support for the latest bill, let's hope the Council does right by the citizens it represents.

Reason 1: A definitional claim supported with examples: Car alarms belong in the category of things that harass.

Every day, car alarms harass thousands of New Yorkers—rousing sleepers, disturbing readers, interrupting conversations and contributing to quality-of-life concerns that propel many weary residents to abandon the city for the suburbs. According to the Census Bureau, more New Yorkers are now bothered by traffic noise, including car alarms, than by any other aspect of city life, including crime or the condition of schools.

So there must be a compelling reason for us to endure all this aggravation, right? Amazingly, no. Many car manufacturers, criminologists and

Reason 2: An evaluation claim

insurers agree that car alarms are ineffective. When the nonprofit Highway Loss Data Institute surveyed insurance-claims data from 73 million vehicles nationwide in 1997, they concluded that cars with alarms "show no overall reduction in theft losses" compared with cars without alarms.

Criteria and evidence supporting the evaluation claim

There are two reasons they don't prevent theft. First, the vast majority of blaring sirens are false alarms, set off by passing traffic, the jostling of urban life or nothing at all. City dwellers quickly learn to disregard these cars crying wolf; a recent national survey by the Progressive Insurance Company found that fewer than 1 percent of respondents would call the police upon hearing an alarm.

5   In 1992, a car alarm industry spokesman, Darrell Issa (if you know his name that's because he would later spearhead the recall of Gov. Gray Davis in California), told the New York City Council that an alarm is effective "only in areas where the sound causes the dispatch of the police or attracts the owner's attention." In New York, this just doesn't happen.

Car alarms also fail for a second reason: they are easy to disable. Most stolen cars are taken by professional car thieves, and they know how to deactivate an alarm in just a few seconds.

Reason 3: A causal claim developed with causal links

Perversely, alarms can encourage more crime than they prevent. The New York Police Department, in its 1994 booklet "Police Strategy No. 5," explains how alarms (which "frequently go off for no apparent reason") can shatter the sense of civility that makes a community safe. As one of the "signs that no one cares," the department wrote, car alarms "invite both further disorder and serious crime."

I've seen some of my neighbors in Washington Heights illustrate this by taking revenge on alarmed cars: puncturing tires, even throwing a toaster oven through a windshield. False alarms enrage otherwise lawful citizens, and alienate the very people car owners depend on to call the police. In other words, car alarms work about as well as fuzzy dice at deterring theft while irritating entire neighborhoods.

Humorous resemblance claim sums up problem

Main proposal claim, restated as evalution claim and supported by three criteria

The best solution is to ban them, as proposed by the sponsors of the City Council legislation, John Liu and Eva Moskowitz. The police could simply ticket or tow offending cars. This would be a great improvement over the current laws, which include limiting audible alarms to three minutes—something that has proved to be nearly impossible to enforce.

10   Car owners could easily comply: more than 50 car alarm installation shops throughout the city have already pledged to disable alarms at no cost, according to a survey by the Center for Automotive Security Innovation.

And there is a viable alternative. People worried about protecting their cars can buy what are called silent engine immobilizers. Many European cars and virtually every new General Motors and Ford vehicle use the technology, in which a computer chip in the ignition key communicates with the engine. Without the key, the only way to steal the car is to tow it away, something most thieves don't have the time for. In the meantime, the rest of us could finally get some sleep.

Thus writers enlist other claim type subarguments in building main arguments. This knowledge can help you increase your flexibility and effectiveness as an arguer. In the following chapters in Part Four, we discuss each of the claim types in more detail, showing how they work and how you can develop skills and strategies for supporting each type of claim.

For additional writing, reading, and research resources, go to www.mycomplab.com

Definition and Resemblance Arguments

11

Case 1 Is Our Love of Oil Like Adam and Eve's Love of the Apple?

This political cartoon by Pulitzer Prize–winning cartoonist Michael Ramirez uses a resemblance argument to link our desire for petroleum to Adam and Eve's desire for the apple. This analogy creates a thoughtful lens for viewing our love affair with SUVs and other gas-guzzling vehicles. Particularly, it raises questions like these: How was life during the era of cheap oil like Paradise? To what extent are Americans "seduced" by gasoline? Is the cartoonist correct in suggesting a theological dimension to the energy crisis?

"AS A MATTER OF FACT, WE JUST BOUGHT ANOTHER SUV...."

Case 2 Is a Frozen Embryo a Person or Property?

An infertile couple conceived several embryos in a test tube and then froze the fertilized embryos for future use. During the couple's divorce, they disagreed about the disposition of the embryos. The woman wanted to use the frozen embryos to try to get pregnant, and the man wanted to destroy them. When the courts were asked to decide what should be done with the embryos, several questions of definition arose: Should the frozen embryos be categorized as "persons," thus becoming analogous to children in custody disputes? Or should they be divided up as "property," with the man getting half and the woman getting the other half? Or should a new legal category be created for them that regards them as more than property but less than actual persons? The judge decided that frozen embryos "are not, strictly speaking, either 'persons' or 'property,' but occupy an interim category that entitles them to special respect because of their potential for human life."*

Arguments about definition or resemblance concern disputes about what category something belongs to, either directly by definition or indirectly or metaphorically through comparison or resemblance. They are among the most common argument types you will encounter. In this chapter you will learn to:

- Analyze questions about the category to which something belongs
- Use criteria-match reasoning to construct your own definition arguments
- Use reasoning about precedents or analogies to construct your own resemblance arguments

An Overview of Definition and Resemblance Arguments

Definition and resemblance arguments occur whenever you claim that a particular person, thing, act, or phenomenon should be identified with a certain category. Here are some examples:

Claims Involving Categories

Claim	This specific phenomenon ...	... belongs to (or is similar to) this category
Piping loud rap music into a prison cell twenty-four hours a day constitutes torture.	Constant, loud rap music	Torture
Graffiti is often art, rather than vandalism.	Graffiti	Art (not vandalism)
Women's obsession with thinness serves the same cultural function as footbinding in ancient China.	Women's obsession with thinness	Footbinding in ancient China

Much is at stake when we place things into categories because the category that something belongs to can have real consequences. Naming the category that something belongs to makes an implicit mini-argument.

---

*See Vincent F. Stempel, "Procreative Rights in Assisted Reproductive Technology: Why the Angst?" *Albany Law Review* 62 (1999), 1187.

Consequences Resulting from Categorical Claims

To appreciate the consequences of categorical claims, consider the competing categories proposed for whales in the international controversy over commercial whaling. What category does a whale belong to? Some arguers might say that "whales are sacred animals," implying that their intelligence, beauty, grace, and power mean they should never be killed. Others might argue that "whales are a renewable food resource" like tuna, crabs, cattle, and chickens. This category implies that we can harvest whales for food the same way we harvest tuna for tuna fish sandwiches or cows for beef. Still others might argue that "whales are an endangered species"—a category that argues for the preservation of whale stocks but not necessarily for a ban on controlled hunting of individual whales. Each of these whaling arguments places whales in a separate, different category that implicitly urges the reader to adopt that category's perspective on whaling.

Significant consequences can also result from resemblance claims. Consider the way that media analysts tried to make sense of the September 11, 2001, terrorist attacks on the World Trade Center and the Pentagon by comparing them to different kinds of previous events. Some commentators said, "The September 11 attacks are like Timothy McVeigh's bombing of the Alfred P. Murrah Federal Building in Oklahoma City in 1995"—an argument that framed the terrorists as criminals who must be brought to justice. Others said, "The September 11 attacks are like the 1941 Japanese attack on Pearl Harbor"—an argument suggesting that the United States should declare war on some as-yet-to-be-defined enemy. Still others said, "The September 11 attacks are like an occasionally disastrous earthquake or an epidemic," arguing that terrorists will exist as long as the right conditions breed them and that it is useless to fight them using the strategies of conventional war. Under this analogy, the "war on terror" is a metaphorical war like the "war on poverty" or the "war against cancer." Clearly, each of these resemblance claims had high-stakes consequences. In 2001, the Pearl Harbor claim prevailed, and the United States went to war, first in Afghanistan and then in Iraq. Many critics of these wars continue to say that war is an inappropriate strategy for fighting the "disease of terrorism."

The Rule of Justice: Things in the Same Category Should Be Treated the Same Way

As you can see, the category we place something into—either directly through definition or indirectly through comparison—can have significant implications for people's actions or beliefs. To ensure fairness, philosophers refer to the *rule of justice*, which states that "beings in the same essential category should be treated in the same way." For example, the problem of how the courts should treat the users or sellers of marijuana depends on the category marijuana belongs to. Marijuana might be placed in the same category as tobacco and alcohol, in which case the possession and sale of marijuana would be legal but subject to regulation and taxes. Or marijuana could be placed in the same category as meth, cocaine, and heroin; in this case, it would be an illegal drug subject to criminal prosecution. Some states have placed marijuana in the same category as penicillin and insulin, making it a legal drug so long as it is obtained from a licensed dispensary with a doctor's prescription. Many states are not happy with any of these categories and are trying to define marijuana in some fourth way.

Such "rule of justice" issues occur regularly. Consider some more examples: Fans of first-person-shooter games have a stake in whether *Grand Theft Auto* or *Postal 2* is in the same category as a slasher film (in which case it is constitutionally protected free speech) or—as claimed by opponents of violent video games in a recent Supreme Court case—in the same category as pornography or even child pornography. If defined as child pornography, violent video games could be banned outright; if defined as pornography but not child pornography, their sale could be restricted to those eighteen and older. At a more familiar level, suppose your professor says that absence from an exam can be excused for emergencies only. How would you define "emergency"? Is attending your best friend's wedding an "emergency"? How about missing an exam because your

EXAMINING VISUAL ARGUMENTS

Claims about Categories (Definition or Resemblance)

When airport security introduced new, full-body X-ray scanners, persons who opted out of the scanner check were subject to "enhanced TSA pat downs." The topic of enhanced pat-downs became fodder for late-night comedy shows and cartoonists. In the first cartoon, Andy Marlette, cartoonist for the *Pensacola News Journal*, creates a resemblance argument comparing a grown male traveler upset by an enhanced pat-down to a child in a sex-abuse therapy session. In the second cartoon, Pat Begley, a cartoonist for Utah's *Salt Lake Tribune*, plays with definition arguments about waterboarding and rape. What is each cartoonist's attitude toward the TSA pat-downs? How does each cartoon work visually and conceptually to make its argument in the enhanced pat-down controversy?

car wouldn't start? Although your interests might be best served by a broad definition of emergency, your professor might prefer a narrow definition, which would permit fewer exemptions.

The rule of justice becomes especially hard to apply when we consider contested cases marked by growth or slow change through time. At what point does a child become an adult? When does a binge drinker become an alcoholic, an Internet poker player a compulsive gambler, or a fetus a human person? Although we may be able arbitrarily to choose a particular point and declare that "adult" means someone at least eighteen years old or that "human person" means a fetus at conception, or at three months, or at birth, in the everyday world the distinction between child and adult, between fetus and person, between Friday-night poker playing and compulsive gambling seems an evolution, not a sudden and definitive step. Nevertheless, our language requires an abrupt shift between categories. In short, applying the rule of justice often requires us to adopt a digital approach to reality (switches are either on or off, either a fetus is a human person or it is not), whereas our sense of life is more analogical (there are numerous gradations between on and off; there are countless shades of gray between black and white).

As we can see from the preceding examples, the promise of language to structure what psychologist William James called "the buzz and confusion of the world" into an orderly set of categories turns out to be elusive. In most category debates, an argument, not a quick trip to the dictionary, is required to settle the matter.

■ ■ ■   **FOR CLASS DISCUSSION**   Applying the Rule of Justice

Suppose your landlord decides to institute a "no pets" rule. The rule of justice requires that all pets have to go—not just your neighbor's barking dog, but also Mrs. Brown's cat, the kids' hamster downstairs, and your own pet tarantula. That is, all these animals have to go, unless you can argue that some of them are not "pets" for purposes of the landlord's "no pets" rule.

1. Working in small groups or as a whole class, define *pets* by establishing the criteria an animal would have to meet to be included in the category "pets." Consider your landlord's "no pets" rule as the cultural context for your definition.
2. Based on your criteria, which of the following animals is definitely a pet that would have to be removed from the apartment? Based on your criteria, which animals could you exclude from the "no pets" rule? How would you make your argument to your landlord?
   - a German shepherd
   - a small housecat
   - a tiny, well-trained lapdog
   - a gerbil in a cage
   - a canary
   - a tank of tropical fish
   - a tarantula

Types of Definition Arguments

Unlike resemblance arguments, which assert that one phenomenon is like another, definition arguments make a more direct claim: they argue that a disputed phenomenon is (or is not) a member of a certain category. Because such disputes always depend on the category that something belongs to, they are sometimes called categorical arguments. Such arguments can be divided into two kinds:

1. **Simple categorical arguments,** in which the writer and an audience already agree on the definition of the category, and
2. **Definition arguments,** in which there is a dispute about the boundaries of the category and hence of its definition.

Simple Categorical Arguments

A categorical argument can be said to be "simple" if there is no disagreement about the definition of the category. For example, suppose you argue that regular milk is healthier than soy milk because soy milk is not calcium-rich. Your supporting reason ("soy milk is not calcium-rich") is a simple categorical claim. You assume that everyone agrees on what *calcium-rich* means; the point of contention is whether soy milk does or does not contain calcium.

As shown in the following chart, the basic procedure for supporting (or rebutting) a simple categorical claim is to supply examples and other data that show how the contested phenomenon fits or doesn't fit into the category:

Strategies for Supporting or Rebutting Simple Categorical Claims

Categorical Claim	Strategies for Supporting Claim	Strategies for Rebutting Claim
Joe is too bossy.	Show examples of his bossy behavior (for example, his poor listening skills, his shouting at people, or his making decisions without asking the committee).	Show counterexamples revealing his ability to listen and create community; reinterpret bossiness as leadership behavior, putting Joe in better light.
Low-carb diets are dangerous.	Cite studies showing the dangers; explain how low-carb diets produce dangerous substances in the body; explain their harmful effects.	Show design problems in the scientific studies; cite studies with different findings; cite counter examples of people who lost weight on low-carb diets with no bad health effects.
Little Green Footballs is a conservative blog.	Give examples of the conservative views it promotes; show the conservative leanings of pundits often cited on the blog.	Give examples from the blog that don't fit neatly into a conservative perspective.

■ ■ ■   **FOR CLASS DISCUSSION**   Supporting and Rebutting Categorical Claims

Working individually or in small groups, consider how you would support the following categorical claims. What examples or other data would convince readers that the specified case fits within the named category? Then discuss ways you might rebut each claim.

1. Bottled water is environmentally unfriendly. [That is, bottled water belongs in the category of "environmentally unfriendly things."]
2. Nelly is a gangsta rapper.
3. Americans today are obsessed with their appearance. [That is, Americans belong in the category of "people obsessed with their appearance."]
4. Barack Obama is a centrist, not a socialist.
5. Competitive cheerleading is physically risky.   ■ ■ ■

Definition Arguments

Simple categorical arguments morph into definition arguments whenever stakeholders disagree about the boundaries of a category. Suppose in the previous exercise that you had said about Nelly, "Well, that depends on how you define 'gangsta rapper.'" The need to define the term "gangsta rapper" adds a new layer of complexity to your arguments about Nelly. To understand full-blown definition arguments, one must distinguish between cases where definitions are *needed* and cases where definitions are *disputed.* Many arguments require a definition of key terms. If you are arguing, for example, that therapeutic cloning might lead to cures for various diseases, you would probably need to define *therapeutic cloning* and distinguish it from *reproductive cloning.* Writers regularly define key words for their readers by providing synonyms, by citing a dictionary definition, by offering their own definition, or by some other means.

In the rest of this chapter, we focus on arguments in which the meaning of a key term is disputed. Consider, for example, the environmental controversy over the definition of *wetland.* Section 404 of the federal Clean Water Act provides for federal protection of wetlands, but it leaves the task of defining *wetland* to administrative agencies and the courts. Currently, about 5 percent of the land surface of the contiguous forty-eight states is potentially affected by the wetlands provision, and 75 percent of this land is privately owned. Efforts to define *wetland* have created a battleground between pro-environment and pro-development (or pro–private property rights) groups. Farmers, homeowners, and developers often want a narrow definition of wetlands so that more property is available for commercial or private use. Environmentalists favor a broad definition in order to protect different habitat types and maintain the environmental safeguards that wetlands provide (control of water pollution, spawning grounds for aquatic species, floodwater containment, and so forth).

The problem is that defining *wetland* is tricky. For example, one federal regulation defines a wetland as any area that has a saturated ground surface for twenty-one consecutive days during the year. But how would you apply this law to a pine flatwood ecosystem that was wet for ten days this year but thirty days last year? And how should the courts react to lawsuits claiming that the regulation itself is either too broad or too narrow? One can see why the wetlands controversy provides hefty incomes for lawyers and congressional lobbyists.

The Criteria-Match Structure of Definition Arguments

As the wetlands example suggests, definition arguments usually have a two-part structure—(1) a definition part that tries to establish the boundaries of the category (What do we mean by *wetland*?) and (2) a match part that argues whether a given case meets that definition (Does this thirty-acre parcel of land near Swan Lake meet the criteria for a wetland?). To describe this structure, we use the term *criteria-match*. Here is an example:

> **Definition issue:** In a divorce proceeding, is a frozen embryo a "person" rather than "property"?
>
> **Criteria part:** What criteria must be met for something to be a "person"?
>
> **Match part:** Does a frozen embryo meet these criteria?

Developing the Criteria-Match Structure for a Definition Argument

To show how a definition issue can be developed into a claim with supporting reasons, let's look more closely at this example:

> **Definition issue:** For purposes of my feeling good about buying my next pair of running shoes, is the Hercules Shoe Company a socially responsible company?
>
> **Criteria part:** What criteria must be met for a company to be deemed "socially responsible"?
>
> **Match part:** Does the Hercules Shoe Company meet these criteria?

Let's suppose you work for a consumer information group that wishes to encourage patronage of socially responsible companies while boycotting irresponsible ones. Your group's first task is to define *socially responsible company*. After much discussion and research, your group establishes three criteria that a company must meet to be considered socially responsible:

> *Your definition:* A company is socially responsible if it (1) avoids polluting the environment, (2) sells goods or services that contribute to the well-being of the community, and (3) treats its workers justly.

The criteria section of your argument would explain and illustrate these criteria.

The match part of the argument would then try to persuade readers that a specific company does or does not meet the criteria. A typical thesis statement might be as follows:

Your thesis statement: Although the Hercules Shoe Company is nonpolluting and provides a socially useful product, it is not a socially responsible company because it treats workers unjustly.

Toulmin Framework for a Definition Argument

Here is how the core of the preceding Hercules definition argument could be displayed in Toulmin terms. Note how the reason and grounds constitute the match argument while the warrant and backing constitute the criterion argument.

Toulmin Analysis of the Hercules Shoe Company Argument

ENTHYMEME

CLAIM The Hercules Shoe Company is not a socially responsible company

REASON because it treats workers unjustly.

GROUNDS

Evidence of unjust treatment:

- Evidence that the company manufactures its shoes in East Asian sweatshops

- Evidence of the inhumane conditions in these shops

- Evidence of hardships imposed on displaced American workers

CONDITIONS OF REBUTTAL

Attacking reasons and grounds

- Possible counter evidence that the shops maintain humane working conditions

- Possible questioning of statistical data about hardships on displaced workers

WARRANT

Socially responsible companies treat workers justly.

BACKING

- Arguments showing that just treatment of workers is right in principle and also benefits society

- Arguments that capitalism helps society as a whole only if workers achieve a reasonable standard of living, have time for leisure, and are not exploited

CONDITIONS OF REBUTTAL

Attacking warrant and backing

Justice needs to be considered from an emerging nation's standpoint:

- The wages paid workers are low by American standards but are above average by East Asian standards.

- Displacement of American workers is part of the necessary adjustment of adapting to a global economy and does not mean that a company is unjust.

As this Toulmin schema illustrates, the warrant and backing constitute the criteria section of the argument by stating and defending "just treatment of workers" as a criterion for a socially responsible company. The reason and grounds constitute the match section of the argument by arguing that the Hercules Shoe Company does not treat its workers justly. How much emphasis you need to place on justifying each criterion and supporting each match depends on your audience's initial beliefs. The conditions of rebuttal help you imagine alternative views and see places where opposing views need to be acknowledged and rebutted.

■ ■ ■ **FOR CLASS DISCUSSION**   Identifying Criteria and Match Issues
Consider the following definition claims. Working individually or in small groups, identify the criteria issue and the match issue for each of the following claims.

> **Definition issue:** A Honda assembled in Ohio is (is not) an American-made car.
>
> **Criteria part:** What criteria have to be met before a car can be called "American made"?
>
> **Match part:** Does a Honda assembled in Ohio meet these criteria?

1. American Sign Language is (is not) a "foreign language" for purposes of a college graduation requirement.
2. The violence in *Grand Theft Auto* is (is not) constitutionally protected free speech.
3. Bungee jumping from a crane is (is not) a "carnival amusement ride" subject to state safety inspections.
4. For purposes of a state sales tax on "candy," a Twinkie is (is not) candy.
5. A skilled video game player is (is not) a true athlete.

■ ■ ■

Kinds of Definitions

In this section we discuss two methods of definition: Aristotelian and operational.

Aristotelian Definitions

Aristotelian definitions, regularly used in dictionaries, define a term by placing it within the next larger class or category and then showing the specific attributes that distinguish the term from other terms within the same category. For example, according to a legal dictionary, *robbery* is "the felonious taking of property" (next larger category) that differs from other acts of theft because it seizes property "through violence or intimidation." Legal dictionaries often provide specific examples to show the boundaries of the term. Here is one example:

> There is no robbery unless force or fear is used to overcome resistance. Thus, surreptitiously picking a man's pocket or snatching something from him without resistance on his part is *larceny,* but not robbery.

Many states specify degrees of robbery with increasingly heavy penalties. For example, *armed robbery* involves the use of a weapon to threaten the victim. In all cases, *robbery* is distinguished from the lesser crime of *larceny,* in which no force or intimidation is involved.

As you can see, an Aristotelian definition of a term identifies specific attributes or criteria that enable you to distinguish it from other members of the next larger class. We created an Aristotelian definition in our example about socially responsible companies. A socially responsible company, we said, is any company (next larger class) that meets three criteria: (1) it doesn't pollute the environment; (2) it creates goods or services that promote the well-being of the community; and (3) it treats its workers justly.

In constructing Aristotelian definitions, you may find it useful to employ the concept of accidental, necessary, and sufficient criteria.

- An *accidental criterion* is a usual but not essential feature of a concept. For example, armed robbers frequently wear masks, but wearing a mask is an accidental criterion because it has no bearing on the definition of *robbery.* In our example about socially responsible companies, "makes regular contributions to charities" might be an accidental criterion; most socially responsible companies contribute to charities, but some do not. And many socially irresponsible companies also contribute to charities—often as a public relations ploy.

- A *necessary criterion* is an attribute that *must* be present for something to belong to the category being defined. To be guilty of robbery rather than larceny, a thief must have used direct force or intimidation. The use of force is thus a necessary criterion for robbery. However, for a robbery to occur, another criterion must also be met: the robber must also take property from the victim.

- *Sufficient criteria* are all the criteria that must be present for something to belong to the category being defined. Together, the use of force plus the taking of property are *sufficient criteria* for an act to be classified as robbery.

Consider again our defining criteria for a "socially responsible" company: (1) the company must avoid polluting the environment; (2) the company must create goods or services that contribute to the well-being of the community; **and** (3) the company must treat its workers justly. In this definition, each criterion is necessary, but none of the criteria alone is sufficient. In other words, to be defined as socially responsible, a company must meet all three criteria at once, as the word *and* signals. It is not enough for a company to be nonpolluting (a necessary but not sufficient criterion); if that company makes a shoddy product or treats its workers unjustly, it fails to meet the other necessary criteria and can't be deemed socially responsible. Because no one criterion by itself is sufficient, all three criteria together must be met before a company can be deemed socially responsible.

In contrast, consider the following definition of *sexual harassment* as established by the U.S. Equal Employment Opportunity Commission in its 1980 guidelines:

> Unwelcome sexual advances, requests for sexual favors, and other verbal or physical conduct of a sexual nature constitute sexual harassment when (1) submission to such conduct is made either explicitly or implicitly a term or condition of an individual's employment,

(2) submission to or rejection of such conduct by an individual is used as the basis for employment decisions affecting such individual, **or** (3) such conduct has the purpose or effect of unreasonably interfering with an individual's work performance or creating an intimidating, hostile, or offensive working environment.*

Here each of these criteria is sufficient, but none is necessary. In other words, an act constitutes sexual harassment if any one of the three criteria is satisfied, as the word *or* indicates.

■ ■ ■ **FOR CLASS DISCUSSION** Working with Criteria
Working individually or in small groups, try to determine whether each of the following is a necessary criterion, a sufficient criterion, an accidental criterion, or no criterion for defining the indicated concept. Be prepared to explain your reasoning and to account for differences in points of view.

Criterion	Concept to Be Defined
Presence of gills	Fish
Profane and obscene language	R-rated movie
Line endings that form a rhyming pattern	Poem
Disciplining a child by spanking	Child abuse
Diet that excludes meat	Vegetarian
Killing another human being	Murder
Good sex life	Happy marriage

Operational Definitions

In some rhetorical situations, particularly those arising in the physical and social sciences, writers need precise, *operational definitions* that can be measured empirically and are not subject to problems of context and disputed criteria. A social scientist studying the effects of television on aggression in children needs a precise, measurable definition of *aggression.* Typically, the scientist might measure "aggression" by counting the number of blows a child gives to an inflatable bobo doll over a fifteen-minute period when other play options are available. In our wetlands example, a federal authority created an operational definition of *wetland:* a wetland is a parcel of land that has a saturated ground surface for twenty-one consecutive days during the year.

---

*Quoted in Stephanie Riger, "Gender Dilemmas in Sexual Harassment Policies and Procedures," *American Psychologist* 46 (May 1991), 497–505.

Such operational definitions are useful because they are precisely measurable, but they are also limited because they omit criteria that may be unmeasurable but important. Thus, we might ask whether it is adequate to define a *superior student* as someone with a 3.5 GPA or higher or a *successful sex-education program* as one that results in a 25 percent reduction in teenage pregnancies. What important aspects of a superior student or a successful sex-education program are not considered in these operational definitions?

Conducting the Criteria Part of a Definition Argument

In constructing criteria to define your contested term, you can either research how others have defined your term or make your own definitions. If you take the first approach, you turn to standard or specialized dictionaries, judicial opinions, or expert testimony to establish a definition based on the authority of others. A lawyer defining a wetland based on twenty-one consecutive days of saturated ground surface would be taking the first approach, using federal regulation as his or her source. The other approach is to use your own critical thinking to make your own definition, thereby defining the contested term yourself. Our definition of a socially responsible company, specifying three criteria, is an example of an individual's own definition created through critical thinking. This section explains these approaches in more detail.

Approach 1: Research How Others Have Defined the Term

When you take this approach, you search for authoritative definitions acceptable to your audience yet favorable to your case. When the state of Washington tried to initiate a new sales tax on candy, lawyers and legislators wrestled with a definition. They finally created the following statute available to the public on a government Web site:

What Is the Definition of Candy?

"Candy" is a preparation of sugar, honey, or other natural or artificial sweeteners combined with chocolate, fruits, nuts, or other ingredients or flavorings in the form of bars, drops, or pieces. Candy does not require refrigeration, and does not include flour as an ingredient.

"Natural or artificial sweeteners" include, but are not limited to, high fructose corn syrup, dextrose, invert sugar, sucrose, fructose, sucralose, saccharin, aspartame, stevia, fruit juice concentrates, molasses, evaporated cane juice, and rice syrup.

"Flour" includes any flour made from a grain, such as wheat flour, rice flour, and corn flour.

Items that require "refrigeration," either before or after opening, are not candy. For example, popsicles, ice cream bars, and fruits in sweetened syrups are not candy.

This definition made it easy for state officials to exclude from the "candy tax" any snack food that contained flour. Thus Twinkies, Froot Loops cereal, and chocolate-covered pretzels were exempt from the tax. But considerable debate occurred over cough drops and halvah (a traditional dessert in India and Mediterranean countries). The state decided to exclude cough drops if the package contained a "drug facts" panel and a list of active ingredients. (Such cough drops were then classified as "over the counter drugs.") The state ruled that nut-butter halvah was taxable but that flour-based halvah was not taxable; even so, many kinds of halvah didn't fit neatly into these two categories.

Turning to established definitions is thus a first step for many definition arguments. Common sources of these definitions are specialized dictionaries such as *Black's Law Dictionary*, which form a standard part of the reference holdings of any library. Other sources of specialized definitions are state and federal appellate court decisions, legislative and administrative statutes, and scholarly articles examining a given definition conflict. Lawyers use this research strategy exhaustively in preparing court briefs. They begin by looking at the actual text of laws as passed by legislatures or written by administrative authorities. Then they look at all the court cases in which the laws have been tested and examine the ways courts have refined legal definitions and applied them to specific cases. Using these refined definitions, lawyers then apply them to their own case at hand.

If your research uncovers definitions that seem ambiguous or otherwise unfavorable to your case, you can sometimes appeal to the "original intentions" of those who defined the term. For example, if a scientist is dissatisfied with definitions of *wetlands* based on consecutive days of saturated ground surface, she might proceed as follows: "The original intention of Congress in passing the Clean Water Act was to preserve the environment." What Congress intended, she could then claim, was to prevent development of those wetland areas that provide crucial habitat for wildlife or that inhibit water pollution. She could then propose an alternative definition based on criteria other than consecutive days of ground saturation.

Approach 2: Create Your Own Extended Definition*

Often, however, you need to create your own definition of the contested term. An effective strategy is to establish initial criteria for your contested term by thinking of hypothetical cases that obviously fit the category you are trying to define and then by altering one or more variables until the hypothetical case obviously doesn't fit the category. You can then test and refine your criteria by applying them to borderline cases. For example, suppose you work at a homeless agency where you overhear street people discuss an incident that strikes you as potential "police brutality." You wonder whether you should write to your local paper to bring attention to the incident.

---

*The defining strategies and collaborative exercises in this section are based on the work of George Hillocks and his research associates at the University of Chicago. See George Hillocks Jr., Elizabeth A. Kahn, and Larry R. Johannessen, "Teaching Defining Strategies as a Mode of Inquiry: Some Effects on Student Writing," *Research in the Teaching of English* 17 (October 1983), 275–84. See also Larry R. Johannessen, Elizabeth A. Kahn, and Carolyn Calhoun Walter, *Designing and Sequencing Prewriting Activities* (Urbana, IL: NCTE, 1982).

A Possible Case of Police Brutality

Two police officers confront an inebriated homeless man who is shouting obscenities on a street corner. The officers tell the man to quiet down and move on, but he keeps shouting obscenities. When the officers attempt to put the man into the police car, he resists and takes a wild swing at one of the officers. As eyewitnesses later testified, this officer shouted obscenities back at the drunk man, pinned his arms behind his back in order to handcuff him, and lifted him forcefully by the arms. The man screamed in pain and was later discovered to have a dislocated shoulder. Is this officer guilty of police brutality?

To your way of thinking, this officer seems guilty: An inebriated man is too uncoordinated to be a threat in a fight, and two police officers ought to be able to arrest him without dislocating his shoulder. But a friend argues that because the man took a swing at the officer, the police were justified in using force. The dislocated shoulder was simply an accidental result of using justified force.

To make your case, you need to develop a definition of "police brutality." You can begin by creating a hypothetical case that is obviously an instance of "police brutality":

A Clear Case of Police Brutality

A police officer confronts a drunk man shouting obscenities and begins hitting him in the face with his police baton. *[This is an obvious incidence of police brutality because the officer intentionally tries to hurt the drunk man without justification; hitting him with the baton is not necessary for making an arrest or getting the man into the police car.]*

You could then vary the hypothetical case until it is clearly *not* an instance of police brutality.

Cases That Are Clearly Not Police Brutality

Case 1: The police officer handcuffs the drunk man, who, in being helped into the police car, accidentally slips on the curb and dislocates his arm while falling. *[Here the injury occurs accidentally; the police officer does not act intentionally and is not negligent.]*

Case 2: The police officer confronts an armed robber fleeing from a scene and tackles him from behind, wrestling the gun away from him. In this struggle, the officer pins the robber's arm behind his back with such force that the robber's shoulder is dislocated. *[Here aggressive use of force is justified because the robber was armed, dangerous, and resisting arrest.]*

Using these hypothetical cases, you decide that the defining criteria for police brutality are (1) *intention* and (2) use of *excessive force*—that is, force beyond what was required by the immediate situation. After more contemplation, you are convinced that the officer was guilty of police brutality and have a clearer idea of how to make your argument. Here is how you might write the "match" part of your argument:

Match Argument Using Your Definition

If we define police brutality as the *intentional* use of *excessive* force, then the police officer is guilty. His action was intentional because he was purposefully responding to the homeless man's drunken swing and was angry enough to be shouting obscenities back at the drunk (according to eyewitnesses). Second, he used excessive force in applying the handcuffs. A drunk man taking a wild swing hardly poses a serious danger to two police officers. Putting handcuffs on the drunk may have been justified, but lifting the man's arm violently enough to dislocate a shoulder indicates excessive force. The officer lifted the man's arms violently not because he needed to but because he was angry, and acting out of anger is no justification for that violence. In fact, we can charge police officers with "police brutality" precisely to protect us from being victims of police anger. It is the job of the court system to punish us, not the police's job. Because this officer acted intentionally and applied excessive force out of anger, he should be charged with police brutality.

The strategy we have demonstrated—developing criteria by imagining hypothetical cases that clearly do and do not belong to the contested category—gives you a systematic procedure for developing your own definition for your argument.

■ ■ ■ **FOR CLASS DISCUSSION**   Developing a Definition

1. Suppose you wanted to define the concept of *courage*. Working in groups, try to decide whether each of the following cases is an example of courage:
   a. A neighbor rushes into a burning house to rescue a child from certain death and emerges, coughing and choking, with the child in his arms. Is the neighbor courageous?
   b. A firefighter rushes into a burning house to rescue a child from certain death and emerges with the child in her arms. The firefighter is wearing protective clothing and a gas mask. When a newspaper reporter calls her courageous, she says, "Hey, this is my job." Is the firefighter courageous?
   c. A teenager rushes into a burning house to recover a memento given to him by his girlfriend, the first love of his life. Is the teenager courageous?
   d. A parent rushes into a burning house to save a trapped child. The fire marshal tells the parent to wait because there is no chance that the child can be reached from the first floor. The fire marshal wants to try cutting a hole in the roof to reach the child. The parent rushes into the house anyway and is burned to death. Was the parent courageous?
2. As you make your decisions on each of these cases, create and refine the criteria you use.
3. Make up your own series of controversial cases, like those given previously for "courage," for one or more of the following concepts:
   a. cruelty to animals
   b. child abuse
   c. true athlete
   d. sexual harassment
   e. free speech protected by the First Amendment

Then, using the strategy of making up hypothetical cases that do and do not belong to each category, construct a definition of your chosen concept.

Conducting the Match Part of a Definition Argument

In conducting a match argument, you need to supply examples and other evidence showing that your contested case does (does not) meet the criteria you established in your definition. In essence, you support the match part of your argument in much the same way you would support a simple categorical claim.

For example, if you were developing the argument that the Hercules Shoe Company is not socially responsible because it treats its workers unjustly, your match section would provide evidence of this injustice. You might supply data about the percentage of shoes produced in East Asia, about the low wages paid these workers, and about the working conditions in these factories. You might also describe the suffering of displaced American workers when Hercules closed its American factories and moved operations to Asia, where the labor is nonunion and cheap. The match section should also summarize and respond to opposing views.

Types of Resemblance Arguments

Whereas definition arguments claim that a particular phenomenon belongs to a certain category, resemblance arguments simply compare one thing to another. In general, there are two types of resemblance arguments:

1. **Arguments by analogy**, in which the arguer likens one thing to another by using a metaphor or imaginative comparison
2. **Arguments by precedent**, in which the arguer likens a current or proposed event or phenomenon to a previous event or phenomenon

We'll illustrate both types later in this section.

In both kinds of resemblance arguments, the arguer's intention is to transfer the audience's understanding of (or feelings about) the second thing back to the first. Thus when opponents of violent video games compare *Postal 2* to pornography, they intend to transfer the audience's disgust at pornography back to *Postal 2*'s particular kind of violence. The *logos* of resemblance arguments comes from their power to throw unexpected light on a contested phenomenon (seeing how gratuitous violence might be similar to pornography); the *pathos* comes from the audience's feelings, which are already attached to the second phenomenon (our disgust at exposing children to pornography). The risk of resemblance arguments is that the differences between the two things being compared are often so significant that the argument collapses under close examination.

Toulmin Framework for a Resemblance Argument

Like most other argument types, resemblance arguments can be analyzed using the Toulmin schema. Suppose you want to find a startling way to warn teenage girls away from excessive dieting. Simultaneously, you want to argue that excessive dieting is partially caused by a patriarchal construction of beauty that keeps women submissive and powerless. You decide to create a resemblance argument claiming that women's obsessive dieting is like footbinding in ancient China. This argument can be displayed in Toulmin terms as follows:

Toulmin Analysis of the Dieting Argument

ENTHYMEME

CLAIM Women's obsessive dieting in America serves the same harmful function as footbinding in ancient China

REASON because both practices keep women childlike, docile, dependent, and unthreatening to men.

GROUNDS

- Evidence that both practices make women childlike: The "perfect woman" is often made to seem childlike. (Men call beautiful women "dolls" or "babes.") Bound feet, covered with tiny slippers, are like children's feet; excessive dieting keeps women slim like pre-adolescent girls. (Fertility goddesses are fleshy; anorexia stops menstruation.)

- Evidence that both practices keep women weak or nonthreatening: Chinese women were physically maimed, unable to run or walk naturally. American women pursuing the ideal of thinness are psychologically maimed and often weakened by excessive dieting.

- Evidence that both practices make women satisfied with inferior positions in society so long as they are considered "pretty" or "beautiful": Footbinding indicated that the woman was upper class and didn't have to work. Dieting and pursuit of beauty (the expense of beauty products) reduce women's economic power.

POSSIBLE CONDITIONS OF REBUTTAL
Attacking the reason and grounds:

- Women who diet are concerned with health, not pursuit of beauty.

- Concern for healthy weight is "rational," not "obsessive."

- Thin women are often powerful athletes, not at all like Chinese victims of foot binding who can hardly walk.

- Dieting does not cause crippling deformity; a concern for beauty does not make a woman subordinate or satisfied with less pay.

- Dieting is a woman's choice—not something forced on her as a child.

WARRANT

Practices that are like ancient Chinese footbinding are bad.

BACKING

- Arguments that the subordinate position of women evidenced in both footbinding and obsession with weight is related to patriarchal construction of women's roles

- Arguments for why women should free themselves from patriarchal views

CONDITIONS OF REBUTTAL
Attacking the warrant and backing

- Perhaps arguments could be made that Chinese foot binding was not as repressive and patriarchal as the analogy implies (?). [We can't imagine a contemporary argument supporting footbinding.]

- Arguments supporting patriarchy and women's subordination

QUALIFIER: Perhaps the writer should say, *"Under certain conditions obsessive dieting can even seem like Chinese footbinding."*

For many audiences, the comparison of women's dieting to Chinese footbinding will have an immediate and powerful emotional effect perhaps causing them to see attitudes toward weight and food from a new, unsettling perspective. The analogy invites them to transfer their understanding of Chinese footbinding—which seems instantly repulsive and oppressive of women—to their understanding of obsessive concern for losing weight. Whereas social controls in ancient China were overt, the modern practice uses more subtle kinds of social controls, such as the influence of the fashion and beauty industry and peer pressure. But in both cases women feel forced to mold their bodies to a patriarchal standard of beauty—one that emphasizes soft curves, tiny waists, and daintiness rather than strength and power.

But this example also illustrates the dangers of resemblance arguments, which often ignore important differences or *disanalogies* between the terms of comparison. As the "conditions of rebuttal" show, there are many differences between dieting and footbinding. For example, the practice of foot binding was not a conscious choice of young Chinese girls, who were forced to have their feet wrapped at an early age. Dieting, on the other hand, is something one chooses, and it may reveal a healthy and rational choice rather than an obsession with appearance. When the practice degenerates to anorexia or bulimia, it becomes a mental disease, not a physical deformity forced on a girl in childhood. Thus a resemblance argument is usually open to refutation if a skeptic points out important disanalogies.

We now turn to the two types of resemblance arguments: analogy and precedent.

Arguments by Analogy

A common kind of resemblance argument uses analogies—imaginative kinds of comparisons often with subtle persuasive effects. If you don't like your new boss, you can say that she's like a Marine drill sergeant, the cowardly captain of a sinking ship, or a mother hen. Each of these analogies suggests a different management style, clarifying the nature of your dislike while conveying an emotional charge.

Sometimes, as in the "My boss is like a Marine drill sergeant" example, arguers use short, undeveloped analogies for quick rhetorical effect. At other times, arguers develop extended analogies that carry a substantial portion of the argument. As an example of an extended analogy, consider the following excerpt from a professor's argument opposing a proposal to require a writing proficiency exam for graduation. In the following portion of his argument, the professor compares development of writing skills to the development of physical fitness.

> A writing proficiency exam gives the wrong symbolic messages about writing. It suggests that writing is simply a skill, rather than an active way of thinking and learning. It suggests that once a student demonstrates proficiency then he or she doesn't need to do any more writing.
>
> Imagine two universities concerned with the physical fitness of their students. One university requires a junior-level physical fitness exam in which students must run a mile in less than 10 minutes, a fitness level it considers minimally competent. Students at this university see the physical fitness exam as a one-time hurdle. As many as 70 percent of them can pass the exam with no practice; another 10–20 percent need a few months' training; and a few hopeless couch potatoes must go through exhaustive remediation.

After passing the exam, any student can settle back into a routine of TV and potato chips having been certified as "physically fit."

The second university, however, believing in true physical fitness for its students, is not interested in minimal competency. Consequently, it creates programs in which its students exercise 30 minutes every day for the entire four years of the undergraduate curriculum. There is little doubt which university will have the most physically fit students. At the second university, fitness becomes a way of life with everyone developing his or her full potential. Similarly, if we want to improve our students' writing abilities, we should require writing in every course throughout the curriculum.

Thus analogies have the power to get an audience's attention like virtually no other persuasive strategy. But seldom are they sufficient in themselves to provide full understanding. At some point, with every analogy, you need to ask yourself, "How far can I legitimately go with this? At what point are the similarities between the two things I am comparing going to be overwhelmed by their dissimilarities?" Analogies are useful attention-getting devices, but they can conceal and distort as well as clarify.

If you choose to make an analogy argument, you will need to focus on the points of comparison that serve your purposes. In the preceding case, the writer's purpose is to argue that the goal of a writing program is to help students develop their full abilities as writers rather than meet minimalist standards. To keep this focus, the writer avoids the disanalogies between the two elements. (For example, writing requires the use of intellect and may differ substantially from physical fitness, which requires muscles and endurance.) Typically, then, in developing an analogy, writers keep the audience's attention only on the relevant similarities.

■ ■ ■ **FOR CLASS DISCUSSION** Developing Analogies

The following exercise will help you clarify how analogies function in the context of arguments. Working individually or in small groups, think of two analogies for each of the following topics. One analogy should urge readers toward a positive view of the topic; the other should urge a negative view. Write each of your analogies in the following one-sentence format:

_____ is like _____ : A, B, C … (in which the first term is the contested topic being discussed; the second term is the analogy; and A, B, and C are the points of comparison).

Example

Topic: Cramming for an exam
Negative analogy: Cramming for an exam is like pumping iron for ten hours straight to prepare for a weight-lifting contest: exhausting and counterproductive.
Positive analogy: Cramming for an exam is like carbohydrate loading before a big race: it gives your brain a full supply of facts and concepts, all fresh in your mind.

1. Using spanking to discipline children
2. Using racial profiling for airport security
3. Using steroids to increase athletic performance
4. Paying college athletes
5. Eating at fast-food restaurants

Arguments by Precedent

A second kind of resemblance argument uses precedent for its persuasive force. An argument by precedent tries to show that a current situation is like a past situation and that therefore a similar action or decision should be taken or reached. You can refute a precedence argument by showing that the present situation differs substantially from the past situation.

Precedentce arguments are very common. For example, during the debate about health care reform in the first year of Barack Obama's presidency, supporters of a single-payer, "Medicare-for-all" system pointed to Canada as a successful precedent. Supporters said that since a single-payer system was successful in Canada, it would also be successful in the United States. But opponents also used the Canadian precedent to attack a single-payer system. They pointed to problems in the Canadian system as a reason to reject a Medicare-for-all system in the United States.

A good example of an extended precedence argument can be found in an article entitled "The Perils of Ignoring History: Big Tobacco Played Dirty and Millions Died. How Similar Is Big Food?"* The authors argue that the food-processing industry is trying to avoid government regulations by employing the same "dirty tricks" used earlier by Big Tobacco. The authors show how Big Tobacco hired lobbyists to fight regulation, how it created clever advertising to make cigarette smoking seem cool, and how it sponsored its own research to cast doubt on data linking nicotine to lung cancer or asthma to secondhand smoke. The researchers argue that Big Food is now doing the same thing. Through lobbying efforts, coordinated lawsuits, and public relations campaigns, Big Food resists labeling ingredients in food products, casts doubt on scientific evidence about possible carcinogens in processed foods, and uses advertising to create a local, "family farm" image for Big Food. The researchers use this precedence argument to call for stricter government oversight of Big Food.

■ ■ ■ **FOR CLASS DISCUSSION** Using Claims of Precedent

1. Consider the following claims of precedent, and evaluate how effective you think each precedent might be in establishing the claim. How would you develop the argument? How would you cast doubt on it?
   a. To increase alumni giving to our university, we should put more funding into our football program. When University X went to postseason bowls for three years in a row, alumni donations to building programs and academics increased by 30 percent. We can expect the same increases here.
   b. Postwar democracy can be created successfully in Afghanistan because it was created successfully in Germany and Japan following World War II.
2. Advocates for "right to die" legislation legalizing active euthanasia under certain conditions often point to the Netherlands as a country where acceptance of euthanasia works effectively. Assume for the moment that your state legislature is considering a law legalizing euthanasia. Assume further that you are a research

---

*Kelly D. Brownell and Kenneth E. Warner, "The Perils of Ignoring History: Big Tobacco Played Dirty and Millions Died. How Similar Is Big Food?" *The Milbank Quarterly* 87.1 (2009), 259–294.

assistant working for a legislator who hasn't made up her mind how to vote on the issue. She has asked you to research the arguments for and against euthanasia based on the experience of the Netherlands. Working in small groups, make a list of research questions you would want to ask. Your long-range rhetorical goal is to use your research to support (or attack) the legalization of euthanasia.

WRITING ASSIGNMENT   A Definition Argument

The assignment for this chapter focuses on definition disputes about categories. Write an essay in which you argue that a borderline or contested case fits (or does not fit) within a given category. In the opening of your essay, introduce the borderline case you will examine and pose your definition question. In the first part of your argument, define the boundaries of your category (criteria) by reporting a definition used by others or by developing your own extended definition. In the second part of your argument (the match), show how your borderline case meets (or doesn't meet) your definition criteria.

Exploring Ideas

Ideally, in writing this argument you will join an ongoing conversation about a definition issue that interests you. What cultural and social issues that concern you involve disputed definitions? In the public arena, you are likely to find numerous examples simply by looking through news stories—for example, the disputes about defining "candy" in the Washington State sales tax controversy, about the definition of "torture" in interrogating terrorist suspects, or about definitions of "pornography" that might include ultra-violent video games. Often you can frame your own definition issues even if they aren't currently in the news. Is using TiVo to avoid TV commercials a form of theft? Is spanking a form of child abuse? Are cheerleaders athletes? Is flag burning protected free speech? Is a person who downloads instructions for making a bomb a terrorist? Are today's maximum-security prisons "cruel and unusual punishment"? Is Wal-Mart a socially responsible company? Can a model or beauty pageant winner (or a man) be a feminist?

If you have trouble discovering a local or national issue that interests you, you can create fascinating definition controversies among your classmates by asking whether certain borderline cases are "true" or "real" examples of some category: Are highly skilled video game players (race car drivers, synchronized swimmers, marbles players) true athletes? Is a gourmet chef (skilled furniture maker, tagger) a true artist? Is a chiropractor (acupuncturist, naturopathic physician) a "real doctor"? Working as a whole class or in small groups inside or outside class, create an argumentative discussion on one or more of these issues. Listen to the various voices in the controversy, and then write out your own argument.

You can also stimulate definition controversies by brainstorming borderline cases for such terms as *courage* (Is mountain climbing an act of courage?), *cruelty to animals* (Are rodeos [zoos, catch-and-release trout fishing, use of animals for medical research] cruelty to animals?), or *war crime* (Was the American firebombing of Tokyo in World War II a war crime?).

As you explore your definition issue, try to determine how others have defined your category. If no stable definition emerges from your search, create your own definition by deciding what criteria must be met for a contested case to fit within your category. Try using the strategy for creating criteria that we discussed on pages 235–236 with reference to police brutality. Once you have determined your criteria, freewrite for five or ten minutes, exploring whether your contested case meets each of the criteria.

Identifying Your Audience and Determining What's at Stake

Before drafting your argument, identify your targeted audience and determine what's at stake. Consider your responses to the following questions:

- What audience are you targeting? What background do they need to understand your issue? How much do they already care about it?
- Before they read your argument, what stance on your issue do you imagine them holding? What change do you want to bring about in their views?

Organization Plan 1: Definition Argument with Criteria and Match in Separate Sections

Introduce the issue and state your claim.	• Engage reader's interest in your definition issue and show why it is controversial or problematic. • Show what's at stake. • Provide background information needed by your audience. • State your claim.
Present your criteria.	• State and develop criterion 1. • State and develop criterion 2. • Continue with the rest of your criteria. • Anticipate and respond to possible objections to the criteria.
Present your match argument.	• Consider restating your claim for clarity. • Argue that your case meets (does not meet) criterion 1. • Argue that your case meets (does not meet) criterion 2. • Continue with the rest of your match argument. • Anticipate and respond to possible objections to the match argument.
Conclude.	• Perhaps sum up your argument. • Help reader return to the "big picture" of what's at stake. • End with something memorable.

- What will they find new or surprising about your argument?
- What objections might they raise? What counterarguments or alternative points of view will you need to address?
- Why does your argument matter? Who might be threatened or made uncomfortable by your views? What is at stake?

Organizing a Definition Argument

As you compose a first draft of your essay, you may find it helpful to know typical structures for definition arguments. There are two basic approaches, as shown in Organization Plans 1 and 2. You can either discuss the criteria and the match separately or interweave the discussion.

Questioning and Critiquing a Definition Argument

A powerful way to stimulate global revision of a draft is to role-play a skeptical audience. The following questions will help you strengthen your own argument or rebut

Organization Plan 2: Definition Argument with Criteria and Match Interwoven

Introduce the issue and state your claim.	• Engage reader's interest in your definition issue and show why it is problematic or controversial. • Show what's at stake. • Provide background information needed by your audience. • State your claim.
Present series of criterion-match arguments.	• State and develop criterion 1 and argue that your case meets (does not meet) the criterion. • State and develop criterion 2 and argue that your case meets (does not meet) the criterion. • Continue with the rest of your criterion-match arguments.
Respond to possible objections to your argument.	• Anticipate and summarize possible objections. • Respond to the objections through rebuttal or concession.
Conclude.	• Perhaps sum up your argument. • Help reader return to the "big picture" of what's at stake. • End with something memorable.

the definition arguments of others. In critiquing a definition argument, you need to appreciate its criteria-match structure because you can question your criteria argument, your match argument, or both.

Questioning Your Criteria

- Could a skeptic claim that your criteria are not the right ones? Could he or she offer different criteria or point out missing criteria?
- Could a skeptic point out possible bad consequences of accepting your criteria?
- Could a skeptic cite unusual circumstances that weaken your criteria?
- Could a skeptic point out bias or slant in your definition?

Questioning Your Match

- Could a skeptic argue that your examples or data don't meet the STAR criteria (see Chapter 5, pages 90–91) for evidence?
- Could a skeptic point out counterexamples or alternative data that cast doubt on your argument?
- Could a skeptic reframe the way you have viewed your borderline case? ∎

Our first reading, by student writer Arthur Knopf, grew out of his research into agricultural subsidies and the nutritional content of foods. It was written for the assignment on page 243.

Is Milk a Health Food?

ARTHUR KNOPF (STUDENT)

If asked to name a typical health food, most of us would put milk high on our lists. We've all seen the "Got Milk?" ads with their milk-mustached celebrities or the dairy product campaigns entitled "Milk, It Does a Body Good" or "Body By Milk." These ads, featuring well known athletes or trim celebrities, argue visually that milk helps you grow fit and strong. But if you define "health food" based on science rather than on marketing claims, and if you include in your definition of health food concerns for the planet as well as for individual bodies, then milk might not fit the category of health food at all.

My first criterion for a "health food" is that the food should have a scientifically supported health benefit with minimal risks. Based on the food pyramid from the United States Department of Agriculture (USDA), milk at first glance seems to fit this criterion. On the *MyPyramid* Web site the dairy group (milk, yogurt, cheese) is one of the essential components of a healthy diet (United States Dept. of Agriculture). All elements of the milk group provide calcium, which is important for healthy bones and the prevention of osteoporosis. Dairy products also provide important vitamins. But the Web site entry under the dairy group specifies in a footnote, "Choose fat-free or low-fat milk, yogurt, and cheese." One cup of whole milk, according to the Web site, contains 70 more calories than a cup of skim milk (147 calories compared to 83). The extra 70 calories are potentially harmful saturated fats and sugar, linked to heart disease and obesity. We can say then that "non-fat milk" fits my first criterion for a health food, but that the rest of the milk group may not.

So how do dairy products in general get listed as essential ingredients on the food pyramid rather than just low fat milk or yogurt? The answer to this question brings us to my second criterion for a health food: Potentially unhealthy aspects of the food should be widely disclosed, not hidden by marketing. Because we are bombarded daily by conflicting nutrition claims, many people turn to the U.S. government for neutral, unbiased information. But the place of dairy products on the USDA food pyramid may be itself a result of marketing. The USDA's mandate isn't directly to promote health, but to promote agriculture and to help farmers flourish economically. In recommending three servings of dairy products per day, the food pyramid serves the interests of dairy farmers by promoting the whole class of dairy products, not just skim milk. According to the Environmental Working Group's Farm Subsidies Database, the USDA spent $4.8 billion in dairy subsidies between 1995 and 2009 ("Dairy Program Subsidies"). All these policies invest public dollars to create a steady consumption of dairy products and fundamentally depend on the premise that dairy products are good for us.

As we have seen, skim milk may be good for us but dairy products in general are more problematic. When the fat in whole milk is removed to make skim milk, it is not thrown away. It is used to make high calorie, high fat products like cheese and ice cream. Revealing its true ambivalence to public nutrition, the USDA warns against saturated fats in its food pyramid site while simultaneously working with companies like Domino's Pizza, to increase the amount of cheese in their products. According to the *New York Times* (Moss), the USDA helped Domino's create a pizza with 40 percent more cheese and paid for a $12 million ad campaign to promote it. The *New York Times* further writes that Americans now consume almost three times as much cheese as we did in 1970. At a time of a national obesity epidemic, the promotion of dairy products either directly or indirectly introduces high calorie, high saturated fat foods into our diet while making many persons think they are eating healthfully.

5   Finally, I would like to suggest a third criterion for health food. A true health food should be good not only for our bodies but also for the earth. Milk, as it is currently produced in the United States, clearly does not meet this criterion. According to environmental writer Jim Motavalli, both "the front and rear ends of a cow" compete with coal plant smokestacks and vehicle tail pipes as "iconic" causes of global warming and environmental degradation (27). Drawing on statistical sources from both the United Nations and the USDA, Motavalli states that livestock in the United States consume 90 percent of the soy crop and more than 70 percent of the corn and grain crops—foods that could otherwise be used for people and could be grown in a more environmentally friendly way. Not only do cattle consume much of the world's grain supply, the need to clear space for grazing contributes to the destruction of rain forests. The other end of the cow, says Motavalli, is equally destructive. While chewing their cuds, cows directly emit methane gas (according to Motavalli, methane has a greenhouse effect 23 times more potent than carbon dioxide) and the concentration of their manure in factory farm sludge ponds produces ammonia, nitrous oxide, and additional methane. According to Motavalli, cows produce a staggering amount of manure ("five tons of waste for every U.S. citizen" [27]), producing 18 percent of the world's greenhouse gases—more than all of the world's cars, trains, and planes (27). Motavalli also cites additional health risks posed by cows, including dangers of disease from unsafe processing of manure and from antibiotic-resistant bacteria (half of the world's antibiotics are given to cattle instead of humans [28]).

In sum, there is no doubt that skim milk, along with low fat yogurt and cheese, is a vital source of bone-building calcium and belongs on our list of health foods. But for most people, "milk" evokes dairy products in general, all of which we tend to associate with health. What we don't picture is the extra sugar and saturated fat in whole milk and cheese nor the environmental dangers of the dairy and livestock industries in general. From the perspective of the earth, perhaps dairy products should not be considered a health food at all.

Works Cited

"Dairy Program Subsidies." *Farm Subsidies Database*. Environmental Working Group, Jan. 2009. Web. 21 Jan. 2011.

Moss, Michael. "While Warning about Fat, U.S. Pushes Cheese Sales." *New York Times*. New York Times, 6 Nov. 2010. Web. 2 Jan. 2011.

Motavalli, Jim. "The Meat of the Matter: Our Livestock Industry Creates More Greenhouse Gas than Transportation Does." *Environmental Magazine* July–Aug. 2008: 29–31. *Academic Search Complete*. Web. 11 Jan. 2011.

United States. Dept. of Agriculture. *MyPyramid.gov: Steps to a Healthier You.* Jan. 2011. Web. 20 Jan. 2011.

Critiquing "Is Milk a Health Food?"

1. Identify the following features of Arthur's essay: (1) his implied definition of "health food"; (2) his criteria for determining whether a borderline case is a health food; (3) his "match" arguments showing whether milk fits each of the criteria.
2. Do you agree with Arthur's criterion that a true health food ought to be good for the planet as well as good for the body?
3. Based on Arthur's argument, do you think the inclusion of dairy products in the USDA's recommendations for a healthy diet is still justified? Visit the USDA's new nutrition Web site, www.choosemyplate.gov. Would you suggest changes to these USDA recommendations? If so, what and why?

The second reading, by student Kathy Sullivan, was also written for the definition assignment on page 243. The definition issue that she addresses—"Are the Menasee photographs obscene?"—was a local controversy in the state of Washington when the state liquor control board threatened to revoke the liquor license of a Seattle gay bar, the Oncore, unless it removed a series of photographs that the board deemed obscene.

Oncore, Obscenity, and the Liquor Control Board

KATHY SULLIVAN (STUDENT)

In early May, Geoff Menasee, a Seattle artist, exhibited a series of photographs with the theme of "safe sex" on the walls of an inner city, predominantly homosexual restaurant and lounge called the Oncore. Before hanging the photographs, Menasee had to consult with the Washington State Liquor Control Board because, under the current state law, art work containing material that may be considered indecent has to be approved by the board before it can be exhibited. Of the almost thirty photographs, six were rejected by the board because they partially exposed "private parts" of the male anatomy. Menasee went ahead and displayed the entire series of photographs, placing Band-Aids over the "indecent" areas, but the customers continually removed the Band-Aids.

The liquor control board's ruling on this issue has caused controversy in the Seattle community. The *Seattle Times* has provided news coverage, and a "Town Meeting" segment was filmed at the restaurant. The central question is this: Should an establishment that caters to a predominantly homosexual clientele be enjoined from displaying pictures promoting "safe sex" on the grounds that the photographs are obscene?

Before I can answer this question, I must first determine whether the art work should truly be classified as obscene. To make that determination, I will use the definition of obscenity in *Black's Law Dictionary:*

> Material is "obscene" if to the average person, applying contemporary community standards, the dominant theme of material taken as a whole appeals to prurient interest, if it is utterly without redeeming social importance, if it goes substantially beyond customary limits of candor in description or representation, if it is characterized by patent offensiveness, and if it is hard core pornography.

An additional criterion is provided by Pember's *Mass Media Laws:* "A work is obscene if it has a tendency to deprave and corrupt those whose minds are open to such immoral influences (children for example) and into whose hands it might happen to fall" (394). The art work in question should not be prohibited from display at predominantly homosexual establishments like the Oncore because it does not meet the above criteria for obscenity.

First of all, to the average person applying contemporary community standards, the predominant theme of Menasee's photographs is not an appeal to prurient interests. The first element in this criterion is "average person." According to Rocky Breckner, manager of the Oncore, 90 percent of the clientele at the Oncore is made up of young white homosexual males. This group therefore constitutes the "average person" viewing the exhibit. "Contemporary community standards" would ordinarily be the standards of the Seattle community. However, this art work is aimed at a particular group of people—the homosexual community. Therefore, the "community standards" involved here are those of the gay community rather than the city at large. Since the Oncore is not an art museum or gallery, which attracts a broad spectrum of people, it is appropriate to restrict the scope of "community standards" to that group who voluntarily patronize the Oncore.

5   Second, the predominant theme of the photographs is not "prurient interest" nor do the photographs go "substantially beyond customary limits of candor." There are no explicit sexual acts found in the photographs; instead, their theme is the prevention of AIDS through the practice of safe sex. Homosexual displays of affection could be viewed as "prurient interest" by the larger community, but same-sex relationships are the norm for the group at whom the exhibit is aimed. If the exhibit were displayed at McDonald's or even the Red Robin it might go "substantially beyond customary limits of candor," but it is unlikely that the clientele of the Oncore would find the art work offensive. The manager stated that he received very few complaints about the exhibit and its contents.

Nor is the material pornographic. The liquor control board prohibited the six photographs based on their visible display of body parts such as pubic hair and naked buttocks, not on the basis of sexual acts or homosexual orientation. The board admitted that the photographs depicted no explicit sexual acts. Hence, it can be concluded that they did not consider the suggestion of same-sex affection to be hard-core pornography. Their sole objection was that body parts were visible. But visible genitalia in art work are not necessarily pornographic. Since other art work, such as Michelangelo's sculptures, explicitly depict both male and female genitalia, it is arguable that pubic hair and buttocks are not patently offensive.

It must be conceded that the art work has the potential of being viewed by children, which would violate Pember's criterion. But once again the incidence of minors frequenting this establishment is very small.

But the most important reason for saying these photographs are not obscene is that they serve an important social purpose. One of *Black*'s criteria is that obscene material is "utterly without redeeming social importance." But these photographs have the explicit purpose of promoting safe sex as a defense against AIDS. Recent statistics reported in the *Seattle Times* show that AIDS is now the leading cause of death of men under forty in the Seattle area. Any methods that can promote the message of safe sex in today's society have strong redeeming social significance.

Those who believe that all art containing "indecent" material should be banned or covered from public view would most likely believe that Menasee's work is obscene. They would disagree that the environment and the clientele should be the major determining factor when using criteria to evaluate art. However, in the case of this exhibit I feel that the audience and the environment of the display are factors of overriding importance. Therefore, the exhibit should have been allowed to be displayed because it is not obscene.

Critiquing "Oncore, Obscenity, and the Liquor Control Board"

1. Kathy Sullivan here uses authoritative definitions for *obscenity*. Based on the definitions of *obscenity* in *Black's Law Dictionary* and Pember's *Mass Media Laws*, what criteria for obscenity does Kathy use?
2. How does she argue that the Menasee photographs do *not* meet the criteria?
3. Working as a whole class or in small groups, share your responses to the following questions: (a) If you find Kathy's argument persuasive, which parts were particularly influential or effective? (b) If you are not persuaded, which parts of her argument do you find weak or ineffective? (c) How does Kathy shape her argument to meet the concerns and objections of her audience? (d) How might a lawyer for the liquor control board rebut Kathy's argument?

Our last readings are a political cartoon and a letter to the editor written in response to that cartoon. The cartoon, by Pulitzer Prize winner Clay Bennett, makes a resemblance argument linking laws against gay marriage to earlier laws against interracial marriage. The occasion for the cartoon was a California Supreme Court decision legalizing gay marriage in California. The cartoon first appeared in the *Chattanooga Times Free Press* on June 18, 2008, and was reprinted in the *Seattle Times*. The responding letter to the editor, by Beth Reis, appeared in the *Seattle Times* on June 20, 2008.

Just Emancipated

CLAY BENNETT

Toon Offensive

BETH REIS

Don't get me wrong. I'm excited about California recognizing same-sex couples' right to marriage equality. I was a plaintiff in a Washington state marriage lawsuit. But the cartoon car with the words "just emancipated" on it, equating this development to the ending of slavery, especially on Juneteenth—the anniversary of the freeing of slaves after generations of brutality, forced labor, and families being separated and sold—is so offensive!

Yes, I feel a little more equal under the law this week. Yes, it matters that some people are now first class citizens, entitled to the same rights and held to the same responsibilities as other couples. Yes, the word *marriage* is honorable and understandable and right.

But, please: How is that like outlawing slavery, exactly 146 years ago today? How is it like 143 years ago, when Texans were told that for the last three years they'd been enslaved illegally and were actually free? How is it like being told, nearly a century later, that they could finally vote?

I am proud to be gay, but not at all proud to have this week's small victory equated with the emancipation of slaves and the enfranchisement of their descendants.

Critiquing "Just Emancipated" and "Toon Offensive"

1. How does the cartoon use an analogy to praise the California gay marriage decision? What is the cartoon's implied claim?
2. How does Beth Reis's letter to the editor point out disanalogies as a method of refuting the cartoon's argument?
3. One strategy often used to support the legalization of same-sex marriage is to point out its similarities to earlier court decisions legalizing interracial marriages. What are the analogies and disanalogies between interracial marriage and same-sex marriage?
4. Analyze Beth Reis's rhetorical appeals to *logos, ethos,* and *pathos.*

For additional writing, reading, and research resources, go to www.mycomplab.com

Causal Arguments

12

Case 1 What Causes Global Warming?

One of the early clues linking global warming to atmospheric carbon dioxide (CO_2) came from side-by-side comparisons of graphs plotting atmospheric carbon dioxide and global temperatures over time. These graphs show that increases in global temperature parallel increases in the percentage of carbon dioxide in the atmosphere. However, the graphs show only a correlation, or link, between increased carbon dioxide and higher average temperature. To argue that an increase in CO_2 could *cause* global warming, scientists needed to expalin the links in a causal chain. They could do so by comparing the earth to a greenhouse. Carbon dioxide, like glass in a greenhouse, lets some of the earth's heat radiate into space but also reflects some of it back to the earth. The higher the concentration of carbon dioxide, the more heat is reflected back to the earth.

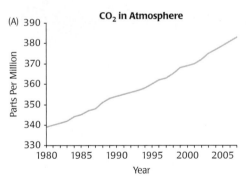

(A)

Source: Data from Dr. Pieter Tans, NOAA/ESRL

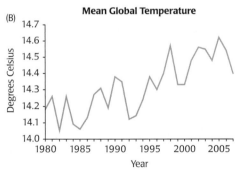

(B)

Source: Data from NASA Goddard Institute for Space Studies Surface Temperature Analysis

Case 2 What Has Caused the Crime Rate to Decline Since the Early 1990s?

Beginning in the 1990s, the crime rate in the United States dropped precipitously. For example, the number of murders in New York City decreased from 2,245 in 1990 to 494 in 2007. Similar reductions for all kinds of crime, ranging from murders to assaults to auto thefts, were reported across the nation. What caused this sudden and unexpected decline?

Many causal theories were debated in social science journals and the popular media. Among the proposed causes were innovative policing strategies, increased incarceration of criminals, an aging population, tougher gun control laws, a strong economy, and more police officers. However, economist Steven Levitt proposed that the primary cause was *Roe v. Wade,* the 1973 Supreme Court decision that legalized abortion.* According to Levitt's controversial theory, the crime rate began dropping because the greatest source of criminals—unwanted children entering their teens and twenties—were largely absent from the cohort of young people coming of age in the 1990s and 2000s; they had been aborted rather than brought up in the crime-producing conditions of unstable families, poverty, and neglect.

We encounter causal issues all the time. What are the causes of global warming? What caused the sudden decline in the U.S. crime rate beginning in the 1990s? Why did rap music become popular? Why are white teenage girls seven times as likely to smoke as African American teenage girls? Why do couples who live together before marriage have a higher divorce rate than those who don't? In addition to asking causal questions like these, we pose consequence questions as well: What might be the consequences of legalizing heroin and other hard drugs, of closing our borders to immigrants, or of overturning *Roe v. Wade?* What have been the consequences—expected or unexpected—of the invasion of Iraq or the emerging popularity of YouTube? What might be the consequences—expected or unexpected—of aggressively combating global warming as opposed to adapting to it? Often, arguments about causes and consequences have important stakes because they shape our view of reality and influence government policies and individual decisions.

In this chapter, you will learn to:

- Analyze causal methods and mechanisms
- Use causal reasoning to construct your own causal arguments

An Overview of Causal Arguments

Typically, causal arguments try to show how one event brings about another. When causal investigation focuses on material objects—for example, one billiard ball striking another—the notion of causality appears fairly straightforward. But when humans become the focus of a causal argument, the nature of causality becomes more vexing. If we say that something happened that "caused" a person to act in a certain way, what do we mean? Do we mean that she was "forced" to act in a certain way, thereby negating her free will (as in, an undiagnosed brain tumor caused her to act erratically), or do we mean more simply that she was "motivated" to act in a certain way (as in, her anger at her parents caused her to act erratically)? When we argue about causality in human

---

*Steven D. Levitt and Stephen J. Dubner, "Where Have All the Criminals Gone?" In *Freakonomics: A Rogue Economist Explores the Hidden Side of Everything* (New York: HarperCollins, 2005), 117–44.

beings, we must guard against confusing these two senses of "cause" or assuming that human behavior can be predicted or controlled in the same way that nonhuman behavior can. A rock dropped from a roof will always fall at thirty-two feet per second squared, and a rat zapped for turning left in a maze will always quit turning left. But if we raise interest rates, will consumers save more money? If so, how much? This is the sort of question we debate endlessly.

Kinds of Causal Arguments

Arguments about causality can take a variety of forms. Here are three typical kinds:

- **Speculations about possible causes.** Sometimes arguers speculate about possible causes of a phenomenon. For example, whenever a shooter opens fire on innocent bystanders (as in the 2011 attempted assassination of Arizona Representative Gabrielle Giffords in a Tucson parking lot), social scientists, police investigators, and media commentators begin analyzing the causes. One of the most heavily debated shooting incidents occurred in 1999 at Columbine High School in Littleton, Colorado, when two male students opened fire on their classmates, killing thirteen people, wounding twenty-three others, and then shooting themselves. Figure 12.1 illustrates some of the proposed theories for the Columbine shootings. What was at stake was not only our desire to understand the sociocultural sources of school violence but also our desire to institute policies to prevent future school shootings. If a primary cause is the availability of guns, then we might push for more stringent gun control laws. But if the primary cause is the disintegration of the traditional family, the shooters' alienation

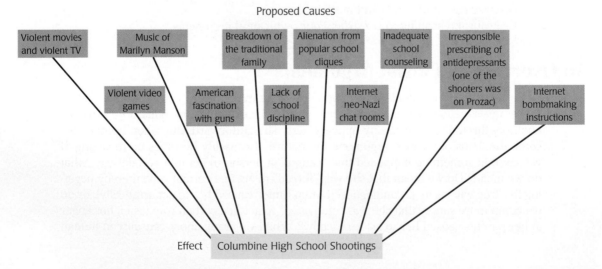

FIGURE 12.1 Speculation about possible causes: Columbine High School massacre

from high school cliques, or the dangerous side effects of Prozac, then we might seek different solutions.

■ **Arguments for an unexpected or surprising cause.** Besides sorting out possible causes of a phenomenon, sometimes arguers try to persuade readers to see the plausibility of an unexpected or surprising cause. This was the strategy used by syndicated columnist John Leo, who wanted readers to consider the role of violent video games as a contributing cause to the Columbine massacre.* After suggesting that the Littleton killings were partly choreographed on video game models, Leo suggested the causal chain shown in Figure 12.2.

■ **Predictions of consequences.** Still another frequently encountered kind of causal argument predicts the consequences of current, planned, or proposed actions or events. Consequence arguments have high stakes because we often judge actions on whether their benefits outweigh their costs. As we will see in Chapter 14, proposal arguments usually require writers to predict the consequences of a proposed action, do a cost/benefit analysis, and persuade readers that no unforeseen negative consequences will result. Just as a phenomenon can have multiple causes, it can also have multiple consequences. Figure 12.3

Many youngsters are left alone for long periods of time (because both parents are working).

↓

They play violent video games obsessively.

↓

Their feelings of resentment and powerlessness "pour into the killing games."

↓

The video games break down a natural aversion to killing, analogous to psychological techniques employed by the military.

↓

Realistic touches in modern video games blur the "boundary between fantasy and reality."

↓

Youngsters begin identifying not with conventional heroes but with sociopaths who get their kicks from blowing away ordinary people ("pedestrians, marching bands, an elderly woman with a walker").

↓

Having enjoyed random violence in the video games, vulnerable youngsters act out the same adrenaline rush in real life.

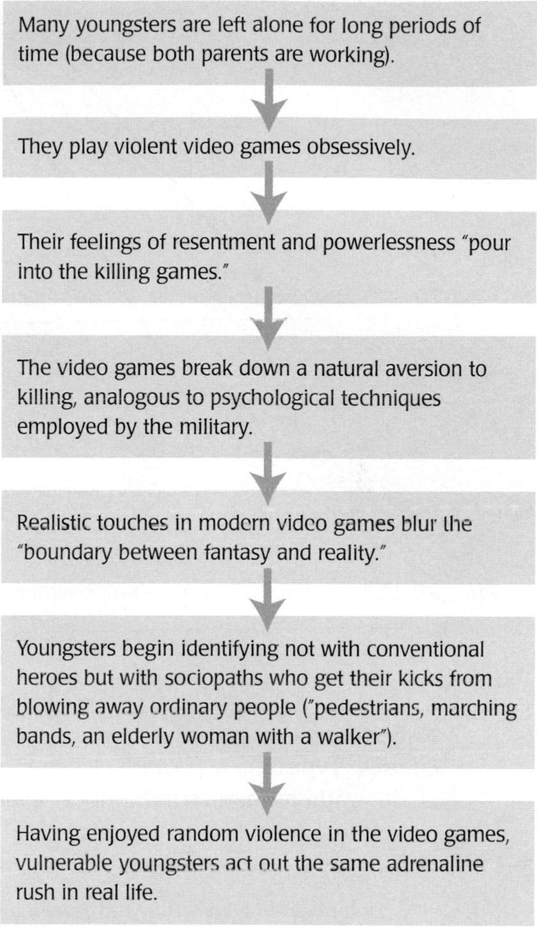

FIGURE 12.2 Argument for a surprising cause: Role of violent video games in the Columbine massacre

shows the consequence arguments considered by environmentalists who propose eliminating several dams on the Snake River in order to save salmon runs.

Toulmin Framework for a Causal Argument

Because causal arguments can involve lengthy or complex causal chains, they are often harder to summarize in *because* clauses than are other kinds of arguments. Likewise, they are not as likely to yield quick analysis through the Toulmin schema.

---

*John Leo, "Kill-for-Kicks Video Games Desensitizing Our Children," *Seattle Times* 27 April 1999, B4.

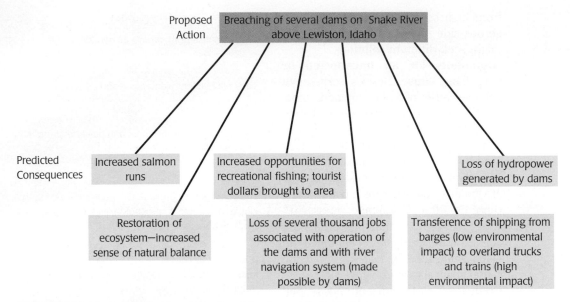

FIGURE 12.3 Predictions of consequences: Breaching dams on the Snake River

Nevertheless, a causal argument can usually be stated as a claim with *because* clauses. Typically, a *because* clause pinpoints one or two key elements in the causal chain rather than summarizes every link. John Leo's argument linking the Columbine massacre to violent video games could be summarized in the following claim with a *because* clause:

> Violent video games may have been a contributing cause to the Littleton massacre because playing these games can make random, sociopathic violence seem pleasurable.

Once stated as an enthymeme, the argument can be analyzed using Toulmin's schema. It is easiest to apply Toulmin's schema to causal arguments if you think of the grounds as the observable phenomena at any point in the causal chain and the warrants as the shareable assumptions about causality that join links together.

Toulmin Analysis of the Violent Video Games Argument

ENTHYMEME

CLAIM Violent video games may have been a contributing cause to the Columbine school shooting

REASON because playing these games can make random, sociopathic violence seem pleasurable.

Qualifiers

GROUNDS

- Evidence that the killers, like many young people, played violent video games
- Evidence that the games are violent
- Evidence that the games involve random, sociopathic violence (not good guys versus bad guys) such as killing ordinary people—marching bands, little old ladies, etc.
- Evidence that young people derive pleasure from these games

CONDITIONS OF REBUTTAL
Attacking the reason and grounds

- Perhaps the killers didn't play violent video games.
- Perhaps the video games are no more violent than traditional kids' games such as cops and robbers.
- Perhaps the video games do not feature sociopathic killing.

WARRANT

If young people derive pleasure from random, sociopathic killing in video games, they can transfer this pleasure to real life, thus leading to the Columbine shooting.

BACKING

- Testimony from psychologists
- Evidence that violent video games desensitize people to violence
- Analogy to military training in which video games are used to "make killing a reflex action"
- Evidence that the distinction between fantasy and reality becomes especially blurred for unstable young people

CONDITIONS OF REBUTTAL
Attacking the warrant and backing

- Perhaps kids are fully capable of distinguishing fantasy from reality.
- Perhaps the games are just fun with no transference to real life.
- Perhaps the games are substantially different from military training games.

■ ■ ■   **FOR CLASS DISCUSSION**   Developing Causal Chains

1. Working individually or in small groups, create a causal chain to show how the item on the left could help lead to the item on the right.

a. High price of oil	Redesign of cities
b. Invention of the automobile	Changes in sexual mores
c. Invention of the telephone	Loss of sense of community in neighborhoods
d. Origin of rap in the black urban music scene	The popularity of rap spreads from urban black audiences to white middle-class youth culture
e. Development of way to prevent rejections in transplant operations	Liberalization of euthanasia laws

2. For each of your causal chains, compose a claim with an attached *because* clause summarizing one or two key links in the causal chain—for example, "The high price of oil is causing homeowners to move from the suburbs into new high-density urban communities because the expense of gasoline is making people value easy access to their work."

■ ■ ■

Two Methods for Arguing that One Event Causes Another

One of the first things you need to do when preparing a causal argument is to note exactly what sort of causal relationship you are dealing with—a onetime phenomenon, a recurring phenomenon, or a puzzling trend. Here are some examples.

Kind of Phenomenon	Examples
Onetime phenomenon	▪ 2007 collapse of a freeway bridge in Minneapolis, Minnesota ▪ Firing of a popular teacher at your university ▪ Your friend's sudden decision to join the army
Recurring phenomenon	▪ Eating disorders ▪ Road rage ▪ Someone's tendency to procrastinate
Puzzling trend	▪ Rising popularity of extreme sports ▪ Declining audience for TV news ▪ Increases in diagnosis of autism

With recurring phenomena or with trends, one has the luxury of being able to study multiple cases, often over time. You can interview people, make repeated observations, or study the conditions in which the puzzling phenomenon occurs. But with a onetime occurrence, one's approach is more like that of a detective than a scientist.

EXAMINING VISUAL ARGUMENTS

A Causal Claim

This ad campaign, "Kill a Child, Destroy a Family," from the Pedestrian Council of Australia, makes a causal argument against careless driving. How does the ad work visually to suggest the links in a causal chain? Place into your own words the argument implied by this ad. You can see the other ads in the campaign online. Why do you think this ad campaign won awards for its effective advocacy?

Because one can't repeat the event with different variables, one must rely only on the immediate evidence at hand, which can quickly disappear.

Having briefly stated these words of caution, let's turn now to two main ways that you can argue that one event causes another.

First Method: Explain the Causal Mechanism Directly

The most convincing kind of causal argument identifies every link in the causal chain, showing how an initiating cause leads step by step to an observed effect. A causes B, which causes C, which causes D. In some cases, all you have to do is fill in the missing links. In other cases—when your assumptions about how one step leads to the next may seem questionable to your audience—you have to argue for the causal connection with more vigor.

A careful spelling out of each step in the causal chain is the technique used by science writer Robert S. Devine in the following passage from his article "The Trouble with Dams." Although the benefits of dams are widely understood (they produce pollution-free electricity while providing flood control, irrigation, barge transportation, and recreational boating), the negative effects are less commonly known and understood. In this article, Devine tries to persuade readers that dams have serious negative consequences. In the following passage, he explains how dams reduce salmon flows by slowing the migration of smolts (newly hatched, young salmon) to the sea.

Causal Argument Describing a Causal Chain

Such transformations lie at the heart of the ongoing environmental harm done by dams. Rivers are rivers because they flow, and the nature of their flows defines much of their character. When dams alter flows, they alter the essence of rivers.

Consider the erstwhile river behind Lower Granite (a dam on Idaho's Snake River). Although I was there in the springtime, when I looked at the water it was moving too slowly to merit the word "flow"—and Lower Granite Lake isn't even one of the region's enormous storage reservoirs, which bring currents to a virtual halt. In the past, spring snowmelt sent powerful currents down the Snake during April and May. Nowadays hydropower operators of the Columbia and Snake systems store the runoff behind the dams and release it during the winter, when demand—and the price—for electricity rises. Over the ages, however, many populations of salmon have adapted to the spring surge. The smolts used the strong flows to migrate, drifting downstream with the current. During the journey smolts' bodies undergo physiological changes that require them to reach salt water quickly. Before dams backed up the Snake, smolts coming down from Idaho got to the sea in six to twenty days; now it takes from sixty to ninety days, and few of the young salmon reach salt water in time. The emasculated current is the single largest reason that the number of wild adult salmon migrating up the Snake each year has crashed from predevelopment runs of 100,000–200,000 to what was projected to be 150–75 this year.*

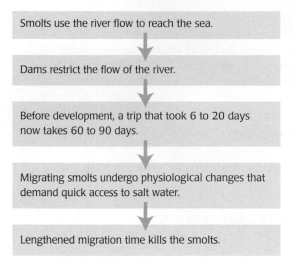

Smolts use the river flow to reach the sea.

Dams restrict the flow of the river.

Before development, a trip that took 6 to 20 days now takes 60 to 90 days.

Migrating smolts undergo physiological changes that demand quick access to salt water.

Lengthened migration time kills the smolts.

This tightly constructed passage connects various causal chains to explain the decline of salmon runs.

Describing each link in the causal chain—and making each link seem as plausible as possible—is the most persuasive means of convincing readers that a specific cause leads to a specific effect.

Second Method: Infer Causal Links Using Inductive Reasoning

If we can't explain a causal link directly, we often employ a reasoning strategy called *induction*. Through induction we infer a general conclusion based on a limited number of specific cases. For example, if on several occasions you got a headache after drinking red wine but not after drinking white wine, you would be likely to conclude inductively that red wine causes you to get headaches, although

*Robert S. Devine, "The Trouble with Dams," *Atlantic* (August 1995), 64–75. The example quotation is from page 70.

you can't explain directly how it does so. However, because there are almost always numerous variables involved, inductive reasoning gives only probable truths, not certain ones.

Three Ways of Thinking Inductively   When your brain thinks inductively, it sorts through data looking for patterns of similarity and difference. In this section we explain three ways of thinking inductively: looking for a common element, looking for a single difference, and looking for correlations.

1. **Look for a common element.** One kind of inductive thinking places you on a search for a common element that can explain recurrences of the same phenomenon. For example, psychologists attempting to understand the causes of anorexia have discovered that many anorexics (but not all) come from perfectionist, highly work-oriented homes that emphasize duty and responsibility. This common element is thus a suspected causal factor leading to anorexia.

2. **Look for a single difference.** Another approach is to look for a single difference that may explain the appearance of a new phenomenon. When infant death rates in the state of Washington shot up in July and August 1986, one event making these two months different stood out: increased radioactive fallout over Washington from the April Chernobyl nuclear meltdown in Ukraine. This single difference led some researchers to suspect radiation as a possible cause of the increase in infant deaths.

3. **Look for correlations.** Still another method of induction is *correlation,* which means that two events or phenomena tend to occur together but doesn't imply that one causes the other. For example, there is a correlation between nearsightedness and intelligence. (That is, in a given sample of nearsighted people and people with normal eyesight, the nearsighted group will have a somewhat higher mean IQ score.) But the direction of causality isn't clear. It could be that high intelligence causes people to read more, thus ruining their eyes (high intelligence causes nearsightedness). Or it could be that nearsightedness causes people to read more, thus raising their intelligence (nearsightedness causes high intelligence). Or it could be that some unknown phenomenon, perhaps a gene, is related to both nearsightedness and intelligence. So keep in mind that correlation is not causation—it simply suggests possible causation.

Beware of Common Inductive Fallacies that Can Lead to Wrong Conclusions
Largely because of its power, informal induction can often lead to wrong conclusions. You should be aware of two common fallacies of inductive reasoning that can tempt you into erroneous assumptions about causality. (Both fallacies are treated more fully in the Appendix.)

■ **Post hoc fallacy:** The *post hoc, ergo propter hoc* fallacy ("after this, therefore because of this") mistakes sequence for cause. Just because event A regularly precedes event B doesn't mean that event A causes event B. The same reasoning that tells us that flipping a switch causes the light to go on can make us believe that low levels of radioactive fallout from the Chernobyl nuclear disaster caused a sudden rise in infant death rates in the state of Washington. The nuclear disaster clearly preceded the rise in death rates. But did it clearly *cause* it? Our point is that precedence alone is no proof of causality and that we are guilty of this fallacy whenever we are swayed to believe that one thing causes another just because it comes first.

■ **Hasty generalization:** The *hasty generalization* fallacy occurs when you make a generalization based on too few cases or too little consideration of alternative explanations: You flip the switch, but the lightbulb doesn't go on. You conclude—too hastily—that the lightbulb has burned out. (Perhaps the power has gone off or the switch is broken.) How many trials does it take before you can make a justified generalization rather than a hasty generalization? It is difficult to say for sure.

Both the *post hoc* fallacy and the hasty generalization fallacy remind us that induction requires a leap from individual cases to a general principle and that it is always possible to leap too soon.

■ ■ ■ **FOR CLASS DISCUSSION**   Developing Plausible Causal Chains Based on Correlations
Working individually or in small groups, develop plausible causal chains that may explain the relationship between the following pairs of phenomena:

a. A person who registers a low stress level on an electrochemical stress meter	does daily meditation
b. A white female teenager	is seven times as likely to smoke as a black female teenager
c. A person who grew up in a house with two bathrooms	is likely to have higher SAT scores than a person who grew up in a one-bathroom home
d. A person who buys lots of ashtrays	is more likely to develop lung cancer
e. A member of the National Rifle Association	supports the death penalty

■ ■ ■

Glossary of Terms Encountered in Causal Arguments

Because causal arguments are often easier to conduct if writer and reader share a few specialized terms, we offer the following glossary for your convenience.

■ **Fallacy of oversimplified cause.** One of the great temptations is to look for *the* cause of something, as if a phenomenon had only one cause rather than multiple causes. For example, in recent years the number of persons in the United States sending out Christmas cards has declined substantially. Many commentators attribute the decline to the increasing use of Facebook, which keeps old friends in touch year-round, eliminating the need for holiday "family letters." But there

may be other causes also, such as a decline in the number of nuclear families, fewer networks of long-term friends, or generational shifts away from older traditions. When you make a causal argument, be especially careful how you use words such as *all, most, some, the,* or *in part.* For example, to say that *all* the decline in Christmas cards is caused by Facebook is to make a universal statement about Facebook as *the* cause. An argument will be stronger and more accurate if the arguer makes a less sweeping statement: *Some* of the cause for the decline in Christmas cards can be attributed to Facebook. Arguers sometimes deliberately mix up these quantifiers to misrepresent and dismiss opposing views.

- **Immediate and remote causes.** Every causal chain extends backward indefinitely into the past. An immediate cause is the closest in time to the event being examined. Consider the causes for the release of nuclear contaminants around the Fukushima nuclear power plant following the 2011 earthquake off the coast of Japan. The immediate cause was loss of power to the water pumps that cooled the reactor's fuel rods, causing the rods to overheat and partially melt. A slightly less immediate cause (several days earlier) was the earthquake-produced tsunami that had swept away the diesel fuel tanks needed to run the backup generators. These immediate causes can be contrasted with a remote cause—in this case, a late-1960s design decision that used backup diesel generators to power the water pumps in case of an electrical power loss to the reactor facility. Still more remote causes were the economic and regulatory systems in the late 1960s that led to this particular design.

- **Precipitating and contributing causes.** These terms are similar to *immediate* and *remote* causes but don't designate a temporal link going into the past. Rather, they refer to a main cause emerging out of a background of subsidiary causes. If, for example, a husband and wife decide to separate, the *precipitating cause* may be a stormy fight over money, after which one of the partners (or both) says, "I've had enough." In contrast, *contributing causes* would be all the background factors that are dooming the marriage—preoccupation with their careers, disagreement about priorities, in-law problems, and so forth. Note that contributing causes and the precipitating cause all coexist at the same time.

- **Constraints.** Sometimes an effect occurs because some stabilizing factor—a *constraint*—is removed. In other words, the presence of a constraint may keep a certain effect from occurring. For example, in the marriage we have been discussing, the presence of children in the home may be a constraint against divorce; as soon as the children graduate from high school and leave home, the marriage may well dissolve.

- **Necessary and sufficient causes.** A *necessary cause* is one that has to be present for a given effect to occur. For example, fertility drugs are necessary to cause the conception of septuplets. Every couple who has septuplets must have used fertility drugs. In contrast, a *sufficient cause* is one that always produces or guarantees a given effect. Smoking more than a pack of cigarettes per day is sufficient to raise the cost of one's life insurance policy. This statement means that if you are a smoker, no matter how healthy you appear to be, life insurance companies will always place you in a higher risk bracket and charge you a higher

premium. In some cases, a single cause can be both necessary and sufficient. For example, lack of ascorbic acid is both a necessary and a sufficient cause of scurvy. (Think of those old-time sailors who didn't eat fruit for months.) It is a necessary cause because you can't get scurvy any other way except through absence of ascorbic acid; it is a sufficient cause because the absence of ascorbic acid always causes scurvy.

■ ■ ■ **FOR CLASS DISCUSSION** **Brainstorming Causes and Constraints**
The terms in the preceding glossary can be effective brainstorming tools for thinking of possible causes of an event. For the following events, try to think of as many causes as possible by brainstorming possible *immediate causes, remote causes, precipitating causes, contributing causes,* and *constraints:*

1. Working individually, make a list of different kinds of causes/constraints for one of the following:
   a. Your decision to attend your present college
   b. An important event in your life or your family (a job change, a major move, etc.)
   c. A personal opinion you hold that is not widely shared
2. Working as a group, make a list of different kinds of causes/constraints for one of the following:
   a. Why women's fashion and beauty magazines are the most frequently purchased magazines in college bookstores
   b. Why American students consistently score below Asian and European students in academic achievement
   c. Why the number of babies born out of wedlock has increased dramatically in the last thirty years

■ ■ ■

WRITING ASSIGNMENT   A Causal Argument

Choose an issue about the causes or consequences of a trend, event, or other phenomenon. Write an argument that persuades an audience to accept your explanation of the causes or consequences of your chosen phenomenon. Within your essay you should examine alternative hypotheses or opposing views and explain your reasons for rejecting them. You can imagine your issue either as a puzzle or as a disagreement. If a puzzle, your task will be to create a convincing case for an audience that doesn't have an answer to your causal question already in mind. If a disagreement, your task will be more overtly persuasive because your goal will be to change your audience's views.

Exploring Ideas

Arguments about causes and consequences abound in public, professional, or personal life, so you shouldn't have difficulty finding a causal issue worth investigating and arguing.

In response to a public controversy over why there are fewer women than men on science and math faculties, student writer Julee Christianson argued that culture, not biology, is the primary cause (see pages 272–277). Student writer Carlos Macias, puzzled by the ease with which college students are issued credit cards, wrote a researched argument disentangling the factors leading young people to bury themselves in debt (see pages 281–284). Other students have focused on causal issues such as these: Why do kids join gangs? What are the consequences of mandatory drug testing (written by a student who has to take amphetamines for narcolepsy)? What has happened since 1970 to cause young people to delay getting married? (This question was initiated by the student's interest in the statistical table in Chapter 9, page 203.)

If you have trouble finding a causal issue to write about, you can often create provocative controversies among your classmates through the following strategies:

- **Make a list of unusual likes and dislikes.** Think about unusual things that people like or dislike. You could summarize the conventional explanations that people give for an unusual pleasure or aversion and then argue for a surprising or unexpected cause. What attracts people to extreme sports? How do you explain the popularity of the tricked-out Cadillac Escalade as a dream car for urban youth?
- **Make a list of puzzling events or trends.** Another strategy is to make a list of puzzling phenomena and then try to explain their causes. Start with onetime events (a curriculum change at your school, the sudden popularity of a new app). Then list puzzling recurring events (failure of knowledgeable teenagers to practice safe sex). Finally, list some recent trends (growth of naturopathic medicine, increased interest in tattoos). Engage classmates in discussions of one or more of the items on your list. Look for places of disagreement as entry points into the conversation.
- **Brainstorm consequences of a recent or proposed action.** Arguments about consequences are among the most interesting and important of causal disputes. If you can argue for an unanticipated consequence of a real or proposed action, whether good or bad, you can contribute importantly to the conversation. What might be the consequences, for example, of placing "green taxes" on coal-produced electricity; of legalizing marijuana; of overturning *Roe v. Wade;* or of requiring national public service for all young adults?

Identifying Your Audience and Determining What's at Stake

Before drafting your argument, identify your targeted audience and determine what's at stake. Consider your responses to the following questions:

- What audience are you targeting? What background do they need to understand your issue? How much do they already care about it?
- Before they read your argument, what stance on your issue do you imagine them holding? What change do you want to bring about in their views?

- What will they find new or surprising about your argument?
- What objections might they raise? What counterarguments or alternative points of view will you need to address?
- Why does your argument matter? Who might be threatened or made uncomfortable by your views? What is at stake?

Organizing a Causal Argument

At the outset, it is useful to know some of the standard ways that a causal argument can be organized. Later, you may decide on a different organizational pattern, but the standard ways shown in Organization Plans 1, 2, and 3 on pages 269–270 will help you get started.

Plans 2 and 3 are similar in that they examine numerous possible causes or consequences. Plan 2, however, tries to establish the relative importance of each cause or consequence, whereas Plan 3 aims at rejecting the causes or consequences normally assumed by the audience and argues for an unexpected, surprising cause or consequence. Plan 3 can also be used when your purpose is to change your audience's mind about a cause or consequence.

Questioning and Critiquing a Causal Argument

Knowing how to question and critique a causal argument will help you anticipate opposing views in order to strengthen your own. It will also help you rebut another person's causal argument. Here are some useful questions to ask:

- When you explain the links in a causal chain, can a skeptic point out weaknesses in any of the links?
- If you speculate about the causes of a phenomenon, could a skeptic argue for different causes or arrange your causes in a different order of importance?
- If you argue for a surprising cause or a surprising consequence of a phenomenon, could a skeptic point out alternative explanations that would undercut your argument?
- If your argument depends on inferences from data, could a skeptic question the way the data were gathered or interpreted? Could a skeptic claim that the data weren't relevant (for example, research done with lab animals might not apply to humans)?
- If your causal argument depends on a correlation between one phenomenon and another, could a skeptic argue that the direction of causality should be reversed or that an unidentified, third phenomenon is the real cause?

Organization Plan 1: Argument Explaining Links in a Causal Chain

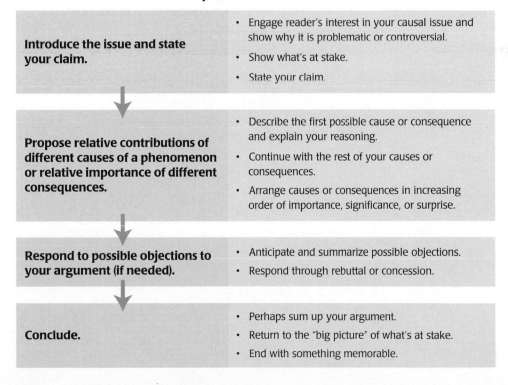

Introduce the issue and state your claim.	• Engage reader's interest in your causal issue and show why it is controversial or problematic. • Show what's at stake. • State your claim.
Explain the links in the chain going from cause to effect.	• Explain the links and their connections in order. • Anticipate and respond to possible objections if needed.
Conclude.	• Perhaps sum up your argument. • Return to the "big picture" of what's at stake. • End with something memorable.

Organization Plan 2: Argument Proposing Multiple Causes or Consequences of a Phenomenon

Introduce the issue and state your claim.	• Engage reader's interest in your causal issue and show why it is problematic or controversial. • Show what's at stake. • State your claim.
Propose relative contributions of different causes of a phenomenon or relative importance of different consequences.	• Describe the first possible cause or consequence and explain your reasoning. • Continue with the rest of your causes or consequences. • Arrange causes or consequences in increasing order of importance, significance, or surprise.
Respond to possible objections to your argument (if needed).	• Anticipate and summarize possible objections. • Respond through rebuttal or concession.
Conclude.	• Perhaps sum up your argument. • Return to the "big picture" of what's at stake. • End with something memorable.

Organization Plan 3: Argument Proposing a Surprising Causes or Consequence

Introduce the issue and state your claim.	• Engage reader's interest in your causal issue and show why it is problematic or controversial. • Show what's at stake. • State your claim.
Reject commonly assumed causes or consequences.	• Describe the first commonly assumed cause or consequence and show why you don't think the explanation is adequate. • Continue with the rest of your commonly assumed causes or consequences.
Argue for your surprising cause or consequence.	• Describe your surprising cause or consequence. • Explain your causal reasoning. • Anticipate and respond to possible objections if needed.
Conclude.	• Perhaps sum up your argument. • Return to the "big picture" of what's at stake. • End with something memorable.

Our first reading, by student Julee Christianson, was written in response **READINGS** to the assignment in this chapter. Julee was entering an intense public debate about the underrepresentation of women on prestigious math and science faculties, a controversy initiated by Lawrence Summers, then president of Harvard, who suggested the possibility of a genetic cause for this phenomenon. A furious reaction ensued. The Web site of the Women in Science and Engineering Leadership Institute has extensive coverage of the controversy, including Summers' original speech.

Julee's argument illustrates the format and documentation system for a paper following the guidelines of the American Psychological Association (APA). For further discussion of the APA documentation system, see pages 397–403.

APA

Why Lawrence Summers Was Wrong: Culture Rather than Biology
Explains the Underrepresentation of Women in Science and Mathematics
Julee Christianson
December 8, 2008

Why Lawrence Summers Was Wrong: Culture Rather
than Biology Explains the Underrepresentation of
Women in Science and Mathematics

In 2005, Harvard University's president, Lawrence H. Summers, gave a controversial speech that suggested that the underrepresentation of women in tenured positions in math and science departments is partly caused by biological differences. In his address, Summers proposed three hypotheses explaining why women shy away from math and science careers. First, he gave a "high-powered job hypothesis" that stated that women naturally want to start a family and therefore will not have the time or desire to commit to the high-stress workload required for research in math and science. His second hypothesis was that genetic differences between the sexes cause more males than females to have high aptitude for math and science. Lastly, he mentioned the hypothesis that women are underrepresented because of discrimination, but he dismissed discrimination as an insignificant factor. It was Summers's second hypothesis about biological differences that started a heated national debate. The academic world seems split over this nature/nurture issue. Although there is some evidence that biology plays a role in determining math ability, I argue that culture plays a much larger role, both in the way that women are socialized and in the continued existence of male discrimination against women in male-dominated fields.

Evidence supporting the role of biology in determining math ability is effectively presented by Steven Pinker (2005), a Harvard psychologist who agrees with Summers. In his article "The Science of Difference: Sex Ed," Pinker focuses extensively on Summers's argument. According to Pinker, "in many traits, men show greater variance than women, and are disproportionately found at both the low and high ends of the distribution" (p. 16). He explains that males and females have similar average scores on math tests but that there are more males than females in the top and the bottom percentiles. This greater variance means that there are disproportionately more male than female math geniuses (and math dunces) and thus more male than female candidates for top math and science positions at major research universities. Pinker explains this greater variance through evolutionary biology: men can pass on their genes to dozens of offspring, whereas women can pass on their genes to only a few. Pinker also argues that men and women have different brain structures that result in different kinds of thinking. For example, Pinker cites research that shows that on average men are better at mental rotation of figures and mathematical word problems, while women are better at remembering locations, doing mathematical calculations,

APA

reading faces, spelling, and using language. Not only do males and females think differently, but they release different hormones. These hormones help shape gender because males release more testosterone and females more estrogen, meaning that men are more aggressive and apt to take risks, while women "are more solicitous to their children" (p. 16). One example Pinker uses to support his biological hypothesis is the case of males born with abnormal genitals and raised as females. These children have more testosterone than normal female children, and many times they show characteristically male interests and behavior. Pinker uses these cases as evidence that no matter how a child is raised, the child's biology determines the child's interests.

Although Pinker demonstrates that biology plays some role in determining math aptitude, he almost completely ignores the much larger role of discrimination and socialization in shaping the career paths of women. According to an editorial from *Nature Neuroscience* ("Separating," 2005), "[t]he evidence to support [Summers's] hypothesis of 'innate difference' turns out to be quite slim" (p. 253). The editorial reports that intercultural studies of the variance between boys' and girls' scores on math tests show significant differences between countries. For example, in Iceland girls outscore boys on math tests. The editorial also says that aptitude tests are not very good at predicting the future success of students and that the "SATs tend to underpredict female and over-predict male academic performance" (p. 253). The editorial doesn't deny that men and women's brains work differently, but states that the differences are too small to be blamed for the underrepresentation of women in math and science careers.

If biology doesn't explain the low number of women choosing math and science careers, then what is the cause? Many believe the cause is culture, especially the gender roles children are taught at a very young age. One such believer is Deborah L. Rhode (1997), an attorney and social scientist who specializes in ethics and gender, law, and public policy. Rhode describes the different gender roles females and males are expected to follow from a very young age. Gender roles are portrayed in children's books and television shows. These gender roles are represented by male characters as heroes and problem solvers, while the female characters are distressed damsels. Another example of gender roles is that only a very small number of these shows and books portray working mothers or stay-at-home fathers. Rhodes also discusses how movies and popular music, especially rap and heavy metal, encourage violence and objectify women. As girls grow up, they face more and more gender stereotypes from toys to magazines. Parents give their boys interactive, problem-solving toys such as chemistry sets and telescopes, while girls are left with dolls. Although more organizations such as the Girl Scouts of America, who sponsor the Website (Girls Go Tech.org) are trying to interest girls in science and math and advertise careers in those fields to girls, the societal forces working against this encouragement are also still pervasive. For example, magazines for teenage girls encourage attracting male attention and the importance of looks, while being smart and successful is considered unattractive. Because adolescents face so many gender stereotypes, it is no wonder that these stereotypes shape the career paths they choose later in life. The gender roles engraved in our adolescents' minds cause discrimination against women later in life. Once women are socialized to see themselves as dependent and not as smart as males, it becomes very difficult to break away from these gender stereotypes. With gender bias so apparent in our society, it is hard for females to have high enough self-confidence to continue to compete with males in many fields.

The effect of socialization begins at a very early age. One study (Clearfield & Nelson, 2006) shows how parents unconsciously send gendered messages to their infants and toddlers. This study examined differences in mothers' speech patterns and play behaviors based on the gender of infants ranging from six months to fourteen months. Although there was no difference in the actual play behavior of male and female infants, the researchers discovered interesting differences in the way mothers interacted with daughters versus sons. Mothers of daughters tended to ask their daughters more questions, encouraging social interaction, whereas mothers of sons were less verbal, encouraging their sons to be more independent. The researchers concluded that "the mothers in our study may have been teaching their infants about gender roles through modeling and reinforcement....Thus girls may acquire the knowledge that they are 'supposed' to engage in higher levels of interaction with other people and display more verbal behavior than boys....In contrast, the boys were reinforced for exploring on their own" (p. 136).

One of the strongest arguments against the biological hypothesis comes from a transgendered Stanford neurobiologist, Ben A. Barres (2006), who has been a scientist first as a woman and then as a man. In his article "Does Gender Matter?" Barres states that "there is little evidence that gender differences in [mathematical] abilities exist, are innate or are even relevant to the lack of advancement of women in science" (p. 134). Barres provides much anecdotal evidence of the way women are discriminated against in this male-dominated field. Barres notes that simply putting a male name rather than a female name on an article or résumé increases its perceived value. He also describes research showing that men and women do equally well in gender-blind academic competitions but that men win disproportionately in contests where gender is revealed.

As Barres says, "The bar is unconsciously raised so high for women and minority candidates that few emerge as winners" (p. 134). In one study reported by Barres, women applying for a research grant needed more than twice the productivity of men in order to be considered equally competent. As a female-to-male transgendered person, Barres has personally experienced discrimination when trying to succeed in the science and math fields. When in college, Barres was told that her boyfriend must have done her homework, and she later lost a prestigious fellowship competition to a male even though she was told her application was stronger and she had published "six high-impact papers," while the man that won published only one. Barres even notices subtle differences, such as the fact that he can now finish a sentence without being interrupted by a male.

Barres urges women to stand up publicly against discrimination. One woman he particularly admires as a strong female role model is MIT biologist Nancy Hopkins, who sued the MIT administration for discrimination based on the lesser amount of lab space allocated to female scientists. The evidence from this study was so strong that even the president of MIT publicly admitted that discrimination was a problem (p. 134). Barres wants more women to follow Hopkins's lead. He believes that women often don't realize they are being discriminated against because they have faith that the world is equal. Barres explains this tendency as a "denial of personal disadvantage" (p. 134). Very few women will admit to seeing or experiencing discrimination. Until discrimination and sexism are addressed, women will continue to be oppressed.

As a society, we should not accept Lawrence Summers's hypothesis that biological differences are the reason women are not found in high-prestige tenured jobs in math and science. In fact, in another generation the gap between men and women in math and science might completely disappear. In 2003–2004, women received close to one-third of all doctorates in mathematics, up from 15 percent of doctorates in the early 1980s ("American Mathematical Society," 2005). Although more recent data are not yet available, the signs point to a steadily increasing number of women entering the fields of math, science, and engineering. Blaming biology for the lack of women in these fields and refusing to fault our culture is taking the easy way out. Our culture can change.

WHY LAWRENCE SUMMERS WAS WRONG   6
References

American Mathematical Society. (2005, July 6). *Women in Mathematics: Study shows gains*. Retrieved from http://www/ams.org/news?news_id=489

Barres, B. A. "Does gender matter?" *Nature* 44.7 (2006): 133–36. doi:10.1038/442133a

Clearfield, M. W., and Nelson, N. M. (2006). Sex differences in mothers' speech and play behavior with 6-, 9-, and 14-month-old infants. *Sex Roles* 54.1–2 : 127–37. doi:.10.1007/s11199-005-8874-1

Pinker, S. (2005 February 14). The science of difference: Sex ed. *New Republic*. 232, 15–17.

Rhode, D. L. (1997) *Speaking of sex: The denial of gender inequality*. Cambridge, MA: Harvard University Press.

Separating science from stereotype. [Editorial]. (2005) *Nature Neuroscience* 8(3) 253. doi:10.1038/nn0305-253

Summers. L. H. (2005 January 14). Remarks at NBER conference on diversifying the science and engineering workforce. Retrieved from http://designintelligences.wordpress.com/lawrence-h-summers-remarks-at-nber-conference/

APA

Critiquing "Why Lawrence Summers Was Wrong"

1. The controversy sparked by Harvard President Lawrence Summers' remarks was a highly politicized version of the classic nature/nurture problem. Liberal commentators claimed that women were underrepresented in science because of cultural practices that discouraged young girls from becoming interested in math and science and that blocked women Ph.D.s from advancing in their scientific careers. In contrast, conservative commentators—praising Summers' courage for raising a politically incorrect subject—took the "nature" side of this argument by citing studies pointing to innate cognitive differences between human males and females. How would you characterize Christianson's position in this controversy?

2. How does Christianson handle opposing views in her essay?

3. Do you regard Christianson's essay as a valuable contribution to the controversy over the reasons for the low numbers of women in math and science? Why or why not?

4. How would you characterize Christianson's *ethos* as a student writer in this piece? Does her *ethos* help convince you that her argument is sound? Explain.

Our second reading, by evolutionary biologist Olivia Judson of Imperial College in London, was published as an op-ed piece in the *New York Times*. In this causal argument, a distinguished scientist looks at the scientific evidence bearing on Summers' remarks.

Different but (Probably) Equal

OLIVIA JUDSON

Hypothesis: males and females are typically indistinguishable on the basis of their behaviors and intellectual abilities.

This is not true for elephants. Females have big vocabularies and hang out in herds; males tend to live in solitary splendor, and insofar as they speak at all, their conversation appears mostly to consist of elephant for "I'm in the mood, I'm in the mood … "

The hypothesis is not true for zebra finches. Males sing elaborate songs. Females can't sing at all. A zebra finch opera would have to have males in all the singing roles.

And it's not true for green spoon worms. This animal, which lives on the sea floor, has one of the largest known size differences between male and female: the male is 200,000 times smaller. He

spends his whole life in her reproductive tract, fertilizing eggs by regurgitating sperm through his mouth. He's so different from his mate that when he was first discovered by science, he was not recognized as being a green spoon worm; instead, he was thought to be a parasite.

5   Is it ridiculous to suppose that the hypothesis might not be true for humans either?

No. But it is not fashionable— as Lawrence Summers, president of Harvard University, discovered when he suggested this month that greater intrinsic ability might be one reason that men are over-represented at the top levels of fields involving math, science, and engineering.

There are—as the maladroit Mr. Summers should have known—good reasons it's not fashionable. Beliefs that men are intrinsically better at this or that have repeatedly led to discrimination and prejudice, and then they've been proved to be nonsense. Women were thought not to be world-class musicians. But when American symphony orchestras introduced blind auditions in the 1970s—the musician plays behind a screen so that his or her gender is invisible to those listening—the number of women offered jobs in professional orchestras increased.

Similarly, in science, studies of the ways that grant applications are evaluated have shown that women are more likely to get financing when those reading the applications do not know the sex of the applicant. In other words, there's still plenty of work to do to level the playing field; there's no reason to suppose there's something inevitable about the status quo.

All the same, it seems a shame if we can't even voice the question. Sex differences are fascinating— and entirely unlike the other biological differences that distinguish other groups of living things (like populations and species). Sex differences never arise in isolation, with females evolving on a mountaintop, say, and males evolving in a cave. Instead, most genes—and in some species, all genes—spend equal time in each sex. Many sex differences are not, therefore, the result of *his* having one gene while *she* has another. Rather, they are attributable to the way particular genes behave when they find themselves in *him* instead of *her*.

The magnificent difference between male and female green spoon worms, for example, has nothing to do with their having different genes: each green spoon worm larva could go either way. Which sex it becomes depends on whether it meets a female during its first three weeks of life. If it meets a female, it becomes male and prepares to regurgitate; if it doesn't, it becomes female and settles into a crack on the sea floor.

What's more, the fact that most genes occur in both males and females can generate interesting sexual tensions. In male fruit flies, for instance, variants of genes that confer particular success—which on Mother Nature's abacus is the number of descendants you have—tend to be detrimental when they occur in females, and vice versa. Worse: the bigger the advantage in one sex, the more detrimental those genes are in the other. This means that, at least for fruit flies, the same genes that make a male a Don Juan would also turn a female into a wall-flower; conversely, the genes that make a female a knockout babe would produce a clumsy fellow with the sex appeal of a cake tin.

But why do sex differences appear at all? They appear when the secret of success differs for males and females: the more divergent the paths to success, the more extreme the physiological differences. Peacocks have huge tails and strut about because peahens prefer males with big tails. Bull elephant seals grow to five times the mass of females because big males are better at monopolizing the beaches where the females haul out to have sex and give birth.

Meanwhile, the crow-like jackdaw has (as far as we can tell) no obvious sex differences and appears to lead a life of devoted monogamy. Here, what works for him also seems to work for her, though the female is more likely to sit on the eggs. So by studying the differences—and similarities— among men and women, we can potentially learn about the forces that have shaped us in the past.

And I think the news is good. We're not like green spoon worms or elephant seals, with males and females so different that aspiring to an egalitarian society would be ludicrous. And though we may not be jackdaws either—men and women tend to look different, though even here there's overlap—it's obvious that where there are intellectual differences, they are so slight they cannot be prejudged.

15   The interesting questions are, is there an average intrinsic difference? And how extensive is the variation? I would love to know if the averages are the same but the underlying variation is different—with members of one sex tending to be either superb or dreadful at particular sorts of thinking while members of the other are pretty good but rarely exceptional.

Curiously, such a result could arise even if the forces shaping men and women have been identical. In some animals—humans and fruit flies come to mind—males have an X chromosome and a Y chromosome while females have two Xs. In females, then, extreme effects of genes on one X chromosome can be offset by the genes on the other. But in males, there's no hiding your X. In birds and butterflies, though, it's the other way around: females have a Z chromosome and a W chromosome, and males snooze along with two Zs.

The science of sex differences, even in fruit flies and toads, is a ferociously complex subject. It's also famously fraught, given its malignant history. In fact, there was a time not so long ago when I would have balked at the whole enterprise: the idea there might be intrinsic cognitive differences between men and women was one I found insulting. But science is a great persuader. The jackdaws and spoon worms have forced me to change my mind. Now I'm keen to know what sets men and women apart—and no longer afraid of what we may find.

Critiquing "Different but (Probably) Equal"

1. What parts of Judson's article tend to support the "nurture" view that cultural practices account for women's underrepresentation in math and science? What parts tend to support the "nature" view?
2. Judson's argument relies heavily on analogies between humans and the animal world. In your own words, explain why the green spoon worm and the jackdaw (crow) are important to Judson's argument. Why does she say that the interesting questions involve "average intrinsic difference" and the extensiveness of "variation"?
3. How would you characterize Judson's *ethos* in this article? Pay particular attention to the narrative embedded in the last paragraph—her claim that she is no longer afraid of what we might find. How important is it that we know the author is a woman?

Our final causal argument, by student writer Carlos Macias, examines the phenomenon of credit card debt among college students. Note how Macias intermixes personal experiences and research data in order to make his case.

"The Credit Card Company Made Me Do It!"—The Credit Card Industry's Role in Causing Student Debt

CARLOS MACIAS (STUDENT)

One day on spring break this year, I strolled into a Gap store. I found several items that I decided to buy. As I was checking out, the cute female clerk around my age, with perfect hair and makeup, asked if I wanted to open a GapCard to save 10 percent on all purchases I made at Gap, Banana Republic, and Old Navy that day. She said I would also earn points toward Gap gift certificates in the future. Since I shop at the Gap often enough, I decided to take her up on her offer. I filled out the form she handed me, and within seconds I—a jobless, indebted-from-student-loans, full-time college student with no substantial assets or income whatsoever—was offered a card with a $1000 credit line. Surprised by the speed at which I was approved and the amount that I was approved for, I decided to proceed to both Banana Republic and Old Navy that day to see if there was anything else I might be interested in getting (there was). By the end of the day, I had rung up nearly $200 in purchases.

I know my $200 shopping spree on credit is nothing compared to some of the horror stories I have heard from friends. One of my friends, a college sophomore, is carrying $2000 on a couple of different cards, a situation that is not unusual at all. According to a May 2005 study by Nellie Mae, students with credit cards carry average balances of just under $3000 by the time they are seniors ("Undergraduate"2). The problem is that most students don't have the income to pay off their balances, so they become hooked into paying high interest rates and fees that enrich banks while exploiting students who have not yet learned how to exercise control on their spending habits.

Who is to blame for this situation? Many people might blame the students themselves, citing the importance of individual responsibility and proclaiming that no one forces students to use credit cards. But I put most of the blame directly on the credit card companies. Credit cards are enormously profitable; according to a *New York Times* article, the industry made $30 billion in pretax profits in 2003 alone (McGeehan). Hooking college students on credit cards is essential for this profit, not only because companies make a lot of money off the students themselves, but because hooking students on cards creates a habit that lasts a lifetime. Credit card companies' predatory lending practices—such as using exploitive advertising, using credit scoring to determine creditworthiness, disguising the real cost of credit, and taking advantage of U.S. government deregulation—are causing many unwitting college students to accumulate high levels of credit card debt.

First of all, credit card companies bombard students with highly sophisticated advertising. College students, typically, are in an odd "in-between" stage where they are not necessarily teens anymore, provided for by their parents, but neither are they fully adults, able to provide entirely for themselves. Many students feel the pressures from family, peers and themselves to assume adult roles in terms of their dress and jobs, not relying on Mom or Dad for help. Card companies know about these pressures. Moreover, college students are easy to target because they are concentrated on campuses and generally consume the same media. I probably get several mailings a month offering me a preapproved credit card. These advertisements are filled with happy campus scenes featuring students wearing just the right clothes, carrying their books in just the right backpack, playing music on their iPods or opening their laptop computers. They also appeal to students' desire to feel like responsible adults by emphasizing little emergencies that college students can relate to such as car breakdowns on a road trip. These advertisements illustrate a point made by a team of researchers in an article entitled "Credit Cards as Lifestyle Facilitators": The authors explain how credit card companies want consumers to view credit cards as "lifestyle facilitators" that enable "lifestyle building" and "lifestyle signaling" (Bernthal, Crockett, and Rose). Credit cards make it easy for students to live the lifestyle pictured in the credit card ads.

5   Another contributing cause of high credit card debt for college students is the method that credit card companies use to grant credit—through credit scoring that does not consider income. It was credit scoring that allowed me to get that quadruple-digit credit line at the Gap while already living in the red. The application I filled out never asked my income. Instead, the personal information I listed was used to pull up my credit score, which is based on records of outstanding debts and payment history. Credit scoring allows banks to grant credit cards based on a person's record of responsibility in paying bills rather than on income. According to finance guru Suze Orman, "Your FICO [credit] score is a great tool to size up how good you will be handling a new loan or credit card" (21). Admittedly, credit scoring has made the lending process as a whole much fairer, giving individuals such as minorities and women the chance to qualify for credit even if they have minimal incomes. But when credit card companies use credit scoring to determine college students' creditworthiness, many students are unprepared to handle a credit line that greatly exceeds their ability to pay based on income. In fact, the Center for Responsible Lending, a consumer advocacy organization in North Carolina, lobbied Congress in September 2003 to require credit card companies to secure proof of adequate income for college-age customers before approving credit card applications ("Credit Card Policy Recommendations"). If Congress passed such legislation, credit card companies would not be able to as easily take advantage of college students who have not yet learned how to exercise control on their spending habits. They would have to offer students credit lines commensurate to their incomes. No wonder these companies vehemently opposed this legislation.

Yet another contributing cause of high levels of credit card debt is the high cost of having this debt, which credit card companies are especially talented at disguising. As credit card debt increases, card companies compound unpaid interest, adding it to the balance that must be repaid. If this balance is not repaid, they charge interest on unpaid interest. They add exorbitant fees for small slip-ups like making a late payment or exceeding the credit limit. While these costs are listed on statements when first added to the balance, they quickly vanish into the "New Balance" number on all subsequent statements, as if these fees were simply past purchases that have yet to be repaid. As the balance continues to grow, banks spike interest rates even higher. In his 2004 article

"Soaring Interest Is Compounding Credit Card Pain for Millions," Patrick McGeehan describes a "new era of consumer credit, in which thousands of Americans are paying millions of dollars each month in fees that they did not expect … lenders are doubling or tripling interest rates with little warning or explanation." These rate hikes are usually tucked into the pages of fine print that come with credit cards, which many consumers are unable to fully read, let alone understand. Usually, a credit card company will offer a very low "teaser rate" that expires after several months. While this industry practice is commonly understood by consumers, many do not understand that credit card companies usually reserve the right to raise the rate at any time for almost any reason, causing debt levels to rise further.

Admittedly, while individual consumers must be held accountable for any debt they accumulate and should understand compound and variable interest and fees, students' ignorance is welcomed by the credit card industry. In order to completely understand how the credit card industry has caused college students to amass high amounts of credit card debt, it is necessary to explain how this vicious monster was let loose during banking deregulation over the past 30 years. In 1978, the Supreme Court opened the floodgates by ruling that the federal government could not set a cap on interest rates that banks charged for credit cards; that was to be left to the states. With Uncle Sam no longer protecting consumers, Delaware and South Dakota passed laws that removed caps on interest rates, in order to woo credit card companies to conduct nationwide business there (McGeehan). Since then, the credit card industry has become one of the most profitable industries ever. Credit card companies were given another sweet deal from the U.S. Supreme Court in 1996, when the Court deregulated fees. Since then, the average late fee has risen from $10 or less, to $39 (McGeehan). While a lot of these fees and finance charges are avoidable if the student pays the balance in full, on time, every month, for college students who carry balances for whatever reason, these charges are tacked on, further adding to the principal on which they pay a high rate of compounded interest. (Seventy-nine percent of the students surveyed in the Nellie Mae study said that they regularly carried a balance on their cards [8].) Moreover, the U.S. government has refused to step in to regulate the practice of universal default, where a credit card company can raise the rate they charge if a consumer is late on an unrelated bill, like a utility payment. Even for someone who pays his or her bills in full, on time, 99% of the time, one bill-paying slip-up can cause an avalanche of fees and frustration, thanks to the credit card industry.

Credit card companies exploit college students' lack of financial savvy and security. It is no secret that most full-time college students are not independently wealthy; many have limited means. So why are these companies so willing to issue cards to poor college students? Profits, of course! If they made credit cards less available to struggling consumers such as college students, consumers would have a more difficult time racking up huge balances, plain and simple. It's funny that Citibank, one of the largest, most profitable credit card companies in the world, proudly exclaims "Live richly" in its advertisements. At the rate that it and other card companies collect interest and fees from their customers, a more appropriate slogan would be "Live poorly."

Works Cited

Bernthal, Matthew J., David Crockett, and Randall L. Rose. "Credit Cards as Lifestyle Facilitators." *Journal of Consumer Research* 32.1 (2005): 130–45. *Research Library Complete.* Web. 18 June 2005.

"Credit Card Policy Recommendations." *Center for Responsible Lending.* Center for Responsible Lending, Sept. 2003. Web. 18 June 2005.

McGeehan, Patrick. "Soaring Interest Is Compounding Credit Card Pain for Millions." *New York Times.* New York Times, 21 Nov. 2004. Web. 3 July 2005.

Nellie Mae. "Undergraduate Students and Credit Cards in 2004: An Analysis of Usage Rates and Trends." *Nellie Mae.* SLM Corporation, May 2005. Web. 3 July 2005.

Orman, Suze. *The Money Book for the Young, Fabulous and Broke.* New York: Riverhead, 2005. Print.

Critiquing 'The Credit Card Company Made Me Do It!'

1. How effective is Macias's argument that the predatory practices of banks and credit card companies are the primary cause of credit card debt among college students?

2. Suppose that you wanted to join this conversation by offering a counterview with a thesis something like this: "Although Macias is partially correct that banks and credit card companies play a role in producing credit card debt among college students, he underestimates other important factors." What would you emphasize as the causes of credit card debt? How would you make your case?

For additional writing, reading, and research resources, go to www.mycomplab.com

Evaluation and Ethical Arguments

13

Case 1 What Is the Value of Immigrants?

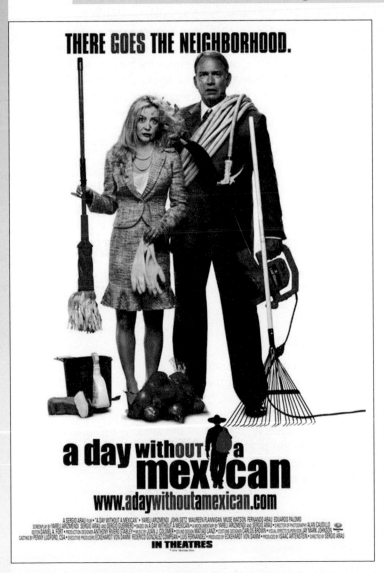

As we explored in Chapter 2, the United States has been embroiled in an ongoing controversy over the influx of illegal immigrants, mostly from Mexico and Central America. While some Americans want to offer citizenship as soon as possible to these immigrants, others want to close off the border between Mexico and the United States and to reduce the number of undocumented workers through deportation or through a crackdown on employers. This marketing image for the movie *A Day without a Mexican* makes a humorous evaluation argument in favor of Mexican immigrants. It argues that the labor provided by immigrants is valuable—so valuable, in fact, that Californians could hardly endure a day without them. The image of the wealthy white couple having to

285

do their own housekeeping, yard work, and tomato picking is an ironic reminder that the standard of living many Americans take for granted depends on the cheap labor of immigrants.

Case 2   What Is a "Good Organ" for a Transplant? How Can an Ill Person Ethically Find an Organ Donor?

In the United States some 87,000 sick people have been waiting as long as six years for an organ transplant, with a portion of these dying before they can find a donor. The problem of organ shortages raises two kinds of evaluation issues. First, doctors are reevaluating the criteria by which they judge a "good organ"—that is, a good lung, kidney, or liver suitable for transplanting. Formerly, people who were elderly or obese or who had engaged in risky behaviors or experienced heart failure or other medical conditions were not considered sources of good organs. Now doctors are reconsidering these sources as well as exploring the use of organs from pigs. Second, the shortage of organs for donation has raised numerous ethical issues: Is it ethical for people to bypass the national waiting list for organs by advertising on billboards and Web sites (see the billboard advertising for a liver on page 211)? Is it morally right for people to sell their organs? Is it right for patients and families to buy organs or in any way remunerate living organ donors? Some states are passing laws that allow some financial compensation to living organ donors.

In our roles as citizens and professionals, we are continually expected to make difficult evaluations and to persuade others to accept them. In this chapter, you will learn to:

- Analyze questions about the worth or value of something by using a criteria-match thinking strategy
- Analyze ethical questions from the perspective of principles or consequences
- Use these analytical tools to make your own evaluation or ethical arguments

An Overview of Evaluation Arguments

In this chapter we explain strategies for conducting two different kinds of evaluation arguments. First, we examine categorical evaluations of the kind "Is this thing a good member of its class?"* (Is Ramon a good committee chair?) In such an evaluation, the writer determines the extent to which a given something possesses the qualities or standards of its class. Second, we examine ethical arguments of the kind "Is this action right (wrong)?" (Was it right or wrong to drop atomic bombs on Hiroshima and Nagasaki in World War II?) In these arguments, the writer evaluates a given act from the perspective of some system of morality or ethics.

---

*In addition to the term *good*, a number of other evaluative terms involve the same kind of thinking— *effective, successful, workable, excellent, valuable,* and so forth.

Criteria-Match Structure of Categorical Evaluations

A categorical evaluation uses a criteria-match structure similar to the structure we examined in definition arguments (see Chapter 11). A typical claim-with-reasons frame for an evaluation argument has the following structure:

> This thing/phenomenon is/is not a good member of its class because it meets (fails to meet) criteria A, B, and C.

The main conceptual difference between an evaluation argument and a definition argument is the nature of the contested category. In a definition argument, one argues whether a particular thing belongs within a certain category. (Is this swampy area a *wetland?*) In an evaluation argument, we know what category something belongs to. For example, we know that this 2002 Ford Escort is a *used car.* For an evaluation argument, the question is whether this 2002 Ford Escort is a *good used car.* Or, to place the question within a rhetorical context, is this Ford Escort a *good used car for me to buy for college?*

Toulmin Framework for an Evaluation Argument

As an illustration of the criteria-match structure of an evaluation argument, let's continue with the Ford Escort example. Suppose you get in a debate with Parent or Significant Other about the car you should buy for college. Let's say that Parent or Significant Other argues that the following criteria are particularly important: (1) initial value for the money, (2) dependability, (3) safety, and (4) low maintenance costs. (Note: You would strenuously reject these criteria if you were looking for a muscle car, coolness, or driving excitement. This is why establishing criteria is a crucial part of evaluation arguments.) A Toulmin analysis of how Parent or Significant Other might make the case for "initial value for the money" is shown on page 288. Note how the warrant is a criterion while the stated reason and grounds assert that the specific case meets the criterion.

As the Toulmin analysis shows, Parent or Significant Other needs to argue that getting high value for the initial money is an important consideration (the criterion argument) and that this 2002 Ford Escort meets this criterion better than competing choices (the match argument). If you can't see yourself driving a Ford Escort, you've got to either argue for other criteria (attack the warrant) or accept the criterion but argue that the Ford Escort's projected maintenance costs undermine its initial value (attack the reason and grounds).

Conducting a Categorical Evaluation Argument

Now that you understand the basic criteria-match structure of a categorical evaluation, let's look at some thinking strategies you can use to develop your criteria and to argue whether the thing you are evaluating meets the criteria.

Toulmin Analysis of the Ford Escort Argument

ENTHYMEME

CLAIM The Ford Escort is a good used car for you at college

REASON because it provides the most initial value for the money.

GROUNDS

- Evidence that Escorts are dependable

- Evidence that Escorts are not in very high demand, so you can get a 2002 Escort for $5,000 less than a 2002 Honda Civic with the same mileage

- Evidence that a 2002 Civic for the same price would have double the miles

- Low initial mileage means years of dependable use without large repair bills.

CONDITIONS OF REBUTTAL
Attacking the reason and grounds

A 2002 Escort is not as great a value as it seems:

- My research suggests there are high maintenance costs after 60,000 miles.

- The initial savings may be blown on high repair costs.

WARRANT

High value for the initial money is an important criterion for buying your college car.

BACKING

Arguments showing why it is important to get high value for the money:

- Money saved on the car can be used for other college expenses.

- Buying in this thrifty way meets our family's image of being careful shoppers.

CONDITIONS OF REBUTTAL
Attacking the warrant and backing

Other criteria are more important to me:

- Great handling and acceleration

- The fun of driving

- The status of having a cool car

Developing Your Criteria

To help you develop your criteria, we suggest a three-step thinking process:

1. Place the thing you are evaluating in the smallest relevant category so that you don't compare apples to oranges.
2. Develop criteria for your evaluation based on the purpose or function of this category.
3. Determine the relative weight of your criteria.

Let's look at each of these steps in turn.

Step 1: Place the Thing You Are Evaluating in the Smallest Relevant Category
Placing your contested thing in the smallest category is a crucial first step. Suppose, for

example, that you want one of your professors to write you a letter of recommendation for a summer job. The professor will need to know what kind of summer job. Are you applying to become a camp counselor, a law office intern, a retail sales clerk, or a tour guide at a wild animal park in your state? Each of these jobs has different criteria for excellence. Or to take a different example, suppose that you want to evaluate e-mail as a medium of correspondence. To create a stable context for your evaluation, you need to place e-mail in its smallest relevant category. You may choose to evaluate e-mail as medium for business communication (by contrasting e-mail with direct personal contact, phone conversations, or postal mail), as a medium for staying in touch with high school friends (in contrast, say, to text messaging or Facebook), or as a medium for carrying on a long-distance romance (in contrast, say, to old-fashioned "love letters"). Again, criteria will vary across these different categories.

By placing your contested thing in the smallest relevant class, you avoid the apples-and-oranges problem. That is, to give a fair evaluation of a perfectly good apple, you need to judge it under the class "apple" and not under the next larger class, "fruit," or a neighboring class such as "orange." And to be even more precise, you may wish to evaluate your apple in the class "eating apple" as opposed to "pie apple" because the latter class is supposed to be tarter and the former class juicier and sweeter.

Step 2: Develop Criteria for Your Evaluation Based on the Purpose or Functions of This Category   Suppose that the summer job you are applying for is tour guide at a wild animal park in your state. The functions of a tour guide are to drive the tour buses, make people feel welcome, give them interesting information about the wild animals in the park, make their visit pleasant, and so forth. Criteria for a good tour guide would thus include reliability and responsibility, a friendly demeanor, good speaking skills, and knowledge of the kinds of animals in the wild animal park. In our e-mail example, suppose that you want to evaluate e-mail as a medium for business communication. The purpose of this class is to provide a quick and reliable means of communication that increases efficiency, minimizes misunderstandings, protects the confidentiality of internal communications, and so forth. Based on these purposes, you might establish the following criteria:

A good medium for business communication:

- Is easy to use, quick, and reliable
- Increases employee efficiency
- Prevents misunderstandings
- Maintains confidentiality where needed

Step 3: Determine the Relative Weight of Your Criteria   In some evaluations all the criteria are equally important. However, sometimes a phenomenon to be evaluated is strong in one criterion but weak in another—a situation that forces the evaluator to decide which criterion takes precedence. For example, the supervisor interviewing candidates for tour guide at the wild animal park may find one candidate who is very knowledgeable about the wildlife but doesn't have good speaking skills. The supervisor would need to decide which of these two criteria gets more weight.

EXAMINING VISUAL ARGUMENTS

An Evaluation Claim

This photograph of Stephen Colbert and Jon Stewart of *The Colbert Report* and *The Daily Show* was taken at the October 30, 2010 "Rally to Restore Sanity 'or Fear,'" on the Washington D.C. National Mall, an event that drew thousands of people. The event followed by two months the "Restoring Honor Rally" led by conservative Fox News talk show celebrity Glenn Beck on August 28, 2010. Political commentators debated whether the Colbert and Stewart rally was simply a satirical entertainment mocking the Beck rally or whether it was serious political activism supporting the liberal left. If your goal was to portray this event as serious political activism, would this photograph be a good image to accompany your argument? What criteria would you establish for selecting a photograph to support your argument that Colbert and Stewart are effective political activists and not simply entertainers?

Making Your Match Argument

Once you've established and weighed your criteria, you'll need to use examples and other evidence to show that the thing being evaluated meets or does not meet the criteria. For example, your professor could argue that you would be a good wildlife park tour guide because you have strong interpersonal skills (based on your work on a college orientation committee), that you have good speaking skills (based on a speech you gave in the professor's class), and that you have quite a bit of knowledge about animals and ecology (based on your major in environmental science).

In our e-mail example, you might establish the following working thesis:

> Despite its being easy to learn, quick, and reliable, e-mail is not an effective medium for business communication because it reduces worker efficiency, leads to frequent misunderstandings, and often lacks confidentiality.

You could develop your last three points as follows:

- **E-mail reduces worker efficiency.** You can use personal anecdotes and research data to show how checking e-mail is addictive and how it eats into worker time (one research article says that the average worker devotes ten minutes of every working hour to reading and responding to e-mail). You might also show how e-mail frequently diverts workers from high-priority to low-priority tasks. Some research even suggests that workers don't relax as much away from work because they are always checking their e-mail.
- **E-mail leads to misunderstandings.** Because an e-mail message is often composed rapidly without revision, e-mail can cause people to state ideas imprecisely, to write something they would never say face-to-face, or to convey an unintended tone. Without the benefits of tone of voice and body language available in face-to-face conversation, e-mail can be easily misread. You could give a personal example of a high-consequence misunderstanding caused by e-mail.
- **E-mail often lacks confidentiality.** You could provide anecdotal or research evidence of cases in which a person clicked on the "reply to all" button rather than the "reply" button, sending a message intended for one person to a whole group of people. Stories also abound of employers who snoop through employees' e-mail messages or workers who forward e-mails without permission from the sender. Perhaps most troubling is the way that e-mail messages are archived forever, so that messages that you thought were deleted may show up years later in a lawsuit.

As these examples illustrate, the key to a successful match argument is to use sufficient examples and other evidence to show how your contested phenomenon meets or does not meet each of your criteria.

■ ■ ■ **FOR CLASS DISCUSSION   Developing Criteria and Match Arguments**
The following small-group exercise can be accomplished in one or two class hours. It gives you a good model of the process you can go through in order to write your own categorical evaluation.

1. Choose a specific controversial person, thing, or event to evaluate (your school's computer services help desk, the invite-a-professor-to-lunch program in your dormitory, Harvey's Hamburger Haven). To help you think of ideas, try brainstorming controversial members of the following categories: *people* (athletes, political leaders, musicians, clergy, entertainers, businesspeople); *science and technology* (weapons systems, word-processing programs, spreadsheets, automotive advancements, treatments for diseases); *media* (a newspaper, a magazine or journal, a TV program, a radio station, a Web site, an advertisement); *government and world affairs* (an economic policy, a Supreme Court decision, a law or legal practice, a government custom or practice, a foreign policy); *the arts* (a movie, a book, a building, a painting, a piece of music); *your college or university* (a course, a teacher, a textbook, a curriculum, an administrative policy, the financial aid system); *the world of work* (a job, a company operation, a dress policy, a merit pay system, a hiring policy, a supervisor); or any other categories of your choice.

2. Place your controversial person or thing within the smallest relevant class, thus providing a rhetorical context for your argument and showing what is at stake. Do you want to evaluate Harvey's Hamburger Haven in the broad category of *restaurants,* in the narrow category of *hamburger joints,* or in a different narrow category such as *late-night study places?* If you are evaluating a recent film, are you evaluating it as *a chick flick,* as a possible *Academy Award nominee,* or as a *political filmmaking statement?*

3. Make a list of the purpose or function of that class, and then list the criteria that a good member of that class would need to have in order to accomplish the purpose or function. (What is the purpose or function of a computer services help desk, a late-night study place, or a chick flick? What criteria for excellence can you derive from these purposes or functions?)

4. If necessary, rank your criteria from most to least important. (For a late-night study place, what is more important: good ambience, Wi-Fi availability, good coffee, or convenient location?)

5. Provide examples and other evidence to show how your contested something matches or does not match each of your criteria. (As a late-night study place, Carol's Coffee Closet beats out Harvey's Hamburger Haven. Although Harvey's Hamburger Haven has the most convenient location, Carol's Coffee Closet has Wi-Fi, an ambience conducive to studying, and excellent coffee.)

An Overview of Ethical Arguments

A second kind of evaluation argument focuses on moral or ethical issues, which can often merge or overlap with categorical evaluations. For example, many apparently straightforward categorical evaluations can turn out to have an ethical dimension. Consider again the criteria for buying a car. Most people would base their evaluations on cost, safety, comfort, and so forth. But some people may feel morally obligated to buy the most fuel-efficient car, to buy an American car, or not to buy a car from a manufacturer whose labor policies they find morally repugnant. Depending on how large a role ethical considerations play in the evaluation, we may choose to call this an ethical argument based on moral considerations rather than a categorical evaluation based on the purposes of a class or category.

As the discussion so far has suggested, disagreements about an ethical issue often stem from different systems of values that make the issue irresolvable. It is precisely this problem—the lack of shared assumptions about value—that makes it so important to confront issues of ethics with rational deliberation. The arguments you produce may not persuade others to your view, but they should make others think seriously about it, and they should help you work out more clearly the reasons and warrants for your own beliefs. By writing about ethical issues, you see more clearly what you believe and why you believe it. Although the arguments demanded by ethical issues require rigorous thought, they force us to articulate our most deeply held beliefs and our richest feelings.

Major Ethical Systems

When we are faced with an ethical issue, we must move from arguments of good or bad to arguments of right or wrong. The terms *right* and *wrong* are clearly different from the terms *good* and *bad* when the latter terms mean, simply, "effective" (meets purposes of class, as in "This is a good laptop") or "ineffective" (fails to meet purposes of class, as in "This is a bad cookbook"). But *right* and *wrong* often also differ from what seems to be a moral use of the terms *good* and *bad*. We may say, for example, that sunshine is good because it brings pleasure and that cancer is bad because it brings pain and death, but that is not quite the same thing as saying that sunshine is "right" and cancer is "wrong." It is the problem of "right" and "wrong" that ethical arguments confront.

For example, from a nonethical standpoint, you could say that certain people are "good terrorists" in that they fully realize the purpose of the class "terrorist": they cause great anguish and damage with a minimum of resources, and they bring much attention to their cause. However, if we want to condemn terrorism on ethical grounds, we have to say that terrorism is wrong. The ethical question is not whether a person fulfills the purposes of the class "terrorist," but whether it is wrong for such a class to exist.

There are many schools of ethical thought—too many to cover in this brief overview—so we'll limit ourselves to two major systems: arguments from consequences and arguments from principles.

Consequences as the Base of Ethics

Perhaps the best-known example of evaluating acts according to their ethical consequences is utilitarianism, a down-to-earth philosophy that grew out of nineteenth-century British philosophers' concern to demystify ethics and make it work in the practical world. Jeremy Bentham, the originator of utilitarianism, developed the goal of the greatest good for the greatest number, or "greatest happiness," by which he meant the most pleasure for the least pain. John Stuart Mill, another British philosopher, built on Bentham's utilitarianism by using predicted consequences to determine the morality of a proposed action.

Mill's consequentialist approach allows you readily to assess a wide range of acts. You can apply the principle of utility—which says that an action is morally right if it produces a greater net value (benefits minus costs) than any available alternative action—to virtually any situation, and it will help you reach a decision. Obviously, however, it's not always easy to make the calculations called for by this approach because, like any prediction of the future, an estimate of consequences is conjectural. In particular, it's often very hard to assess the long-term consequences of any action. Too often, utilitarianism seduces us into a short-term analysis of a moral problem simply because long-term consequences are difficult to predict.

Principles as the Base of Ethics

Any ethical system based on principles will ultimately rest on moral tenets that we are duty bound to uphold, no matter what the consequences. Sometimes the moral tenets come from religious faith—for example, the Ten Commandments. At other times, however, the principles are derived from philosophical reasoning, as in the case of German philosopher Immanuel Kant. Kant held that no one should ever use another person as a means to his own ends and that everyone should always act as if his acts are the basis of universal law. In other words, Kant held that we are duty bound to respect other people's sanctity and to act in the same way that we would want all other people to act. The great advantage of such a system is its clarity and precision. We are never overwhelmed by a multiplicity of contradictory and difficult-to-quantify consequences; we simply make sure we are following (or not violating) the principles of our ethical system and proceed accordingly.

Constructing an Ethical Argument

To show you how to conduct an ethical argument, let's now apply these two strategies to an example. In general, you can conduct an ethical evaluation by using the frame for either a principles-based argument or a consequences-based argument or a combination of both.

> **Principles-Based Frame:** An act is right (wrong) because it follows (violates) principles A, B, and C.
>
> **Consequences-Based Frame:** An act is right (wrong) because it will lead to consequences A, B, and C, which are good (bad).

To illustrate how these frames might help you develop an ethical argument, let's use them to develop arguments for or against capital punishment.

Constructing a Principles-Based Argument

A principles-based argument looks at capital punishment through the lens of one or more guiding principles. Kant's principle that we are duty bound not to violate the sanctity of other human lives could lead to arguments opposing capital punishment. One might argue as follows:

> *Principles-based argument opposing capital punishment:* The death penalty is wrong because it violates the principle of the sanctity of human life.

You could support this principle either by summarizing Kant's argument that one should not violate the selfhood of another person or by pointing to certain religious systems such as Judeo-Christian ethics, where one is told, "Vengeance is mine, saith the Lord" or "Thou shalt not kill." To develop this argument further, you might examine two exceptions in which principles-based ethicists may allow killing—self-defense and war—and show how capital punishment does not fall in either category.

Principles-based arguments can also be developed to support capital punishment. You may be surprised to learn that Kant himself—despite his arguments for the sanctity of life—supported capital punishment. To make such an argument, Kant evoked a different principle about the suitability of the punishment to the crime:

> There is no sameness of kind between death and remaining alive even under the most miserable conditions, and consequently there is no equality between the crime and the retribution unless the criminal is judicially condemned and put to death.

Stated as an enthymeme, Kant's argument is as follows:

> *Principles-based argument supporting capital punishment:* Capital punishment is right because it follows the principle that punishments should be proportionate to the crime.

In developing this argument, Kant's burden would be to show why the principle of proportionate retribution outweighs the principle of the supreme worth of the individual. Our point is that a principles-based argument can be made both for and against capital punishment. The arguer's duty is to make clear what principle is being evoked and then to show why this principle is more important than opposing principles.

Constructing a Consequences-Based Argument

Unlike a principles-based argument, which appeals to certain guiding maxims or rules, a consequences-based argument looks at the consequences of a decision and measures the positive benefits against the negative costs. Here is the frame that an arguer might use to oppose capital punishment on the basis of negative consequences:

> *Consequences-based argument opposing capital punishment:* Capital punishment is wrong because it leads to the following negative consequences:

- The possibility of executing an innocent person
- The possibility that a murderer who may repent and be redeemed is denied that chance
- The excessive legal and political costs of trials and appeals
- The unfair distribution of executions so that one's chances of being put to death are much greater if one is a minority or is poor

To develop this argument, the reader would need to provide facts, statistics, and other evidence to support each of the stated reasons.

A different arguer might use a consequences-based approach to support capital punishment:

Consequences-based argument supporting capital punishment: Capital punishment is right because it leads to the following positive consequences:

- It may deter violent crime and slow down the rate of murder.
- It saves the cost of lifelong imprisonment.
- It stops criminals who are menaces to society from committing more murders.
- It helps grieving families reach closure and sends a message to victims' families that society recognizes their pain.

It should be evident, then, that adopting an ethical system doesn't lead to automatic answers to one's ethical dilemmas. A system offers a way of proceeding—a way of conducting an argument—but it doesn't relieve you of personal responsibility for thinking through your values and taking a stand. When you face an ethical dilemma, we encourage you to consider both the relevant principles and the possible consequences the dilemma entails. In many arguments, you can use both principles-based and consequences-based reasoning as long as irreconcilable contradictions don't present themselves.

■ ■ ■ **FOR CLASS DISCUSSION**   Developing Ethical Arguments

Working as individuals or in small groups, construct an ethical argument (based on principles, consequences, or both) for or against the following actions:

1. Eating meat
2. Buying a hybrid car
3. Legalizing assisted suicide for the terminally ill
4. Selling organs
5. Generating state revenue through lotteries   ■ ■ ■

Common Problems in Making Evaluation Arguments

When conducting evaluation arguments (whether categorical or ethical), writers can bump up against recurring problems that are unique to evaluation. In some cases these problems complicate the establishment of criteria; in other cases they complicate the match argument. Let's look briefly at some of these common problems.

- **The problem of standards—what is commonplace versus what is ideal:** In various forms, we experience the dilemma of the commonplace versus the ideal all the time. Is it fair to get a ticket for going seventy miles per hour on a sixty-five-mile-per-hour freeway when most of the drivers go seventy miles per hour or faster? (Does what is *commonplace*—going seventy—override what is *ideal*—obeying the law?) Is it better for high schools to pass out free contraceptives to students because students are having sex anyway (what's *commonplace*), or is it better not to pass them out in order to support abstinence (what's *ideal*)?

- **The problem of mitigating circumstances:** This problem occurs when an arguer claims that unusual circumstances should alter our usual standards of judgment. Ordinarily, it is fair for a teacher to reduce a grade if you turn in a paper late. But what if you were up all night taking care of a crying baby? Does that count as a *mitigating circumstance* to waive the ordinary criterion? When you argue for mitigating circumstances, you will likely assume an especially heavy burden of proof. People assume the rightness of usual standards of judgment unless there are compelling arguments for abnormal circumstances.

- **The problem of choosing between two goods or two bads:** Often an evaluation issue forces us between a rock and a hard place. Should we cut pay or cut people? Put our parents in a nursing home or let them stay at home, where they have become a danger to themselves? In such cases one has to weigh conflicting criteria, knowing that the choices are too much alike—either both bad or both good.

- **The problem of seductive empirical measures:** The need to make high-stakes evaluations has led many people to seek quantifiable criteria that can be weighed mathematically. Thus we use grade point averages to select scholarship winners, student evaluation scores to decide merit pay for teachers, and combined scores of judges to evaluate figure skaters. In some cases, empirical measures can be quite acceptable, but they are often dangerous because they discount important nonquantifiable traits. The problem with empirical measures is that they seduce us into believing that complex judgments can be made mathematically, thus rescuing us from the messiness of alternative points of view and conflicting criteria.

- **The problem of cost:** A final problem in evaluation arguments is cost. Something may be the best possible member of its class, but if it costs too much, we have to go for second or third best. We can avoid this problem somewhat by placing items into different classes on the basis of cost. For example, a Mercedes will exceed a Kia on almost any criterion, but if we can't afford more than a Kia, the comparison is pointless. It is better to compare a Mercedes to a Lexus and a Kia to an equivalent Ford. Whether costs are expressed in dollars, personal discomfort, moral repugnance, or some other terms, our final evaluation of an item must take cost into account.

WRITING ASSIGNMENT   An Evaluation or Ethical Argument

Write an argument in which you try to change your readers' minds about the value, worth, or ethics of something. Choose a phenomenon to be evaluated that is controversial so that your readers are likely at first to disagree with your evaluation or at least to be surprised by it. Somewhere in your essay you should summarize alternative views and either refute them or concede to them (see Chapter 7).

Exploring Ideas

Evaluation issues are all around us. Think of disagreements about the value of a person, thing, action, or phenomenon within the various communities to which you belong—your dorm, home, or apartment community; your school community, including clubs or organizations; your academic community, including classes you are currently taking; your work community; and your city, state, national, and world communities. For further ideas, look at the categories listed in the For Class Discussion exercise on pages 291–292. Once you have settled on a controversial thing to be evaluated, place it in its smallest relevant category, determine the purposes of that category, and develop your criteria. If you are making an ethical evaluation, consider your argument from the perspective of both principles and consequences.

Identifying Your Audience and Determining What's at Stake

Before drafting your argument, identify your targeted audience and determine what's at stake. Consider your responses to the following questions:

- What audience are you targeting? What background do they need to understand your issue? How much do they already care about it?
- Before they read your evaluation argument, what stance on your issue do you imagine them holding? What change do you want to bring about in their view?
- What will they find new or surprising about your argument?
- What objections might they raise? What counterarguments or alternative points of view will you need to address?
- Why does your evaluation matter? Who might be threatened or made uncomfortable by your views? What is at stake?

Organizing an Evaluation Argument

As you write a draft, you may find useful the following prototypical structures for evaluation arguments shown in Organization Plans 1 and 2 on pages 299 and 300. Of course, you can always alter these plans if another structure better fits your material.

Questioning and Critiquing a Categorical Evaluation Argument

Here is a list of questions you can use to critique a categorical evaluation argument:

Will a skeptic accept my criteria? Many evaluative arguments are weak because the writers have simply assumed that readers will accept their criteria. Whenever your audience's acceptance of your criteria is in doubt, you will need to argue for your criteria explicitly.

Will a skeptic accept my general weighting of criteria? Another vulnerable spot in an evaluation argument is the relative weight of the criteria. How much anyone weights a given criterion is usually a function of his or her own interests relative to your contested something. You should always ask whether some particular group might have good reasons for weighting the criteria differently.

Organization Plan 1: Criteria and Match in Separate Sections

Introduce the issue and state your claim.	• Engage reader's interest in your evaluation issue and show why it is controversial or problematic. • Show what's at stake. • Provide background information needed by your audience. • State your claim.
Present your criteria.	• State and develop criterion 1. • State and develop criterion 2. • Continue with the rest of your criteria. • Anticipate and respond to possible objections to the criteria.
Present your match argument.	• Consider restating your claim for clarity. • Argue that your case meets (does not meet) criterion 1. • Argue that your case meets (does not meet) criterion 2. • Continue with the rest of your match argument. • Anticipate and respond to possible objections to the match argument.
Conclude.	• Perhaps sum up your argument. • Help reader return to the "big picture" of what's at stake. • End with something memorable.

Will a skeptic accept my criteria but reject my match argument? The other major way of testing an evaluation argument is to anticipate how readers may object to your stated reasons and grounds. Will readers challenge you by showing that you have cherry-picked your examples and evidence? Will they provide counterexamples and counterevidence?

Organization Plan 2: Criteria and Match Interwoven

Introduce the issue and state your claim.	• Engage reader's interest in your evaluation issue and show why it is controversial or problematic. • Show what's at stake. • Provide background information needed by your audience. • State your claim.
Present series of criterion-match arguments.	• State and develop criterion 1 and argue that your case meets (does not meet) the criterion. • State and develop criterion 2 and argue that your case meets (does not meet) the criterion. • Continue with the rest of your criterion-match arguments.
Respond to possible objections to your argument.	• Anticipate and summarize possible objections. • Respond to the objections through rebuttal or concession.
Conclude.	• Perhaps sum up your argument. • Help reader return to the "big picture" of what's at stake. • End with something memorable.

Critiquing an Ethical Argument

Ethical arguments can be critiqued through appeals to consequences or principles. If an argument appeals primarily to principles, it can be vulnerable to a simple cost analysis. What are the costs of adhering to this principle? There will undoubtedly be some, or else there would be no real argument. If the argument is based strictly on consequences, we should ask whether it violates any rules or principles, particularly such commandments as the Golden Rule—"Do unto others as you would have others do unto you"—which most members of our audience adhere to. By failing to mention these alternative ways of thinking about ethical issues, we undercut not only our argument but our credibility as well. ■

Our first reading, by student writer Sam Isaacson, was written for the assignment on page 297. It joins a conversation about whether the legalization of same-sex marriage would be good for our society. However, Isaacson, a gay writer, limits the question to whether legalization of same-sex marriage would be *good for the gay community.* Earlier in this text (see Chapter 7, page 127), we discussed Isaacson's rhetorical choices as he considered the audience for his essay. Isaacson's decision was to address this paper to the readers of a gay magazine such as *Harvard Gay and Lesbian Review* or *The Advocate.*

Would Legalization of Gay Marriage Be Good for the Gay Community?

SAM ISAACSON (STUDENT)

For those of us who have been out for a while, nothing seems shocking about a gay pride parade. Yet at this year's parade, I was struck by the contrast between two groups— the float for the Toys in Babeland store (with swooning drag queens and leather-clad, whip-wielding, topless dykes) and the Northwest chapters of Integrity and Dignity (Episcopal and Catholic organizations for lesbians and gays), whose marchers looked as conservative as the congregation of any American church.

These stark differences in dress are representative of larger philosophical differences in the gay community. At stake is whether or not we gays and lesbians should act "normal." Labeled as deviants by many in straight society, we're faced with various opposing methods of response. One option is to insist that we are normal and work to integrate gays into the cultural mainstream. Another response is to form an alternative gay culture with its own customs and values; this culture would honor deviancy in response to a society which seeks to label some as "normal" and some as "abnormal." For the purposes of this paper I will refer to those who favor the first response as "integrationists" and those who favor the second response as "liberationists." Politically, this ideological clash is most evident in the issue of whether legalization of same-sex marriage would be good for the gay community. Nearly all integrationists would say yes, but many liberationists would say no. My belief is that while we must take the objections of the liberationists seriously, legalization of same-sex marriage would benefit both gays and society in general.

Let us first look at what is so threatening about gay marriage to many liberationists. Many liberationists fear that legalizing gay marriage will reinforce current social pressures that say monogamous marriage is the normal and right way to live. In straight society, those who choose not to marry are often viewed as self-indulgent, likely promiscuous, and shallow—and it is no coincidence these are some of the same stereotypes gays struggle against. If gays begin to marry, married life will be all the more the norm and subject those outside of marriage to even greater marginalization. As homosexuals, liberationists argue, we should be particularly sensitive to the tyranny of the majority. Our sympathies should lie with the deviants—the transsexual, the fetishist, the drag queen, and the leather-dyke. By choosing marriage, gays take the easy route into "normal" society; we not only abandon the sexual minorities of our community, we strengthen society's narrow notions of what is "normal" and thereby further confine both straights and gays.

Additionally, liberationists worry that by winning the right to marry, gays and lesbians will lose the distinctive and positive characteristics of gay culture. Many gay writers have commented on how as a marginalized group, gays have been forced to create different forms of relationships that often allow for a greater and often more fulfilling range of life experiences. Writer Edmund White, for instance, has observed that there is a greater fluidity in the relationships of gays than straights. Gays, he says, are more likely than straights to stay friends with old lovers, are more likely to form close friendships outside the romantic relationship, and are generally less likely to become compartmentalized into isolated couples. It has also been noted that gay relationships are often characterized by more equality and better communication than are straight relationships. Liberationists make the reasonable assumption that if gays win the right to marry, they will be subject to the same social pressure to marry that straights are subject to. As more gays are pressured into traditional life patterns, liberationists fear the gay sensibility will be swallowed up by the established attitudes of the broader culture. All of society would be the poorer if this were to happen.

5   I must admit that I concur with many of the arguments of the liberationists that I have outlined above. I do think if given the right, gays would feel social pressure to marry; I agree that gays should be especially sensitive to the most marginalized elements of society; and I also agree that the unique perspectives on human relationships that the gay community offers should not be sacrificed. However, despite these beliefs, I feel that legalizing gay marriage would bring valuable benefits to gays and society as a whole.

First of all, I think it is important to put the attacks the liberationists make on marriage into perspective. The liberationist critique of marriage claims that marriage in itself is a harmful institution (for straights as well as gays) because it needlessly limits and normalizes personal freedom. But it seems clear to me that marriage in some form is necessary for the well-being of society. Children need a stable environment in which to be raised. Studies have shown that children whose parents divorce often suffer long-term effects from the trauma. Studies have also shown that people tend to be happier in stable long-term relationships. We need to have someone to look after us when we're old, when we become depressed, when we fall ill. All people, gay or straight, parents or nonparents, benefit from the stabilizing force of marriage.

Second, we in the gay community should not be too quick to overlook the real benefits that legalizing gay marriage will bring. We are currently denied numerous legal rights of marriage that the straight community enjoys: tax benefits, insurance benefits, inheritance rights, and the right to have a voice in medical treatment or funeral arrangements for a dying partner.

Further, just as important as the legal impacts of being denied the right to marriage is the socially symbolic weight this denial carries. We are sent the message that while gay sex in the privacy of one's home will be tolerated, gay love will not be respected. We are told that it is not important to society whether we form long-term relationships or not. We are told that we are not worthy of forming families of our own. By gaining the same recognitions by the state of our relationships and all the legal and social weight that recognition carries, the new message will be that gay love is just as meaningful as straight love.

Finally, let me address what I think is at the heart of the liberationist argument against marriage—the fear of losing social diversity and our unique gay voice. The liberationists are wary of society's normalizing forces. They fear that if gays win the right to marry, gay relationships will simply become imitations of straight relationships—the richness gained through the gay experience will be lost. I feel, however, this argument unintentionally plays into the hands of conservatives. Conservatives argue that marriage is, by definition, the union between man and woman. As a consequence, to the broad culture gay marriage can only be a mockery of marriage. As gays and lesbians we need to argue that conservatives are imposing arbitrary standards on what is normal and not normal in society. To fight the conservative agenda, we must suggest instead that marriage is, in essence, a contract of love and commitment between two people. The liberationists, I think, unwittingly feed into conservative identification and classification by pigeonholing gays as outsiders. Reacting against social norms is simply another way of being held hostage by them.

10   We need to understand that the gay experience and voice will not be lost by gaining the right to marry. Gays will always be the minority by simple biological fact and this will always color the identity of any gay person. But we can only make our voice heard if we are seen as full-fledged members of society. Otherwise we will remain an isolated and marginalized group. And only when we have the right to marry will we have any say in the nature and significance of marriage as an institution. This is not being apologetic to the straight culture, but is a demand that we not be excluded from the central institutions of Western culture. We can help merge the fluidity of gay relationships with the traditionally more compartmentalized married relationship. Further, liberationists should realize that the decision *not* to marry makes a statement only if one has the ability to choose marriage. What would be most radical, most transforming, is two women or two men joined together in the eyes of society.

Critiquing "Would Legalization of Gay Marriage Be Good for the Gay Community?"

1. Who is the audience that Sam Isaacson addresses in this argument?
2. Ordinarily when we think of persons opposing gay marriage, we imagine socially conservative heterosexuals. However, Sam spends little time addressing the antigay marriage arguments of straight society. Rather, he addresses the antimarriage arguments made by "liberationist" gay people. What are these arguments? How well does Sam respond to them?
3. What are the criteria Sam uses to argue that legalizing gay marriage would be good for the gay community?
4. How persuasive do you think Sam's argument is to the various audiences he addresses?

Our second reading, by student writer Christopher Moore, grew out of class discussions about what constitutes a "good news media" and about whether today's college students are informed about the news.

Information Plus Satire:
Why *The Daily Show* and *The Colbert Report* Are Good Sources of News for Young People

CHRISTOPHER MOORE (STUDENT)

Media commentators often complain that college-age students, along with much of the older population, are uninformed about the news. Fewer people today read mainstream newspapers or watch network news than in the past. Hard-core news junkies often get their news online from blog sites or from cable news. Meanwhile, less informed people use social networking tools like Twitter and Facebook for instant, unofficial news, often about popular culture or their favorite celebrities. Another possible source of news is *The Daily Show* and *The Colbert Report.* By presenting information and entertainment together, these shows attract a young audience, especially college-age students who shy away from newspapers or news networks like Fox or CNN. But are these actually good news sources? I will argue that they are, especially for a young audience, because they cover each day's important news and because their satire teaches viewers how to read the news rhetorically. The content on these shows provides up-to-date news stories and compels consumers to recognize that all news has an angle of vision demanding thoughtful processing, not simply blind consumption.

The first thing a good news source does is keep consumers up-to-date on the most important worldwide news. Since *The Daily Show* and *The Colbert Report* both air every weekday except Friday, they constantly present viewers with up-to-date news. Furthermore, all broadcasts are available online, as well as archived—if you missed Tuesday's episode, it's easy to backtrack so that you can stay current. Content published in these shows is trimmed to about 22 minutes (to allow for commercial time), so only the most pertinent information is presented. Consider, for example, the content published in January and February of 2011, which focused almost exclusively on the revolutions in Egypt and the volatile political climate in Tunisia. In these episodes, the shows pulled information from different news sources, both liberal and conservative, showing clips, news anchor commentary, or primary sources just the way other news sources do. In one episode during the turmoil in the Middle East, Stewart interviewed CNN reporter Anderson Cooper, who had just returned from reporting on the revolution from inside Egypt. Viewers watching Stewart might have had more insight into the controversial issues surrounding these revolutions than watchers of network news.

Skeptics, however, may argue that *The Daily Show* and *The Colbert Report* aren't providing real news but just satire. After all, the shows air on Comedy Central. Yet even a satirist needs material to satirize, and these satires always focus on current events, politics, or social trends. Moreover, watching *The Daily Show* offers deeper coverage than many network news programs because it focuses on what is most significant or important in the news. Whereas network news broadcasts tend to move quickly toward sports, weather, humanitarian "feel good" stories, or "breaking news" such as fires, robberies, or traffic accidents, Stewart and Colbert keep their satirical focus on major events with social or political significance.

The satirical methods used by Stewart and Colbert lead to my second and most important reason that *The Daily Show* and *The Colbert Report* are good sources of news: The satire teaches audiences how to "read" the news rhetorically. Unlike conventional news sources, the satire in these two shows unmasks the way that traditional news is packaged and framed, encouraging viewers to be skeptical of news. The satire in these shows functions by pointing out a news source's angle of vision, which promotes specific ideologies and presents news with an agenda. Consider the satirical character played by Stephen Colbert, who presents at one moment a far-right conservative ideology, only to compromise these beliefs at the next moment. His dramatization helps viewers see how rhetorical strategies create an angle of vision. For example, in an interview with Julian Assange, the founder of WikiLeaks, Colbert told his audience that he would show two versions of the interview: one of the unaltered footage and one that deliberately edited the footage to serve an agenda. Network news programs often employ the same tactics as Colbert, but in a much more subtle fashion. Editing may be one strategy, but opinion show hosts like Bill O'Reilly and other conservative news commentators employ a variety of tactics, like selective interviewing, cherry-picking news topics, following "fair and balanced" news with tacit conservative thinking, or any number of other methods. Showing the two versions of Colbert's interview is just one example that reminds viewers that information can be manipulated, presented out of context, edited, or reshaped. Foregrounding these strategies helps viewers criticize and analyze the news they digest.

5   The satire on these shows also points out the absurdities and pretensions of politicians, media commentators, and other public figures. An episode that discussed the Wisconsin labor protests in early 2011 focused on newly elected Republican Governor Scott Walker's decision to slash union benefits and collective bargaining rights to cover deficits in the state budget. When protestors took to the streets, Stewart showed clips from CNN, MSNBC and CBS, that called these protests "inspired by" or "having strong parallels to" revolutionary political action in Egypt or Cairo. However, Stewart rejected this comparison. He pointed out that "no citizens have died, no reporters have been abused, and Republican Governor Scott Walker was elected with 52 percent of the vote—dictators like Mubarak typically hold about 92 percent favor." Stewart's point, in other words, is that comparing two dissimilar things, as traditional news media had done, is unjust to both the Wisconsin protestors and the Tunisian and Egyptian rebels. It belittles those Tunisians or Egyptians who had the courage to raise their voices against dictators just as it distorts the very different political and economic issues and motivations at work in Wisconsin.

Satire also points out inconsistencies in news reporting, or the logical pitfalls into which politicians regularly stumble. In a skit in which Jon Stewart interviewed a conservative political candidate, he exposed inconsistencies in ideological views about when life begins. On the abortion issue, the candidate argued that life begins at conception, but on constitutional issues of citizenship, he argued that life begins at birth. Stewart took these two conflicting Republican ideologies and used a humorous either/or fallacy to show their inconsistency. Stewart argued that Obama was conceived by his mother in Hawaii. Therefore, if pro-life Republicans believe life begins at conception, then logically Obama is a natural citizen of Hawaii. Either Obama is a citizen, or life does not begin at conception, contradicting the fundamental right-to-life belief. Arguments like these help show how poorly constructed arguments or logical fallacies are common tools of news media for political discussions, facilitating a certain agenda or ideological perspective.

Viewers of *The Daily Show* or *The Colbert Report* will not get the same kind of news coverage that they would get from reading hard-copy news or an online newspaper, but they learn a healthy skepticism about the objective truthfulness of news. To many young people, entering a discussion on current affairs can be intimidating. Both Stephen Colbert and Jon Stewart make it easier for younger audiences to analyze the rhetorical dimension of news stories, thus allowing the viewer to see bias and angle of vision. The use of satire is a means of allowing entertainment and information to mingle together on a critical level. These approaches to delivering news are energizing, providing an alternative to lackluster news sources that can make us feel like we're drowning in a sea of information. The conservative Fox News commentator Bill O'Reilly once called my generation "a bunch of stone slackers" who sit at home unengaged in politics and watching *The Daily Show* and *The Colbert Report*. Yeah, right. But I wonder, where did he get his information?

Critiquing "Information Plus Satire"

1. Christopher Moore's first criterion for a good news source is that it should keep viewers up-to-date with significant and important news rather than with ephemeral events like traffic accidents or celebrity divorces. Do you agree with Moore that *The Daily Show* and *The Colbert Report* keep viewers up-to-date with important news?

2. Moore's second criterion is the thought-provoking claim that a good news source teaches viewers to read the news rhetorically. What does he mean by reading the news rhetorically? How does he make his case? Are you persuaded?

3. Much of Christopher Moore's argument is topical in that it refers to events happening at the time he was drafting his essay (for example, the references to revolutions in Egypt or the release of government documents on WikiLeaks). One of his topical events concerns the "birther movement"—claims made by "birthers" that Barack Obama was born in Kenya rather than in Hawaii and therefore was constitutionally ineligible to be president. (Several months after Moore's essay was written, Obama released his long-form Hawaiian birth certificate, reducing the impact of the "birther movement.") How does this additional background information help you understand Moore's paragraph on "inconsistencies in ideological views on when life begins" (paragraph 6).

Our third reading is a political cartoon by Adey Bryant, a self-taught British cartoonist. In this whimsical visual argument, Bryant reinforces one of the environmental complaints against wind energy—the danger posed to migrating birds.

Well, It Bloody Wasn't There Last Year!

ADEY BRYANT

Critiquing "Well, It Bloody Wasn't There Last Year!"

1. Through the use of image and text, political cartoons can powerfully condense a complex argument into a brief statement with a claim and an implied line of reasoning. In your own words, what is the claim and implied supporting argument made by this cartoon?
2. How do the drawing, action, and words call attention to this drawback of wind energy?
3. What background knowledge about wind energy do readers need to possess before they understand this cartoon?

Our final readings are a guest opinion piece and a subsequent letter to the editor, both appearing in the *New York Times* in March 2011. The op-ed piece is by Christian Longo, a prisoner on death row in the Oregon State Penitentiary, convicted of the gruesome murder of his wife and three children. Longo's op-ed sparked wide debate in the blogosphere—partly because of the ethical issues raised by his argument and partly because of his bizarre history: he fled to Mexico after his crime and stole the identity of a *New York Times* reporter. In prison, Longo founded the organization GAVE (Gifts of Anatomical Value from Everyone). The responding letter to the editor (one of four that appeared in the *New York Times* on March 13, 2011) is by Dr. Kenneth Prager, a professor of clinical medicine and chairman of the Medical Ethics Committee at New York–Presbyterian Hospital/Columbia University Medical Center.

Giving Life after Death Row

CHRISTIAN LONGO

Salem, Ore. Eight years ago I was sentenced to death for the murders of my wife and three children. I am guilty. I once thought that I could fool others into believing this was not true. Failing that, I tried to convince myself that it didn't matter. But gradually, the enormity of what I did seeped in; that was followed by remorse and then a wish to make amends.

I spend 22 hours a day locked in a 6 foot by 8 foot box on Oregon's death row. There is no way to atone for my crimes, but I believe that a profound benefit to society can come from my circumstances. I have asked to end my remaining appeals, and then donate my organs after my execution to those who need them. But my request has been rejected by the prison authorities.

According to the United Network for Organ Sharing, there are more than 110,000 Americans on organ waiting lists. Around 19 of them die each day. There are more than 3,000 prisoners on death row in the United States, and just one inmate could save up to eight lives by donating a healthy heart, lungs, kidneys, liver and other transplantable tissues.

There is no law barring inmates condemned to death in the United States from donating their organs, but I haven't found any prisons that allow it. The main explanation is that Oregon and most other states use a sequence of three drugs for lethal injections that damages the organs. But Ohio and Washington use a larger dose of just one drug, a fast-acting barbiturate that doesn't destroy organs. If states would switch to a one-drug regimen, inmates' organs could be saved.

5 Another common concern is that the organs of prisoners may be tainted by infections, H.I.V. or hepatitis. Though the prison population does have a higher prevalence of such diseases than do non-prisoners, thorough testing can easily determine whether a prisoner's organs are healthy. These tests would be more reliable than many given to, say, a victim of a car crash who had signed up to be a donor; in the rush to transplant organs after an accident, there is less time for a full risk analysis.

There are also fears about security—that, for example, prisoners will volunteer to donate organs as part of an elaborate escape scheme. But prisoners around the country make hospital trips for medical reasons every day. And in any case, executions have to take place on prison grounds, so the organ removal would take place 10 there as well.

Aside from these logistical and health concerns, prisons have a moral reason for their reluctance to allow inmates to donate. America has a shameful history of using prisoners for medical experiments. In Oregon, for example, from 1963 to 1973, many inmates were paid to "volunteer" for research into the effects of radiation on testicular cells. Some ethicists believe that opening the door to voluntary donations would also open the door to abuse. And others argue that prisoners are simply unable to make a truly voluntary consent.

But when a prisoner initiates a request to donate with absolutely no enticements or pressure to do so, and if the inmate receives the same counseling afforded every prospective donor, there is no question in my mind that valid organ-donation consent can be given.

I am not the only condemned prisoner who wants the right to donate his organs. I have discussed this issue with almost every one of the 35 men on Oregon's death row, and nearly half of them expressed a wish to have the option of donating should their appeals run out.

I understand the public's apprehension. And I know that it could look as if what I really want are extra privileges or a reduction in my sentence. After all, in a rare and well-publicized case last December, Gov. Haley Barbour of Mississippi released two sisters who had been sentenced to life in prison so that one could donate a kidney to the other. But I don't expect to leave this prison alive. I am seeking nothing but the right to determine what happens to my body once the state has carried out its sentence.

If I donated all of my organs today, I could clear nearly 1 percent of my state's organ waiting list. I am 37 years old and healthy; throwing my organs away after I am executed is nothing but a waste.

And yet the prison authority's response to my latest appeal to donate was this: "The interests of the public and condemned inmates are best served by denying the petition."

Many in the public, most inmates, and especially those who are dying for lack of a healthy organ, would certainly disagree.

A Death Row Donation of Organs?

KENNETH PRAGER

The most important argument against carrying out Mr. Longo's altruistic wish to donate his organs for transplantation after he is executed is an ethical one. This would come too close to violating what ethicists call the dead-donor rule, which states that a person must never be killed for the purpose of removing organs for transplant.

Although his execution would be punishment for a quadruple

homicide, its linkage to organ removal would be too close to pass ethical muster. It would be reminiscent of an egregious violation of human rights, as when the Chinese executed scores of prisoners and harvested their organs to fuel a lucrative trade in organ transplants.

Moreover, the exploitation of prisoners for the ostensibly laudable reason of furthering medical knowledge should give us further pause before trying to wring benefit from an act of execution.

Organ donation from dead patients will always be a sensitive moral enterprise. We must not risk ethically sullying this practice by harvesting organs from executed prisoners.

Critiquing "Giving Life after Death Row" and "A Death Row Donation of Organs?"

1. Longo's proposal to allow organ donation from executed prisoners is supported by both categorical evaluation arguments and ethical arguments. How does Longo make the categorical case that his organs will be healthy? How does he make the ethical case that it is right for executed prisoners to be able to donate their organs? Besides his appeals to *logos*, how does he also try to create appeals to *ethos* and *pathos*?
2. What opposing arguments does Longo address? How well does he refute these opposing arguments?
3. In his responding letter to the editor, what objection does Kenneth Prager make to Longo's proposal? How do Longo's op-ed and Prager's response illustrate the ethical conflict between arguments from principle and arguments from consequences?

For additional writing, reading, and research resources, go to www.mycomplab.com

Proposal Arguments

14

Case 1 Should the Supreme Court Overturn *Roe v. Wade?*

Among the most heated debates in the United States is whether the due process and privacy protections of the Fourteenth Amendment can be extended to a woman's right to an abortion. The right-to-life movement has intensified its efforts to restrict access to abortions at the state level and to overturn *Roe v. Wade* in the U.S. Supreme Court. Meanwhile, pro-choice advocates such as Planned Parenthood have vigorously defended a woman's right to an abortion. Both sides make effective use of visual arguments. Right-to-life groups

When
*your right
to an abortion
is taken away,
what are you
going to
do*

Reproductive rights are under attack. The Pro-Choice Public Education Project. It's pro-choice or no choice.
1(688)253-CHOICE or www.protect.choice.org

frequently use posters showing ultrasound images of unborn babies (often not using the word "fetus"). The poster on the previous page, sponsored by Planned Parenthood, features a starkly black question mark that on second look is seen to be made from a coat hanger. It makes an implied proposal claim ("Abortion should remain legal") and supports it with a consequence argument: If abortions are outlawed, women will have abortions anyway—using coat hangers instead of medically safe procedures. The image of the coat hanger (reminiscent of horror stories about abortions prior to *Roe v. Wade*) appeals simultaneously to *logos* and *pathos*.

> ## Case 2   How Should the United States Reduce Its Dependence on Foreign Oil?
>
> In 2010, the United States imported approximately 70 percent of its oil, much of it from the Middle East. Not only did this dependency threaten our economy and harm the environment, it also threatened national security. Conservatives often propose solving this problem through more drilling of domestic oil, particularly in offshore sites and in the Arctic National Wildlife Refuge. Liberals and environmentalists, meanwhile, pin their hopes on conservation and renewable sources such as wind and solar energy. Almost everyone is nervous about nuclear power, which has the advantage of not promoting global warming but carries enormous risk, as shown when radioactivity escaped from the Fukushima nuclear plant after Japan's 2011 earthquake and tsunami. With no large-scale technological solutions in sight, concerned citizens have proposed dozens of ideas for reducing domestic consumption of oil. Among the proposals are the following: placing a "green tax" on gasoline; requiring auto manufacturers to increase the fuel efficiency of their fleets; giving tax credits for buying a fuel-efficient car; increasing incentives for carpooling or taking public transportation; increasing the cost of parking; subsidizing hybrid or all-electric cars; charging different gas prices at the pump, with higher prices for less fuel-efficient cars; promoting telecommuting; and rebuilding cities so that housing is closer to worksites.

Although proposal arguments are the last type of argument we examine, they are among the most common arguments that you will encounter or be called on to write. In this chapter, you will learn to:

- Develop proposal arguments using a typical problem-solution-justification structure
- Use the claim-types strategy and the stock issues strategy to develop supporting reasons for your proposal argument
- Use words and images to create a one-page advocacy poster or advertisement

An Overview of Proposal Arguments

The essence of proposal arguments is that they call for action. In reading a proposal, the audience is enjoined to make a decision and then to act on it—to *do* something. Proposal arguments are sometimes called *should* or *ought* arguments because those helping verbs express the obligation to act: "We *should* do this [action]" or "We *ought* to do this [action]."

For instructional purposes, we will distinguish between two kinds of proposal arguments even though they are closely related and involve the same basic arguing strategies. The first kind we will call *practical proposals,* which propose an action to solve some kind of local or immediate problem. A student's proposal to change the billing procedures for scholarship students would be an example of a practical proposal, as would an engineering firm's proposal for the design of a new bridge being planned by a city government. The second kind we will call *policy proposals,* in which the writer offers a broad plan of action to solve major social, economic, or political problems affecting the common good. An argument that the United States should adopt a national health insurance plan or that the electoral college should be abolished would be an example of a policy proposal.

The primary difference is the narrowness versus breadth of the concern. *Practical* proposals are narrow, local, and concrete; they focus on the nuts and bolts of getting something done in the here and now. They are often concerned with the exact size of a piece of steel, the precise duties of a new person to be hired, or a close estimate of the cost of paint or computers to be purchased. *Policy* proposals, in contrast, are concerned with the broad outline and shape of a course of action, often on a regional, national, or even international issue. What government should do about overcrowding of prisons would be a problem addressed by policy proposals. How to improve the security alarm system for the county jail would be addressed by a practical proposal.

Learning to write both kinds of proposals is valuable. Researching and writing a *policy* proposal is an excellent way to practice the responsibilities of citizenship, which require the ability to understand complex issues and to weigh positive and negative consequences of policy choices. In your professional life, writing *practical* proposals may well be among your most important duties on the job. Effective proposal writing is the lifeblood of many companies and also constitutes one of the most powerful ways you can identify and help solve problems.

The Structure of Proposal Arguments

Proposal arguments, whether practical proposals or policy proposals, generally have a three-part structure: (1) description of a problem, (2) proposed solution, and (3) justification for the proposed solution. In the justification section of your proposal argument, you develop *because* clauses of the kinds you have practiced throughout this text.

Toulmin Framework for a Proposal Argument

The Toulmin schema is particularly useful for proposal arguments because it helps you find good reasons and link them to your audience's beliefs, assumptions, and values. Suppose that your university is debating whether to banish fraternities and sororities. Suppose further that you are in favor of banishing the Greek system. One of your arguments is that eliminating the Greek system will improve your university's academic reputation. The chart on page 315 shows how you might use the Toulmin schema to make this line of reasoning as persuasive as possible.

Special Concerns for Proposal Arguments

In their call for action, proposal arguments entail certain emphases and audience concerns that you don't generally face with other kinds of arguments. Let's look briefly at some of these special concerns.

- **The need for presence**. To persuade people to *act* on your proposal, particularly if the personal or financial cost of acting is high, you must give your argument presence as well as intellectual force. By *presence* we mean an argument's ability to grip your readers' hearts and imaginations as well as their intellects. You can give presence to an argument through appeals to *pathos* such as effective use of details, provocative statistics, dialogue, illustrative narratives, and compelling examples that show the reader the seriousness of the problem you are addressing or the consequences of not acting on your proposal.

- **The need to overcome people's natural conservatism**. Another difficulty with proposals is the innate conservatism of all human beings, whatever their political persuasion, as suggested by the popular adage "If it ain't broke, don't fix it." The difficulty of proving that something needs fixing is compounded by the fact that frequently the status quo appears to be working. So sometimes when writing a proposal, you can't argue that what we have is bad, but only that what we could have would be better. Often, then, a proposal argument will be based not on present evils but on the evils of lost potential. And getting an audience to accept lost potential may be difficult indeed, given the inherently abstract nature of potentiality.

- **The difficulty of predicting future consequences**. Further, most proposal makers will be forced to predict consequences of their proposed action. As the "law of unintended consequences" suggests, few major decisions lead neatly to their anticipated results without surprises along the way. So when we claim that our proposal will lead to good consequences, we can expect our audience to be skeptical.

- **The problem of evaluating consequences**. A final problem for proposal writers is the difficulty of evaluating consequences. In government and industry, managers often use a *cost-benefit analysis* to reduce all consequences to a single-scale comparison, usually money. Although this scale may work well in some circumstances, it can lead to grotesquely inappropriate conclusions in other situations. Just how does one balance the environmental benefits of high gasoline prices against the suffering of drivers who can't afford to get to work or the benefits of pollution-free nuclear power against the costs of a potential nuclear accident? Also, what will be a cost for one group will often be a benefit for others. For example, if Social Security benefits are cut, current workers will have smaller retirement incomes, but the savings can be used to reduce the national debt.

Toulmin Analysis of the Greek System Argument

ENTHYMEME

CLAIM Our university should eliminate the Greek system

REASON because doing so will improve our university's academic reputation.

GROUNDS

Evidence that eliminating the Greek system will improve our academic reputation:

• Excessive party atmosphere of some Greek houses emphasizes social life rather than studying—we are known as a party school.

• Last year the average GPA of students in fraternities and sororities was lower than the GPA of non-Greek students.

• New pledges have so many house duties and initiation rites that their studies suffer.

• Many new students think about rush more than about the academic life.

CONDITIONS OF REBUTTAL
Attacking the reason and grounds

• Many of the best students are Greeks. Last year's highest-GPA award went to a sorority woman, and several other Greeks won prestigious graduate school scholarships.

• Statistics on grades are misleading. Many houses had a much higher average GPA than the university average. Total GPA was brought down by a few rowdy houses.

• Many other high-prestige universities have Greek systems.

• There are ways to tone down the party atmosphere on campus without abolishing the Greek system.

• Greeks contribute significantly to the community through service projects.

WARRANT

It is good for our university to achieve a better academic reputation.

BACKING

• The school would attract more serious students, leading to increased prestige.

• Campus would be more academically focused and attract better faculty.

• Losing the "party-school" reputation would put us in better light for taxpayers and legislators.

• Students would graduate with more skills and knowledge.

CONDITIONS OF REBUTTAL
Attacking the warrant and backing

• No one will argue that it is not good to have a strong academic reputation.

• However, skeptics may say that eliminating sororities and fraternities won't improve the university's academic reputation but will hurt its social life and its wide range of living options.

These, then, are some of the general difficulties facing someone who sets out to write a proposal argument. Although these difficulties may seem daunting, the rest of this chapter offers strategies to help you overcome them and produce a successful proposal.

Developing a Proposal Argument

Writers of proposal arguments must focus in turn on three main phases or stages of the argument: showing that a problem exists, explaining the proposed solution, and offering a justification.

Convincing Your Readers that a Problem Exists

There is one argumentative strategy generic to all proposal arguments: calling your reader's attention to a problem. In some situations, your intended audience may already be aware of the problem and may have even asked for solutions. In such cases, you do not need to develop the problem extensively or motivate your audience to solve it. But in most situations, awakening your readers to the existence of a problem—a problem they may well not have recognized before—is your first important challenge. You must give your problem presence through anecdotes, telling statistics, or other means that show readers how the problem affects people or otherwise has important stakes. Your goal is to gain your readers' intellectual assent to the depth, range, and potential seriousness of the problem and thereby motivate them to want to solve it.

Typically, the arguer develops the problem in one of two places in a proposal argument—either in the introduction prior to the presentation of the arguer's proposal claim or in the body of the paper as the first main reason justifying the proposal claim. In the second instance the writer's first *because* clause has the following structure: "We should do this action *because* it addresses a serious problem."

Here is how one student writer gave presence to a proposal, addressed to the chair of the mathematics department at her school, calling for redesign of the first-year calculus curriculum in order to slow its pace. She wants the chair to see the problem from her perspective.

Example Passage Giving Presence to a Problem

For me, who wants to become a high school math teacher, the problem with introductory calculus is not its difficulty but its pace. My own experience in the Calculus 134 and 135 sequence last year showed me that it was not the learning of calculus that was difficult for me. I was able to catch on to the new concepts. My problem was that it went too fast. Just as I was assimilating new concepts and feeling the need to reinforce them, the class was on to a new topic before I had full mastery of the old concept. … Part of the reason for the fast pace is that calculus is a feeder course for computer science and engineering. If prospective engineering students can't learn the calculus rapidly, they drop out of the program. The high dropout rate benefits the Engineering School because they use the math course to weed out an overabundance of engineering applicants. Thus the pace of the calculus course is geared to the needs of the engineering curriculum, not to the needs of someone like me, who wants to be a high school mathematics teacher and who believes that my own difficulties with math—combined with my love for it—might make me an excellent math teacher.

By describing the fast pace of the math curriculum from the perspective of a future math teacher rather than an engineering student, this writer brings visibility to a problem. What before didn't look like a problem (it is good to weed out weak engineering majors) suddenly became a problem (it is bad to weed out future math teachers). Establishing herself as a serious student genuinely interested in learning calculus, she gave presence to the problem by calling attention to it in a new way.

Showing the Specifics of Your Proposal

Having decided that there is a problem to be solved, you should lay out your thesis, which is a proposal for solving the problem. Your goal now is to stress the feasibility of your solution, including costs. The art of proposal making is the art of the possible. To be sure, not all proposals require elaborate descriptions of the implementation process. If you are proposing, for example, that a local PTA chapter buy new tumbling mats for the junior high gym classes, the procedures for buying the mats will probably be irrelevant. But in many arguments the specifics of your proposal—the actual step-by-step methods of implementing it—may be instrumental in winning your audience's support.

You will also need to show how your proposal will solve the problem either partially or wholly. Sometimes you may first need to convince your reader that the problem is solvable, not something intractably rooted in "the way things are," such as earthquakes or jealousy. In other words, expect that some members of your audience will be skeptical about the ability of any proposal to solve the problem you are addressing. You may well need, therefore, to "listen" to this point of view in your refutation section and to argue that your problem is at least partially solvable.

In order to persuade your audience that your proposal can work, you can follow any one of several approaches. A typical approach is to lay out a causal argument showing how one consequence will lead to another until your solution is effected. Another approach is to turn to resemblance arguments, either analogy or precedent. You try to show how similar proposals have been successful elsewhere. Or, if similar things have failed in the past, you try to show how the present situation is different.

The Justification: Convincing Your Readers that Your Proposal Should Be Enacted

The justification phase of a proposal argument will need extensive development in some arguments and minimal development in others, again depending on your particular problem and the rhetorical context of your proposal. If your audience already acknowledges the seriousness of the problem you are addressing and has simply been waiting for the right solution to come along, then your argument will be successful so long as you can convince your audience that your solution will work and that it won't cost too much. Such arguments depend on the clarity of your proposal and the feasibility of its being implemented.

But what if the costs are high? What if your readers don't think the problem is serious? What if they don't appreciate the benefits of solving the problem or the bad consequences of not solving it? In such cases you have to develop persuasive reasons for enacting your proposal. You may also have to determine who has the power to act on your proposal and apply arguments directly to that person's or agency's immediate interests. You need to know to whom or to what your power source is beholden or responsive and what values your power source holds that can be appealed to. You're looking, in short, for the best pressure points.

Proposal Arguments as Advocacy Posters or Advertisements

A frequently encountered kind of proposal argument is the one-page newspaper or magazine advertisement often purchased by advocacy groups to promote a cause. Such arguments also appear as Web pages or as posters or fliers. These condensed advocacy arguments are marked by their bold, abbreviated, tightly planned format. The creators of these arguments know they must work fast to capture our attention, give presence to a problem, advocate a solution, and enlist our support. Advocacy advertisements frequently use photographs, images, or icons that appeal to a reader's emotions and imagination. In addition to images, they often use different type sizes and styles. Large-type text in these documents frequently takes the form of slogans or condensed thesis statements written in an arresting style. To outline and justify their solutions, creators of advocacy ads often put main supporting reasons in bulleted lists and sometimes enclose carefully selected facts and quotations in boxed sidebars. To add an authoritative *ethos,* the arguments often include fine-print footnotes and bibliographies. (For more detailed discussion of how advocacy posters and advertisements use images and arrange text for rhetorical effect, see Chapter 9 on visual argument.)

Another prominent feature of these condensed, highly visual arguments is their appeal to the audience through a direct call for a course of action: go to an advocacy Web site to find more information on how to support the cause; cut out a postcardlike form to send to a decision maker; vote for or against the proposition or the candidate; write a letter to a political representative; or donate money to a cause.

An example of a student-produced advocacy advertisement is shown in Figure 14.1. Here student Lisa Blattner joins a heated debate in her city on whether to close down all-ages dance clubs. Frustrated because the evening dance options for under-twenty-one youth were threatened in Seattle, Lisa directed her ad toward the general readership of regional newspapers, with the special intention of reaching adult voters and parents. Lisa's ad uses three documentary-like, emotionally loaded, and disturbing photographs to give immediacy and presence to the problem. The verbal text in the ad states the proposal claim and provides three reasons in support of the claim. Notice how the reasons also pick up the ideas in the three photo images. The final lines of text memorably reiterate the claim and call readers to action. The success of this ad derives from the collaboration of layout, photos, and verbal text in conveying a clear, direct argument.

What Is Left for Teenagers to Do When the Teen Ordinance Bans Them from Dance Clubs?

Take Ecstasy
at Raves

Drink at Places with
No Adult Supervision

Roam the Streets

Is There an Answer to These Problems?

Yes! Through your support of the All Ages Dance Ordinance, teens will have a safe place to go where:

- **No hard drugs, like ecstasy and cocaine, are present**
- **Responsible adults are watching over everyone**
- **All of their friends can hang out in one place indoors, instead of outside with drug dealers, criminals, and prostitutes**

Give Your Child a Safe Place to Have Fun at Night

Let the Seattle City Committee Know That You Support the All Ages Dance Ordinance

FIGURE 14.1 Student advocacy advertisement

Now that you have been introduced to the main elements of a proposal argument, including condensed visual arguments, we explain in the next two sections two invention strategies you can use to generate persuasive reasons for a proposal argument and to anticipate your audience's doubts and reservations. We call these the "claim type strategy" and the "stock issues strategy."

Using the Claim Types Strategy to Develop a Proposal Argument

In Chapter 10 we explained how claim type theory can help you generate ideas for an argument. Specifically, we explained how evaluation and proposal claims often depend for their supporting reasons on claims about category, cause, or resemblance. This fact leads to a powerful idea-generating strategy based on arguments from category (which also includes argument from principle), on arguments from consequences, or on arguments from resemblance. This "claim types" strategy is illustrated in the following chart:

Explanation of Claim Types Strategy for Supporting a Proposal Claim

Claim Type	Generic Template	Example from Biotechnology Issue
Argument from principle or category	We should do this action ■ because doing so adheres to this good principle [or] ■ because this action belongs to this good category	We should support genetically modified foods ■ because doing so values scientific reason over emotion [or] ■ because genetically modified foods are safe
Argument from consequences	■ because this action will lead to these good consequences	■ because biotech crops can reduce world hunger ■ because biotech crops can improve the environment by reducing use of pesticides
Argument from resemblance	■ because this action has been done successfully elsewhere [or] ■ because this action is like this other good action	■ because genetic modification is like natural crossbreeding that has been accelerated [or] ■ because genetic modification of food is like scientific advancements in medicine

Before we give you some simple strategies for using this approach, let's illustrate it with another example.

Insurance companies should pay for long-term psychological counseling for anorexia (proposal claim)

■ because paying for such counseling is a demonstration of commitment to women's health. (principle/category)

■ because paying for such counseling may save insurance companies from much more extensive medical costs at a later date. (consequence)

■ because paying for anorexia counseling is like paying for alcoholism or drug counseling, which is already covered by insurance. (resemblance)

Note how each of these supporting reasons appeals to the value system of the audience. The writer hopes to show that covering the cost of counseling is within the class of things that the audience already values (commitment to women's health), will lead to consequences desired by the audience (reduced long-term costs), and is similar to something the audience already values (drug and alcohol counseling). The claim types strategy for generating ideas is easy to apply in practice. The following chart shows you how.

Suggestions for Applying the Claim Types Strategy to Your Proposal

Claim Type	Your Goal	Thinking Strategy
Argument from principle or category	Show how your proposed action follows a principle valued by your audience or belongs to a category valued by your audience.	■ Think of how your proposed action adheres to a rule or principle. ■ Use this template: "because doing this action is" and then fill in the blank with a noun or adjective: *kind, just, loving, courageous, merciful, legal, fair, democratic, constitutional, an act of hope, an illustration of the golden rule, faithful to the principle of limited government.* ■ If you are opposing a proposal, search for negative rather than positive principles/categories.
Argument from consequences	Show how your proposed action will lead to consequences valued by your audience.	■ Brainstorm consequences of your proposal and identify those that the audience will agree are good. ■ If you are opposing a proposal, search for negative consequences.
Argument from resemblance	Show how your proposed action has been done successfully elsewhere or is like another action valued by your audience.	■ Brainstorm places or times when your proposal (or something similar to it) has been done successfully. ■ Brainstorm analogies that compare your proposed action to something the audience already values. ■ If you are opposing a proposal, think of places or times where similar actions have failed or construct a negative analogy.

■ ■ ■   **FOR CLASS DISCUSSION**   Generating Ideas Using the Claim Types Strategy

1. Working individually or in small groups, use the strategies of principle/category, consequence, and resemblance to create *because* clauses that support each of the following claims. Try to have at least one *because* clause from each of the categories, but generate as many reasons as possible. Don't worry about whether any individual reason exactly fits the category. The purpose is to stimulate thinking, not fill in the slots.

Example

Congress should not pass gun control laws (proposal claim)

- because the Second Amendment guarantees the right to own guns (principle or category)
- because owning a gun allows citizens to protect themselves, their homes, and their loved ones from intruders (consequence)
- because laws to ban guns will be as ineffective as laws to ban alcohol during Prohibition (resemblance)

  a. Marijuana should be legalized.

  b. Division I college athletes should receive salaries.

  c. High schools should pass out free contraceptives.

  d. Violent video games should be made illegal.

  e. Parents should be heavily taxed for having more than two children.

2. Repeat the first exercise, taking a different position on each issue.

Using the "Stock Issues" Strategy to Develop a Proposal Argument

Another effective way to generate ideas for a proposal argument is to ask yourself a series of questions based on the "stock issues" strategy. Suppose, for example, you wanted to develop the following argument: "In order to solve the problem of students who won't take risks with their writing, the faculty should adopt a pass/fail method of grading in all writing courses." The stock issues strategy invites the writer to consider "stock" ways (that is, common, usual, frequently repeated ways) that such arguments can be conducted.

Stock issue 1: *Is there really a problem here that needs to be solved?* Is it really true that a large number of student writers won't take risks in their writing? Is this problem more serious than other writing problems such as undeveloped ideas, lack of organization, and poor sentence structure? This stock issue invites the writer to convince her audience that a true problem exists. Conversely, an opponent to the proposal may argue that a true problem does not exist.

Stock issue 2: *Will the proposed solution really solve this problem?* Is it true that a pass/fail grading system will cause students to take more risks with their writing? Will more interesting, surprising, and creative essays result from pass/fail grading? Or will students simply put less effort into their writing? This stock issue prompts a supporter to demonstrate that the proposal will solve the problem; in contrast, it prompts the opponent to show that the proposal won't work.

Stock issue 3: *Can the problem be solved more simply without disturbing the status quo?* An opponent of the proposal may agree that a problem exists and that the proposed solution might solve it. However, the opponent may say, "Are there not less radical ways to solve this problem? If we want more creative and risk-taking student essays, can't we just change our grading criteria so that we reward risky papers and penalize conventional ones?" This stock issue prompts supporters to show that *only* the proposed solution will solve the problem and that no minor tinkering with the status quo will be adequate. Conversely, opponents will argue that the problem can be solved without acting on the proposal.

Stock issue 4: *Is the proposed solution really practical? Does it stand a chance of actually being enacted?* Here an opponent to the proposal may agree that the proposal would work but contends that it involves pie-in-the-sky idealism. Nobody will vote to change the existing system so radically; therefore, it is a waste of our time to debate it. Following this prompt, supporters would have to argue that pass/fail grading is workable and that enough faculty members are disposed to it that the proposal is worth debating. Opponents may argue that the faculty is so traditional that pass/fail has utterly no chance of being accepted, despite its merits.

Stock issue 5: *What will be the unforeseen positive and negative consequences of the proposal?* Suppose we do adopt a pass/fail system. What positive or negative consequences may occur that are different from what we at first predicted? Using this prompt, an opponent may argue that pass/fail grading will reduce the effort put forth by students and that the long-range effect will be writing of even lower quality than we have now. Supporters would try to find positive consequences—perhaps a new love of writing for its own sake rather than for the sake of a grade.

■ ■ ■ **FOR CLASS DISCUSSION** **Brainstorming Ideas for a Proposal**
The following collaborative task takes approximately two class days to complete. The exercise takes you through the process of creating a proposal argument.

1. In small groups, identify and list several major problems facing students in your college or university.
2. Decide among yourselves which are the most important of these problems and rank them in order of importance.
3. Take your group's number one problem and explore answers to the following questions. Group recorders should be prepared to present their group's answers to the class as a whole:
   a. Why is the problem a problem?
   b. For whom is the problem a problem?
   c. How will these people suffer if the problem is not solved? (Give specific examples.)
   d. Who has the power to solve the problem?
   e. Why hasn't the problem been solved up to this point?
   f. How can the problem be solved? (That is, create a proposal.)
   g. What are the probable benefits of acting on your proposal?
   h. What costs are associated with your proposal?
   i. Who will bear those costs?

j. Why should this proposal be enacted?

k. Why is it better than alternative proposals?

4. As a group, draft an outline for a proposal argument in which you

   a. describe the problem and its significance.

   b. propose your solution to the problem.

   c. justify your proposal by showing how the benefits of adopting that proposal outweigh the costs.

5. Recorders for each group should write their group's outline on the board and be prepared to explain it to the class.

EXAMINING VISUAL ARGUMENTS

IF YOU DON'T PICK IT UP THEY WILL.

A Proposal Claim

This advocacy poster, sponsored by the Endangered Wildlife Trust, presents a photograph of a dead baby albatross on a beach on Midway Island, a main nesting ground for albatrosses. The photo is part of environmental photographer Chris Jordan's 2009 exhibit "Midway: Message from the Gyre." In this exhibit, Jordan exposes the effects of increasing volumes of ocean garbage on albatrosses, who mistake the garbage for food. What policy proposal is the Endangered Wildlife Trust making in this poster? What action is it asking people to take? The colorful, plastic-filled carcass of the baby albatross creates a complex appeal to *pathos* in its effort to give presence to the problem. How does the verbal text help to interpret this appeal while driving home the *logos* of the argument?

WRITING ASSIGNMENT   A Proposal Argument

Option 1: A Practical Proposal Addressing a Local Problem   Write a practical proposal offering a solution to a local problem. Your proposal should have three main sections: (1) description of the problem, (2) proposed solution, and (3) justification. Proposals are usually accompanied by a *letter of transmittal*—a one-page business letter that introduces the proposal to its intended audience and provides some needed background about the writer.

Document design is important in practical proposals, which are aimed at busy people who have to make many decisions under time constraints. An effective design helps establish the writer's *ethos* as a quality-oriented professional and helps make the reading of the proposal as easy as possible. For a student example of a practical proposal, see Megan Johnson's argument on pages 330–333.

Option 2: A Policy Proposal as a Guest Editorial   Write a two- to three-page policy proposal suitable for publication as a feature editorial in a college or city newspaper or in a publication associated with a particular group, such as a church newsletter or employee bulletin. The voice and style of your argument should be aimed at readers of your chosen publication. Your editorial should have the following features:

1. The identification of a problem (Persuade your audience that this is a genuine problem that needs solving; give it presence.)
2. A proposal for action that will help alleviate the problem
3. A justification of your solution (the reasons why your audience should accept your proposal and act on it)

Option 3: A Researched Argument Proposing Public Policy   Write an eight- to twelve-page proposal argument as a formal research paper, using researched data for development and support. In business and professional life, this kind of research proposal is often called a *white paper*, which recommends a course of action internally within an organization or externally to a client or stakeholder. An example of a researched policy proposal is student writer Juan Vazquez's "Why the United States Should Adopt Nuclear Power" on pages 334–338.

Option 4: Multimedia Project: A One-Page Advocacy Advertisement   Using the strategies of visual argument discussed in Chapter 9 and on pages 318–319 of this chapter, create a one-page advocacy advertisement urging action on a public issue. Your advertisement should be designed for publication in a newspaper or for distribution as a poster or flier. An example of a student-produced advocacy advertisement is shown in Figure 14.1 on page 319.

Option 5: Multimedia Project: A Proposal Speech with Visual Aids   Deliver a proposal argument as a prepared but extemporaneous speech of approximately five to eight minutes, supported with visual aids created on presentation software such as PowerPoint. Your speech should present a problem, propose a solution, and justify the solution with reasons and evidence. Use visual aids to give "presence" to the problem and to enhance appeals to *logos*, *ethos*, and *pathos*. Good aids use visual strategies to create encapsulated visual arguments; they are not simply bullet point outlines of your speech. Sandy Wainscott's speech outline and selected PowerPoint slides (pages 341–343) illustrate this genre.

Exploring Ideas

Because *should* or *ought* issues are among the most common sources of arguments, you may already have ideas for proposal issues. To think of ideas for practical proposals, try making an idea map of local problems you would like to see solved. For initial spokes, try trigger words such as the following:

- Problems at my university (dorms, parking, registration system, financial aid, campus appearance, clubs, curriculum, intramural program, athletic teams)
- Problems in my city or town (dangerous intersections, ugly areas, inadequate lighting, parks, police policy, public transportation, schools)
- Problems at my place of work (office design, flow of customer traffic, merchandise display, company policies)
- Problems related to my future career, hobbies, recreational time, life as a consumer, life as a homeowner

If you can offer a solution to the problem you identify, you may make a valuable contribution to some phase of public life.

To find a topic for policy proposals, stay in touch with the news, which will keep you aware of current debates on regional and national issues. Also, visit the Web sites of your congressional representatives to see what issues they are currently investigating and debating. You might think of your policy proposal as a white paper for one of your legislators.

Once you have decided on a proposal issue, we recommend you explore it by trying one or more of the following activities:

- Explore ideas by using the claim types strategy (see pages 320–322).
- Explore ideas by using the "stock issues" strategy (see pages 322–323).
- Explore ideas using the eleven questions (a–k) on pages 323–324.

Identifying Your Audience and Determining What's at Stake

Before drafting your argument, identify your targeted audience and determine what's at stake. Consider your responses to the following questions:

- What audience are you targeting? What background do they need to understand your problem? How much do they already care about it? How could you motivate them to care?
- After they read your argument, what stance do you imagine them holding? What change do you want to bring about in their view or their behavior?
- What will they find uncomfortable or threatening about your proposal? Particularly, what costs will they incur by acting on your proposal?

- What objections might they raise? What counterarguments or alternative solutions will you need to address?
- Why does your proposal matter? What is at stake?

Organizing a Proposal Argument

When you write your draft, you may find it helpful to have at hand an organization plan for a proposal argument. The plan on page 328 shows a typical structure for a proposal argument. In some cases, you may want to summarize and rebut opposing views before you present the justification for your own proposal.

Designing a One-Page Advocacy Advertisement

As an alternative to a traditional written argument, your instructor may ask you to create a one-page advocacy advertisement. The first stage of your invention process should be the same as that for a longer proposal argument. Choose a controversial public issue that needs immediate attention or a neglected issue about which you want to arouse public passion. As with a longer proposal argument, consider your audience in order to identify the values and beliefs on which you will base your appeal.

When you construct your argument, the limited space available demands efficiency in your choice of words and in your use of document design. Your goal is to have a memorable impact on your reader in order to promote the action you advocate. The following questions may help you design and revise your advocacy ad:

1. How could photos or other graphic elements establish and give presence to the problem?
2. How can type size, typestyle, and layout be used to present the core of your proposal, including the justifying reasons, in the most powerful way for the intended audience?
3. Can any part of this argument be presented as a memorable slogan or catchphrase? What key phrases could highlight the parts or the main points of this argument?
4. How can document design clarify the course of action and the direct demand on the audience this argument is proposing?
5. How can use of color enhance the overall impact of your advocacy argument? (Note: One-page advertisements are expensive to reproduce in color, but you might make effective use of color if your advocacy ad were to appear as a poster or Web page.)

Designing PowerPoint Slides or Other Visual Aids for a Speech

In designing visual aids, your goal is to increase the persuasive effect of your speech rather than to demonstrate your technical wizardry. A common mistake with PowerPoint presentations is to get enamored with the program's bells and whistles. If you find yourself thinking about special effects (animations, fade-outs, flashing letters) rather than about "at a glance" visual appeals to *logos* or *pathos*, you may be on the wrong track. Another common mistake is to use slides simply to project a bullet point outline of your speech. Our best advice in designing slides is thus to "think visual argument."

Organization Plan for a Proposal Argument

Introduce and develop the problem.	• Engage readers' interest in your problem. • Provide background, including previous attempts to solve the problem. • Give the problem "presence" by showing who is affected and what is at stake. • Argue that the problem is solvable (optional).
Present your proposed solution to the problem.	• First, state your proposal concisely to serve as your thesis statement or claim. • Then, explain the specifics of your proposal.
Justify your proposed solution through a series of supporting reasons.	• Restate your claim and forecast your supporting reasons. • Present and develop reason 1. • Present and develop reason 2. • Present and develop additional reasons.
Respond to objections or to alternative proposals.	• Anticipate and summarize possible objections or alternative ways to solve the problem. • Respond appropriately through rebuttal or concession.
Conclude.	• Sum up your argument and help readers return to the "big picture" of what's at stake. • Call readers to action. • End with something memorable.

In terms of visual argument, effective presentation slides can usually be placed in three design categories:

- Slides using images (photographs, drawings) to enhance *pathos* or to create snapshot visual clarity of a concept (*logos*)
- Slides using graphs or other visual displays of numbers to make numeric arguments
- Slides using bulleted (all-text) subpoints for evidence

All the strategies for visual arguments discussed in Chapter 9 and in this chapter under "Proposal Arguments as Advocacy Posters or Advertisements" (pages 318–319) apply equally to presentation slides.

In most cases, the "title" of the slide should put into words the "take-away point" of the slide—a verbal summary of the slide's visual argument. Most rhetoricians suggest that the title of a slide be a short sentence that makes a point rather than just a topic phrase.

Topic as Title (Weak)	Point as Title (Strong)
Coal and the Environment	Burning Coal Produces Dangerous Greenhouse Gases
The Effect of Money on Happiness	More Money Doesn't Mean More Happiness

Student writer Sandy Wainscott tried to follow these principles in her speech and accompanying PowerPoint slides, shown on pages 341–343. ■

Questioning and Critiquing a Proposal Argument

As we've suggested, proposal arguments need to overcome the innate conservatism of people, the difficulty of anticipating all the consequences of a proposal, and so forth. What questions, then, can we ask about proposal arguments to help us anticipate these problems?

Will a skeptic deny that my problem is really a problem? Be prepared for skeptics who aren't bothered by your problem, who see your problem as limited to a small group of people, or who think you are exaggerating.

Will a skeptic doubt the effectiveness of my solution? A skeptic might agree that your problem is indeed important and worth solving, but will not be convinced that your solution will work. For these skeptics, you'll need to provide evidence that your solution is feasible and workable. Also be prepared for skeptics who focus on the potential negative or unintended consequences of your proposed solution.

Will a skeptic think my proposal costs too much? The most commonly asked question of any proposal is simply, "Do the benefits of enacting the proposal outweigh the costs?" Be wary of the (understandable) tendency to underestimate the costs and exaggerate the benefits of a proposal. Honesty will enhance your *ethos*.

Will a skeptic suggest counterproposals? Once you've convinced readers that a problem exists, they are likely to suggest solutions different from yours. It only makes sense to anticipate alternative solutions and to work out ways to argue why your solution is better. And who knows, you may end up liking the counterproposal better and changing your mind about what to propose!

Our first reading, by student writer Megan Johnson, is a practical proposal **READINGS** addressing the problem of an inequitable meal plan on her campus—one that she claims discriminates against women. As a practical proposal, it uses headings and other elements of document design aimed at giving it a finished and professional appearance. When sent to the intended audience, it is accompanied by a single-spaced letter of transmittal following the conventional format of a business letter.

A Practical Proposal
MEGAN JOHNSON (STUDENT)

Ms. Jane Doe

Vice-President for Budgeting and Finance

Certain University

Certain City

Certain State, Zip

Dear Ms. Doe:

Enclosed is a proposal that addresses our university's minimum meal plan requirements for students living on campus. My proposal shows the problems associated with this requirement and suggests a workable solution for the university.

The enclosed proposal suggests a modest plan for allowing students to use their campus cards to purchase items off campus. Currently, students are required to purchase a minimum meal plan of $1,170, even though women eat less than men and often have to donate unspent meal funds back to the university. This proposal would give students the option to spend some of their meal plan money off campus. The benefits of my plan include more fairness to women students, fewer incentives toward binge eating, more opportunities for student bonding, and better relations with the nearby business community.

Through web research, I have discovered that other universities have systems in place similar to what I am proposing. I hope that my proposal is received well and considered as a workable option. A change in the minimum meal plan requirement might make our university a more desirable option for more prospective students as well as ultimately benefit the general welfare of the current student body.

Thank you for your time.

Sincerely,
Megan Johnson (Student)

A Proposal to Allow Off-Campus Purchases with a Meal Card
Submitted by Megan Johnson (Student)

Problem

The problem with this university's required meal plan is that it is too large for many students, particularly women. For example, at the end of Winter Quarter, my final balance on my meal card was $268.50, all of which, except for $100, I had to donate back to the university. As the current system stands, students have to purchase a minimum meal plan for living on campus. The minimum meal plan totals $1,170 per quarter. During the academic year an amount of $100 may be rolled into the next quarter. At the end of the quarter any remaining funds, excluding the $100, will be removed from the meal plan. Therefore, if students do not spend the money on their meal plans, it will be wasted. As a woman, I am frustrated about having to decide whether to give my money back to the university or to use up my meal card by binge eating at the end of each quarter.

Proposed Solution

I propose that our university create a system in which students are able to use their campus meal plans at local businesses off campus such as local drug stores, grocery stores, and restaurants. As I will note later in this proposal, other universities have such a system, so the technical difficulties should be easy to solve. Basically, the card works as a debit card loaded with the amount of money the student places on the card. Local businesses would swipe a student's card the same way as the on-campus food service currently does, deducting the current charge against the amount still available on the card. It would probably be possible to limit the total number of dollars available for spending off campus.

Justification

My proposal would allow on-campus residential students to use some of their meal plan money on groceries, on non-food related items such as toiletries, or on an occasional off-campus meal at a local restaurant. This proposal would resolve the problem of gender bias in the current system, promote opportunities for more bonding among students, and ultimately help create a healthier student body. Moreover, it would show the university's commitment to its students' welfare.

First of all, the current meal plan policy tends to discriminate against women. All students on campus are required to have a minimum meal plan, even though men and women have clearly different eating habits. Men tend to eat much more than women and frequently have to add money to their meal plans to get through the quarter. In contrast, many women, like myself, don't use up their prepaid amounts. For example, my friend James ran out of his meal plan by the eighth week of the quarter whereas my roommate Blaire still had over $400 left on her card at the end of the quarter. She and I, like many other women, will have to donate our money back to the school. Therefore, women often feel cheated out of their money while men do not. It is discriminatory to require all students, regardless of gender, to have the same minimum meal plan. However, if the university is going to require all students to have the same minimum meal plan, then the university needs to give women more options to spend their money on things other than food purchased in the school dining halls.

5   In addition, my proposal would create more opportunities for bonding. For example, it would allow persons who love to cook, such as me, to use the residence hall kitchens to create "home-cooked meals" for floor mates, thus creating more friendships among students. Personally, I have had the pleasure of helping create such bonds among the women on my floor by cooking a "family dinner" in our floor's kitchen. The aroma of the roasted chicken and homemade mashed potatoes drew the students on the fifth floor into the lounge. After our shared dinner, it seemed as if our floor felt more comfortable being around each other in a more family-like way. I think that cooking on campus gives students a sense of comfort that they do not get when they go to the dining halls and have food pre-made for them. While I would love to cook dinner for my floor more often, the bottom line is that ingredients are too expensive to pay for on my regular credit card when I have already purchased from the university more food than I can eat. If the school were to implement a system where we could use a portion of our meal plans off campus, students would be able to buy groceries from local stores and to put to better use the kitchens already built into the residence halls.

In addition to creating closer bonds between students, an off-campus option for our meal cards would help women eat more healthfully. The current system promotes bad eating habits causing women to overeat or even to binge in order to use up their extra meal plan money. For example, with the left over money on my card at the end of Fall Quarter, I bought cases of energy drinks which are filled with high fructose corn syrup and other empty calories. As another example, my friend Amber purchases multiple meals such as pizza and a burger for dinner because she doesn't want to waste her money. Overeating is obviously unhealthy and could eventually lead to an increase in obesity or eating disorders. However, if students were able to use their meal card off campus, they could buy items such as shampoo or other toiletries, which would be more beneficial for women than overeating to avoid losing money.

Despite all these benefits of a new meal plan system, some administrators might be skeptical of the benefits and focus on the drawbacks instead. The biggest drawback is the potential loss of revenue to food services. As it is now, women help subsidize food costs for men. Without that subsidy, the food service might not be able to break even, forcing them to raise food costs for everyone. I don't have the financial expertise to know how to compute these costs. Clearly, however, other universities have thought about these issues and decided that allowing students to spend some of their food money off campus was a benefit worth providing for students. For example, the University of Texas, the University of Minnesota, and the University of Florida allow their meal cards to be used as debit cards at local businesses. As stated on their website, the University of Texas has a system called Bevo Bucks in which students can "purchase food, goods and services at participating locations, both on and off campus" by loading money onto their ID cards. Also according to the University of Minnesota's website, students have a system called FlexDine connected to their ID cards. FlexDine gives students the "convenience … [to eat] at PAPA JOHN's for residence hall residents." If other schools can implement off campus use of dining cards, then the plan is feasible. It might also be possible to limit the number of dollars that could be spent each quarter off campus in order to assure a minimum level of revenue for the food service.

Even if my proposal would be costly in terms of lost revenue to the food service, the benefits of my plan might still outweigh the costs. A revised meal card system might become a recruiting point for prospective students because they would feel as if the university is more personalized to fit the students' needs rather than just the university's needs. My proposal might help prospective students see how close the students at our university are and might draw more students to apply here. (Our website and view books could even include pictures of students' cooking in the resident hall kitchens or eating at a local restaurant.) Moreover local off-campus businesses would welcome the opportunity for more student customers and might offer special promotions for students. A new meal card system might even improve the relationship between the university and the surrounding community.

Based on all these reasons, I believe that the university community as a whole would benefit if my proposal were enacted. The new plan would be especially appreciated by women students, many of whom now subsidize the food costs of men. In addition, the new system would bring students closer together by encouraging more creative use of the residence hall kitchens for community meals and by reducing the incentive toward binge eating at the end of each quarter. Finally, if other universities can use this system then our university should be able to use it as well. Although the food service may lose money to local businesses, the university would ultimately benefit by creating a more flexible and attractive meal option—especially for women—and by showing administrative concern for student welfare.

Critiquing "A Proposal to Allow Off-Campus Purchases with a University Meal Card"

1. In your own words, summarize briefly the problem that Megan Johnson addresses, her proposed solution, and her justifying reasons.
2. Megan addresses her proposal to Ms. Jane Doe, an administrator who has the power to change policy. To what extent does Megan develop audience-based reasons that resonate for this audience of university administrators? How effectively does she anticipate and respond to objections her audience might raise?
3. How does Megan establish a positive *ethos* in this argument? To what extent does she appeal to *pathos* as well as *logos*?
4. How effective is Megan's proposal?

Our second reading, by student writer Juan Vazquez, is a researched public policy proposal written in response to the option 3 assignment on page 325. Vazquez's argument is based on library and Internet research he conducted into the problem of fossil fuels and climate change. It is formatted as a formal research paper using the documentation style of the Modern Language Association (MLA). A full explanation of this format is given in Chapter 17.

Juan Vazquez

Professor Bean

English 210

15 July 2008

Why the United States Should Adopt Nuclear Power

Thousands of studies conducted by scientists to measure climate change over the last one hundred years have accumulated substantial evidence that global warming is occurring unequivocally. According to the NASA *Earth Observatory* web site, greenhouse gas emissions caused the average surface temperature of the Earth to increase by 0.6 to 0.9 degrees Celsius between 1906 and 2006. If fossil fuel energy continues to be burned relentlessly, scientists are predicting that the average surface temperatures could rise between 2°C and 6°C by the end of the twenty-first century (Riebeek). A prevalent consensus among scientists is that humans are a major culprit in global warming by burning fossil fuels such as coal and petroleum, with coal-fired power plants being one of the major problems. Lately, discussion has focused on what governments in developed countries can do to tackle climate change.

One solution, advocated by scientist William Sweet writing for the magazine *Discover*, is that the United States should expand its long-ignored nuclear power industry. However, many people—especially environmentalists—are afraid of nuclear power and believe that we can solve global warming through other alternatives. Despite these fears and counter-arguments, I believe that Sweet is right about nuclear energy. The United States should as quickly as possible phase out coal-burning power plants and replace them with nuclear power and other green technologies.

Before we look at the advantages of nuclear power, it is important to see why many people are opposed to it. First, opponents argue that nuclear power plants aren't safe. They regularly cite the Three Mile Island accident in 1979 and the disastrous Chernobyl meltdown in 1986. A more exhaustive list of recent small scale but worrisome nuclear accidents is provided by an editorial from the *Los Angeles Times,* which describes how a July 2007 magnitude 6.8 earthquake in Japan "caused dozens of problems at the world's biggest nuclear plant, leading to releases of radioactive elements into the air and ocean and an indefinite shutdown" ("No to Nukes"). Opponents also argue that nuclear plants are attractive terrorist targets. A properly placed explosive could spew radioactive material over wide swathes of densely populated areas. Nuclear power plants also provide opportunities for terrorists to steal plutonium for making their own nuclear weapons.

MLA

Second, while agreeing that nuclear power plants don't produce greenhouse gases, opponents remind us that radioactive waste cannot be stored safely and that radioactive waste remains hazardous for tens of thousands of years. The heavy walled concrete containers used to enclose nuclear waste will eventually develop cracks. If the planned disposal facility at Yucca Mountain, Nevada—where wastes would be stored in concrete and steel containers deep underground—ever becomes operational, it would ease the waste issue for the United States but would not eliminate it. The dangerous nuclear waste would still have to be trucked to Nevada, and even the Nevada site might not be completely impervious to earthquake damage or to the possibility that future generations would dig it up accidentally.

Finally, opponents claim that nuclear power plants are extremely expensive and the process of building them is extremely slow so that this method won't provide any short-term solutions for climate change. According to the "No to Nukes" editorial from the *Los Angeles Times,* the average nuclear plant is estimated to cost about $4 billion, making nuclear-generated energy about 25% to 75% more expensive than old-fashioned coal. At the same time, the regulatory process for building nuclear power plants is slow and unpredictable, making investors hesitant about supplying the capital needed. Opponents of nuclear energy argue that these high costs and long waiting period would make it impossible to launch a massive construction of nuclear power plants that would have an immediate impact on global warming.

So in the face of these risks, why should we support Sweet's proposal for expanding nuclear technology? One answer is that some of the fears about nuclear plants are overstated, fabricated, or politicized. It is true that in the past there have been accidents at nuclear power plants, but improvements in technology make such disasters in the future very unlikely. According to Sweet, changes in the design of nuclear reactors in the United States make them "virtually immune to the type of accident that occurred at Chernobyl in April 1986" (62). Furthermore, Sweet points out, the oft-cited Three Mile Island accident didn't injure a single person and led to a better regulatory system that makes new reactors much safer than old ones. According to Sweet, today's "coal fired power plants routinely kill tens of thousands of people in the United States each year by way of lung cancer, bronchitis, and other ailments; the U.S. nuclear economy kills virtually no one in a normal year" (62). In addition, management of power plants has improved. As for the fear of terrorist threats and nuclear proliferation, these concerns have been blown out of proportion. As Sweet argues, if any terrorists are seeking to produce bombs, their access to plutonium will not depend on how

MLA

many nuclear power plants the U.S. is building. Because nuclear power plants must be housed within concrete containment barriers to prevent damage from earthquakes, hurricanes, and floods, they are also resistant to terrorist attacks. A study carried out by the Electric Power Research Institute and reported in a major study of nuclear power by scientists from MIT showed that an airplane crashing into a U.S. nuclear power plant would not breech the containment barriers (*Future of Nuclear Power* 50). Moreover, nuclear scientists say that the safe containment of nuclear waste is not a technical problem but a political problem.

Although nuclear reactors are not risk free, they are much safer for people's health and for the environment than are coal-fired plants with their pollution-spewing greenhouse gases. According to the MIT study on nuclear power, since the first commercial nuclear reactor was built in the United States in 1957 (there are now currently 100 nuclear reactors in the United States), there has been only one accident that caused core damage (Three Mile Island). Using statistical analysis, the researchers estimate that the current safety regulations and design specifications will limit core damage frequency to about 1 accident per 10,000 reactor-per-years. They also believe that the technology exists to reduce the rate of serious accidents to 1 in 100,000 reactor-years (*Future of Nuclear Power* 48). The benefits of nuclear power for reducing global warming therefore outweigh the real but very low risks of using nuclear energy.

As to the problem of nuclear power's expense, it is true that nuclear plants are more expensive than coal plants, but it is important to understand that the high initial cost of building a nuclear power plant is being compared to the artificially low cost of coal power. If we were to tax coal-burning plants through a cap and trade system so that coal plants would have to pay for social and environmental costs of pollution and production of greenhouse gases, nuclear power would become more competitive. As Sweet argues, we need a tax or equivalent trading scheme that would increase the cost of coal-generated electricity to encourage a switch from cheap coal to more environmentally friendly nuclear power plants.

Nuclear power plants are not the perfect or sole alternative to burning coal to generate energy, but they are certainly the most effective for combating global warming. Without nuclear power plants, we can't generate enough electricity to meet U.S. demands while also reducing carbon emissions. There are other alternatives such as wind technology, but this is also more expensive than coal and not nearly as reliable as nuclear power. Wind turbines only generate energy about a third of the time, which would not be enough to meet peak demands, and the problem of building enough wind towers and creating a huge distribution system to transmit the power from remote windy regions to cities where the power is needed is overwhelming. Currently wind power generates less than 1% of the nation's electricity whereas nuclear power currently generates 20 percent (Sweet). According to Jesse Ausubel, head of the Program for the Human Environment at Rockefeller University, "To reach the scale at which they would contribute importantly to meeting global energy demand, renewable sources of energy such as wind, water, and biomass cause serious environmental harm. Measuring renewables in watts per square meter, nuclear has astronomical advantages over its competitors."

To combat global warming we need to invest in strategies that could make a large difference fairly quickly. The common belief that we can slow global warming by switching to fluorescent light bulbs, taking the bus to work, and advocating for wind or solar energy is simply wrong. According to science writer Matt Jenkins, the climate problem is solvable. "But tackling it is going to be a lot harder than you've been led to believe" (39). Jenkins summarizes the work of Princeton researchers Stephen Pacala and Robert Socolow, who have identified a "package of greenhouse gas reduction measures" (44), each measure of which they call a "stabilization wedge." Each wedge would reduce carbon gas emissions by one gigaton. Pacala and Socolow have identified 15 possible stabilization wedges and have shown that adopting 7 of these wedges will reduce carbon emissions to the levels needed to halt global warming. One of Pacala and Socolow's wedges could be achieved by raising the fuel economy of 2 billion cars from 30 mpg to 60 mpg (Jenkins 44). Another wedge would come from building 50 times more wind turbines than currently exist in the world or 700 times more solar panels. In contrast, we could achieve a wedge simply by doubling the number of nuclear power plants in the world. Nuclear power is clearly not the only solution to climate change. In Pacala and Socolow's scheme, it is at most one-seventh of the solution, still forcing us to take drastic measures to conserve energy, stop the destruction of rain forests, develop clean-burning coal, and create highly fuel-efficient automobiles. But nuclear energy produces the quickest, surest, and most dramatic reduction of the world's carbon footprint. If we do not take advantage of its availability, we will need to get equivalent carbon-free power from other sources, which may not be possible and will certainly be more expensive. Therefore expanded use of nuclear technology has to be part of the solution to stop global warming. We should also note that other countries are already way ahead of us in the use of nuclear technology. France gets almost 80% of its electricity from nuclear power and Sweden

Vazquez 5

almost 50% ("World Statistics"). These countries have accepted the minimal risks of nuclear power in favor of a reduced carbon footprint and a safer environment.

In sum, we should support Sweet's proposal for adopting nuclear power plants as a major national policy. However, there are other questions that we need to pursue. Where are we going to get the other necessary wedges? Are we going to set gas mileage requirements of 60 mpg on the auto industry? Are we going to push research and development for ways to burn coal cleanly by sequestering carbon emissions in the ground? Are we going to stop destruction of the rain forests? Are we going to fill up our land with wind towers to get one more wedge? If all these questions make climate change seem unsolvable, it will be even more difficult if we cannot factor in nuclear technology as a major variable in the equation.

Vazquez 6

Works Cited

Ausubel, Jesse H. "Renewable and Nuclear Heresies." Canadian Nuclear Association. Ottowa, CA. 10 Mar. 2005. Plenary Address. *Nuclear Green.* Web. 20 June 2008.

The Future of Nuclear Power: An Interdisciplinary MIT Study. Massachusetts Institute of Technology, 29 July 2003. Web. 20 June 2008.

Jenkins, Matt. "A Really Inconvenient Truth." *Miller McClune* April-May 2008: 38-49. Print.

"No to Nukes." Editorial. *Los Angeles Times.* Los Angeles Times, 23 July 2007. Web. 1 July 2008.

Riebeek, Holli. "Global Warming." *Earth Observatory.* NASA, 11 May 2007. Web. 18 June 2008.

Sweet, William. "Why Uranium Is the New Green." *Discover* Aug. 2007: 61-62. Print.

"World Statistics: Nuclear Energy around the World." *Resources and Stats.* Nuclear Energy Institute, 2008. Web. 19 June 2008.

Critiquing "Why the United States Should Adopt Nuclear Power"

1. What are Juan Vazquez's major reasons for building more nuclear power plants? Which of these reasons do you feel is most persuasive?
2. What are your own major objections to building more nuclear power plants? Do you have any objections that Vazquez fails to summarize?
3. To what extent does Vazquez respond persuasively to your objections? Which of his refutations of the anti-nuke arguments is weakest?
4. How effective is Vazquez's use of audience-based reasons? How would you evaluate his overall appeal to *logos, ethos,* and *pathos*?

Our third reading is the one-page paid advocacy advertisement on page 340. This is the second in a series of ads produced by the Center for Children's Health and the Environment, located at Mount Sinai School of Medicine in New York. The ads were intended to work in concert with the organization's Web site, http://www.childenvironment.org, which provides backup documentation including access to the scientific studies on which the ads' arguments are based. All the ads can be downloaded as PDF files from the Web site. The ads' purpose is to call public attention to environmental dangers to children and to urge public action.

Critiquing the Advocacy Ad from the Center for Children's Health and the Environment

1. A difficulty faced by many proposal writers is awakening the audience to the existence of the problem. The doctors and researchers who founded the Center for Children's Health and the Environment felt that a series of full-page newspaper ads was the best way to awaken the public to a problem that Americans either denied or didn't know existed.

    a. In your own words, what is the problem that this proposal addresses?
    b. How does the ad give presence to the problem?

2. How does this ad use the strategies of visual argument (use of images, arrangement of text, type size, and so forth) discussed in Chapter 9? The ad makers probably had available thousands of pictures to use in this ad. Why did they choose this photograph? Try to reconstruct the thinking of the ad makers when they decided on their use of type sizes and fonts. How is the message in different parts of the ad connected to the visual presentation of the words?
3. How effective is the verbal argument of this advertisement? Why does it place "Toxic chemicals appear linked to rising rates of some cancers" in boldface type at the beginning of the text?
4. Most of this ad is devoted to presentation of the problem. What does the ad actually propose?
5. Overall, how effective do you find this advocacy advertisement? If you were thumbing through a newspaper, would you stop to read this ad? If so, what would hook you?

#2 IN A SERIES

More kids are getting brain cancer.
Why?

Toxic chemicals appear linked to rising rates of some cancers.

As scientists and physicians, we've seen a drop in the death rates of many adult and childhood cancers because of earlier detection and better treatment. But we are also seeing a disturbing rise in the reported *incidence* of cancer among young children and adolescents, especially brain cancer, testicular cancer, and acute lymphocytic leukemia. In fact, after injuries and violence, cancer is the leading cause of death in our children.

The increase in childhood cancers may be explained in part by better detection or better access to medical care. But evidence suggests the rise in these childhood cancers, as well as in cancers like non-Hodgkin's lymphoma and multiple myeloma among adults, may also be partially explained by exposure to chemicals in the environment, chemicals found in many products, from paints and pesticides to dark-colored hair dyes.

What We Know

Pound for pound, kids are exposed to more toxic chemicals in food, air, and water than adults, because children breathe twice as much air, eat three to four times more food, and drink as much as two to seven times more water. Recent epidemiologic studies have shown that as children's exposures to home and garden pesticides increase, so does their risk of non-Hodgkin's lymphoma, brain cancer, and leukemia. Yet, right now, you can go to your hardware store and buy lawn pesticides, paint thinner and weed killers, all containing toxic chemicals linked to these diseases.

In both children and adults, the incidence rate for non-Hodgkin's lymphoma has increased thirty percent since 1950. The disease has been linked to industrial chemicals, chemicals found in agricultural, home, and garden pesticides, as well as dark hair dyes.

Studies have shown that Vietnam veterans and chemical workers exposed to Agent Orange, a phenoxy herbicide, are especially at risk for non-Hodgkin's lymphoma. American farmers who use phenoxy herbicides have an increased risk of the cancer. A Swedish study showed that among the general population, the risk of non-Hodgkin's lymphoma rises with increased exposure to these herbicides. And, a study in Southern California found that children of parents who use home pesticides have seven times the risk of non-Hodgkin's lymphoma. Multiple myeloma, a bone marrow cancer,

is also associated with toxic chemicals. Its incidence has tripled since 1950. Farmers are especially at risk: a recent analysis of thirty-two studies worldwide showed "consistent, positive findings" of an association between farming and multiple myeloma.

What We Can Do

There is much that parents can do to protect their children from carcinogenic chemicals, beginning with the elimination of many pesticides both outside and in the home. And, of course, the cessation of smoking. There are more suggestions on our website, www.childenvironment.org.

But more needs to be done. As a society, we've done much to protect people, especially children, from the toxic chemicals in cigarettes. But too many toxic chemicals are being marketed without adequate testing. We should demand that new chemicals undergo the same rigorous testing as medicines before being allowed on the market. And we should phase out those chemicals linked with a wide range of health problems from neurological impairment to cancer in children.

A summary of the supporting scientific evidence, and a list of scientific endorsers, can be found at www.childenvironment.org.

Center for Children's Health and the Environment

MOUNT SINAI SCHOOL OF MEDICINE

Box 1043, One Gustave Levy Place, New York, NY 10029 • **www.childenvironment.org**

Our fourth reading, by student Sandy Wainscott, illustrates option 5, a proposal speech supported by visual aids. We have reproduced Sandy's outline for her speech, along with six of her ten PowerPoint slides. Her final slide was a bibliography of the sources she used in her speech. Note how she has constructed her slides as visual arguments supporting a point (stated in the slide title) as opposed to using her slides to reproduce her speech outline.

Why McDonald's Should Sell Meat and Veggie Pies: A Proposal to End Subsidies for Cheap Meat

SANDY WAINSCOTT (STUDENT)

Introduction: McDonald's hamburgers are popular because they're satisfying and pretty darn cheap. It's quite amazing, when you think about it, that McDonald's can sell a double cheeseburger on their 99 cent menu. The average American wage earner can buy this burger after just 3 minutes of work. But I will argue that the hamburger is cheap because the American taxpayer subsidizes the cost of meat. Uncle Sam pays agribusiness to grow feed corn while not requiring agribusiness to pay the full cost for water or for cleaning up the environmental damage caused by cattle production. If meat producers had to recover the true cost of their product, the cost of meat would be substantially higher, but there would be offsetting benefits: a healthier environment, happier lives for cows and chickens, and healthier diets for all of us.

1. Meat is cheap partly because
   a. U.S. taxpayers give farmers money to grow feed corn, which is fed to cows
   b. U.S. taxpayers provide farmers with cheap water
2. Keeping meat cheap creates significant costs to our health, to the environment, and to animals
   a. Cheap meat threatens health
      (i) Factory-style farms significantly reduce effectiveness of antibiotics
      (ii) Antibiotic-resistant pathogens are potentially huge killers
      (iii) Factory farms are likely sources of new swine and bird flus
      (iv) Meat-related food poisoning harms millions of people per year with thousands of deaths
   b. Cheap meat threatens the environment
      (i) Factory farms create 130 times more sewage than humans
         (1) This sewage is not treated
         (2) It is held in open-air lagoons and releases large amounts of ammonium nitrate into the atmosphere and water supply

FIGURE 14.2 Sandy's title slide

FIGURE 14.3 Slide using Sandy's humorous drawing to illustrate a point

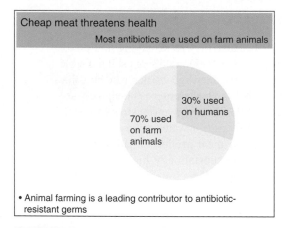

FIGURE 14.4 Slide using graphic for support

FIGURE 14.5 Slide using photograph for support

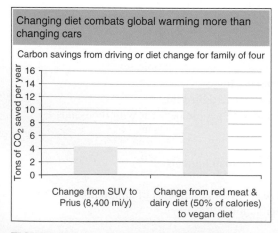

FIGURE 14.6 Slide using graphic for support

FIGURE 14.7 Slide using photograph for support

(ii) Animal farming contributes more to global warming than all forms of human transportation combined
(1) Most people think the way to combat global warming is by changing our driving habits (driving fuel-efficient cars, carpooling, taking the bus) or doing more conservation (fluorescent light bulbs, insulation, recycling)
(2) More impact would be achieved by reducing amount of meat in our diets
(iii) Animal farming uses much of the world's land and water
(1) Cattle consume 14 times more calories in grain than they produce in meat
(2) 80% of grain produced in the U.S. is eaten by livestock, not people
(3) It requires 125 times as much water to produce a calorie of beef as a calorie of potatoes
(4) The amount of land required to grow the plants to feed the animals leads to deforestation
c. Cheap meat requires cruelty to animals
(1) 98% of egg-laying hens in the U.S. spend their entire lives in stacked 9" × 9" × 9" cages
(2) Cruel conditions also exist for pigs and cows

Conclusion: If we quit giving farmers taxpayer subsidies and required them to pay for the pollution they cause, the cost of meat would be much higher—but with great benefits to our health and to our environment. A restaurant like McDonald's would likely adjust its menus. McDonald's would move the burger off its 99 cent menu and replace it with something like a meat pie, a similarly warm, quick, and satisfying choice, but with a lower proportion of meat than a burger. In a fair market, we should have to pay more for a hamburger than for a meat pie or a stir fry. But we would have the benefit of a healthier earth.

Critiquing "Why McDonald's Should Sell Meat and Veggie Pies: A Proposal to End Subsidies for Cheap Meat"

1. Although it is common to design PowerPoint slides that use topics and bullets to reproduce the speaker's outline, most public speaking experts prefer the approach that Sandy takes in this speech. She uses photographs, drawings, and graphics to create a visual argument that reinforces rather than simply reproduces the verbal message of her speech. How do her slides operate visually to create arguments from both *logos* and *pathos*?
2. Note that the top heading of each slide is a complete sentence making a point rather than a topic phrase without a subject and verb. For example, Figure 14.5 might have had the heading "Cost to Environment" or "Cheap Meat and the Environment." Do you agree with most experts, who would say that the complete sentence version ("Cheap meat hurts the environment") is more effective? Why or why not?
3. How effective do you find Sandy's speech?

Our final reading appeared in the *Wall Street Journal* on February 19, 2011. The authors are both professors of entomology at Wageningen University in the Netherlands. In 2007, Marcel Dicke was awarded the NWO-Spinoza award, often called the Dutch Nobel Prize. He gives speeches (summaries of which are available on the Web) arguing that humans should eat insects rather than meat as one solution to the environmental degradation caused by the meat industry. Coauthor Arnold Van Huis coordinates a research consortium of scientists investigating the nutritional value of insects. He also gives cooking classes featuring bug recipes.

The Six-Legged Meat of the Future

MARCEL DICKE AND ARNOLD VAN HUIS

At the London restaurant Archipelago, diners can order the $11 Baby Bee Brulee: a creamy custard topped with a crunchy little bee. In New York, the Mexican restaurant Toloache offers $11 chapulines tacos: two tacos stuffed with Oaxacan-style dried grasshoppers.

Could beetles, dragonfly larvae and water bug caviar be the meat of the future? As the global population booms and demand strains the world's supply of meat, there's a growing need for alternate animal proteins. Insects are high in protein, B vitamins and minerals like iron and zinc, and they're low in fat. Insects are easier to raise than livestock, and they produce less waste. Insects are abundant. Of all the known animal species, 80% walk on six legs; over 1,000 edible species have been identified. And the taste? It's often described as "nutty."

Worms, crickets, dung beetles—to most people they're just creepy crawlers. To Brooklyn painter and art professor Marc Dennis, they're yummy ingredients for his Bug Dinners.

The vast majority of the developing world already eats insects. In Laos and Thailand, weaver-ant pupae are a highly prized and nutritious delicacy. They are prepared with shallots, lettuce, chilies, lime and spices and served with sticky rice. Further back in history, the ancient Romans considered beetle larvae to be gourmet fare, and the Old Testament mentions eating crickets and grasshoppers. In the 20th century, the Japanese emperor Hirohito's favorite meal was a mixture of cooked rice, canned wasps (including larvae, pupae and adults), soy sauce and sugar.

Will Westerners ever take to insects as food? It's possible. We are entomologists at Wageningen University, and we started promoting insects as food in the Netherlands in the 1990s. Many people laughed—and cringed—at first, but interest gradually became more serious. In 2006 we created a "Wageningen—City of Insects" science festival to promote the idea of eating bugs; it attracted more than 20,000 visitors.

Over the past two years, three Dutch insect-raising companies, which normally produce feed for animals in zoos, have set up special production lines to raise locusts and mealworms for human consumption. Now those insects are sold, freeze-dried, in two dozen retail food outlets that cater to restaurants. A few restaurants in the Netherlands have already placed insects on the menu, with locusts and mealworms (beetle larvae) usually among the dishes.

Insects have a reputation for being dirty and carrying diseases—yet less than 0.5% of all known insect species are harmful to people, farm animals or crop plants. When raised under hygienic conditions—eating bugs

straight out of the backyard generally isn't recommended—many insects are perfectly safe to eat.

Meanwhile, our food needs are on the rise. The human population is expected to grow from six billion in 2000 to nine billion in 2050. Meat production is expected to double in the same period, as demand grows from rising wealth. Pastures and fodder already use up 70% of all agricultural land, so increasing livestock production would require expanding agricultural acreage at the expense of rain forests and other natural lands. Officials at the United Nations Food and Agriculture Organization recently predicted that beef could become an extreme luxury item by 2050, like caviar, due to rising production costs.

Raising insects for food would avoid many of the problems associated with livestock. For instance, swine and humans are similar enough that they can share many diseases. Such co-infection can yield new disease strains that are lethal to humans, as happened during a swine fever outbreak in the Netherlands in the late 1990s. Because insects are so different from us, such risks are accordingly lower.

Insects are also cold-blooded, so they don't need as much feed as animals like pigs and cows, which consume more energy to maintain their body temperatures. Ten pounds of feed yields one pound of beef, three pounds of pork, five pounds of chicken and up to six pounds of insect meat.

Insects produce less waste, too. The proportion of livestock that is not edible after processing is 30% for pork, 35% for chicken, 45% for beef and 65% for lamb. By contrast, only 20% of a cricket is inedible.

Raising insects requires relatively little water, especially as compared to the production of conventional meat (it takes more than 10 gallons of water, for instance, to produce about two pounds of beef). Insects also produce far less ammonia and other greenhouse gases per pound of body weight. Livestock is responsible for at least 10% of all greenhouse gas emissions.

Raising insects is more humane as well. Housing cattle, swine or chickens in high densities causes stress to the animals, but insects like mealworms and locusts naturally like to live in dense quarters. The insects can be crowded into vertical stacked trays or cages. Nor do bug farms have to be restricted to rural areas; they could sprout up anywhere, from a suburban strip mall to an apartment building. Enterprising gourmets could even keep a few trays of mealworms in the garage to ensure a fresh supply.

The first insect fare is likely to be incorporated subtly into dishes, as a replacement for meat in meatballs and sauces. It also can be mixed into prepared foods to boost their nutritional value—like putting mealworm paste into a quiche. And dry-roasted insects can be used as a replacement for nuts in baked goods like cookies and breads.

We continue to make progress in the Netherlands, where the ministry of agriculture is funding a new $1.3 million research program to develop ways to raise edible insects on food waste, such as brewers' grain (a byproduct of beer brewing), soyhulls (the skin of the soybean) and apple pomace (the pulpy remains after the juice has been pressed out). Other research is focusing on how protein could be extracted from insects and used in processed foods.

Though it is true that intentionally eating insects is common only in developing countries, everyone already eats some amount of insects. The average person consumes about a pound of insects per year, mostly mixed into other foods. In the U.S., most processed foods contain small amounts of insects, within limits set by the Food and Drug Administration. For chocolate, the FDA limit is 60 insect fragments per 100 grams. Peanut butter can have up to 30 insect parts per 100 grams, and fruit juice can have five fruit-fly eggs and one or two larvae per 250 milliliters (just over a cup). We also use many insect products to dye our foods, such as the red dye cochineal in imitation crab sticks, Campari and candies. So we're already some of the way there in making six-legged creatures a regular part of our diet.

Not long ago, foods like kiwis and sushi weren't widely known or available. It is quite likely that in 2020 we will look back in surprise at the era when our menus didn't include locusts, beetle larvae, dragonfly larvae, crickets and other insect delights.

Critiquing "The Six-Legged Meat of the Future"

1. On page 314 we note that a problem faced by all proposal writers is "the need to overcome people's natural conservatism." Their readers' natural conservatism is a major constraint for co-authors Dicke and Van Huis ("Hey, I've never eaten bugs before! If four-legged meat was good enough for my parents, it's good enough for me!") How do the authors use the appeals of *logos, ethos*, and *pathos* to try to overcome this natural conservatism?

2. Although this journalistic piece does not have a tightly closed-form structure with transitions and because clauses marking each reason, it still provides a logical progression of separate reasons in support of eating insects. Convert this argument into a bulleted list of because clauses in support of the claim "Westerners should eat insects as a major source of protein."

3. Are you persuaded by this argument? Would you try some mealworm spaghetti or a handful of fried crickets? Why or why not?

For additional writing, reading, and research resources, go to www.mycomplab.com

PART FIVE

The Researched Argument

Smart Cars, two-seater vehicles less than nine feet long, can now be seen in dozens of countries. Made by the Mercedes Car Group, these cars get around 40 miles per gallon of gasoline and, with their titanium structure, are purported to have good crash ratings. The Smart Car emerged at the *kairotic* moment when consumers began rethinking their car-buying habits with respect to fuel economy and concern for the enviornment. This photo, which juxtaposes a Hummer, the king of the SUVs, with this new, "greener" vehicle, emphasizes the parking advantage of going green.

15 Finding and Evaluating Sources

Although the "research paper" is a common writing assignment in college, students are often baffled by their professor's expectations. The problem is that students often think of research writing as presenting information rather than creating an argument. One of our business school colleagues calls these sorts of research papers "data dumps" (as in, "Here's your pickup load of info on 'world poverty,' Professor, I've dumped it into this paper for you").

But a research paper shouldn't be a data dump. Like any other argument, it should use information to support a contestable claim. In academic settings (as opposed to arguments in many business or civic settings), a distinguishing feature of a researched argument is its formal documentation. By **documentation**, we mean the in-text citations and accompanying list of references that allow readers to identify and locate the researcher's sources for themselves. In academic culture, authors gain credibility for new findings and ideas by showing the roots of their work and by explaining how they reached their conclusions. By documenting their sources according to appropriate conventions, research writers establish a credible *ethos* for their work while also providing a valuable resource for others who wish to consult the same sources.

Fortunately, writing an argument as a formal research paper draws on the same argumentation skills you have already been using—the ability to pose a question at issue within a community, to formulate a contestable claim, and to support your claim with audience-based reasons and evidence. What additional skills are required for a formal researched argument? The main ones are finding appropriate sources, evaluating those sources, incorporating them into your writing, and documenting them properly.

The three chapters in Part Five should help you develop these skills. In the present chapter, you will learn to:

- Pose a research question
- Unlock the resources of your library and the Web
- Evaluate your sources by reading them rhetorically

Chapter 16 then shows you how to incorporate your sources skillfully into your own prose using the academic conventions for ethical research. (Knowing and using these conventions will free you from any fears of plagiarism.) Finally, in Chapter 17 we explain the nitty-gritty details of in-text citations and end-of-paper lists of sources.

Formulating a Research Question Instead of a "Topic"

The best way to use your research time efficiently is to pose a question rather than a topic. To appreciate this difference, suppose a friend asks you what your research paper is about. Consider the differences in the following responses:

Topic focus: I'm doing a paper on gender-specific children's toys.

Question focus: I'm researching the effects of gender-specific toys on children's intellectual development. Do boys' toys develop intellectual skills more than girls' toys do?

Topic focus: I'm doing a paper on eating disorders.

Question focus: I'm trying to sort out what the experts say is the best way to treat severe anorexia nervosa. Is inpatient or outpatient treatment more effective?

As these scenarios suggest, a topic focus invites you to collect information without a clear point or purpose—an open road toward data dumping. In contrast, a question focus requires you to make an argument in which you support a claim with reasons and evidence.

A good way to formulate a research question is to use the exploration methods we suggested in Chapter 2. We suggest that you freewrite for ten minutes or so, reflecting on recent readings that have provoked you, on controversies within the communities to which you belong, or on personal experiences that may open up onto public issues. Your goal is to create an issue question about which reasonable persons may disagree. In many cases, you might not know where you stand yourself. Your research thus becomes a process of inquiry and clarification.

Thinking Rhetorically about Kinds of Sources

To be an effective researcher, you need to think rhetorically about the different kinds of sources that you might encounter while doing your research. In Chapter 2, we identified the various genres of argument and also explained who writes arguments and why (see pages 31–36). When you do research, you need to ask yourself, "What genre of argument is this source? Who wrote it and why?" In this section we'll extend our Chapter 2 discussion by explaining ways to distinguish among different kinds of sources. (See Table 15.1 for a rhetorical overview of kinds of sources.) Your payoff will be an increased ability to read sources rhetorically and to use them purposefully in your research writing.

To help you appreciate some of the distinctions made in Table 15.1, consider the following questions about each source's degree of editorial review, stability, advocacy, and authority.

Degree of Editorial Review

Note that Table 15.1 begins with "peer-reviewed scholarly sources," which are published by nonprofit academic presses and written for specialized audiences. "**Peer review**" is a highly prized concept in academia. It refers to the rigorous and competitive

TABLE 15.1   A Rhetorical Overview of Sources

Type of Source	Author and Angle of Vision	How to Recognize Them
Peer-Reviewed Scholarly Sources		
ARTICLES IN SCHOLARLY JOURNALS Examples: articles in *Journal of Abnormal Psychology; American Journal of Botany*	**Author:** Professors, industry researchers, independent scholars **Angle of vision:** Scholarly advancement of knowledge; presentation of research findings; development of new theories and applications	• Not sold on magazine racks • No commercial advertising • Academic style with documentation and bibliography • Cover often lists table of contents • Found through licensed online databases
SCHOLARLY BOOKS Example: *Shakespearean Negotiations: The Circulation of Social Identity in Renaissance England* by Stephen Greenblatt	**Author:** Professors, industry researchers, independent scholars **Angle of vision:** Scholarly advancement of knowledge; presentation of research findings; development of new theories and applications	• University press or other academic publisher on title page • Academic style with documentation and bibliography • Found in academic libraries; may be available as e-book
SCHOLARLY WEB SITES Example: http://seasia.museum.upenn.edu (Southeast Asian Archeology Scholarly Web site)	**Author:** Professors or institute scholars **Angle of vision:** Dissemination of research findings; informative access to primary sources	• Usually have an .edu Web address or address of professional scholarly organization • Clearly identified with an academic institution • Material is usually peer reviewed, but may include reports on work-in-progress or links to primary sources
REFERENCE WORKS Example: *The Farmer's Almanac; Statistical Abstract of the United States*	**Author:** Commissioned scholars **Angle of vision:** Balanced, factual overview	• Titles containing words such as *encyclopedia, dictionary, atlas,* and so forth • Found in library reference section or online
Public Affairs Sources		
NEWSPAPERS AND NEWS MAGAZINES Examples: *Time, Newsweek, Washington Post, Los Angeles Times*	**Author:** Staff writers and occasional free-lance journalists **Angle of vision:** News reports aimed at balance and objectivity; editorial pages reflect perspective of editors; op-ed pieces reflect different perspectives	• Readily familiar by name, distinctive cover style • Widely available on newsstands, by subscription, and on the Web • Ads aimed at broad, general audience
ARTICLES IN PUBLIC AFFAIRS PERIODICALS Examples: *Harper's, Commonweal, National Review*	**Author:** Staff writers, freelancers, scholars **Angle of vision:** Aims to deepen general public's understanding of issues; magazines often have political bias	• Long, well-researched articles reviewed by editors • Ads aimed at upscale professionals • Often have reviews of books, theater, film, and the arts • Often can be found in online databases or on the Web

Type of Source	Author and Angle of Vision	How to Recognize Them
ORGANIZATIONAL WHITE PAPERS Examples: "Congressional White Paper on a National Policy for the Environment" (on Web) or "Reform Suggestions for Core Curriculum" (in-house document at a university)	**Author:** Organizational stakeholders; problem-solvers for a client **Angle of vision:** Informative document for client or argumentative paper for influencing policy or improving operations	• Desktop-published, internal documents aimed at problem solving; may also be written for clients • Internal documents generally not made available to public • Sometimes posted to Web or published in print medium
BLOGS Examples: dailykos.com (liberal blog site); michellemalkin.com (conservative blog site); theladysportswriter.blogspot.com (sports commentary)	**Author:** Anyone; some bloggers are practicing journalists **Angle of vision:** Varies from personal diaries to in-depth commentary on a subject or issues; wide range of views from conservative to liberal	• Usually published on time-stamped blog sites; most sites post responses from readers • Bloggers sometimes use pseudonyms • Often combines text with images or linked videos
NONFICTION TRADE BOOKS Example: *Cheap: The High Cost of Discount Culture* by Ellen Ruppell Shell (a journalism professor)	**Author:** Journalists, freelancers, scholars aiming at popular audience **Angle of vision:** Varies from informative to persuasive; often well researched and respected, but sometimes shoddy and aimed for quick sale	• Published by commercial presses for profit • Popular style; covers designed for marketing appeal • Usually documented in an informal rather than an academic style • May be available as an e-book
DOCUMENTARY FILMS Examples: Michael Moore, *Sicko*; Louie Psihoyos, *The Cove*	**Writer/Director:** Filmmakers, screenwriters trained in nonfiction documentaries **Angle of vision:** Varies from informative "science" documentaries to strong advocacy	• Specifically identified as "documentary" or "nonfiction" • Combines Interviews and voice-overs with subject-matter footage

Advocacy Sources

Type of Source	Author and Angle of Vision	How to Recognize Them
NEWSPAPER EDITORIALS, COMMENTARY, AND LETTERS TO THE EDITOR Examples: editorial page, letters to the editor, and op-ed pages of *Washington Post, Los Angeles Times, Wall Street Journal,* and some magazines	**Author:** Editorial writers; citizens writing letters to editor; syndicated or guest columnists **Angle of vision:** Advocacy for certain positions or public policies	• Located in the editorial/op-ed sections of a newspaper • Editorials are often unsigned—they advocate positions held by owners or publishers of the newspaper • Letters and op-ed pieces are signed
EDITORIAL CARTOONS Examples: see www.cagle.com/politicalcartoons/	**Cartoonist:** Usually syndicated artists who specialize in cartoons **Angle of vision:** Varies from conservative to liberal	• Usually located in the op-ed section of newspapers • Occasionally political cartoonists are treated as comics (*Doonesbury*)
ADVOCACY ORGANIZATION WEB SITES, BLOGS, AND ADVERTISEMENTS Examples: NRA.org (National Rifle Association); csgv.org (Coalition to Stop Gun Violence)	**Author/Site Sponsor:** Advocacy organizations; staff writers/researchers; Web developers; guest writers; often hard to identify individual writers	• .org in URL—denotes advocacy or nonprofit status • Sometimes doesn't announce advocacy clearly on home page • Facts/data selected and filtered by site's angle of vision

(continued)

TABLE 15.1 Continued

Type of Source	Author and Angle of Vision	How to Recognize Them
	Angle of vision: Strong advocacy for the site's viewpoint; often encourage donations through site	• Often uses visuals for emotional appeals • Site often includes blogs (or links to blogs) that promote same angle of vision
Government Sources		
GOVERNMENT AGENCY WEB SITES Example: www.energy.gov (site of the U.S. Dept. of Energy)	**Author:** Development teams employed by agency; sponsoring agency is usually the author (corporate authorship); may include material by individual authors **Angle of vision:** Varies—informational sites publish data and objective documents; agency sites also advocate for agency's agenda	• .gov or .mil in URL—denotes government or military sites • Are often layered and complex with hundreds of links to other sites
LEGAL AND COURT DOCUMENTS	**Author:** Lawyers, judges, persons deposed for trials, trial testimony **Angle of vision:** Trial lawyers take strong advocacy positions; testifiers vow to tell the whole truth; judges defend decisions	• Legal briefs have distinctive formats • Court records can be accessed through www.pacer.gov (public access to court electronic records—requires user to establish an account)
POLITICAL AND LEGISLATIVE SPEECHES	**Author:** Politicians, political candidates, researchers, and aides **Angle of vision:** Reflects politics of speaker	• Widely available through newspapers, Web sites, YouTube videos, congressional records
Commercial Sources		
TRADE MAGAZINES Examples: *Advertising Age, Automotive Rebuilder, Farm Journal*	**Author:** Staff writers, industry specialists **Angle of vision:** Informative articles for practitioners; advocacy for the profession or trade	• Title indicating trade or profession • Articles on practical industry concerns • Ads geared toward a particular trade or profession
POPULAR NICHE MAGAZINES Examples: *Seventeen, People, TV Guide, Car and Driver, Golf Digest*	**Author:** Staff or freelance writers **Angle of vision:** Varies—focuses on interests of targeted audience; in some cases content and point of view are dictated by advertisers or the politics of the publisher	• Glossy paper, extensive ads, lots of visuals • Popular; often distinctive style • Short, undocumented articles • Credentials of writer often not mentioned
COMMERCIAL WEB SITES AND ADVERTISEMENTS	**Author:** Development teams, in-house writers, contracted developers; advertising agencies **Angle of vision:** Varies from information to advocacy; promotes the viewpoint of the business	• .com or .biz in URL—denotes "commercial" • Advertisements or Web sites often promote corporate image as well as products • Frequent use of visuals as well as text
PERSONAL WEB SITES, BLOGS, OR CORRESPONDENCE	**Author:** Anyone can create a personal Web site or blog or write personal letters/e-mails **Angle of vision:** Varies from person to person	• Researcher using these sources is responsible for citing credentials of source or revealing bias of source

selection process by which scholarly manuscripts get chosen for publication. When manuscripts are submitted to an academic publisher, the editor removes the names of the authors and sends the manuscripts to experienced scholars who judge the rigor and accuracy of the research and the significance and value of the argument. The most distinguished scholarly journals publish only a small percentage of the manuscripts submitted to them. Other kinds of scholarly material, such as news about research in progress, working papers, or papers submitted at conferences but not yet published, are sometimes made available on scholarly Web sites created and maintained by research centers within a university.

In contrast, the other types of sources listed in Table 15.1, in many cases published for profit, are not peer reviewed but may have undergone rigorous editorial review by a publishing house. Trade books and freelance or commissioned magazine articles (whether in print or online versions) are selected for publication by editors whose business is to make a profit by appealing to targeted readers. Fortunately, it can be profitable for popular presses to publish superbly researched and argued intellectual material written for the general reader rather than for highly specialized scholars. These can be excellent sources for undergraduate research, but you need to separate the trash from the treasure.

Degree of Stability

Print sources (books, scholarly journals, magazines, newspapers), which can be stored in archives and retrieved many years later, are more stable than Web-only material, which may change hourly. What complicates the distinction between "print" and "Web only" is that many documents retrievable on the Web are also stable—either because they were originally print sources and made available online in pdf or html formats or because they are produced by a reputable company as e-books, e-journals, or online newspapers that will be archived digitally. As a quick example of a stable versus nonstable source, suppose you write a "letter to the editor" that was published in a major newspaper. Your letter will be archived permanently and retrievable just as you wrote it long into the future. But if instead you post a comment on blog site, that comment (and the whole blog site) might disappear at any time.

When evaluating and citing your sources, you must therefore pay attention to whether a source retrieved electronically was originally a print source made available on the Web, is an e-book or e-journal that has the same stability as a print source, or is in fact a more ephemeral, Web-only source. You'll need to know this information in order to read the source rhetorically, evaluate its trustworthiness, and cite it properly.

When you retrieve print sources electronically, be aware that you may lose important contextual clues about the author's purpose and angle of vision—clues that would be immediately apparent if you looked at the original print source. (These clues would come from physical layout of the pages, adjacent articles, product advertisements, and so forth. Clues based on original layout of the page can still be obtained electronically if you can access the article in *pdf* format.)

Degree of Advocacy

In Chapter 1 we explained how arguments combine truth seeking and persuasion. To illustrate these concepts, we charted a continuum from exploratory essays at one end of the continuum to outright propaganda at the other end (see Figure 1.7, page 12). To read a source rhetorically, you should try to determine where on this continuum your source resides. In Table 15.1, we identify as "advocacy sources" those sources that clearly announce their persuasive intentions. But other kinds of sources such as an article in a public affairs magazine, a trade book, a legal brief, a documentary film, or a political speech can have a strong advocacy stance. (See pages 363–364 for further discussion of how to evaluate the degree of advocacy in a source.)

Degree of Authority

Sometimes you turn to a source because you just want the facts. News stories from reputable newspapers (as opposed to feature stories, editorials, or op-ed pieces) are good sources for day-to-day reporting on "what happened." Other kinds of excellent fact-checking sources include encyclopedias, statistical abstracts, or other reference works that provide distilled background or overview information on many topics.

You should be aware, however, of the difference between a commissioned reference article and an article in the online source Wikipedia. Professional encyclopedia companies such as Encyclopedia Britannica commission highly regarded scholars with particular expertise in a subject to write that subject's encyclopedia entry. Usually the entry is signed so that the author can be identified. In contrast, all forms of wikis—including Wikipedia—are communal projects using collaborative wiki software. Wikipedia, the Free Encyclopedia (its official name) is written communally by volunteers; anyone who follows the site's procedures can edit an entry. An entry's accuracy and angle of vision thus depend on collective revisions by interested readers.

Wikipedia is a fascinating cultural product that provides rapid overview information, but it is not a reliable academic source. It is often accused of inaccurate information, editorial bias, and shifting content because of constant revisions by readers. Most instructors will not accept Wikipedia as a factual or informative source.

■ ■ ■ **FOR CLASS DISCUSSION**   Identifying Types of Sources

Your instructor will bring to class a variety of print sources—different kinds of books, scholarly journals, magazines, and so forth—and may also show you various kinds of sources retrieved online. Working individually or in small groups, decide to which category in Table 15.1 each piece belongs. Be prepared to justify your decisions on the basis of the clues you used to make your decision.   ■ ■ ■

Searching Libraries, Databases, and Web Sites

In the previous section, we explained differences among the kinds of sources you may uncover in a research project. In this section, we explain how to find these sources by using your campus library's resources (both its print and multimedia collections and its extensive online databases) as well as Web search engines for finding material on the World Wide Web.

Checking Your Library's Home Page

We begin by focusing on the specialized resources provided by your campus library. Your starting place and best initial research tool will be your campus library's home page. This portal will lead you to two important resources: (1) the library's online catalog for its own holdings of books, periodicals, films, multimedia materials, reference works, and other resources and (2) direct links to the many digital databases leased by the library. These licensed databases include exhaustive listings of articles (many of which are available in full-text format) as well as direct-access reference materials such as statistical abstracts, biographies, dictionaries, and encyclopedias.

In addition to checking your library's home page, make a personal visit to your library to learn its features and to meet your library's reference librarians, who are a researcher's best friends.

Finding Articles in Magazines, News Sources, and Scholarly Journals: Searching a Licensed Database

For many research projects, the most useful sources are articles that may be immediately available in your library's periodical collection or online through databases. In either case, you discover the existence of these articles by searching licensed databases leased by your library.

What Is a Licensed Database?   Electronic databases of periodical sources are produced by for-profit companies that index the articles appearing in thousands of periodicals. You can search the database by author, title, subject, keyword, date, genre, and other characteristics. In most cases the database contains an abstract of each article, and in many cases it contains the full text of the article, which you can download and print. These databases are referred to by several different generic names: "licensed databases" (our preferred term), "periodical databases," or "subscription services." Because access to these databases is restricted to fee-paying customers, they can't be searched through Web engines like Google. Most university libraries allow students to access these databases from a remote computer by using a password. You can therefore use the Internet to connect your computer to licensed databases as well as to the World Wide Web (see Figure 15.1).

Although the methods of accessing licensed databases vary from institution to institution, we can offer some widely applicable guidelines. Most likely your library has online one or more of the following databases:

- **Academic Search Complete (Ebsco)**: Indexes nearly 8,000 periodicals, including full text of nearly 7,000 peer-reviewed journals. It features a mix of interdisciplinary scholarly journals, magazines, newspapers, and books.

- **Research Library Complete (ProQuest)**: Similar to Academic Search Complete except that it includes trade publications and more business and industry materials.
- **LexisNexis Academic Universe**: Is primarily a full-text database covering current events, business, and financial news; includes company profiles and legal, medical, and reference information.
- **JSTOR**: Offers full text of scholarly journal articles across many disciplines; you can limit searches to specific disciplines.

Generally, one of these databases is the "default database" chosen by your library for most article searches. Your reference librarian will be able to direct you to the most useful licensed database for your purpose.

Licensed Databases versus Google Scholar   Currently, Google is developing a free online service called "Google Scholar," which attempts to duplicate the services of licensed databases. However, Google doesn't make available to the public the names of the journals it indexes, and no one knows for sure how current or thorough it is. Google Scholar is a potentially useful substitute for researchers who do not have access to the online databases licensed by university libraries.

Keyword Searching   To use an online database, you need to be adept at keyword searching. When you type a word or phrase into a search box, the computer will find sources that contain the same words or phrases. If you want the computer to search for a phrase, put it in quotation marks. Thus if you type "*street people*" using quotation marks, the computer will search for those two words occurring together. If you type in *street people* without quotation marks, the computer will look for the word *street* and the word *people* occurring in the same document but not necessarily together. Use your imagination to try a number of related terms. If you are researching gendered toys and you get too many hits using the keyword *toys,* try *gender toys, Barbie, G.I. Joe, girl toys, boy toys, toys psychology,* and so forth.

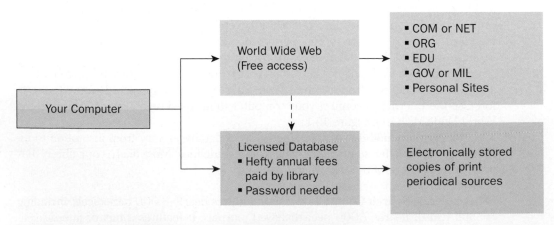

FIGURE 15.1 Licensed database versus free-access portions of internet

Finding Cyberspace Sources: Searching the World Wide Web

Another valuable resource is the World Wide Web. Web search engines, such as Google, search only the "free-access," ever-changing portions of the Internet known as the World Wide Web (see Figure 15.1). When you type keywords into a Web search engine, it searches for matches in material made available on the Web by all the users of the world's network of computers—government agencies, corporations, advocacy groups, information services, individuals with their own Web sites, and many others. Because different Web search engines search the Web in different ways, your reference librarian can give you good advice on what works well for particular kinds of searches. On the Web, an additional resource is NoodleTools.com, which offers lots of good advice for choosing the best search engine.

The following example will quickly show you the difference between a licensed database search and a Web search. When one of our students was investigating the impact of the Navy's sonar-detection systems on the hearing of whales, she entered the keywords "Navy sonar" and "whales" into Google and received 299,000 hits. In contrast, when she entered the same keywords into Academic Search Complete, she received sixty-nine hits. When she limited her Academic Search Complete search to articles appearing in peer-reviewed journals between 2000 and 2010, she received thirteen hits. Clearly the search tools are searching different fields. Google picks up, in addition to all the articles that someone may have posted on the Web, all references to Navy sonar and whales that appear in advocacy Web sites, government publications, newspapers, blogs, chat rooms, student papers posted on the Web, and so forth. In contrast, Academic Search Complete searches for articles primarily in scholarly journals and public affairs magazines.

Evaluating Your Sources by Reading Rhetorically

So far we have explained the importance of posing a good research question, understanding the different kinds of sources, and using purposeful strategies for searching libraries, licensed databases, and the Web. In this final section we explain how to read your sources rhetorically. Particularly, we show you how to read your sources with your own goals in mind, take purposeful notes, and evaluate sources for reliability, credibility, angle of vision, and degree of advocacy. We also provide some additional advice for evaluating Web sources.

Reading with Your Own Goals in Mind

How you read a source depends to a certain extent on where you are in the research process. Early in the process, when you are in the thesis-seeking, exploratory stage, your goal is to achieve a basic understanding about your research problem. You need to become aware of different points of view, learn what is unknown or controversial about your research question, see what values or assumptions are in conflict, and build up your store of background knowledge.

Given these goals, at the early stages of research you should select overview kinds of sources to get you into the conversation. In some cases, even an encyclopedia or specialized reference work can be a good start for getting general background.

As you get deeper into your research, your questions become more focused, and the sources you read become more specialized. Once you formulate a thesis and plan a structure for your paper, you can determine more clearly the sources you need and read them with purpose and direction.

Reading with Rhetorical Awareness

To read your sources rhetorically, you should keep two basic questions in mind:

1. What was the source author's purpose in writing this piece?
2. What might be my purpose in using this piece?

Table 15.2 sums up the kinds of questions a rhetorical reader typically considers.

Table 15.2 reinforces a point we've made throughout this text: all writing is produced from an angle of vision that privileges some ways of seeing and filters out other

TABLE 15.2   Questions Asked by Rhetorical Readers

What was the source author's purpose in writing this piece?	What might be my purpose in using this piece in my own argument?
• Who is this author? What are his or her credentials and affiliations? • What audience is this person addressing? • What is the genre of this piece? (if you downloaded the piece from the World Wide Web, did it originally appear in print?) • If this piece appeared in print, what is the reputation and bias of the journal, magazine, or press? Was the piece peer reviewed? • If this piece appeared only on the Web, who or what organization sponsors the Web site (check the home page)? What is the reputation and bias of the sponsor? • What is the author's thesis or purpose? • How does this author try to change his or her audience's view? • What is this writer's angle of vision or bias? • What is omitted or censored from this text? • How reliable and credible is this author? • What facts, data, and other evidence does this author use and what are the sources of these data? • What are this author's underlying values, assumptions, and beliefs?	• How has this piece influenced or complicated my own thinking? • How does this piece relate to my research question? • How will my own intended audience react to this author? • How might I use this piece in my own argument? • Is it an opposing view that I might summarize? • Is it an alternative point of view that I might compare to other points of view? • Does it have facts and data that I might use? • Would a summary of all or part of this argument support or oppose one or more of my own points? • Could I use this author for testimony? (If so, how should i indicate this author's credentials?) • If I use this source, will I need to acknowledge the author's bias and angle of vision?

ways. You should guard against reading your sources as if they present hard, undisputed facts or universal truths. For example, if one of your sources says that "Saint-John's-wort [an herb] has been shown to be an effective treatment for depression," some of your readers might accept that statement as fact—but many wouldn't. Skeptical readers would want to know who the author is, where his views have been published, and what he uses for evidence. Let's say the author is someone named Samuel Jones. Skeptical readers would ask whether Jones is relying on published research, and if so, whether the studies have been peer reviewed in reputable, scholarly journals and whether the research has been replicated by other scientists. They would also want to know whether a trade association for herbal supplements sponsored the research and whether Jones has financial connections to companies that produce herbal remedies and supplements. Rather than settling the question about Saint-John's-wort as a treatment for depression, a quotation from Jones may open up a heated controversy about medical research.

Reading rhetorically is thus a way of thinking critically about your sources. It influences the way you take notes, evaluate sources, and shape your argument.

Taking Purposeful Notes

Many beginning researchers opt not to take notes—a serious mistake, in our view. Instead, they simply photocopy or print articles, perhaps using a highlighter to mark passages. This practice, which experienced researchers almost never use, reduces your ability to engage the ideas in a source and to find your own voice in a conversation. When you begin drafting your paper, you'll have no notes to refer to, no record of your thinking-in-progress. Your only recourse is to revisit all your sources, thumbing through them one at a time—a practice that leads to passive cutting and pasting (and possible plagiarism).

Good note taking includes recording bibliographic information for each source, recording information and ideas from each source, and responding to each source with your own ideas and exploratory writing.

Recording Bibliographic Information   To take good research notes, begin by making a bibliographic entry for each source, following the documentation format assigned by your instructor. Although you will be tempted to put off doing this mechanical task, there are two reasons to do it immediately:

- Doing it now, while the source is in front of you, will save you time in the long run. Otherwise you'll have to try to retrieve the source, in a late-night panic, just before the paper is due.
- Doing it now will make you look at the source rhetorically. Is this a peer-reviewed journal article? A magazine article? An op-ed piece? A blog? Making the bibliographic entry forces you to identify the source's genre.

Chapter 17 explains in detail how to make bibliographic entries for both MLA (called "Works Cited") and APA (called "References").

Recording Ideas and Information and Responding to Each Source To take good research notes, follow the reading habits of summary and exploration discussed in Chapter 2, weaving back and forth between walking in the shoes of the source author and then standing back to believe and doubt what the source says.

- **Your informational notes on each source:** Using the skills of summary writing explained in Chapter 2, summarize each source's argument and record useful information. To avoid the risk of plagiarism later, make sure that you put quotation marks around any passages that you copy word for word (be sure to copy *exactly*). When you summarize or paraphrase passages, be sure to put the ideas entirely into your own words. (For more on quoting, summarizing, and paraphrasing sources, see Chapter 16, pages 370–376.)
- **Your own exploratory notes as you think of ideas:** Write down your own ideas as they occur to you. Record your thinking-in-progress as you mull over and speak back to your sources.

An approach that encourages both modes of writing is to keep a dialectic or double-entry journal. Divide a page in half; enter your informational notes on one side and your exploratory writing on the other. If you use a computer, you can put your informational notes in one font and your own exploratory writing in another.

Taking effective notes is different from the mechanical process of copying out passages or simply listing facts and information. Rather, make your notes purposeful by imagining how you might use a given source in your research paper. Table 15.3 shows the different functions that research sources might play in your argument and highlights appropriate note-taking strategies for each function.

Evaluating sources

When you read sources for your research project, you need to evaluate them as you go along. As you read each potential source, ask yourself questions about the author's reliability, credibility, angle of vision, and degree of advocacy.

Reliability "Reliability" refers to the accuracy of factual data in a source. If you check a writer's "facts" against other sources, do you find that the facts are correct? Does the writer distort facts, take them out of context, or otherwise use them unreasonably? In some controversies, key data are highly disputed—for example, the frequency of date rape or the risk factors for many diseases. A reliable writer acknowledges these controversies and doesn't treat disputed data as fact. Furthermore, if you check out the sources used by a reliable writer, they'll reveal accurate and careful research—respected primary sources rather than hearsay or secondhand reports. Journalists of reputable newspapers (not tabloids) pride themselves on meticulously checking out their facts, as do editors of serious popular magazines. Editing is often minimal for Web sources, however, and they can be notoriously unreliable. As you gain knowledge of your research question, you'll develop a good ear for writers who play fast and loose with data.

TABLE 15.3   Strategies for Taking Notes According to Purpose

Function that Source Might Play in Your Argument	Strategies for Informational Notes	Strategies for Exploratory Notes
Provides background about your problem or issue	• Summarize the information. • Record specific facts and figures useful for background.	• Speculate on how much background your readers will need.
Gives an alternative view that you will mention briefly	• Summarize the source's argument in a couple of sentences; note its bias and perspective. • Identify brief quotations that sum up the source's perspective.	• Jot down ideas on how and why different sources disagree. • Begin making an idea map of alternative views.
Provides an alternative or opposing view that you might summarize fully and respond to	• Summarize the article fully and fairly (see Chapter 2 on summary writing). • Note the kinds of evidence used.	• Speculate about why you disagree with the source and whether you can refute the argument, concede to it, or compromise with it. • Explore what research you'll need to support your own argument.
Provides information or testimony that you might use as evidence	• Record the data or information. • If using authorities for testimony, quote short passages. • Note the credentials of the writer or person quoted.	• Record new ideas as they occur to you. • Continue to think purposefully about additional research you'll need.
Mentions information or testimony that counters your position or raises doubts about your argument	• Note counterevidence. • Note authorities who disagree with you.	• Speculate how you might respond to counterevidence.
Provides a theory or method that influences your approach to the issue	• Note credentials of the author. • Note passages that sparked ideas.	• Freewrite about how the source influences your method or approach.

Credibility   "Credibility" is similar to "reliability" but is based on internal rather than external factors. It refers to the reader's trust in the writer's honesty, goodwill, and trustworthiness and is apparent in the writer's tone, reasonableness, fairness in summarizing opposing views, and respect for different perspectives. Audiences differ in how much credibility they will grant to certain authors. Nevertheless, a writer can achieve a reputation for credibility, even among bitter political opponents, by applying to issues a sense of moral courage, integrity, and consistency of principle.

Angle of Vision and Political Stance   By "angle of vision," we mean the way that a piece of writing is shaped by the underlying values, assumptions, and beliefs of its author, resulting in a text that reflects a certain perspective, worldview, or belief system. Of paramount importance are the underlying values or beliefs that the writer assumes his or her readers will share. You can get useful clues about a writer's angle of vision and intended audience by doing some quick research into the politics and reputation of the author on the Internet or by analyzing the genre, market niche, and political reputation of the publication in which the material appears.

Determining Political Stance   Your awareness of angle of vision and political stance is especially important if you are doing research on contemporary cultural or political issues. In Table 15.4, we have categorized some well-known political commentators, publications, policy research institutes (commonly known as *think tanks*), and blogs across the political spectrum from left/liberal to right/conservative.

TABLE 15.4   **Angles of Vision in U.S. Media and Think Tanks: A Sampling Across the Political Spectrum[1]**

Commentators				
Left	**Left Center**	**Center**	**Right Center**	**Right**
Barbara Ehrenreich	E. J. Dionne	David Ignatius	David Brooks	Charles Krauthammer
Bob Herbert	Leonard Pitts	Thomas Friedman	Peggy Noonan	Cal Thomas
Michael Moore (filmmaker)	Eugene Robinson	Kathleen Hall Jamieson	Jonah Goldberg	Glenn Beck (radio/TV)
Bill Moyers (television)	Nicholas Kristof	Kevin Phillips	Andrew Sullivan	Rush Limbaugh (radio/TV)
Paul Krugman	Maureen Dowd	David Broder	George Will	Bill O'Reilly (radio/TV)
Thom Hartman (radio)	Mark Shields	William Saletan	Ruben Navarrette, Jr.	Kathleen Parker
Rachel Maddow (radio)	Frank Rich	Mary Sanchez		Thomas Sowell

Newspapers and Magazines[2]		
Left/Liberal	**Center**	**Right/Conservative**
The American Prospect	*Atlantic Monthly*	*American Spectator*
Harper's	*Business Week*	*Fortune*
Los Angeles Times	*Commentary*	*National Review*
Mother Jones	*Commonweal*	*Reader's Digest*
The Nation	*Foreign Affairs*	*Reason*
New York Times	*New Republic*	*Wall Street Journal*
The New Yorker	*Slate*	*Washington Times*
Salon	*Washington Post*	*Weekly Standard*
Sojourners		

Blogs		
Liberal/Left	**Center**	**Right/Conservative**
americablog.com	donklephant.com	conservativeblogger.com
atrios.blogspot.com	newmoderate.blogspot.com	drudgereport.com
crooksandliars.com	politics-central.blogspot.com	instapundit.com
dailykos.com	rantingbaldhippie.com	littlegreenfootballs.com
digbysblog.blogspot.com	stevesilver.net	michellemalkin.com
firedoglake.com	themoderatevoice.com	polipundit.com
huffingtonpost.com	washingtonindependent.com	powerlineblog.com
mediamatters.com	watchingwashington.blogspot.com	sistertoldjah.com
talkingpointsmemo.com		redstate.com
wonkette.com		townhall.com

Think Tanks

Left/Liberal	Center	Right/Conservative
Center for American Progress	The Brookings Institution	American Enterprise Institute
Center for Media and Democracy (sponsors Disinfopedia.org)	Carnegie Endowment for International Peace	Cato Institute (Libertarian)
	Council on Foreign Relations	Center for Strategic and International Studies
Institute for Policy Studies	Jamestown Foundation	Heritage Foundation (sponsors Townhall.com)
Open Society Institute (Soros Foundation)	National Bureau of Economic Research	Project for the New American Century
Progressive Policy Institute		
Urban Institute		

[1] *For further information about the political leanings of publicatios or think tanks, ask your librarian about* Gale Directory of Publications and Broadcast Media *or* NIRA World Directory of Think Tanks.
[2] *Newspapers are categorized according to positions they take on their editorial page; any reputable newspaper strives for objectivity in news reporting and includes a variety of views on its op-ed pages. Magazines do not claim and are not expected to present similar breadth and objectivity.*

Although the terms *liberal* and *conservative* or *left* and *right* often have fuzzy meanings, they provide convenient shorthand for signaling a person's overall views about the proper role of government in relation to the economy and social values. Liberals, tending to sympathize with those potentially harmed by unfettered free markets (workers, consumers, plaintiffs, endangered species), are typically comfortable with government regulation of economic matters while conservatives, who tend to sympathize with business interests, typically assert faith in free markets and favor a limited regulatory role for government. On social issues, conservatives tend to espouse traditional family values and advocate laws that would maintain these values (for example, promoting a constitutional amendment limiting marriage to a bond between a man and a woman). Liberals, on the other hand, tend to espouse individual choice regarding marital partnerships and a wide range of other issues. Some persons identify themselves as economic conservatives but social liberals; others side with workers' interests on economic issues but are conservative on social issues.

Finally, many persons regard themselves as "centrists." In Table 15.4 the column labeled "Center" includes commentators who seek out common ground between the left and the right and who often believe that the best civic decisions are compromises between opposing views. Likewise, centrist publications and institutes often approach issues from multiple points of view, looking for the most workable solutions.

Degree of Advocacy   By "degree of advocacy" we mean the extent to which an author unabashedly takes a persuasive stance on a contested position as opposed to adopting a more neutral, objective, or exploratory stance. For example, publications affiliated with advocacy organizations (the Sierra Club, the National Rifle Association) will have a clear editorial bias. When a writer has an ax to grind, you need to weigh carefully the writer's selection of evidence, interpretation of data, and fairness to opposing views. Although no one can be completely neutral, it is always useful to seek out authors who offer a balanced assessment of the evidence. Evidence from a more detached and neutral writer may be more trusted by your readers than the arguments of a committed advocate. For example, if you want to persuade corporate executives of the dangers of global warming, evidence from scholarly journals may be more persuasive than evidence from an environmentalist Web site or from a freelance writer for a leftist popular magazine such as *Mother Jones*.

Criteria for Evaluating a Web Source   When you evaluate a Web source, we suggest that you ask five different kinds of questions about the site in which the source appeared, as shown in Table 15.5. These questions, developed by scholars and librarians as points to consider when you are evaluating Web sites, will help you determine the usefulness of a site or source for your own purposes.

As a researcher, the first question you should ask about a potentially useful Web source should be, "Who placed this piece on the Web and why?" You can begin

TABLE 15.5   Criteria for Evaluating Web Sites

Criteria	Questions to Ask
1. Authority	• Is the document author or site sponsor clearly identified? • Does the site identify the occupation, position, education, experience, or other credentials of the author? • Does the home page or a clear link from the home page reveal the author's or sponsor's motivation for establishing the site? • Does the site provide contact information for the author or sponsor such as an e-mail or organization address?
2. Objectivity or Clear Disclosure of Advocacy	• Is the site's purpose clear (for example, to inform, entertain, or persuade)? • Is the site explicit about declaring its point of view? • Does the site indicate whether the author is affiliated with a specific organization, institution, or association? • Does the site indicate whether it is directed toward a specific audience?
3. Coverage	• Are the topics covered by the site clear? • Does the site exhibit a suitable depth and comprehensiveness for its purpose? • Is sufficient evidence provided to support the ideas and opinions presented?
4. Accuracy	• Are the sources of information stated? • Do the facts appear to be accurate? • Can you verify this information by comparing this source with other sources in the field?
5. Currency	• Are dates included in the Web site? • Do the dates apply to the material itself, to its placement on the Web, or to the time the site was last revised and updated? • Is the information current, or at least still relevant, for the site's purpose? For your purpose?

answering this question by analyzing the site's home page, where you will often find navigational buttons linking to "Mission," "About Us," or other identifying information about the site's sponsors. You can also get hints about the site's purpose by asking, "What kind of Web site is it?" Different kinds of Web sites have different purposes, often revealed by the domain identifier following the site name:

- **.com sites:** These are commercial sites designed to promote a business's image, attract customers, market products and services, and provide customer service. Their angle of vision is to promote the view of the corporation or business. Often material has no identified author. (The sponsoring company is often cited as the author.)
- **.org sites:** These are sites for nonprofit organizations or advocacy groups. Some sites provide accurate, balanced information related to the organization's mission work (Red Cross, World Vision), while others promote political views (Heritage Foundation) or advocate a cause (People for the Ethical Treatment of Animals).
- **.edu sites:** These sites are associated with a college or university. Home pages aim to attract prospective students and donors and provide a portal into the site. Numerous subsites are devoted to research, pedagogy, libraries, and so forth. The angle of vision can vary from strong advocacy on issues (a student paper, an on-campus advocacy group) to the objective and scholarly (a university research site).
- **.gov or .mil sites:** These sites are sponsored by a government agency or military units. They can provide a range of basic data about government policy, bills in Congress, economic forecasts, census data, and so forth. Their angle of vision varies from objective informational sites to sites that promote the agency's agenda.

Because of a new rule by the agency that controls domain identifiers, people and organizations will be able to buy their own unique domain identifiers. Sites with unique identifiers are likely to be commercial sites since the identifiers cost thousands of dollars each.

■ ■ ■   **FOR CLASS DISCUSSION**   Analyzing the Rhetorical Elements of Two Home Pages
Using a Web search engine, find the home pages for Women Against Gun Control and Million Mom March. Working in small groups or as a whole class, try to reach consensus answers to the following questions about how these Web sites seek to draw in readers.

1. How are the images of women in the Women Against Gun Control site different from those on the Million Mom March page? How do pieces of text (such as "Ladies of High-Caliber" on the Women Against Gun Control site or one of the "facts" on the Million Mom March site) contribute to the visual-verbal effects of the home pages?
2. In the Women Against Gun Control (WAGC) page, what seems to be the Web designer's intention in the use of color, curved background lines, and images?
3. How does the home page for each site use *logos, ethos,* and *pathos* to sway readers toward its point of view?

■ ■ ■

Conclusion

This chapter has explained the need to establish a good research question; to understand the key differences among different kinds of sources; to use purposeful strategies
for searching libraries, databases, and Web sites; and to use your rhetorical knowledge
when you read and evaluate sources and take purposeful notes. It has also discussed
briefly the special problems of evaluating a Web site. In the next chapter we focus on
how to integrate research sources into your own prose.

For support in learning this chapter's content, follow this path
in **MyCompLab:** Resources ⟹ The Research Assignment ⟹
Finding Sources and ⟹ Evaluating Sources. Review the
Instruction and Multimedia resources about finding and evaluating sources, and then complete the Exercises
and click on Gradebook to measure your progress.

Incorporating Sources into Your Own Argument 16

The previous chapter helped you pose a good research question, unlock the resources of your library's collections, use online databases, search the World Wide Web wisely, and evaluate your sources by reading them rhetorically. This chapter teaches you how to incorporate sources smoothly into your own argument. You will learn how to:

- Use your sources for your own purposes
- Summarize, paraphrase, and quote a source
- Signal your use of sources through rhetorically effective attributive tags
- Punctuate quotations correctly
- Avoid plagiarism

Using Sources for Your Own Purposes

To illustrate the purposeful use of sources, we will use the following short argument from the Web site of the American Council on Science and Health (ACSH)—an organization of doctors and scientists devoted to providing scientific information on health issues and to exposing health fads and myths. Please read the argument carefully in preparation for the discussions that follow.

Is Vegetarianism Healthier than Nonvegetarianism?

Many people become vegetarians because they believe, in error, that vegetarianism is uniquely conducive to good health. The findings of several large epidemiologic studies indeed suggest that the death and chronic-disease rates of vegetarians—primarily vegetarians who consume dairy products or both dairy products and eggs—are lower than those of meat eaters....

The health of vegetarians may be better than that of nonvegetarians partly because of nondietary factors: Many vegetarians are health-conscious. They exercise regularly, maintain a desirable body weight, and abstain from smoking. Although most epidemiologists have attempted to take such factors into account in their analyses, it is possible that they did not adequately control their studies for nondietary effects.

People who are vegetarians by choice may differ from the general population in other ways relevant to health. For example, in Western countries most vegetarians are more affluent than nonvegetarians and thus have better living conditions and more access to medical care.

An authoritative review of vegetarianism and chronic diseases classified the evidence for various alleged health benefits of vegetarianism:

- The evidence is "strong" that vegetarians have (a) a lower risk of becoming alcoholic, constipated, or obese and (b) a lower risk of developing lung cancer.
- The evidence is "good" that vegetarians have a lower risk of developing adult-onset diabetes mellitus, coronary artery disease, hypertension, and gallstones.
- The evidence is "fair to poor" that vegetarianism decreases risk of breast cancer, colon cancer, diverticular disease, kidney-stone formation, osteoporosis, and tooth decay.

For some of the diseases mentioned above, the practice of vegetarianism itself probably is the main protective factor. For example, the low incidence of constipation among vegetarians is almost certainly due to their high intakes of fiber-rich foods. For other conditions, nondietary factors may be more important than diet. For example, the low incidence of lung cancer among vegetarians is attributable primarily to their extremely low rate of cigarette smoking. Diet is but one of many risk factors for most chronic diseases.

How you might use this article in your own writing would depend on your research question and purpose. To illustrate, we'll show you three different hypothetical examples of writers who have reason to cite this article.

Writer 1: A Causal Argument Showing Alternative Approaches to Reducing Risk of Alcoholism

Writer 1 argues that vegetarianism may be an effective way to resist alcoholism. She uses just one statement from the ACSH article for her own purpose and then moves on to other sources.

Another approach to fighting alcoholism is through naturopathy, holistic medicine, and vegetarianism. Vegetarians generally have better health than the rest of the population and particularly have, according to the American Council on Science and Health, "a lower risk of becoming alcoholic." This lower risk has been borne out by other studies showing that the benefits of the holistic health movement are particularly strong for persons with addictive tendencies. … [goes on to other arguments and sources]	Writer's claim Identification of source Quotation from ACSH

Writer 2: A Proposal Argument Advocating Vegetarianism

Writer 2 proposes that people become vegetarians. Parts of his argument focus on the environmental costs and ethics of eating meat, but he also devotes one paragraph to the health benefits of vegetarianism. As support for this point he summarizes the ACSH article's material on health benefits.

Not only will a vegetarian diet help stop cruelty to animals, but it is also good for your health. According to the American Council on Science and Health, vegetarians have longer life expectancy than nonvegetarians and suffer from fewer chronic diseases. The Council cites "strong" evidence from the scientific literature showing that vegetarians have reduced risk of lung cancer, obesity, constipation, and alcoholism. The Council also cites "good" evidence that they have a reduced risk of adult-onset diabetes, high blood pressure, gallstones, and hardening of the arteries. Although the evidence isn't nearly as strong, vegetarianism may also lower the risk of certain cancers, kidney stones, loss of bone density, and tooth decay.

Writer's claim

Identification of source

Summary of ACSH material

Writer 3: An Evaluation Argument Looking Skeptically at Vegetarianism

Here, Writer 3 uses portions of the same article to make an opposite case from that of Writer 2. She focuses on those parts of the article that Writer 2 consciously excluded.

The link between vegetarianism and death rates is a classic instance of correlation rather than causation. While it is true that vegetarians have a longer life expectancy than nonvegetarians and suffer from fewer chronic diseases, the American Council on Science and Health has shown that the causes can mostly be explained by factors other than diet. As the Council suggests, vegetarians are apt to be more health conscious than nonvegetarians and thus get more exercise, stay slender, and avoid smoking. The Council points out that vegetarians also tend to be wealthier than nonvegetarians and see their doctors more regularly. In short, they live longer because they take better care of themselves, not because they avoid meat.

Writer's claim

Identification of source

Paraphrased points from ACSH

■ ■ ■   **FOR CLASS DISCUSSION**   Using a Source for Different Purposes

Each of the hypothetical writers uses the short ACSH argument in different ways for different purposes. Working individually or in small groups, respond to the following questions; be prepared to elaborate on and defend your answers.

1. How does each writer use the original article differently and why?
2. If you were the author of the article from the American Council on Science and Health, would you think that your article is used fairly and responsibly in each instance?
3. Suppose your goal were simply to summarize the argument from the American Council on Science and Health. Write a brief summary of the argument and then explain how your summary is different from the partial summaries by Writers 2 and 3.

Using Summary, Paraphrase, and Quotation

As a research writer, you need to incorporate sources gracefully into your own prose. Depending on your purpose, you might (1) summarize all or part of a source author's argument, (2) paraphrase a relevant portion of a source, or (3) quote small passages from the source directly. To avoid plagiarism, you'll need to reference the source with an in-text citation, put quotation marks around quoted passages, and convert paraphrases and summaries entirely into your own words. Table 16.1 gives you an overview of summary, paraphrase, and quotation as ways of incorporating sources into your own prose. With practice, you'll be able to use all these strategies smoothly and effectively. (For an explanation of in-text citations, see Chapter 17; for more on plagiarism in academic writing and how to avoid it, see pages 378–382.)

Summarizing

Detailed instructions on how to write a summary of an article and incorporate it into your own prose are provided in Chapter 2 (pages 39–42). Summaries can be as short as a single sentence or as long as a paragraph. Make the summary as concise as possible so that you don't distract the reader from your own argument. In many cases, writers summarize only parts of a source, depending on what is relevant to their own argument. Writer 3's summary of the article by the American Council on Science and Health is a good example of a partial summary.

Paraphrasing

Unlike a summary, which is a condensation of a source's whole argument, a **paraphrase** translates a short passage from a source's words into the writer's own words. Writers often choose to paraphrase when the details of a source passage are particularly important or when the source is overly technical and needs to be simplified for the intended audience. When you paraphrase, be careful to avoid reproducing the original writer's grammatical structure and syntax. If you mirror the original sentence structure while replacing occasional words with synonyms or small structural changes, you will be doing what composition specialists call "**patchwriting**"—that is,

TABLE 16.1   Incorporating Sources into Your Own Prose

Strategy	What to Do	When to Use This Strategy
Summarize the source.	Condense a source writer's argument by keeping main ideas and omitting details (see Chapter 2, pages 39–42).	• When the source writer's whole argument is relevant to your purpose • When the source writer presents an alternative or opposing view that you want to push against • When the source writer's argument can be used in support of your own
Paraphrase the source.	Reproduce an idea from a source writer but translate the idea entirely into your own words; a paraphrase should be approximately the same length as the original.	• When you want to incorporate factual information from a source or to use one specific idea from a source • When the source passage is overly complex or technical for your targeted audience • When you want to incorporate a source's point in your own voice without interrupting the flow of your argument
Quote short passages from the source using quotation marks.	Work brief quotations from the source smoothly into the grammar of your own sentences (see pages 373–376).	• When you need testimony from an authority (state the authority's credentials in an attributive tag—see pages 376–378) • In summaries, when you want to reproduce a source's voice, particularly if the language is striking or memorable • In lieu of paraphrase when the source language is memorable
Quote long passages from the source using the block method.	Results in a page with noticeably lengthy block quotations	• When you intend to analyze or critique the quotation—the quotation is followed by your detailed analysis of its ideas or rhetorical features • When the flavor and language of testimonial evidence is important

patching some of your language onto someone else's writing.* Patchwriting is a form of academic dishonesty because you aren't fully composing your own sentences and are thus misrepresenting both your own work and that of the source writer. An acceptable paraphrase needs to be entirely in your own words. To understand patchwriting more fully, track the differences between unacceptable patchwriting and acceptable paraphrase in the following examples.

---

*We are indebted to the work of Rebecca Moore Howard and others who have led composition researchers to reexamine the use of sources and plagiarism from a cultural and rhetorical perspective. See especially Rebecca Moore Howard, *Standing in the Shadow of Giants: Plagiarists, Authors, Collaborators* (Stamford, CT: Ablex Pub., 1999).

Original

- The evidence is "strong" that vegetarians have (a) a lower risk of becoming alcoholic, constipated, or obese and (b) a lower risk of developing lung cancer.
- The evidence is "good" that vegetarians have a lower risk of developing adult-onset diabetes mellitus, coronary artery disease, hypertension, and gallstones.

Unacceptable Patchwriting

According to the American Council on Science and Health, there is strong evidence that vegetarians have a lower risk of becoming alcoholic, constipated, or obese. The evidence is also strong that they have a lower risk of lung cancer. The evidence is good that vegetarians are less apt to develop adult-onset diabetes, coronary artery disease, hypertension, or gallstones.

Identification of source

Note phrases taken word for word from original.

Acceptable Paraphrase

The Council summarizes "strong" evidence from the scientific literature showing that vegetarians have reduced risk of lung cancer, obesity, constipation, and alcoholism. The council also cites "good" evidence that they have a reduced risk of adult-onset diabetes, high blood pressure, gallstones, or hardening of the arteries.

Identification of source

Doesn't follow original sentence structure

Quotes "strong" and "good" to indicate distinction made in original

Both the patchwriting example and the acceptable paraphrase reproduce the same ideas as the original in approximately the same number of words. But the writer of the acceptable paraphrase has been more careful to change the sentence structure substantially and not copy exact phrases. In contrast, the patchwritten version contains longer strings of borrowed language without quotation marks.

Among novice writers, the ease of copying Web sources can particularly lead to patchwriting. You may be templed to copy and paste a Web-based passage into your own draft and then revise it slightly by changing some of the words. Such patchwriting won't occur if you write in your own voice—that is, if you convert information from a source into your own words in order to make your own argument.

When you first practice paraphrasing, try paraphrasing a passage twice to avoid patchwriting:

- The first time, read the passage carefully and put it into your own words, looking at the source as little as possible.
- The second time, paraphrase your own paraphrase. Then recheck your final version against the original to make sure you have eliminated similar sentence structures or word-for-word strings.

We'll return to the problem of patchwriting in our discussion of plagiarism (pages 378–382).

Quoting

Besides summary and paraphrase, writers often choose to quote directly in order to give the reader the flavor and style of the source author's prose or to make a memorable point in the source author's own voice. Be careful not to quote a passage that you don't fully understand. (Sometimes novice writers quote a passage because it sounds impressive.) When you quote, you must reproduce the source author's original words exactly without change, unless you indicate changes with ellipses or brackets. Also be careful to represent the author's intention and meaning fairly; don't change the author's meaning by taking quotations out of context.

Because the mechanics of quoting offers its own difficulties, we devote the following sections to it. These sections answer the nuts-and-bolts questions about how to punctuate quotations correctly. Additional explanations covering variations and specific cases can be found in any good handbook.

Quoting a Complete Sentence   In some cases, you will want to quote a complete sentence from your source. Typically, you will include an attributive tag that tells the reader who is being quoted. At the end of the quotation, you usually indicate its page number in parentheses (see our later discussion of in-text citations, Chapter 17).

Original Passage

Many people become vegetarians because they believe, in error, that vegetarianism is uniquely conducive to good health. [found on page 367 of source].*

Writer's Quotation of This Passage

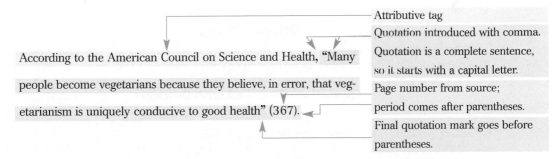

According to the American Council on Science and Health, "Many people become vegetarians because they believe, in error, that vegetarianism is uniquely conducive to good health" (367).

Attributive tag

Quotation introduced with comma.

Quotation is a complete sentence, so it starts with a capital letter.

Page number from source; period comes after parentheses.

Final quotation mark goes before parentheses.

Quoting Words and Phrases   Instead of quoting a complete sentence, you often want to quote only a few words or phrases from your source and insert them into your own sentence. In these cases, make sure that the grammatical structure of the quotation fits smoothly into the grammar of your own sentence.

---

*The cited page is from this text. When quoting from print sources or other sources with stable page numbers, you indicate the page number as part of your citation. To illustrate how to punctuate page citations, we'll assume throughout this section that you found the American Council on Science and Health article in this textbook rather than on the Web, in which case it would not be possible to cite page numbers

Original Passage

The health of vegetarians may be better than that of nonvegetarians partly because of nondietary factors: Many vegetarians are health-conscious. They exercise regularly, maintain a desirable body weight, and abstain from smoking. [found on page 367]

Quoted Phrase Inserted into Writer's Own Sentence

The American Council on Science and Health argues that the cause of vegetarians' longer life may be "nondietary factors." The Council claims that vegetarians are more "health-conscious" than meat eaters and that they "exercise regularly, maintain a desirable body weight, and abstain from smoking" (367).

Attributive tag

Quotation marks show where quotation starts and ends.

No comma or capital letter: Punctuation and capitalization determined by grammar of your own sentence.

Period comes after parentheses containing page number.

Modifying a Quotation   Occasionally you may need to alter a quotation to make it fit your own context. Sometimes the grammar of a desired quotation doesn't match the grammar of your own sentence. At other times, the meaning of a quoted word is unclear when it is removed from its original context. In these cases, use brackets to modify the quotation's grammar or to add a clarifying explanation. Place your changes or additions in brackets to indicate that the bracketed material is not part of the original wording. You should also use brackets to show a change in capitalization.

Original Passage

Many vegetarians are health-conscious. They exercise regularly, maintain a desirable body weight, and abstain from smoking. [found on page 367]

Quotations Modified with Brackets

The American Council on Science and Health hypothesizes that vegetarians maintain better health by "exercis[ing] regularly, maintain[ing] a desirable body weight, and abstain[ing] from smoking" (367).

Attributive tag

Brackets show change in quotation to fit grammar of writer's sentence.

Page number from source

According to the American Council on Science and Health, "They [vegetarians] exercise regularly, maintain a desirable body weight, and abstain from smoking" (367).

Attributive tag

Brackets show that writer has added a word to explain what "they" stands for.

Omitting Something from a Quoted Passage   Another way that writers modify quotations is to leave words out of the quoted passage. To indicate an omission, use three spaced periods called an **ellipsis** (…). Placement of the ellipsis depends on where the omitted material occurs. In the middle of a sentence, each of the periods should be preceded and followed by a space. When your ellipsis comes at the boundary between sentences, use an additional period to mark the end of the first sentence. When a parenthetical page number must follow the ellipsis, insert it before the final (fourth) period in the sequence.

Original Passage

People who are vegetarians by choice may differ from the general population in other ways relevant to health. For example, in Western countries most vegetarians are more affluent than nonvegetarians and thus have better living conditions and more access to medical care. [found on page 368]

Quotations with Omitted Material Marked by Ellipses

According to the American Council on Science and Health, "people

who are vegetarians by choice may differ . . . in other ways relevant to health. For example, in Western countries most vegetarians are more affluent than nonvegetarians . . ." (368).

> Three spaced periods mark omitted words in middle of sentence. Note spaces between each period.
>
> Three periods form the ellipsis. (Omitted material comes before the end of the sentence.)
>
> This period ends the sentence.

Quoting Something That Contains a Quotation   Occasionally a passage that you wish to quote will already contain quotation marks. If you insert the passage within your own quotation marks, change the original double marks (") into single marks (') to indicate the quotation within the quotation. The same procedure works whether the quotation marks are used for quoted words or for a title. Make sure that your attributive tag signals who is being quoted.

Original Passage

The evidence is "strong" that vegetarians have (a) a lower risk of becoming alcoholic, constipated, or obese and (b) a lower risk of developing lung cancer. [found on page 368]

Use of Single Quotation Marks to Identify a Quotation within a Quotation

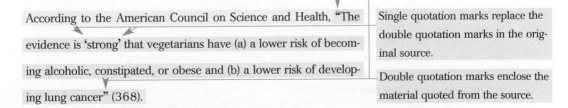

According to the American Council on Science and Health, "The evidence is 'strong' that vegetarians have (a) a lower risk of becoming alcoholic, constipated, or obese and (b) a lower risk of developing lung cancer" (368).

> Single quotation marks replace the double quotation marks in the original source.
>
> Double quotation marks enclose the material quoted from the source.

Using a Block Quotation for a Long Passage   If you quote a long source passage that will take four or more lines in your own paper, use the block indentation method rather than quotation marks. Block quotations are generally introduced with an attributive tag followed by a colon. The indented block of text, rather than quotation marks, signals that the material is a direct quotation. As we explained earlier, block quotations occur rarely in scholarly writing and are used primarily in cases where the writer intends to analyze the text being quoted. If you overuse block quotations, you simply produce a collage of other people's voices.

Original Passage

The health of vegetarians may be better than that of nonvegetarians partly because of nondietary factors: Many vegetarians are health-conscious. They exercise regularly, maintain a desirable body weight, and abstain from smoking. Although most epidemiologists have attempted to take such factors into account in their analyses, it is possible that they did not adequately control their studies for nondietary effects. [found on page 367]

Block Quotation

The American Council on Science and Health suggests that vegetarians may be healthier than nonvegetarians not because of their diet but because of their more healthy lifestyle: ◄————— Block quotation introduced with a colon

> Many vegetarians are health-conscious. They exercise regularly, maintain a desirable body weight, and abstain from smoking. Although most epidemiologists have attempted to take such factors into account in their analyses, it is possible that they did not adequately control their studies for nondietary effects. (367) ◄—————

No quotation marks

Block indented 1 inch on left

Page number in parentheses. (Note that parentheses come after the closing period preceded by a space.)

Creating Rhetorically Effective Attributive Tags

Throughout the previous examples we've been using attributive tags to indicate words or ideas taken from a source. *Attributive tags* are phrases such as "according to the American Council on Science and Health … ," "Smith claims that … ," or "the author continues … ." Such phrases signal to the reader that the material immediately following the tag is from the cited source. In this section we'll show you why attributive tags are often clearer and more powerful than other ways of signaling a source, such as a parenthetical citation. Particularly, they can also be used rhetorically to shape your reader's response to a source.

Attributive Tags versus Parenthetical Citations

Instead of attributive tags, writers sometimes indicate a source only by citing it in parentheses at the end of the borrowed material—a common practice in the social sciences and some other kinds of academic writing. However, the preferred practice when writing to nonspecialized audiences is to use attributive tags.

Less Preferred: Indicating Source through Parenthetical Citation

Vegetarians are apt to be more health-conscious than nonvegetarians (American Council on Science and Health).*

More Preferred: Indicating Source through Attributive Tag

According to the American Council on Science and Health, vegetarians are apt to be more health-conscious than nonvegetarians.

A disadvantage of the parenthetical method is that it requires readers to wait until the end of the source material before the source is identified. Attributive tags, in contrast, identify the source the moment it is first used, thus marking more clearly the beginning of borrowed material. Another disadvantage of the parenthetical method is that it tends to treat the borrowed material as "fact" rather than as the view of the source author. In contrast, attributive tags call attention to the source's angle of vision. An attributive tag reminds the reader to put on the glasses of the source author—to see the borrowed material as shaped by the source author's biases and perspectives.

Creating Attributive Tags to Shape Reader Response

Attributive tags can be used not only to identify a source but also to shape your readers' attitude toward the source. For example, if you wanted your readers to respect the expertise of a source, you might say, "According to noted chemist Marjorie Casper ...." If you wanted your readers to discount Casper's views, you might say, "According to Marjorie Casper, an industrial chemist on the payroll of a major corporate polluter ...."

When you compose an initial tag, you can add to it any combination of the kinds of information in Table 16.2, depending on your purpose, your audience's values, and your sense of what the audience already knows about the source. Our point here is that you can use attributive tags rhetorically to help your readers understand the significance and context of a source when you first introduce it and to guide your readers' attitudes toward the source.

---

*This parenthetical citation is in MLA form. If this had been a print source rather than a Web source, a page number would also have been given as follows: (American Council on Science and Health 43). APA form also indicates the date of the source: (American Council on Science and Health, 2002, p. 43). We explain MLA and APA styles for citing and documenting sources in Chapter 17.

TABLE 16.2   Modifying Attributive Tags to Shape Reader Response

Add to Attributive Tags	Examples
Author's credentials or relevant specialty (enhances credibility)	Civil engineer David Rockwood, a noted authority on stream flow in rivers
Author's lack of credentials (decreases credibility)	City Council member Dilbert Weasel, a local politician with no expertise in international affairs
Author's political or social views	Left-wing columnist Alexander Cockburn [has negative feeling]; Alexander Cockburn, a longtime champion of labor [has positive feeling]
Title of source if it provides context	In her book *Fasting Girls: The History of Anorexia Nervosa,* Joan Jacobs Brumberg shows that [establishes credentials for comments on eating disorders]
Publisher of source if it adds prestige or otherwise shapes audience response	Dr. Carl Patrona, in an article published in the prestigious *New England Journal of Medicine*
Historical or cultural information about a source that provides context or background	In his 1960s book popularizing the hippie movement, Charles Reich claims that
Indication of source's purpose or angle of vision	Feminist author Naomi Wolfe, writing a blistering attack on the beauty industry, argues that

Avoiding Plagiarism

In the next chapter, we proceed to the nuts and bolts of citing and documenting sources—a skill that will enhance your *ethos* as a skilled researcher and as a person of integrity. Unethical use of sources—called **plagiarism**—is a major concern not only for writing teachers but for teachers in all disciplines. To combat plagiarism, many instructors across the curriculum use plagiarism-detection software like turnitin.com. Their purpose, of course, is to discourage students from cheating. But sometimes students who have no intention of cheating can fall into producing papers that look like cheating. That is, they produce papers that might be accused of plagiarism even though the students had no intention of deceiving their readers.* Our goal in this section is to explain the concept of plagiarism more fully and to sum up the strategies needed to avoid it.

Why Some Kinds of Plagiarism May Occur Unwittingly

To understand how unwitting plagiarism might occur, consider Table 16.3, where the middle column—"Misuse of Sources"—shows common mistakes of novice writers.

---

*See Rebecca Moore Howard, *Standing in the Shadow of Giants: Plagiarists, Authors, Collaborators* (Stamford, CT: Ablex Pub., 1999).

TABLE 16.3   Plagiarism and the Ethical Use of Sources

Plagiarism		Ethical Use of Sources
Fraud	**Misuse of Sources (Common Mistakes Made by New Researchers)**	
The writer	The writer	The writer
• buys paper from a paper mill • submits someone else's work as his own • copies chunks of text from sources with obvious intention of not being detected • fabricates data or makes up evidence • intends to deceive	• copies passages directly from a source, references the source with an in-text citation, but fails to use quotation marks or block indentation • in attempting to paraphrase a source, makes some changes, but follows too closely the wording of the original ("patchwriting") • fails to indicate the sources of some ideas or data (often is unsure what needs to be cited or has lost track of sources through poor note taking) • in general, misunderstands the conventions for using sources in academic writing	• writes paper entirely in her own words or uses exact quotations from sources • indicates all quotations with quotation marks or block indentation • indicates her use of all sources through attribution, in-text citation, and an end-of-paper list of works cited

Everyone agrees that the behaviors in the "Fraud" column constitute deliberate cheating and deserve appropriate punishment. Everyone also agrees that good scholarly work meets the criteria in the "Ethical Use of Sources" column. Novice researchers, however, may find themselves unwittingly in the middle column until they learn the academic community's conventions for using research sources.

You might appreciate these conventions more fully if you recognize how they have evolved from Western notions of intellectual property and patent law associated with the rise of modern science in the seventeenth and eighteenth centuries. A person not only could own a house or a horse, but also could own an idea and the words used to express that idea. You can see these cultural conventions at work—in the form of laws or professional codes of ethics—whenever a book author is disgraced for lifting words or ideas from another author or whenever an artist or entrepreneur is sued for stealing song lyrics, publishing another person's photographs without permission, or infringing on some inventor's patent.

This understanding of plagiarism may seem odd in some non-Western cultures where collectivism is valued more than individualism. In these cultures, words written or spoken by ancestors, elders, or other authority figures may be regarded with reverence and shared with others without attribution. Also in these cultures, it might be disrespectful to paraphrase certain passages or to document them in a way that would suggest the audience didn't recognize the ancient wisdom.

However, such collectivist conventions won't work in research communities committed to building new knowledge. In the academic world, the conventions separating ethical from unethical use of sources are essential if research findings are to win the community's confidence. Effective research can occur only within ethical and responsible research communities, where people do not fabricate data and where current researchers respect and acknowledge the work of those who have gone before them.

Strategies for Avoiding Plagiarism

Table 16.4 will help you review the strategies presented throughout Chapters 15 to 17 for using source material ethically and avoiding plagiarism.

TABLE 16.4   Avoiding Plagiarism or the Appearance of Plagiarism

What to Do	Why to Do It
At the beginning	
Read your college's policy on plagiarism as well as statements from your teachers in class or on course syllabi.	Understanding policies on plagiarism and academic integrity will help you research and write ethically.
Pose a research question rather than a topic area.	Arguing your own thesis gives you a voice, establishes your *ethos,* and urges you to write ethically.
At the note-taking stage	
Create a bibliographic entry for each source.	This action makes it easy to create an end-of-paper bibliography and encourages rhetorical reading.
When you copy a passage into your notes, copy word for word and enclose it within quotation marks.	It is important to distinguish a source's words from your own words.
When you enter summaries or paraphrases into your notes, avoid patchwriting.	If your notes contain any strings of a source's original wording, you might later assume that these words are your own.
Distinguish your informational notes from your personal exploratory notes.	Keeping these kinds of notes separate will help you identify borrowed ideas when it's time to incorporate the source material into your paper.
When writing your draft	
Except for exact quotations, write the paper entirely in your own words.	This strategy keeps you from patchwriting when you summarize or paraphrase.
Indicate all quotations with quotation marks or block indentation. Use ellipses or brackets to make changes to fit your own grammar.	Be careful to represent the author fairly; don't change meaning by taking quotations out of context.

When you summarize or paraphrase, avoid patchwriting.	Word-for-word strings from a source must either be avoided or placed in quotation marks. Also avoid mirroring the source's grammatical structure.
Never cut and paste a Web passage directly into your draft. Paste it into a separate note file and put quotation marks around it.	Pasted passages are direct invitations to patchwrite.
Inside your text, use attributive tags or parenthetical citations to identify all sources. List all sources alphabetically in a concluding Works Cited or References list.	This strategy makes it easy for readers to know when you are using a source and where to find it.
Cite with attributive tags or parenthetical citations all quotations, paraphrases, summaries, and any other references to specific sources.	These are the most common in-text citations in a research paper.
Use in-text citations to indicate sources for all visuals and media such as graphs, maps, photographs, films, videos, broadcasts, and recordings.	The rules for citing words and ideas apply equally to visuals and media cited in your paper.
Use in-text citations for all ideas and facts that are not common knowledge.	Although you don't need to cite widely accepted and noncontroversial facts and information, it is better to cite them if you are unsure.

■ ■ ■ **FOR CLASS AND DISCUSSION**   Avoiding Plagiarism

Reread the original article from the American Council on Science and Health (pages 367–368) and Writer 3's use of this source in her paragraph about how nondietary habits may explain why vegetarians are healthier than nonvegetarians (page 369). Then read the paragraph below by Writer 4, who makes the same argument as Writer 3 but crosses the line from ethical to nonethical use of sources. Why might Writer 4 be accused of plagiarism?

Writer 4's Argument (Example of Plagiarism)

According to the American Council on Science and Health, the health of vegetarians may be better than that of nonvegetarians partly because of nondietary factors. People who eat only vegetables tend to be very conscious of their health. They exercise regularly, avoid getting fat, and don't smoke. Scientists who examined the data may not have adequately controlled for these nondietary effects. Also in Western countries most vegetarians are more affluent than nonvegetarians and thus have better living conditions and more access to medical care.

Working in small groups or as a whole class, respond to the following questions.

1. How does this passage cross the line into plagiarism?
2. The writer of this passage might say, "How can this be plagiarism? I cited my source." How would you explain the problem to this writer?

3. Psychologically or cognitively, what may have caused Writer 4 to misuse the source? How might this writer's note-taking process or composing process have differed from that of Writer 3 on page 369? In other words, what happened to get this writer into trouble?

Conclusion

This chapter has shown you how to use sources for your own purposes; how to summarize, paraphrase, and quote a source; how to signal your use of sources through rhetorically effective attributive tags; and how to punctuate quotations correctly. It has also explained how to use sources ethically to avoid plagiarism and create a professional ethos. In the next chapter we will provide guidelines and formats for citing and documenting your sources.

For support in learning this chapter's content, follow this path in **MyCompLab:** Resources ⇒ Research ⇒ The Research Assignment ⇒ Integrating Sources. Review the Instruction and Multimedia resources about integrating sources, and then complete the Exercises and click on Gradebook to measure your progress.

Citing and Documenting Sources

The previous chapter showed you how to use sources ethically, incorporating them into your own prose so as to further your argument as well as to avoid plagiarism. In this chapter, you will learn to:

- Cite and document your sources using the style and format of the Modern Language Association
- Cite and document your sources using the style and format of the American Psychological Association

The Connection between In-Text Citations and the End-of-Paper List of Cited Works

The most common forms of documentation use what are called in-text citations that match an end-of-paper list of cited works (as opposed to footnotes or endnotes). An **in-text citation** identifies a source in the body of the paper at the point where it is summarized, paraphrased, quoted, inserted, or otherwise referred to. At the end of your paper you include a list—alphabetized by author (or by title if there is no named author)—of all the works you cited. Both the Modern Language Association (MLA) system, used primarily in the humanities, and the American Psychological Association (APA) system, used primarily in the social sciences, follow this procedure. In MLA, your end-of-paper list is called **Works Cited.** In APA it is called **References.**

Whenever you place an in-text citation in the body of your paper, your reader knows to turn to the Works Cited or References list at the end of the paper to get the full bibliographic information. The key to the system's logic is this:

- Every source in Works Cited or References must be mentioned in the body of the paper.
- Conversely, every source mentioned in the body of the paper must be included in the end-of-paper list.
- The first word in each entry of the Works Cited or References list (usually an author's last name) must also appear in the in-text citation. In other words, there must be a one-to-one correspondence between the first word in each entry in the end-of-paper list and the name used to identify the source in the body of the paper.

Suppose a reader sees this phrase in your paper: "According to Debra Goldstein...." The reader should be able to turn to your Works Cited list and find an alphabetized entry beginning with "Goldstein, Debra." Similarly, suppose that in looking over your Works Cited list, your reader sees an article by "Guillen, Manuel." This means that the name "Guillen" has to appear in your paper in one of two ways:

- As an attributive tag: Economics professor Manuel Guillen argues that....
- As a parenthetical citation, often following a quotation: "...changes in fiscal policy" (Guillen 49).

Because this one-to-one correspondence is so important, let's illustrate it with some complete examples using the MLA formatting style:

If the body of your paper has this:	Then the Works Cited list must have this:
According to linguist Deborah Tannen, political debate in America leaves out the complex middle ground where most solutions must be developed.	Tannen, Deborah. *The Argument Culture: Moving from Debate to Dialogue.* New York: Random, 1998. Print.
In the 1980s, cigarette advertising revealed a noticeable pattern of racial stereotyping (Pollay, Lee, and Carter-Whitney).	Pollay, Richard W., Jung S. Lee, and David Carter-Whitney. "Separate, but Not Equal: Racial Segmentation in Cigarette Advertising." *Journal of Advertising* 21.1 (1992): 45–57. Print.
On its Web site, the National Men's Resource Center offers advice to parents on how to talk with children about alcohol and drugs ("Talking").	"Talking with Kids about Alcohol and Drugs." *Menstuff.* National Men's Resource Center, 1 Mar. 2007. Web. 26 June 2007.

How to format an MLA in-text citation and a Works Cited list entry is the subject of the next section. The APA system is similar except that it emphasizes the date of publication in both the in-text citation and the References entry. APA formatting is discussed on pages 397–403.

MLA Style

An in-text citation and its corresponding Works Cited entry are linked in a chicken-and-egg system: You can't cite a source in the text without first knowing how the source's entry will be alphabetized in the Works Cited list. However, since most Works Cited entries are alphabetized by the first author's last name, for convenience we start with in-text citations.

In-Text Citations in MLA Style

A typical in-text citation contains two elements: (1) the last name of the author and (2) the page number of the quoted or paraphrased passage. However, in some cases a work is identified by something other than an author's last name, and sometimes no page number is required. Let's begin with the most common cases.

Typically, an in-text citation uses one of these two methods:

■ **Parenthetical method.** Place the author's last name and the page number in parentheses immediately after the material being cited.

> The Spanish tried to reduce the status of Filipina women, who had been able to do business, get divorced, and sometimes become village chiefs (Karnow 41).

■ **Attributive tag method.** Place the author's name in an attributive tag at the beginning of the source material and the page number in parentheses at the end.

> According to Karnow, the Spanish tried to reduce the status of Filipina women, who had been able to do business, get divorced, and sometimes become village chiefs (41).

Once you have cited an author and it is clear that the same author's material is being used, you need cite only the page numbers in parentheses in subsequent citations. A reader who wishes to look up the source will find the bibliographic information in the Works Cited section by looking for the entry under "Karnow."

Let's now turn to the variations. Table 17.1 identifies the typical variations and shows again the one-to-one connection between the in-text citation and the Works Cited list.

TABLE 17.1   In-Text Citations in MLA Style

Type of Source	Works Cited Entry at End of Paper (*Construct the entry while taking notes on each source.*)	In-Text Citation in Body of Paper (*Use the first word of the Works Cited entry in parentheses or an attributive tag; add page number at end of quoted or paraphrased passage.*)
One author	Pollan, Michael. *The Omnivore's Dilemma: A Natural History of Four Meals*. New York: Penguin, 2006. Print.	…(Pollan 256). OR According to Pollan,…(256).
More than one author	Pollay, Richard W., Jung S. Lee, and David Carter-Whitney. "Separate, but Not Equal: Racial Segmentation in Cigarette Advertising." *Journal of Advertising* 21.1 (1992): 45–57. Print.	… race" (Pollay, Lee, and Carter-Whitney 52). OR Pollay, Lee, and Carter-Whitney have argued that "advertisers…race" (52). *For the in-text citation, cite the specific page number rather than the whole range of pages given in the Works Cited entry.*
Author has more than one work in Works Cited list	Dombrowski, Daniel A. *Babies and Beasts: The Argument from Marginal Cases*. Urbana: U of Illinois P, 1997. Print. —. *The Philosophy of Vegetarianism*. Amherst: U of Massachusetts P, 1984. Print.	…(Dombrowski, *Babies* 207).… …(Dombrowski, *Philosophy* 328). OR According to Dombrowski,…(*Babies* 207). Dombrowski claims that…(*Philosophy* 328). *Because author has more than one work in Works Cited, include a short version of title to distinguish between entries.*

(continued)

TABLE 17.1   Continued

Type of Source	Works Cited Entry at End of Paper	In-Text Citation in Body of Paper
Corporate author	American Red Cross. *Standard First Aid*. St. Louis: Mosby Lifeline, 1993. Print.	…(American Red Cross 102). OR Snake bite instructions from the American Red Cross show that…(102).
No named author (Work is therefore alphabetized by title.)	"Ouch! Body Piercing." *Menstuff*. National Men's Resource Center, 1 Feb. 2001. Web. 17 July 2004.	…("Ouch!"). According to the National Men's Resource Center,…("Ouch!"). • Add "Ouch!" in parentheses to show that work is alphabetized under "Ouch!" not "National." • No page numbers are shown because Web site pages aren't stable.
Indirect citation of a source that you found in another source *Suppose you want to use a quotation from Peter Singer that you found in a book by Daniel Dombrowski. Include Dombrowski but not Singer in Works Cited.*	Dombrowski, Daniel A. *Babies and Beasts: The Argument from Marginal Cases*. Urbana: U of Illinois P, 1997. Print.	Animal rights activist Peter Singer argues that …(qtd. in Dombrowski 429). • Singer is used for the attributive tag, but the in-text citation is to Dombrowski. • "qtd. in" stands for "quoted in."

When to Use Page Numbers in In-Text Citations   When the materials you are citing are available in print or in pdf format, you can provide accurate page numbers for parenthetical citations. If you are working with Web sources or HTML files, however, do not use the page numbers obtained from a printout because they will not be consistent from printer to printer. If the item has numbered paragraphs, cite them with the abbreviation *par.* or *pars.*—for example, "(Jones, pars. 22–24)." In the absence of reliable page numbers for the original material, MLA says to omit page references

Include a page number in the in-text citation:	Do not include a page number:
If the source has stable page numbers (print source or pdf version of print source): • If you quote something • If you paraphrase a specific passage • If you refer to data or details from a specific page or range of pages in the source	• If you are referring to the argument of the whole source instead of a specific page or passage • If the source does not have stable page numbers (articles on Web sites, HTML text, and so forth)

from the parenthetical citation. The chart on the previous page summarizes the use of page numbers in in-text citations.

Works Cited List in MLA Style

In the MLA system, you place a complete Works Cited list at the end of the paper. The list includes all the sources that you mention in your paper. However, it does *not* include works you read but did not use. Entries in the Works Cited list follow these general guidelines:

- Entries are arranged alphabetically by author, or by title if there is no author.
- Each entry includes the medium of publication of the source you consulted—for example, *Print, Web, DVD, Performance, Oil on canvas,* and so on.
- If there is more than one entry per author, the works are arranged alphabetically by title. For the second and all additional entries, type three hyphens and a period in place of the author's name.

Dombrowski, Daniel A. *Babies and Beasts: The Argument from Marginal Cases.* Urbana: U
>of Illinois P, 1997. Print.

—. *The Philosophy of Vegetarianism.* Amherst: U of Massachusetts P, 1984. Print.

You can see a complete, properly formatted Works Cited list on the last pages of Juan Vazquez's paper (pages. 334–338).

The remaining pages in this section show examples of MLA citation formats for different kinds of sources and provide explanations and illustrations as needed.

Works Cited Citation Models

Print Articles in Scholarly Journals

General Format for Print Article in Scholarly Journal

Author. "Article Title." *Journal Title* volume number.issue number (year): page numbers. Print.

Note that all scholarly journal entries include both volume number and issue number, regardless of how the journal is paginated. For articles published in a scholarly Web journal, see page 393. For scholarly journal articles retrieved from an online database, see page 391.

One author

Herrera-Sobek, Maria. "Border Aesthetics: The Politics of Mexican Immigration in Film and Art."
>*Western Humanities Review* 60.2 (2006): 60–71. Print.

Two or three authors

Pollay, Richard W., Jung S. Lee, and David Carter-Whitney. "Separate, but Not Equal: Racial
>Segmentation in Cigarette Advertising." *Journal of Advertising* 21.1 (1992): 45–57. Print.

Four or more authors

Either list all the authors in the order in which they appear, or use "et al." (meaning "and others") to replace all but the first author.

Buck, Gayle A., et al. "Examining the Cognitive Processes Used by Adolescent Girls and Women
Scientists in Identifying Science Role Models: A Feminist Approach." *Science Education*
92.4 (2008): 688–707. Print.

Print Articles in Magazines and Newspapers   If no author is identified, begin the entry with the title or headline. Distinguish between news stories and editorials by putting the word "Editorial" after the title. If a magazine comes out weekly or biweekly, include the complete date ("27 Sept. 2011"). If it comes out monthly, then state the month only ("Sept. 2011").

General Format for Magazines and Newspapers

Author. "Article Title." *Magazine Title* day Month year: page numbers. Print.

(Note: If the article continues in another part of the magazine or newspaper, add "+" to the number of the first page to indicate the nonsequential pages.)

Magazine article with named author

Snyder, Rachel L. "A Daughter of Cambodia Remembers: Loung Ung's Journey." *Ms.* Aug.–Sept.
2001: 62–67. Print.

Magazine article without named author

"Daddy, Daddy." *New Republic* 30 July 2001: 2–13. Print.

Review of book, film, or performance

Schwarz, Benjamin. "A Bit of Bunting: A New History of the British Empire Elevates Expediency
to Principle." Rev. of *Ornamentalism: How the British Saw Their Empire*, by David
Cannadine. *Atlantic Monthly* Nov. 2001: 126–35. Print.

Kaufman, Stanley. "Polishing a Gem." Rev. of *The Blue Angel*, dir. Josef von Sternberg. *New
Republic* 30 July 2001: 28–29. Print.

Lahr, John. "Nobody's Darling: Fascism and the Drama of Human Connection in *Ashes to Ashes*."
Rev. of *Ashes to Ashes*, by Harold Pinter. The Roundabout Theater Co. Gramercy Theater,
New York. *New Yorker* 22 Feb. 1999: 182–83. Print.

Newspaper article

Henriques, Diana B. "Hero's Fall Teaches Wall Street a Lesson." *Seattle Times* 27 Sept. 1998:
A1+. Print.

Page numbers in newspapers are typically indicated by a section letter or number as well as a page number. The "+" indicates that the article continues on one or more pages later in the newspaper.

Newspaper editorial

"Dr. Frankenstein on the Hill." Editorial. *New York Times* 18 May 2002, natl. ed.: A22. Print.

Letter to the editor of a magazine or newspaper

Tomsovic, Kevin. Letter. *New Yorker* 13 July 1998: 7. Print.

Print Books

General Format for Print Books

Author. *Title.* City of publication: Publisher, year of publication. Print.

One author

Pollan, Michael. *The Omnivore's Dilemma: A Natural History of Four Meals.* New York: Penguin,
     2006. Print.

Two or more authors

Dombrowski, Daniel A., and Robert J. Deltete. *A Brief, Liberal, Catholic Defense of Abortion.*
     Urbana: U of Illinois P, 2000. Print.

Belenky, Mary, et al. *Women's Ways of Knowing: The Development of Self, Voice, and Mind.* New
     York: Basic, 1986. Print.

If there are four or more authors, you have the choice of listing all the authors in the order
in which they appear on the title page or using "et al." (meaning "and others") to replace all
but the first author. Your Works Cited entry and the parenthetical citation should match.

Second, later, or revised edition

Montagu, Ashley. *Touching: The Human Significance of the Skin.* 3rd ed. New York: Perennial,
     1986. Print.

In place of "3rd ed.," you can include abbreviations for other kinds of editions:
"Rev. ed." (for "Revised edition") or "Abr. ed." (for "Abridged edition").

*Republished book (for example, a paperback published after the original hardback edition
or a modern edition of an older work)*

Hill, Christopher. *The World Turned Upside Down: Radical Ideas During the English Revolution.*
     1972. London: Penguin, 1991. Print.

Wollstonecraft, Mary. *The Vindication of the Rights of Woman, with Strictures on Political and Moral
     Subjects.* 1792. Rutland: Tuttle, 1995. Print.

The date immediately following the title is the original publication date of the work.

Multivolume work

Churchill, Winston S. *A History of the English-Speaking Peoples.* 4 vols. New York: Dodd,
     1956–58. Print.

MLA

Churchill, Winston S. *The Great Democracies*. New York: Dodd, 1957. Print. Vol. 4 of *A History of
the English-Speaking Peoples*. 4 vols. 1956–58.

Use the first method when you cite the whole work; use the second method when you
cite one individually titled volume of the work.

Article in familiar reference work

"Mau Mau." *The New Encyclopaedia Britannica*. 15th ed. 2002. Print.

Article in less familiar reference work

Ling, Trevor O. "Buddhism in Burma." *Dictionary of Comparative Religion*. Ed. S. G. F. Brandon.
New York: Scribner's, 1970. Print.

Translation

De Beauvoir, Simone. *The Second Sex*. 1949. Trans. H. M. Parshley. New York: Bantam, 1961.
Print.

Illustrated book

Jacques, Brian. *The Great Redwall Feast*. Illus. Christopher Denise. New York: Philomel, 1996.
Print.

Graphic novel

Miyazaki, Hayao. *Nausicaa of the Valley of Wind*. 4 vols. San Francisco: Viz, 1995–97. Print.

Corporate author (a commission, committee, or other group)

American Red Cross. *Standard First Aid*. St. Louis: Mosby Lifeline, 1993. Print.

No author listed

The New Yorker Cartoon Album: 1975–1985. New York: Penguin, 1987. Print.

Whole anthology

O'Connell, David F., and Charles N. Alexander, eds. *Self Recovery: Treating Addictions Using
Transcendental Meditation and Maharishi Ayur-Veda*. New York: Haworth, 1994.
Print.

Anthology article

Royer, Ann. "The Role of the Transcendental Meditation Technique in Promoting Smoking
Cessation: A Longitudinal Study." *Self Recovery: Treating Addictions Using Transcendental
Meditation and Maharishi Ayur-Veda*. Ed. David F. O'Connell and Charles N. Alexander.
New York: Haworth, 1994. 221–39. Print.

When you cite an individual article, give the inclusive page numbers for the article at
the end of the citation, before the medium of publication.

Articles or Books from an Online Database

General Format for Material from Online Databases

Author. "Title." *Periodical Name* Print publication data including date and volume/issue numbers: pagination. *Database.* Web. Date Month year you obtained the article from the database.

Journal article from online database

Matsuba, M. Kyle. "Searching for Self and Relationships Online." *CyberPsychology and Behavior* 9.3 (2006): 275–84. *Academic Search Complete.* Web. 14 Apr. 2007.

To see where each element in this citation was found, see Figure 17.1, which shows the online database screen from which the Matsuba article was accessed. For articles in databases, follow the formats for print newspapers, magazines, or scholarly journals, as relevant. When the database text provides only the starting page number of a multi-page article, insert a plus sign after the number, before the period.

Broadcast transcript from online database

Conan, Neal. "Arab Media." *Talk of the Nation.* With Shibley Telhami. 4 May 2004. Transcript. *LexisNexis.* Web. 31 July 2004.

The label "Transcript" after the broadcast date indicates a text (not audio) version.

Matsuba, M. Kyle. "Searching for Self and Relationships Online." *CyberPsychology and Behavior* 9.3 (2006): 275–84. *Academic Search Complete.* Web. 14 Apr. 2007.

FIGURE 17.1 Article downloaded from an online database, with elements identified for an MLA-style citation

E-book from online database

Hanley, Wayne. *The Genesis of Napoleonic Propaganda, 1796–1799*. New York: Columbia UP,
    2002. *Gutenberg-e*. Web. 31 July 2010.

Machiavelli, Niccolo. *Prince*. 1513. *Bibliomania*. Web. 31 July 2009.

Information about the original print version, including a translator if relevant and
available, should be provided.

Other Internet Sources

General Format for Web Sources

Since Web sources are often unstable, MLA recommends that you download
or print out your Web sources. The goal in citing these sources is to enable readers
to locate the material. To that end, use the basic citation model and adapt it as
necessary.

Author, editor, director, narrator, performer, compiler, or producer of the work, if available. *Title*
    of a long work, italicized. OR "Title of page or document that is part of a larger work, in
    quotation marks". *Title of the overall site, usually taken from the home page, if this is different*
    from the title of the work. Publisher or sponsor of the site (if none, use n.p.), day Month year
    of publication online or last update of the site (if not available, use n.d.). Web. day Month
    year you obtained the article from the database.

Saucedo, Robert. "A Bad Idea for a Movie." *theeagle.com*. Bryan College Station Eagle, 1 July
    2010. Web. 7 July 2010.

To see where each element of the Saucedo citation comes from, see the Web article in
Figure 17.2.

    MLA assumes that readers will use a search engine to locate a Web source, so do
not include a URL *unless* the item would be hard to locate without it. If you do include
a URL, it goes at the end of the citation, after the access date. Enclose it in angle
brackets < > followed by a period. If you need to break the URL from one line to the
next, divide it only after a slash. Do not hyphenate a URL. See the home page entries
on page 395 for examples of citations with URLs.

Entire Web site

BlogPulse. Intelliseek, n.d. Web. 24 July 2011.

Padgett, John B., ed. *William Faulkner on the Web*. U of Mississippi, 26 Mar. 2007. Web. 25 June 2010.

Documents within a Web site

Marks, John. "Overview: Letter from the President." *Search for Common Ground*. Search for
    Common Ground, n.d. Web. 25 June 2007.

Gourlay, Alexander S. "Glossary." *The William Blake Archive*. Lib. of Cong., 2005. Web. 21 Jan. 2011.

Site title
Date posted
Article title
Author of the article

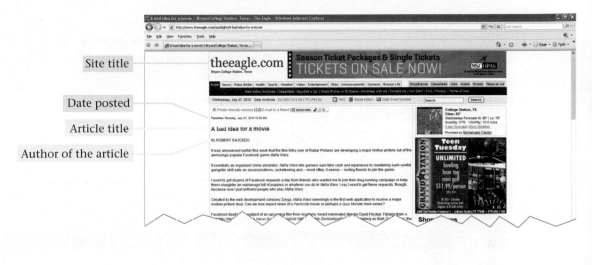

Site sponsor

Saucedo, Robert. "A Bad Idea for a Movie." *theeagle.com*. Bryan College Station Eagle,
1 July 2010. Web. 7 July 2010.

FIGURE 17.2 An article published on the Web, with elements identified for an MLA-style citation

"Ouch! Body Piercing." *Menstuff*. National Men's Resource Center, 1 Feb. 2001. Web. 17 July
    2004.

Article from a newspaper or newswire site

Bounds, Amy. "Thinking Like Scientists." *Daily Camera* [Boulder]. Scripps Interactive Newspaper
    Group, 26 June 2007. Web. 26 June 2007.

"Great Lakes: Rwanda Backed Dissident Troops in DRC-UN Panel." *IRIN*. UN Office for the
    Coordination of Humanitarian Affairs, 21 July 2004. Web. 31 July 2004.

Article from a scholarly e-journal

Welch, John R., and Ramon Riley. "Reclaiming Land and Spirit in the Western Apache
    Homeland." *American Indian Quarterly* 25.4 (2001): 5–14. Web. 19 Dec. 2011.

Broadcast transcript from a Web site

Woodruff, Judy, Richard Garnett, and Walter Dellinger. "Experts Analyze Supreme Court Free
    Speech Rulings." Transcript: Background and discussion. *Online NewsHour*. PBS, 25 June
    2007. Web. 26 June 2010.

MLA

Blog posting

Dyer, Bob, and Ella Barnes. "The 'Greening' of the Arctic." *Greenversations*. U.S. Environmental
Protection Agency, 7 Oct. 2008. Web. 11 Oct. 2010. <http://blog.epa.gov/blog/2008/
10/07/the-greening-of-the-arctic/>.

To see where each element of this citation comes from, refer to Figure 17.3.

Podcast

"The Long and Winding Road: DNA Evidence for Human Migration." *Science Talk.* Scientific
American, 7 July 2008. Web. 21 July 2011.

MLA

Dyer, Bob, and Ella Barnes. "The 'Greening' of the Arctic." *Greenversations*. U.S. Environmental Protection Agency,
7 Oct. 2008. Web. 11 Oct. 2008. <http://blog.epa.gov/blog/2008/10/07/the-greening-of-the-arctic/>.

FIGURE 17.3 A blog posting from the Web, with citation elements identified

Web video

Beck, Roy. "Immigration Gumballs." *YouTube*. YouTube, 2 Nov. 2006. Web. 23 July 2009.

For films and DVDs, see below.

Home pages

Agatucci, Cora. *Culture and Literature of Africa*. Course home page. Humanities Dept., Central
    Oregon Community College, Jan. 2007–May 2007. Web. 31 July 2007. <http://web
    .cocc.edu/cagatucci/classes/hum211/>.

African Studies Program. Home page. School of Advanced International Study, Johns Hopkins U,
    n.d. Web. 31 July 2011.

Sharpe, William F. Home page. May 2004. Web. 31 July 2004. <http://www.stanford.edu/
    ~wfsharpe/>.

E-mail

Daffinrud, Suo. "Scoring Guide for Class Participation." Message to the author. 12 Dec. 2011. E-mail.

Use the subject line as the title of the e-mail. Use "E-mail" as the medium of publication and omit your access date.

Miscellaneous Sources

Television or radio program

Begin with the episode name, if any, in quotation marks, followed by the program
name, italicized. Use "Television" or "Radio" as the medium of publication.

"Lie Like a Rug." *NYPD Blue*. Dir. Steven Bochco and David Milch. ABC. KOMO, Seattle. 6 Nov.
    2001. Television.

If you accessed a program on the Web, give the basic citation information without the
original medium of publication; then include the Web publication information with an
access date.

Ashbrook, Tom. "Turf Wars and the American Lawn." *On Point*. Natl. Public Radio, 22 July
    2008. Web. 23 July 2009.

For podcasts, see page 394.

Film or video recording

Shakespeare in Love. Dir. John Madden. Perf. Joseph Fiennes and Gwyneth Paltrow. Screenplay by
    Marc Norman and Tom Stoppard. Universal Miramax, 1998. Film.

Use "DVD" or "Videocassette" rather than "Film" as the medium of publication if that
is the medium you consulted. If you accessed a film or video on the Web, omit the
original medium of publication, include the Web site or database name (italicized), the
sponsor and posting date, "Web" as medium of publication, and the date of access.

Shakespeare in Love. Dir. John Madden. Perf. Joseph Fiennes and Gwyneth Paltrow. Screenplay by
    Marc Norman and Tom Stoppard. Universal Miramax, 1998. *Netflix*. Netflix, n.d. Web. 9
    Mar. 2010.

For videos published originally on the Web, see page 395.

Sound recording

Begin the entry with what your paper emphasizes—for example, the artist's, com-
poser's, or conductor's name—and adjust the elements accordingly. List the medium—
CD, LP, Audiocassette—last.

Dylan, Bob. "Rainy Day Women #12." *Blonde on Blonde*. Columbia, 1966. LP.

If you accessed the recording on the Web, drop the original medium of publication
and include the Web site or database name (italicized), "Web" as the medium of publication, and the access date.

Dylan, Bob. "Rainy Day Women #12." *Blonde on Blonde*. Columbia, 1966. *Lala*. La La Media,
    n.d. Web. 10 Mar. 2011.

Cartoon or advertisement

Trudeau, Garry. "Doonesbury." Comic strip. *Seattle Times* 19 Nov. 2011: B4. Print.

Banana Republic. Advertisement. *Details* Oct. 2001: 37. Print.

Interview

Castellucci, Marion. Personal interview. 7 Oct. 2010.

Lecture, speech, or conference presentation

Sharples, Mike. "Authors of the Future." Conference of European Teachers of Academic Writing.
    U of Groningen. Groningen, Neth. 20 June 2001. Lecture.

Government publications

In general, follow these guidelines:

- Usually cite as author the government agency that produced the document. Begin
  with the highest level and then branch down to the specific agency:

  United States. Dept. of Justice. FBI.

  Idaho. Dept. of Motor Vehicles.

- Follow this with the title of the document, italicized.
- If a specific person is clearly identified as the author, you may begin the citation
  with that person's name, or you may list the author (preceded by the word "By")
  after the title of the document.
- Follow standard procedures for citing publication information for print sources or
  Web sources.

United States. Dept. of Justice. FBI. *The School Shooter: A Threat Assessment Perspective*. By Mary
    Ellen O'Toole. 2000. Web. 16 Aug. 2001.

MLA-Style Research Paper

As an illustration of a student research paper written in MLA style, see Juan Vazquez's argument about nuclear power on pages 334–338.

APA Style

In many respects, the APA style and the MLA style are similar and their basic logic is the same. In the APA system, the list where readers can find full bibliographic information is titled "References"; as in MLA format, it includes only the sources cited in the body of the paper. The distinguishing features of APA citation style are highlighted in the following sections.

In-Text Citations in APA Style

A typical APA-style in-text citation contains three elements: (1) the last name of the author, (2) the date of the publication, and (3) the page number of the quoted or paraphrased passage. Table 17.2 identifies some typical variations and shows again the one-to-one connection between the in-text citation and the References list.

References List in APA Style

The APA References list at the end of a paper presents entries alphabetically. If you cite more than one item for an author, repeat the author's name each time and arrange the items in chronological order, beginning with the earliest. In cases where two works by an author appeared in the same year, arrange them in the list alphabetically by title, and then add a lowercase "a" or "b" (etc.) after the date so that you can distinguish between them in the in-text citations:

Smith, R. (1999a). *Body image in non-Western cultures, 1750–present.* London, England: Bonanza
Press.

Smith, R. (1999b). Eating disorders reconsidered. *Journal of Appetite Studies, 45,* 295–300.

A formatted References list appears on page 277.

References Citation Models

Print Articles in Scholarly Journals

General Format for Print Article in Scholarly Journal

Author. (Year of Publication). Article title. *Journal Title, volume number,* page numbers.
doi:xx.xxxx/x.xxxx.xx

If there is one, include the **DOI** (digital object identifier), a number that is uniquely assigned to many journal articles. Note the style for capitalizing article titles and for italicizing the volume number.

TABLE 17.2 In-Text Citations in APA Style

Type of Source	References Entry at End of Paper	In-Text Citation in Body of Paper
One author	Pollan, M. (2006). *The omnivore's dilemma: A natural history of four meals*. New York, NY: Penguin.	…(Pollan, 2006, p. 256). OR According to Pollan (2006),…(p. 256).
Two authors	Kwon, O., & Wen, Y. (2010). An empirical study of the factors affecting social network service use. *Computers in Human Behavior, 26,* 254–263. doi:10.1016 /j.chb.2009.04.011	…(Kwon & Wen, 2010, p. 262). OR Kwon and Wen (2010) claimthat …(p. 262).
Three to five authors	Pollay, R. W., Lee, J. S., & Carter-Whitney, D. (1992). Separate, but not equal: Racial segmentation in cigarette advertising. *Journal of Advertising, 21*(1), 45–57.	…race" (Pollay, Lee, & Carter-Whitney, 1992, p. 52). OR Pollay, Lee, and Carter-Whitney have argued that "advertisers…race" (1992, p. 52). *For subsequent citations, use Pollay et al. For a quotation, use the specific page number, not the whole range of pages.*
Author has more than one work in References list	Dombrowski, D. A. (1984). *The philosophy of vegetarianism*. Amherst, MA: University of Massachusetts Press. Dombrowski, D. A. (1997). *Babies and beasts: The argument from marginal cases*. Urbana: University of Illinois Press.	…(Dombrowski, 1984, p. 207). …(Dombrowski, 1997, p. 328). OR Dombrowski (1984) claims that…(p. 207). According to Dombrowski (1997),…(p. 328).
Indirect citation of a source that you found in another source *You use a quotation from Peter Singer from a book by Dombrowski. Include Dombrowski, not Singer, in References.*	Dombrowski, D. A. (1997). *Babies and beasts: The argument from marginal cases*. Urbana: University of Illinois Press.	Animal rights activist Peter Singer argues that…(as cited in Dombrowski, 1997, p. 429). *Singer is used for the attributive tag, but the intext citation is to Dombrowski.*

One author

Herrera-Sobek, M. (2006). Border aesthetics: The politics of Mexican immigration in film and art. *Western Humanities Review, 60,* 60–71. doi:10.1016/j.chb.2009.04.011

Two to seven authors

Kwon, O., & Wen, Y. (2010). An empirical study of the factors affecting social network service use. *Computers in Human Behavior, 26,* 254–263.

When a source has more than seven authors, list the first six and the last one by name, separated by an ellipsis (…) to indicate the authors whose names have been omitted.

Scholarly journal that restarts page numbering with each issue

Pollay, R. W., Lee, J. S., & Carter-Whitney, D. (1992). Separate, but not equal: Racial segmentation in cigarette advertising. *Journal of Advertising, 21*(1), 45–57.

Note that the issue number and the parentheses are *not* italicized.

Print Articles in Magazines and Newspapers

General Format for Print Article in Magazine or Newspaper

Author. (Year, Month Day). Article title. *Periodical Title, volume number*, page numbers.

If page numbers are discontinuous, identify every page, separating numbers with a comma.

Magazine article with named author

Hall, S. S. (2001, March 11). Prescription for profit. *The New York Times Magazine*, 40–45, 59, 91–92, 100.

Magazine article without named author

Daddy, daddy. (2001, July 30). *New Republic, 225*, 12–13.

Review of book or film

Schwarz, B. (2001, November). A bit of bunting: A new history of the British empire elevates expediency to principle [Review of the book *Ornamentalism: How the British saw their empire*]. *Atlantic Monthly, 288*, 126–135.

Kaufman, S. (2001, July 30). Polishing a gem [Review of the motion picture *The blue angel*]. *New Republic, 225*, 28–29.

Newspaper article

Henriques, D. B. (1998, September 27). Hero's fall teaches Wall Street a lesson. *The Seattle Times*, pp. A1, A24.

Newspaper editorial

Dr. Frankenstein on the hill [Editorial]. (2002, May 18). *The New York Times*, p. A22.

Letter to the editor of a magazine or newspaper

Tomsovic, K. (1998, July 13). Culture clash [Letter to the editor]. The New Yorker, 7.

Print Books

General Format for Print Books

Author. (Year of publication). *Book title: Subtitle.* City, State [abbreviated]: Name of Publisher.

Brumberg, J. J. (1997). *The body project: An intimate history of American girls.* New York, NY:
Vintage.

If the publisher's name indicates the state in which it is located, list the city but omit the state.

Reid, H., & Taylor, B. (2010). *Recovering the commons: Democracy, place, and global justice.*
Champaign: University of Illinois Press.

Second, later, or revised edition

Montagu, A. (1986). *Touching: The human significance of the skin* (3rd ed.). New York, NY:
Perennial Press.

Republished book (for example, a paperback published after the original hardback edition or a modern edition of an older work)

Wollstonecraft, M. (1995). *The vindication of the rights of woman, with strictures on political and
moral subjects.* Rutland, VT: Tuttle. (Original work published 1792)

The in-text citation should read: (Wollstonecraft, 1792/1995).

Multivolume work

Churchill, W. S. (1956–1958). *A history of the English-speaking peoples* (Vols. 1–4). New York, NY:
Dodd, Mead.

This is the citation for all the volumes together. The in-text citation should read: (Churchill, 1956–1958).

Churchill, W. S. (1957). *A history of the English-speaking peoples: Vol. 4. The great democracies.*
New York, NY: Dodd, Mead.

This is the citation for a specific volume. The in-text citation should read: (Churchill, 1957).

Article in reference work

Ling, T. O. (1970). Buddhism in Burma. In S. G. F. Brandon (Ed.), *Dictionary of comparative
religion.* New York, NY: Scribner's.

Translation

De Beauvoir, S. (1961). *The second sex* (H. M. Parshley, Trans.). New York, NY: Bantam Books.
(Original work published 1949)

The in-text citation should read: (De Beauvoir, 1949/1961).

Corporate author (a commission, committee, or other group)

American Red Cross. (1993). *Standard first aid.* St. Louis, MO: Mosby Lifeline.

Anonymous author

The New Yorker cartoon album: 1975–1985. (1987). New York, NY: Penguin Books.

The in-text citation is (*New Yorker*, 1987).

Whole anthology

O'Connell, D. F., & Alexander, C. N. (Eds.). (1994). *Self recovery: Treating addictions using transcendental meditation and Maharishi Ayur-Veda.* New York, NY: Haworth Press.

Anthology article

Royer, A. (1994). The role of the transcendental meditation technique in promoting smoking cessation: A longitudinal study. In D. F. O'Connell & C. N. Alexander (Eds.), *Self recovery: Treating addictions using transcendental meditation and Maharishi Ayur-Veda* (pp. 221–239). New York, NY: Haworth Press.

Articles or Books from an Online Database

Article from database with digital object identifier (DOI)

Scharrer, E., Daniel, K. D., Lin, K.-M., & Liu, Z. (2006). Working hard or hardly working? Gender, humor, and the performance of domestic chores in television commercials. *Mass Communication and Society, 9*(2), 215–238. doi.10.1207/s15327825mcs0902_5

Omit the database name. If an article or other document has been assigned a digital object identifier (DOI), include the DOI at the end.

Article from database without DOI

Highland, R. A., & Dabney, D. A. (2009). Using Adlerian theory to shed light on drug dealer motivations. *Applied Psychology in Criminal Justice, 5*(2), 109–138. Retrieved from http://www.apcj.org

Omit the database name. Instead, use a search engine to locate the publication's home page, and cite that URL. If you need to break a URL at the end of a line, do not use a hyphen. Instead, break it *before* a punctuation mark or *after* http://.

Other Internet Sources

General Format for Web Documents

Author, editor, director, narrator, performer, compiler, or producer of the work, if available. (Year, Month Day of posting). *Title of web document, italicized.* Retrieved from Name of website if different from author or title: URL of home page

Barrett, J. (2007, January 17). *MySpace is a natural monopoly.* Retrieved from ECommerce Times
website: http://www.ecommercetimes.com

Marks, J. (n.d.). "Overview: Letter from the president." Retrieved June 3, 2010, from the Search
for Common Ground website: http://www.sfcg.org

Entire Web site

BlogPulse. (n.d.). Retrieved September 3, 2010, from the Intelliseek website: http://
www.intelliseek.com

Article from a newspaper site

Bounds, A. (2007, June 26). Thinking like scientists. *Daily Camera* [Boulder]. Retrieved from
http://www.dailycamera.com

Article from a scholarly e-journal

Welch, J. R., & Riley, R. (2001). Reclaiming land and spirit in the western Apache homeland.
American Indian Quarterly, 25, 5–14. Retrieved from http://muse.jhu.edu/journals
/american_indian_quarterly

Reference material

Cicada. (2004). In *Encyclopaedia Britannica.* Retrieved from http://www.britannica.com

E-book

Hoffman, F. W. (1981). *The literature of rock: 1954–1978.* Retrieved from http://www.netlibrary.com

E-mail, interviews, and personal correspondence

Cite personal correspondence in the body of your text, but not in the References list:
"Daffinrud (personal communication, December 12, 2001) claims that...."

Blog Posting

Dyer, B., & Barnes, E. (2008, October 7). The "greening" of the Arctic [Web log post]. Retrieved
from http://blog.epa.gov/blog/2008/10/07/the-greening-of-the-arctic

To see where each element of this citation comes from, refer to Figure 17.3.

Web video

Beck, R. (2006, November 2). Immigration gumballs [Video file]. Retrieved from
http://www.youtube.com/watch?v=n7WJeqxuOfQ

Podcast

Funke, E. (Host). (2007, June 26). *ArtScene* [Audio podcast]. National Public Radio. Retrieved
from http://www.npr.org

Miscellaneous Sources

Television program

Bochco, S., & Milch, D. (Directors). (2001, November 6). Lie like a rug [Television series episode].
    In *NYPD blue.* New York, NY: American Broadcasting Company.

Film

Madden, J. (Director). (1998). *Shakespeare in love* [Motion picture]. United States: Universal
    Miramax.

Sound recording

Dylan, B. (1966). Rainy day women #12. On *Blonde on blonde* [Record]. New York, NY:
    Columbia.

Government publications

O'Toole, M. (2000). *The school shooter: A threat assessment perspective.* Washington, DC: U.S.
    Federal Bureau of Investigation. Retrieved from http://www.fbi.gov/publications
    /school/school2.pdf

APA-Style Research Paper

An example of a paper in APA style is shown on pages 272–277.

Conclusion

This chapter has shown you the nuts and bolts of citing and documenting sources in
both the MLA and APA styles. It has explained the logic of parenthetical citation systems, showing you how to match sources cited in your text with those in your concluding bibliography. It has also shown you the documentation formats for a wide range of
sources in both MLA and APA styles.

PEARSON
mycomplab

For support in learning this chapter's content, follow this path
in **MyCompLab:** Resources ⇒ Research ⇒ Citing Sources.
Review the Instruction and Multimedia resources about citing
sources, and then complete the Exercises and click on Gradebook to measure your progress.

Informal Fallacies

In this appendix, we look at ways of assessing the legitimacy of an argument within a real-world context of probabilities rather than within a mathematical world of certainty. Whereas formal logic is a kind of mathematics, the informal fallacies addressed in this appendix are embedded in everyday arguments, sometimes making fallacious reasoning seem deceptively persuasive, especially to unwary audiences. We begin by looking at the problem of conclusiveness in arguments, after which we give you an overview of the most commonly encountered informal fallacies.

The Problem of Conclusiveness in an Argument

In real-world disagreements, we seldom encounter arguments that are absolutely conclusive. Rather, arguments are, to various degrees, "persuasive" or "nonpersuasive." In the pure world of formal logic, however, it is possible to have absolutely conclusive arguments. For example, an Aristotelian syllogism, if it is validly constructed, yields a certain conclusion. Moreover, if the first two premises (called the "major" and "minor" premises) are true, then we are guaranteed that the conclusion is also true. Here is an example:

Valid Syllogism

Major premise: All ducks are feathered animals.

Minor premise: Quacko is a duck.

Conclusion: Therefore Quacko is a feathered animal.

This syllogism is said to be valid because it follows a correct form. Moreover, because its premises are true, the conclusion is guaranteed to be true. However, if the syllogism follows an incorrect form (and is therefore invalid), we can't determine whether the conclusion is true.

Invalid Syllogism

Major premise: All ducks are feathered animals.

Minor premise: Clucko is a feathered animal.

Conclusion: Therefore Clucko is a duck.

In the valid syllogism, we are guaranteed that Quacko is a feathered animal because the minor premise states that Quacko is a duck and the major premise places ducks within the larger class of feathered animals. But in the invalid syllogism, there is no guaranteed conclusion. We know that Clucko is a feathered animal but we can't know whether he is a duck. He may be a duck, but he may also be a buzzard or a chicken. The invalid syllogism thus commits a "formal fallacy" in that its form doesn't guarantee the truth of its conclusion even if the initial premises are true.

From the perspective of real-world argumentation, the problem with formal logic is that it isn't concerned with the truth of premises. For example, the following argument is logically valid even though the premises and conclusion are obviously untrue:

Valid Syllogism with Untrue Major and Minor Premises

Major premise: The blood of insects can be used to lubricate lawn mower engines.

Minor premise: Vampires are insects.

Conclusion. Therefore the blood of vampires can be used to lubricate lawn mower engines.

Even though this syllogism meets the formal requirements for validity, its argument is ludicrous.

In this appendix, therefore, we are concerned with "informal" rather than "formal" fallacies because informal fallacies are embedded within real-world arguments addressing contestable issues of truth and value. Disputants must argue about issues because they can't be resolved with mathematical certainty; any contestable claim always leaves room for doubt and alternative points of view. Disputants can create only more or less persuasive arguments, never conclusive ones.

An Overview of Informal Fallacies

The study of informal fallacies remains the murkiest of all logical endeavors. It's murky because informal fallacies are as unsystematic as formal fallacies are rigid and systematized. Whereas formal fallacies of logic have the force of laws, informal fallacies have little more than explanatory power. Informal fallacies are quirky; they identify classes of less conclusive arguments that recur with some frequency, but they do not contain formal flaws that make their conclusions illegitimate no matter what the terms may say. Informal fallacies require us to look at the meaning of the terms to determine how much we should trust or distrust the conclusion. In evaluating arguments with informal fallacies, we usually find that arguments are "more or less" fallacious, and determining the degree of fallaciousness is a matter of judgment.

Knowledge of informal fallacies is most useful when we run across arguments that we "know" are wrong, but we can't quite say why. They just don't "sound right." They look reasonable enough, but they remain unacceptable to us. Informal fallacies are a sort of compendium of symptoms for arguments flawed in this way. We must be careful, however, to make sure that the particular case before us "fits" the descriptors for the fallacy that seems to explain its problem. It's much easier, for example, to find informal fallacies in a hostile argument than in a friendly one simply because we are more likely to expand the limits of the fallacy to make the disputed case fit.

In arranging the fallacies, we have, for convenience, put them into three categories derived from classical rhetoric: *pathos, ethos,* and *logos.* Fallacies of *pathos* rest on flaws in the way an argument appeals to the audience's emotions and values. Fallacies of *ethos* rest on flaws in the way the argument appeals to the character of opponents or of sources and witnesses within an argument. Fallacies of *logos* rest on flaws in the relationship among statements in an argument.

Fallacies of Pathos

Argument to the People (Appealing to Stirring Symbols)   This is perhaps the most generic example of a *pathos* fallacy. Arguments to the people appeal to the fundamental beliefs, biases, and prejudices of the audience in order to sway opinion through a feeling of solidarity among those of the group. Thus a "Support Our Troops" bumper sticker, often including the American flag, creates an initial feeling of solidarity among almost all citizens of goodwill. But the car owner may have the deeper intention of actually meaning "support our president" or "support the war in _____." The stirring symbol of the flag and the desire shared by most people to support our troops is used fallaciously to urge support of a particular political act. Arguments to the people often use visual rhetoric, as in the soaring eagle used in Wal-Mart corporate ads or images of happy families in marketing advertisements.

Appeal to Ignorance   This fallacy persuades an audience to accept as true a claim that hasn't been proved false or vice versa. "Jones must have used steroids to get those bulging biceps because he can't prove that he hasn't used steroids." Appeals to ignorance are particularly common in the murky field of pseudoscience. "UFOs (ghosts, abominable snowmen) do exist because science hasn't proved that they don't exist." Sometimes, however, it is hard to draw a line between a fallacious appeal to ignorance and a legitimate appeal to precaution: "Genetically modified organisms must be dangerous to our health because science hasn't proved that they are safe."

Appeal to Popularity—Bandwagon   To board the bandwagon means (to use a more contemporary metaphor) to board the bus or train of what's popular. Appeals to popularity are fallacious because the popularity of something is irrelevant to its actual merits. "Living together before marriage is the right thing to do because most couples are now doing it." Bandwagon appeals are common in advertising where the claim that a product is popular substitutes for evidence of the product's excellence. There are times, however, when popularity may indeed be relevant: "Global warming is probably caused by human activity because a preponderance of scientists now hold this position." (Here we assume that scientists haven't simply climbed on a bandwagon themselves, but have formed their opinions based on research data and well-vetted, peer-reviewed papers.)

Appeal to Pity   Here the arguer appeals to the audience's sympathetic feelings in order to support a claim that should be decided on more relevant or objective grounds. "Honorable judge, I should not be fined $200 for speeding because I was distraught from hearing news of my brother's illness and was rushing to see him in the hospital." Here the argument is fallacious because the arguer's reason, while evoking sympathy, is not a relevant justification for speeding (as it might have been, for instance, if the arguer had been rushing an injured person to the emergency room). In many cases, however, an arguer can legitimately appeal to pity, as in the case of fund-raising for victims of a tsunami or other disaster.

Red Herring   This fallacy's funny name derives from the practice of using a red herring (a highly odiferous fish) to throw dogs off a scent that they are supposed to be tracking. It refers to the practice of throwing an audience offtrack by raising an unrelated or irrelevant point. "Debating a gas tax increase is valuable, but I really think there should be an extra tax on SUVs." Here the arguer, apparently uncomfortable with the gas tax issue, diverts the conversation to the emotionally charged issue of owning SUVs. A conversant who noted how the argument has gotten offtrack might say, "Stop talking, everyone. The SUV question is a red herring; let's get back to the topic of a gas tax increase."

Fallacies of Ethos

Appeal to False Authority   Arguers appeal to false authority when they use famous people (often movie stars or other celebrities) to testify on issues about which these persons have no special competence. "Joe Quarterback says Gooey Oil keeps his old tractor running sharp; therefore, Gooey Oil is a good oil." Real evidence about the quality of Gooey Oil would include technical data about the product rather than testimony from an actor or hired celebrity. However, the distinction between a "false authority" and a legitimate authority can become blurred. Consider the Viagra ads by former senator Bob Dole during the first marketing years of this impotence drug. As a famous person rather than a doctor, Dole would seem to be a false authority. But Dole was also widely known to have survived prostate cancer, and he may well have used Viagra. To the extent a person is an expert in a field, he or she is no longer a "false authority."

Ad Hominem   Literally, *ad hominem* means "to the person." An *ad hominem* argument is directed at the character of an opponent rather than at the quality of the opponent's reasoning. Ideally, arguments are supposed to be *ad rem* ("to the thing"), that is, addressed to the specifics of the case itself. Thus an *ad rem* critique of a politician would focus on her voting record, the consistency and cogency of her public statements, her responsiveness to constituents, and so forth. An *ad hominem* argument would shift attention from her record to features of her personality, life circumstances, or the company she keeps. "Senator Sweetwater's views on the gas tax should be discounted because her husband works for a huge oil company" or "Senator Sweetwater supports tax cuts for the wealthy because she is very wealthy herself and stands to gain." But not all *ad hominem* arguments are *ad hominem* fallacies. Lawyers, for example, when questioning expert witnesses who give damaging testimony, often make an issue of their honesty, credibility, or personal investment in an outcome.

Poisoning the Well   This fallacy is closely related to *ad hominem.* Arguers poison the well when they discredit an opponent or an opposing view in advance. "Before I yield the floor to the next speaker, I must remind you that those who oppose my plan do not have the best interests of working people in their hearts."

Straw Man   The straw man fallacy occurs when you oversimplify an opponent's argument to make it easier to refute or ridicule. Rather than summarizing an opposing view fairly and completely, you basically make up the argument you wish your opponent had made because it is so much easier to knock over, like knocking over a straw man or scarecrow in a corn field. See pages 128–129 for a fuller discussion of the straw man fallacy.

Fallacies of *Logos*

Hasty Generalization   This fallacy occurs when someone makes a broad generalization on the basis of too little evidence. Generally, the evidence needed to support a generalization persuasively must meet the STAR criteria (sufficiency, typicality, accuracy, and relevance) discussed in Chapter 5 (pages 90–91). But what constitutes a sufficient amount of evidence? The generally accepted standards of sufficiency in any given field are difficult to determine. The Food and Drug Administration (FDA), for example, generally proceeds cautiously before certifying a drug as "safe." However, if people are harmed by the side effects of an FDA-approved drug, critics often accuse the FDA of having made a hasty generalization. At the same time, patients eager to have access to a new drug and manufacturers eager to sell a new product may lobby the FDA to quit "dragging its feet" and get the drug to market. Hence, the point at which a hasty generalization passes over into the realm of a prudent generalization is nearly always uncertain and contested.

Part for the Whole   Sometimes called by its Latin name *pars pro toto,* this fallacy is closely related to hasty generalization. In this fallacy, arguers pick out a part of the whole or a sample of the whole (often not a typical or representative part or sample) and then claim that what is true of the part is true for the whole. If, say, individuals wanted to get rid of the National Endowment for the Arts (NEA), they might focus on several controversial programs funded by the NEA and use them as justification for wiping out all NEA programs. The flip side of this fallacy occurs when an arguer picks only the best examples to make a case and conveniently forgets about examples that may weaken the case.

Post Hoc, Ergo Propter Hoc   The Latin name of this fallacy means "after this, therefore because of this." The fallacy occurs when a sequential relationship is mistaken for a causal relationship. (See Chapter 12, pages 263–264), where we discuss this fallacy in more depth.) For example, you may be guilty of this fallacy if you say, "Cramming for a test really helps because last week I crammed for my psychology test and I got an A on it." When two events occur frequently in conjunction with each other, we've got a good case for a causal relationship. But until we can show how one causes the other and until we have ruled out other causes, we cannot be certain that a causal relationship is occurring. For example, the A on your psych test may have been caused by something other than your cramming. Maybe the exam was easier, or perhaps you were luckier or more mentally alert. It is often difficult to tell when a *post hoc* fallacy occurs. When the New York police department changed its policing tactics in the early 1990s, the crime rate plummeted. Many experts attributed the declining crime rate to the new policing tactics, but some critics proposed other explanations. (See pages 254–255, Case 2, where economist Steven Levitt attributes the declining crime rate to the legalization of abortion in the 1970s.)

Begging the Question—Circular Reasoning   Arguers beg the question when they provide a reason that simply restates the claim in different words. Here is an example: "Abortion is murder because it is the intentional taking of the life of a human being." Because "murder" is defined as "the intentional taking of the life of a human being," the argument is circular. It is tantamount to saying, "Abortion is murder because it is murder." In the abortion debate, the crucial issue is whether a fetus is a "human being" in the legal sense. So in this case the arguer has fallaciously "begged the question" by assuming from the start that the fetus is a legal human being. The argument is similar to saying, "That person is obese because he is too fat."

False Dilemma—Either/Or   This fallacy occurs when an arguer oversimplifies a complex issue so that only two choices appear possible. Often one of the choices is made to seem unacceptable, so the only remaining option is the other choice. "It's my way or the highway" is a typical example of a false dilemma. Here is a more subtle one: "Either we allow embryonic stem cell research, or we condemn people with diabetes, Parkinson's disease, or spinal injuries to a life without a cure." Clearly, there may be other options, including other approaches to curing these diseases. A good extended example of the false dilemma fallacy is found in sociologist Kai Erikson's analysis of President Truman's decision to drop the A-bomb on Hiroshima. His analysis suggests that the Truman administration prematurely reduced numerous options to just two: either drop the bomb on a major city, or sustain unacceptable losses in a land invasion of Japan. Erikson, however, shows there were other alternatives.

Slippery Slope   The slippery slope fallacy is based on the fear that once we put a foot on a slippery slope heading in the wrong direction, we're doomed to slide right out of sight. The controlling metaphor is of a slick mountainside without places to hold on rather than of a staircase with numerous stopping places. Here is an example of a slippery slope: "Once we allow medical use of marijuana, we'll eventually legalize it for everyone, after which we're on a slippery slope toward social acceptance of cocaine and heroin." Slippery slope arguments are frequently encountered when individuals request exceptions to bureaucratic rules: "Look, Blotnik, no one feels worse about your need for open-heart surgery than I do. But I still can't let you turn this paper in late. If I were to let you do it, then I'd have to let everyone turn in papers late." Slippery slope arguments can be very persuasive—and often rightfully so because every slippery slope argument isn't necessarily a slippery slope fallacy. Some slopes really are slippery. The slippery slope becomes a fallacy when we forget that we can often dig a foothold into the slope and stop. For example, we can define procedures for exceptions to rules so that Blotnik can turn in his paper late without allowing everyone to turn in a paper late. Likewise, a state could legalize medical use of marijuana without legalizing it for everyone.

False Analogy   In Chapter 11 on definition and resemblance arguments, we explained that no analogy is perfect (see our discussion of analogies on pages 240–241). Any two things being compared are similar in some ways and different in other ways. Whether an analogy is persuasive or false often depends on the audience's initial degree of skepticism. For example, people opposed to gun control may find the following argument persuasive: "Banning guns on the basis that guns accidentally kill people is like banning cars on the basis that cars accidentally kill people." In contrast, supporters of gun control are likely to call this argument a false analogy on the basis of dissimilarities between cars and guns. (For example, they might say that banning cars would be far more disruptive on our society than would be banning guns.) Just when a persuasive analogy turns into a false analogy is difficult to say.

Non Sequitur   The name of this fallacy means "it does not follow." *Non sequitur* is a catchall term for any claim that doesn't follow from its premises or is supported by irrelevant premises. Sometimes the arguer seems to make an inexplicably illogical leap: "Genetically modified foods should be outlawed because they are not natural." (Should anything that is not natural be outlawed? In what way are they not natural?) At other times there may be a gap in the chain of reasons: "Violent video games have some social value because the army uses them for recruiting." (There may be an important idea emerging here, but too many logical steps are missing.) At still other times an arguer may support a claim with irrelevant reasons: "I should not receive a C in this course because I currently have a 3.8 GPA." In effect, almost any fallacy could be called a *non sequitur* because fallacious reasoning always indicates some kind of disconnect between the reasons and the claim.

Loaded Label or Definition   Sometimes arguers try to influence their audience's view of something by creating a loaded label or definition. For example, people who oppose the "estate tax" (which calls to mind rich people with estates) have relabeled it the "death tax" in order to give it a negative connotation without any markers of class or wealth. Or to take another example, proponents of organic foods could create definitions like the following: "Organic foods are safe and healthy foods grown without any pesticides, herbicides, or other unhealthy additives." "Safe" and "healthy" are evaluative terms used fallaciously in what purports to be a definition. The intended implication is that nonorganic foods are not safe and healthy.

■ ■ ■ **FOR CLASS DISCUSSION** **Persuasive or Fallacious?**

Working individually or in small groups, determine the potential persuasiveness of each of the following argument cores. If fleshed out with supporting evidence, how persuasive do each of these arguments promise to be? If any argument seems doomed because of one or more of the fallacies discussed in this appendix, identify the fallacies and explain how they render the argument nonpersuasive. In your discussion, remember that it is often hard to determine the exact point where fallacious reasoning begins to kick in, especially when you consider different kinds of audiences. So in each case, consider also variations in audience. For which audiences would any particular argument appear potentially fallacious? Which audiences would be more likely to consider the argument persuasive?

1. Either we legalize marijuana or we watch a steady increase in the number of our citizens who break the law.
2. Smoking must cause lung cancer because a much higher percentage of smokers get lung cancer than do nonsmokers.
3. Smoking does not cause cancer because my grandfather smoked two packs per day for fifty years and died in his sleep at age ninety.
4. Society has an obligation to provide housing for the homeless because people without adequate shelter have a right to the resources of the community.
5. Based on my observations of the two renters in our neighborhood, I have concluded that people who own their own homes take better care of them than those who rent. [This arguer provided detailed evidence about the house-caring practices of the two renters and of the homeowners in the neighborhood.]
6. Intelligent design must qualify as a scientific theory because hundreds of scientists endorse it.
7. If we pass legislation requiring mandatory registration of handguns, we'll open the door to eventual confiscation of hunting rifles.
8. Those who support gun control are wrong because they believe that no one should have the right to defend himself or herself in any situation.
9. Most other progressive nations have adopted a program of government-provided health insurance. Therefore it is time for the United States to abandon its present employer-funded insurance system and adopt federally funded universal health insurance.
10. You should discount Dr. Smith's objections to federally funded health care because as a doctor he may face a loss of some income.

■ ■ ■

Credits

Text

Page 5. "Let the Facts Decide, Not Fear: Ban AB 1108" by Louis W. Sullivan. Reprinted with permission of the author.

Page 16. "College Athletes Caught in Tangled Web: Teams Regulations, Free Speech at Odds Over Internet Usage" by Brent Schrotenboer, from *The San Diego Union-Tribune*, May 24, 2006. Copyright © 2005 The San Diego Union-Tribune. Reprinted with permission.

Page 16. "Homeless Hit Street to Protest Proposed Ban" by Linda Keene, from *The Seattle Times,* August 28, 1993. Copyright © 1993 by Linda Keene. Reprinted with permission of The Seattle Times.

Page 38. "Amnesty?" by John F. Kavanaugh from *America,* March 10, 2008. Copyright © 2008 by John F. Kavanaugh. Reprinted with permission of America Press.

Page 45. "Why Blame Mexico?" by Fred Reed, from *The American Conservative,* March 10, 2008. Copyright © 2008 by Fred Reed. Reprinted with permission of The American Conservative.

Page 130. "Recycling Is Garbage" by John Tierney, from *New York Times Magazine*, June 30, 1996. Copyright © 1996 by John Tierney. Reprinted with permission of the author.

Page 161. "Eggheads" by Kathryn Jean Lopez, from *National Review*, September 1, 1998. pp. 26–28 Copyright © 1998 by Kathryn Jean Lopez. Reprinted with permission of National Review.

Page 252. "Toon Offensive" by Beth Reis, from *Seattle Times,* June 20, 2008. Copyright © 2008 by Beth Reis. Reprinted with permission of the author.

Page 309. "A Death Row Donation of Organs?" (Letter to the Editor) by Dr. Kenneth Prager, from *The New York Times*, March 12, 2011. Copyright 2011 by Kenneth Prager. Reprinted with permission of the author.

Page 344. "The Six-Legged Meat of the Future", by Marcel Dicke and Arnold Van Huis from *Wall Street Journal* February 19, 2011 © 2011 Dow Jones & Company. Reprinted by permission.

Page 367. "Is Vegetarianism Healthier Than Nonvegetarianism?" from *Priorities*, from American Council on Science and Health, Volume 9(3). Reprinted with permission of American Council on Science and Health.

Images

Page 1 (left). Adrian Alonso, 2007. TM & Fox Searchlight. All rights reserved/courtesy Everett Collection.

Page 1 (right). Kate del Castillo, 2007. TM & Fox Searchlight. All rights reserved/courtesy Everett Collection.

Page 4. United Steelworkers (USW)

Page 6. Gail Shumway/Getty Images

Page 7 (top). Jason Kottke

Page 7 (bottom). Signe Wilkinson Editorial Cartoon used with the permission of Signe Wilkinson, the Washington Post Writers Group and the Cartoonist Group. All rights reserved.

Page 8 (top). TOLES © 2010 The Washington Post. Reprinted with permission of UNIVERSAL UCLICK. All rights reserved.

Page 8 (bottom). RJ Matson Cartoon/St. Louis Dispatch

Page 26 (top). UPI Photo/Earl S. Cryer/Landov

Page 26 (bottom). Jim Ruymen/UPI /Landov

Page 27 (top). Kenny Be

Page 27 (bottom). Nick Anderson Editorial Cartoon used with the permission of Nick Anderson, the Washington Post Writers Group and the Cartoonist Group. All rights reserved.

Page 57. Andreas Rentz/Getty Images

Page 68 (top). AP Images/Delphinus Riviera Maya

Index

Our Versatile Verbs

CHAPTER PREVIEW

It's probably impossible to count the number of verbs in English. We regularly add new ones when new technology and new ideas require them, and we seem to have no qualms about making verbs out of nouns: We *text* and *fax* and *e-mail* our friends; we *google* to find information. We also have a wide array of affixes we can use to change other word classes into verbs: beaut*ify*, lega*lize*, dark*en*, activ*ate*, *en*courage, *be*friend, *de*rail.

Not only do we have countless verbs, old and new, we have numerous ways of expanding them with auxiliary verbs for expressing subtle variations in time. In the examples and exercises you have seen in the first two chapters, the verbs have been limited to the one-word variety, the simple **present** and **past tenses.** We begin this chapter by examining expansions of those forms, with an outline of the meaning that the auxiliary verbs convey. We also emphasize the importance of choosing effective verbs and of using the passive voice judiciously.

THE EXPANDED VERB

As you are well aware, many of the predicates we use in writing and speech go beyond the simple present and past tenses to include **auxiliary verbs,** also called **helping verbs.** You'll find the auxiliary—sometimes more than one—in the position before the main verb:

> Cassie *is serving* vegetable lasagna at her party.
>
> My little brother *has read* all the Harry Potter books three times.
>
> Jamal *has been* volunteering at the food bank on Saturdays.

Sometimes the auxiliaries are separated by an adverb:

I *will* probably *be* <u>taking</u> the bus home this weekend.

Although the way auxiliaries are combined with main verbs may seem chaotic, in fact, it's very systematic. To understand this system, you must be able to distinguish between the two ways verb tenses are labeled. The first is perhaps familiar to you: Verbs are labeled according to time as *present, past,* or *future.* The second is probably less familiar: Verbs are also labeled as *simple, progressive, perfect,* or *perfect progressive.* The following chart shows how these two different ways of labeling combine to create the traditional names for our wide array of tenses. In the chart we use the verb *eat* as our example. (In this chart you will find the five forms of *eat* that you saw in Chapter 1, page 10.) Note that the three columns designate time.

Verb Tenses			
	PRESENT	PAST	FUTURE
Simple	eat, eats (simple present)	ate (simple past)	*will* eat (simple future)
Progressive	*am* (*is, are*) eating (present progressive)	*was* (*were*) eating (past progressive)	*will be* eating (future progressive)
Perfect	*has* (*have*) eaten (present perfect)	*had* eaten (past perfect)	*will have* eaten (future perfect)
Perfect progressive	*has* (*have*) been eating (present perfect progressive)	*had been* eating (past perfect progressive)	*will have been* eating (future perfect progressive)

As you can see, in the first row, a verb in the simple present or simple past does not team up with an auxiliary. A verb in the simple future, though, does take an auxiliary, the **modal auxiliary** *will* (which is discussed further on page 43). In the second row, you will find that the **present participle** (the *-ing* form of the verb) appears in all progressive tenses along with *be*, the form of which is determined by the time: *am, is,* and *are* for the present tense, *was* and *were* for the past tense, and *will be* for the future tense. Similarly, in the third row, the **past participle** appears in all the perfect tenses along with a form of the auxiliary *have: Has* and *have* are in the present tense, *had* is in the past tense, and *will have* is in the future tense. The fourth row is a combination of the previous two: In each of the perfect-progressive tenses, you will see *been,* the past participle of *be,* as one auxiliary followed by the main verb, the present participle *eating;* the first auxiliary in the string is a form of *have.*

You may be wondering why there is more than one auxiliary listed in each cell. The form of the auxiliary verb depends on the subject of the sentence. For example, when *I* is the subject, the verb in the present progressive will be *am eating;* the verb will be *are eating* when *you, we,* or *they* is the subject; *he, she,* or *it* as subject calls for *is eating.* (These variations will come up again in connection with point of view in Chapter 7; you'll also read about personal pronouns in Chapter 12.)

Using the Expanded Verbs

In this section, you will be encouraged to pay attention to the verb tenses used in prose. Consider the verb forms in the following paragraph from Scott Turow's essay "An Odyssey That Started with Ulysses":

> At the age of eighteen, after my freshman year in college, I worked as a mailman. This was merely a summer job. My life's calling, I had decided, was to be a novelist, and late at night I was already toiling on my first novel.

This passage includes five main verbs: *work, be, decide, be,* and *toil.* They occur, however, in different tenses:

worked—simple past,

was—simple past,

had decided—past perfect,

was—simple past,

was toiling—past progressive.

When you check the chart on page 39, you'll discover they are all in the "Past" column. By using the past tense throughout the paragraph, Turow is able to provide a consistent **time frame** for his narrative. This point may seem obvious. But sometimes, amid the fury of producing that first draft, the writer may inadvertently shift tenses.

> Because the library was open long hours, he spends his free time there.

Something sounds off beat here. You might be asking yourself why the verb *was* is in the past tense, but *spends* is present. Is the library still open long hours? Does the writer still go there? This is the type of confusion that can happen when verb tenses are inconsistent.

You may remember hearing the rule to "avoid shifting tenses" in your writing. What does it mean? Don't writers shift tenses all the time? Yes and no. It's true that Scott Turow has shifted from simple past to past perfect to simple past to past progressive. But as we pointed out, he has stayed in one time frame: All of his verbs fit in the past column. A more accurate statement of the rule is "avoid shifting *time frames* when writing." As long as you use one time frame (present, past, or future), your tenses will be consistent.

There are times, however, when you may want to shift from one time frame to another. You can do this by using a time marker, very likely an adverbial, such as *today, yesterday, soon, in 2002, when I was younger.*

> We <u>take</u> our old magazines to a recycling center. *Soon,* however, we <u>will leave</u> them in curbside recycling bins.

The tense in the first of these two sentences is present; the tense in the second is future. The time marker *soon* signals the shift in time frame.

It is also possible, for writers to shift time frames without using a specific time marker—but only when the reason for shifting is easily understood. The second sentence in the following pair of sentences provides historical information to support the assertion in the first sentence, so the shift from a present time frame to a past time frame is appropriate.

> Our recycling center <u>has moved</u>. The owners of the barn housing the center <u>refused</u> to renew our lease.

Another common shift occurs when a writer wants to add a comment that might aid the reader's understanding. In this example, the opening sentence is in the past tense, but the second sentence, the comment, is in the present.

> We recently <u>established</u> a Web site for reporting local air quality.
>
> Our reports <u>are</u> important to citizens with respiratory diseases.

◀ FOR GROUP DISCUSSION

1. Read the passage below from Robert Grudin's *Time and the Art of Living.*

> In the late November of 1968, I <u>spent</u> a few days in a hotel just off the Piazza San Marco in Venice. At 6 one morning, hearing the loud warning bells, I <u>jumped</u> out of bed, <u>grabbed</u> my camera and <u>rushed</u> out to see the famous Venetian flood. I <u>stood</u> in the empty and as yet dry Piazza and <u>looked</u> out toward the Gulf, for I <u>expected</u> the flood tides to come in from the open water. Many minutes <u>passed</u> before I <u>turned</u> to see that the Piazza <u>was</u> <u>flooding</u>, not directly from the Gulf, but up through its

own sewers. The indented gratings in the pavement <u>had</u> <u>all but</u> <u>disappeared</u> under calm, flat silver puddles, which <u>grew</u> slowly and silently until their peripheries <u>touched</u> and the Piazza <u>had become</u> a lake. That morning I <u>experienced</u> vividly, if almost subliminally, the reality of change itself: how it <u>fools</u> our sentinels and <u>undermines</u> our defenses, how careful we <u>are</u> to look for it in the wrong places, how it <u>does</u> <u>not</u> <u>reveal</u> itself until it <u>is</u> beyond redress, how vainly we <u>search</u> for it around us and <u>find</u> too late that it <u>has occurred</u> within us.

Notice how Grudin begins with one time frame—then shifts to another. Why does he make this shift? Is it effective? Why or why not?

2. Reread Annie Dillard's weasel paragraph at the opening of Chapter 2 with time frames in mind. You'll find that she too has shifted. Did she have a good reason? Does it work? Why or why not?

Special Uses of the Present Tense

Although you might assume that the present tense is used only to refer to present time, this is not the case. In some rhetorical situations writers use the present tense to refer to past events. For example, fiction writers sometimes use the simple present tense to make action more immediate or suspenseful. The following passage is from the first chapter of William Trevor's novel *Felicia's Journey*. In this scene Felicia is riding on a train:

The train <u>judders</u> on, rattling on the rails, slowing almost to a halt, gathering speed again. Felicia <u>opens</u> her eyes. A hazy dawn <u>is distributing</u> farmhouses and silos and humped barns in shadowy fields. Later, there <u>are</u> long lines of motor cars creeping slowly on nearby roads, and blank early-morning faces at railway stations.

The present tense is also used in the analysis of literature. In this passage, John Elder discusses Robert Frost's poem "Directive":

Frost's opening lines not only <u>point</u> up to the ridge above Bristol, they also <u>identify</u> a tension fundamental to America's environmental movement. We <u>long</u> to save wild beauty from heedless development, to guarantee a modicum of biodiversity in the world of internal combustion engines and electronic monoculture.

We also use the simple present form of the verb to refer to habitual actions:

> The news comes on at six o'clock.
>
> I always vote a straight party ticket.

And we use the present in reference to propensities of nature:

> Beavers build dams.
>
> Bears hibernate in winter.
>
> Thunder follows lightning.

Other Auxiliaries

Do-Support. So far we have looked at three auxiliary verbs: *be, have,* and *will.* Another common auxiliary is *do.* We call on *do,* or one of its other two forms, *does* and *did,* when we need an auxiliary for converting a positive sentence into a negative or turning a statement into a question or for carrying the emphasis—but only when the sentence has no other auxiliary:

> I *don't like* horseradish.
>
> *Do* you *like* horseradish?
>
> Jose *does like* horseradish.
>
> *Do* sit down.

This auxiliary use of *do* is called **do-support.** In other words, *do* comes to the rescue when an auxiliary is needed. Like *be* and *have, do* can also serve as a main verb; in fact, all three are among our most common verbs.

Modal Auxiliaries. You're already familiar with one of the **modal auxiliaries:** *will,* sometimes called "the sign of the future." Unlike *be, have,* and *do,* the job of the modals is to add nuances to the meaning of the main verb. The other modal auxiliaries are equally familiar: *can, could, may, might, must, shall, should, would, ought to.* These verbs signal a variety of meanings:

> This weekend I <u>*can* go</u> to the library. (ability)
>
> This weekend I <u>*might* go</u> to the library. (possibility)
>
> This weekend I <u>*should* go</u> to the library. (advisability)
>
> This weekend I <u>*must* go</u> to the library. (obligation)

THE PASSIVE VOICE

You're probably familiar with the definition of a verb as an "action word," a description commonly applied to both intransitive and transitive verbs:

> The baby cried. (Pattern 4)
>
> My roommate wrote the play. (Pattern 5)

In these sentences the subjects are performing the action; they are making something happen. Linguists use the term **agent** for this "doer" of the verbal action. Another term that describes this relationship of the subject to the verb is **active voice.**

What happens when we turn the Pattern 5 sentence around, when we remove the agent from the subject position and give that role to the original direct object, *the play?*

> The play was written by my roommate.

This reversal has changed the sentence from active to **passive voice.** However, while *my roommate* is no longer the sentence subject, it is still the agent; and while *the play* is no longer the direct object, it is still the so-called receiver of the action. What has changed are their functions, their roles, in the sentence, not their relationship to each other.

The transformation from active to passive involves three steps:

1. The direct object becomes the subject.
2. A form of *be* is added as an auxiliary (in this case the past form *was,* because *wrote* is past); it joins the past participle of the main verb.
3. The original agent, if mentioned, becomes the object of the preposition *by* (or, in some cases, *for*).

If you think about the first step in the list, you'll understand why the other example of an action verb, *The baby cried,* is not being used to illustrate the passive voice: Intransitive verbs, such as *cry,* cannot be made passive because they have no direct object.

The passive voice has an important purpose: to shift the focus of the sentence, changing the topic under discussion. This shift is an important tool for sentence cohesion, a feature of writing you will explore in Chapter 5.

Using the Passive Voice

The core of the passive verb is the auxiliary *be* and the past participle. Here is an abbreviated form of the tense chart you studied earlier; this time, though, it is filled with verbs in the passive voice.

Verb Tenses (Passive Voice)			
	PRESENT	PAST	FUTURE
Simple	*am, is, are* assigned	*was, were* assigned	*will be* assigned
Progressive	*am, is, are being* assigned	*was, were being* assigned	*will be, being* assigned
Perfect	*has, have been* assigned	*had been* assigned	*will have been* assigned

We can cite good reasons for using the passive voice, as you will see in Chapter 5, where we discuss the role of the passive in cohesion. The passive voice may also be called for when the agent is unknown or has no bearing on the discussion:

> So far as we know, from Einstein's Special Theory of Relativity, the universe is constructed in such a way (at least around here) that no material object and no information can be transmitted faster than the velocity of light.
> —Carl Sagan (*Broca's Brain*)

> The Vikings have had a bad press. Their activities are equated with rape and pillage and their reputation for brutality is second only to that of the Huns and the Goths. Curiously, they also have been invested with a strange glamour which contradicts in many ways their fearsome image.
> —James Graham-Campbell and Dafydd Kidd
> (*The Vikings*)

The authors' purpose in the last passage is not to explain who equates the Vikings with rape and pillage or who invests them with glamour. The use of the passive puts these statements in the category of accepted beliefs. In some cases the passive voice is simply more straightforward:

> Joe was wounded in Iraq.

And sometimes, in order to add modifiers to the agent, we put it where we can do so more conveniently, at the end of the sentence:

> Early this morning a campus van was hit by a delivery truck traveling at high speed through the intersection of James Avenue and Water Street.

Note that if we switched the agent to the subject position, the result would be a fairly wide separation of the subject headword and the verb:

> Early this morning a delivery truck traveling at high speed
>   through the intersection of James Avenue and Water Street hit
>   a campus van.

The choice, of course, also depends on where the main focus should be.

The passive voice is especially common—and deliberate—in technical and scientific writing, in legal documents, and in lab reports, where the researcher is the agent, but to say so would be inappropriate:

> *Active:* I increased the heat to 450° and allowed it to remain at that temperature for twenty minutes.
>
> *Passive:* The heat was increased to 450° and allowed to remain at that temperature for twenty minutes.

EXERCISE 7

It's important to recognize the passive voice when you see it—so that you'll know when you've used it and thus will use it deliberately and effectively. In the first section of this exercise, you'll transform active sentences into the passive voice; in the second part you'll do the opposite—change the passive into the active. And in the third part, the voice of the sentence is not identified: You'll have to figure it out.

A. Transform the following active sentences into the passive voice; remember that the direct object of the active functions as the subject in the passive.

   1. My roommate wrote the lead article in today's *Collegian*.
   2. Bach composed some of our most intricate fugues.
   3. Our homecoming committee has organized an elaborate celebration.
   4. I should have washed the car before our trip.
   5. The county commissioners are proposing a new tax-collection system this year.
   6. Your positive attitude pleases me.

B. Transform the following passive sentences into the active voice; remember that the subject of the passive is the direct object in the active. (Note: If the agent is missing, you will have to supply one to act as the subject for the active.)

1. This year's cheerleading squad was chosen by a committee last spring.
2. Bill's apartment was burglarized last weekend.
3. The election of the class officers will be held on Tuesday.
4. Your car's oil should be changed on a regular basis.
5. The suspect is being kept in solitary confinement.
6. The kidnap victim has been found unharmed.

C. First decide if the following sentences are active or passive; then transform them.

1. Barack Obama was elected president in 2008.
2. You should read the next six chapters before Monday.
3. The cities in the Northeast have been affected by migration in recent years.
4. After the dot-com bubble burst, many employees of financial institutions were cheated out of their retirement savings.
5. Our company is trying out a new vacation schedule this year.
6. The streetlights on campus are finally being repaired.

FOR GROUP DISCUSSION

Surely the most famous words in our country's history are those written by Thomas Jefferson in the Declaration of Independence. Here is the opening of the Declaration's second paragraph:

> We hold these truths to be self-evident, that all men are created equal, that they are endowed by their Creator with certain unalienable Rights, that among these are Life, Liberty and the pursuit of Happiness. That to secure these rights, Governments are instituted among Men, deriving their just powers from the consent of the governed. That whenever any Form of Government becomes destructive of these ends, it is the Right of the People to alter or to abolish it, and to institute a new government, laying its foundation on such principles and organizing its powers in such form, as to them shall seem most likely to effect their Safety and Happiness. Prudence, indeed, will dictate that Governments long established should not be changed for light and transient causes; and accordingly all experience hath shown, that mankind are more disposed to suffer, while evils are sufferable, than to right themselves by abolishing the forms to which they are accustomed.

Underline the passive sentences. Rewrite all or some of them in the active voice and compare the two versions.

The Obscure Agent

Certainly the passive voice has a place in every kind of writing; it is a legitimate tool—but like any tool it must be right for the job. Too often the purpose of the passive voice is simply to obscure the agent. For example, one of the most common responses that governmental investigative committees hear from individuals accused of mismanagement is

> "Yes, Senator, mistakes were made."

And the passive is common in the "official" style used by bureaucrats:

> It was reported today that the federal funds to be allocated for the power plant would not be forthcoming as early as had been anticipated. Some contracts on the preliminary work have been canceled and others renegotiated.

Such "officialese" or "bureaucratese" takes on a nonhuman quality because the agent role has completely disappeared from the sentences. In the foregoing example we do not know who is reporting, allocating, anticipating, canceling, or renegotiating.

This kind of agentless passive is especially common in official news conferences, where press secretaries and other government officials explain what is happening without revealing who is responsible for making it happen:

> Recommendations <u>are being made</u> to the Mexican government concerning drug enforcement.

> A tax hike <u>has been proposed</u>, but several other solutions to the federal deficit <u>are</u> also <u>being considered</u>.

> The president <u>has been advised</u> that certain highly placed officials <u>are being investigated</u>.

The faceless passive does an efficient job of obscuring responsibility, but it is neither efficient nor graceful for the writing that most of us do in school and on the job.

Sometimes writers use the passive to avoid the first-person *I,* perhaps because the paper has too many *I*'s already or because the teacher has ruled out the first-person point of view:

> The incessant sound of foghorns <u>could be heard</u> along the waterfront.

But remember that English is a versatile language; first person is not the only alternative to the passive. You don't have to write, "I [or we] heard the sound of foghorns. . . ." Here's a version of the sentence using *sound* as the verb:

> The foghorns <u>sounded</u> along the waterfront.

And here's one that describes the movement of the sound:

> The incessant sound of foghorns <u>floated</u> across the water.

Many times, of course, the writer simply doesn't realize that the passive voice may be the culprit producing the vagueness or wordiness of that first draft. For example, a student writer ended his family Christmas story with an impersonal, inappropriate passive:

> That visit from Santa was an occurrence that <u>would never be forgotten by the family</u>.

Clearly, he needed to ask himself, "Who was doing what?"

> <u>The family would never forget</u> that visit from Santa.

And if for purposes of transition or rhythm he had wanted to retain *visit* as the subject, he could easily have done so in an active way:

> That <u>visit</u> from Santa <u>became</u> part of our family legend.

EXERCISE 8

1. The writer of the following passage has managed to avoid using the first-person point of view but in doing so has obliterated any resemblance to a personal voice. Revise the passage, avoiding both the passive and the first person. Remember to think about the agent as subject.

   > The woods in the morning seemed both peaceful and lively. Birds could be heard in the pines and oaks, staking out their territory. Squirrels could be seen scampering across the leaves that covered the forest floor, while in the branches above, the new leaves of the birches and maples were outlined by the sun's rays. The leaves, too, could be heard, rustling to the rhythm of the wind.

2. Identify the passive verbs in the following passage from *Stalking the Wild Asparagus* by Euell Gibbons. Why do you think he chose the passive instead of the active voice? Can you improve the passage by revising some or all of the sentences?

> Wild food is used at our house in a unique method of entertaining. Our "wild parties," which are dinners where the chief component of every dish is some foraged food, have achieved a local fame. Many different meals can be prepared almost wholly from wild food without serving anything that will be refused by the most finicky guest. Such dinners are remembered and talked about long after the most delicious of conventional dinners have been forgotten.

WELL-CHOSEN VERBS: SHOWING, NOT TELLING

When writing teachers promote the virtues of "showing" rather than "telling," what do they mean? They mean that you don't have to tell us that the old woman on the park bench is sad; you can show us:

> The old woman on the park bench wept quietly.

You don't even have to tell us that she's old:

> Wearing a shawl around her shoulders, the woman on the park bench wept quietly, wisps of gray hair escaping the woolen cap, frail bony fingers clutching her handkerchief.

Annie Dillard doesn't tell us that building a road through the Everglades between Miami and Tampa was an arduous job; she shows us:

> To build the road, men stood sunk in muck to their armpits. They fought off cottonmouth moccasins and six-foot alligators. They slept in boats, wet. They blasted muck with dynamite, cut jungle with machetes; they laid logs, dragged drilling machines, hauled dredges, heaped limestone. The road took fourteen years to build up by the shovelful.
>
> —*An American Childhood*

And Barbara Ehrenreich doesn't tell us that she was glad her day of hard work as a housecleaner was over; she shows us:

> I rush home to the Blue Haven [Motel] at the end of the day, pull down the blinds for privacy, strip off my uniform in the

kitchen—the bathroom being too small for both a person and her discarded clothes—and stand in the shower for a good ten minutes, thinking all this water is *mine*. I have paid for it. In fact, I have earned it.

—*Nickel and Dimed*

A well-chosen verb not only heightens the drama of a sentence and makes its meaning clear, it also sends a message to the reader that the writer has crafted the sentence carefully, that the idea matters. We certainly get that message from the examples of prose we have just seen.

The overuse of the linking-*be* is a common signal that a writer is telling rather than showing: "The old woman *is* sad." "The old woman *is* old." "Building a road through the Everglades between Miami and Tampa *was* an arduous job." "She *was* glad her day of hard work as a housecleaner *was* over."

You saw in Chapter 2 that the *be* patterns commonly serve not only as topic sentences but also as supporting sentences throughout the paragraph. You may be surprised, in checking a paragraph or two of your own prose, at how often you've used a form of *be* as the main verb. An abundance of such examples—say, more than two or three in a paragraph—constitutes a clear "revise" message.

Certainly, the potential drama and meaning of your prose are weakened or missing altogether when the verbs don't pull their weight. Sometimes the culprit is one of our other common, garden-variety verbs, such as *have, make, go, do, say, get, take*. Because these verbs have so many nuances of meaning, you can often find a more precise one. For example, where you have selected the verb *make*, you could probably express yourself more exactly with *constitute, render, produce, form, complete, compel,* or *create*, all of which are indexed under *make* in *Roget's Thesaurus*, along with *make believe, make good* (demonstrate), *make out* (discover, know, interpret), and *make up* (complete).

It's important to note, too, that these alternatives to *make* are not uncommon or esoteric words; they're certainly a part of your active vocabulary. Unfortunately, however, the precise verb doesn't always come to mind when you need it—especially when you're composing the first draft. Rather than stop right there in midsentence or midparagraph to find it, just circle the word you've used—or highlight it with boldface type if you're using a word processor. Then, during the revision stage you can take time to think about it again. At that point, in fact, you may want to consult your dictionary or thesaurus just to remind yourself of some of these more specific verbs.

(*A word of warning:* Every word in the thesaurus is not for you. If it's not your word, if you're not sure of it, if it doesn't sound natural in your voice, then don't use it. Sometimes the dictionary is a better reminder: It often provides synonyms in context, along with the distinctive meanings of each.)

EXERCISE 9

Find time today to watch someone doing something for five or ten minutes. Then write a paragraph-long description of the person in action. Try to use as few *be* patterns as possible. The next time you're in class, compare your paragraphs with those of your friends, paying special attention to the verbs.

....

KEY TERMS

Active voice	Intransitive verb	Present participle
Agent	Linking-*be*	Present tense
Auxiliary verb	Modal auxiliary	Showing
Be patterns	Passive voice	Telling
Do-support	Past participle	Time frame
Helping verb	Past tense	Transitive verb

RHETORICAL REMINDERS

Have I remembered to show, not tell?

Have I kept my use of the linking-*be* to a minimum?

Have I put the agent in subject position whenever possible?

Have I used the passive voice effectively?

Have I used time frames consistently?

Are the shifts I make in time frames signaled by a time marker? If they aren't, will my readers understand why I have made the shifts?

Coordination and Subordination

CHAPTER PREVIEW

In Chapter 2 we introduced basic sentence patterns, emphasizing the separate units of each; here we examine the ways in which we expand units and even sentences themselves, using **coordination, subordination,** or both. The technique of coordination, of putting together like structures in sentences, is old hat; you've been using it all your life. Coordination is a natural part of language, one that develops early in speech. If you pay attention to sentence structure the next time you're within hearing distance of a small child, you'll hear the **coordinating conjunction** *and* used frequently to link parts of sentences:

> We built a new snow fort <u>and</u> threw snowballs.
>
> Robbie is mean, <u>and</u> I'm not going to play with him anymore.

Coordination shows up early and often in writing as well. Certainly in this book you can't read very far without coming to a coordinating conjunction—an *and* or a *but* or an *or.* Your own writing is probably filled with these conjunctions, too.

Subordination is another technique you use or encounter frequently without even realizing that it has a special name. When you come across the following types of newspaper announcements, you're reading sentences that contain **subordinating conjunctions** such as *because* and *after:*

> School was canceled <u>because</u> many roads were closed.
>
> All games will be rescheduled <u>after the strike is over.</u>

So why do we need to study coordination and subordination? Because they're so essential to communication! Any technique that we use as often as we do coordination or subordination needs to be under our control. Remember, a written sentence is there to be looked at and pondered, to be read over and over again. We want to be sure that every one of our sentences containing coordinate or subordinate structures is grammatical and logical. And, equally important, we want to use the most efficient and accurate conjunctions possible.

This chapter is also about punctuation. Make no mistake, it is important to follow the conventions of punctuation; the effectiveness of your prose diminishes with every error the reader notices. As we're sure you know, punctuation rules can seem complicated in sentences with coordinate or subordinate structures. You already know how to use these structures in your sentences; it's also important to know when they require a special punctuation mark, usually a comma. Having punctuation under control will give you the confidence to construct long sentences. And, just as important, such control will send a message to your reader that you are a writer with authority.

COORDINATION WITHIN THE SENTENCE

In this chapter you'll find it useful to think again about the sentence parts you studied in Chapters 1 and 2. Most of the coordination that takes place within the sentence results from compounding one or more of those parts. *Compounding* means simply "joining" or "linking." Here we've compounded the subject:

> Gino's father *and* my uncle flew helicopters in Vietnam.

In the following sentence the complete predicate is compounded:

> The kids played outdoors all morning *but* stayed inside all afternoon.

In the following sentence, only the direct object is compounded

> He usually drinks a cappuccino *or* a latte before class.

Now is a good time to review the important punctuation rule you learned in Chapter 2:

> **Do not mark boundaries of the required sentence units with punctuation.**

Here's another, a non-comma rule of sorts, that describes the sample sentences you have just seen:

> **Use *no* comma with a coordinating conjunction when it joins a two-part compound *within* a sentence.**

The connectors in the preceding examples—*and, but, or*—are the three primary coordinating conjunctions we use for connecting both full sentences and their parts; you can think of them as "the big three."

You may have had a teacher in elementary or middle school who taught you a list of seven conjunctions—and perhaps helped you remember them with an acronym: *fanboys.* (The *a, b,* and *o* of *fanboys,* of course, stand for *and, but,* and *or.*) That list includes *for,* which has features of both a coordinating conjunction and a subordinating conjunction; it also includes *yet* and *so,* which share features of **conjunctive adverbs** (words like *however,* defined later in this chapter). The *n* of *fanboys* is even further removed from the big three in that it has a built-in negative meaning and is generally used only with its partner, *neither,* or, sometimes, *not.* (You'll read more about the **correlative conjunction** *neither–nor* later in the chapter.) All of these lesser conjunctions are certainly words you use in writing from time to time, but their in-between status means they do not have the wide range of use that the big three have.

Although the non-comma rule will apply to most of your sentences containing coordinate pairs, you may at times want to give special emphasis to the second part of the pair, in which case, a comma can be used to signal a slight pause:

> I didn't believe her, and said so.
>
> The running back charged ahead, but missed the goal line by an inch.

The emphasis is even stronger with a dash instead of a comma:

> I didn't believe her—and said so.
>
> The running back charged ahead—but missed the goal line by an inch.

The dash also sends the message that the punctuation was deliberate—not a comma error, a judgment some readers might make. Because an emphatic comma can be misjudged, be sure to use it with care.

Parallel Structure

One of your most important writer's tools is the concept of **parallel structure,** or **parallelism.** A coordinate structure is parallel only when the parts are of the same form. The parallel structure is an effective one—and this feature is just as important—only when the two ideas are equal, when they belong together. Annie Dillard clearly understood the effectiveness of parallel forms when she wrote this sentence:

> We could live under the wild rose as weasels, <u>mute</u> and <u>uncomprehending</u>.

For contrast, examine this compound structure that is unparallel in form:

> *<u>My new exercise program</u> and <u>going on a strict diet</u> will make me stronger and healthier.

Here the conjunction *and* connects the parts of a compound subject. The first part (*My new exercise program*) is a noun phrase in form; the second (*going on a strict diet*) is a special type of verb phrase, a **gerund.** (*Gerund* is the label we give an *-ing* verb when it is used as a noun. Gerunds are discussed further in Chapter 10.) In this case the ideas are equal, so in that sense they belong together. But for the sentence to be grammatical, the two parts of the compound must be the same form:

> <u>My new exercise program</u> **and** <u>a strict diet</u> (NP + NP)
> <u>Sticking to my exercise program</u> **and** <u>going on a diet</u> (VP + VP)

You may be thinking that these unparallel structures sound perfectly normal—like sentences you hear every day. And you're right: They do sound normal. We use sentences like these in our conversation all the time—and no one accuses us of being ungrammatical. But writing is different. We want to be as precise and effective as possible. And as writers we have a second (and third and fourth!) chance to improve our sentences. We don't have to show that first draft to anyone. Sentences with unparallel features can always be improved.

Coordination of the Series

In the **series**—a coordinate structure with three or more components—we use commas to separate the parallel coordinate elements:

> Among the lands on the frozen fringes of the Arctic Ocean are Alaska, Canada, and Greenland.

These commas represent the pauses and slight changes of pitch that occur in the production of the series. You can hear the commas in your voice

---

*An asterisk marks the sentence as ungrammatical or of questionable usage.

when you compare the series of three with a two-part structure, which of course has no comma:

> Among the lands on the frozen fringes of the Arctic Ocean are
> Alaska and Canada.

You probably noticed a leveling of your voice in reading the pair, a certain smoothness that the series does not have.

Some writers—and some publications as a matter of policy—leave out the **serial comma,** the one immediately before the coordinating conjunction. One such publication is *The New York Times.* Here is the sentence from which the previous example was taken, as published in the *Times:*

> Unlike Antarctica, a continent surrounded by ocean, the Arctic
> is mostly ocean ringed by land—the frozen, inhospitable fringes
> of Alaska, Canada, Greenland, Iceland, Scandinavia and Russia.
> —Darcy Frey

The open, or light, punctuation style leaves out the comma where a boundary is otherwise marked. Here, of course, the conjunction *and* marks the final boundary of the series.

This punctuation style, however, does have a drawback: It may imply a closer connection than actually exists between the last two elements of the series, such as the connection in the following sentence:

> Throughout college Herbie survived on pizza, ramen, and
> <u>macaroni and cheese.</u>

Climax. In addition to parallelism, a second structural principle should be emphasized in connection with the series: **climax,** the arrangement of words or phrases or clauses in the order of increasing scope, length, or importance. Consider the three-part series in this sentence:

> With <u>his bright sunflowers, searing wheat fields and blazing
> yellow skies,</u> Vincent van Gogh was fanatic about light.
> —Paul Trachtman

This parallel series consists of three noun phrases functioning as the object of the preposition *with.* Notice also the climactic ordering of these phrases, starting with *sunflowers,* moving to *wheat fields,* and ending with *skies.* When you use climactic ordering, you might think of yourself as a photographer, shifting a camera's focus from close-up to wide angle. To get a sense of the effect when a sentence follows neither of these principles, compare Trachtman's sentence with the following version:

> With his searing wheat fields, bright sunflowers, and skies that are blazing yellow, Vincent van Gogh was fanatic about light.

In this example, the first two elements in the series begin with adjectives (*searing* and *bright*), but the third begins with a noun (*skies*). The third element makes the series unparallel; the climactic ordering has also been lost, the series now beginning with wheat fields instead of sunflowers.

Let's return now to coordination that *is* effective. The next two sentences, with coordination in a series, exemplify both principles, parallelism and climax:

> Thus political language has to consist largely of euphemism, question-begging and sheer cloudy vagueness.
>
> —George Orwell

Note that Orwell, like Trachtman, omits the serial comma, but his ordering is impeccable: first one, then two, then three words. The parallel items in the following sentence are also ordered according to length:

> Those of us who manage the public's dollar will be held to account—to spend wisely, reform bad habits, and do our business in the light of day—because only then can we restore the vital trust between a people and their government.
>
> —Barack Obama

You can probably hear the special rhythm in these examples with **triplets,** the three-item series. Clearly, there must be something special about triplets, a natural inclination of some kind that encourages writers to write them and satisfies the readers who read them.

FOR GROUP DISCUSSION

If you read extensively, you're bound to note many sentences that include parallel forms; sometimes, however, you'll find a sentence such as the following. Find the form that is not parallel with its partners.

> But it is her [Francine du Plessix Gray's] voice that says the most about her: deep, earthy and so in love with words that

her syllables roll up against one another like Vouvray on a vintner's tongue.

Did you choose the long phrase *so in love with words that her syllables roll up against one another like Vouvray on a vintner's tongue?* The principle of climax is certainly at work here. The last element in a series is often longer and more important than the other elements. Why do you suppose the writer, Marie Arana, used this form in her sentence? Would you agree that she broke the parallelism rule to good effect?

Coordination with Correlative Conjunctions

In Chapter 6 you will learn about "power words," words that command special attention; among them are the correlative conjunctions:

both–and	*either–or*
not only–but also	*neither–nor*

The power of the correlatives lies in their ability to change the rhythm and focus of the sentence and so set up different expectations in the reader. Read these two sentences aloud and listen to the change in your voice when you add *both:*

Individuals <u>and</u> nations must learn to think about the environment.

<u>Both</u> individuals <u>and</u> nations must learn to think about the environment.

The change may seem like a small one. But notice what the added *both* does: It shifts the emphasis from the predicate to the subject, which normally gets little, if any. Now the reader expects to read on about the response of individuals and nations. Here's another example of the difference that *both–and* can make in contrast to *and* alone. This is a revised version of a sentence you just read:

The power of the correlatives lies in their ability to change <u>both</u> the rhythm <u>and</u> the focus of the sentence and so set up different expectations in the reader.

If you listen carefully, you'll notice that the addition of *both* adds stress, or loudness, to *and*. The same kind of change in emphasis occurs with *not only–but also* (or *not only–but . . . as well*):

> As citizens of this global village, we must be concerned <u>not only</u> with our own health and safety <u>but</u> with the needs of others <u>as well</u>.
>
> As citizens of this global village, we must be concerned <u>not only</u> with our own health and safety <u>but also</u> with the needs of others.

In reading these two sentences aloud, you'll notice that in the second there is less emphasis on *others;* the main focus falls on *also*.

Probably the least common correlative is *neither–nor;* and it's probably accurate to say that inexperienced writers avoid it. But because it is rare, it sends a strong message, one that says the writer has constructed the sentence carefully:

> <u>Neither</u> individuals <u>nor</u> nations can afford to ignore what is happening to the environment.

The use of *both–and* carries a restriction the other correlatives do not have: It cannot connect full sentences. The other correlatives are more versatile in that they can connect both sentences and the units within the sentence.

> I should *either* spend more time studying *or* get a part-time job.
>
> *Either* I should spend more time studying, *or* I should get a part-time job.

As with other compound structures, the two parts connected by the correlatives will be parallel in structure: two noun phrases, two prepositional phrases, two verb phrases, and so on. In the case of correlative conjunctions, the problem of unparallel structure is usually easy to spot and easy to fix: It's a matter of paying attention to the conjunctions. *Either* signals that *or* is on the way—and your reader knows it! Just be sure that the same form follows both parts of the correlative, because that's what the reader is expecting. The writer of the following sentence suffered a lapse in attention:

> *I will **either** <u>take the train</u> **or** <u>the bus</u>.

Here we have a verb phrase (*take the train*) connected to a noun phrase (*the bus*). To correct this unparallel structure, simply move *either:*

> I will take **either** <u>the train</u> **or** <u>the bus</u>.

Now the same form, a noun phrase, follows both *either* and *or*.

EXERCISE 10

Revise the following sentences by substituting correlatives for the coordinating conjunctions. In your revisions, use all four of the correlatives at least once: (*both–and, either–or, neither–nor, not only–but also*).

1. Tea and coffee contain caffeine.

2. Caffeine quickens metabolism and increases the heart rate.

3. Some people drink coffee or tea, but not both.

4. Coffee and tea cannot make you intelligent, but a little caffeine can help you concentrate for a short period of time.

5. Japanese blue-collar workers work more hours per day than American workers do and typically do so with more dedication and energy.

6. Workers and schoolchildren in Japan put in more time than their American counterparts.

7. Blue-collar workers and students in the United States do not spend as much time at their respective jobs as their Japanese counterparts.

SUBJECT-VERB AGREEMENT

The topic of **subject–verb agreement** is often at issue in sentences that have compound subjects. The concept can perhaps best be illustrated by looking at examples where the subject and verb "disagree":

> We was at the movies last night.
>
> He don't work here anymore.

The subject-verb pairings in these sentences, though acceptable in some dialects, differ from what is expected in standard English—*We were; He doesn't*.

	Singular	**Plural**	**Singular**	**Plural**
1st	I was	we were	I do	we do
2nd	you were	you were	you do	you do
3rd	she was	they were	he does	they do

A comparison of these differences highlights the importance of understanding when to use the *-s* form of the verb, the third-person singular. The first comparison—*we was* versus *we were*—shows that in the nonstandard dialect, *was* is the only form of the verb *be* used to indicate past tense. In standard English, however, *be* has two forms for the past tense, both *was* and *were*. The second comparison—*don't* versus *doesn't*—reveals a similar pattern. The nonstandard dialect has just one form of negative *do* in the present tense (*don't*), whereas standard English has two (*don't* and *doesn't*). When your writing situation calls for standard English (not all writing situations do), be sure to use the two past-tense forms of *be* and the two present-tense forms of *do*.

In writing, too, the issue of subject–verb agreement is concerned with the *-s* form of the verb and the number (whether singular or plural) of the subject. In standard English, we use the *-s* form only when the subject is singular *and* third person (a subject that can be replaced by *he, she,* or *it*). But when subjects are compound, agreement can get a bit tricky.

When nouns or noun phrases in the subject position are joined by *and* or by the correlative *both–and,* the subject is plural:

> <u>My friends and relatives</u> **are** coming to the wedding.

However, the coordinating conjunction *or* and the correlatives *either–or* and *neither–nor* do not have the additive meaning of *and*. In compound subjects with these conjunctions, the verb is determined by the closer member of the pair:

> Neither the speaker nor <u>the listeners</u> **<u>were</u>** intimidated by the protestors.
> Either the class officers or <u>the faculty adviser</u> **<u>makes</u>** the final decision.

If the correct sentence sounds awkward because of the verb form, you can simply reverse the compound pair:

> Either the faculty adviser or <u>the class officers</u> **<u>make</u>** the final decision.

When both members of the pair are alike, of course, there is no question:

> Either <u>the president or the vice president</u> **is** going to introduce the speaker.
> Neither <u>the union members nor the management representatives</u> **<u>were</u>** willing to compromise.

For most verb forms, there is no decision to be made about subject–verb agreement; the issue arises only when the present tense *-s* form of the verb or auxiliary is involved. In the following sentences with the past tense, there is no choice:

> Either the class officers or the faculty adviser <u>made</u> the final decision.
>
> Either the faculty adviser or the class officers <u>made</u> the final decision.

Another situation that sometimes causes confusion about number—that is, whether the subject is singular or plural—occurs with subjects that include a phrase introduced by *in addition to* or *along with:*

> *The sidewalk, in addition to the driveway, need to be repaired.
>
> *Mike, along with his friend Emilio, often help out at the bakery on weekends.

These additions to the subject are parenthetical; they are not treated as part of the subject. In both sentences, the subjects are singular; the verb should be the *-s* form—*needs* and *helps.* To make the subject compound— to include the additions—the writer could use a coordinating conjunction, such as *and:*

> The sidewalk <u>and</u> the driveway <u>need</u> to be repaired.
>
> Mike <u>and</u> his friend Emilio often <u>help</u> out at the bakery on weekends.

EXERCISE 11

Choose the verb that agrees in number and in person with the subject. If a compound subject is joined by *either . . . or* or *neither . . . nor*, the verb should agree with the closer member.

1. The students in Biology 101 (goes/go) on a field trip each spring for a full day.

2. Either the students or the instructor (chooses/choose) a site in the region to explore.

3. Neither the instructor nor the students (goes/go) to any other classes that day.

4. A lunch, along with plenty of water, (is/are) essential for the trip.

5. A field guide, as well as a writer's notebook, (finds/find) a place in most students' backpacks.

COMPOUND SENTENCES

The sentence patterns you learned in Chapter 2 can also be called *clause patterns:* The two words **clause** and **sentence** are close in meaning. First, we'll define *clause* as a structure that contains a subject and a predicate. That definition, of course, conforms precisely to the illustration of *sentence* shown in Chapter 1. When a clause functions independently, we call it an **independent clause.** When it begins with a capital letter and ends with a period (or other terminal mark of punctuation), we call it a **simple sentence:**

> A weasel is wild.

As you well know, however, not all sentences in the English language are simple. Often we want to show that the ideas expressed in two independent clauses are related, so we join them together into a **compound sentence:**

> Acupuncture has been effective in healing muscular disorders, **and** it has no side effects.
>
> Acupuncture is cheaper than conventional medicine, **but** most Americans do not understand how it works.

The punctuation convention for compound sentences calls for a comma at the end of the first clause, signaling that another independent clause is on the way. Here, then, is the second punctuation rule in connection with coordination:

> **Use a comma before the coordinating conjunction joining the two independent clauses of a compound sentence.**

As you can see, it's important to understand exactly what it is you're compounding: If it's only two words or phrases within the sentence, then no comma is called for; if it's two independent clauses, then the conjunction needs a comma to send a signal to the reader that a second independent clause is on the way. It's not unusual to see in published works compound sentences without the comma, especially when both independent clauses are short. However, most professional writers follow the rule consistently.

◀ ### FOR GROUP DISCUSSION

You may remember hearing a rule for writers that warns, "Never begin a sentence with *and* or *but.*" Is it true? Does it accurately describe how writers write? Frankly, no. According to the fifteenth edition of *The Chicago*

Manual of Style, "a substantial percentage (often as many as 10 percent) of the sentences in first-rate writing begin with conjunctions" (193).

The reason for this common usage is that starting a sentence with a coordinating conjunction can provide a rhetorical punch, as in this example from the Introduction to *Earth: The Sequel* by Fred Krupp and Miriam Horn:

> A revolution is on the horizon: a wholesale transformation of the world economy and the way people live. This revolution will depend on industrial technology—capital-intensive, shovel-in-the-ground industries—and will almost certainly create the great fortunes of the twenty-first century. But this new industrial revolution holds a more important promise: securing the world against the dangers of global warming.

A. Rewrite their last sentence, following the so-called rule. Has your revision changed the impact of the sentence?

B. To see if the estimate of sentence-opening conjunctions given in *The Chicago Manual of Style* is accurate, check the textbooks or other readings you have done for your classes. Also check daily newspapers and/or weekly newsmagazines.

Conjunctive Adverbs and Transitional Phrases

In Chapter 5, on the topic of cohesion, you will read about *metadiscourse,* a term that refers to certain signals that help the reader understand the writer's message. Among the most useful of such signals are the conjunctive adverbs, also known as adverbial conjunctions. As their name suggests, conjunctive adverbs join sentences to form coordinate structures as other conjunctions do, but they do so in a different way. The following list includes some of the most common adverbs that function as sentence connectors:

Addition: moreover, furthermore, further, also
Time: meanwhile, then, afterwards, previously
Contrast: however, instead, rather
Result: therefore, consequently, thus
Concession: though
Reinforcement: indeed, nevertheless, still

Conjunctive adverbs differ from other conjunctions in that, like ordinary adverbs, most of them are movable; they need not only introduce their clause. It is that movability that makes them such an important tool for writers:

> We worked hard for the Consumer Party candidates; <u>however,</u> we knew they didn't stand a chance.
>
> We worked hard for the Consumer Party candidates; we knew, <u>however,</u> that they didn't stand a chance.
>
> We worked hard for the Consumer Party candidates; we knew they didn't stand a chance, <u>however.</u>

Bear in mind, though, that the farther along in the sentence the conjunctive adverb appears, the less value it has as a connector. If the reader needs the signal that the connector carries—such as the message of *however,* indicating that a contrast is coming—you will probably want the reader to get it in a timely fashion, not wait until the end, especially when the second clause is fairly long.

A different emphasis occurs when the conjunctive adverb is used with no punctuation. Read these pairs of sentences aloud and note where you put the main stress in the second clause of each:

> Our main speaker canceled at the last minute; the rally was <u>therefore</u> postponed until the following weekend.
>
> Our main speaker canceled at the last minute; the rally, <u>therefore,</u> was postponed until the following weekend.

In the versions *without* commas, it is the word *following* the conjunctive adverb that gets main stress; *with* commas, it's the word *preceding.*

This punctuation choice occurs with only a limited number of the conjunctive adverbs; most of them require the commas to send their message. And it's also important to recognize that without punctuation they lose some of their connective power, functioning more like adverbials, less like conjunctions. In the example without commas, *therefore* seems more like a modifier of the word *postponed* rather than a comment relating to the clause as a whole.

You'll also want to consider the tone that conjunctive adverbs tend to convey. Some of them—such as *moreover, nevertheless, therefore,* and even the fairly common *however*—may strike the reader as formal, perhaps even stiff. You can often diminish that formality by using coordinating conjunctions: Instead of *however,* use *but;* instead of *moreover,* use *and;* for *nevertheless,* use *yet.*

Many prepositional phrases are also used as sentence connectors. They are called **transitional phrases.** Note that they serve the same purposes as conjunctive adverbs:

> *Addition:* in addition to
> *Time:* in the meantime
> *Contrast:* in contrast, on the contrary
> *Result:* as a result, in the end
> *Concession:* of course, at any rate, at least
> *Reinforcement:* in fact, above all, in particular

And like conjunctive adverbs, many of these prepositional phrases can appear at various points in a sentence.

> The campaign contributions we had been counting on didn't materialize; <u>in fact,</u> the campaign was broke.
> The campaign contributions we had been counting on didn't materialize; the campaign, <u>in fact,</u> was broke.
> The campaign contributions we had been counting on didn't materialize; the campaign was broke, <u>in fact.</u>

Unless you want to stress the word following the connector, the rule to remember when using either conjunctive adverbs or transitional phrases is as follows:

> **Use commas to set off conjunctive adverbs and transitional phrases.**

Compound Sentences with Semicolons

You've seen a great many semicolons used in the discussions throughout these chapters. And in the previous section you saw them in sentences illustrating the use of conjunctive adverbs. However, you can't assume from these examples that you'll find them in great numbers everywhere. Some people manage to go through life without ever making their acquaintance. If you belong to that group of non-users, you can be sure of one thing: Your punctuation is not as effective as it could and should be. But take heart! The semicolon is easy to use.

In her book *Woe Is I,* Patricia T. O'Conner calls the semicolon the flashing red of punctuation traffic signals:

> If a comma is a yellow light and a period is a red light, the semicolon is a flashing red—one of those lights you drive through after a brief pause. (139)

Think of the semicolon as the equivalent of the comma-plus-conjunction that connects compound sentences. You could even put this relationship into a formula:

$$(, + and) = (;)$$

In the last section you saw semicolons in compound sentences with conjunctive adverbs, but don't get the idea that the conjunctive adverb is required. Semicolons can be used with no conjunction at all:

> There was silence; I stood awkwardly, then moved to the door.
> There was silence; white faces were looking strangely at me.
> —Richard Wright

In compound sentences like these, the semicolon sends a message to the reader: "Notice the connection." To understand the importance of the semicolon, imagine these sentences without the semicolons, with periods instead. The connection of the silence to what follows in each case would be lost.

These two uses of the semicolon to connect clauses—by itself and with a conjunctive adverb—are perhaps the most common; but there are times when you will want to use a coordinating conjunction along with the semicolon, as in this compound sentence you are reading. As you can see, the second clause includes a comma, so we use a semicolon before the conjunction *but* to signal clearly the boundary between the two independent clauses. In Chapter 10 you will read about the one other place we use the semicolon: to separate the parts of a series when the individual parts include punctuation of their own. Here's an example:

> The study of language includes three main areas: phonology, the study of sounds; morphology, the study of meaningful combinations of sounds; and syntax, the study of sentences.

Because each of the three items in the series includes an explanatory phrase set off by commas, the use of semicolons between them helps keep the reader on track.

Compound Sentences with Colons

Inexperienced writers often avoid using semicolons simply because they don't understand them; even less understood is the colon as a sentence connector. In Chapter 10 you will read about the colon in its more familiar role—as a signal of a list of items:

> Three committees were set up to plan the convention: program, finance, and local arrangements.

In this sentence the message of the colon is "Here it comes, the list of committees I promised."

In connecting two complete sentences, the message of the colon is similar. As with the list in the preceding example, the independent clause following a colon also completes or explains or illustrates the idea in the first clause:

> Rats and rabbits, to those who injected, weighed and dissected them, were little different from cultures in a petri dish: they were just things to manipulate and observe.
>
> —Steven Zak

> It's not that Japanese consumers are eager to throw their money away: to judge by the way shoppers prowl through the neighborhood supermarket and electronics store, they are extremely cost conscious.
>
> —James Fallows

> I came to a conclusion that I want to pass on to you, and I hope nobody gets too mad: Medical science does everything it can.
>
> —Carolyn See

The preceding examples are all taken from essays in popular magazines. The following sentence is from fiction:

> Jem and I found our father satisfactory: he played with us, read to us, and treated us with courteous detachment.
>
> —Harper Lee (*To Kill a Mockingbird*)

Notice how the first clause sets up an expectation in the reader. The colon says, "Here comes the information you're expecting," or "Here's what

I promised." In the second passage, the *not* in the first clause sets the reader up for a contrast in the second. In general, if you can mentally insert *namely* or *that is* or *in fact,* as you can in the preceding examples, you should consider using a colon to connect the sentences.

It's important to recognize that this way of connecting two clauses is quite different from the connection with semicolons. The two clauses connected with the semicolon have parallel ideas. And unless you include a signal to the contrary, your reader will expect the relationship to be an additive one, an *and* connection. If you try to replace the colon with *and,* you'll see that it won't work.

Two other common structures that the colon signals are questions and direct quotations:

> Everyone at the news conference wondered what was coming next: Would the senator actually admit her part in the cover-up?
> A Northwestern University psychiatrist explained the purpose of brain chemicals rather poetically: "A person's mood is like a symphony, and serotonin is like the conductor's baton."
>
> —*Time*

Another situation that calls for the colon as a signal, which you are probably familiar with, is the block quotation—the long indented quotation.

There is one detail of punctuation in these compound sentences that varies. Except in the case of the direct quotation, you have the choice of using either a capital or a lowercase letter following the colon. (The first word of a direct quotation following a colon is generally capitalized.) Some publications capitalize all independent clauses following colons (the style of this book); others capitalize only questions; some use lowercase for all independent clauses except direct quotations. Whichever style of punctuation you choose, be consistent.

Punctuation Pitfalls

If you've ever encountered a teacher's "CS" or "FS" or "RO" notation in the margin of an essay, you're in good company. The **comma splice** and the **fused sentence,** sometimes called a **run-on sentence,** are among the most common—and probably the most perplexing to teachers—of all the punctuation errors that writers make. They are perplexing because they are based on such a straightforward and common situation: a sentence with two independent clauses.

Consider again the sentence patterns you saw in Chapter 2—those simple *subject–verb–complement* sentences. When you write one of those—when you begin it with a capital letter and end it with a period—you've created an independent clause, actually a sentence that can stand on its own. It's true, of course, that most of the sentences we write aren't as simple as the bare sentence patterns—and often not as easy to identify. Every subject and every complement can be expanded with all sorts of structures; further, there are all shapes and sizes of adverbials that can be added to the beginning and the end of the sentence. So the key is first to recognize a sentence pattern when you see it—to recognize the boundaries of its various units—bearing in mind that certain units can themselves be clauses (which we'll discuss in more detail later). Let's examine again a sentence we discussed earlier in this chapter.

> Acupuncture has been effective in healing muscular disorders, **and** it has no side effects.

The punctuation in this sentence follows the highlighted rule you saw in the last section:

> **Use a comma before the coordinating conjunction joining the two independent clauses of a compound sentence.**

What happens if we leave out the conjunction?

> *Acupuncture has been effective in healing muscular disorders, it has no side effects.

We've produced a *comma splice*. In other words, we've spliced, or joined, two independent clauses together with a comma. But a comma alone is not strong enough: It needs the support of a conjunction. *Remember, we want the reader to know that another independent clause is coming.*

If you have ever committed a comma splice—left out the *and* (well, maybe *committed* is too strong a word!)—you may have done so for what you thought was a good reason: to create a tighter connection. The sentence may have sounded or looked better. It's true that sometimes the conjunction adds a certain flabbiness, and maybe the sentence would be better off without it. There is a solution, though, and it's often a good one—the semicolon. Notice how slim and trim the following sentence is with a semicolon instead of *and:*

> It's true that sometimes the conjunction adds a certain flabbiness; maybe the sentence would be better off without it.

In the version with the semicolon, the reader will give more emphasis to the second clause.

However, if we were feeling miserly and decided to leave out the semicolon as well, we would be creating a fused sentence—two sentences run together without any punctuation—another error best to avoid.

At this point you may be asking yourself, "How about the conjunction by itself? Is that ever allowed in a compound sentence?"

> *It's true that sometimes the conjunction adds a certain flabbiness and maybe the sentence would be better off without it.

Again, the wrong message—another fused sentence of sorts, although not as serious as the one with neither conjunction nor comma. The use of *and* without the comma tells the reader that a coordinate structure *within the sentence* is coming—not that a new independent clause is coming.

In an earlier section, you saw examples of the semicolon used to join sentences beginning with a conjunctive adverb or transitional phrase:

> We worked hard for the Consumer Party candidates; <u>however,</u> we knew that they didn't stand a chance.
>
> The campaign contributions we had been counting on didn't materialize; <u>in fact,</u> the campaign was broke.

Inexperienced writers sometimes use a comma in these sentences where the semicolon should be, thus creating a sentence with a comma splice. When you use a conjunctive adverb to begin a clause, be sure that it follows a semicolon (as shown previously) or a period (as in the following):

> We worked hard for the Consumer Party candidates. However, we knew that they didn't stand a chance.
>
> The campaign contributions we had been counting on didn't materialize. In fact, the campaign was broke.

It's certainly possible to find examples in both contemporary and older prose of two sentences, usually short ones, put together with the conjunction alone or with the comma alone—deliberate deviations from conventional punctuation practices. However, most academic and business writing assignments call for the compound sentence to follow the rules stated earlier—*comma-plus-conjunction* or *semicolon-plus-conjunctive adverb/transitional phrase*—so that the punctuation provides the reader with information about the kinds of structures that will come after it. These are the rules followed in this book.

The importance of accurate punctuation cannot be overemphasized. Not only will readers be guided efficiently through your ideas, they will also gain confidence in you as a writer—and as an authority on your topic. It's easy for a reader to conclude—perhaps subconsciously and, yes, perhaps unfairly—that slipshod punctuation equals slipshod thinking.

Your image, your credibility as a writer, can only be enhanced when you make accurate, effective, and helpful punctuation choices.

THE COMPOUND SENTENCE: PUNCTUATION REVIEW

We have seen five styles of punctuation for joining the clauses in compound sentences. Every writer should understand all five and be able to use them effectively.

1. COMMA-PLUS-CONJUNCTION

> Every ride at an amusement park has a history, and the history of the roller coaster begins with the Russian Ice Slides of the seventeenth century.

Remember that the comma by itself is not strong enough to make that connection; without the conjunction, the result is a comma splice. Without either the conjunction or the comma, the sentence becomes a fused sentence.

2. SEMICOLON

> Every ride at an amusement park has a history; the history of the roller coaster begins with the Russian Ice Slides of the seventeenth century.

You can think of this connection as a tighter version of the comma with *and.*

3. SEMICOLON-PLUS-CONJUNCTION

> Every ride at an amusement park has a history; and the history of the roller coaster begins with the Russian Ice Slides of the seventeenth century, located primarily in the area around present-day St. Petersburg.

A semicolon, instead of a comma, is used between two independent clauses, especially when one of the clauses already includes a comma.

4. SEMICOLON-PLUS-CONJUNCTIVE ADVERB/TRANSITIONAL PHRASE

The inclusion of a conjunctive adverb has the advantage of being movable, so you can manipulate the rhythm pattern to focus the emphasis on different words. You can decide how the reader reads the sentence:

> Every ride at an amusement park has a history; <u>however,</u> the roller coaster has one of the most unusual stories to tell.

Every ride at an amusement park has a history; the roller coaster, <u>however,</u> has one of the most unusual stories to tell.

Strong stress falls on the word preceding the comma.

5. Colon

Many of the ice slides built in Russia were quite elaborate: Some rose to eighty feet and accommodated several large sleds at once.

Here the colon is saying, "Here it comes, the elaboration you're expecting." Note that the full sentence following the colon does not always begin with a capital letter, as it does here. Some publications prefer lowercase in this position.

These, then, are the five ways we connect the two clauses of a compound sentence. Be sure to take time to understand all of them. Using them correctly also means understanding the structure of clauses, their parameters. These two concepts—the structure of clauses and the conventions for connecting them—are basic tools that every writer needs for every writing task.

Exercise 12

Add punctuation to the following passages, if necessary. In some cases there may be more than one possibility.

1. The Smithsonian Institution comprises nineteen museums nine research centers and the National Zoo.

2. Most of the museums are located on the National Mall in Washington, DC but the National Air and Space Museum has two locations.

3. You can find one of the museums on the National Mall and the other near Dulles International Airport.

4. The National Air and Space Museum on the National Mall contains in its collection the Wright Flyer Sputnik 1 and the Apollo 11 lunar module.

5. The museum on the National Mall opened in 1976 however, its collection was so large that an additional museum was built near Dulles International Airport.

6. Visitors to the Steven F. Udvar-Hazy Center can view the Boeing B-29 Superfortress *Enola Gay* the MacCready *Gossamer Albatross* and the space shuttle *Enterprise*.

7. Together, these two museums maintain a vast collection of air- and spacecraft they also sponsor vital research into aviation and related technologies.

8. These museums share the same mission they are dedicated to the commemoration of the nation's aeronautic history.

9. Approximately 260 employees work at the museums but the museums could not open their doors without the help of their 500 volunteers, whose tasks range from staffing the information desk to serving as docents.

10. Admission to both these spectacular museums is free but donations are accepted.

SUBORDINATION: THE DEPENDENT CLAUSES

So far we've discussed sentences in terms of independent clauses: The simple sentence consists of one independent clause; the compound sentence consists of two, sometimes three or more, independent clauses. But a clause need not be independent. It can also function within a sentence as a **dependent clause,** also called a *subordinate clause.*

In Chapter 2 we saw examples of dependent clauses functioning as adverbials:

Because a weasel is wild, it should be approached with great caution.

Yesterday the teacher called the students lazy when they complained about their assignment.

Remember that movability is a good clue that a structure is functioning as an adverbial. And as you can see in the first example, when an adverbial clause opens the sentence, it is followed by a comma. We'll discuss this comma rule in more depth in Chapter 8.

Another type of dependent clause functions adjectivally, as the modifier of a noun. In the following sentence a *who*-clause is a modifier of the subject *the man:*

The man who lives upstairs bothers the neighbors.

Again you can recognize the three units of the sentence when you substitute pronouns for the noun phrases:

He	bothers	them.
(subject)	(verb)	(object)

Recall that a pronoun stands in for the entire noun phrase, including all the modifiers. Because this type of dependent clause functions as an adjective to modify a noun, it is called an **adjectival clause.** Like the prepositional phrases you saw in Chapter 1, the adjectival clause follows the headword of the noun phrase:

the man	who lives upstairs
our new neighbors	across the hall

Dependent clauses can also function as **nominals,** filling noun phrase positions. For example, we could use our original weasel clause as a direct object following a transitive verb like *say,* creating a Pattern 5 sentence:

Annie Dillard says *that a weasel is wild.*

This sentence has the same three units as this sample Pattern 5 sentence from Chapter 2:

My roommate	borrowed	my laptop.
Annie Dillard	says	something.

But in the Annie Dillard sentence, the "something" in the direct object position is a clause, not a noun phrase. This type of dependent clause is called a **nominal clause** because it functions as a noun. Note that the term *nominal,* the *–al* form of *noun,* is the name of a function, not a form, just as *adverbial* and *adjectival* are. (In Chapter 1 you learned that the terms *adverbial* and *adjectival* apply to all forms that function the way adverbs and adjectives do.)

These then are the three roles that dependent clauses fill in sentences, their three functions: adverbial, adjectival, and nominal. You will learn more about the functional categories in Chapters 8, 9, and 10.

EXERCISE 13

In his textbook *Classical Rhetoric for the Modern Student,* Professor Edward P. J. Corbett reports on a study of style he conducted in his Honors Freshman English class. His students compared the length of their own sentences and paragraphs with those of a professional writer, F. L. Lucas. They selected eight paragraphs from an essay by Lucas, avoiding short transitional paragraphs and any that contained two or more sentences of quoted material. Then they calculated the average number of words per sentence (20.8) and the average number of sentences per paragraph (7.6). In addition, they calculated the percentage of sentences that were ten words longer than the average (17 percent) and the percentage that were five words shorter than average (40 percent). Then they did the same with an expository theme of their own.

We cannot, of course, judge the effectiveness of a paragraph on the basis of statistics. However, data gathered can sometimes show us our strengths (or perhaps bad habits); they can also point out structures we might consider using.

Do a contrastive study of your own writing style and that of a professional, following Professor Corbett's model. For the analysis, choose eight paragraphs from an article published in a magazine (e.g., *Harper's, Atlantic Monthly, The New Yorker, Smithsonian, Nature*) or from an article published in a professional journal in your major field. For purposes of this analysis, a sentence is defined as "a group of words beginning with a capital letter and ending with some mark of end punctuation." In some cases these sentences will be fragments; even so, you should include them in your analysis. However, among the eight do not include short transitional paragraphs or any paragraph that contains two or more sentences of quoted material. Do the same analysis with eight paragraphs from an expository essay of your own.

	PROFESSIONAL	STUDENT
1. Total number of words	_____	_____
2. Total number of sentences	_____	_____
3. Longest sentence (in # of words)	_____	_____
4. Shortest sentence (in # of words)	_____	_____
5. Average sentence length	_____	_____
6. Number of sentences with more than ten words *over* the average length	_____	_____
7. Percentage of sentences with more than ten words *over* the average	_____	_____
8. Number of sentences with more than five words *below* the average	_____	_____
9. Percentage of sentences with more than five words *below* the average	_____	_____
10. Paragraph length	_____	_____
longest paragraph (in # of sentences)	_____	_____
shortest paragraph (in # of sentences)	_____	_____
average paragraph (in # of sentences)	_____	_____

REVISING COMPOUND STRUCTURES

In compound sentences, as well as sentences with compound predicates, verb forms that are unparallel can sometimes produce a kind of fuzziness. Notice in the following sentence that only one of the two verbs includes an auxiliary:

> Experts in sports medicine <u>emphasize</u> the importance of water intake and <u>are recommending</u> a half-ounce per day for every pound of body weight.

A related source of fuzziness can occur in the compound sentence. Our example could easily be turned into a compound sentence with the simple addition of a second subject:

> Experts in sports medicine emphasize the importance of water intake , and
>
> <u>they</u> are recommending a half-ounce per day for every pound of body weight.

The sentence is now parallel in *form*. But a question remains: Are the two *ideas* parallel? Do they belong together as equal partners? (And remember, that's what the message of *and* is: "These two structures are equal partners.")

If the two ideas were fuzzy partners as predicates—a judgment suggested by the form of the verbs—then they are just as likely to be fuzzy partners as sentences. The problem is not just that one verb has an auxiliary and the other doesn't (*are recommending* and *emphasize*); it's the underlying reason for that difference. We generally use the simple present tense (*emphasize*) to describe an accepted truth or timeless quality; we use the present progressive tense (*are recommending*) for an ongoing action. It's not that the two ideas don't belong together: They do—but not as equal partners. *And* is simply the wrong connection.

Because the sentence is out of context, we don't know which of the two ideas should be emphasized, but a good guess would be the recommendation:

> Experts in sports medicine, who emphasize the importance of water intake, are recommending a half-ounce per day for every pound of body weight.

Here we've used a dependent clause for one of the two ideas. Another possibility is the **participial phrase** to open the sentence. (An *-ing* verb used as an adjective is called a **participle** or, as in this case, a participial phrase.)

> Emphasizing the importance of water intake, experts in sports medicine recommend a half-ounce per day for every pound of body weight.

We will look at both of these noun modifiers—the adjectival clause and the participial phrase—in Chapter 9.

You may find it helpful to think in terms of **foregrounding** and **backgrounding** when you have two ideas to combine. Which idea should get the foreground, the prominence of the main clause? Which should be thought of as background and given the supporting role of the dependent clause? This concept is related to the concept of known and new information, which you will study in the next chapter.

The following sentence illustrates another common coordination problem: a fact and a conclusion based on that fact put together as parallel ideas.

> The African killer bees are less predictable than European bees and tend to attack in vast swarms.

One clue that the two predicates don't belong together is a difference in verb classes: linking and transitive. Again, we need context to know which idea should get the main focus, which idea should be foreground, and which should be treated as the background:

> The African killer bees, which are less predictable than European bees, tend to attack in vast swarms.
>
> The African killer bees, which tend to attack in vast swarms, are less predictable than European bees.

A mismatch in verb forms certainly doesn't guarantee a problem, but it's the kind of sentence you'll want to notice when you're revising.

EXERCISE 14

Revise the following sentences, paying particular attention to the unparallel structures.

1. At the new recreation center, students have the privilege of deciding whether to lift weights or swimming in an Olympic-size pool.

2. The Baltimore Orioles' stadium at Camden Yards has all the virtues of the beloved ballparks of another era and is in the great tradition of classic baseball architecture.

3. I neither enjoy flying across the country nor particularly want to take the train.

4. The movie's starting time and whether we could afford the tickets were both more important to us than were the opinions of the reviewers.

5. The academic adviser introduced a number of programs and said that we could make individual appointments to see her.

6. Lance Armstrong won the Tour de France seven times but is also known for his philanthropy.

7. I almost never watch television: There is either nothing on that appeals to me, or the picture disappears at a crucial moment.

8. Blue whales are the largest of all animals and up to 80 percent of them congregate seasonally in Antarctic waters.

FOR GROUP DISCUSSION

The following excerpt is from Malcolm Gladwell's *Outliers: The Story of Success*. Comment on the uses of coordination, subordination, and parallelism. Be sure to go beyond finding examples to discuss the effects the author's choices have on his message and on you, the reader.

You can't buy your way into Major Junior A hockey. It doesn't matter who your father or mother is, or who your grandfather was, or what business your family is in. Nor does it matter if you live in the most remote corner of the most northerly province in Canada. If you have ability, the vast network of hockey scouts and talent spotters will find you, and if you are willing to work to develop that ability, the system will reward you. Success in hockey is based on *individual merit*—and both of these words are important. Players are judged on their own performance, not on anyone else's, and on the basis of their ability, not on some other arbitrary fact.
Or are they?

KEY TERMS

Adjectival clause
Backgrounding
Clause
Climax
Colon
Comma
Comma splice
Compound sentence
Conjunction
Conjunctive adverb
Coordinating
    conjunction
Coordination

Correlative
    conjunction
Dependent clause
Foregrounding
Fused sentence
Gerund
Independent clause
Nominal
Nominal clause
Parallelism
Parallel structure
Participial phrase
Participle

Run-on sentence
Semicolon
Sentence
Serial comma
Series
Simple sentence
Subject–verb
    agreement
Subordinating
    conjunction
Subordination
Transitional phrase
Triplet

RHETORICAL REMINDERS

Parallelism

Do the coordinate structures within the sentence belong together? (Are the ideas equal? Are the forms the same?)

Climax

When writing a series, have I ordered phrases or clauses in the order of increasing importance, scope, or length?

Coordinating Conjunctions

Have I used coordinating conjunctions to begin sentences when I would like to stress addition or contrast?

Correlatives

Have I taken advantage of the strong focus that the correlatives provide: *either–or, neither–nor, both–and, not only–but also?*

Conjunctive Adverbs

Have I used the versatile conjunctive adverbs to good advantage?

Have I placed them where I want the reader to focus?

Colons

Have I used the colon to connect those sentences that set up an expectation in the reader?

PUNCTUATION REMINDERS

Have I remembered that in the case of a two-part compound within the sentence no comma is required?

Have I used commas between elements in a series?

Have I used a comma with the conjunction joining the two independent clauses of a compound sentence?

Have I used commas to set off conjunctive adverbs and transitional phrases, especially when they begin a clause?

Have I used a comma after a dependent clause at the beginning of a sentence?

Have I made good use of a semicolon to connect clauses when it would effectively signal a close connection?

Have I used a colon effectively to signal the expected information that follows in a second independent clause?

Have I used a dash (or dashes) to lighten the comma load?

PART II

Controlling the Message

Good prose is a kind of speech, more deliberate and shapely than the words we utter aloud, yet still akin to the living voice.
—SCOTT RUSSELL SANDERS

The writer's toolkit that you brought to this course already had a good many tools in it. As you studied the previous four chapters, you learned the names of many of those tools, along with some new ones. You can think of the next three chapters as the training manual for their use:

Chapter 5: Cohesion
Chapter 6: Sentence Rhythm
Chapter 7: The Writer's Voice

These three chapters all focus on helping you gain control of your prose and its effects on your reader: controlling your message. They will help you feel confident in making choices as you draft and revise. And having that control, that confidence, means more than simply avoiding error: It means creating sentences that flow, that work together to send your readers the message you want them to hear.

In these chapters, you will learn the *what*s and the *whys*—what options are available to you and why they have the effects they do. By the end of Chapter 7, you'll be able to use your tools to develop your own repertoire of writer's voices, one to suit each of the writing situations you encounter.

CHAPTER 5

Cohesion

CHAPTER PREVIEW

Cohesion refers to the connection of sentences to one another, to the flow of a text, to the ways in which a paragraph of separate sentences becomes a unified whole. In Chapter 4 we discussed the role coordinating conjunctions, subordinating conjunctions, conjunctive adverbs, and transitional phrases play in connecting clauses. They may signal that the content in the second of two adjoining clauses contrasts with the content in the first. *But, while, however*, and *on the contrary* all indicate contrast. Other connections commonly signaled by conjunctions, conjunctive adverbs, and transitional phrases include addition, result, time, concession, and reinforcement.

In our examination of cohesion in this chapter, we first look at **reader expectation,** which means, simply, imagining yourself—you, as writer—in your reader's shoes. Then we examine three important features of cohesive writing:

- **Repetition:** key words and phrases that keep the reader on course.
- The **known-new contract:** a simple but powerful concept that reflects one aspect of reader expectation—that a sentence will have both known, or old, information as well as new and that the known information will precede the new.
- **Parallelism:** the repetition of structures of the same form for purposes of clarity and emphasis. In the previous chapter you looked for parallel forms within a sentence; in this chapter you will study parallel forms across sentences.

By studying these topics, you are essentially learning to put labels on features of the language that often make the difference between merely adequate prose and genuinely effective prose. When you recognize them and learn to manipulate them, they become writing tools at your disposal.

In every aspect of rhetoric—especially in the matter of connections—the writer must keep the reader and the reader's expectations in mind. So before taking up the separate features of cohesion, we will look at this important concept affecting all the connections: reader expectation.

READER EXPECTATION

Have you ever come across a teacher's "awk" noted in the margin of a written assignment, or have you yourself ever judged a piece of writing as awkward? Perhaps in reading a composition of your own or one written by a classmate, you have felt that something was amiss—but you couldn't quite put your finger on the something. Such problems can often be traced to thwarted expectations. Something may have struck you as awkward simply because you weren't expecting it.

Both in reading and in conversation our language is loaded with expectations; we have a sense of direction about language. Although we may not know exactly what's coming next, when we hear it—or read it—we recognize if it's appropriate. It's when the ideas take an unexpected turn that the "awk" response can set in, when a passage fails to fit that expectation, that sense of appropriateness: "I didn't know exactly what was coming next—but I certainly didn't expect *that!*"

In conversation, we can call a halt to the speaker: "Wait! What was that you just said?" But as readers, we don't have that option. Instead, we find ourselves thinking, "Why am I reading this now?" Even though it's only a fleeting thought, it doesn't take many such interruptions—the pause, the second thought, the backtracking—to obstruct the cohesive flow of a piece of writing.

Where do a reader's expectations come from? Obviously, from what has gone before, from the prior text, or, in the case of an opening paragraph, from the title or, possibly, from the author's reputation. Within a paragraph, reader expectation begins with the opening sentence. The writer, of course, has all manner of possibilities for setting up that expectation. The first sentence of this paragraph, because it is a question, sets up the expectation of an answer—or perhaps a second question.

Following is the opening sentence from a paragraph in an article about the "most glamorous sweepstakes in sports"—the Triple Crown of thoroughbred racing. This paragraph follows the article's opening section discussing the eleven horses that have successfully swept the three races of the Triple Crown since its inception in 1914, the most recent being

Affirmed in 1978. The paragraph is preceded by a subheading: "Three races become the ultimate test."

> The sweep is so rare and difficult because each race has unique demands and the series as a whole requires unusual ruggedness.

This opening sentence has no doubt set up an expectation in you about what is coming next, something about the difficulties, demands, and/or ruggedness of the Triple Crown sweep. Now read the complete paragraph:

> The sweep is so rare and difficult because each race has unique demands and the series as a whole requires unusual ruggedness. Racehorses usually do best with about a month between races. In the Triple Crown they must race three times in 36 days, over three different tracks, and at three different distances, all longer than most have ever tried before.
> —Steven Crist (*USAir Magazine*)

That second sentence is surely a letdown: We were expecting something else. The topic has shifted. Not that this new topic is unimportant. But the writer did not prepare us to expect this shift from the ruggedness of the race to the ideal interval between races.

The effective topic sentence nearly always suggests the direction the paragraph will take, calling up a response in the reader: "Prove it" or "Tell me more." The following sentence opens a paragraph in *Time* about the friendship between Abraham Lincoln and Frederick Douglass, the third paragraph in an article by John Stauffer entitled "Across the Great Divide":

> Despite the immense racial gulf separating them, Lincoln and Douglass had a lot in common.

After reading that statement, we expect to read facts that prove the point. The writer meets our expectations, first with what we might call a subtopic sentence and then the supporting details:

> They were the two preeminent self-made men of their era. Lincoln was born dirt poor, had less than a year of formal schooling and became one of the nation's greatest Presidents. Douglass spent the first 20 years of his life as a slave, had no formal schooling— in fact, his masters forbade him to read or write—and became one of the nation's greatest writers and activists.

The paragraph ends with two additional sentences about Douglass as writer and activist. As you can see, the promise of the topic sentence has been kept. It led us to believe we would be given proof of its proposition—and the rest of the paragraph does just that.

While you're in the early drafting stage of your essay, you have lots of details to think about: deciding which ideas should be emphasized, which main ideas require support, and which words convey meaning most effectively. At this early stage the response of your reader may not even occur to you. But certainly at the various revision stages along the way—and, by the way, revision does go on all the time—you'll want to think about the reader's expectations.

Remember that, as with many other facets of language, a reader's expectations are not necessarily conscious thoughts. A thwarted expectation may constitute only a fleeting break in concentration, a momentary blip in the flow. But remember, too, it's that blip that produces the "awk."

Active readers do more than simply process the words and meanings of a particular sentence as they are reading it. They also fit the ideas of the current sentence into what they already know: knowledge garnered both from previous sentences and from their own experience. At the same time, they are developing further expectations.

To become aware of the reader's expectations means to put yourself in the reader's shoes—or head. It requires the ability to read your own ideas objectively, to see and hear your own words as someone else might read them. All the sections that follow in this chapter, covering various features of cohesion, emphasize this relationship between writer and reader.

FOR GROUP DISCUSSION

1. Look again at the weasel paragraph at the opening of Chapter 2. Delete the second sentence, the question. Discuss how that deletion alters reader expectation. In what way does the presence of the question change the expectation set up by the opening sentence? Compose an alternative second sentence in the form of a statement, rather than a question. Compare your version to Dillard's in terms of its effect on a reader's expectation.

2. Revise the second sentence of the Triple Crown paragraph to eliminate that blip of awkwardness. In other words, prepare the reader for the information about the time between races; prepare the reader to expect it.

3. The following excerpt comes from a paragraph in *The Life and Wars of General Phil Sheridan* by Roy Morris, Jr. For this exercise, the excerpt is divided into four separate sentences. Take a slip of paper and cover all the sentences but the first. Then, read the first and discuss what you expect to follow. Do the same with the second and third sentences. Are the sentences in this excerpt cohesive? Is there anything that could be done to make them more cohesive?

Before 1870, large buffalo herds still roamed the Southern plains, and many thousands of Native people still lived as they preferred, with the buffalo at the base of their economies.

The slaughter of the vast buffalo herd that roamed the plains and prairies until the 1840s reached a million animals a year during the 1870s.

Along the newly opened tracks, the railroads ran special excursions from which self-styled sportsmen shot buffalo from the comfort of their seats.

General Phil Sheridan remarked that the buffalo hunters had done more in two years to defeat the Indians than the entire regular Army had been able to do in the previous thirty years.

REPETITION

Instead of "Repetition," this discussion could be headed **"Lexical Cohesion,"** a term that refers to the contribution of particular words to the cohesion, or continuity, of text. (*Lexicon,* the noun form of *lexical,* means the words of the language; you can think of your lexicon as the dictionary in your head.) The repetition of words from one sentence to another is an obvious cohesive link, one that logically occurs in a paragraph on a particular topic.

In *Constructing Texts,* George Dillon characterizes the conflicting advice about repetition that student writers often encounter as a "no-man's land":

> [A] no-man's-land where they are caught in the crossfire of Never Use the Same Word Twice on a Page and Repeat Key Terms, Use Your Thesaurus to Find Synonyms and Avoid Needless ('Elegant') Variation. (p. 96)

Dillon notes that the journalism class is more often the source of "Never Use the Same Word Twice" and the English class the source of "Repeat Key Terms." He points out that sportswriters are especially good at avoiding repetition, at finding synonyms. In the following paragraph from a *New York Times* description of the 2009 Super Bowl, notice the variety of verbs:

> On the Steelers' first drive, on the offense's second play, Roethlisberger <u>faked</u> a handoff to Willie Parker, <u>rolled</u> right and <u>fired</u> a strike to receiver Hines Ward that <u>gained</u> 38 yards. Two plays later, he <u>found</u> tight end Heath Miller for 21 yards up a seam on the left side of the field.

—Greg Bishop

Here is another example from the *Times*, a paragraph from the Associated Press's "National League Roundup" column about a Cubs-Cardinals game:

> [Derrek Lee's] two-run shot off Matt Morris (11–3) with two outs in the fifth sailed over the visitors' bullpen in left before clanging off a guardrail, a drive estimated at 421 feet that put the Cubs ahead, 5–3. Morris gave up all three homers and has allowed 10 this season after surrendering 35 last year.

In the first sentence, the batter's successful hit is referred to as both a *shot,* and a *drive;* and the three verbs in the last sentence—*gave up, has allowed, surrendering*—are all synonyms for delivering a home-run pitch. In fact, among the major word classes in the paragraph—nouns, verbs, adjective, and adverbs—there's not a single repeated word!

It's not only the sports reporters who avoid repetition. News writers in other departments also rely on synonyms. During the 2008 election campaign, for example, we often read news reports that started off with "John McCain," then changed to "the Republican candidate," then "the nominee," then "the senator from Arizona" in successive sentences or paragraphs. And political writers often use "the White House," "the administration," and "the executive branch" as alternatives to "the president."

On the other hand, you'll find that the paragraphs you've been reading in this textbook reflect the English-class advice that Dillon identifies: "Repeat Key Terms." For example, the second paragraph in Chapter 2, headed "Chapter Preview," includes the word *sentence* eight times in its five sentences and the word *pattern* three times, with no synonyms for either word—simply because there are no synonyms that would do the job as well. And, of course, it makes sense to repeat key concepts in a book designed to teach those concepts. But you'll also find from time to time alternative phrasing for the sake of variety or for the purpose of adding a new dimension to the discussion. In the writing you do for your English class, the best advice is probably the middle ground. It would certainly be a mistake to conclude that repetition should be avoided. In fact, the opposite is true: Repetition strengthens cohesion.

But what happens when your teacher writes "rep" in the margin of your essay, a comment usually aimed at unnecessary repetition? How can you tell the difference between the good kind, the repetition that enhances cohesion, and the kind that calls negative attention to itself? Unnecessary repetition goes by the name of **redundancy.** It's possible that the redundant word the teacher noticed is part of a redundant sentence, one that adds nothing new to the discussion. As you'll read in the next section, most sentences contain both known (old) and new information. The lack of new information may be the source of that "rep" comment.

Lexical cohesion also refers to synonyms and other related words, not just actual repetition: *birds/robins, rodents/mice, meal/supper, friend/companion, vacation/trip/holiday.* And of course our grammar itself calls for the use of pronouns in lieu of repeating a noun or noun phrase. Such substitutes constitute strong cohesive ties.

THE KNOWN-NEW CONTRACT

Seeing the sentence as a series of units, as you did in Chapter 2, will help you understand the feature of cohesion called the **known–new contract.** It relates to both what the reader knows and what the reader expects.

The first sentence in a paragraph, like the first paragraph of a chapter or an essay, sets up expectations in the reader about what is coming. Certainly one of those expectations is that the following sentences will stick to the topic. Another is that the sentence will have new information, not just a repeat of what the reader already knows.

The term *known-new* also describes the most common order for that information, with the known information coming first, generally in the subject position, and the new information—the reason for the sentence—in the predicate, where the main emphasis of the sentence naturally occurs. This pattern is obvious in the Lincoln/Douglass paragraph you read earlier in this chapter, with *Lincoln and Douglass* as the subject of the topic sentence, *they* as the subject of the second, and their separate names as subjects in the sentences that follow. In the Triple Crown paragraph, that blip of awkwardness we encountered occurred in the subject position of the second sentence. We expected a known subject, old information, such as *each race;* instead we encountered *racehorses.*

The repeated known information is not always repeated in the exact words, as it is in the Lincoln/Douglass example—as the sports reports in the preceding section clearly demonstrate. We saw another example in the paragraph about dams in Chapter 2, where the known information in the second sentence is a paraphrase of the topic in the first:

> Shaping up as an important milestone is <u>the demolition of two large dams</u> in Washington State's Elwha River, which flows from the mountains of Olympic National Park into the Juan de Fuca Strait. <u>Their removal</u>, scheduled to begin in 2008, would occur in stages, and if it goes as planned, the Pacific Northwest will lose only a tiny amount of hydropower and regain a legendary salmon fishery.

In other words, *removal* is another way of saying *demolition.*

The Lincoln/Douglass example illustrates a common pattern wherein the repeated topic, information that the reader knows, remains fairly constant throughout the paragraph, in subject position. In some paragraphs, however, the new information that appears in the predicate of one sentence becomes the known information in the next, functioning as the subject. Here, for example, is a newspaper paragraph written by a meteorologist in response to a reader's question about thunderstorms; it begins with a one-sentence paragraph:

> Thunderstorms can be categorized as single cell or multicell.

> Basically, *a single-cell thunderstorm* is the lone thunderstorm that forms <u>on a hot humid day</u>. The *heat and humidity of the day* is the only trigger for the storm. This type of storm forms in an environment with little difference in the wind speed and direction—or wind shear—between the surface and cloud level.
> —Joe Murgo (*Centre Daily Times*)

Here's another paragraph in which you can find known-new links:

> This desire to deepen my alternate language [Ojibwe] puts me in an odd relationship to my first love, <u>English</u>. *It* is, after all, the language stuffed into my mother's ancestors' mouths. English is the reason she didn't speak her native language and the reason I can barely limp along in mine. English is <u>an all-devouring language that has moved across North America like the fabulous plagues of locusts that darkened the sky and devoured even the handles of rakes and hoes</u>. Yet *the omnivorous nature of a colonial language* is a writer's gift. Raised in the English language, I partake of a mongrel feast.
> —Louise Erdrich ("Two Languages in Mind, but Just One in the Heart")

The ⟶ in these examples highlight this pattern: The new information in the predicate of one sentence (underlined) becomes the known information (italicized) in the next one.

In another paragraph pattern, or information pattern, the proposition in the topic sentence is followed by supporting details suggested by the topic and expected by the reader. This pattern of development is fairly standard for writing various kinds of description, where the topic sentence sets up the expectation of the details that will prove its point, specific examples to support the generalization in the topic sentence:

> *Our trip to Florida for spring break* turned out to be a disaster. <u>The hotel room</u> we rented was miserable—shabby and stuffy and downright depressing. <u>The food</u> we could afford made our dining hall remembrances from campus seem positively gourmet. <u>The daily transportation</u> to the beach we had been promised showed up only once and even then was an hour late. . . .

Here the subjects of the supporting sentences are what we can think of as subtopics of the main subject, "our trip to Florida for spring break." Paragraphs like this one generally cry out for more details, and the place to add them is under those subtopic sentences, with specifics of the room and the food and other events that make the trip come alive for the reader—in other words, another layer of detail. If, after finishing the disaster details, you decide to add some happy events of the trip, either in the same paragraph or in the next one (assuming there were indeed some happy events), you'll have to signal that change to your reader with "on the other hand" or "however" or "but" or some other indication that you're shifting gears.

If you are writing a descriptive essay about your apartment, perhaps to let a future roommate know what to expect, chances are you'd use this same pattern. You might begin with an overall assessment of the apartment's adequacy or inadequacy, its efficiency or lack thereof, in your topic sentence. The subjects of the sentences that follow would support that assessment with details about cost, location, furnishings, neighbors, and so on.

It might appear that the sentences of such a paragraph, like those in the description of spring break, contain no known information, when each brings up a new topic, or subtopic. But in both cases the subtopics really are known information; they are all part of the domain, the sphere, of apartment living—or of spring breaks in Florida. We can think of them as essentially given information, information that a reader can be expected to recognize as relevant.

FOR GROUP DISCUSSION

The following paragraphs are from Chapter 15 of *Undaunted Courage* by Stephen E. Ambrose, the story of the Lewis and Clark expedition. The passage here describes an event in October 1804, a year into the trip. As you read the sentences, note the information patterns and cohesive ties that Ambrose has used. You might begin by marking the known information in each sentence and noting its connection to the preceding text:

> Beginning in October, as the expedition made its way through present northern South Dakota, it passed numerous abandoned villages, composed of earth-lodge dwellings and cultivated fields. Some of the fields, although unattended, still had squash and corn growing in them. These had once been home to the mighty Arikara tribe. About thirty thousand persons strong in the year the United States won its independence, the tribe had been reduced by smallpox epidemics in the 1780s to not much more than one-fifth that size. Another epidemic

swept through in 1803–4, devastating the tribe. What had been eighteen villages the previous year had been reduced to three by the time Lewis arrived.

EXERCISE 15

Revise the following passages to improve their cohesion. Think especially about reader expectation and the known-new contract.

1. The Gateway Arch at the edge of the Mississippi River in St. Louis is the world's tallest monument. Eero Saarinen designed the stainless steel structure that commemorates the Westward Movement.

2. Psychologists believe that color conveys emotional messages. Advertisers routinely manipulate consumers using color psychology. The pure white backgrounds and bold primary colors of detergent boxes are thought to influence buyers. Cleanliness and strength are associated with those colors.

3. The relentless heat of California's great Central Valley makes the summer almost unbearable at times. Over 110° is not an unusual temperature reading from June through September. Bakersfield often records the hottest temperature in the valley.

4. Getting chilled or getting your feet wet won't cause a cold. Weather is not the culprit that causes the common cold. Viruses are to blame.

5. The federal witness-protection service began in 1968. The U.S. Marshal Service directs the program. Over four thousand people have been relocated under the program. New identities are created for people in the program. The people are in extreme danger because they have testified against criminals.

The Role of Pronouns

Personal Pronouns. Perhaps our most common known element, equally as strong as the repeated noun phrase, is the pronoun. In Chapter 1, you'll recall, we used personal pronouns—*he, she, it, they, we*—to identify the boundaries of noun phrase units. When we use those pronouns in writing (and we often do use a pronoun instead of repeating a noun phrase), we call that noun phrase the pronoun's **antecedent.** You can think of the antecedent as the pronoun's back-up system. And because it has that back-up noun phrase, the pronoun is, by definition, known information.

But the pronoun will work only when its antecedent is clear to the reader, in the foreground of the reader's consciousness.

Let's look at a portion of the weasel paragraph we saw in Chapter 2:

> (1) A weasel is wild. (2) Who knows what **he** thinks? (3) **He** sleeps in **his** underground den, **his** tail draped over **his** nose. (4) Sometimes **he** lives in **his** den for two days without leaving. (5) Outside, **he** stalks rabbits, mice, muskrats, and birds, killing more bodies than **he** can eat warm, and often dragging the carcasses home.

The pronoun *he* connects the second sentence to the first—only that one word, but clearly a strong grammatical tie. The third sentence repeats *he*. The fourth and fifth sentences both begin with *he*.

As you learned in Chapter 1, personal pronouns in the **possessive case,** such as *his* in the third and fourth sentences of the weasel passage, function as **determiners,** or noun signalers. These **possessive pronouns** also signal a link between new and known information. In the following passage, the possessive pronoun *its* provides strong cohesive ties:

> Portland, sixty miles from the Pacific Ocean, is by no means immune to the suburbanization that has sapped the vitality from many cities. **Its** suburbs now contain about two thirds of the area's 1.4 million residents and about half of the area's jobs. Yet as the suburbs have grown, the downtown has become more attractive and popular than ever.
>
> Downtown Portland has distinct edges. **Its** eastern border is the deep, navigable Willamette River, lined for more than a mile by Tom McCall Waterfront Park, a grassy, mostly level expanse suited to events that draw thousands such as the Rose Festival (Portland calls itself the "City of Roses"), a blues festival, and a summer symphony series. **Its** western border is the steep West Hills, which contain Washington Park, home of the International Rose Test Gardens, where more than 400 varieties of roses are cultivated, and Forest Park, whose 4,800 acres of Douglas fir, alder, and maple constitute one of the largest nature preserves and hiking areas in any American city.
> —Philip Langdon (*The Atlantic Monthly*)

In the weasel paragraph, *he* constitutes the entire subject; in the Portland paragraph, in all three cases, *its* stands for the possessive noun *Portland's* and acts as a signal for the headwords: *suburbs, eastern border,* and *western border.* But no matter how it functions—whether it occurs by itself or acts as a determiner—the pronoun represents known information.

It is this known information that helps provide the cohesive tie between sentences. The three *its* sentences here are typical, with the known information in the subject, the new information in the predicate.

Demonstrative Pronouns. Like the personal pronouns, the **demonstrative pronouns**—*this, that, these,* and *those*—take the place of a noun phrase; in doing so, they provide a strong cohesive tie. And, like the possessive pronouns, they also serve as determiners:

> <u>That</u> sounds like a good plan. (noun phrase replacement)
> <u>That</u> plan sounds good to me. (determiner for *plan*)

When you read the second sentence aloud, you can hear the special focusing quality that the demonstrative adds to the noun *plan,* a focus that the determiner *the* would not have:

> The plan sounds good to me.

The demonstratives include the feature of proximity, in reference to both space and time, with *this* and *these* indicating closeness, *that* and *those* more distance. You'll find many sentences in these chapters (note the use of *these*) that demonstrate the close proximity indicated by *these* and *this* in their roles as determiners.

In the following example from Chapter 2, the demonstrative pronoun *these* occurs without a noun headword:

> <u>These</u> seven [sentence patterns] represent the underlying skeletal
>   structure of nearly all our sentences.

When a writer uses a pronoun, the reader has the right to assume that the antecedent is not just known information but that, in fact, the information is located in the foreground of his or her consciousness. The demonstratives, especially *this* and *these,* represent extra emphasis for foregrounding. We saw an example of this emphasis in the Ambrose passage about Lewis and Clark:

> Some of the fields, although unattended, still had squash and corn
>   growing in them. <u>These</u> had once been home to the mighty
>   Arikara tribe.

And in the sentence introducing the quote you just read, there's another example: *this emphasis.*

Writers can easily introduce weak spots when a pronoun has no clear antecedent. For example, in the following sentence there is no specific noun phrase to back up either the demonstrative pronoun *this* or the personal pronoun *it:*

> My roommate told me she has decided to drop out of school and look for a job. <u>This</u> has taken me completely by surprise, and I know <u>it</u> will shock her parents.

The problem here is not one of communication; we can easily figure out what the sentence means. But notice the absence of a specific noun in the first sentence to which the demonstrative *this* refers; rather, the pronoun refers to the idea in the sentence as a whole. This use of the pronoun is called **broad reference.** And while this example may not cause the reader to stumble, sometimes the understood antecedent is a bit troublesome to figure out. The point is that we, as readers, shouldn't have to do the figuring: That job belongs to the writer. Often the best way to fix a vague *this* or *that* is to turn the pronoun into a determiner and supply the missing headword:

> <u>This decision of hers</u> took me completely by surprise.

By turning *this* into a complete noun phrase, we also provide the vague *it* with a backup antecedent.

When you're revising the first draft of your essay—or perhaps rereading a sentence you just wrote—always pay attention to those sentences with a lone pronoun as subject, especially the demonstratives. Make sure that the antecedent of *this* or *that* or *these* or *those* is clear to the reader. If the noun phrase the pronoun stands for is not obvious, consider using the pronoun as a determiner and adding a headword. Pay special attention to *it* and *they* as well. It's important to recognize that pronouns without clear antecedents are in violation of the known–new contract.

FOR GROUP DISCUSSION

You could make the argument that a bare *this, that, these,* or *those* is perfectly capable of communicating without a noun headword, as the example in the Lewis and Clark passage by Steven Ambrose demonstrates. In fact, the original draft of the sentence that introduces the quotation also had a bare determiner: "We saw an example of *this* in the Lewis and Clark passage."

Do you think the revised version with the word *emphasis* added is an improvement? Would the addition of *fields* improve the Ambrose passage? And how about the roommate example? Did it really need the headword added? Check some of your reading material from this or another class to find out how common it is for demonstratives to appear without headwords. Are the missing headwords obvious, easy to retrieve?

EXERCISE 16

Revise the following passages to eliminate the vague pronouns. In some cases the most effective revision will be to turn *this* or *that* into a determiner. Another possibility is to combine the sentences.

1. Many women in the nineteenth century joined the fight for equal legal and political status. This eventually led to the establishment in 1890 of the National American Woman Suffrage Association.

2. Women in the labor force protested against long hours and poor working conditions. The National Consumers' League, founded in 1899, tried to improve that.

3. Some married women in the 1830s were able to have their own property, but it didn't mean they could vote.

4. Elizabeth Cady Stanton and Susan B. Anthony insisted that the fourteenth amendment gave women the rights of citizenship; because of this, they also argued that the fifteenth amendment should be expanded to guarantee a woman's right to vote.

5. In 1920 the Constitution was finally amended to give women the right to vote. That did not, however, provide *all* women with the right to vote: In some states, many African American women (and men) had to pass tests in order to vote.

6. Today equal rights are still denied to women in many countries either because of their sex, their ethnic identity, or their economic status. This will not change without pressure from international organizations dedicated to promoting and protecting human rights.

The Role of the Passive Voice

It's possible that everything you've heard about the **passive voice** up to now has been negative; English teachers often declare it out of bounds. Such edicts come about—those "pass" comments appear in the margins—because writers so often use passives when they shouldn't. And it's true that ineffective passives do stand out. But there's a great deal of misunderstanding about the passive. All good prose includes both active and passive voice.

In Chapter 3 you practiced changing active sentences to passive by making the direct object of the active sentence the subject of the passive. That shift of focus is one of the main strengths of the passive voice, one of its purposes: It allows known information to be in the subject position. Here, for example, is the beginning of a paragraph from a *Time* article by

Michael D. Lemonick about the destruction of the Brazilian rain forests. Note how the subject of the passive second sentence provides a cohesive tie:

> If Americans are truly interested in saving the rain forests, they should move beyond rhetoric and suggest *policies* that are practical—and acceptable—to the understandably wary Brazilians. <u>*Such policies* cannot be presented as take-them-or-leave-them propositions</u>. If the U.S. expects better performance from Brazil, Brazil has a right to make demands in return. In fact, the U.S. and Brazil need to engage in face-to-face negotiations as part of a formal dialogue on the environment between the industrial nations and the developing countries. [Emphasis added.]

In the first sentence, *policies* is new information; in the second it is known. You'll note that the agent is missing from the passive sentence; however, "by the Americans" is clearly understood. Note also how the information patterns work in the two sentences following the passive, with the known information, *U.S.* and *Brazil*—the agents—in subject position and the new information in the predicates.

The following example of the passive voice appears in a sentence you read earlier in this chapter in the discussion of the known–new contract. It opens a paragraph:

> In another paragraph pattern, or information pattern, the proposition in the topic sentence <u>is followed</u> by supporting details suggested by the topic and expected by the reader.

Here the term *supporting details* is the new information, so it belongs in the predicate, where it gets the main emphasis. You'll be reading more about this important feature—the connection of information and sentence rhythm—in the next chapter.

Other Sentence Inversions

As you have seen, the *passive transformation,* as the passive voice is called, inverts the active word order, with the original direct object shifted to subject position. Another, much more common, method of rearranging information is to open the sentence with an adverbial modifier, as you saw in Chapter 2 under the heading "The Optional Adverbials" (page 28). Adverbials are called optional because, with few exceptions, sentences are grammatical without them. However, when we do add them—and adverbials are very common indeed—they are considered modifiers of the verb; that is, they are part of the predicate. But they don't have to stay in the predicate position. Here are two opening adverbials from the discussion in Chapter 2, the first a prepositional phrase and the second a dependent clause:

> <u>During the Vietnam War</u>, Gino's dad was a pilot.
>
> <u>Because a weasel is wild</u>, it should be approached with great caution.

In that discussion of adverbials, these examples were presented without context. But let's assume that the second one is the opening of a paragraph following our old standby weasel passage. You probably remember its opening sentence: *A weasel is wild.* Clearly, if our *because* clause opened a second paragraph on weasels, the clause itself would be adding no new information, so we don't want it at the end of the sentence. We want to save the sentence end for the new idea—in this case, the idea of great caution. The *because* clause, with its known information, provides the transition from the previous sentence; it is the glue that connects them. One of the main points of the adverbial discussion in Chapter 2 is the movability—and thus the versatility—of the optional adverbial. When you put that feature together with the concept of the known–new contract, you can appreciate how important a tool movable adverbials can be for you as a writer.

Still another inversion of information involves switching the position of the subject and the predicate. Here's the topic sentence of a paragraph you've seen before:

> Shaping up as an important milestone is the demolition of two large dams in Washington State's Elwha River, which flows from the mountains of Olympic National Park into the Juan de Fuca Strait.

Here's the underlying subject-predicate structure:

> The demolition of two large dams . . . is shaping up as an important milestone.

The writer's purpose for making that subject-predicate switch is connected to the previous paragraphs in the article, which relate the history and consequences of dam removal. The word *milestone* refers to that history, so it becomes the transition to the new information about these two particular dams. It's an unusual grammatical situation, for the old information to occur in the verb phrase, the predicate. Using her inversion tool, the writer has set aside the subject-predicate order so that the new information is in line for emphasis. The position at the end of the sentence also makes it easier to add those two long modifiers, a prepositional phrase and a *which*-clause.

We look more closely at word-order variations in Chapter 11.

FOR GROUP DISCUSSION

The following paragraph is the beginning of a short description of
Thomas Jefferson by Lee A. Jacobus:

> Thomas Jefferson, an exceptionally accomplished and well-
> educated man, is probably best known for writing the Decla-
> ration of Independence, a work composed under the eyes of
> Benjamin Franklin, John Adams, and the Continental Con-
> gress, which spent two and a half days going over every word.
> The substance of the document was developed in committee,
> but Jefferson, because of the grace of his style, was chosen to
> do the actual writing. The result is one of the most memorable
> statements in American history.

Explain why the author used the passive voice where he did. Try writing
a version of the paragraph using only the active voice. Is it equally
effective?

PARALLELISM

Early in this chapter you read that it's okay to repeat words, that repetition
can have a positive effect on the reader. In this section we look at a specific
kind of repetition called **parallelism,** the repetition of whole structures,
such as phrases and clauses. Parallelism is usually thought of as a device
for enhancing a writer's style—and indeed it is that—as you learned in
Chapter 4. It can certainly add polish and flavor to prose that otherwise
might be the plain vanilla variety. But it can also provide cohesion, especially when the repeated elements extend through a paragraph or from
one paragraph to the next.

Parallelism refers to repeated grammatical elements, often combined
with repeated words. The quality of being parallel means that the repeated
elements have the same structure, such as noun phrases with noun
phrases, prepositional phrases with prepositional phrases. One of the
most famous sentences in President Kennedy's inaugural address includes
parallel verb phrases: "pay any price, bear any burden, meet any hardship,
support any friend, oppose any foe." And we're all familiar with Lincoln's
"of the people, by the people, and for the people."

Parallelism becomes an especially strong cohesive device when a structure echoes a structure from a previous sentence or paragraph. In the
second paragraph of the Portland passage on page 94, the subject "Its

eastern border" names one of the "distinct edges" referred to in the opening sentence. The next sentence not only fulfills the reader's expectation with the word *western,* it does so using parallel structure:

> Its eastern border is the deep, navigable Willamette River . . . .
> Its western border is the steep West Hills . . . .

In the following passage the author's use of repetition adds intensity and drama to his argument:

> That knowledge has become the key resource means that there is a world economy, and that the world economy, rather than the national economy, is in control. <u>Every country, every industry, and every business</u> will be in an increasingly competitive environment. <u>Every country, every industry, and every business</u> will, in its decisions, have to consider its competitive standing in the world economy and the competitiveness of its knowledge competencies.
> —Peter F. Drucker (*The Atlantic Monthly*)

The two repeated series as subjects are the most obvious repetitions, but note also in the first sentence two instances of *world economy* contrasted with *national economy* and a third repetition of *world economy* in the last sentence. And in the second and third sentences we read *competitive standing, competitive environment,* and *competitiveness.*

The repeated series in this paragraph by Stephen Jay Gould from *Ever Since Darwin* illustrates another fairly common feature of parallelism, that of **antithesis,** the introduction of contrasting, or dissimilar, ideas:

> Why imagine that specific genes for <u>aggression, dominance, or spite</u> have any importance when we know that the brain's enormous flexibility permits us to be <u>aggressive or peaceful, dominant or submissive, spiteful or generous?</u> <u>Violence, sexism, and general nastiness</u> are biological since they represent one subset of a possible range of behaviors. But <u>peacefulness, equality, and kindness</u> are just as biological—and we may see their influence increase if we can create social structures that permit them to flourish.
> —Stephen Jay Gould (*Ever Since Darwin*)

Note in the following passage how the point of view changes in the middle of the paragraph where the parallel *it* clauses begin. Each of them introduces a clause in the second person, one with *you* as the subject.

> A thin broken strand of islands curves out into the Atlantic Ocean and then back again in a sheltering embrace of North Carolina's mainland coast and its offshore sounds. These are the Outer Banks of North Carolina. For thousands of years these barrier islands have survived the onslaught of wind and sea. Today their long stretches of beach, sand dunes, marshes, and woodlands are set aside as Cape Hatteras National Seashore. <u>It can be a lonely place</u>; you may walk along the beach unseen except by shore birds searching for a meal. <u>It can be a place of discovery</u>; you may visit the 1870 Cape Hatteras Lighthouse, one of many monuments to man's encounter with the sea. <u>It can be a wild place</u>; you may be buffeted by an approaching gale or surprised by the honking of large flocks of migrating geese. <u>And it can be an exciting place</u>, where you may explore many opportunities for recreation: surf fishing, sunbathing, swimming, beach combing, canoeing, sailing, surfing, snorkeling. Part land, part sea, Cape Hatteras offers rewards from each.
>
> —National Park Service Brochure

From all of these examples it should be clear that parallelism is more than mere stylistic décor: The parallel structures are, in fact, among the strongest cohesive ties that the writer has available. They highlight those ideas that should be in the foreground of the reader's consciousness, sending the message that the parallel structures are not only connected but also significant.

Repetition Versus Redundancy

Rather than commending these authors for effective parallelism, you may be tempted to accuse them of unnecessary repetition, a problem that goes by the label **redundancy.** How do we distinguish between them? How do we tell the difference between good repetition and bad?

Parallelism of the kind we see here—parallelism as a stylistic device— invariably calls attention to itself. Did these authors intend to do that, to call attention to these structures? Clearly, the answer is "Yes—and for good reason." In both passages, the use of repetition has added a dramatic dimension to the prose.

The repetition in these passages might also tempt you to accuse the authors of wordiness; their sentences certainly don't pass the test of brevity or conciseness, features of writing so often touted in composition textbooks. Clarity, of course, is always a goal. And, yes, sometimes clarity calls for brevity, for a lean version of a sentence. But there are many occasions that call for a celebration of words. We certainly don't expect the president to be brief in an inaugural address; neither should we expect a writer to be brief in describing Cape Hatteras or in explaining the concept of a world economy or in arguing for the biological basis of kindness.

In Chapter 8 redundancy is addressed in a section called "The Proliferating Prepositional Phrase." And the use of repetition as a stylistic device is discussed further in Chapter 11, "Making Stylistic Choices."

FOR GROUP DISCUSSION

Find the parallel structures in the following paragraph from Jay Wink's *The Great Upheaval* and explain how they provide cohesion:

> Soldiers marched that day in Manhattan. For almost as long as anyone could remember, the sight of soldiers had invariably meant the same thing, whether they were French or Russian, Austrian or English, whether they belonged to kings or were battle-hardened mercenaries, whether they moved in great formations or galloped along on horseback. Too often their presence was ominous, signaling that the campaign was beginning and the war was deepening, that the dead would increase and the bloodshed would continue, and the suffering would go on. But today their footsteps were unique, booming out the rites of nationhood. They called out a celebration of victory and the raising of the flag—the American flag. It was November 25, 1783. Evacuation Day in New York City.

KEY TERMS

Antecedent	Determiner	Possessive case
Antithesis	Known–new contract	Possessive pronouns
Broad reference	Lexical cohesion	Pronouns
Cohesion	Parallelism	Reader expectation
Demonstrative	Passive voice	Redundancy
pronouns	Personal pronouns	Repetition

RHETORICAL REMINDERS

Have I anticipated my reader's expectations?

Do my paragraphs profit from lexical cohesion, the repetition of words?

Is the known information in the beginning of the sentence, where it can provide a cohesive tie to the previous sentence, with the new information in end-focus position?

Have I taken advantage of parallelism as a cohesive device?

CHAPTER 7

The Writer's Voice

CHAPTER PREVIEW

In the first six chapters we looked at the structure and connection of sentences, including options the writer has for controlling the way the reader reads and interprets those sentences. This chapter continues that discussion, focusing on features of language that affect the writer's **voice** and, thus, the reader's interpretation. Think of your writer's voice as the identity you create through choosing words and arranging them on the page. Just as different facets of your identity appear during the day, depending on whom you're talking to, your writing voice or identity will vary according to your imagined readers. Sometimes your voice will be angry, sometimes friendly, other times meditative. You can easily come up with a list of the various voices you assume on a regular basis. The key in writing is to be able to control your voice so that you convey the message you want to. You can gain this control by understanding certain features of language: **tone,** the writer's stance, or attitude toward the topic; **diction,** the choice of words; **point of view,** the perspective from which the writer views the topic; and **metadiscourse,** the signals that help guide the reader through the text as well as communicate the writer's credibility and authority.

As you would expect, all of these features depend on the writing situation: the audience, the purpose, and the topic. Your writer's voice in a personal letter, for example, will be quite different from the voice in a letter to a prospective employer. Your voice in a personal essay for your composition class will be different from the voice you choose for a history research paper. In all of your writing, however, your writer's voice should be your voice, your **personal voice.**

123

TONE

In conversation there's nothing very mysterious about tone of voice and its contribution to meaning:

> "He was his usual cheerful self."
>
> "She's got attitude."
>
> "I think he was kidding."

In a face-to-face encounter, of course it's not only the voice that communicates the tone: There's the red face, the raised eyebrows, the rolling eyes, the smile, the smirk, the pleased expression.

But even on the telephone, without visual cues, we usually have no trouble drawing conclusions about tone. A person's voice may exude confidence or trepidation, hostility or pleasure, anger, bitterness, indifference. "How did she sound?" is a question someone might ask you about a phone conversation—not only, "What did she say?"

But how does your *writer's* voice sound? What determines its tone? Indeed, what does *tone* mean when there is no sound, only words on paper?

To answer these questions, consider what you read in the Introduction about rhetoric—about the choices we make based not only on the topic we're writing about but also on the audience and purpose. In that discussion we compared your writer's voice in a text message to your best friend with a letter to the dean of your college. Or consider the words you would use in a letter to a prospective employer. You would choose words to convey an earnest and confident and businesslike tone—and of course you'd be careful to dot every *i* and cross every *t*, so to speak.

Clearly, it's the rhetorical situation—the topic, the purpose, and the audience—that determines the tone. For example, newspapers and newsmagazines generally call for a neutral, objective voice. But apparently not always—not in this Associated Press article about rodent fossils discovered in South America:

> Eeek! Imagine a rodent that weighed a ton and was as big as a bull.
>
> Uruguayan scientists say they have uncovered fossil evidence of the biggest species of rodent ever found, one that scurried across wooded areas of South America about 4 million years ago, when the continent was not connected to North America.
>
> A herbivore, the beast may have been a contemporary, and possibly prey, of saber-toothed cats—a prehistoric version of Tom and Jerry.
>
> For those afraid of rodents, forget hopping on a chair. Its huge skull, more than 20 inches long, suggested a beast more

than eight feet long and weighing between 1,700 and 3,000 pounds.

Although British newspapers variously described it as a mouse or a rat, researchers say the animal, named Josephoartigasia monesi, actually was more closely related to a guinea pig or porcupine.

—Raphael G. Satter

The author's tongue-in-cheek tone here is anything but neutral. His opening with the interjection *eek* is a sure way to signal a playful tone. His use of the imperative—*imagine a rodent, forget hopping on a chair*—invites our participation, our agreement; his choice of details—*big as a bull, a prehistoric version of Tom and Jerry*—keeps us interested.

And in the following short piece, one of several in "Parade's Special Intelligence Report," a regular feature of *Parade* magazine, the use of the word *snafu* in the headline sets the reader up to expect that same kind of flippant tone:

Social Security Snafu

The federal government had to cough up cash last month and mail a "letter of explanation" to 51 million Americans who were short-changed on their Social Security checks. It seems the Bureau of Labor Statistics was supposed to give them 2.5% cost-of-living increases but only added 2.4%, due to faulty math. Recipients won't get rich: It's about $12 to $19 more. (We wonder what it cost to calculate the difference, then print and mail all those letters.) But the blunders didn't stop there: Some folks were sent financial data about their neighbors.

As you can see, the writer fulfills the headline's expectations. It's the choice of words that does it: *cough up, short-changed, faulty math, blunders.* You can be quite sure that a news release on the topic sent by the Bureau of Labor Statistics would have used different words.

In each of these examples, the writer's attitude toward the topic, the writer's take on the topic, clearly sets the tone: tongue-in-cheek, flippant, facetious, derisive.

EXERCISE 19

1. Rewrite the "Snafu" paragraph in a neutral tone, as the Bureau of Labor Statistics might have done in a news release. In addition to the informal words mentioned, you'll also want to consider the

appropriateness of *It seems* in the second sentence, the reference to getting rich in the third, and the sentence in parentheses.

2. These five short paragraphs open an article by Jeff Gammage entitled "One Significant Swede" about Carl Linnaeus in the magazine section of the *Philadelphia Inquirer* (June 28, 2005):

> At the Swedish museum in South Philadelphia, the staff is getting ready for a gala, year-long celebration of the 300th birthday of Carl Linnaeus.
>
> They face just one pesky problem: Most people don't know who the heck he is.
>
> And that's a shame, sponsors say. Because Linnaeus is not just another guy in a powdered wig.
>
> The Scandinavian scientist came up with a big, world-changing idea, a way to tidy up the clutter of the natural universe: He invented a system to name and categorize everything that lives, has lived or will live. And then he got people to follow his rules.
>
> Remember your high school biology teacher pounding *kingdom-phylum-class* into your head? You can thank—or blame—Carl Linnaeus

As you can see, the first paragraph covers the standard *who-what-when-where-why* of journalistic reporting in a straightforward way. What has the writer done to change the tone of the last four paragraphs?

A. Revise the last four paragraphs so that they conform to the straight reporting of the first paragraph.

B. Then, revise the opening paragraph so that it conforms in tone to the final four paragraphs.

For the revisions, you might want to combine paragraphs into perhaps just one or two.

DICTION

All of the published examples in the preceding section, besides illustrating tone, show clearly the connection between tone and **diction,** the choice of words: They are two sides of the same coin. Both are connected to the writing situation as well as to the essential sense of the words. And it may take only a few words to change the tone from neutral to ironic or bitter or skeptical or enthusiastic—depending, of course, on their meanings.

Where do those meanings come from? While the dictionary can give the core meaning of a word—its **denotation**—its essential sense resides in the language user and in the written or spoken context in which it is used. This special sense, association, or overtone carried by the word is called its **connotation.** For example, *economical* and *cheap* are synonyms: They both mean "thrifty." However, their connotations differ. While *an economical car* has a positive connotation, suggesting good gas mileage, *a cheap car* has a negative connation, bringing to mind the hassles of needing multiple car repairs. Communication takes place when the essential sense of a word is shared between speaker and listener, writer and reader.

Groups of synonyms can often be organized according to levels of formality. You would no doubt be able to sense that of the three verbs *choose, select,* and *pick out* (a phrasal verb), *pick out* is least formal and *select* is most formal. The words you choose are effective only when they are appropriate in the writing situation, appropriate for the audience and purpose, when they convey your message accurately and comfortably. The idea of comfort may seem out of place in connection with diction, but, in fact, words, especially those with negative connotations, can sometimes cause the reader to feel uncomfortable. You've probably experienced such feelings yourself as a listener—hearing a speaker whose words for one reason or another strike you as inappropriate and make you feel uncomfortable. Writing can provoke those same feelings in a reader.

As a reader yourself, you undoubtedly spot an inappropriate word simply because it commands attention—negative, uncomfortable attention. And when words are inappropriate, they set up communication barriers. As a writer you must learn to spot your own inappropriate words. One of the most common such attention-getters is the word that is too formal for the situation. Sometimes, of course, the opposite problem occurs: a word too informal for its purpose. But student writers are more likely to have the mistaken notion that writing calls for a sophisticated vocabulary. And so they look for words that demonstrate that sophistication.

One consequence of that inappropriate word choice is the loss of a personal voice. If what you've written doesn't sound like something you'd actually say, then you should reconsider your choice of words or style of phrasing. This is not to suggest that writing is exactly like speech; it's not, of course. In our everyday conversation with family and friends, we use informal words and phrases that we rarely see in writing, and we commonly use sentence fragments. Further, in writing we use certain modifiers and connectors, such as the *further* at the beginning of this sentence, that we rarely use in speaking. But even when we include such structures, we should be able to recognize our words as our own.

The following passage is the opening of a law school applicant's short essay in response to the question "Why do you want to study law?"

> It has long been a tenet of my value system that as a capable individual I have a social and moral duty to contribute to the improvement of the society in which I live. It seems that the way to make a valuable contribution is by choosing the means that will best allow me to utilize my abilities and facilitate my interests.

In spite of the **first person** point of view—the use of *I*—there's nothing personal in those lines. Here the writer's voice simply doesn't fit the rhetorical situation. If she had been asked in a face-to-face interview why she wanted to go to law school, she certainly would not have begun her answer with "It has long been a tenet of my value system." Never in her life has she begun a sentence that way. Instead, she would have said "I believe" or "I've always thought." But like many inexperienced writers, she associated formal writing with lofty phrases and uncommon words.

A personal voice does not preclude the use of big words or uncommon words. Nor does the expression "big words" refer to the number of syllables. It means pretentious or fancy words, words that call attention to themselves. Pretentious words send the message that the writer is trying too hard. The word *tenet,* as used in the law school statement, is one such pretentious word; it's out of place. Even the Declaration of Independence, with its formal, ceremonial language, uses the simple word *truths:*

> We hold these truths to be self-evident.

Chances are that Thomas Jefferson didn't consider, even in his first draft,

> We hold these tenets of our value system to be self-evident.

There are times, of course when an uncommon word is called for, a word with the precise meaning you want. All of us have in our passive vocabulary words that we rarely, if ever, use in speaking; and using them when they're called for does not mean giving up our personal voice. The mere fact that a word is infrequent does not make it pretentious. In the opening sentence of the previous paragraph, for example, the verb is *preclude.* It's not a common word, but there's certainly nothing fancy or pretentious about it: It's simply the most precise word for the job.

Another problem with pretentious language is the flabbiness that it produces, such as "utilize my abilities and facilitate my interests." Verbs like *utilize* and *facilitate* may sound impressive, but what do they really mean? *Utilize* simply means *use:* "to use my abilities." And it would probably surprise the law school applicant to learn that *facilitate* does not mean "to carry out," as she apparently assumed; it means "to make easier." So "facilitate my interests" is not only pretentious; it is meaningless.

FOR GROUP DISCUSSION

1. Words are powerful. As a writer you can use to advantage the power that words hold to call up images in the mind of the reader. But to use words effectively, you have to understand the meanings, the associations, they are likely to have for the reader. Consider the following sets of related words: What features do the members have in common? What features separate them? In what context would one be more effective than another?

companion/friend/buddy	careful/stingy/thrifty/tight
picky/careful/prudent	slumber/sleep/snooze
cocky/confident	foolhardy/daring/rash/bold
slender/skinny/scrawny	

2. Bertrand Russell is credited with the following "conjugation of an irregular verb":

   I am firm. You are obstinate. He is pigheaded.

   Using some of the groups of words in Part 1, and adding to them as necessary, try your own conjugations.

   Example: I am slender; you are skinny; he is scrawny.

3. One characteristic of ineffective diction is the overuse of **clichés,** many of which are **similes,** comparisons that transfer the qualities of one thing (or person or animal) to another. Such comparisons become clichés when the reader knows exactly what's coming—that is, when there is no new information involved. Unlike the message of pretentious words, trying too

hard, clichés send the message that the writer isn't trying hard enough. The comparison is much more effective when it evokes a fresh image, when it helps the reader see something or someone in a new way.

Chances are you and most of your classmates can complete the following phrases with identical words:

quiet as a _____	mean as _____
hot as _____	light as _____
cold as _____	pretty as _____
scared as a _____	weak as _____
strong as _____	ugly as _____
fast as _____	tough as _____
avoid like the _____	sell like _____

Now, instead of using the expected word, find one that creates a fresh image. For example, you might say, "Quiet as a sealskin coat."

Note: You'll find it interesting and instructive to compare the answers given by the nonnative speakers of English in the class with those of native speakers.

Verbs and Formality

As you might expect, the level of formality in our prose is determined in large part by our choice of verbs—the pivotal unit in the sentence. Among the verbs that send an informal signal to the reader are **phrasal verbs,** common verbs combined with one or more **particles,** or preposition-like words. Some of the verb-plus-particle combinations form **idioms.** The term *idiom* refers to a set phrase whose meaning cannot be predicted from the separate meanings of the words. The meaning of the idiom *give up,* for example, is different from the combined meanings of *give* and *up:* It means "surrender" or "abandon."

Our language is filled with such idioms: *turn down, bring about, bring on, put up with, stand for, think up, take off, take up, look down on, brush aside, get on with, walk out on, come down with, swear off, write off*—the list goes on and on. As you can see, these are common verbs, part of our everyday speech. They lend an air of familiarity, a conversational tone to the writer's voice.

Idioms are certainly appropriate in informal contexts—for example, in a personal essay or narrative, or for a general audience, such as you might address in a letter to the editor of a newspaper. But for research papers or technical reports—and certainly for résumés and letters to prospective employers—a more formal verb may be called for. One way of adding formality, then, is to look carefully at (*scrutinize*) your sentences and do away with (*eliminate*) or at least cut down on (*reduce*) the number of idioms.

EXERCISE 20

A. Substitute a single word for each of the idioms listed in the second paragraph of the preceding discussion. In some cases there will be more than one possibility.

B. The idioms we have used in writing this book certainly influence its level of formality. Here are some of the sentences you have seen so far. Come up with a more formal version of each.

 1. <u>Come up with</u> a more formal version of each.

 2. The punctuation convention <u>calls for</u> a comma. . . .

 3. There are three steps we follow in <u>turning</u> the active voice <u>into</u> passive.

 4. All sentences are <u>made up of</u> one or more independent clauses.

 5. The first sentence in a paragraph <u>sets up</u> expectations in the reader about what is coming.

 6. We can easily <u>figure out</u> what the sentence means.

 7. We can <u>think of</u> it as part of the contract between writer and reader.

 8. You can be sure that in reading their own prose, whether silently or aloud, they are <u>paying attention to</u> sentence rhythm.

 9. The pronoun <u>stands in for</u> the entire noun phrase.

 10. We <u>call on</u> *do* when we need an auxiliary. . . .

Nominalized Verbs and Abstract Subjects

One common feature of formal writing, especially academic writing, is the use of **nominalized verbs**—verbs that have been turned into nouns: *occur →* *occurrence, succeed → success, combine → combination, remove → removal.*

Writers take advantage of this feature to link sentences together; they use the verb (actually the entire predicate) to present new information and the nominalized verb, often preceded by a demonstrative *this, that, these,* or *those,* to establish known information:

> The grammar of the written language <u>differs</u> greatly from that of the spoken language. <u>This difference</u> is attributable to the constant innovations of spoken language.

In this example *differ* and *difference* affirm the known-new contract.

Though nominalized verbs contribute to cohesion, they should be used with care. Because they are so common and so easy to produce, they can become a trap for the unwary writer, introducing abstraction where concrete ideas belong. It's during the revision stage of writing that you'll want to be on the lookout. Ask yourself, is the **agent**—the initiator of the action—there and, if so, is it functioning as the subject? In other words, does the sentence explain *who is doing what?* If the answer is no, your sentence may be a prime candidate for revision. Can you find the agent in the following sentence?

> High student achievement led to the creation of the Gifted Students Program.

Although *high student achievement* is the subject, it is an abstraction. The agent could be *students,* or it could be the unnamed creators of the program. Here is one possible revision:

> The School Board created the Gifted Students Program for high achievers.

Another possible source of confusion is the sentence with a verb phrase or a clause as subject, rather than the usual noun phrase. When you study these structures in Chapter 10, you'll see that they are common substitutes for noun phrases. But because they are abstractions, they too may be pitfalls for the unwary writer. Again, the source of the problem may be that of the misplaced or missing agent:

> The <u>buying</u> of so many American companies and so much real estate by the Japanese caused concern on Wall Street.
> <u>Analyzing</u> the situation in China shows that opportunities for investment are growing.

Although we need context to tell us the best way to revise these sentences, we can see and hear a problem. The sentences seem to be about actions— but they can't show the action in a strong and concrete way because the agents of those actions are not there in subject position. This kind of agentless sentence should send up a red flag—a signal that here's a candidate for revision.

EXERCISE 21

Revise the following passages, paying special attention to unnecessary nominalizations and problems of agency. The first two items are the examples from the preceding discussion. Remember to ask yourself, "Who is doing what?"

1. The buying of so many American companies and so much real estate by the Japanese caused concern on Wall Street.

2. Analyzing the situation in China showed that opportunities for investment were growing.

3. In the biography of Lyndon Johnson by Robert Caro, the account of the Senate election of 1948 is described in great detail.

4. One of the requirements for the completion of the application for a scholarship was the submission of a financial statement by the student's parents.

5. The overuse of salt in the typical American diet has had the result of obscuring the natural taste of many foods. Nutritionists maintain that a reduction in people's dependence on salt would lead to an enhancement of taste and heightened enjoyment of food.

Contractions

Contractions affect the rhythm of sentences and, in doing so, affect the reader's perception of the writer's voice. That voice will probably strike the reader as more conversational, less formal, when contractions are part of the message. Contractions help to close the distance between writer and reader.

Although contractions are often seen as too conversational, most writers, even in formal contexts, will contract the negative *not* in such words as *don't* and *can't:*

> If you use ready-made phrases, you not only <u>don't</u> have to hunt about for words; you also <u>don't</u> have to bother with the rhythms of your sentences, since these phrases are generally so arranged as to be more or less euphonious.
> —George Orwell ("Politics and the English Language")

Other frequent contractions are those with the auxiliary verbs *have, had, will, would, is, am,* and *are.* Here are some common examples:

Negatives: can't, don't, won't, couldn't, doesn't, isn't

Auxiliaries: I'd, she'll, they're, we've, he's, it's

The contracted forms of *be* can also occur when they function as the main verb:

<u>You're</u> happy.
<u>I'm</u> sad.

The contracted *is* is especially common with *it* and *there:*

<u>It's</u> a nice day today.
<u>There's</u> a storm due tomorrow.

If you think about—and listen for—sentence rhythm, you'll understand the contribution that contractions make in eliminating or greatly diminishing a syllable. As you read the following passages, consider how different the sentences would be without the contractions they include:

Cats, I surmise, seem unsocial to us only because we <u>aren't</u> good at recognizing the signals of other species. We interpret cat signals as telling us, for instance, that the cat <u>doesn't</u> care about us and <u>doesn't</u> miss us when <u>we're</u> gone. If people were giving off similar signals, our interpretation would probably be right. But <u>they're</u> not people, and <u>we're</u> wrong.
—Elizabeth Marshall Thomas (*The Atlantic Monthly*)

You may have noticed that none of the examples, either in the lists or in the quoted passages, involve nouns—only pronouns. Contractions with nouns—"My <u>dog'll</u> eat anything"; "The <u>Senate's</u> accomplished a lot lately"—are fairly common in conversation and in written quotations and dialogue, but they are rare in most writing situations. However, contractions with pronouns are anything but rare.

The advice against using contractions that you may have heard or read simply does not reflect actual usage. Even fairly formal written prose commonly includes the contracted *not,* as the Orwell passage illustrates. And in negative questions, the contracted form is essentially required:

Hasn't the winter weather been wonderful?
Shouldn't the tax laws be revised?

In the uncontracted form, the *not* predominates, changing the intended emphasis, if not the meaning:

> Has the winter weather not been wonderful?
> Should the tax laws not be revised?

An interesting feature in negative statements is that often the writer has more than one contraction to choose from.

> She is not here. → She's not here *or* She isn't here.

Both contracted forms are less formal than the original, but there's also a difference between the two: In the version with the diminished *not (isn't)*, the reader will probably put more emphasis on *here*—and may then expect a different follow-up sentence:

> She isn't here. She's in class.
> She's not here. I don't know where she is.

If you want to ensure that the reader puts strong stress on the negative, you can use the uncontracted *not*—with or without the contracted *is*. Another difference between these two contracted versions is the number of syllables. The sentence with *isn't* has four syllables; the one with *not* has only three—a rhythm difference that in a given situation may be important.

In some cases where there's a choice of contractions, you may also notice a difference in formality, with the uncontracted *not* on the more formal side:

> I won't be there. / I'll not be there.
> I haven't finished. / I've not finished.
> I wouldn't go there if I were you. / I'd not go there if I were you.

Even though the second version in each case includes a contraction, it has a rather formal tone.

It's important to recognize the connection between the level of formality and the use of contractions: In general, the more formal the writing, the fewer contractions you'll find, or want to use, especially contracted auxiliaries. However, in most of the writing you do for school or on the job, the occasional contraction will certainly be appropriate. It's important to recognize the contribution that contractions can make to your personal voice.

FOR GROUP DISCUSSION

Consider the personal voice that you hear in the following advertisements, which appeared during the same week in two different publications. How would you characterize the tone and the diction? In each case the opening paragraph shown is the headline for the ad.

Rewrite each of the ads using the voice and tone of the other one.

1. Looks like this winter will be warmer than the last. Lands' End introduces the newest—and driest—in Polartec outerwear.

   Have you met Polartec yet? If you're into winter sports, betcha you have.

   It's the original man-made fleece. A nubby fabric that weighs nothing—yet keeps you warm when it's umpteen below.

   Well, the folks at Malden Mills who dreamed up Polartec have outdone themselves now.

   They've not only created an even cozier warmer version—they've made it more water repellent, too.

   So much so, that it inspired us at Lands' End to introduce a whole bunch of new Polartec outerwear.

   —*The Atlantic Monthly*

2. A perfect dinner party requires hours of planning and preparation. Having decent appliances doesn't hurt, either.

   Fresh herbs as opposed to dry. Going to the butcher instead of the supermarket. The wedding china, not everyday.

   Her dinner party was that special. Perhaps the brilliant shine of stainless steel inspired her, from a kitchen that was special too. Filled with restaurant-quality appliances—aka the Pro-Style Collection from Jenn-Air.

   From the quintessential cooktop to the matching refrigerator and dishwasher, they're all sleek, gleaming and state-of-the-art. The crème de la crème, as they say.

   True, throwing the perfect dinner party is a major project. But if you've got the perfect kitchen, it's a labor of love.

   —*The New Yorker*

Metaphor

As you have seen, the choice of words affects the reader's response to the message and no doubt to the writer as well. The use of contractions tends to close the distance between writer and reader. Another technique for closing that distance is the use of *metaphor,* the application of words from one sphere to another.

You were introduced to the grammar of metaphor in Chapter 2 when you read about the linking-*be* followed by a noun phrase as subject complement. A "something is something" sentence becomes metaphor when that equation is figurative rather than literal—in other words, when the two "somethings" belong to different spheres or domains. Shakespeare's

All the world's a stage

and Charlie Brown's (Charles Schulz's)

Happiness is a warm puppy

illustrate the wide range of possibilities—from the profound to the commonplace.

But *be* sentences, like these examples, are by no means the only form of metaphor, or even the most common. In our everyday language we apply words from one domain to another, creating metaphor with just a simple modifier. Language itself is often described metaphorically: flowery prose, gutter journalism, bathroom words, hard-boiled detective novels. Newsmagazines abound with metaphors, many of them overworked. *Time* reported on "an industrial dinosaur like General Motors" the same week that *Newsweek* described the company as "a sinking ship." In *Time's* story the head of the company "doesn't like sitting in the back seat"; in *Newsweek's* he's helping to steer "a treasure galleon."

Metaphor can often illuminate and lighten a serious or technical discussion. In the following extended metaphor, *New York Times* writers explain the issue of class. This paragraph is from an article by Janny Scott and David Leonhardt called "The Shadowy Lines That Still Divide," the first installment of an eleven-part series called "Class in America":

> One way to think of a person's position in society is to imagine a hand of cards. Everyone is dealt four cards, one from each suit: education, income, occupation and wealth, the four commonly used criteria for gauging class. Face cards in a few categories may land a player in the upper middle class. At first, a person's class is his parents' class. Later, he may pick up a new hand of his own; it is likely to resemble that of his parents, but not always.

The following passage opens the third paragraph of a long article by Lauren Resnick and Chris Zurawsky in *American Education,* a publication of the American Federation of Teachers, describing the standards movement in American schools. The two preceding paragraphs introduce the topic in straightforward academic prose.

> At about fifteen years of age, the standards movement is in its adolescence, and many are already preparing to kick it out of the house. Before we give up on our unruly teen, however, let's take a clear look at what we have to be proud of, what flaws we need to address, and what might be the benefits of pressing ahead.

After just two sentences of the teenager metaphor, however, the reader is back to serious business, with the questions that the article goes on to address. Undoubtedly, though, in both of these examples, the metaphor has made the reader stop and think about the topic in a new way.

METADISCOURSE

Metadiscourse refers to certain signals that help the reader understand the writer's message. The word *metadiscourse* actually means discourse about discourse—signals that clarify the purpose or direction of a particular passage, acting as guideposts for the reader. For example, a word like *thus* tells the reader that what follows is a summary. And when a sentence opens with *for example*, as the previous one does, you know the sentence will discuss an example of the concept just mentioned. The phrase may not be necessary—many examples go unmarked—but sometimes that help is very important.

Some of our most common and useful metadiscourse signals are the conjunctive adverbs you read about in Chapter 4: *however, so, nevertheless,* and prepositional phrases such as *in other words, in addition,* and *in fact* (see the list on pages 65 and 67). Other text connectors you're familiar with, such *as first, in the first place, second, next, finally,* and *in conclusion,* clearly add to the ease of reading, the flow of the text. Those that signal contrasting pairs of ideas—*on the one hand/on the other hand*—are especially helpful. Signals like these contribute to the sense of cohesion, the flow of the paragraph—and sometimes to its accurate interpretation—by keeping the reader informed of the writer's intentions.

We can think of these text connectors as primarily informational, to help the reader understand the message.

Other structures that we label as metadiscourse have a different purpose and a different effect: They offer guidance for reading the text, informing the reader of the writer's own attitude about the content of the message.

As you read the following passages, think about the role played by the underlined words. If the sentences look familiar, it's because they have all appeared in earlier sections of this book.

1. <u>The point is</u> that we, as readers, shouldn't have to do the figuring.
2. Parallelism is usually thought of as a device for enhancing a writer's style—<u>and indeed it is that</u>—as you learned in Chapter 4.
3. You've <u>probably</u> been told at one time or another to avoid *I or you* or the passive voice—and, <u>very possibly</u>, the *it*-cleft as well.

All of these underlined structures qualify as metadiscourse.

The opener, *the point is,* in (1) emphasizes our take on the importance and validity of the proposition. The inserted sentence in (2) calls attention to the truth of the statement about parallelism that could be taken wrong, given the wording "is usually thought of." The paragraph goes on to emphasize the importance of parallelism to cohesion.

The use of *probably* and *very possibly* in (3) is called hedging: There's no way we could know for sure that you've been told those things, so we don't want to sound too positive. We don't want you, the reader, to be stopped by a bold statement when it may not be valid in your case. And we certainly don't want you to lose confidence in our authority to write on this topic. Other hedging terms are words like *perhaps,* verbs like *seem* or *indicate* or *suggest* and phrases like *to a certain extent,* as well as the modal auxiliaries *might* and *may* and *could.*

Although you might think that using words like *perhaps* and *probably* would communicate doubt about the author's authority and the reliability of the information, such **hedges** actually have the opposite effect on the reader. In *Constructing Texts,* George Dillon maintains that they "certify the writer as a modest, careful scholar whose tentative conclusions are probably of wider application and greater likelihood than he feels he can claim" (p. 91).[1]

There are many other kinds of metadiscourse markers that affect the writer's personal voice: Some of them comment on the content of the sentence; some of them allow the writer to address the reader directly; some comment on what is coming next—or what the reader has already learned. Here are some further examples, also taken from earlier sections of the book:

<u>As you probably noticed,</u> the only difference between the two passages is in the rhythm pattern of the last sentence in each.

---

[1]Dillon's book is listed in the Bibliography under "Composition Theory."

The following passive sentence, <u>which may look familiar,</u> closes the first paragraph of the section in Chapter 2 called "Sentence Patterns". . . .

<u>It is important to recognize</u> that pronouns without antecedents are in violation of the known–new contract.

<u>And you can be sure</u> that in reading their own prose, whether silently or aloud, they are paying attention to sentence rhythm.

In the following paragraph, from *Saga of Chief Joseph* by Helen Addison Howard, the author translates "Nez Perce" in a parenthetical comment, a type of metadiscourse called a **code gloss,** a term applied when the writer clarifies the meaning of a word or phrase. You'll see other obvious metadiscourse signals as well:

> After Lewis and Clark passed through their country (about which more later), French-Canadian trappers came to trade the white man's guns, cloth, metal articles, and trinkets for their pelts of beaver. The French traders, it is claimed, applied the name "Nez Perce" (Pierced Nose) to these Indians because a few members of the tribe used to pierce their noses to insert a shell for ornament. This habit was not a tribal custom, but the name clung to them.

Still another example of metadiscourse appears in the first sentence of the paragraph introducing the previous quotation: The sentence beginning "In the following paragraph" is called an **attributor,** the source of the quoted information. Attributors add authority to the text. In the previous discussion of Dillon's comment about hedges, the attributor phrase begins "In *Constructing Texts*"; the opening "According to" is another common lead-in for an attributor.

All of these metadiscourse markers send messages to the reader from and about the writer. They say, in effect, "I'm helping you out here, trying to make your job of reading and understanding easier."

The Overuse of Metadiscourse

It can happen, as you would expect, that inexperienced writers sometimes get carried away with metadiscourse, with those helpful messages, to the detriment of their primary message. The following paragraph is from a paper written by a student participating in a research study on the effectiveness of teaching metadiscourse. The underlined segments were identified as metadiscourse by the researchers:

> In the beginning the television <u>was posed</u> as a real asset for families with children because it would be a big influence in the home. <u>Basically this is what Marie Winn discussed in her article "The Plug-In Drug."</u> <u>As a young adult today</u> I can safely say that the hours one person sits in front of the television has greatly increased from what it was forty years ago. <u>So yes Winn is correct in stating</u> that the television is a major influence on children these days.[2]

FOR GROUP DISCUSSION

Consider the use of metadiscourse in the following paragraph, the first paragraph in Chapter 9 of Thomas S. Kuhn's *The Structure of Scientific Revolutions.* This chapter is entitled "The Nature and Necessity of Scientific Revolutions."

> These remarks permit us at last to consider the problems that provide this essay with its title. What are scientific revolutions, and what is their function in scientific development? Much of the answer to these questions has been anticipated in earlier sections. In particular, the preceding discussion has indicated that scientific revolutions are here taken to be those non-cumulative developmental episodes in which an older paradigm is replaced in whole or in part by an incompatible new one. There is more to be said, however, and an essential part of it can be introduced by asking one further question. Why should a change of paradigm be called a revolution? In the face of the vast and essential differences between political and scientific development, what parallelism can justify the metaphor that finds revolutions in both?

Identify all the uses of metadiscourse in the paragraph; characterize their purpose and their effect on the reader.

---

[2]Quoted in the article by Chang and Steffensen listed in the Bibliography under "Metadiscourse."

EXERCISE 22

A. Continue the survey of your writing style.

	Professional	Student
1. Number of sentences with first person pronouns	_____	_____
2. Number with second person: *you* or *your*	_____	_____
3. Number of transitional phrases	_____	_____
4. Number of hedging words	_____	_____
5. Number of code glosses	_____	_____
6. Number of attributors	_____	_____

B. What do your statistics tell you? Do they tell you anything about the kinds of metadiscourse expected in a specific writing situation? Do they suggest any types of metadiscourse that you might consider using in the future? If they do, what is it about your writing situation that makes you think these metadiscourse signals would be appropriate?

POINT OF VIEW

In discussing **point of view**—the perspective from which the writer views the topic—we again take up the discussion of **personal pronouns.** In Chapter 1 we saw personal pronouns as stand-ins for noun phrases and used them to determine those phrase boundaries; in Chapter 5 we recognized their role as cohesive devices. Here we look at their relationship to point of view. The writer's decision about point of view is essentially a choice about **person,** a feature of personal pronouns: Shall I write in **first person**? **Second person**? A combination? Or shall I stick strictly to **third person**?

In the following chart, the first forms shown are **subjective case,** the form used when the pronoun functions as the subject or subject complement in its sentence. The forms shown in parentheses are variations of case **(possessive, objective):** The possessive case is used when the pronoun functions as a determiner; the objective case is used in three complement positions (direct object, indirect object, object complement) and as the object of a preposition.

PERSON	NUMBER	
	__Singular__	__Plural__
1st	I (my, me)	we (our, us)
2nd	you (your, you)	you (your, you)
3rd	he (his, him) she (her, her) it (its, it)	they (their, them)

(The case of personal pronouns is discussed further on pages 249–251.)

Many kinds of essays are written in first person—more than you might think. Personal narratives, of course, are nearly always first person, but so are many other essays. In fact, it would probably be accurate to say that most essay writers use first person somewhere in their text—an occasional *we* or *our* or *us*. The exceptions are business and scientific reports and historical essays, which are often strictly third person. Newspapers and newsmagazines also stick to third person when they report the news. But writers of editorials and syndicated columns and feature stories regularly use both first and second person. And in textbooks it's certainly common to see both first and second person. In this one you'll find sentences with *we* or *our* or *you* or *your* on every page.

If it's true that first person is a common point of view, then why do teachers so often rule it unacceptable in the essays they assign? You may have had an English teacher in high school or college who required you to stick to third person. One reason for that proscription against first person is undoubtedly the bad writing that so often results, with *I* turning up as the subject of almost every sentence—as if the writer, the "I," were the topic being discussed.

The most common use of first person in professional writing is the plural—*we* and *us* and *our* rather that *I* and *me* and *my*. The result is a kind of collective first person (sometimes referred to as the "royal *we*" or the "editorial *we*"). You'll find that collective first person in the preamble to the Constitution: "We the people . . . for ourselves and our posterity . . . ." The *we* in this book is also often that collective *we*, though at times it refers just to the two authors of this book. Following is another example of the collective *we*, a first-person passage from *A Brief History of Time* by Stephen W. Hawking:

> Now at first sight, all this evidence that the universe looks the same whichever direction <u>we</u> look in might seem to suggest there is something special about <u>our</u> place in the universe. In particular, it might seem that if <u>we</u> observe all other galaxies to

be moving away from <u>us,</u> then <u>we</u> must be at the center of the universe.

Here the first-person plural is especially effective, where the writer wants the reader to be included in his description of the universe.

Another point of view that teachers sometimes rule out is the second person, the use of *you*. But it too is common for many writing occasions. You'll notice that many of the sentences in the foregoing paragraphs, as well as the sentence you're reading now, include *you* as the subject. This use of *you* not only gets the attention of the reader, it actually involves the reader in the subject matter.

But *you* does not always address the reader; it is often used in a more general sense, with a meaning more like that of the third person. Notice the use of *you* in this passage from *Broca's Brain* by Carl Sagan, describing an excursion into the back rooms of the Museum of Man in Paris:

> Most of the rooms were evidently used for storage of anthropological items, collected from decades to more than a century ago. <u>You</u> had the sense of a museum of the second order, in which were stored not so much materials that might be of interest as materials that had once been of interest. <u>You</u> could feel the presence of nineteenth-century museum directors engaged, in their frock coats, in goniometrie and craniologie, busily collecting and measuring everything, in the pious hope that mere quantification would lead to understanding.

Here *you* takes the place of "one" or "a person"; it is not "you the reader."
Some teachers, however, prefer *one* to this general *you:*

> When <u>one</u> sees the Golden Gate Bridge for the first time, the sight is simply breathtaking.

The use of *one* adds a formality, a distance that *you* does not have. The sentence sounds formal and British, like something Prince Charles would say. In American English, we're more likely to use *you* rather than *one* to convey that third-person indefinite sense:

> When <u>you</u> see the Golden Gate Bridge for the first time, the sight is simply breathtaking.

This use of *you* is technically second person, but the meaning is closer to the indefinite third-person *one.*

It is not at all unusual to mix the point of view. A first- or second-person passage always includes pronouns in the third person. And many essays that are essentially third person have an occasional *we* or *our* or *you*. There is no rule that says good writing should not have that versatility of view.

FOR GROUP DISCUSSION

1. Revise the point of view in the paragraph by Carl Sagan. What version—first-person, second-person, or third-person—do you prefer? Why?

2. Next, revise the point of view in the paragraph by Stephen H. Hawking. Which version sounds better to you? Why?

3. Now, change the point of view of one of your own paragraphs and discuss the differences you find.

KEY TERMS

Abstract subject
Agent
Attributor
Cliché
Code gloss
Connotation
Contraction
Denotation
Diction
First person

Hedge
Idiom
Metadiscourse
Metaphor
Nominalized verb
Objective cass
Particle
Person
Personal pronoun
Personal voice

Phrasal verb
Point of view
Possessive case
Second person
Simile
Subjective case
Third person
Tone
Voice

RHETORICAL REMINDERS

What is there in my sentence structure and word choice that has established my tone? Have I avoided words that contradict my tone?

Can I hear my personal voice in the words I've written? Have I avoided unusual words that don't really sound like me—words I probably wouldn't use in speech?

Have I been accurate and complete in attributing the ideas and words of outside sources and in using quotation marks for passages that are not my own?

Are my contractions appropriate, given the level of formality I want to achieve? Are my contractions attached only to pronouns (*she's*) and auxiliaries (*can't*)—not to nouns (*John'll go with us; The teacher's talking*)?

Have I used hedging words appropriately, where I need to hedge? Emphatic words where I want to show emphasis? Have I guided the reader where such guidance would help?

PUNCTUATION REMINDERS

Have I set off metadiscourse markers with commas where an emphasis on the marker would be useful?

Have I included apostrophes in contractions to indicate where a letter or letters have been left out?

Have I used quotation marks correctly (e.g., outside the period at the end of a sentence)? (*Note:* See pages 278–279 in the Glossary of Punctuation.)

CHAPTER 9

Choosing Adjectivals

CHAPTER PREVIEW

The traditional definition of *adjective* is "a word that modifies a noun." Like the word *adverb,* however, *adjective* refers to a word class with particular characteristics, not to a grammatical function. That traditional definition, then, turns out to be a definition not of *adjective* but rather of **adjectival,** the topic of this chapter. And as you saw on the Form and Function chart on page 148, there are many forms that do the work of adjectives, a variety of words, phrases, and clauses that add information to nouns. Given the diversity of forms available for expanding noun phrases, along with the number of roles in the sentence that noun phrases play, you can see that opportunities abound for writers to enhance and enrich their prose in choosing adjectivals.

THE NOUN PHRASE

As you learn about the various forms that function as adjectivals, it is useful to put them in the context of the noun phrase, to picture them in relation to the noun headword. Each of the forms has its designated place, with the headword noun occupying the central position; the single-word modifiers—determiners, adjectives, and nouns—come before the noun headword; the phrases and clauses follow:

determiner   adjective   noun   HEADWORD   phrase   clause

We will take up each of these positions, beginning with the determiners.

PREHEADWORD MODIFIERS

Determiners

Most nouns require a **determiner,** the noun signaler that occupies the opening position in the noun phrase. The determiner class includes articles, possessive nouns, possessive pronouns, demonstrative pronouns, and numbers, as well as a variety of other common words. In both speech and writing you select most determiners automatically. But sometimes in your writing you will want to give that selection deliberate thought.

As the first word in the noun phrase, and thus frequently the first word of the sentence and even of the paragraph, the determiner can provide a bridge between ideas. The selection of that bridge can make subtle but important differences in emphasis, providing transition for the reader—and it can certainly change the rhythm of the sentence:

> The decision that Ben made was the right one.
>
> That decision of Ben's was the right one.
>
> Ben's decision was the right one.
>
> Every such decision Ben made . . .
>
> His decision . . .
>
> Such a decision might have been questionable . . .
>
> A decision like that . . .

In selecting determiners, then, writers have the opportunity to make subtle distinctions and to help their readers move easily from one idea to the next in a meaningful way.

In Chapter 5 we looked at the special problem of the demonstrative pronouns used as subjects when they would be better used as determiners. As with other pronouns, the four demonstratives—*this, that, these, those*—always refer to known information. Any pronoun can become a problem when it has no clear referent—that is, when the information it represents is not, in fact, known. In the case of demonstratives, the problem can be solved by providing a headword and using the pronoun as a determiner. Here is a sentence from Chapter 5 that illustrates the problem:

> My roommate told me she has decided to drop out of school.
>
> *This* took me completely by surprise.

The problem is easily solved:

> *This decision* took me completely by surprise.

We probably don't give much thought to determiners, either as readers or as writers. But with all the choices available, as writers we certainly should. And sometimes determiners need our special attention.

FOR GROUP DISCUSSION

In Chapter 12 we look briefly at the semantic features of nouns that regulate our selection of determiners. For example, the indefinite article *a* signals only countable nouns, while the definite *the* can signal both countables and noncountables.

All the determiners are missing from the following passages. Add them to all the nouns that need them. You'll discover, when you compare your versions with those of your classmates, that for some nouns there are choices—not only a choice of determiner but in some cases a choice of whether or not to use a determiner.

A. Dorothy was little girl who lived on farm in Kansas. Tornado struck farm and carried her over rainbow to land of Munchkins. Soon afterwards she met scarecrow who wanted brain, tin man who wanted heart, and lion who wanted courage. On way to Emerald City four friends met wicked witch who cast spell on them in field of flowers. Witch wanted magic shoes that Dorothy was wearing. When they reached city, as you recall, they met wizard. Story has happy ending.

B. Planet has wrong name. Ancestors named it Earth, after land they found all around them. So far as they thought about planet as whole, they believed for centuries that surface consisted almost entirely of rocks and soil, except for smallish bodies of water like Mediterranean Sea and Black Sea. They knew about Atlantic, of course, but they regarded it as relatively narrow river running around rim of world. If ancients had known what earth was really like they undoubtedly would have named it Ocean after tremendous areas of water that cover 70.8 percent of surface.

—adapted from *The Sea* (Time-Life Books)

There were several nouns in those passages that you left bare, without determiners. Why? How do they differ from the nouns that needed them? In how many cases did you have a choice of adding a determiner or not?

Did you notice a relationship between your use of the articles (*a* vs. *the*) and information—that is, whether known or new information? Which article did you use when a noun was mentioned for the first time? Which for subsequent mentions? What conclusions can you draw about the indefinite *a* and the definite *the?*

Adjectives and Nouns

Adjectives and nouns fill the position between the determiner and the headword. When the noun phrase includes both, they appear in that order:

Determiner	Adjective	Noun	Headword
a	dismal	weather	forecast
the	new	pizza	shop
your	important	career	decision

We frequently use more than one adjective:

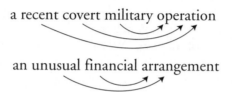

You'll notice that there are no commas in the preceding noun phrases, even though there are several modifiers in a row. But sometimes commas are called for. A good rule of thumb is to use a comma if it's possible to insert *and* between the modifiers. We would not say *a recent and covert and military operation* or *an unusual and financial arrangement.* However, we would say *an exciting and innovative concept,* so in writing that phrase without *and,* we would use a comma: *an exciting, innovative concept.*

In general, our punctuation system calls for a comma between two adjectives when they are of the same class—for instance, when they are both subjective qualities like "festive" and "exciting" and "innovative." However, in the noun phrases we saw without commas—*covert military operation* and *unusual financial arrangement*—the two adjectives in each pair are different kinds of qualities. The easiest way to decide on punctuation is to remember *and:*

> **Use a comma between prenoun modifiers if it's possible to use *and.***

Sometimes prenoun modifiers are themselves modified or qualified:

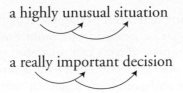

a highly unusual situation

a really important decision

When the first modifier is an *-ly* adverb, as in these two examples, we do not connect it with a hyphen. With other adverbs, however, and with nouns and adjectives as modifiers, we do use a hyphen for these prenoun compound modifiers:

> the English-speaking world
>
> a four-door minivan

Here the hyphen makes clear that *English* modifies *speaking* rather than *world* and that *four* modifies *door*, not *minivan*.

Here are some other examples of hyphens with prenoun modifiers:

a problem-solving approach	a bases-loaded home run
a poor inner-city neighborhood	a small-town high school teacher
a fuel-injected engine	a well-developed paragraph

Another occasion for hyphens in preheadword position occurs when we use a complete phrase in the adjective slot:

an off-the-wall idea	the end-of-the-term party

Modifier Noun Proliferation. There's a pitfall for writers in this system of prenoun modifiers: the temptation to string together too many adjectives or nouns. It's easy to do. For example, the curriculum committee of the faculty is known as the "faculty curriculum committee." And when the committee meets, it has a "faculty curriculum committee meeting." The minutes of that meeting then become the "faculty curriculum committee meeting minutes." And so on. Such strings are not ungrammatical, but they easily become unreadable.

You can make such noun phrases somewhat easier to read by using an *of* phrase in place of the last modifier in the string:

> a meeting of the faculty curriculum committee
>
> the minutes of the faculty curriculum committee meeting

EXERCISE 27

Punctuate the following sentences, paying particular attention to commas and hyphens that might be needed in prenoun position. Remember the rule about those commas: If you can add *and*, you probably need a comma. Remember also to apply what you know about punctuating compound sentences and compounds within sentences. You may also have to correct some fused sentences.

1. The administration's recent clean air proposals have been criticized as inadequate not only by environmental groups but also by highly placed government officials from several states.

2. A high ranking federal employee testified at a Congressional hearing on Monday.

3. The stock market reached an all time high last week and will probably keep going up.

4. There was a splendid old table for sale at the auction.

5. A big yellow delivery truck is blocking the driveway and its driver is nowhere to be seen.

6. There was not enough firefighting equipment available this summer for the widespread devastating forest fires in the Northwest.

7. I found an expensive looking copper colored bracelet in the locker room and immediately turned it in to the coach.

8. A commonly held notion among my cynical friends is that big business lobbyists run the country they could be right.

9. I have back to back exams on Wednesday.

10. The highly publicized paper recycling program has finally become a reality on our campus this fall after a year long surprisingly acrimonious discussion.

POSTHEADWORD MODIFIERS

Prepositional Phrases

The adjectival prepositional phrase, which follows the headword noun, is our most frequently occurring postnoun modifier. It is identical in form to the adverbial prepositional phrase we saw in Chapter 7; only its function is different. It's there to add a distinguishing feature to the noun, often defining "which one":

> The security guard <u>in our building</u> knows every tenant personally.
>
> We had delicious fish and chips at the new seafood restaurant <u>near the marina</u>.
>
> The meeting <u>during our lunch hour</u> was a waste of time.
>
> Ed finally found an occasion to meet that beautiful girl <u>with the long red hair</u> <u>in our math class.</u>

Because prepositional phrases are so common, both as adverbials and as adjectivals, they can easily get out of hand. In Chapter 8, you may recall, we pointed out the problem of the proliferating prepositional phrase: the tendency for writers to string them together. Such proliferation can easily obscure the sentence focus. One of the examples in that discussion included a string of five prepositional phrases at the end of the sentence, four of which are adjectival:

> You can undoubtedly find many such sentences in the pages <u>of this book</u> <u>about the grammar</u> <u>of English</u> <u>for writers</u>.

The last three of those four adjectival phrases are not only unnecessary, they obscure the focus of the sentence, which was intended to be on "this book." Those three superfluous phrases add nothing but words—no new information at all.

In place of certain adjectival prepositional phrases, the writer may have the option of using a prenoun modifier:

> an elderly lady with white hair = an elderly white-haired lady
>
> guests for dinner = dinner guests
>
> the soliloquy in the second act = the second-act soliloquy
>
> the problems with the budget = the budget problems
>
> the final exam in calculus = the calculus final

And sometimes revision may be just a matter of choosing a more precise word:

> a bunch of flowers = a bouquet
>
> the main character of the story = the protagonist
>
> birds that fly south in the winter = migratory birds

Adjective Phrases

We have described the usual position for an adjective: between the determiner and the noun headword. However when the adjective is expanded into a phrase with qualifiers or is compounded, it will occupy a position following the headword, where it will be set off by commas:

> The hot, tired Boy Scouts trudged the last mile to their campsite.
>
> The Boy Scouts, <u>hot and tired,</u> trudged the last mile to their campsite.
>
> This highly unusual banking crisis calls for extraordinary measures.
>
> This banking crisis, <u>highly unusual,</u> calls for extraordinary measures.

And in one of the weasel sentences in Chapter 2, we saw an opening adjective phrase when the subject was a personal pronoun:

> Obedient to instinct, he bites his prey at the neck.

In this case, the opening position is the only one that sounds natural; personal pronouns rarely have modifiers in postheadword position.

Unlike the previous examples of adjective phrases, which simply comment on the subject, in the following sentence the adjective phrase in postnoun position clarifies the referent of the noun:

> The students <u>unable to attend the audition</u> will have to make special arrangements with the play director.

Here the modifier tells which students will have to make arrangements. The punctuation of postnoun modifiers is taken up later in this chapter.

Participial Phrases

One of our most versatile adjectivals is the **participial phrase,** a verb phrase headed by the present or past participle form of the verb.

> The **<u>helicopter</u>** <u>hovering over the roof</u> frightened the dogs.
>
> We were shocked to see all the homeless **<u>people</u>** <u>living on the streets of Los Angeles.</u>
>
> The **<u>travelers</u>** <u>going through airport security</u> do not look happy.

You'll notice that these noun phrases with participial modifiers resemble sentences; the only thing missing is an auxiliary:

> the helicopter [is] hovering over the roof
>
> the homeless people [are] living on the streets of Los Angeles
>
> the travelers [are] going through airport security

In other words, the noun and the participle that modifies it have a subject–predicate relationship. This is an important feature of participial phrases for you to understand, as you will see later in the discussion of dangling participles.

Why do we use participles? Like adjectives and prepositional phrases, participles add information about the noun headword; and because they are verb phrases in form, they add a whole verbal idea, just as the predicate does. In the first example, the subject, *helicopter,* is the subject of two verb phrases: *hovering over the roof* and *frightened the dogs.* The two verb phrases could have been expressed with a compound predicate:

> The helicopter hovered over the roof and frightened the dogs.

or with a main clause and a dependent clause:

> The helicopter frightened the dogs as it hovered over the roof.

The participial phrase, however, allows the writer to include both verbal ideas in a more concise way. Even more important than conciseness is the clear focus of the sentence with a single predicating verb.

The Prenoun Participle. When the participle is a single word—the verb with no complements or modifiers—it usually occupies the adjective pre-headword position:

> Our <u>snoring</u> visitor kept the household awake.
> The <u>barking</u> dog next door drives us crazy.
> I should replace that <u>broken</u> hinge.
> The old hound growled at every <u>passing</u> stranger.

And, as we saw in the earlier discussion of hyphens, an adverb sometimes modifies the participle:

> a <u>fast-moving</u> object
> a <u>well-developed</u> paragraph

Remember, too, that if the adverb in that prenoun modifier is an *-ly* adverb, there will be no hyphen:

> a carefully conceived plan
> a fully grown dog

The Movable Participle. We can think of the position following the headword in the noun phrase as the home base of the participial phrase, as it is of the adjectival prepositional phrase. However, the participial phrase can be moved to the beginning of the sentence—*but only if it modifies the subject and if it is set off by commas:*

> <u>Looking out the window,</u> my mother waved to me.
>
> <u>Carrying all of their supplies,</u> the Boy Scouts trudged up the mountain in search of a campsite.
>
> <u>Laughing uproariously,</u> the audience stood and applauded.
>
> <u>Shifting his weight from one foot to the other,</u> the man looked impatient as he waited by the fountain.
>
> <u>Pressured by Congress,</u> the president agreed to support an increase in the minimum wage.

Only those participial phrases that are set off by commas can undergo this shift—that is, only those that are nonrestrictive. (Punctuation of phrases and clauses is discussed on pages 185–187.)

While the single-word participle generally fills the preheadword adjective position, it too can sometimes open the sentence—and with considerable drama:

> <u>Exasperated,</u> she made the decision to leave immediately.
>
> <u>Outraged,</u> the entire committee resigned.

You'll note that both of these openers are past participles, rather than the *-ing* present participle form; they are, in fact, the passive voice. The last participial phrase in the previous set of examples, *"Pressured by Congress,"* is also passive. There the *by* phrase offers a clue. (Underlying it is the sentence *"Congress pressured the president."*) In the case of the single-word participles here, the *by* phrase is understood.

That same participial phrase—the nonrestrictive phrase that modifies the subject—can also come at the end of the sentence:

> The Boy Scouts trudged up the mountain in search of a campsite, <u>carrying all of their supplies on their backs.</u>
>
> The audience stood and applauded, <u>laughing uproariously.</u>
>
> The man looked impatient as he waited by the fountain, <u>shifting his weight from one foot to the other.</u>

The reason for choosing one position over another has to do with sentence rhythm and focus. At the end of the sentence the participle gets much more attention than it would at the beginning or in the home-base position. At sentence end, participial phrases have great flexibility; there's room to spread out and expand, so it's not unusual to see more than one and to see them with embedded modifiers of their own. In opening and closing position they are sometimes called **free modifiers.**

The first two examples are from Jeff Shaara's Civil War story *The Last Full Measure:*

> He [Robert E. Lee]'d been awake even before that, staring up at the dark and thinking of Jackson.
>
> He [Grant]'d been up front again this morning, correcting one officer's mistake, adjusting lines of infantry that had dug in too close to the mouths of their own big guns. The men on the front lines had become wary of the rebel sharp-shooters, stayed low, flinching from the small bits of lead whistling overhead, sent at them from a hidden enemy very far away.

The following passage is from J. M. Coetzee's *Waiting for the Barbarians:*

> They live in settlements of two or three families along the banks of the river, fishing and trapping for most of the year, paddling to the remote southern shores of the lake in the autumn to catch redworms and dry them, building flimsy reed shelters, groaning with cold through the winter, dressing in skins.

And many of the details we learned about weasels in Chapter 2 came by way of participial phrases:

> Outside, he stalks rabbits, mice, muskrats, and birds, killing more bodies than he can eat warm, and often dragging the carcasses home. Obedient to instinct he bites his prey at the neck, either splitting the jugular vein at the throat or crunching the brain at the base of the skull, and he does not let go.

The Dangling Participle. The participial phrase provides a good way to change the focus of the sentence, as we have seen in these variations—but it carries an important restriction:

> **The participle can open or close the sentence *only* if it modifies the subject—that is, when the subject of the participle is also the subject of the sentence and is in regular subject position. Otherwise, the participle will dangle.**

Remember, a participle modifies its own subject. Simply stated, a dangling participle is a verb without a subject:

> *Carrying all of our supplies for miles, the campground was a
> welcome sight.
>
> *Having swung his five-iron too far to the left, Joe's ball landed
> precisely in the middle of a sand trap.
>
> * Furiously filling in the bubbles on the answer sheet, the time was
> up before I could finish the test.

The campground, of course, did not do the carrying; nor did Joe's ball swing the five-iron; and I was the one filling in those bubbles, not "the time." You can fix such sentences (and avoid them in the first place) by making sure that the subject of the sentence is also the subject of the participle:

> Having carried all of our supplies for miles, *we* were exhausted by
> the time we reached the campground.
>
> Having swung his five-iron too far to the left, *Joe* once again hit the
> ball into the sand trap.
>
> Furiously filling in the bubbles on the answer sheet, *I* still wasn't
> able to finish the test before time was up.

Another common source of the dangling participle, and other dangling modifiers as well, is the sentence with a delayed subject—a *there*-transformation, for example, or an *it*-cleft:

> *Having moved all the outdoor furniture into the garage, there was
> no room left for the car.
>
> *Knowing how much work I had to do, it was good of you to come
> and help.

In the second sentence, *you* is the subject of the participle, so it's there in the sentence, but it's not in the usual subject position. Sometimes the most efficient way to revise such sentences is to expand the participial phrase into a complete clause. That expansion adds the missing subject:

> <u>After we moved all the outdoor furniture into the garage,</u> there was
> no room left for the car.
>
> It was good of you to come and help <u>when you learned how much
> work I had to do.</u>

Even though there is often no problem of communication with dangling and misplaced modifiers—that is, the reader probably knows what you mean—you may in fact be communicating something you hadn't intended: You may be sending a message that says, "Fuzzy thinking."

Our language includes a few participial phrases that we use in sentence-opening position that are not dangling, even though the subject of the sentence is not their subject. They function as sentence modifiers rather than as noun modifiers. The most common are the "speaking of" phrases:

> <u>Speaking of</u> old movies, have you seen *Gaslight?*
>
> <u>Speaking of</u> the weather, we should probably cancel the picnic.

There are other *-ing* words that have the status of prepositions. They often open a sentence in order to set up the topic:

> <u>Regarding</u> your job interview, the supervisor called to change the time.
>
> <u>Concerning</u> the recent book about the Kennedys, several reviewers have doubted its credibility.

Because of their common use, such expressions have achieved the status of set phrases. Nevertheless, they may be regarded by some readers as too casual or informal for certain writing situations.

EXERCISE 28

Rewrite the following sentences to eliminate the dangling participles. In some cases you may want to expand the participles into full clauses.

1. Having endured rain all week, the miserable weather on Saturday didn't surprise us.

2. Hoping for the sixth win in a row, there was great excitement in the stands when the band finally played "The Star Spangled Banner."

3. Known for her conservative views on taxes and the role of government, we were not at all surprised when the Republican county commissioner announced her candidacy for the General Assembly.

4. Exhausted by the heat and humidity, it was wonderful to do nothing but lie in the shade and drink iced tea.

5. Having spent nearly all day in the kitchen, everyone agreed that my superb gourmet meal was worth the effort.

6. Feeling pressure from the environmentalists, the Clean Air Act was immediately put on the committee's agenda.

7. Obviously intimidated by a long history of defeats in Morgantown, there seems to be no way that our basketball team can beat the West Virginia Mountaineers on their home court.

8. Arriving unexpectedly on a weekend when I had two papers to finish and a big exam coming up, I didn't feel exactly overjoyed at seeing my parents.

....

Relative Clauses

Another modifier in the noun phrase following the noun is the adjectival dependent clause called the **relative clause,** also called the *adjective clause.* Because it is a clause—that is, a structure with a subject and a predicate— this adjectival modifier is a powerful tool; it enables the writer to embed a complete subject–predicate idea into a noun phrase.

In many respects, the relative clause and the participial phrase are alike. The participial phrase, in fact, is actually a shortened version of the relative clause. All of the examples we saw earlier could easily be expanded into clauses with no change in their meaning:

The helicopter <u>that is hovering over the roof</u> frightened the dogs.

We were shocked to see all the homeless people <u>who are living on the streets of Los Angeles.</u>

The travelers <u>who are going through airport security</u> do not look happy.

One feature the participle has that the clause does not is its movability: The clause rarely moves out of the noun phrase; it almost always follows the noun it modifies.

The Relatives.   The relative clause is introduced by either a **relative pronoun** (*that, who,* or *which*) or a **relative adverb** (*where, when,* or *why*); the relative plays a part in the clause it introduces. In the case of the relative pronoun (the most common introducer), the part will be that of a noun: a subject, direct object, indirect object, subject complement, object of the preposition, or, as possessive nouns generally function, a determiner.

The relative pronoun *who* has different forms depending on its **case,** its role in the clause—*who* (**subjective**), *whose* (**possessive**), and *whom* (**objective**):

The man <u>who called last night</u> wouldn't leave his name.

Here *who* is the subject in its clause.

The student <u>whose notes I borrowed</u> was absent today.

Here the possessive relative, *whose,* is the determiner for *notes.* (You'll recall that "determiner" is a common role for possessive pronouns.) The clause, in normal left-to-right fashion, is "I borrowed whose notes."

> Our dog, Rusty, <u>whom we all dearly loved</u>, was recently killed on the highway.

Here the objective relative, *whom,* is the direct object in its clause: "We all dearly loved whom."

When the relative pronoun is an object in its clause, it can be deleted if the clause is **restrictive**—that is, if the clause is not set off by commas. In the previous example, the clause is **nonrestrictive,** so the relative *whom* cannot be deleted. And you'll notice also that *whom* makes the sentence sound formal, not like something you would say. But in the following example, the *whom* can be omitted, and in speech it certainly would be. Most writers too would probably omit it.

> King Edward VIII gave up the throne of England for the woman <u>(whom)</u> <u>he loved.</u>

The relative pronoun *that* always introduces restrictive clauses; in other words, *that* clauses are never set off by commas:

> You choose a color <u>that you like.</u>
> A boy <u>that I knew in junior high</u> called me last week.
> A truck <u>that was going too fast for road conditions</u> hit our dog.

In the first two preceding sentences, *that* can be omitted. Some writers, in fact, would insist on leaving it out in the second one because it refers to a person; some writers insist on *who* and *whom* in reference to people—not *that.* The easiest and smoothest solution is simply to omit the relative:

> A boy <u>I knew in junior high</u> called me last week.

However, the relative *cannot* be omitted when it functions as the subject in its clause, as in the sentence about the truck. Nor can it be omitted if the clause is nonrestrictive—no matter what role the pronoun fills:

> Rob Miller, <u>whom I knew in junior high,</u> called me last week.

We should note, too, that in speaking this sentence we are more likely to say *who,* even though the objective case of the pronoun is called for; most listeners wouldn't notice the difference. (*Who* actually sounds correct because it's at the beginning of the clause, where the subjective case is found.)

The relative pronoun *which* is generally reserved for nonrestrictive clauses—those set off by commas:

> My roommate's financial problems, <u>which he finally told me about,</u> have caused him a lot of stress this semester.

The relative adverbs *where, when,* and *why* also introduce adjectival clauses, modifiers of nouns denoting place (*where* clauses), time (*when* clauses), and of the noun *reason* (*why* clauses):

> Newsworthy events rarely happen in the small *town* <u>where I lived as a child.</u>
>
> We will all feel nervous until next *Tuesday,* <u>when results of the auditions will be posted.</u>
>
> I understand the *reason* <u>why Margo got the lead.</u>

THE BROAD-REFERENCE CLAUSE

As we have seen, the relative clause is part of a noun phrase—and the antecedent of the relative pronoun that introduces it is the headword of that noun phrase:

The **students** <u>who live across the hall</u> are quiet today.

I came to see the **dress** <u>that you bought for the prom.</u>

Joe's **car,** <u>which he bought last week,</u> looks like a gas guzzler to me.

However, the relative clause introduced by *which,* instead of referring to a particular noun, sometimes has what is called **broad reference:**

> Joe bought a gas guzzler, <u>which surprised me.</u>
>
> Tom cleaned up the garage without being asked, <u>which made me suspect that he wanted to borrow the car.</u>

Here the antecedent of *which* in both cases is the idea of the entire main clause, not a specific noun.

One way to revise this vague broad-reference clause is to furnish a noun that sums up the idea of the main clause, so that the clause will have specific, rather than broad, reference. Note in the revisions that the relative *that* has replaced *which,* and the clauses now have nouns to modify:

> Joe bought a gas guzzler, <u>a decision</u> that surprised me.
>
> Tom cleaned up the garage without being asked, <u>a rare event</u> that made me suspect he wanted to borrow the car.

This solution to the vague antecedent is sometimes called a **summative modifier.**

There are other solutions to the broad-reference *which* clause besides the summative modifier. For example, we could revise the following sentence,

> I broke out in a rash, which really bothered me,

in at least three ways. The first is the summative modifier:

> I broke out in a rash, a problem that really bothered me.
>
> Breaking out in a rash really bothered me.
>
> The rash I got last week really bothered me.

The earlier example about the clean garage also has other possibilities:

> When Tom cleaned up the garage without being asked, I suspected that he wanted to borrow the car.
>
> Tom's cleaning of the garage without being asked made me suspect that he wanted to borrow the car.

While it's true that broad-reference clauses often have a vague quality, sending a message of carelessness, there are times when a *which* in reference to the whole clause makes the point clearly—and, in fact, may be preferred:

> The men my two sisters married are brothers, which makes their children double cousins.

EXERCISE 29

Revise the following sentences to eliminate any instances of the broad-reference *which.*

1. My roommate told me she was planning to withdraw from school, which came as a complete surprise.

2. The first snowstorm of the season in Denver was both early and severe, which was not what the weather service had predicted.

3. The college library has finally converted the central card catalog to a computer system, which took over four years to complete.

4. The president had some harsh words for Congress in his recent press conference, which some observers considered quite inappropriate.

5. Wendell didn't want to stay for the second half of the game, which made Harriet rather unhappy.

6. We're having company for dinner three times this week, which probably means hot dogs for the rest of the month.

7. In his State of the Union message, the president characterized the last two years as a period of "unprecedented prosperity," which one economist immediately labeled "sheer hype and hyperbole."

8. The Brazilian government has grudgingly agreed to consider new policies regarding the rain forests, which should come as good news to everyone concerned about the environment.

FOR GROUP DISCUSSION

The following paragraph, the first one in "Revival Road," a short story by Louise Erdrich, contains nine sentences, with a total of sixteen clauses, seven of which are either adjectival or adverbial. You'll notice, however, that there are many more than sixteen verbs in the sentence. List all the verbs that you find; name their function. Then consider their effect on the overall description.

From the air, our road must look like a length of rope flung down haphazardly, a thing of inscrutable loops and half-finished question marks. But there is a design to Revival Road. The beginning of the road is paved, though with a material inferior to that of the main highway, which snakes south from our college town into the villages and factory cities of New Hampshire. When the town has the money, the road is also coated with light gravel. Over the course of a summer, those bits of stone are pressed into the softened tar, making a smooth surface on which the cars pick up speed. By midwinter, though, the frost has crept beneath the road and flexed, creating heaves that force the cars to slow again. I'm glad when that happens, for children walk down this road to the bus stop below. They walk past our house with their dogs, wearing puffy jackets of saturated brilliance—hot pink, hot yellow, hot blue. They change shape and grow before my eyes, becoming the young drivers of fast cars that barely miss the smaller children, who, in their turn, grow up and drive away from here.

PUNCTUATION OF PHRASES AND CLAUSES

Does this modifier need to be set off by commas? That's the question to be answered about the punctuation of participial phrases and relative clauses in the noun phrase. The question also comes up in the case of certain appositives, which are discussed in Chapter 10.

The answer to the question has to do with the purpose of the modifier: Is it there to identify the referent of the noun being modified—that is, to restrict its meaning—or simply to comment on it. (The traditional terms for the difference are *restrictive* and *nonrestrictive*.)

You may recall back in Chapter 2 you saw the word *referent* in the discussion of sentence patterns: When the subject complement in the *be*-pattern or the linking-verb pattern is a noun or noun phrase, it has the same referent as the subject (*Mary is my sister*). *Referent* means the thing (or person, event, concept, and so on) that the noun or noun phrase stands for: *Mary* and *my sister* refer to the same person. The term *referent* is useful here, too, in thinking about the purpose of the modifier as well as the knowledge of the reader: Is the referent of the noun clear to the reader without the modifier?

In the following sentence, with no other context, the relative clause is needed to identify the referent of the noun phrase *the president:*

> The president <u>who was elected in 1932</u> faced problems that would have overwhelmed the average person.

Ordinarily we would say that the noun phrase *the president* has many possible referents; the *who* clause is needed to make the referent clear; it defines and restricts *the president* to a particular man, the one elected in 1932. But what if the reader already knows the referent from previous context?

> Franklin Delano Roosevelt took office at a time when the outlook for the nation was bleak indeed. The president, <u>who was elected in 1932,</u> faced decisions that would have overwhelmed the average person.

In this context the referent of *the president* is already defined by the time the reader gets to it: The clause is simply commenting, so it needs to be set off by commas. In other words, the commas are sending the message that the *who* clause is extra information, just a comment. You don't need this information to know who is being discussed here. In contrast, the lack of commas in the earlier sentence without context sends the message that the *who* clause is needed to identify the referent of *president*. In other words,

> Restrictive (no commas) = identifying
>
> Nonrestrictive (commas) = commenting[1]

---

[1]*Comment* and *identify* are terms that Francis Christensen introduced in his book *Notes Toward a New Rhetoric.* It is listed under "Punctuation" in the Bibliography.

Punctuation of participial phrases works the same way. When the participial phrase provides information for identifying, or defining the referent, there are no commas:

The merchants <u>holding the sidewalk sales</u> are hoping for good weather.

This lack of commas, then, implies that not all merchants are concerned about the weather—only those who are holding the sidewalk sales. The *holding* phrase is there to tell which merchants are hoping for good weather. In other words, there's another group of merchants who may or may not be concerned about the weather. The lack of commas identifies a particular subgroup of merchants—in this case, those concerned about the weather.

> **Use commas around a nonrestrictive modifier when the modifier is only commenting on the noun rather than identifying it—when the reader already knows the referent or if there is only one possible referent.**

In the punctuation of relative clauses, the relative pronoun provides clues:

1. The *that* clause is always restrictive; it is never set off by commas.
2. The *which* clause is generally nonrestrictive; it is set off by commas. If you want to figure out if your *which* clause needs commas, try substituting *that*. If you can do so without changing the meaning, then the commas can, and perhaps should, be omitted.
3. If the relative pronoun can be deleted, the clause is restrictive:

   The bus (that) I ride to work is always late.
   The woman (whom) I work with is always early.

The next two rules of thumb apply to both clauses and phrases:

4. After any proper noun, the modifier is nonrestrictive:

   Willamette University, which was established seven years before the Gold Rush of 1849, is within walking distance of Oregon's capitol.
   In Alaska, where the distance between some cities is vast, many businesses and individuals own private planes.

5. After any common noun that has only one possible referent, the modifier will be nonrestrictive:

The highest mountain in the world, which resisted the
efforts of climbers until 1953, looks truly forbidding
from the air.
Mike's twin brother, who lives in Austin, has a personality
just like Mike's.
My mother, sitting by the window, is talking to herself.

EXERCISE 30

Decide whether the participial phrases in the following sentences are restrictive
(defining) or nonrestrictive (commenting) and punctuate them accordingly.

1. Many coal miners in West Virginia refused to approve two sections
   of the contract offered by management last week. They maintain
   that the sections covering wages and safety represent no improvement over their present contract expiring on Friday at midnight.

2. A group of students held a protest rally in front of the administration building yesterday. The students hoping for a meeting with
   the provost were demonstrating against the tuition hike recently
   approved by the trustees. The increase expected to take effect in
   September will raise tuition almost 15 percent.

3. The senator and her husband sitting next to her on the speaker's
   platform both looked calm as they waited for the mayor to finish the
   introduction. Then the mayor turning to look directly at the senator
   shocked both the audience and the listeners on the platform.

EXERCISE 31

Combine the following groups of sentences into single sentences by
embedding some of the ideas as modifiers. You will probably want to use
adverbial modifiers as well as adjectivals—participial phrases and relative
clauses you have just been studying in this chapter. In some cases you may
have to make other changes in the wording as well.

1. In many parts of the country, citizens are mobilizing against
   crime and drugs.
   They are driving drug dealers out of their neighborhoods.

2. More and more public officials are supporting the legalization of
   certain drugs.
   They argue that there is no other way to win the drug war.

3. Fingerprints have been used for criminal identification since 1891.
   A police officer in Argentina introduced the method.

The computer has revolutionized the storage and retrieval of fingerprints.

4. The leaning tower of Pisa is 179 feet high.
It is over 800 years old.
It leans 17 feet off the perpendicular.

5. In 1997 an earthquake struck the Assisi region of Italy.
Many priceless mosaics from the 14th century were destroyed.
The mosaics decorated the walls and ceiling of the Basilica of St. Francis.

6. The highest incidence of colon cancer in the United States occurs in the Northeast.
The Northeast also has the highest levels of acid rain.
Cancer researchers suspect that there is a causal link between the two.

7. The rate of colon cancer is related to the amount of carbon dioxide in the air.
Carbon dioxide absorbs ultraviolet light.
Ultraviolet light fuels the body's production of vitamin D.

8. Influenza, or flu, is a viral infection.
It begins as an upper respiratory infection and then spreads to other parts of the body.
Flu causes aches and pains in the joints.

9. Flu viruses mutate constantly.
We cannot build up our immunity.
New varieties spread from person to person and from place to place.

10. The sodium intake of the average American is far higher than necessary.
The recommended level is 400 to 3,300 mg per day.
The average American consumes over 4,000 mg per day.

A Punctuation Rule Revisited

The very first punctuation lesson you learned in this book, back in Chapter 2, concerned the boundaries between parts of the sentence

> Do not use a single comma to separate the required units in the basic sentence.

The punctuation lessons in this chapter perhaps explain why the word *single* was included in that rule. In this chapter you have seen sentences in which a modifier that falls between two units is set off with two commas:

> My mother, sitting by the window, is talking to herself.

You may be tempted to think that here the subject and predicate are separated by a single comma, the comma after *window.* But they are not. It's important to recognize that the second comma has a partner and that the purpose of these commas is to allow the participial phrase into the noun phrase as a modifier. *That particular participle wouldn't be allowed without its two commas.* In other words, that comma is not *between* sentence units: It is part of the subject.

You have learned a great many punctuation rules so far in this book—and there are more to come in the next chapter! Learning those rules in connection with the expansion of sentences, as you are doing, should help you recognize their purposes and use them well. And you can be sure that using punctuation well—using it to help the reader and doing so according to the standard conventions—will go a long way in establishing your authority.

EXERCISE 32

Continue your style inventory. This time count the kinds of sentences you have used in your essay, whether simple, compound, or complex. (The latter refers to a sentence that includes a dependent clause—that is, a clause that functions as an adjectival or adverbial or one that fills a nominal position.) Compare your essay with one written by a professional—perhaps an essay that you've read in your English class or one that your instructor suggests.

	Your Essay	Professional
1. Total number of simple sentences	_____	_____
2. Total number of compound sentences	_____	_____
a. number connected with *and*	_____	_____
b. number connected with *but*	_____	_____
c. number with other conjunctions	_____	_____
d. number with semicolons	_____	_____
3. Number of complex sentences	_____	_____
4. Number with adjectival clauses	_____	_____
5. Number with participial phrases	_____	_____
a. at sentence opening	_____	_____
b. at sentence end	_____	_____
6. Number of opening adverbial clauses	_____	_____
7. Number of other adverbial openers	_____	_____

KEY TERMS

Adjectival
Adjective
Adjective phrase
Broad-reference clause
Commenting modifier
Dangling participle
Defining modifier

Determiner
Free modifier
Headword
Nonrestrictive
    modifier
Noun phrase
Participial phrase

Participle
Prepositional phrase
Relative adverb
Relative clause
Relative pronoun
Restrictive modifier
Summative modifier

RHETORICAL REMINDERS

Prenoun Modifiers

Have I paid attention to commas and hyphens in the noun phrase?

Have I avoided strings of nouns as modifiers?

Postnoun Modifiers

Do opening and closing participles modify the subject of the sentence?

Have I thought about sentence focus in placing the participles?

Does the punctuation distinguish between restrictive (defining) and nonrestrictive (commenting) phrases and clauses?

Have I made a conscious choice in my use of participles and clauses?

Have I avoided fuzzy broad-reference *which* clauses?

PUNCTUATION REMINDERS

Have I used a comma between prenoun modifers where it's possible to use *and?*

Have I used commas around a nonrestrictive modifier when the modifier is only commenting on the noun rather than defining it—when the reader already knows its referent or if it has only one possible referent?

Have I used a comma to set off a verb phrase that opens the sentence? And have I made sure that the subject of the sentence is also the subject of the verb in that verb phrase?

Other Stylistic Variations

Everything we say, we say "with **style**," in one sense of the word—when the word refers simply to an individual's way of writing. You have your own style of writing, just as you have your own style of walking and whistling and wearing your hair. We also use the word *style* to characterize the overall impression of a piece of writing, such as the plain style, the pompous style, the grand style, the official style. When you follow advice about being brief and using simple words, the outcome will be a plain style; words that are too fancy will probably result in a pompous style.

The word *style* is also used in connection with variations in sentence structure, with the structural and punctuation choices that you as a writer can use to advantage. For example, in the second sentence of the previous paragraph, three verb phrases in a series are connected with two *and*s and no commas:

> walking and whistling and wearing your hair

It could have been written with two commas and only one *and:*

> walking, whistling, and wearing your hair

Or only commas:

> walking, whistling, wearing your hair

Such stylistic variations have traditionally occupied an important place in the study of rhetoric. In fact, the Greeks had names for every deviation from ordinary word order or usage, and Greek orators practiced using them. Some of the more common ones, you're familiar with, such as **figures of speech** as simile, metaphor, and personification. But many of them, you probably don't even notice—such as the shift, in both this sentence and the previous one, of the direct object to opening position. The Greeks called this inversion of usual word order **anastrophe** (pronounced a-NAS-tro-fee).

In studying this chapter you will use your understanding of grammar as you study stylistic choices. You'll look more closely at variations in the series, along with repetition, ellipsis, antithesis, and sentence fragments.

For some of these variations you'll learn the term the Greeks used. But is that important—to learn their labels? Yes and no. Yes, it's important to know, simply, that they have labels. It's important to know that stylistic choices like these are used deliberately by good speakers and writers. But no, it's not really important that you remember their names. It's enough that you make their acquaintance, that you recognize them when you see them again, and feel comfortable using them.

We begin this chapter with a description of a structure you saw way back on the first page of Chapter 2, but one you haven't seen often since then in these pages: the **absolute phrase.** Rather than an adverbial or adjectival, the absolute is considered a sentence modifier because it functions as a kind of loner, standing beyond the sentence. It has a familiar form—that of noun phrase—but it fills none of the noun phrase positions. We include it here in the discussion of stylistic variations not only because it lends a special flair to a descriptive or narrative passage but also because the well-chosen absolute phrase sends the reader a message, a message about the writer's craftsmanship and ability and style.

The purpose of this chapter, then, is to raise your consciousness about style, to encourage you to make the kinds of stylistic choices that send a message to your reader: "Pay attention! Read this carefully. It's important."

ABSOLUTE PHRASES

You saw two absolute phrases on the first page of Chapter 2 in our old familiar weasel paragraph:

> A weasel is wild. Who knows what he thinks? He sleeps in his underground den, <u>his tail draped over his nose. . . .</u> One naturalist refused to kill a weasel who was socketed into his hand deeply as a rattlesnake. The man could in no way pry the tiny weasel off, and he had to walk half a mile to water, <u>the weasel dangling from his palm,</u> and soak him off like a stubborn label.

If you recall the formula for the noun phrase that opened Chapter 9, you'll recognize that both of these examples follow the pattern:

> determiner + noun headword + participial phrase

Absolute phrases are, indeed, noun phrases. This pattern, with a participial phrase as the postheadword modifier, is our most common form of the absolute, although sometimes that modifier is itself a noun phrase, sometimes a prepositional phrase.

Our two weasel examples illustrate one of the two styles of absolutes, the phrase that adds a detail or point of focus to the idea stated in the main clause. Notice in the third sentence how the main clause describes the overall scene, the weasel asleep in his underground den; the absolute phrase moves the reader in for a close-up view, focusing on a detail, just as a filmmaker uses the camera. The example in the last sentence works the same way: The main clause gives us the long shot of the man walking; the absolute focuses on the weasel dangling from his palm.

With only one small addition to these absolutes, the relationship of the noun headword and its modifier becomes clear:

> His tail (is) draped over his nose.
> The weasel (is) dangling from his palm.

In other words, the absolute actually adds a subject–predicate relationship to its sentence, but does so without actually adding another clause. That third sentence,

> The weasel sleeps in his underground den, his tail draped over
> his nose,

is neither "compound" nor "complex"; in fact, it would be classified as "simple" in traditional grammar, since it has only one clause. However, you can see that it has the impact of a complex sentence, given that it includes what is essentially a subordinate subject–predicate construction.

As you read the sentences containing these two examples, you can probably hear your voice giving emphasis to the noun headword of the absolute phrase. The absolute invariably calls attention to itself, sending a "Pay attention!" message to the reader. For that reason, writers often reserve the absolute for important details. It also sends a more subtle message: "I have crafted this sentence carefully; I know what I'm doing." Even though a reader may not be able to name, perhaps not even to consciously recognize, the absolute phrase, that reader will certainly recognize a writer in control. The well-chosen absolute can add to the writer's authority.

The absolute phrase that adds a focusing detail is especially common in fiction writing, much more common than in expository writing—such as the prose in this textbook and probably your texts for other classes. In the following passages, all from works of fiction, some have a participle as the postnoun modifier, just as Annie Dillard has in her weasel description; however, you'll also see some with noun phrases, others with prepositional phrases.

> There was no bus in sight and Julian, <u>his hands still jammed in his pockets and his head thrust forward,</u> scowled down the empty street.
>
> —Flannery O'Connor
> ("Everything That Rises Must Converge")

> He smiled a little to himself as he ran, holding the ball lightly in front of him with his two hands, <u>his knees pumping high, his hips twisting in the almost girlish run of a back in a broken field.</u>
>
> —Irwin Shaw ("The Eighty-Yard Run")

In this series of three absolutes, the first and third have noun phrases as the postnoun modifiers: tiny ribbons of light; a purple hollow. . . :

> He saw the city spread below like a glittering golden ocean, <u>the streets tiny ribbons of light, the planet curving away at the edges, the sky a purple hollow extending to infinity.</u>
>
> —Anne Tyler (*The Accidental Tourist*)

And these two examples have prepositional phrases:

> Silently they ambled down Tenth Street until they reached a stone bench that jutted from the sidewalk near the curb. They stopped there and sat down, <u>their backs to the eyes of the two men in white smocks who were watching them.</u>
>
> —Toni Morrison (*Song of Solomon*)

> The man stood laughing, <u>his weapons at his hips.</u>
> —Stephen Crane ("The Bride Comes to Yellow Sky")

In this example, the first absolute phrase adds a detail to the dining event with a prepositional phrase as the modifier; the second, rather than focusing on a detail, explains the significance of the scene described:

> Most days she left the adding machine set up on the kitchen table, so we cleared space around it when we ate, <u>usually just</u>

one or two of us at a time, <u>family dinners long since a thing</u>
<u>of the past.</u>

—Richard Russo (*Bridge of Sighs*)

A second style of absolute phrase, rather than focusing on a detail, explains a cause or condition:

<u>Our car having developed engine trouble,</u> we stopped for the night
   at a roadside rest area.

We decided to have our picnic, <u>the weather being warm and clear.</u>

<u>Victory assured,</u> the fans stood and cheered during the last five
   minutes of the game.

The first example could be rewritten as a *because*- or *when*- clause:

<u>When our car developed engine trouble,</u> we stopped . . .

or

<u>Because our car developed engine trouble,</u> we stopped . . .

The absolute allows the writer to include the information without the explicitness of the complete clause; the absolute, then, can be thought of as containing both meanings, both *when* and *because*. The absolute about the weather in the second example suggests an attendant condition rather than a cause.

Here's a familiar (and hotly debated) absolute of this style:

A well-regulated militia being necessary to the security of a free state,
   the right of the people to keep and bear arms shall not be infringed.

This rendering of the Second Amendment does not include two commas that appear in the original: one following *militia* and one following *arms*. Punctuation conventions have changed in the past two centuries.

As you can probably hear, this second style of absolute adds a formal tone to the sentence, formal almost to the point of stiffness. It's certainly not a structure that's used in speech. In fact, neither of these two styles of absolute phrases is used in speech—in speeches, perhaps, but certainly not in everyday speech.

FOR GROUP DISCUSSION

We could add *with* to most, if not all, of the examples, thus turning the absolute phrases into prepositional phrases:

The man stood laughing, <u>with his weapons at his hips.</u>

There was no bus in sight and Julian, <u>with his hands still jammed in his pockets and his head thrust forward,</u> scowled down the empty street.

Try the other examples as well, with the added *with.*

How would you characterize the difference in the two styles? Has the meaning changed at all?

EXERCISE 36

Expand the following sentences by adding the modifiers called for. (You might want to review participial phrases and relative clauses in Chapter 9.)

1. Add a *who-* clause that tells what one of your relatives is usually like: My cousin (aunt, uncle, sister, etc.), who _____

   _____,

   surprised everyone at the family reunion.

Now add a dependent clause that explains what your relative did that was so surprising. Now add an absolute phrase at the end of the sentence—a close-up detail.

2. Add a series of participial phrases that tell what the cyclists were doing: From the window we watched the cyclists _____

   _____.

Now add an appositive at the end of the sentence as a comment on the whole scene.

3. Use an appositive to describe the trucker: At the far end of the counter sat a trucker, _____

   _____.

Now add two prenoun modifiers to explain what sort of counter it is so that the reader will be better able to picture the scene—and an absolute at the end that provides a close-up detail.

4. Start this sentence with an adverbial clause or phrase that tells when: _____

   _____,

   endless cars jammed the freeway.

Now add a series of absolute phrases that describe the cars.

> 5. Write a sentence or paragraph describing your classroom or campus. Use the modifiers you have been practicing with.

THE COORDINATE SERIES

Many of the variations that writers use for special effects occur in connection with coordinate structures—pairs and series of sentences and their parts. One of those changes is a deviation in the use of conjunctions. Let's go back to the variations possible for the second sentence in the Chapter Preview:

> You have your own style of writing, just as you have your own style of walking and whistling and wearing your hair.

This style, with that extra *and*, was labeled **polysyndeton** by the Greek rhetoricians. You'll recall from the discussion of the serial comma in Chapter 4 that the usual punctuation for the series includes commas until the final *and:*

> walking, whistling, and wearing your hair

Opposite of the extra *and* is the series with no conjunction at all, just commas, a style called **asyndeton:**

> walking, whistling, wearing your hair

The differences are subtle but meaningful. Polysyndeton puts emphasis on each element of the series with a fairly equal beat: _____ and _____ and _____. As Arthur Quinn notes in *Figures of Speech* (see the Bibliography), polysyndeton slows us down, perhaps adds a sense of formality, while asyndeton speeds us up. And asyndeton, the variation with no *ands*, also suggests that the list is open-ended. It seems to suggest, "I could go on and on; I could tell you much more."

In the following passage, Winston Churchill describes Stonewall Jackson using asyndeton in both series; he has embedded one such series within another:

> His character was stern, his manner reserved and unusually forbidding, his temper Calvinistic, his mode of life strict, frugal, austere.

The omission of the conjunctions contributes to the strictness and frugality of style that echo the words themselves. With conjunctions, the sentence would lose that echo:

> His mode of life was strict and frugal and austere.

In the following sentence from *A Not Entirely Benign Procedure: Four Years as a Medical Student,* Perri Klass uses asyndeton to help convey the pressure of medical school:

> The general pressure in medical school is to push yourself ahead into professionalism, to start feeling at home in the hospital, in the operating room, to make medical jargon your native tongue—it's all part of becoming efficient, knowledgeable, competent.

And in the following sentence by Annie Dillard, this one from her memoir, *An American Childhood,* she uses both stylistic variations: asyndeton in the opening and the final series; polysyndeton in the series with *or:*

> As for loss, as for parting, as for bidding farewell, so long, thanks, to love or a land or a time—what did I know of parting, of grieving, mourning, loss?

Perhaps the series is not a feature of language that you've thought much about in your writing. But as these examples illustrate, a well-constructed series can add a great deal of stylistic flair. And while it's not important that you remember their labels, now that you know about polysyndeton and asyndeton, you can add these devices to your collection of writers' tools with the assurance that using them will make the reader pay attention and, what's even more important, recognize your competence and authority as a writer.

REPETITION

Repetition has come up before in these pages—in both a positive and a negative sense. On the positive side, repetition gives our sentences cohesion: The known–new contract calls for the repetition, if not of words, then of ideas. It is part of the glue that holds paragraphs together. But we also have a negative label for repetition when it has no purpose, when it gets in the reader's way: Then we call it *redundancy.* You may recall the discussion of redundancy in connection with flabby prepositional phrases that added nothing but words to the sentence and kept the reader from focusing on the new information.

If you've heard warnings about redundancy, if you've seen "red" in the margins of your essays, you might hesitate to use repetition deliberately. But don't hesitate. It's easy to distinguish redundancy from good repetition, from repetition as a stylistic tool. You saw examples of good repetition in the discussion of parallelism as a cohesive device in Chapter 5.

In an essay on redundancy and ellipsis as writing strategies, listed in the Bibliography, Keith Grant-Davie reports that redundancy "is widely seen as a kind of linguistic cholesterol, clogging the arteries of our prose and impeding the efficient circulation of knowledge" (455). On the other hand, effective redundancy contributes "good cholesterol," especially in the field of technical writing.

While "good cholesterol" was not a term they used, the Greek rhetoricians had a label for every conceivable kind of good repetition—from the repetition of sounds and syllables to that of words and phrases in various locations in the sentence. We confine our discussion to repetition in coordinate structures that make the reader sit up and take notice. Again, to emphasize their importance as tools, we use their ancient labels.

Consider the Gettysburg Address. Which of Lincoln's words, other than "Fourscore and seven years ago," do you remember? Probably "government of the people, by the people, and for the people." It's hard to imagine those words without the repetition: "Of, by, and for the people" just wouldn't have the same effect. Lincoln's repetition of the same grammatical form is called **isocolon.** And think about President Kennedy's stirring words, with his repetition of *any* to signal five noun phrases:

> [We] shall pay any price, bear any burden, meet any hardship, support any friend, oppose any foe to assure the survival and the success of liberty.

Notice, too, Kennedy's use of asyndeton. He seems to be saying, "I could go on and on with my list."

You don't have to be a president to use that kind of repetition, nor do you have to reserve it for formal occasions. Whenever you use a coordinate structure, there's an opportunity for you to add to its impact with repetition, simply by including words that wouldn't have to be included. The following sentence, from an essay in *Time* by Charles Krauthammer, could have been more concise, but it would have lost its drama:

> There is not a single Western standard, there are two: what we demand of Western countries at peace and what we demand of Western countries at war.

The following example of isocolon, the repetitions in the *of-* phrases, is part of a paragraph from Virginia Woolf's essay "How Should One Read a Book?" Notice also the asyndeton in the paragraph's opening sentence:

> It is simple enough to say that since books have classes—fiction, biography, poetry—we should separate them and take from each what it is right that each should give us. Yet few people ask from books what books can give us. Most commonly we come to books with blurred and divided minds,

asking of fiction that it shall be true, of poetry that it shall be false, of biography that it shall be flattering, of history that it shall enforce our own prejudices. If we could banish all such preconceptions when we read, that would be an admirable beginning.

A series of clauses too can be dramatized by repetition. The following sentence by Terrence Rafferty is from a review of the movie *Mountains of the Moon,* which appeared in the *New Yorker.* Here too the repetition helps to persuade the reader of the accuracy of the description "an intellectual adventurer":

> He [Sir Richard Burton] <u>had travelled</u> widely, in Europe, Asia, and Africa; <u>he had mastered</u> a couple of dozen languages; <u>he had written</u> seven books; and <u>he had made</u> a reputation as an intellectual adventurer, a man whose joy was to immerse himself in other cultures, to experience everything—even (or perhaps especially) things that his countrymen loathed and feared.

The Greeks called this repetition of clause openings **anaphora.**

The repetitions we have seen so far are contained within sentences, in compound structures—verb phrases in Kennedy's speech, clauses in the Krauthammer and Rafferty sentences, prepositional phrases in the Woolf passage. But whole sentences with obvious repeated elements not only add a stylistic flair beyond the sentence level, they contribute a great deal to the cohesion of a paragraph and beyond. We saw a number of examples in Chapter 5. You may recall the paragraph about Portland (page 94) where one sentence begins with *Its eastern border is* and the following one with *Its western border is.* In a paragraph illustrating parallelism on page 102, four successive sentences begin with *It can be.* These are both examples of anaphora, the repetition of clause openings.

These kinds of repetition are obviously not the artery-clogging kind of redundancy. Rather than hindering the flow of the sentence or paragraph, they enhance it. And they certainly send a message to the reader that the writer has crafted the work with care.

FOR GROUP DISCUSSION

Shakespeare, of course, was a master of all kinds of stylistic variations. If you've read *The Merchant of Venice,* you may remember these well-known words, spoken by Shylock in Act III, Scene I:

> He hath disgrac'd me, and hind'red me half a million, laugh'd at my losses, mock'd at my gains, scorn'd my nation, thwarted

my bargains, cool'd my friends, heated mine enemies; and what's his reason? I am a Jew. Hath not a Jew eyes? Hath not a Jew hands, organs, dimensions, senses, affections, passions? Fed with the same food, hurt with the same weapons, subject to the same diseases, heal'd by the same means, warm'd and cool'd by the same winter and summer, as a Christian is? If you prick us, do we not bleed? If you tickle us, do we not laugh? If you poison us, do we not die? And if you wrong us, shall we not revenge?

A. Identify the various rhetorical figures that Shakespeare has used here. In what ways does the sentence style enhance the meaning of Shylock's words?

B. Examine your own use of compound structures or those of a classmate in a peer review session. Look for places where one or more of the stylistic variations you have read about here—polysyndeton, asyndeton, isocolon, and anaphora—would enhance the effectiveness of the writing. For example, you might add details by turning a compound structure into a series. You'll want to bear in mind that these variations can affect the focus and rhythm.

WORD-ORDER VARIATION

A number of the classical rhetorical schemes have to do with variation in normal subject-verb-complement word order, as we saw in the examples of *anastrophe* in the Chapter Preview. Such deviations are especially common in poetry. In reading poetry, we're always on the lookout for subjects and predicates in unexpected places. Here, for example, is the opening of Robert Frost's famous poem "Stopping by Woods on a Snowy Evening":

Whose woods these are, I think I know.

In this line the opening clause is the direct object of *know:*

I think I know *something.*

This inversion of word order can also be effective in prose, mainly because we're not looking for it. It can put stress on the verb, just as it did in Frost's line. In one of the earlier examples cited from this chapter,

But many of them, you probably don't even notice,

the verb is in line for end focus. And in the following sentence, Charles Dickens made sure that the reader would hear the contrast between *has* and *has not:*

> Talent, Mr. Micawber has; money, Mr. Micawber has not.

Another variation in word order occurs with certain adverbs in opening position, when a shift of subject and auxiliary is required:

> Never before <u>had I seen</u> such an eerie glow in the night sky.
> Rarely <u>do I hear</u> such words of praise.

You'll notice that the opening adverbial is a peak of stress. The reader will focus on that opening negative—and will pay attention.

The following sentence, written by Winston Churchill, illustrates yet another kind of shift in word order. Here the very last noun phrase in the sentence is the grammatical subject:

> Against Lee and his great Lieutenant [Stonewall Jackson], united for a year of intense action in a comradeship which recalls that of Marlborough and Eugene, were now to be marshalled the overwhelming forces of the Union.

When you read this sentence aloud, you can hear your voice building to a crescendo on *overwhelming forces,* just as Churchill planned. In fact, it's hard to read the sentence without sounding Churchillian. The sentence leaves the reader in suspense until the end.

The inversion in this passage, from *The Templars* by Piers Paul Read, produces something of that same Churchillian effect:

> The conversion of Constantine was of momentous consequence for Christianity. Equally significant for the future of the Empire was his decision to move its capital from Rome to Byzantium on the Bosphorus.

In Chapter 9 we saw another variation in the expected word order when we shifted adjective phrases from their usual preheadword position:

> <u>Hot and tired,</u> the Boy Scouts trudged the last mile to their campsite.
> The Boy Scouts, <u>hot and tired,</u> trudged the last mile to their campsite.

> <u>Highly unusual,</u> the situation called for extraordinary measures.
> The situation, <u>highly unusual,</u> called for extraordinary measures.

These shifts are less dramatic than Churchill's, but they do change the emphasis and call attention to themselves. In both versions, they put the strong stress on the subject, rather than on the predicate, its usual place. The reader of the Boy Scout sentence will not be surprised to read on about the physical condition of the boys. If the writer had not called attention to the adjectives, the reader might have expected to read about the campsite in the next sentence. Likewise, in the other example, both versions put strong stress on the subject. Read them aloud, then compare your reading with this version:

> The highly unusual situation called for extraordinary measures.

You probably heard the highest peak of stress on the word *extraordinary* rather than on the subject. The reader of this version will expect to learn more about those measures; in the other two versions the reader probably expects to read more about the situation and what makes it unusual.

All of these word order variations change the rhythm patterns and thus the messages that the reader will get. As a writer, you will want to construct your sentences with the reader and the reader's expectations in mind.

FOR GROUP DISCUSSION

In the following paragraph, the opening paragraph of Chapter 5 in Daniel J. Boorstin's *The Discoverers,* you'll find two sentences that illustrate anastrophe:

> While man allowed his time to be parsed by the changing cycles of daylight, he remained a slave to the sun. To become the master of his time, to assimilate night into the day, to slice his life into neat, usable portions, he had to find a way to mark off precise small portions—not only equal hours, but even minutes and seconds and parts of seconds. He would have to make a machine. It is surprising that machines to measure time were so long in coming. Not until the fourteenth century did Europeans devise mechanical timepieces. Until then, as we have seen, the measuring of time was left to the shadow clock, the water clock, the sandglass, and the miscellaneous candle clocks and scent clocks. While there was remarkable progress five thousand years ago in measuring the year, and useful week clusters of days were long in use, the subdivided day was another matter. Only in modern times did we begin to live by the hour, much less by the minute.

A. You'll notice that the two sentences illustrating anastrophe also include the shift of the subject and the auxiliary verb. What do they have in common with those examples with *never before* and *rarely* in the discussion? Note as well other figures of speech that Boorstin uses here.

B. Note the variation in sentence length. Where do you find the topic sentence in this paragraph?

C. In Chapter 7 you read about metadiscourse; you'll find two examples in this paragraph. What effect do they have on you as a reader?

ELLIPSIS

Another fairly common stylistic variation—another that the Greeks used in their oratory—is **ellipsis,** which refers to a sentence in which a part is simply left out, or understood. As you might expect, they had many names for this variation, depending on the kind of structure deleted. We use the umbrella term *ellipsis* for all of them.

One example we've already seen is Churchill's description of Stonewall Jackson:

> His character was stern, his manner reserved and unusually forbidding, his temper Calvinistic, his mode of life strict, frugal, and austere.

And you saw this sentence as an illustration of the series without conjunctions, asyndeton; however, it's also a good example of ellipsis, where all the clauses except the first are missing the verb: "his manner [was] reserved . . . his temper [was] Calvinistic," and so on. Here are some other, similar, examples, where part of the second clause or phrase is left out to avoid repetition:

> The first day of our vacation was wonderful; the second, miserable.
>
> For breakfast we had eggs; for lunch, eggs; and for dinner, eggs again.
>
> Some of our games this season were awesome; others awful.
>
> Percy always orders the extra-large latte for himself; for me, the medium. He gets his with sugar; I get mine without.

Note that within the sentence a comma sometimes signals the omission, depending on the rhythm, where the pause produced by the comma may be needed to help the reader. As you can hear when you read these sentences, this use of ellipsis gives them a tight, controlled quality that would be missing if the clauses were complete.

In some clauses of comparison, the ellipsis is required by our grammar:

I'm a week older than Terry [is old].
My sister isn't as tall as I [am tall].

or

I'm a week older than Terry is [old].
My sister isn't as tall as I am [tall].

These structures are not a problem for native speakers; we use them automatically. But some elliptical clauses are not quite as obvious; they can be left dangling, as we saw in the discussion on pages 163–164.

*While waiting for the bus, the police arrested a pickpocket at the edge of the crowd.

As you may recall from Chapter 8, the subject of that *while-* clause must be the same as the subject of the main clause:

While [we were] waiting for the bus, we saw the police arrest a pickpocket at the edge of the crowd.

In this case, if you prefer to stay with *the police* as the subject of the main clause, there's an easy solution: Simply get rid of the ellipsis; write out the clause in full:

While we were waiting for the bus, the police arrested . . .

When well used, ellipsis can create a bond of sorts between the writer and the reader. The writer is saying, in effect, I needn't spell everything out for you; I know you'll understand.

You may be thinking at this point that if you actually used such sentences in your essays your teacher would mark them as sentence fragments and ask you to correct them. But that's not likely. Clearly, these elliptical sentences are not accidental; in fact, the opposite message will get through to the reader: "Pay attention. I crafted this sentence carefully."

We should note that *ellipsis* is also the term we use to refer to the string of periods, or *ellipsis points,* that indicate to the reader that we have left something out of quoted material. You can read more about this punctuation convention on page 276 in the Glossary of Punctuation.

ANTITHESIS

In his book on classical rhetoric, referred to in an earlier chapter (also listed in the Bibliography), Edward P. J. Corbett defines **antithesis** as "the juxtaposition of contrasting ideas, often in parallel" (464); among his examples illustrating this figure of speech are the words of Neil Armstrong as he stepped on the moon in 1969:

> That's one small step for a man, one giant leap for mankind.

This example is from George W. Bush's second inaugural address:

> Across the generations we have proclaimed the imperative of self-government because no one is fit to be a master and no one deserves to be a slave.

Benjamin Franklin included this example of antithesis in a letter he wrote in 1783:

> There never was a good war, or a bad peace.

Don't get the idea that world-changing events and presidential speeches are the only occasions for antithesis. Advertisers often use the same kind of juxtaposition of contrasting ideas. Here are some headlines from magazine ads published in *Atlantic* and *Harper's*:

> Before our engineers design our cars, our racing programs design our engineers.
>
> Felt but not seen. Because our miracle is on the inside . . . [mattress ad]
>
> We only live once. But we sit many, many times. [chair ad]
>
> You can't see the innovative technology. But you can certainly hear it. [sound system]

The first one is a clever play on words; in the last three, the negative comment is there to contrast with, and thus enhance, the positive quality being promoted. Earlier we saw an example of antithesis in a quotation from Dickens used to illustrate word order variation:

> Talent, Mr. Micawber has; money, Mr. Micawber has not.

The following example is a portion of the paragraph that follows the Boorstin paragraph about clocks quoted in the Group Discussion activity on page 217. It includes the kind of antithesis that you are likely to see in works you are reading—and also to use—where contrasts are included to emphasize the point:

> The first steps toward the mechanical measurement of time, the beginnings of the modern clock in Europe, came not from farmers or shepherds, nor from merchants or craftsmen, but from religious persons anxious to perform promptly and regularly their duties to God. Monks needed to know the times for their appointed prayers. In Europe the first mechanical clocks were designed not to *show* the time but to *sound* it. . . . [author's emphasis]

In his autobiography, *Long Walk to Freedom,* Nelson Mandela uses antithesis to explain the importance of education:

> Education is the great engine of personal development. It is through education that <u>the daughter of a peasant can become a doctor,</u> that <u>the son of a mineworker can become the head of the mine,</u> that <u>a child of farmworkers can become the president of a great nation.</u> It is what we make out of <u>what we have, not what we are given,</u> that separates one person from another.

In the discussion of cohesion in Chapter 5 we also saw antithesis, where Stephen Jay Gould contrasts "violence, sexism, and general nastiness" with "peacefulness, equality, and kindness." And the Virginia Woolf example of anaphora we saw earlier also illustrates antithesis: "asking of fiction that it shall be true, of poetry that it shall be false. . . ."

THE DELIBERATE FRAGMENT

The sentence fragments used for their stylistic effect are not the kind that teachers mark with a marginal "frag"; those are usually the result of punctuation errors, often a dependent clause punctuated as a full sentence. But experienced writers know how to use fragments deliberately and effectively—noun phrases or verb phrases that add a detail without a full sentence and invariably call attention to themselves. Here are two examples from the novels of John le Carré:

> Our Candidate begins speaking. <u>A deliberate, unimpressive opening.</u>
>
> —*A Perfect Spy*

> He began packing up his desk. <u>Precisely.</u> <u>Packing to leave.</u> <u>Opening and shutting drawers.</u> <u>Putting his file trays into his steel cupboard and locking it.</u> <u>Absently smoothing back his hair between moves, a tic that Woodrow had always found particularly irritating in him.</u>
>
> —*The Constant Gardener*

Barack Obama opens Chapter 5 of his memoir, *Dreams from My Father,* with three sentence fragments in two sentences. The second sentence has two fragments, an absolute phrase and a noun phrase:

> Three o'clock in the morning. The moon-washed streets empty, the growl of a car picking up speed down a distant road.

In the following paragraph from *Love Medicine* by Louise Erdrich, we are hearing fragmented thoughts—ideal candidates for sentence fragments. You'll notice that some are simple noun phrases, some are absolutes—a noun with a modifier following—and some are dependent clauses. But, obviously, all are deliberate:

<u>Northern lights.</u> Something in the cold, wet atmosphere brought them out. I grabbed Lipsha's arm. We floated into the field and sank down, crushing green wheat. We chewed the sweet kernels and stared up and were lost. Everything seemed to be one piece. <u>The air, our faces, all cool, moist, and dark, and the ghostly sky.</u> Pale green licks of light pulsed and faded across it. <u>Living lights.</u> Their fires lobbed over, higher, higher, then died out in blackness. At times the whole sky was ringed in shooting points and puckers of light gathering and falling, pulsing, fading, rhythmical as breathing. <u>All of a piece.</u> <u>As if the sky were a pattern of nerves and our thought and memories traveled across it.</u> <u>As if the sky were one gigantic memory for us all.</u> <u>Or a dance hall.</u> And all the world's wandering souls were dancing there. I thought of June. She would be dancing if there was a dance hall in space. She would be dancing a two-step for wandering souls. <u>Her long legs lifting and falling.</u> <u>Her laugh an ace.</u> <u>Her sweet perfume the way all grown-up women were supposed to smell.</u> <u>Her amusement at both the bad and the good.</u> <u>Her defeat.</u> <u>Her reckless victory.</u> Her sons.

And in the following passage from *The Shipping News,* E. Annie Proulx conveys a tentative quality of the characters' feelings:

Wavey came down the steps pulling at the sleeves of her home-made coat, the color of slushy snow. She got in, glanced at him. <u>A slight smile.</u> <u>Looked away.</u>
   <u>Their silence comfortable.</u> <u>Something unfolding.</u> But what? <u>Not love, which wrenched and wounded.</u> <u>Not love, which came only once.</u>

Both ellipsis and sentence fragments contribute to that tentativeness.

EXERCISE 37

Examine the style of one of your essays or, if working in groups, an essay written by a classmate.

1. Calculate the average length of the sentences. Then count the number that surpass the average length by at least ten words and the number at least five words below the average.

2. Note any series of three or more structures. Do they follow the order of climax, with the longest and/or most important member last in the string? Do any have variations in their punctuation, either asyndeton or polysyndeton?

3. Are there any places where a compound structure could be expanded into a series to add stylistic interest or further information?

4. Is there any clause-level punctuation other than commas and periods—semicolons, colons, dashes? Are there places where alternative punctuation might enhance the effectiveness?

5. How many sentences begin with opening phrases or clauses that precede the subject? Check for other word-order variation, such as subject–verb shifts?

6. Count the instances of any repetition, ellipsis, and antithesis.

7. Count the number of appositive and absolute phrases.

Write an evaluation of the essay based on these findings.

FOR GROUP DISCUSSION

The writers of the following passages have used a great many stylistic tools to good advantage. Identify the places where they have sent that special message to the reader: "Pay attention! I've crafted this sentence carefully."

[George Caleb] Bingham's greatest paintings depend upon an open rhetoric, an uncannily frank relation to their audience. We view his subjects from a perspective that includes us within the painting, and the direct looks we meet there usually recall the openness of Bingham's own disposition, itself characteristically American. Looking at *Fur Traders Descending the Missouri* as if from a canoe or from the Missouri's bank, we are obliged to remember that rivers have mouths and sources. *Fur Traders* can certainly be read as a painting in which the wilderness is brought into the frame of civilization, tending ever downriver. But it is more ambiguous than that, and ambiguity is an important source of its effect. Backlit by the diffuse light of the rising sun, offset by an island still in shadow, barely accented by a line of ducks wheeling over the far shore, these exotic figures are just as redolent of where they have been as of where they are going. And as time moves the viewer farther and farther downstream from the wilderness, it seems more and more as if this painting leads us upstream in imagination to the wilder country from which this man and boy have just descended.

—Verlyn Klinkenborg
(*Smithsonian*)

The general pressure in medical school is to push yourself ahead into professionalism, to start feeling at home in the hospital, in the operating room, to make medical jargon your native tongue—it's all part of becoming efficient, knowledgeable, competent. You want to leave behind that green, terrified medical student who stood awkwardly on the edge of the action, terrified of revealing limitless ignorance, terrified of killing a patient. You want to identify with the people ahead of you, the ones who know what they're doing. And instead, I have found it necessary to retain some of the greenness, so I could explain the hospital to people for whom it was not familiar turf.

—Perri Klass (*A Not Entirely Benign Procedure*)

(*Note:* You saw the opening sentence of this paragraph in the discussion of asyndeton)

It is so known through the length and breadth of its watershed. The Bay. There is no possible confusion with any other body of water, no need for more precise description. It is, after all, the continent's largest estuary. Its waters are rich, the main supply of oysters, crabs, clams and other seafoods for much of the Atlantic seaboard. Its shorelines cradled our first settlements. It is the Chesapeake.

—William W. Warner (*Beautiful Swimmers*)

(*Note*: This paragraph opens the book's first chapter, "The Bay.")

On two occasions, the contractor hired a group of Mexican aliens. They were employed to cut down some trees and haul off debris. In all, there were six men of varying age. The youngest in his late twenties; the oldest (his father?) perhaps sixty years old. They came and they left in a single old truck. Anonymous men. They were never introduced to the other men at the site. Immediately upon their arrival they would follow the contractor's directions, starting working—rarely resting—seemingly driven by a fatalistic sense that work which had to be done was best done as quickly as possible.

I watched them sometimes. Perhaps they watched me. The only time I saw them pay me much notice was one day at lunchtime when I was laughing with the other men. The

Mexicans sat apart when they ate, just as they worked by themselves. Quiet. I rarely heard them say much to each other. All I could hear were their voices calling out sharply to one another, giving directions. Otherwise, when they stood briefly resting, they talked among themselves in voices too hard to overhear.

—Richard Rodriguez (*Hunger of Memory*)

Thornton's command cracked out like a pistol shot. Buck threw himself forward, tightening the traces with a jarring lunge. His whole body was gathered compactly together in the tremendous effort, the muscles writhing and knotting like live things under the silky fur. His great chest was low to the ground, his head forward and down, while his feet were flying like mad, the claws scarring the hard-packed snow in parallel grooves. The sled swayed and trembled, half-started forward. One of his feet slipped, and one man groaned aloud. The sled lurched ahead in what appeared a rapid succession of jerks, though it never really came to a dead stop again . . . half an inch . . . an inch . . . two inches . . . The jerks perceptibly diminished; as the sled gained momentum, he caught them up, till it was moving steadily along.

—Jack London (*The Call of the Wild*)

The mass movement of the Scandinavian peoples between the years AD 750 and 1050, one of the great migrations of European history, began as plunder-raids and ended as conquest and settlement. People from what is now known as Sweden established a kingdom in part of European Russia. Adventurers from Norway colonized parts of the British Isles, the Faroes, and Iceland, pushed on to Greenland and eventually the coast of Labrador. And the Danes—also called Norsemen— conquered northern France (which became Normandy) and finally England. Collectively, these peoples are referred to as the Vikings, a name which is thought to come either from the Norse *vik* (a bay, indicating "one who frequents inlets of the sea") or from the Old English *wic,* a camp, the formation of temporary encampments being a prominent feature of Viking raids. In the past, the Vikings have been described as daring pirates but, while there is obviously much truth to the stereotype, recent scholarship likes to emphasize the long-term peaceful benefits of the Norse landings. It has been suggested, too, that the native Anglo-Saxons took advantage of the Viking raids to settle old scores with each other. Unlike the

Anglo-Saxon race war against the Celts, which preserved virtually no trace of the Celtic languages in English, the Danish settlers had a profound influence on the development of Old English.

—Robert McCrum, Robert MacNeil,
and William Cran *(The Story of English)*

KEY TERMS

Absolute phrase	Ellipsis	Redundancy
Anaphora	Figures of speech	Repetition
Anastrophe	Fragment	Style
Antithesis	Isocolon	Word-order variation
Asyndeton	Polysyndeton	

RHETORICAL REMINDERS

Have I taken advantage of the stylistic possibilities of absolute phrases and of various kinds of repetition, word-order variation, antithesis, and ellipsis to heighten the drama and/or call attention to particular passages?

In my series of three or more structures, have I considered order of importance and/or length?

PUNCTUATION REMINDERS

Have I used any punctuation variations for any series, such as asyndeton or polysyndeton?

Do my punctuation choices help the reader, especially in long sentences with internal punctuation?

Have I used colons, semicolons, and dashes accurately and effectively?

Answers to the Exercises

Chapter 1

Exercise 1, page 9
1. The(d) students(H)   their(d) long trip(H)
3. Mickey's(d) roommate(H)   the(d) library(H)   rainy weekends(H)
5. This(d) new lasagna recipe(H)   an(d) enormous crowd(H)

Exercise 2, page 13
1. Our county commissioners (They)
3. The mayor (She)
5. The merchants in town (They)

Exercise 3, page 17
1. Adverbial
3. Adjectival, Adverbial
5. Adverbial

Chapter 2

Exercise 4, page 23
1. The bus from Flagstaff / arrived / at two o'clock (P 4)
3. The . . . grill / smells / wonderful (P 3)
5. AD / is / a . . . nature (P 2)
7. Our . . . meeting / is / in the library (P 1)

Exercise 5, page 29
A1. Many people / now / consider (trans) / the penny / a nuisance coin
A3. During World War II / the government / required (trans) / large amounts of copper / for war production
A5. The Philadelphia Mint / unwittingly / produced (trans) / twelve copper pennies / that year / in addition to the new model
A7. Those twelve 1943 copper pennies / soon / became (linking) / valuable collectors' items

Here are some possible revisions of the sentences in the first part:
B1. Now many people consider . . .
B3. The government required large amounts of copper for war production during World War II.

B5. Unwittingly, the Philadelphia Mint . . .

B7. Soon those twelve 1943 copper pennies . . .

Exercise 6, page 32

1. In 1747 / a physician in the British Navy / conducted / an experiment / to discover a cure for scurvy. (P 5)

3. Dr. James Lind / fed / six groups of scurvy victims / six different remedies. (P 6)

5. Although . . . findings, / it / finally / ordered / a daily dose of fresh lemon juice / for every British seaman. (P 6)

7. The British / called / lemons / "limes" / in the eighteenth century. (P 7).

Chapter 3

Exercise 7, page 46

Active to Passive:

1. The lead article in today's *Collegian* was written by my roommate.

3. An elaborate celebration has been organized by our homecoming committee.

5. A new tax-collection system is being proposed by the county commissioners this year.

Passive to Active:

1. A committee chose this year's cheerleading squad last spring.

3. We will hold the election of the class officers on Tuesday.

5. The police are keeping the suspect in solitary confinement.

Either:

1. We elected Barack Obama president in 2008. (Passive to Active)

3. Migration has affected the cities in the Northeast in recent years. (P to A)

5. A new vacation schedule is being tried out this year by our company. (A to P)

Exercise 8, page 49

Answers will vary.

Exercise 9, page 52

Answers will vary.

Chapter 4

Exercise 10, page 61

Answers may vary.

1. Both tea and coffee contain caffeine.

3. Some people drink either coffee or tea, but not both.

5. Japanese blue-collar workers not only work more hours per day than American workers but also typically do so with more dedication and energy.

7. In the U.S. neither blue-collar workers nor students spend as much time at their respective jobs as do their Japanese counterparts.

Exercise 11, page 63

1. go

3. go

5. finds

Exercise 12, page 74

1. The Smithsonian Institution comprises nineteen museums, nine research centers, and the National Zoo.

3. No extra punctuation necessary.

5. The museum . . . in 1976; however, its collection . . . Airport.

7. Together . . . air- and spacecraft; they also sponsor vital research into aviation and related technologies.

9. Approximately . . . museums, but the museums . . . as docents.

Exercise 13, page 76
Answers will vary.

Exercise 14, page 79
Here are some of the problems:

1. Unparallel verb phrases: *to lift* and *swimming*
3. Unparallel verb phrases: *enjoy flying* and *want to take*
5. Unparallel complements: *introduced + noun phrase* and *said + nominal clause*
7. Unparallel complements: *either + noun phrase* and *or + independent clause*

Chapter 5

Exercise 15, page 93

1. At the edge of the Mississippi River in St. Louis stands the Gateway Arch, the world's tallest monument. The stainless steel structure, designed by Eero Saarinen, commemorates the Westward Movement.

3. [No change in the first sentence.] It's not unusual for the temperature to reach 110° in Bakersfield, often the hottest spot in the valley. [Note that *summer* in the first sentence makes *June through September* redundant.]

5. Directed by the U.S. Marshal Service, the federal witness-protection service began in 1968. This program has relocated and created new identities for over four thousand people in extreme danger because they have testified against criminals.

Exercise 16, page 97

1. Many women . . . political status. This effort . . . .
3. Some married women . . . property, but this right . . . .
5. In 1920 the Constitution . . . vote. That amendment . . . .

Chapter 6

Exercise 17, page 109
There are, of course, no right and wrong answers for the question of main stress. The answers here are based on our readings of the passages—words that are likely candidates for strong stress:

1. Sentence 1. <u>understand</u> and <u>salesperson</u>; 2. <u>buyer</u>, <u>sellee</u>; 3. <u>want</u>, <u>vacuum</u>, <u>buy</u>; 4. <u>else</u>, <u>selling</u>

3. Sentence 1. <u>hazards</u> and <u>easy</u>; 2. <u>literature</u> and <u>body</u> and <u>one</u> conclusion and <u>contradicts</u>; 3. <u>out</u> and <u>steady</u>.

Exercise 18, page 113
Answers will vary. Here are some possibilities:

1. It was in 1912 that the *Titanic* hit . . .
3. There were hundreds of angry parents protesting the senator's position . . .
5. There have been countless travelers who have lost . . .

Chapter 7

Exercise 19, page 125
Remember! You won't be using the word *snafu!*

Exercise 20, page 131

A. Here are some possibilities for the first five in the list: turn down/reject; bring about/cause; bring on/induce; put up with/tolerate; stand for/represent, tolerate

B. (1) suggest, offer, propose; (3) replacing with, transforming into; (5) establishes, creates, produces; (7) consider; (9) replaces/represents

Exercise 21, page 133
1. Investors on Wall Street are concerned because the Japanese are buying so many American companies and so much real estate.
3. In his biography of Lyndon Johnson, Robert Caro provides a detailed account of the Senate election of 1948.
5. The overuse of salt in the typical American diet obscures the natural taste of many foods. Nutritionists maintain that if people reduced their dependence on salt they would find their food tastier and more enjoyable.

Exercise 22, page 142
Answers will vary.

Chapter 8
Exercise 23, page 154
Answers will vary.

Exercise 24, page 159
Answers will vary

Exercise 25, page 162
(*Note:* You may have come up with even tighter versions using other kinds of modifiers.)
1. Even though the famous Gateway Arch is in St. Louis, it is Kansas City that claims the title "Gateway to the West."
3. Thomas Jefferson acquired the Ozark Mountains for the United States when he negotiated the Louisiana Purchase with Napoleon in 1803.
5. When the neighbors added a pit bull to their pet population, now numbering three unfriendly four-legged creatures, we decided to fence in our backyard.
7. Fad diets that severely restrict the intake of carbohydrates are not only ineffective but also often dangerous, because carbohydrates are the body's prime source of energy.

Exercise 26, page 164
1. *To save money* (infinitive/reason); *often* (adverb/frequency); *at my desk* (prep phr/place)
3. *After . . . navy* (clause/time); *from the navy* (prep phr/place)
5. *As soon as the guests left* (clause/time); *in a heap* (prep phr/manner); *on the couch* (prep phr/place)
7. *When October came* (clause/time)
9. *slowly* (adverb/manner); *northward* (adverb/direction)
11. *home* (noun/place); *last night* (noun phr/time); *because of the snowstorm* (prep phr/reason)

Chapter 9
Exercise 27, page 172
1. The administration's recent clean-air proposals have been criticized as inadequate not only by . . . .
3. The stock market reached an all-time high last week and will probably keep going up.
5. A big yellow delivery truck is blocking the driveway, and its driver . . . .
7. I found an expensive-looking copper-colored bracelet . . . .
9. I have back-to-back exams on Wednesday.

Exercise 28, page 179

1. Having endured rain all week, we weren't surprised by the miserable weather on Saturday. [or "we weren't surprised when the weather turned miserable on Saturday."]
3. We were not at all surprised when the Republican county commissioner, known for her conservative views . . . , announced her candidacy . . . .
5. After I spent nearly all day in the kitchen, everyone agreed . . . .
7. Obviously intimidated by a long history of defeats in Morgantown, our basketball team just can't seem to beat the Virginia Mountaineers on their home court.

Exercise 29, page 183

1. My roommate's announcement that she is planning to withdraw from school came as a complete surprise.

   or

   When my roommate told me she is planning to withdraw from school, I was completely surprised.
3. Converting the central card catalog in the college library to a computer system took over four years.
5. Harriett was rather unhappy when Wendell didn't want to stay for the second half of the game.
7. When the president characterized the last two years as a period of "unprecedented prosperity" in his State of the Union message, one economist immediately labeled his statement "sheer hype and hyperbole."

Exercise 30, page 187

1. Sentence 2: . . . contract, expiring . . .
3. . . . husband, sitting . . . platform, both . . . . Then the mayor, turning . . . senator, shocked . . . .

Exercise 31, page 187

1. Citizens in many parts of the country, mobilizing against crime and drugs, are driving drug dealers out of their neighborhoods. [or . . . are mobilizing to drive drug dealers out of their neighborhoods.]
3. The computer has revolutionized the storage and retrieval of fingerprints, which have been used for criminal identification since 1891, when a police officer in Argentina introduced the method.
5. In 1997 an earthquake that struck the Assisi region of Italy destroyed many priceless fourteenth-century mosaics decorating the walls and ceiling of the Basilica of St. Francis. [or . . . an earthquake struck the Assisi region of Italy, destroying many priceless mosaics from the fourteenth century, which decorated the walls . . . .]
7. The amount of carbon dioxide in the air affects the rate of colon cancer because carbon dioxide absorbs ultraviolet light, which fuels the body's production of vitamin D.
9. We cannot build up our immunity to flu viruses because they mutate constantly, producing new varieties that spread from person to person and from place to place.

Exercise 32, page 189

Answers will vary.

Chapter 10

Exercise 33, page 194

1. simple ballads sung to guitar music
3. An offbeat film about illegal trash dumping
5. a contemporary folk singer and songwriter; *Soul Journey* and *Time* (*The Revelator*)

Exercise 34, page 200
1. <u>to tell the truth,</u> infinitive (subjective complement)
3. <u>To ignore . . . order,</u> infinitive (subject)
5. <u>to buy up . . . stocks,</u> infinitive (appositive)
7. <u>Raising . . . profile,</u> gerund (subject)
9. <u>your proofreading . . . me,</u> gerund

Exercise 35, page 203
1. The neighbors never suspected <u>that we had a pet boa constrictor in our house.</u> (nom cl, d.o.)
3. <u>Mark's complaining about his grades</u> is getting tiresome. (gerund ph, subj)
5. His problem is <u>getting accepted</u> (gerund ph, sub comp)
7. The knowledge <u>that spring break is almost here</u> makes me happy. (nom cl, appositive)
9. It's almost impossible <u>to predict what will be on the final exam.</u> (inf ph, app to it, a delayed subj) (nom clause, d.o. of inf. ph)

Chapter 11
Exercise 36, page 210
Here are some examples:
1. My sister, who is one of the most conservative people I know, surprised everyone at the family reunion when she showed up in a 1920s-style dress trimmed with beads and feathers, her normally blonde hair dyed red.
3. At the far end of the diner's chrome and plastic counter sat a trucker, an old man with long grey hair, his leathery face a pattern of creases and scars, his fringed jacket worn nearly through at the elbows.

Exercise 37, page 222
Answers will vary.

Chapter 12
Exercise 38, page 235
1. The <u>statement</u> . . . <u>was</u> . . .
3. Apparently the <u>use</u> of robots . . . <u>has</u> . . .
5. Correct

Exercise 39, page 239
1. grief, grieve, grievous, grievously
3. ability, enable, able, ably
5. quickness, quicken, quick, quickly
7. type, typify, typical, typically
9. critic (criticism/critique), criticize (critique), critical, critically
11. appreciation, appreciate, appreciable, appreciably
13. acceptance (acceptability), accept, acceptable, acceptably
15. stealth, steal, stealthy, stealthily

Exercise 40, page 242
Answers will vary. Here are some possibilities.
1. meticulous
3. brusque
5. futile
7. exhausted
9. enthusiastic

Exercise 41, page 244

1. <u>in</u> a relatively short period of time (noun phrase)
3. <u>to</u> what the guide told us about the trail leading into the canyon (nominal clause) *and* <u>about</u> the trail leading into the canyon (noun phrase) *and* <u>into</u> the canyon (noun phrase)

Exercise 42, page 253

1. Claire has always been interested in children and, when she graduates, plans to work with them. Both she and I are majoring in early childhood education.
3. When . . . , I had no idea Beth was sick . . . . Our grandmother took one look at her called the doctor, and drove her to the hospital. That decision turned out to be a good one: Beth's cramps turned out to be appendicitis.

Exercise 43, page 256

1. I recall with great pleasure the good times that we had at our annual family reunions when I was young. With our cousins and younger aunts and uncles, we played volleyball and softball until dark. Those games were a lot of fun.
3. It seemed to my cousin Terry and me that the grownups were different people at those family reunions. Such memories of family reunions may be true for people everywhere.

Chapter 13

Exercise 44, page 266

Here are some examples:

1. The cost of repairs to the nation's public transportation facilities—roads, bridges, and railroads—is an expenditure that cannot be delayed much longer if the system is to survive.
3. Normally living in the coastal waters of Japan, the paper nautilus octopus, a rare marine animal, was found recently in the squid nets off Santa Catalina in California.

Exercise 45, page 269

Management is still taught in most business schools as a bundle of techniques, such as budgeting and personnel relations. To be sure, management, like any other work, has its own tools and its own techniques. But just as the essence of medicine is not urinalysis (important though that is) the essence of management is not techniques and procedures. The essence of management is to make knowledge productive. Management, in other words, is a social function. And in its practice management is truly a liberal art. [Note: If you put a comma after *practice* in the last sentence, you have improved on the original! A comma would make the sentence easier to read.]

The old communities—family, village, parish, and so on—have all but disappeared in the knowledge society. Their place has largely been taken by the new unit of social integration, the organization. Where community was fate, organization is voluntary membership. Where community claimed the entire person, organization is a means to a person's ends, a tool. For 200 years a hot debate has been raging, especially in the West: are communities "organic" or are they simply extensions of the people of which they are made? Nobody would claim that the new organization is "organic." It is clearly an artifact, a creation of man, a social technology.